Nissan Qashqai
Owner's Workshop Manual

Pete Gill

(6463 - 400)

Models covered

Nissan Qashqai (2nd generation) SUV/crossover with front-wheel-drive (2WD)

Petrol: 1.2 litre (1199cc) DIG-T
Turbo-diesel: 1.5 litre (1461cc) & 1.6 litre (1598cc) dCi

Does NOT cover models with 1.3 litre, 1.6 litre or 2.0 litre petrol engines or 2.0 litre diesel engine

Does NOT cover models with four-wheel-drive (4WD) or automatic transmission

© Haynes Publishing 2020

A book in the Haynes Owners Workshop Manual Series

ABCDE
FGHIJ
KLMNO
PQRST

ISBN 978 1 78521 463 9

British Library Cataloguing in Publication Data
A catalogue record for this book is available from the British Library.

Printed in Malaysia

Haynes Publishing
Sparkford, Yeovil, Somerset BA22 7JJ, England

Haynes North America, Inc
859 Lawrence Drive, Newbury Park, California 91320, USA

T0364802

Contents

LIVING WITH YOUR NISSAN QASHQAI

MAINTENANCE

Routine maintenance and servicing

Contents

The Nissan Qashqai (J10) 5-door hatchback, known as a "Crossover" vehicle was first introduced in the UK in February 2007. During the course of production, various trim levels were introduced and in August 2008 the +2 version (7-seater) was launched. In 2010 the Qashqai (J10) had a facelift, which involved some small changes to the external and internal appearance of the vehicle. In February 2014, the Nissan Qashqai (J11), was introduced and that will be the model covered in this manual. In 2017 the Qashqai (J11) had a mild facelift, which involved some small changes to the external and internal appearance of the vehicle.

Covered in this manual is the 1.2 litre petrol engine, being of double overhead camshaft (DOHC) 16-valve design. The engine features a multi-point fuel injection and is equipped with emissions control systems. Also covered in this manual are the 1.5 litre and 1.6 litre diesel engines, both being of double overhead camshaft (DOHC) 16-valve design. The 1.5 litre Renault diesel engine, is of a well-proven design and has been used previously in Nissan/Renault vehicles.

Fully independent front and rear suspension units are fitted, with MacPherson strut type at the front and multi-link suspension used at the rear.

A six-speed, manual transmission is fitted as standard across the range, with a six-speed automatic transmission optionally available on 1.6 litre diesel models.

A wide range of standard and optional equipment is available within the Qashqai range including central locking, electric windows, an electric sunroof, an anti-lock braking system and supplementary restraint system.

For the home mechanic, the Qashqai is a straightforward vehicle to maintain, and most of the items requiring frequent attention are easily accessible.

Your Nissan Qashqai Manual

The aim of this manual is to help you get the best value from your vehicle. It can do so in several ways. It can help you decide what work must be done (even should you choose to get it done by a garage), provide information on routine maintenance and servicing, and give a logical course of action and diagnosis when random faults occur. However, it is hoped that you will use the manual by tackling the work yourself. On simpler jobs, it may even be quicker than booking the car into a garage and going there twice, to leave and collect it. Perhaps most important, a lot of money can be saved by avoiding the costs a garage must charge to cover its labour and overheads.

The manual has drawings and descriptions to show the function of the various components, so that their layout can be understood. Then the tasks are described and photographed in a clear step-by-step sequence.

References to the 'left' or 'right' are in the sense of a person in the driver's seat, facing forward.

Acknowledgements

Thanks are due to Draper Tools Limited, who provided some of the workshop tools, and to all those people at Sparkford who helped in the production of this manual.

We take great pride in the accuracy of information given in this manual, but vehicle manufacturers make alterations and design changes during the production run of a particular vehicle of which they do not inform us. No liability can be accepted by the authors or publishers for loss, damage or injury caused by any errors in, or omissions from, the information given.

Dimensions and weights

Note: *All figures are approximate, and may vary according to model. Refer to manufacturer's data for exact figures.*

Dimensions

Overall length	4377 mm
Overall width	1806 to 1838 mm
Overall height (unladen):	
Without roof rails	1587 to 1590 mm
With roof rails	1607 to 1624 mm
Wheelbase	2646 mm
Front track	1560 to 1585 mm
Rear track	1560 to 1580 mm

Weights

Vehicle weights are listed on the VIN label on the driver's side door pillar **(see illustration)**.

First (kg) figure is	Gross vehicle weight
Second (kg) figure is	Gross vehicle weight + Gross trailer weight
Third (kg) figure is	Gross axle weight (front)
Fourth (kg) figure is	Gross axle weight (rear)

Working on your car can be dangerous. This page shows just some of the potential risks and hazards, with the aim of creating a safety-conscious attitude.

General hazards

Scalding

• Don't remove the radiator or expansion tank cap while the engine is hot.
• Engine oil, transmission fluid or power steering fluid may also be dangerously hot if the engine has recently been running.

Burning

• Beware of burns from the exhaust system and from any part of the engine. Brake discs and drums can also be extremely hot immediately after use.

Crushing

• When working under or near a raised vehicle, always supplement the jack with axle stands, or use drive-on ramps. *Never venture under a car which is only supported by a jack.*

• Take care if loosening or tightening high-torque nuts when the vehicle is on stands. Initial loosening and final tightening should be done with the wheels on the ground.

Fire

• Fuel is highly flammable; fuel vapour is explosive.
• Don't let fuel spill onto a hot engine.
• Do not smoke or allow naked lights (including pilot lights) anywhere near a vehicle being worked on. Also beware of creating sparks (electrically or by use of tools).
• Fuel vapour is heavier than air, so don't work on the fuel system with the vehicle over an inspection pit.
• Another cause of fire is an electrical overload or short-circuit. Take care when repairing or modifying the vehicle wiring.
• Keep a fire extinguisher handy, of a type suitable for use on fuel and electrical fires.

Electric shock

• Ignition HT and Xenon headlight voltages can be dangerous, especially to people with heart problems or a pacemaker. Don't work on or near these systems with the engine running or the ignition switched on.

• Mains voltage is also dangerous. Make sure that any mains-operated equipment is correctly earthed. Mains power points should be protected by a residual current device (RCD) circuit breaker.

Fume or gas intoxication

• Exhaust fumes are poisonous; they can contain carbon monoxide, which is rapidly fatal if inhaled. Never run the engine in a confined space such as a garage with the doors shut.
• Fuel vapour is also poisonous, as are the vapours from some cleaning solvents and paint thinners.

Poisonous or irritant substances

• Avoid skin contact with battery acid and with any fuel, fluid or lubricant, especially antifreeze, brake hydraulic fluid and Diesel fuel. Don't syphon them by mouth. If such a substance is swallowed or gets into the eyes, seek medical advice.
• Prolonged contact with used engine oil can cause skin cancer. Wear gloves or use a barrier cream if necessary. Change out of oil-soaked clothes and do not keep oily rags in your pocket.
• Air conditioning refrigerant forms a poisonous gas if exposed to a naked flame (including a cigarette). It can also cause skin burns on contact.

Asbestos

• Asbestos dust can cause cancer if inhaled or swallowed. Asbestos may be found in gaskets and in brake and clutch linings. When dealing with such components it is safest to assume that they contain asbestos.

Special hazards

Hydrofluoric acid

• This extremely corrosive acid is formed when certain types of synthetic rubber, found in some O-rings, oil seals, fuel hoses etc, are exposed to temperatures above 4000C. The rubber changes into a charred or sticky substance containing the acid. *Once formed, the acid remains dangerous for years. If it gets onto the skin, it may be necessary to amputate the limb concerned.*
• When dealing with a vehicle which has suffered a fire, or with components salvaged from such a vehicle, wear protective gloves and discard them after use.

The battery

• Batteries contain sulphuric acid, which attacks clothing, eyes and skin. Take care when topping-up or carrying the battery.
• The hydrogen gas given off by the battery is highly explosive. Never cause a spark or allow a naked light nearby. Be careful when connecting and disconnecting battery chargers or jump leads.

Air bags

• Air bags can cause injury if they go off accidentally. Take care when removing the steering wheel and trim panels. Special storage instructions may apply.

Diesel injection equipment

• Diesel injection pumps supply fuel at very high pressure. Take care when working on the fuel injectors and fuel pipes.

⚠️ *Warning: Never expose the hands, face or any other part of the body to injector spray; the fuel can penetrate the skin with potentially fatal results.*

Remember...

DO

• Do use eye protection when using power tools, and when working under the vehicle.

• Do wear gloves or use barrier cream to protect your hands when necessary.

• Do get someone to check periodically that all is well when working alone on the vehicle.

• Do keep loose clothing and long hair well out of the way of moving mechanical parts.

• Do remove rings, wristwatch etc, before working on the vehicle – especially the electrical system.

• Do ensure that any lifting or jacking equipment has a safe working load rating adequate for the job.

DON'T

• Don't attempt to lift a heavy component which may be beyond your capability – get assistance.

• Don't rush to finish a job, or take unverified short cuts.

• Don't use ill-fitting tools which may slip and cause injury.

• Don't leave tools or parts lying around where someone can trip over them. Mop up oil and fuel spills at once.

• Don't allow children or pets to play in or near a vehicle being worked on.

Vehicle identification numbers

1 The vehicle identification number is stamped into the bulkhead behind the plastic scuttle panel and there is an additional sticker on the driver's side door pillar. The VIN is also visible through the windscreen, at the lower left hand corner **(see illustrations)**.

2 The engine number is stamped on a machined surface on the front side of the cylinder block, at the flywheel end on petrol engines **(see illustrations)**. On diesel engines, the number is stamped on a plate on the front of the cylinder block. The first part of the engine number gives the engine code – e.g. R9M.

3 The transmission number is on a label on top of the transmission housing **(see illustration)**.

5.1a VIN plate location on driver's side B-pillar

5.1b Unclip the trim panel to access the VIN on the rear bulkhead panel

5.1c The VIN is also on a plate visible through the base of the windscreen

5.2a Engine number (HRA2) - on front of cylinder block

5.2b Engine number (R9M) - on top of coolant pump housing in the cylinder block

5.3 Transmission number on the label

Buying spare parts

Spare parts are available from many sources, including maker's appointed garages, accessory shops, and motor factors. To be sure of obtaining the correct parts, it will sometimes be necessary to quote the vehicle identification number. If possible, it can also be useful to take the old parts along for positive identification. Items such as starter motors and alternators may be available under a service exchange scheme – any parts returned should be clean.

Our advice regarding spare parts is as follows.

Officially appointed garages

This is the best source of parts which are peculiar to your car, and which are not otherwise generally available (e.g. badges, interior trim, certain body panels, etc). It is also the only place at which you should buy parts if the vehicle is still under warranty.

Accessory shops

These are very good places to buy materials and components needed for the maintenance of your car (oil, air and fuel filters, light bulbs, drivebelts, greases, brake pads, touch-up paint, etc). Components of this nature sold by a reputable shop are usually of the same standard as those used by the car manufacturer.

Besides components, these shops also sell tools and general accessories, usually have convenient opening hours, charge lower prices, and can often be found close to home. Some accessory shops have parts counters where components needed for almost any repair job can be purchased or ordered.

Motor factors

Good factors will stock the more important components, which wear out comparatively quickly, and can sometimes supply individual components needed for the overhaul of a larger assembly (e.g. brake seals and hydraulic parts, bearing shells, pistons, valves). They may also handle work such as cylinder block reboring, crankshaft regrinding, etc.

Tyre and exhaust specialists

These outlets may be independent, or members of a local or national chain. They frequently offer competitive prices when compared with a main dealer or local garage, but it will pay to obtain several quotes before making a decision. When researching prices, also be sure to ask what "extras" may be added – for instance, fitting a new valve, balancing the wheel, and checking the tracking (front wheels) are all commonly charged on top of the price of a new tyre.

Other sources

Beware of parts or materials obtained from market stalls, car boot sales or similar outlets. Such items are not invariably sub-standard, but there is little chance of compensation if they do prove unsatisfactory. In the case of safety-critical components such as brake pads, there is the risk not only of financial loss, but also of an accident causing injury or death.

Second-hand components or assemblies obtained from a car breaker can be a good buy in some circumstances, but this sort of purchase is best made by the experienced DIY mechanic.

Modifications are a continuing and unpublicised process in vehicle manufacture, quite apart from major model changes. Spare parts manuals and lists are compiled upon a numerical basis, the individual vehicle identification numbers being essential to correct identification of the component concerned. When ordering spare parts, always give as much information as possible. Quote the car model; year of manufacture, body and engine numbers as appropriate.

Fault finding

Online assistance

1 Haynes.com provides a wealth of information about your vehicle, including repair tips and techniques; however, the specifics of diagnosing an issue on your particular vehicle is sometimes extremely specialised and intricate. If you're having difficulty diagnosing a problem, you may wish to judiciously engage in online research or request assistance from experts.

The source matters!

2 As we're all aware, information on the internet is only as reliable as the person or organisation who provides it. We suggest the following hierarchy when searching:

a) *The manufacturer or related source: Ideally, your source would be associated directly with the vehicle manufacturer or the manufacturer of the affected component(s). They are the most likely to be authoritative and generally have an interest in assuring diagnosis and repair are carried out safely and correctly.*

b) *Fee-based assistance: Some sites employ experts who assist owners with their vehicle diagnostics. Their fees are reasonable in comparison with the diagnostic charges you're likely to encounter at a dealership or repair workshop. Look for popular sites with many positive reviews.*

c) *Recommendation from an expert: Repair workshops who specialise in your vehicle type will likely be aware of online resources for your vehicle. Repair workshops may not readily divulge sources because they want to do the work for you. Nevertheless, they want positive relationships with potential customers and are unlikely to give you false information.*

d) *Owner forums: Information from online forums can be anything from first-rate to entirely wrong. The quality of information is not always obvious. Get involved with forums before you need help so you will know who you can trust. Search for confirmed fixes – If someone trustworthy shared the solution to a problem similar to yours, it might be your solution too.*

Introduction

3 The vehicle owner who does his or her own maintenance according to the recommended service schedules should not have to use this section of the manual very often. Modern component reliability is such that, provided those items subject to wear or deterioration are inspected or renewed at the specified intervals, sudden failure is comparatively rare. Faults do not usually just happen as a result of sudden failure, but develop over a period of time. Major mechanical failures in particular are usually preceded by characteristic symptoms over hundreds or even thousands of miles. Those components which do occasionally fail without warning are often small and easily carried in the vehicle.

4 With any fault finding, the first step is to decide where to begin investigations. Sometimes this is obvious, but on other occasions, a little detective work will be necessary. The owner who makes half a dozen haphazard adjustments or replacements may be successful in curing a fault (or its symptoms), but will be none the wiser if the fault recurs, and ultimately may have spent more time and money than was necessary. A calm and logical approach will be found to be more satisfactory in the long run. Always take into account any warning signs or abnormalities that may have been noticed in the period preceding the fault – power loss, high or low gauge readings, unusual smells, etc – and remember that failure of components such as fuses or spark plugs may only be pointers to some underlying fault.

5 The pages that follow provide an easy-reference guide to the more common problems which may occur during the operation of the vehicle. These problems and their possible causes are grouped under headings denoting various components or systems, such as Engine, Cooling system, etc. The Chapter which deals with the problem is also shown in brackets. Whatever the fault, certain basic principles apply. These are as follows:

Verify the fault. This is simply a matter of being sure that you know what the symptoms are before starting work. This is particularly important if you are investigating a fault for someone else, who may not have described it very accurately.

Don't overlook the obvious. For example, if the vehicle won't start, is there fuel in the tank? (Don't take anyone else's word on this particular point, and don't trust the fuel gauge either). If an electrical fault is indicated, look for loose or broken wires before digging out the test gear.

Cure the disease, not the symptom. Substituting a flat battery with a fully-charged one will get you off the hard shoulder, but if the underlying cause is not attended to, the new battery will go the same way. Similarly, changing oil-fouled spark plugs for a new set will get you moving again, but remember that the reason for the fouling (if it wasn't simply an incorrect grade of plug) will have to be established and corrected.

Don't take anything for granted. Particularly, don't forget that a 'new' component may itself be defective (especially if it's been rattling around in the boot for months), and don't leave components out of a fault diagnosis sequence just because they are new or recently-fitted. When you do finally diagnose a difficult fault, you'll probably realise that all the evidence was there from the start.

Consider what work, if any, has recently been carried out. Many faults arise through careless or hurried work. For instance, if any work has been performed under the bonnet, could some of the wiring have been dislodged or incorrectly routed, or a hose trapped? Have all the fasteners been properly tightened? Were new, genuine parts and new gaskets used? There is often a certain amount of detective work to be done in this case, as an apparently-unrelated task can have far-reaching consequences.

Engine

Engine difficult to start when cold

☐ Battery discharged (Chapter 5 Section 5)
☐ Battery terminal connections loose or corroded (Chapter 5 Section 3)
☐ Worn, faulty or incorrectly-gapped spark plugs (Chapter 1A Section 30)
☐ Fuel injection/engine management system fault (Chapter 6A or Chapter 6B)
☐ Other ignition system fault (Chapter 6A or Chapter 6B)
☐ Low cylinder compressions (Chapter 2D Section 2)

Engine difficult to start when hot

☐ Air filter element dirty or clogged (Chapter 1A or Chapter 1B)
☐ Fuel injection/engine management system fault (Chapter 6A or Chapter 6B)
☐ Other ignition system fault (Chapter 6A Section 7)
☐ Low cylinder compressions (Chapter 2D Section 2)

Starter motor noisy or excessively rough in engagement

☐ Starter pinion or flywheel ring gear teeth loose or broken (Chapter 5)
☐ Starter motor mounting bolts loose or missing (Chapter 5 Section 11)
☐ Starter motor internal components worn or damaged (Chapter 5 Section 11)

Engine starts, but stops immediately

☐ Loose or faulty electrical connections in the ignition circuit (Chapter 6A or Chapter 6B)
☐ Vacuum leak at the throttle housing or inlet manifold (Chapter 4A or Chapter 4B)
☐ Fuel injection/engine management system fault (Chapter 6A or Chapter 6B)

Engine (continued)

Engine idles erratically

- [ ] Air filter element clogged (Chapter 1A, 1B)
- [ ] Vacuum leak at the throttle housing, inlet manifold or associated hoses (Chapter 4A or Chapter 4B)
- [ ] Worn, faulty or incorrectly-gapped spark plugs (Chapter 1A Section 30)
- [ ] Uneven or low cylinder compressions (Chapter 2D Section 2)
- [ ] Camshaft lobes worn (Chapter 2A, Chapter 2B or Chapter 2C)
- [ ] Timing chain/belt incorrectly fitted (Chapter 2B or Chapter 2D)
- [ ] Fuel injection/engine management system fault (Chapter 6A or Chapter 6B)

Engine misfires at idle speed

- [ ] Worn, faulty or incorrectly-gapped spark plugs (Chapter 1A Section 30)
- [ ] Vacuum leak at the throttle housing, inlet manifold or associated hoses (Chapter 4A or Chapter 4B)
- [ ] Fuel injection/engine management system fault (Chapter 6A or Chapter 6B)
- [ ] Uneven or low cylinder compressions (Chapter 2D Section 2)
- [ ] Disconnected, leaking, or perished crankcase ventilation hoses (Chapter 4A or Chapter 4B)

Engine misfires throughout the driving speed range

- [ ] Fuel filter choked (Chapter 1A or Chapter 1B)
- [ ] Fuel pump faulty, or delivery pressure low (Chapter 4A or Chapter 4B)
- [ ] Fuel tank vent blocked, or fuel pipes restricted (Chapter 4A or Chapter 4B)
- [ ] Vacuum leak at the throttle housing, inlet manifold or associated hoses (Chapter 4A or Chapter 4B)
- [ ] Worn, faulty or incorrectly-gapped spark plugs (Chapter 1A Section 30)
- [ ] Faulty ignition coil (Chapter 6A Section 7)
- [ ] Uneven or low cylinder compressions (Chapter 2D Section 2)
- [ ] Fuel injection/engine management system fault (Chapter 6A or Chapter 6B)

Engine hesitates on acceleration

- [ ] Worn, faulty or incorrectly-gapped spark plugs (Chapter 1A Section 30)
- [ ] Vacuum leak at the throttle housing, inlet manifold or associated hoses (Chapter 4A or Chapter 4B)
- [ ] Fuel injection/engine management system fault (Chapter 6A or Chapter 6B)

Engine stalls

- [ ] Vacuum leak at the throttle housing, inlet manifold or associated hoses (Chapter 4A or Chapter 4B)
- [ ] Fuel filter choked (Chapter 1B Section 26)
- [ ] Fuel pump faulty, or delivery pressure low (Chapter 4A Section 6 or Chapter 4B Section 4)
- [ ] Fuel tank vent blocked, or fuel pipes restricted (Chapter 4A Section 7 or Chapter 4B Section 5)
- [ ] Fuel injection/engine management system fault (Chapter 6A or Chapter 6B)

Engine lacks power

- [ ] Timing chain/belt incorrectly fitted (Chapter 2B or Chapter 2D)
- [ ] Fuel filter choked (Chapter 1B Section 26)
- [ ] Fuel pump faulty, or delivery pressure low (Chapter 4A or Chapter 4B)
- [ ] Uneven or low cylinder compressions (Chapter 2D Section 2)
- [ ] Worn, faulty or incorrectly-gapped spark plugs (Chapter 1A Section 30)
- [ ] Vacuum leak at the throttle housing, inlet manifold or associated hoses (Chapter 4A or Chapter 4B)
- [ ] Fuel injection/engine management system fault (Chapter 6A or Chapter 6B)

- [ ] Brakes binding (Chapter 9 Section 1)
- [ ] Clutch slipping – manual transmission (Chapter 8 Section 6)

Engine backfires

- [ ] Timing chain/belt incorrectly fitted (Chapter 2B or Chapter 2D)
- [ ] Vacuum leak at the throttle housing, inlet manifold or associated hoses (Chapter 4A or Chapter 4B)
- [ ] Fuel injection/engine management system fault (Chapter 6A or Chapter 6B)

Oil pressure warning light illuminated with engine running

- [ ] Low oil level, or incorrect oil grade (Chapter 1A or Chapter 1B)
- [ ] Faulty oil pressure warning light switch (Chapter 2A, Chapter 2B or Chapter 2C)
- [ ] Worn engine bearings and/or oil pump (Chapter 2A, Chapter 2B or Chapter 2C)
- [ ] High engine operating temperature (Chapter 3 Section 8)
- [ ] Oil pressure relief valve defective (Chapter 2A, Chapter 2B or Chapter 2C)
- [ ] Oil pick-up strainer clogged (Chapter 2A, Chapter 2B or Chapter 2C)

Engine runs-on after switching off

- [ ] Excessive carbon build-up in engine (Chapter 2A, Chapter 2B or Chapter 2C)
- [ ] High engine operating temperature (Chapter 3 Section 8)
- [ ] Fuel injection/engine management system fault (Chapter 6A or Chapter 6B)

Engine noises

Pre-ignition (pinking) or knocking during acceleration or under load

- [ ] Ignition timing incorrect/ignition system fault (Chapter 6A or Chapter 6B)
- [ ] Incorrect grade of spark plug (Chapter 1A Section 30)
- [ ] Incorrect grade of fuel (Chapter 4A or Chapter 4B)
- [ ] Vacuum leak at the throttle housing, inlet manifold or associated hoses (Chapter 4A or Chapter 4B)
- [ ] Excessive carbon build-up in engine (Chapter 2A, Chapter 2B or Chapter 2C)
- [ ] Fuel injection/engine management system fault (Chapter 6A or Chapter 6B)

Whistling or wheezing noises

- [ ] Leaking inlet manifold or throttle housing gasket (Chapter 4A or Chapter 4B)
- [ ] Leaking exhaust manifold gasket or pipe-to-manifold joint (Chapter 4A or Chapter 4B)
- [ ] Leaking vacuum hose (Chapter 4A or Chapter 4B)
- [ ] Blowing cylinder head gasket (Chapter 2A, Chapter 2B or Chapter 2C)

Tapping or rattling noises

- [ ] Worn valve gear or camshaft (Chapter 2A, Chapter 2B or Chapter 2C)
- [ ] Ancillary component fault (coolant pump, alternator, etc) (Chapter 3 or Chapter 5)

Knocking or thumping noises

- [ ] Worn big-end bearings (regular heavy knocking, perhaps less under load) (Chapter 2D Section 21)
- [ ] Worn main bearings (rumbling and knocking, perhaps worsening under load) (Chapter 2D Section 21)
- [ ] Piston slap (most noticeable when cold) (Chapter 2D Section 25)
- [ ] Ancillary component fault (coolant pump, alternator, etc) (Chapter 2A, Chapter 2B or Chapter 2C)

Cooling system

Overheating

- [ ] Insufficient coolant in system (Chapter 1A or Chapter 1B)
- [ ] Thermostat faulty (Chapter 3 Section 6)
- [ ] Radiator core blocked, or grille restricted (Chapter 3 Section 5)
- [ ] Electric cooling fan faulty (Chapter 3 Section 7)
- [ ] Pressure cap faulty (Chapter 3 Section 4)
- [ ] Ignition timing incorrect/ignition system fault (Chapter 4A or Chapter 4B)
- [ ] Inaccurate temperature gauge sender unit (Chapter 3 Section 8)
- [ ] Airlock in cooling system (Chapter 1A or Chapter 1B)

Overcooling

- [ ] Thermostat faulty (Chapter 3 Section 6)
- [ ] Inaccurate temperature gauge sender unit (Chapter 3 Section 8)

External coolant leakage

- [ ] Deteriorated or damaged hoses or hose clips (Chapter 1A or Chapter 1B)
- [ ] Radiator core or heater matrix leaking (Chapter 3 Section 5)
- [ ] Pressure cap faulty (Chapter 3 Section 4)
- [ ] Coolant pump seal leaking (Chapter 3 Section 9)
- [ ] Boiling due to overheating (Chapter 3 Section 2)
- [ ] Cylinder block core plug leaking (Chapter 2D Section 18)

Internal coolant leakage

- [ ] Leaking cylinder head gasket (Chapter 2A, Chapter 2B or Chapter 2C)
- [ ] Cracked cylinder head or cylinder bore (Chapter 2A, Chapter 2B or Chapter 2C)

Corrosion

- [ ] Infrequent draining and flushing (Chapter 1A or Chapter 1B)
- [ ] Incorrect coolant mixture or inappropriate coolant type (Chapter 1A or Chapter 1B)

Fuel and exhaust systems

Excessive fuel consumption

- [ ] Air filter element dirty or clogged (Chapter 1A or Chapter 1B)
- [ ] Fuel injection/engine management system fault (Chapter 6A or Chapter 6B)
- [ ] Ignition timing incorrect/ignition system fault (Chapter 6A or Chapter 6B)
- [ ] Tyres under-inflated (Chapter 1A or Chapter 1B)

Fuel leakage and/or fuel odour

- [ ] Damaged or corroded fuel tank, pipes or connections (Chapter 4A or Chapter 4B)

Excessive noise or fumes from exhaust system

- [ ] Leaking exhaust system or manifold joints (Chapter 4A or Chapter 4B)
- [ ] Leaking, corroded or damaged silencers or pipe (Chapter 4A or Chapter 4B)
- [ ] Broken mountings causing body or suspension contact (Chapter 1A or Chapter 1B)

Clutch

Pedal travels to floor – no pressure or very little resistance

- [ ] Leaking hydraulic fluid (Chapter 8 Section 2)
- [ ] Faulty slave or master cylinder (Chapter 8 Section 3 or 4)
- [ ] Broken clutch release bearing or fork (Chapter 8 Section 7)
- [ ] Broken diaphragm spring in clutch pressure plate (Chapter 8 Section 6)

Clutch fails to disengage (unable to select gears)

- [ ] Leaking hydraulic fluid (Chapter 8 Section 2)
- [ ] Clutch friction plate sticking on gearbox input shaft splines (Chapter 8 Section 6)
- [ ] Clutch friction plate sticking to flywheel or pressure plate (Chapter 8 Section 6)
- [ ] Faulty pressure plate assembly (Chapter 8 Section 6)
- [ ] Clutch release mechanism worn or incorrectly assembled (Chapter 8 Section 7)

Clutch slips (engine speed increases, with no increase in vehicle speed)

- [ ] Leaking hydraulic fluid (Chapter 8 Section 2)
- [ ] Clutch friction plate linings excessively worn (Chapter 8 Section 6)
- [ ] Clutch friction plate linings contaminated with oil or grease (Chapter 8 Section 6)
- [ ] Faulty pressure plate or weak diaphragm spring (Chapter 8 Section 6)

Judder as clutch is engaged

- [ ] Clutch friction plate linings contaminated with oil or grease (Chapter 8 Section 6)
- [ ] Clutch friction plate linings excessively worn (Chapter 8 Section 6)
- [ ] Leaking hydraulic fluid (Chapter 8 Section 2)
- [ ] Faulty or distorted pressure plate or diaphragm spring (Chapter 8 Section 6)
- [ ] Worn or loose engine or gearbox mountings (Chapter 2A, Chapter 2B or Chapter 2C)
- [ ] Clutch friction plate hub or gearbox input shaft splines worn (Chapter 8 Section 6)

Noise when depressing or releasing clutch pedal

- [ ] Worn clutch release bearing (Chapter 8 Section 4)
- [ ] Worn or dry clutch pedal bushes (Chapter 8 Section 5)
- [ ] Faulty pressure plate assembly (Chapter 8 Section 6)
- [ ] Pressure plate diaphragm spring broken (Chapter 8 Section 6)
- [ ] Broken clutch friction plate cushioning springs (Chapter 8 Section 6)

Manual transmission

Noisy in neutral with engine running

- ☐ Input shaft bearings worn (noise apparent with clutch pedal released, but not when depressed) (Chapter 7 Section 6)*
- ☐ Clutch release bearing worn (noise apparent with clutch pedal depressed, possibly less when released) (Chapter 8 Section 4)

Noisy in one particular gear

- ☐ Worn, damaged or chipped gear teeth (Chapter 7 Section 6)*

Difficulty engaging gears

- ☐ Clutch fault (Chapter 8 Section 6)
- ☐ Oil level low (Chapter 7 Section 2)
- ☐ Worn or damaged gearchange linkage (Chapter 7 Section 3)
- ☐ Worn synchroniser units (Chapter 7 Section 6)*

Jumps out of gear

- ☐ Worn or damaged gearchange linkage (Chapter 7 Section 3)
- ☐ Worn synchroniser units (Chapter 7 Section 6)*
- ☐ Worn selector forks (Chapter 7 Section 6)*

Vibration

- ☐ Lack of oil (Chapter 7 Section 2)
- ☐ Worn bearings (Chapter 7 Section 6)*

Lubricant leaks

- ☐ Leaking driveshaft oil seal (Chapter 7 Section 4)
- ☐ Leaking housing joint (Chapter 7 Section 6)*
- ☐ Leaking input shaft oil seal (Chapter 7 Section 4)*
- ☐ Leaking selector shaft oil seal (Chapter 7 Section 4)

Although the corrective action necessary to remedy the symptoms described is beyond the scope of the home mechanic, the above information should be helpful in isolating the cause of the condition, so that the owner can communicate clearly with a professional mechanic.

Driveshafts

Clicking or knocking noise on turns (at slow speed on full-lock)

- ☐ Lack of constant velocity joint lubricant, possibly due to damaged gaiter (Chapter 8 Section 9)
- ☐ Worn outer constant velocity joint (Chapter 8 Section 8)

Vibration when accelerating or decelerating

- ☐ Worn inner constant velocity joint (Chapter 8 Section 8)
- ☐ Bent or distorted driveshaft (Chapter 8 Section 8)

Braking system

Vehicle pulls to one side under braking

Note: *Before assuming that a brake problem exists, make sure that the tyres are in good condition and correctly inflated, that the front wheel alignment is correct, and that the vehicle is not loaded with weight in an unequal manner. Apart from checking the condition of all pipe and hose connections, any faults occurring on the anti-lock braking system should be referred to a Nissan dealer for diagnosis.*

- ☐ Worn, defective, damaged or contaminated brake pads on one side (Chapter 9 Section 5 or 6)
- ☐ Seized or partially-seized front brake caliper or rear wheel caliper piston (Chapter 9 Section 9 or 10)
- ☐ A mixture of brake pad materials fitted between sides (Chapter 9 Section 5 or 6)
- ☐ Brake caliper or backplate mounting bolts loose (Chapter 9 Section 9 or 10)
- ☐ Worn or damaged steering or suspension components (Chapter 1A Section 20)

Noise (grinding or high-pitched squeal) when brakes applied

- ☐ Brake pad friction lining material worn down to metal backing (Chapter 9 Section 5 or 6)
- ☐ Excessive corrosion of brake disc. (May be apparent after the vehicle has been standing for some time (Chapter 9 Section 7 or 8)
- ☐ Foreign object (stone chipping, etc) trapped between brake disc and shield (Chapter 1A Section 18)

Excessive brake pedal travel

- ☐ Faulty master cylinder (Chapter 9 Section 11)
- ☐ Air in hydraulic system (Chapter 9 Section 3)
- ☐ Faulty vacuum servo unit (Chapter 9 Section 14)

Brake pedal feels spongy when depressed

- ☐ Air in hydraulic system (Chapter 9 Section 3)
- ☐ Deteriorated flexible rubber brake hoses (Chapter 1A Section 15)
- ☐ Master cylinder mounting nuts loose (Chapter 9 Section 11)
- ☐ Faulty master cylinder (Chapter 9 Section 11)

Excessive brake pedal effort required to stop vehicle

- ☐ Faulty vacuum servo unit (Chapter 9 Section 14 or 15)
- ☐ Disconnected, damaged or insecure brake servo vacuum hose (Chapter 9 Section 15)
- ☐ Primary or secondary hydraulic circuit failure (Chapter 9 Section 3)
- ☐ Seized brake caliper piston(s) (Chapter 9 Section 9 or 10)
- ☐ Brake pads incorrectly fitted (Chapter 9 Section 5 or 6)
- ☐ Incorrect grade of brake pads fitted (Chapter 9 Section 5 or 6)
- ☐ Brake pads contaminated (Chapter 9 Section 5 or 6)

Judder felt through brake pedal or steering wheel when braking

- ☐ Excessive run-out or distortion of discs (Chapter 9 Section 7 or 8)
- ☐ Brake pads worn (Chapter 9 Section 5 or 6)
- ☐ Brake caliper or brake backplate mounting bolts loose (Chapter 9 Section 9 or 10)
- ☐ Wear in suspension or steering components or mountings (Chapter 1A Section 20)

Brakes binding

- ☐ Seized brake caliper or wheel cylinder piston(s) (Chapter 9 Section 9 or 10)
- ☐ Faulty master cylinder (Chapter 9 Section 11)

Rear wheels locking under normal braking

- ☐ Rear brake pads contaminated (Chapter 9 Section 6)

Suspension and steering

Vehicle pulls to one side

Note: *Before diagnosing suspension or steering faults, be sure that the trouble is not due to incorrect tyre pressures, mixtures of tyre types, or binding brakes.*

☐ Defective tyre (Chapter 1A or Chapter 1B)
☐ Excessive wear in suspension or steering components (Chapter 1A Section 20)
☐ Incorrect front wheel alignment (Chapter 10 Section 17)
☐ Accident damage to steering or suspension components (Chapter 1A Section 20)

Wheel wobble and vibration

☐ Front roadwheels out of balance (vibration felt mainly through the steering wheel) (Chapter 1A Section 22)
☐ Rear roadwheels out of balance (vibration felt throughout the vehicle) (Chapter 1A Section 22)
☐ Roadwheels damaged or distorted (Chapter 1B Section 23)
☐ Faulty or damaged tyre (Chapter 1A or Chapter 1B)
☐ Worn steering or suspension joints, bushes or components (Chapter 1B Section 21)
☐ Wheel nuts loose (Chapter 1A or Chapter 1B)

Excessive pitching and/or rolling around corners, or during braking

☐ Defective shock absorbers (Chapter 10 Section 3)
☐ Broken or weak spring and/or suspension component (Chapter 10 Section 3)
☐ Worn or damaged anti-roll bar or mountings (Chapter 10 Section 6)

Wandering or general instability

☐ Incorrect front wheel alignment (Chapter 10)
☐ Worn steering or suspension joints, bushes or components (Chapter 1A Section 20)
☐ Roadwheels out of balance (Chapter 10)
☐ Faulty or damaged tyre (Chapter 1A or Chapter 1B)
☐ Wheel nuts loose (Chapter 1A or Chapter 1B)
☐ Defective shock absorbers (Chapter 10 Section 3 or 8)

Excessively-stiff steering

☐ Lack of steering gear lubricant (Chapter 10 Section 14)
☐ Seized track rod end balljoint or suspension balljoint (Chapter 10 Section 16)
☐ Broken or incorrectly-adjusted auxiliary drivebelt – power steering (Chapter 1A or Chapter 1B)
☐ Incorrect front wheel alignment (Chapter 10 Section 17)
☐ Steering rack or column bent or damaged (Chapter 10 Section 14)

Excessive play in steering

☐ Worn steering track rod end balljoints (Chapter 10 Section 16)
☐ Worn rack-and-pinion steering gear (Chapter 10 Section 14)
☐ Worn steering or suspension joints, bushes or components (Chapter 1A Section 20)

Lack of power assistance

☐ Broken or incorrectly-adjusted auxiliary drivebelt (Chapter 1A or Chapter 1B)
☐ Faulty power steering pump/motor (Chapter 10 Section 13)
☐ Faulty rack-and-pinion steering gear (Chapter 10 Section 14)

Tyre wear excessive

Tyres worn on inside or outside edges

☐ Tyres under-inflated (wear on both edges) (Chapter 1A or Chapter 1B)
☐ Incorrect camber or castor angles (wear on one edge only) (Chapter 10 Section 17)
☐ Worn steering or suspension joints, bushes or components (Chapter 1B Section 21)
☐ Excessively-hard cornering.
☐ Accident damage.

Tyre treads exhibit feathered edges

☐ Incorrect toe setting (Chapter 10 Section 17)

Tyres worn in centre of tread

☐ Tyres over-inflated (Chapter 1A or Chapter 1B)

Tyres worn on inside and outside edges

☐ Tyres under-inflated (Chapter 1A or Chapter 1B)

Tyres worn unevenly

☐ Tyres/wheels out of balance (Chapter 10)
☐ Excessive wheel or tyre run-out (Chapter 10)
☐ Worn shock absorbers (Chapter 10 Section 3 or 8)
☐ Faulty tyre (Chapter 1A or Chapter 1B)

Electrical system

Battery will not hold a charge for more than a few days

Note: *For problems associated with the starting system, refer to the faults listed under 'Engine' earlier in this Section.*

☐ Battery defective internally (Chapter 5 Section 4)
☐ Battery terminal connections loose or corroded (Chapter 5 Section 4)
☐ Auxiliary drivebelt worn or incorrectly adjusted (Chapter 1A or Chapter 1B)
☐ Alternator not charging at correct output (Chapter 5 Section 7)
☐ Alternator or voltage regulator faulty (Chapter 5 Section 5)
☐ Short-circuit causing continual battery drain (Chapter 5 Section 3)

Ignition/no-charge warning light remains illuminated with engine running

☐ Auxiliary drivebelt broken, worn, or incorrectly adjusted (Chapter 1A or Chapter 1B)
☐ Alternator brushes worn, sticking, or dirty (Chapter 5 Section 7)
☐ Alternator brush springs weak or broken (Chapter 5 Section 7)
☐ Internal fault in alternator or voltage regulator (Chapter 5 Section 7)
☐ Broken, disconnected, or loose wiring in charging circuit (Chapter 5 Section 5)

Electrical system (continued)

Ignition/no-charge warning light fails to come on

- ☐ Warning light bulb blown (Chapter 12 Section 2)
- ☐ Broken, disconnected, or loose wiring in warning light circuit (Chapter 5 Section 5)
- ☐ Alternator faulty (Chapter 5 Section 7)

Lights inoperative

- ☐ Bulb blown (Chapter 12 Section 5 or 6)
- ☐ Corrosion of bulb or bulbholder contacts (Chapter 12 Section 5 or 6)
- ☐ Blown fuse (Chapter 12 Section 3)
- ☐ Faulty relay (Chapter 12 Section 3)
- ☐ Broken, loose, or disconnected wiring (Chapter 12 Section 2)
- ☐ Faulty switch (Chapter 12 Section 4)

Instrument readings inaccurate or erratic

Fuel or temperature gauges give no reading

- ☐ Faulty gauge sender unit (Chapter 12 Section 9)
- ☐ Wiring open-circuit (Chapter 12 Section 2)
- ☐ Faulty gauge (Chapter 12)

Fuel or temperature gauges give continuous maximum reading

- ☐ Faulty gauge sender unit (Chapter 12)
- ☐ Wiring short-circuit (Chapter 12)
- ☐ Faulty gauge (Chapter 12)

Horn inoperative, or unsatisfactory in operation

Horn operates all the time

- ☐ Horn push either earthed or stuck down (Chapter 12 Section 4)
- ☐ Horn cable-to-horn push earthed (Chapter 10 Section 11)

Horn fails to operate

- ☐ Blown fuse (Chapter 12 Section 3)
- ☐ Cable or cable connections loose, broken or disconnected (Chapter 12)
- ☐ Faulty horn (Chapter 12 Section 10)

Horn emits intermittent or unsatisfactory sound

- ☐ Cable connections loose (Chapter 10 Section 11)
- ☐ Horn mountings loose (Chapter 10 Section 11)
- ☐ Faulty horn (Chapter 12 Section 10)

Windscreen/tailgate wipers inoperative, or unsatisfactory in operation

Wipers fail to operate, or operate very slowly

- ☐ Wiper blades stuck to screen, or linkage seized or binding (Chapter 12 Section 12)
- ☐ Blown fuse (Chapter 12 Section 3)
- ☐ Cable or cable connections loose, broken or disconnected (Chapter 12)
- ☐ Faulty relay (Chapter 12 Section 3)
- ☐ Faulty wiper motor (Chapter 12 Section 12)

Wiper blades sweep over too large or too small an area of the glass

- ☐ Wiper arms incorrectly positioned on spindles (Chapter 12 Section 11)
- ☐ Excessive wear of wiper linkage (Chapter 12 Section 12)
- ☐ Wiper motor or linkage mountings loose or insecure (Chapter 12 Section 12)

Wiper blades fail to clean the glass effectively

- ☐ Wiper blade rubbers worn or perished (Chapter 12 Section 11)
- ☐ Wiper arm tension springs broken, or arm pivots seized (Chapter 12 Section 11)
- ☐ Insufficient windscreen washer additive to adequately remove road film (Chapter 1A or Chapter 1B)

Windscreen/tailgate washers inoperative, or unsatisfactory in operation

One or more washer jets inoperative

- ☐ Blocked washer jet (Chapter 12 Section 14)
- ☐ Disconnected, kinked or restricted fluid hose (Chapter 12 Section 14)
- ☐ Insufficient fluid in washer reservoir (Chapter 1A or Chapter 1B)

Washer pump fails to operate

- ☐ Broken or disconnected wiring or connections (Chapter 12)
- ☐ Blown fuse (Chapter 12 Section 3)
- ☐ Faulty washer switch (Chapter 12 Section 4)
- ☐ Faulty washer pump (Chapter 12 Section 14)

Washer pump runs for some time before fluid is emitted from jets

- ☐ Faulty one-way valve in fluid supply hose (Chapter 12)

Electric windows inoperative, or unsatisfactory in operation

Window glass will only move in one direction

- ☐ Faulty switch (Chapter 12 Section 4)

Window glass slow to move

- ☐ Incorrectly-adjusted door glass guide channels (Chapter 11 Section 13)
- ☐ Regulator seized or damaged, or in need of lubrication (Chapter 11 Section 13)
- ☐ Door internal components or trim fouling regulator (Chapter 11)
- ☐ Faulty motor (Chapter 11 Section 13)

Window glass fails to move

- ☐ Incorrectly-adjusted door glass guide channels (Chapter 11 Section 13)
- ☐ Blown fuse (Chapter 12 Section 3)
- ☐ Faulty relay (Chapter 12 Section 3)
- ☐ Broken or disconnected wiring or connections (Chapter 12)
- ☐ Faulty motor (Chapter 11 Section 13)

Central locking system inoperative, or unsatisfactory in operation

Complete system failure

- ☐ Blown fuse (Chapter 12 Section 3)
- ☐ Faulty relay (Chapter 12 Section 3)
- ☐ Broken or disconnected wiring or connections (Chapter 12)
- ☐ Faulty control unit (Chapter 12)

Latch locks but will not unlock, or unlocks but will not lock

- ☐ Faulty master switch (Chapter 12 Section 4)
- ☐ Broken or disconnected latch operating rods or levers (Chapter 11)
- ☐ Faulty relay (Chapter 12 Section 3)
- ☐ Faulty control unit (Chapter 12)

One solenoid/motor fails to operate

- ☐ Broken or disconnected wiring or connections (Chapter 12)
- ☐ Faulty solenoid/motor (Chapter 11 Section 12)
- ☐ Broken, binding or disconnected latch operating rods or levers (Chapter 11 Section 12)
- ☐ Fault in door latch (Chapter 11 Section 12)

The following pages are intended to help in dealing with common roadside emergencies and breakdowns. You will find more detailed fault finding information on the previoius pages, and repair information in the main chapters.

If your car won't start and the starter motor doesn't turn

- ☐ If it's a model with automatic transmission, make sure the selector is in the P or N position.
- ☐ Open the bonnet and make sure that the battery terminals are clean and tight.
- ☐ Switch on the headlights and try to start the engine. If the headlights go very dim when you're trying to start, the battery is probably flat. Get out of trouble by jump starting (see next page) using a friend's car.

If your car won't start even though the starter motor turns as normal

- ☐ Is there fuel in the tank?
- ☐ Is there moisture on electrical components under the bonnet? Switch off the ignition, and then wipe off any obvious dampness with a dry cloth. Spray a water-repellent aerosol product (WD-40 or equivalent) on ignition and fuel system electrical connectors like those shown in the photos. Pay special attention to the ignition coils wiring connector. (Note that diesel engines do not normally suffer from damp.
- ☐ Is there a fault code stored in the ECU, check for codes using a fault code reader, plugged into the diagnostic plug on the lower part of the facia (see illustration).

Check for fault codes stored in the ECU

Jump starting will get you out of trouble, but you must correct whatever made the battery go flat in the first place. There are three possibilities:

1 *The battery has been drained by repeated attempts to start, or by leaving the lights on.*

2 *The charging system is not working properly (alternator drivebelt slack or broken, alternator wiring fault or alternator itself faulty).*

3 *The battery itself is at fault (electrolyte low, or battery worn out).*

When jump-starting a car, observe the following precautions:

✓ Before connecting the booster battery, make sure that the ignition is switched off.

Caution: Remove the key in case the central locking engages when the jump leads are connected

✓ Ensure that all electrical equipment (lights, heater, wipers, etc) is switched off.
✓ Take note of any special precautions printed on the battery case.
✓ Make sure that the booster battery is the same voltage as the discharged one in the vehicle.

Jump starting

✓ If the battery is being jump-started from the battery in another vehicle, the two vehicles MUST NOT TOUCH each other.

✓ Make sure that the transmission is in neutral (or PARK, in the case of automatic transmission).

Budget jump leads can be a false economy, as they often do not pass enough current to start large capacity or diesel engines. They can also get hot.

1 Connect one end of the red jump lead to the positive (+) terminal of the flat battery.

2 Connect the other end of the red lead to the positive (+) terminal of the booster battery.

3 Connect one end of the black jump lead to the negative (-) terminal of the booster battery.

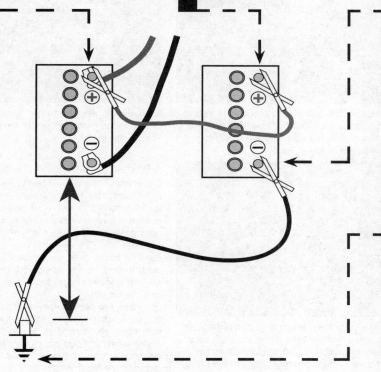

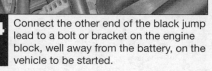

4 Connect the other end of the black jump lead to a bolt or bracket on the engine block, well away from the battery, on the vehicle to be started.

5 Make sure that the jump leads will not come into contact with the fan, drive-belts or other moving parts of the engine.

6 Start the engine using the booster battery and run it at idle speed. Switch on the lights, rear window demister and heater blower motor, then disconnect the jump leads in the reverse order of connection. Turn off the lights etc.

Wheel changing

The following procedure is for early, lower specification models, which have spare wheels supplied. On later high specification models, there is no spare wheel supplied, follow the instructions on the pump in the rear luggage compartment to inflate a punctured wheel.

 Warning: Do not change a wheel in a situation where you risk being hit by another vehicle. On busy roads, try to stop in a lay-by or a gateway. Be wary of passing traffic while changing the wheel – it is easy to become distracted by the job in hand.

Preparation

- ☐ When a puncture occurs, stop as soon as it is safe to do so.
- ☐ Park on firm level ground, if possible, and well out of the way of other traffic.
- ☐ Use hazard warning lights if necessary.
- ☐ If you have one, use a warning triangle to alert other drivers of your presence.
- ☐ Apply the handbrake and engage first or reverse gear (or Park on models with automatic transmission).
- ☐ If the ground is soft, use a flat piece of wood to spread the load under the foot of the jack.
- ☐ Place a chock against the wheel diagonally opposite the wheel to be removed, or use a large stone (or similar) to stop the car rolling

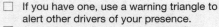

The spare wheel and tools are stored in the luggage compartment, lift up the floor panel/carpet. The tool kit is located to the side of the spare wheel.

Unscrew the centre fastener and remove the spare wheel from the luggage compartment.

Where anti-theft wheel nuts are fitted, unscrew the anti-theft nut using the special tool provided – normally stored in the passenger glovebox or toolkit.

With the vehicle still on the ground, use the tool provided to slacken each wheel nut by half a turn.

Make sure the jack is located on firm ground, and engage the jack head correctly with the sill. Then raise the jack until the wheel is raised clear of the ground.

Unscrew the wheel nuts and remove the wheel. Place the wheel under the vehicle sill in case the jack fails.

Fit the spare wheel and screw in the bolts. Lightly tighten the nuts with the wheel brace then lower the car to the ground.

Securely tighten the wheel nuts in a diagonal sequence then refit the wheel trim/hub cap/wheel nut covers (as applicable). Stow the punctured wheel and tools back in the boot, and secure them in position.

Finally...

- ☐ Remove the wheel chock.
- ☐ Check the tyre pressure on the wheel just fitted. If it is low, or if you don't have a pressure gauge with you, drive slowly to the next garage and inflate the tyre to the correct pressure.
- ☐ The wheel nuts should be slackened and retightened to the specified torque at the earliest possible opportunity (see Chapter 1A or Chapter 1B).
- ☐ Have the damaged tyre or wheel repaired as soon as possible, or another puncture will leave you stranded. **Note:** *If a compact spare wheel is fitted (as pictured), speed and distance restrictions apply. Drive with caution and refit the repaired tyre as soon as possible.*

Towing

When all else fails, you may find yourself having to get a tow home – or of course you may be helping somebody else. Long-distance recovery should only be done by a garage or breakdown service. For shorter distances, DIY towing using another car is easy enough, but observe the following points:

☐ Nissan insist that vehicles with automatic transmission must not be towed with the front wheels on the ground. Consequently, a recovery truck cable of lifting the front of the vehicle must be used.

☐ Use a proper tow-rope – they are not expensive. The vehicle being towed must display an ON TOW sign in its rear window.

☐ Always turn the ignition key to the 'on' position when the vehicle is being towed, so that the steering lock is released, and that the direction indicator and brake lights work.

☐ The towing eye is kept under the rear luggage compartment, with the spare wheel (where supplied – see wheel changing). To fit the eye, unclip the access cover from the relevant bumper and screw the eye firmly into position **(see illustrations)**.

☐ Note that greater-than-usual pedal pressure will be required to operate the brakes, since the vacuum servo unit is only operational with the engine running.

☐ Before being towed, release the parking brake and select neutral on the transmission.

☐ The driver of the car being towed must keep the tow-rope taut at all times to avoid snatching.

☐ Make sure that both drivers know the route before setting off.

☐ Do not exceed 30 mph, or a distance of 30 miles. Drive smoothly and allow plenty of time for slowing down at junctions.

The towing eye is located under the rear luggage compartment

Unclip the front cover and then screw the towing eye in securely. . .

. . . or screw into the rear of the vehicle

Identifying leaks

Puddles on the garage floor or drive, or obvious wetness under the bonnet or underneath the car, suggest a leak that needs investigating. It can sometimes be difficult to decide where the leak is coming from, especially if an engine undershield is fitted. Leaking oil or fluid can also be blown rearwards by the passage of air under the car, giving a false impression of where the problem lies.

 Warning: Most automotive oils and fluids are poisonous. Wash them off skin, and change out of contaminated clothing, without delay.

> **HAYNES HiNT**
> *The smell of a fluid leaking from the car may provide a clue to what's leaking. Some fluids are distinctively coloured. It may help to remove the engine undershield, clean the car carefully and to park it over some clean paper overnight as an aid to locating the source of the leak. Remember that some leaks may only occur while the engine is running.*

Sump oil

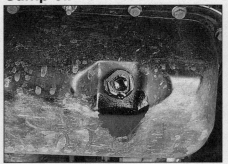

Engine oil may leak from the drain plug...

Oil from filter

...or from the base of the oil filter.

Gearbox oil

Gearbox oil can leak from the seals at the inboard ends of the driveshafts.

Antifreeze

Leaking antifreeze often leaves a crystalline deposit like this.

Brake fluid

A leak occurring at a wheel is almost certainly brake fluid.

Jacking and vehicle support

The jack supplied with the vehicle tool kit should only be used for changing the roadwheels in an emergency – see Wheel changing, previously in this Chapter. When carrying out any other kind of work, raise the vehicle using a hydraulic ('workshop' or 'trolley') jack, and always supplement the jack with axle stands positioned under the vehicle jacking points.

When using a hydraulic jack or axle stands, always position the jack head or axle stand head under one of the relevant jacking points **(see illustration)** (note that the jacking points for use with the vehicle jack are different from those for a hydraulic trolley jack). Nissan recommend the use of adapters when supporting the vehicle with axle stands – the adapters should be grooved, and fit over the sill edge to prevent the vehicle weight damaging the sill. **Do not** jack the vehicle under the sump or any of the steering or suspension components other than those indicated.

Only ever jack the vehicle up on a solid, level surface. If there is even a slight slope, take great care that the vehicle cannot move as the wheels are lifted off the ground. Jacking up on an uneven or gravelled surface is not recommended, as the weight of the vehicle will not be evenly distributed, and the jack may slip as the vehicle is raised.

As far as possible, do not leave the vehicle unattended once it has been raised, particularly if children are playing nearby.

Before jacking up the front of the car, ensure that the handbrake is firmly applied. When jacking up the rear of the car, place wooden chocks in front of the front wheels, and engage first gear (or P).

The jack supplied with the vehicle locates in the position provided in the sill. Ensure that the jack head is correctly engaged before attempting to raise the vehicle.

Note that inexpensive hard rubber inserts are available which locate into the sill jacking point recesses. The use of these inserts minimises the risk of damage to the plastic jacking point mouldings when using axle stands or a trolley/workshop jack.

When jacking or supporting the vehicle at these points, always use a block of wood between the jack head or axle stand, and the vehicle body. It is also considered good practice to use a large block of wood when supporting under other areas, to spread the load over a wider area, and reduce the risk of damage to the underside of the car (it also helps to prevent the underbody coating from being damaged by the jack or axle stand). **Do not** jack the vehicle under any other part of the sill, engine sump, floor pan, subframe, or directly under any of the steering or suspension components.

⚠ *Warning: Never work under, around, or near a raised vehicle, unless it is adequately supported on stands. Do not rely on a jack alone, as even a hydraulic jack could fail under load. Makeshift methods should not be used to lift and support the car during servicing work.*

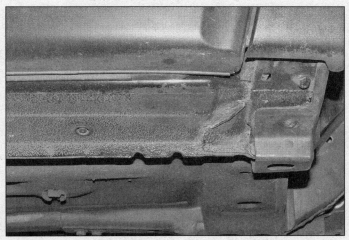

The jacking point as indicated by two cut-outs on the lower edge of the sill

This is a guide to getting your vehicle through the MOT test. Obviously it will not be possible to examine the vehicle to the same standard as the professional MOT tester. However, working through the following checks will enable you to identify any problem areas before submitting the vehicle for the test.

It has only been possible to summarise the test requirements here, based on the regulations in force at the time of printing. Test standards are becoming increasingly stringent, although there are some exemptions for older vehicles.

An assistant will be needed to help carry out some of these checks.

The checks have been sub-divided into four categories, as follows:

1 Checks carried out **FROM THE VEHICLE INTERIOR**

2 Checks carried out **WITH THE VEHICLE ON THE GROUND**

3 Checks carried out **WITH THE VEHICLE RAISED AND THE WHEELS FREE TO TURN**

4 Checks carried out on **YOUR VEHICLE'S EXHAUST EMISSION SYSTEM**

1 Checks carried out **FROM THE VEHICLE INTERIOR**

Handbrake (parking brake)

☐ Test the operation of the handbrake. Excessive travel (too many clicks) indicates incorrect brake or cable adjustment.
☐ Check that the handbrake cannot be released by tapping the lever sideways. Check the security of the lever mountings.

☐ If the parking brake is foot-operated, check that the pedal is secure and without excessive travel, and that the release mechanism operates correctly.
☐ Where applicable, test the operation of the electronic handbrake. The brake should engage and disengage without excessive delay. If the warning light does not extinguish, or a warning message is displayed when the brake is disengaged, this could indicate a fault which will need further investigation.

Footbrake

☐ Depress the brake pedal and check that it does not creep down to the floor, indicating a master cylinder fault. Release the pedal, wait a few seconds, then depress it again. If the pedal travels nearly to the floor before firm resistance is felt, brake adjustment or repair is necessary. If the pedal feels spongy, there is air in the hydraulic system which must be removed by bleeding.

☐ Check that the brake pedal is secure and in good condition. Check also for signs of fluid leaks on the pedal, floor or carpets, which would indicate failed seals in the brake master cylinder.
☐ Check the servo unit (when applicable) by operating the brake pedal several times, then keeping the pedal depressed and starting the engine. As the engine starts, the pedal will move down. If not, the vacuum hose or the servo itself may be faulty.

Steering wheel and column

☐ Examine the steering wheel for fractures or looseness of the hub, spokes or rim.
☐ Move the steering wheel from side to side and then up and down. Check that the steering wheel is not loose on the column, indicating wear or a loose retaining nut. Continue moving the steering wheel as before, but also turn it slightly from left to right.
☐ Check that the steering wheel is not loose on the column, and that there is no abnormal movement of the steering wheel, indicating wear in the column support bearings or couplings.

☐ Check that the ignition lock (where fitted) engages and disengages correctly.
☐ Steering column adjustment mechanisms (where fitted) must be able to lock the column securely in place with no play evident.

Windscreen, mirrors and sunvisor

☐ The windscreen must be free of cracks or other significant damage within the 'swept area' of the windscreen. This is the area swept by the windscreen wipers. A second test area, known as 'Zone A', is the part of the swept area 290 mm wide, centred on the steering wheel centre line. Any damage in Zone A that cannot be contained in a 10 mm diameter circle, or any damage in the remainder of the swept area that cannot be contained in a 40 mm diameter circle, may cause the vehicle to fail the test.

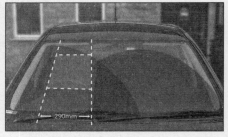

☐ Any items that may obscure the drivers view, such as stickers, sat-navs, anything hanging from the interior mirror, should be removed prior to the test.
☐ Vehicles registered after 1st August 1978 must have a drivers side mirror, and either an interior mirror, or a passenger's side mirror. Cameras (or indirect vision devices) may replace the mirrors, but they must function correctly.
☐ The driver's sunvisor must be capable of being stored in the "up" position.

Seat belts, seats and supplementary restraint systems (SRS)

Note: *The following checks are applicable to all seat belts, front and rear.*

☐ Examine the webbing of all the belts (including rear belts if fitted) for cuts, serious fraying or deterioration. Fasten and unfasten each belt to check the buckles. If applicable, check the retracting mechanism. Check the security of all seat belt mountings accessible from inside the vehicle, ensuring any height adjustable mountings lock securely in place.

☐ Where the seat belt is attached to a seat, the frame and mountings of the seat form part of the belt mountings, and are to be inspected as such.

☐ Any airbag, or SRS warning light must extinguish a few seconds after the ignition is switched on. Failure to do so indicates a fault which must be investigated.

☐ Seat belts with pre-tensioners, once activated, have a "flag" or similar showing on the seat belt stalk. This, in itself, is a reason for test failure.

☐ Check that the original airbag(s) is/are present, and not obviously defective.

☐ The seats themselves must be securely attached and the backrests must lock in the upright position. The driver's seat must also be able to slide forwards/rearwards, and lock in several positions.

Doors

☐ Both front doors must be able to be opened and closed from outside and inside, and must latch securely when closed.

☐ The rear doors must open from the outside.

☐ Examine all door hinges, catches and striker plates for missing, deteriorated, or insecure parts that could effect the opening and closing of the doors.

Speedometer

☐ The vehicle speedometer must be present, and appear operative. The figures on the speedometer must be legible, and illuminated when the lights are switched on.

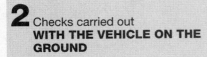

2 Checks carried out WITH THE VEHICLE ON THE GROUND

Vehicle identification

☐ Number plates must be in good condition, secure and legible, with letters and numbers correctly spaced – spacing at (**A**) should be 33 mm and at (**B**) 11 mm. At the front, digits must be black on a white background and at the rear

black on a yellow background. Other background designs (such as honeycomb) are not permitted.

☐ The VIN plate and/or homologation plate must be permanently displayed and legible.

Electrical equipment

☐ Switch on the ignition and check the operation of the horn.

☐ Check the windscreen washers and wipers, examining the wiper blades; renew damaged or perished blades. The wiper blades must clear a large enough area of the windscreen to provide an 'adequate' view of the road, and be able to be parked in a position where they will not affect the drivers' view.

☐ On vehicles first used from 1st September 2009, the headlight washers (where fitted) must operate correctly.

☐ Check the operation of the stop-lights. This includes any lights that appear to be connected – Eg. high-level lights.

☐ Check the operation of the sidelights and number plate lights. The lenses and reflectors must be secure, clean and undamaged.

☐ Check the operation and alignment of the headlights. The headlight reflectors must not be tarnished and the lenses must be undamaged. Where plastic lenses are fitted, check they haven't deteriorated to the extent where they affect the light ouput or beam image. It's often possible to restore the plastic lens using a suitable polish or aftermarket treatment.

☐ Where HID or LED headlights are fitted, check the operation of the cleaning and self-levelling functions.

☐ The headlight main beam warning lamp must be functional.

☐ On vehicles first used from 1st March 2018, the daytime running lights (where fitted) must operate correctly.

☐ Switch on the ignition and check the operation of the direction indicators (including the instrument panel tell-tale) and the hazard warning lights. Operation of the sidelights and stop-lights must not affect the indicators – if it does, the cause is usually a bad earth at the rear light cluster. Indicators should flash at a rate of between 60 and 120 times per minute – faster or slower than this could indicate a fault with the flasher unit or a bad earth at one of the light units.

☐ The hazard warning lights must operate with the ignition on and off.

☐ Check the operation of the rear foglight(s), including the warning light on the instrument panel or in the switch. Note that the foglight

must be positioned in the centre or driver's side of the vehicle. If only the passenger's side illuminates, the test will fail.

☐ The warning lights must illuminate in accordance with the manufacturers' design (this includes any warning messages). For most vehicles, the ABS and other warning lights should illuminate when the ignition is switched on, and (if the system is operating properly) extinguish after a few seconds. Refer to the owner's handbook.

☐ On vehicles first used from 1st September 2009, the reversing lights must operate correctly when reverse gear is selected.

☐ Check the vehicle battery for security and leakage.

☐ Check the visible/accessible vehicle wiring is adequately supported, with no evidence of damage or deterioration that could result in a short-circuit.

Footbrake

☐ Examine the master cylinder, brake pipes and servo unit for leaks, loose mountings, corrosion or other damage. If ABS is fitted, this unit should also be examined for signs of leaks or corrosion.

☐ The fluid reservoir must be secure and the fluid level must be between the upper (**A**) and lower (**B**) markings.

☐ Check the fluid in the reservoir for signs of contamination.

☐ Inspect both front brake flexible hoses for cracks or deterioration of the rubber. Turn the steering from lock to lock, and ensure that the hoses do not contact the wheel, tyre, or any part of the steering or suspension mechanism. With the brake pedal firmly depressed, check the hoses for bulges or leaks under pressure.

Steering and suspension

☐ Have your assistant turn the steering wheel from side to side slightly, up to the point where the steering gear just begins to transmit this movement to the roadwheels. Check for excessive free play between the steering wheel and the steering gear, indicating wear or insecurity of the steering column joints, the column-to-steering gear coupling, or the steering gear itself. With a standard (380 mm diameter) steering wheel, there should be no more than 13 mm of free play for rack-and-pinion systems, and no more than 75 mm for non-rack-and-pinion designs.

☐ Have your assistant turn the steering

wheel more vigorously in each direction, so that the roadwheels just begin to turn. As this is done, examine all the steering joints, linkages, fittings and attachments. Renew any component that shows signs of wear or damage. On vehicles with hydraulic power steering, check the security and condition of the steering pump, drivebelt and hoses.

☐ Note that all movement checks on power steering systems are carried out with the engine running.

☐ Check that the vehicle is standing level, and at approximately the correct ride height.

Exhaust system

☐ Start the engine. With your assistant holding a rag over the tailpipe, check the entire system for leaks. Repair or renew leaking sections.

3 Checks carried out **WITH THE VEHICLE RAISED AND THE WHEELS FREE TO TURN**

Jack up the front and rear of the vehicle, and securely support it on axle stands. Position the stands clear of the suspension assemblies. Ensure that the wheels are clear of the ground and that the steering can be turned from lock to lock.

Steering mechanism

☐ Have your assistant turn the steering from lock to lock. Check that the steering turns smoothly, and that no part of the steering mechanism, including a wheel or tyre, fouls any brake hose or pipe or any part of the body structure.

☐ Examine the steering rack rubber gaiters for damage or insecurity of the retaining clips. If power steering is fitted, check for signs of damage or leakage of the fluid hoses, pipes or connections. Also check for excessive stiffness or binding of the steering, a missing split pin or locking device, or severe corrosion of the body structure within 30 cm of any steering component attachment point.

☐ Check the track rod end ball joint dust covers. Any covers that are missing, seriously damaged, deteriorated or insecure, may fail inspection.

Front and rear suspension and wheel bearings

☐ Starting at the front right-hand side, grasp the roadwheel at the 3 o'clock and 9 o'clock positions and rock gently but firmly. Check for free play or insecurity at the wheel bearings, suspension balljoints, or suspension mountings, pivots and attachments.

☐ Now grasp the wheel at the 12 o'clock and 6 o'clock positions and repeat the previous inspection. Spin the wheel, and check for roughness or tightness of the front wheel bearing.

☐ If excess free play is suspected at a component pivot point, this can be confirmed by using a large screwdriver or similar tool and levering between the mounting and the component attachment. This will confirm whether the wear is in the pivot bush, its retaining bolt, or in the mounting itself (the bolt holes can often become elongated).

☐ Carry out all the above checks at the other front wheel, and then at both rear wheels.

Springs and shock absorbers

☐ Examine the suspension struts (when applicable) for serious fluid leakage, corrosion, or damage to the casing. Also check the security of the mounting points.

☐ If coil springs are fitted, check that the spring ends locate in their seats, and that the spring is not corroded, cracked or broken.

☐ If leaf springs are fitted, check that all leaves are intact, that the axle is securely attached to each spring, and that there is no deterioration of the spring eye mountings, bushes, and shackles.

☐ The same general checks apply to vehicles fitted with other suspension types, such as torsion bars, hydraulic displacer units, etc. Ensure that all mountings and attachments are secure, that there are no signs of excessive wear, corrosion or damage, and (on hydraulic types) that there are no fluid leaks or damaged pipes.

☐ Check any suspension and anti-roll bar link ball joint dust covers. Any covers that are missing, seriously damaged, deteriorated or insecure, may fail inspection.

☐ Examine each shock absorber for signs of leakage, corrosion of the casing, missing, detached or worn pivots and/or rubber bushes.

Driveshafts (fwd vehicles only)

☐ Rotate each front wheel in turn and inspect the inner and outer joint gaiters for splits or damage. Also check that each driveshaft is straight and undamaged.

Braking system

☐ If possible without dismantling, check brake pad wear and disc condition. Ensure that the friction lining material has not worn excessively, (A) and that the discs are not fractured, pitted, scored or badly worn (B). As a general rule, if the friction material is less than 1.5 mm thick, the inspection will fail.

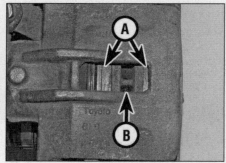

☐ Examine all the rigid brake pipes underneath the vehicle, and the flexible hose(s) at the rear. Look for corrosion, chafing or insecurity of the pipes, and for signs of bulging under pressure, chafing, splits or deterioration of the flexible hoses.

☐ Look for signs of fluid leaks at the brake calipers or on the brake backplates. Repair or renew leaking components.

☐ Slowly spin each wheel, while your assistant depresses and releases the footbrake. Ensure that each brake is operating and does not bind when the pedal is released.

☐ Examine the handbrake mechanism, checking for frayed or broken cables, excessive corrosion, or wear or insecurity of the linkage. Check that the mechanism works on each relevant wheel, and releases fully, without binding.

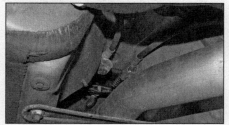

☐ Check the ABS sensors' wiring for signs of damage, deterioration or insecurity.
☐ It is not possible to test brake efficiency without special equipment, but a road test can be carried out later to check that the vehicle pulls up in a straight line.

Fuel and exhaust systems

☐ Inspect the fuel tank (including the filler cap), fuel pipes, hoses and unions. All components must be secure and free from leaks. Locking fuel caps must lock securely and the key must be provided for the MOT test.
☐ Examine the exhaust system over its entire length, checking for any damaged, broken or missing mountings, security of the retaining clamps and rust or corrosion.

☐ If the vehicle was originally equipped with a catalytic converter or particulate filter, one must be fitted.

Wheels and tyres

☐ Examine the sidewalls and tread area of each tyre in turn. Check for cuts, tears, lumps, bulges, separation of the tread, and exposure of the ply or cord due to wear or damage. Check that the tyre bead is correctly seated on the wheel rim, that the valve is sound and properly seated, and that the wheel is not distorted or damaged.
☐ Check that the tyres are of the correct size for the vehicle, that they are of the same size and type on each axle, and that the pressures are correct. The vehicle will fail the test if the tyres are obviously under-inflated.
☐ Check the tyre tread depth. The legal minimum at the time of writing is 1.6 mm over the central three-quarters of the tread width. Abnormal tread wear may indicate incorrect front wheel alignment or wear in steering or suspension components.
☐ Check that all wheel bolts/nuts are present.

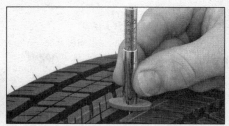

☐ If the spare wheel is fitted externally or in a separate carrier beneath the vehicle, check that mountings are secure and free of excessive corrosion.

Body corrosion

☐ Check the condition of the entire vehicle structure for signs of corrosion in load-bearing areas. (These include chassis box sections, side sills, cross-members, pillars, and all suspension, steering, braking system and seat belt mountings and anchorages.) Any corrosion which has seriously reduced the thickness of a load-bearing area (or is within 30 cm of safety-related components such as steering or suspension) is likely to cause the vehicle to fail. In this case professional repairs are likely to be needed.
☐ Damage or corrosion which causes sharp or otherwise dangerous edges to be exposed will also cause the vehicle to fail.

Towbars

☐ Check the condition of mounting points (both beneath the vehicle and within boot/hatchback areas) for signs of corrosion, ensuring that all fixings are secure and not worn or damaged. There must be no excessive play in detachable tow ball arms or quick-release mechanisms.
☐ Examine the security and condition of the towbar electrics socket. If the later 13-pin socket is fitted, the MOT tester will check its' wiring functions/connections are correct.

General leaks

☐ The vehicle will fail the test if there is a fluid leak of any kind that poses an environmental risk.

4 Checks carried out on
YOUR VEHICLE'S EXHAUST EMISSION SYSTEM

Petrol models

☐ The engine should be warmed up, and running well (ignition system in good order, air filter element clean, etc).
☐ Before testing, run the engine at around 2500 rpm for 20 seconds. Let the engine drop to idle, and watch for smoke from the exhaust. If the idle speed is too high, or if dense blue or black smoke emerges for more than 5 seconds, the vehicle will fail. Typically, blue smoke signifies oil burning (engine wear); black smoke means unburnt fuel (dirty air cleaner element, or other fuel system fault).
☐ An exhaust gas analyser for measuring carbon monoxide (CO) and hydrocarbons (HC) is now needed. If one cannot be hired or borrowed, have a local garage perform the check.

CO emissions (mixture)

☐ The MOT tester has access to the CO limits for all vehicles from 1st August 1992. The CO level is measured at idle speed, and at 'fast idle' (2500 to 3000 rpm). The following limits are given as a general guide:
    At idle speed – Less than 0.3% CO
    At 'fast idle' – Less than 0.2% CO
    Lambda reading – 0.97 to 1.03
☐ If the CO level is too high, this may point to poor maintenance, a fuel injection system problem, faulty lambda (oxygen) sensor or catalytic converter. Try an injector cleaning treatment, and check the vehicle's ECU for fault codes.

HC emissions

☐ The MOT tester has access to HC limits for all vehicles. The HC level is measured at 'fast idle' (2500 to 3000 rpm). The following limits are given as a general guide:
    At 'fast idle' – Less than 200 ppm
☐ Excessive HC emissions are typically caused by oil being burnt (worn engine), or by a blocked crankcase ventilation system ('breather'). If the engine oil is old and thin, an oil change may help. If the engine is running badly, check the vehicle's ECU for fault codes.

Diesel models

☐ If the vehicle was fitted with a DPF (Diesel Particulate Filter) when it left the factory, it will fail the test if the MOT tester can see smoke of any colour emitting from the exhaust, or finds evidence that the filter has been tampered with.
☐ The only emission test for diesel engines is measuring exhaust smoke density, using a calibrated smoke meter.
☐ This test involves accelerating the engine to its maximum unloaded speed a minimum of once, and a maximum of 6 times. With the smoke meter connected, the engine is accelerated quickly to its maximum speed. If the smoke level is at or below the limit specified, the vehicle will pass. If the level is more than the specified limit then two further accelerations are carried out, and an average of the readings calculated. If the vehicle is still over the limit, a further three accelerations are carried out, with the average of the last three calculated after each check.
Note: *On engines with a timing belt, it is VITAL that the belt is in good condition before the test is carried out.*

Vehicles registered after 1st July 2008
Smoke level must not exceed 1.5m-1 – Turbo-charged and non-Turbocharged engines

Vehicles registered before 1st July 2008
Smoke level must not exceed 2.5m-1 – Non-turbo vehicles
Smoke level must not exceed 3.0m-1 – Turbocharged vehicles:
☐ If excess smoke is produced, try fitting a new air cleaner element, or using an injector cleaning treatment. If the engine is running badly, where applicable, check the vehicle's ECU for fault codes. Also check the vehicle's EGR system, where applicable. At high mileages, the injectors may require professional attention.

Introduction

A selection of good tools is a fundamental requirement for anyone contemplating the maintenance and repair of a motor vehicle. For the owner who does not possess any, their purchase will prove a considerable expense, offsetting some of the savings made by doing-it-yourself. However, provided that the tools purchased meet the relevant national safety standards and are of good quality, they will last for many years and prove an extremely worthwhile investment.

To help the average owner to decide which tools are needed to carry out the various tasks detailed in this manual, we have compiled three lists of tools under the following headings: *Maintenance and minor repair, Repair and overhaul*, and *Special*. Newcomers to practical mechanics should start off with the *Maintenance and minor repair* tool kit, and confine themselves to the simpler jobs around the vehicle. Then, as confidence and experience grow, more difficult tasks can be undertaken, with extra tools being purchased as, and when, they are needed. In this way, a *Maintenance and minor repair* tool kit can be built up into a *Repair and overhaul* tool kit over a considerable period of time, without any major cash outlays. The experienced do-it-yourselfer will have a tool kit good enough for most repair and overhaul procedures, and will add tools from the *Special* category when it is felt that the expense is justified by the amount of use to which these tools will be put.

Maintenance and minor repair tool kit

The tools given in this list should be considered as a minimum requirement if routine maintenance, servicing and minor repair operations are to be undertaken. We recommend the purchase of combination spanners (ring one end, open-ended the other); although more expensive than open-ended ones, they do give the advantages of both types of spanner.

☐ *Combination spanners:*
  Metric - 8 to 19 mm inclusive
☐ *Adjustable spanner - 35 mm jaw (approx.)*
☐ *Spark plug spanner (with rubber insert) - petrol models*
☐ *Spark plug gap adjustment tool - petrol models*
☐ *Set of feeler gauges*
☐ *Brake bleed nipple spanner*
☐ *Screwdrivers:*
  Flat blade - 100 mm long x 6 mm dia
  Cross blade - 100 mm long x 6 mm dia
  Torx - various sizes (not all vehicles)
☐ *Combination pliers*
☐ *Hacksaw (junior)*
☐ *Tyre pump*
☐ *Tyre pressure gauge*
☐ *Oil can*
☐ *Oil filter removal tool (if applicable)*
☐ *Fine emery cloth*
☐ *Wire brush (small)*
☐ *Funnel (medium size)*
☐ *Sump drain plug key (not all vehicles)*

Repair and overhaul tool kit

These tools are virtually essential for anyone undertaking any major repairs to a motor vehicle, and are additional to those given in the *Maintenance and minor repair* list. Included in this list is a comprehensive set of sockets. Although these are expensive, they will be found invaluable as they are so versatile - particularly if various drives are included in the set. We recommend the half-inch square-drive type, as this can be used with most proprietary torque wrenches.

The tools in this list will sometimes need to be supplemented by tools from the *Special* list:

☐ *Sockets to cover range in previous list (including Torx sockets)*
☐ *Reversible ratchet drive (for use with sockets)*
☐ *Extension piece, 250 mm (for use with sockets)*
☐ *Universal joint (for use with sockets)*
☐ *Flexible handle or sliding T "breaker bar" (for use with sockets)*
☐ *Torque wrench (for use with sockets)*
☐ *Self-locking grips*
☐ *Ball pein hammer*
☐ *Soft-faced mallet (plastic or rubber)*
☐ *Screwdrivers:*
  Flat blade - long & sturdy, short (chubby), and narrow (electrician's) types
  Cross blade - long & sturdy, and short (chubby) types
☐ *Pliers:*
  Long-nosed
  Side cutters (electrician's)
  Circlip (internal and external)
☐ *Cold chisel - 25 mm*
☐ *Scriber*
☐ *Scraper*
☐ *Centre-punch*
☐ *Pin punch*
☐ *Hacksaw*
☐ *Brake hose clamp*
☐ *Brake/clutch bleeding kit*
☐ *Selection of twist drills*
☐ *Steel rule/straight-edge*
☐ *Allen keys (inc. splined/Torx type)*
☐ *Selection of files*
☐ *Wire brush*
☐ *Axle stands*
☐ *Jack (strong trolley or hydraulic type)*
☐ *Light with extension lead*
☐ *Universal electrical multi-meter*

Sockets and reversible ratchet drive

Brake bleeding kit

Torx key, socket and bit

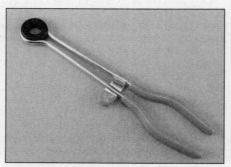

Hose clamp

Angular-tightening gauge

Special tools

The tools in this list are those which are not used regularly, are expensive to buy, or which need to be used in accordance with their manufacturers' instructions. Unless relatively difficult mechanical jobs are undertaken frequently, it will not be economic to buy many of these tools. Where this is the case, you could consider clubbing together with friends (or joining a motorists' club) to make a joint purchase, or borrowing the tools against a deposit from a local garage or tool hire specialist.

The following list contains only those tools and instruments freely available to the public, and not those special tools produced by the vehicle manufacturer specifically for its dealer network. You will find occasional references to these manufacturers' special tools in the text of this manual. Generally, an alternative method of doing the job without the vehicle manufacturers' special tool is given. However, sometimes there is no alternative to using them. Where this is the case and the relevant tool cannot be bought or borrowed, you will have to entrust the work to a dealer.

- ☐ Angular-tightening gauge
- ☐ Valve spring compressor
- ☐ Valve grinding tool
- ☐ Piston ring compressor
- ☐ Piston ring removal/installation tool
- ☐ Cylinder bore hone
- ☐ Balljoint separator
- ☐ Coil spring compressors (where applicable)
- ☐ Two/three-legged hub and bearing puller
- ☐ Impact screwdriver
- ☐ Micrometer and/or vernier calipers
- ☐ Dial gauge
- ☐ Tachometer
- ☐ Fault code reader
- ☐ Cylinder compression gauge
- ☐ Hand-operated vacuum pump and gauge
- ☐ Clutch plate alignment set
- ☐ Brake shoe steady spring cup removal tool
- ☐ Bush and bearing removal/installation set
- ☐ Stud extractors
- ☐ Tap and die set
- ☐ Lifting tackle

Buying tools

Reputable motor accessory shops and superstores often offer excellent quality tools at discount prices, so it pays to shop around.

Remember, you don't have to buy the most expensive items on the shelf, but it is always advisable to steer clear of the very cheap tools. Beware of 'bargains' offered on market stalls, on-line or at car boot sales. There are plenty of good tools around at reasonable prices, but always aim to purchase items which meet the relevant national safety standards. If in doubt, ask the proprietor or manager of the shop for advice before making a purchase.

Care and maintenance of tools

Having purchased a reasonable tool kit, it is necessary to keep the tools in a clean and serviceable condition. After use, always wipe off any dirt, grease and metal particles using a clean, dry cloth, before putting the tools away. Never leave them lying around after they have been used. A simple tool rack on the garage or workshop wall for items such as screwdrivers and pliers is a good idea. Store all normal spanners and sockets in a metal box. Any measuring instruments, gauges, meters, etc, must be carefully stored where they cannot be damaged or become rusty.

Take a little care when tools are used. Hammer heads inevitably become marked, and screwdrivers lose the keen edge on their blades from time to time. A little timely attention with emery cloth or a file will soon restore items like this to a good finish.

Working facilities

Not to be forgotten when discussing tools is the workshop itself. If anything more than routine maintenance is to be carried out, a suitable working area becomes essential.

It is appreciated that many an owner-mechanic is forced by circumstances to remove an engine or similar item without the benefit of a garage or workshop. Having done this, any repairs should always be done under the cover of a roof.

Wherever possible, any dismantling should be done on a clean, flat workbench or table at a suitable working height.

Any workbench needs a vice; one with a jaw opening of 100 mm is suitable for most jobs. As mentioned previously, some clean dry storage space is also required for tools, as well as for any lubricants, cleaning fluids, touch-up paints etc, which become necessary.

Another item which may be required, and which has a much more general usage, is an electric drill with a chuck capacity of at least 8 mm. This, together with a good range of twist drills, is virtually essential for fitting accessories.

Last, but not least, always keep a supply of old newspapers and clean, lint-free rags available, and try to keep any working area as clean as possible.

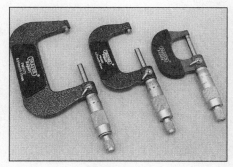

Micrometers

Dial test indicator ("dial gauge")

Oil filter removal tool (strap wrench type)

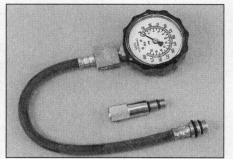

Compression tester

Bearing puller

Fuel economy

Although depreciation is still the biggest part of the cost of motoring for most car owners, the cost of fuel is more immediately noticeable. These pages give some tips on how to get the best fuel economy.

Working it out

Manufacturer's figures

Car manufacturers are required by law to provide fuel consumption information on all new vehicles sold. These 'official' figures are obtained by simulating various driving conditions on a rolling road or a test track. Real life conditions are different, so the fuel consumption actually achieved may not bear much resemblance to the quoted figures.

How to calculate it

Many cars now have trip computers which will

display fuel consumption, both instantaneous and average. Refer to the owner's handbook for details of how to use these.

To calculate consumption yourself (and maybe to check that the trip computer is accurate), proceed as follows.

1. Fill up with fuel and note the mileage, or zero the trip recorder.
2. Drive as usual until you need to fill up again.
3. Note the amount of fuel required to refill the tank, and the mileage covered since the previous fill-up.
4. Divide the mileage by the amount of fuel used to obtain the consumption figure.

For example:

Mileage at first fill-up (a) = 27,903
Mileage at second fill-up (b) = 28,346
Mileage covered (b - a) = 443
Fuel required at second fill-up = 48.6 litres

The half-completed changeover to metric units in the UK means that we buy our fuel

in litres, measure distances in miles and talk about fuel consumption in miles per gallon. There are two ways round this: the first is to convert the litres to gallons before doing the calculation (by dividing by 4.546, or see Table 1). So in the example:

48.6 litres ÷ 4.546 = 10.69 gallons
443 miles ÷ 10.69 gallons = 41.4 mpg

The second way is to calculate the consumption in miles per litre, then multiply that figure by 4.546 (or see Table 2).

So in the example, fuel consumption is:

443 miles ÷ 48.6 litres = 9.1 mpl
9.1 mpl x 4.546 = 41.4 mpg

The rest of Europe expresses fuel consumption in litres of fuel required to travel 100 km (l/100 km). For interest, the conversions are given in Table 3. In practice it doesn't matter what units you use, provided you know what your normal consumption is and can spot if it's getting better or worse.

Table 1: conversion of litres to Imperial gallons

litres	1	2	3	4	5	10	20	30	40	50	60	70
gallons	0.22	0.44	0.66	0.88	1.10	2.24	4.49	6.73	8.98	11.22	13.47	15.71

Table 2: conversion of miles per litre to miles per gallon

miles per litre	5	6	7	8	9	10	11	12	13	14
miles per gallon	23	27	32	36	41	46	50	55	59	64

Table 3: conversion of litres per 100 km to miles per gallon

litres per 100 km	4	4.5	5	5.5	6	6.5	7	8	9	10
miles per gallon	71	63	56	51	47	43	40	35	31	28

Maintenance

A well-maintained car uses less fuel and creates less pollution. In particular:

Filters

Change air and fuel filters at the specified intervals.

Oil

Use a good quality oil of the lowest viscosity specified by the vehicle manufacturer (see *Lubricants and fluids*). Check the level often and be careful not to overfill.

Spark plugs

When applicable, renew at the specified intervals.

Tyres

Check tyre pressures regularly. Under-inflated tyres have an increased rolling resistance. It is generally safe to use the higher pressures specified for full load conditions even when not fully laden, but keep an eye on the centre band of tread for signs of wear due to over-inflation.

When buying new tyres, consider the 'fuel saving' models which most manufacturers include in their ranges.

Driving style

Acceleration

Acceleration uses more fuel than driving at a steady speed. The best technique with modern cars is to accelerate reasonably briskly to the desired speed, changing up through the gears as soon as possible without making the engine labour.

Air conditioning

Air conditioning absorbs quite a bit of energy from the engine – typically 3 kW (4 hp) or so. The effect on fuel consumption is at its worst in slow traffic. Switch it off when not required.

Anticipation

Drive smoothly and try to read the traffic flow so as to avoid unnecessary acceleration and braking.

Automatic transmission

When accelerating in an automatic, avoid depressing the throttle so far as to make the transmission hold onto lower gears at higher speeds. Don't use the 'Sport' setting, if applicable.

When stationary with the engine running, select 'N' or 'P'. When moving, keep your left foot away from the brake.

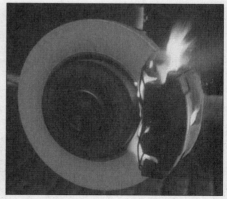

Braking

Braking converts the car's energy of motion into heat – essentially, it is wasted. Obviously some braking is always going to be necessary, but with good anticipation it is surprising how much can be avoided, especially on routes that you know well.

Carshare

Consider sharing lifts to work or to the shops. Even once a week will make a difference.

Fuel economy

Electrical loads

Electricity is 'fuel' too; the alternator which charges the battery does so by converting some of the engine's energy of motion into electrical energy. The more electrical accessories are in use, the greater the load on the alternator. Switch off big consumers like the heated rear window when not required.

Freewheeling

Freewheeling (coasting) in neutral with the engine switched off is dangerous. The effort required to operate power-assisted brakes and steering increases when the engine is not running, with a potential lack of control in emergency situations.

In any case, modern fuel injection systems automatically cut off the engine's fuel supply on the overrun (moving and in gear, but with the accelerator pedal released).

Gadgets

Bolt-on devices claiming to save fuel have been around for nearly as long as the motor car itself. Those which worked were rapidly adopted as standard equipment by the vehicle manufacturers. Others worked only in certain situations, or saved fuel only at the expense of unacceptable effects on performance, driveability or the life of engine components.

The most effective fuel saving gadget is the driver's right foot.

Journey planning

Combine (eg) a trip to the supermarket with a visit to the recycling centre and the DIY store, rather than making separate journeys.

When possible choose a travelling time outside rush hours.

Load

The more heavily a car is laden, the greater the energy required to accelerate it to a given speed. Remove heavy items which you don't need to carry.

One load which is often overlooked is the contents of the fuel tank. A tankful of fuel (55 litres / 12 gallons) weighs 45 kg (100 lb) or so. Just half filling it may be worthwhile.

Lost?

At the risk of stating the obvious, if you're going somewhere new, have details of the route to hand. There's not much point in achieving record mpg if you also go miles out of your way.

Parking

If possible, carry out any reversing or turning manoeuvres when you arrive at a parking space so that you can drive straight out when you leave. Manoeuvering when the engine is cold uses a lot more fuel.

Driving around looking for free on-street parking may cost more in fuel than buying a car park ticket.

Premium fuel

Most major oil companies (and some supermarkets) have premium grades of fuel which are several pence a litre dearer than the standard grades. Reports vary, but the consensus seems to be that if these fuels improve economy at all, they do not do so by enough to justify their extra cost.

Roof rack

When loading a roof rack, try to produce a wedge shape with the narrow end at the front. Any cover should be securely fastened – if it flaps it's creating turbulence and absorbing energy.

Remove roof racks and boxes when not in use – they increase air resistance and can create a surprising amount of noise.

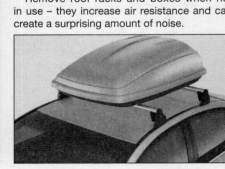

Short journeys

The engine is at its least efficient, and wear is highest, during the first few miles after a cold start. Consider walking, cycling or using public transport.

Speed

The engine is at its most efficient when running at a steady speed and load at the rpm where it develops maximum torque. (You can find this figure in the car's handbook.) For most cars this corresponds to between 55 and 65 mph in top gear.

Above the optimum cruising speed, fuel consumption starts to rise quite sharply. A car travelling at 80 mph will typically be using 30% more fuel than at 60 mph.

Supermarket fuel

It may be cheap but is it any good? In the UK all supermarket fuel must meet the relevant British Standard. The major oil companies will say that their branded fuels have better additive packages which may stop carbon and other deposits building up. A reasonable compromise might be to use one tank of branded fuel to three or four from the supermarket.

Switch off when stationary

Switch off the engine if you look like being stationary for more than 30 seconds or so. This is good for the environment as well as for your pocket. Be aware though that frequent restarts are hard on the battery and the starter motor.

Windows

Driving with the windows open increases air turbulence around the vehicle. Closing the windows promotes smooth airflow and

reduced resistance. The faster you go, the more significant this is.

And finally . . .

Driving techniques associated with good fuel economy tend to involve moderate acceleration and low top speeds. Be considerate to the needs of other road users who may need to make brisker progress; even if you do not agree with them this is not an excuse to be obstructive.

Safety must always take precedence over economy, whether it is a question of accelerating hard to complete an overtaking manoeuvre, killing your speed when confronted with a potential hazard or switching the lights on when it starts to get dark.

Whenever servicing, repair or overhaul work is carried out on the car or its components, observe the following procedures and instructions. This will assist in carrying out the operation efficiently and to a professional standard of workmanship.

Joint mating faces and gaskets

When separating components at their mating faces, never insert screwdrivers or similar implements into the joint between the faces in order to prise them apart. This can cause severe damage which results in oil leaks, coolant leaks, etc upon reassembly. Separation is usually achieved by tapping along the joint with a soft-faced hammer in order to break the seal. However, note that this method may not be suitable where dowels are used for component location.

Where a gasket is used between the mating faces of two components, a new one must be fitted on reassembly; fit it dry unless otherwise stated in the repair procedure. Make sure that the mating faces are clean and dry, with all traces of old gasket removed. When cleaning a joint face, use a tool which is unlikely to score or damage the face, and remove any burrs or nicks with an oilstone or fine file.

Make sure that tapped holes are cleaned with a pipe cleaner, and keep them free of jointing compound, if this is being used, unless specifically instructed otherwise.

Ensure that all orifices, channels or pipes are clear, and blow through them, preferably using compressed air.

Oil seals

Oil seals can be removed by levering them out with a wide flat-bladed screwdriver or similar implement. Alternatively, a number of self-tapping screws may be screwed into the seal, and these used as a purchase for pliers or some similar device in order to pull the seal free.

Whenever an oil seal is removed from its working location, either individually or as part of an assembly, it should be renewed.

The very fine sealing lip of the seal is easily damaged, and will not seal if the surface it contacts is not completely clean and free from scratches, nicks or grooves. If the original sealing surface of the component cannot be restored, and the manufacturer has not made provision for slight relocation of the seal relative to the sealing surface, the component should be renewed.

Protect the lips of the seal from any surface which may damage them in the course of fitting. Use tape or a conical sleeve where possible. Where indicated, lubricate the seal lips with oil before fitting and, on dual-lipped seals, fill the space between the lips with grease.

Unless otherwise stated, oil seals must be fitted with their sealing lips toward the lubricant to be sealed.

Use a tubular drift or block of wood of the appropriate size to install the seal and, if the seal housing is shouldered, drive the seal down to the shoulder. If the seal housing is unshouldered, the seal should be fitted with its face flush with the housing top face (unless otherwise instructed).

Screw threads and fastenings

Seized nuts, bolts and screws are quite a common occurrence where corrosion has set in, and the use of penetrating oil or releasing fluid will often overcome this problem if the offending item is soaked for a while before attempting to release it. The use of an impact driver may also provide a means of releasing such stubborn fastening devices, when used in conjunction with the appropriate screwdriver bit or socket. If none of these methods works, it may be necessary to resort to the careful application of heat, or the use of a hacksaw or nut splitter device. Before resorting to extreme methods, check that you are not dealing with a left-hand thread!

Studs are usually removed by locking two nuts together on the threaded part, and then using a spanner on the lower nut to unscrew the stud. Studs or bolts which have broken off below the surface of the component in which they are mounted can sometimes be removed using a stud extractor.

Always ensure that a blind tapped hole is completely free from oil, grease, water or other fluid before installing the bolt or stud. Failure to do this could cause the housing to crack due to the hydraulic action of the bolt or stud as it is screwed in.

For some screw fastenings, notably cylinder head bolts or nuts, torque wrench settings are no longer specified for the latter stages of tightening, "angle-tightening" being called up instead. Typically, a fairly low torque wrench setting will be applied to the bolts/nuts in the correct sequence, followed by one or more stages of tightening through specified angles.

When checking or retightening a nut or bolt to a specified torque setting, slacken the nut or bolt by a quarter of a turn, and then retighten to the specified setting. However, this should not be attempted where angular tightening has been used.

Locknuts, locktabs and washers

Any fastening which will rotate against a component or housing during tightening should always have a washer between it and the relevant component or housing.

Spring or split washers should always be renewed when they are used to lock a critical component such as a big-end bearing retaining bolt or nut. Locktabs which are folded over to retain a nut or bolt should always be renewed.

Self-locking nuts can be re-used in non-critical areas, providing resistance can be felt when the locking portion passes over the bolt or stud thread. However, it should be noted that self-locking stiffnuts tend to lose their effectiveness after long periods of use, and should then be renewed as a matter of course.

Split pins must always be replaced with new ones of the correct size for the hole.

When thread-locking compound is found on the threads of a fastener which is to be re-used, it should be cleaned off with a wire brush and solvent, and fresh compound applied on reassembly.

Special tools

Some repair procedures in this manual entail the use of special tools such as a press, two or three-legged pullers, spring compressors, etc. Wherever possible, suitable readily-available alternatives to the manufacturer's special tools are described, and are shown in use. In some instances, where no alternative is possible, it has been necessary to resort to the use of a manufacturer's tool, and this has been done for reasons of safety as well as the efficient completion of the repair operation. Unless you are highly-skilled and have a thorough understanding of the procedures described, never attempt to bypass the use of any special tool when the procedure described specifies its use. Not only is there a very great risk of personal injury, but expensive damage could be caused to the components involved.

Environmental considerations

When disposing of used engine oil, brake fluid, antifreeze, etc, give due consideration to any detrimental environmental effects. Do not, for instance, pour any of the above liquids down drains into the general sewage system, or onto the ground to soak away, as this is likely to pollute your local environment. Many local council refuse tips provide a facility for waste oil disposal, as do some garages. You can find your nearest disposal point by calling the Environment Agency on 03708 506 506 or by visiting www.oilbankline.org.uk.

Note: It is illegal and anti-social to dump oil down the drain. To find the location of your local oil recycling bank, call 03708 506 506 or visit www.oilbankline.org.uk.

A

ABS (Anti-lock brake system) A system, usually electronically controlled, that senses incipient wheel lockup during braking and relieves hydraulic pressure at wheels that are about to skid.

Air bag An inflatable bag hidden in the steering wheel (driver's side) or the dash or glovebox (passenger side). In a head-on collision, the bags inflate, preventing the driver and front passenger from being thrown forward into the steering wheel or windscreen.

Air cleaner A metal or plastic housing, containing a filter element, which removes dust and dirt from the air being drawn into the engine.

Air filter element The actual filter in an air cleaner system, usually manufactured from pleated paper and requiring renewal at regular intervals.

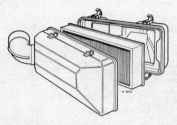

Air filter

Allen key A hexagonal wrench which fits into a recessed hexagonal hole.

Alligator clip A long-nosed spring-loaded metal clip with meshing teeth. Used to make temporary electrical connections.

Alternator A component in the electrical system which converts mechanical energy from a drivebelt into electrical energy to charge the battery and to operate the starting system, ignition system and electrical accessories.

Ampere (amp) A unit of measurement for the flow of electric current. One amp is the amount of current produced by one volt acting through a resistance of one ohm.

Anaerobic sealer A substance used to prevent bolts and screws from loosening. Anaerobic means that it does not require oxygen for activation. The Loctite brand is widely used.

Antifreeze A substance (usually ethylene glycol) mixed with water, and added to a vehicle's cooling system, to prevent freezing of the coolant in winter. Antifreeze also contains chemicals to inhibit corrosion and the formation of rust and other deposits that would tend to clog the radiator and coolant passages and reduce cooling efficiency.

Anti-seize compound A coating that reduces the risk of seizing on fasteners that are subjected to high temperatures, such as exhaust manifold bolts and nuts.

Asbestos A natural fibrous mineral with great heat resistance, commonly used in the composition of brake friction materials. Asbestos is a health hazard and the dust created by brake systems should never be inhaled or ingested.

Axle A shaft on which a wheel revolves, or which revolves with a wheel. Also, a solid beam that connects the two wheels at one end of the vehicle. An axle which also transmits power to the wheels is known as a live axle.

Axleshaft A single rotating shaft, on either side of the differential, which delivers power from the final drive assembly to the drive wheels. Also called a driveshaft or a halfshaft.

B

Ball bearing An anti-friction bearing consisting of a hardened inner and outer race with hardened steel balls between two races.

Bearing The curved surface on a shaft or in a bore, or the part assembled into either, that permits relative motion between them with minimum wear and friction.

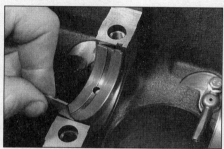

Bearing

Big-end bearing The bearing in the end of the connecting rod that's attached to the crankshaft.

Bleed nipple A valve on a brake wheel cylinder, caliper or other hydraulic component that is opened to purge the hydraulic system of air. Also called a bleed screw.

Brake bleeding Procedure for removing air from lines of a hydraulic brake system.

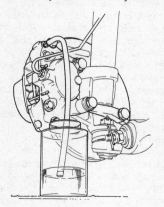

Brake bleeding

Brake disc The component of a disc brake that rotates with the wheels.

Brake drum The component of a drum brake that rotates with the wheels.

Brake linings The friction material which contacts the brake disc or drum to retard the vehicle's speed. The linings are bonded or riveted to the brake pads or shoes.

Brake pads The replaceable friction pads that pinch the brake disc when the brakes are applied. Brake pads consist of a friction material bonded or riveted to a rigid backing plate.

Brake shoe The crescent-shaped carrier to which the brake linings are mounted and which forces the lining against the rotating drum during braking.

Braking systems For more information on braking systems, consult the *Haynes Automotive Brake Manual*.

Breaker bar A long socket wrench handle providing greater leverage.

Bulkhead The insulated partition between the engine and the passenger compartment.

C

Caliper The non-rotating part of a disc-brake assembly that straddles the disc and carries the brake pads. The caliper also contains the hydraulic components that cause the pads to pinch the disc when the brakes are applied. A caliper is also a measuring tool that can be set to measure inside or outside dimensions of an object.

Camshaft A rotating shaft on which a series of cam lobes operate the valve mechanisms. The camshaft may be driven by gears, by sprockets and chain or by sprockets and a belt.

Canister A container in an evaporative emission control system; contains activated charcoal granules to trap vapours from the fuel system.

Canister

Carburettor A device which mixes fuel with air in the proper proportions to provide a desired power output from a spark ignition internal combustion engine.

Castellated Resembling the parapets along the top of a castle wall. For example, a castellated balljoint stud nut.

Castor In wheel alignment, the backward or forward tilt of the steering axis. Castor is positive when the steering axis is inclined rearward at the top.

Catalytic converter A silencer-like device in the exhaust system which converts certain pollutants in the exhaust gases into less harmful substances.

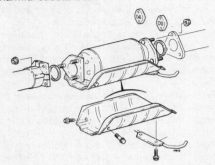

Catalytic converter

Circlip A ring-shaped clip used to prevent endwise movement of cylindrical parts and shafts. An internal circlip is installed in a groove in a housing; an external circlip fits into a groove on the outside of a cylindrical piece such as a shaft.

Clearance The amount of space between two parts. For example, between a piston and a cylinder, between a bearing and a journal, etc.

Coil spring A spiral of elastic steel found in various sizes throughout a vehicle, for example as a springing medium in the suspension and in the valve train.

Compression Reduction in volume, and increase in pressure and temperature, of a gas, caused by squeezing it into a smaller space.

Compression ratio The relationship between cylinder volume when the piston is at top dead centre and cylinder volume when the piston is at bottom dead centre.

Constant velocity (CV) joint A type of universal joint that cancels out vibrations caused by driving power being transmitted through an angle.

Core plug A disc or cup-shaped metal device inserted in a hole in a casting through which core was removed when the casting was formed. Also known as a freeze plug or expansion plug.

Crankcase The lower part of the engine block in which the crankshaft rotates.

Crankshaft The main rotating member, or shaft, running the length of the crankcase, with offset "throws" to which the connecting rods are attached.

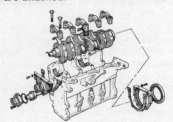

Crankshaft assembly

Crocodile clip See Alligator clip

D

Diagnostic code Code numbers obtained by accessing the diagnostic mode of an engine management computer. This code can be used to determine the area in the system where a malfunction may be located.

Disc brake A brake design incorporating a rotating disc onto which brake pads are squeezed. The resulting friction converts the energy of a moving vehicle into heat.

Double-overhead cam (DOHC) An engine that uses two overhead camshafts, usually one for the intake valves and one for the exhaust valves.

Drivebelt(s) The belt(s) used to drive accessories such as the alternator, water pump, power steering pump, air conditioning compressor, etc. off the crankshaft pulley.

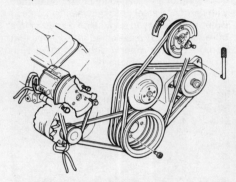

Accessory drivebelts

Driveshaft Any shaft used to transmit motion. Commonly used when referring to the axleshafts on a front wheel drive vehicle.

Drum brake A type of brake using a drum-shaped metal cylinder attached to the inner surface of the wheel. When the brake pedal is pressed, curved brake shoes with friction linings press against the inside of the drum to slow or stop the vehicle.

E

EGR valve A valve used to introduce exhaust gases into the intake air stream.

Electronic control unit (ECU) A computer which controls (for instance) ignition and fuel injection systems, or an anti-lock braking system. For more information refer to the *Haynes Automotive Electrical and Electronic Systems Manual.*

Electronic Fuel Injection (EFI) A computer controlled fuel system that distributes fuel through an injector located in each intake port of the engine.

Emergency brake A braking system, independent of the main hydraulic system, that can be used to slow or stop the vehicle if the primary brakes fail, or to hold the vehicle stationary even though the brake pedal isn't depressed. It usually consists of a hand lever that actuates either front or rear brakes mechanically through a series of cables and linkages. Also known as a handbrake or parking brake.

Endfloat The amount of lengthwise movement between two parts. As applied to a crankshaft, the distance that the crankshaft can move forward and back in the cylinder block.

Engine management system (EMS) A computer controlled system which manages the fuel injection and the ignition systems in an integrated fashion.

Exhaust manifold A part with several passages through which exhaust gases leave the engine combustion chambers and enter the exhaust pipe.

F

Fan clutch A viscous (fluid) drive coupling device which permits variable engine fan speeds in relation to engine speeds.

Feeler blade A thin strip or blade of hardened steel, ground to an exact thickness, used to check or measure clearances between parts.

Feeler blade

Firing order The order in which the engine cylinders fire, or deliver their power strokes, beginning with the number one cylinder.

Flywheel A heavy spinning wheel in which energy is absorbed and stored by means of momentum. On cars, the flywheel is attached to the crankshaft to smooth out firing impulses.

Free play The amount of travel before any action takes place. The "looseness" in a linkage, or an assembly of parts, between the initial application of force and actual movement. For example, the distance the brake pedal moves before the pistons in the master cylinder are actuated.

Fuse An electrical device which protects a circuit against accidental overload. The typical fuse contains a soft piece of metal which is calibrated to melt at a predetermined current flow (expressed as amps) and break the circuit.

Fusible link A circuit protection device consisting of a conductor surrounded by heat-resistant insulation. The conductor is smaller than the wire it protects, so it acts as the weakest link in the circuit. Unlike a blown fuse, a failed fusible link must frequently be cut from the wire for replacement.

G

Gap The distance the spark must travel in jumping from the centre electrode to the side electrode in a spark plug. Also refers to the spacing between the points in a contact breaker assembly in a conventional points-type ignition, or to the distance between the reluctor or rotor and the pickup coil in an electronic ignition.

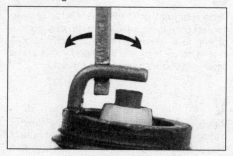

Adjusting spark plug gap

Gasket Any thin, soft material - usually cork, cardboard, asbestos or soft metal - installed between two metal surfaces to ensure a good seal. For instance, the cylinder head gasket seals the joint between the block and the cylinder head.

Gasket

Gauge An instrument panel display used to monitor engine conditions. A gauge with a movable pointer on a dial or a fixed scale is an analogue gauge. A gauge with a numerical readout is called a digital gauge.

H

Halfshaft A rotating shaft that transmits power from the final drive unit to a drive wheel, usually when referring to a live rear axle.

Harmonic balancer A device designed to reduce torsion or twisting vibration in the crankshaft. May be incorporated in the crankshaft pulley. Also known as a vibration damper.

Hone An abrasive tool for correcting small irregularities or differences in diameter in an engine cylinder, brake cylinder, etc.

Hydraulic tappet A tappet that utilises hydraulic pressure from the engine's lubrication system to maintain zero clearance (constant contact with both camshaft and valve stem). Automatically adjusts to variation in valve stem length. Hydraulic tappets also reduce valve noise.

I

Ignition timing The moment at which the spark plug fires, usually expressed in the number of crankshaft degrees before the piston reaches the top of its stroke.

Inlet manifold A tube or housing with passages through which flows the air-fuel mixture (carburettor vehicles and vehicles with throttle body injection) or air only (port fuel-injected vehicles) to the port openings in the cylinder head.

J

Jump start Starting the engine of a vehicle with a discharged or weak battery by attaching jump leads from the weak battery to a charged or helper battery.

L

Load Sensing Proportioning Valve (LSPV) A brake hydraulic system control valve that works like a proportioning valve, but also takes into consideration the amount of weight carried by the rear axle.

Locknut A nut used to lock an adjustment nut, or other threaded component, in place. For example, a locknut is employed to keep the adjusting nut on the rocker arm in position.

Lockwasher A form of washer designed to prevent an attaching nut from working loose.

M

MacPherson strut A type of front suspension system devised by Earle MacPherson at Ford of England. In its original form, a simple lateral link with the anti-roll bar creates the lower control arm. A long strut - an integral coil spring and shock absorber - is mounted between the body and the steering knuckle. Many modern so-called MacPherson strut systems use a conventional lower A-arm and don't rely on the anti-roll bar for location.

Multimeter An electrical test instrument with the capability to measure voltage, current and resistance.

N

NOx Oxides of Nitrogen. A common toxic pollutant emitted by petrol and diesel engines at higher temperatures.

O

Ohm The unit of electrical resistance. One volt applied to a resistance of one ohm will produce a current of one amp.

Ohmmeter An instrument for measuring electrical resistance.

O-ring A type of sealing ring made of a special rubber-like material; in use, the O-ring is compressed into a groove to provide the sealing action.

Overhead cam (ohc) engine An engine with the camshaft(s) located on top of the cylinder head(s).

Overhead valve (ohv) engine

Overhead valve (ohv) engine An engine with the valves located in the cylinder head, but with the camshaft located in the engine block.

Oxygen sensor A device installed in the engine exhaust manifold, which senses the oxygen content in the exhaust and converts this information into an electric current. Also called a Lambda sensor.

P

Phillips screw A type of screw head having a cross instead of a slot for a corresponding type of screwdriver.

Plastigage A thin strip of plastic thread, available in different sizes, used for measuring clearances. For example, a strip of Plastigage is laid across a bearing journal. The parts are assembled and dismantled; the width of the crushed strip indicates the clearance between journal and bearing.

Plastigage

Propeller shaft The long hollow tube with universal joints at both ends that carries power from the transmission to the differential on front-engined rear wheel drive vehicles.

Proportioning valve A hydraulic control valve which limits the amount of pressure to the rear brakes during panic stops to prevent wheel lock-up.

R

Rack-and-pinion steering A steering system with a pinion gear on the end of the steering shaft that mates with a rack (think of a geared wheel opened up and laid flat). When the steering wheel is turned, the pinion turns, moving the rack to the left or right. This movement is transmitted through the track rods to the steering arms at the wheels.

Radiator A liquid-to-air heat transfer device designed to reduce the temperature of the coolant in an internal combustion engine cooling system.

Refrigerant Any substance used as a heat transfer agent in an air-conditioning system. R-12 has been the principle refrigerant for many years; recently, however, manufacturers have begun using R-134a, a non-CFC substance that is considered less harmful to the ozone in the upper atmosphere.

Rocker arm A lever arm that rocks on a shaft or pivots on a stud. In an overhead valve engine, the rocker arm converts the upward movement of the pushrod into a downward movement to open a valve.

Rotor In a distributor, the rotating device inside the cap that connects the centre electrode and the outer terminals as it turns, distributing the high voltage from the coil secondary winding to the proper spark plug. Also, that part of an alternator which rotates inside the stator. Also, the rotating assembly of a turbocharger, including the compressor wheel, shaft and turbine wheel.

Runout The amount of wobble (in-and-out movement) of a gear or wheel as it's rotated. The amount a shaft rotates "out-of-true." The out-of-round condition of a rotating part.

S

Sealant A liquid or paste used to prevent leakage at a joint. Sometimes used in conjunction with a gasket.

Sealed beam lamp An older headlight design which integrates the reflector, lens and filaments into a hermetically-sealed one-piece unit. When a filament burns out or the lens cracks, the entire unit is simply replaced.

Serpentine drivebelt A single, long, wide accessory drivebelt that's used on some newer vehicles to drive all the accessories, instead of a series of smaller, shorter belts. Serpentine drivebelts are usually tensioned by an automatic tensioner.

Serpentine drivebelt

Shim Thin spacer, commonly used to adjust the clearance or relative positions between two parts. For example, shims inserted into or under bucket tappets control valve clearances. Clearance is adjusted by changing the thickness of the shim.

Slide hammer A special puller that screws into or hooks onto a component such as a shaft or bearing; a heavy sliding handle on the shaft bottoms against the end of the shaft to knock the component free.

Sprocket A tooth or projection on the periphery of a wheel, shaped to engage with a chain or drivebelt. Commonly used to refer to the sprocket wheel itself.

Starter inhibitor switch On vehicles with an automatic transmission, a switch that prevents starting if the vehicle is not in Neutral or Park.

Strut See MacPherson strut.

T

Tappet A cylindrical component which transmits motion from the cam to the valve stem, either directly or via a pushrod and rocker arm. Also called a cam follower.

Thermostat A heat-controlled valve that regulates the flow of coolant between the cylinder block and the radiator, so maintaining optimum engine operating temperature. A thermostat is also used in some air cleaners in which the temperature is regulated.

Thrust bearing The bearing in the clutch assembly that is moved in to the release levers by clutch pedal action to disengage the clutch. Also referred to as a release bearing.

Timing belt A toothed belt which drives the camshaft. Serious engine damage may result if it breaks in service.

Timing chain A chain which drives the camshaft.

Toe-in The amount the front wheels are closer together at the front than at the rear. On rear wheel drive vehicles, a slight amount of toe-in is usually specified to keep the front wheels running parallel on the road by offsetting other forces that tend to spread the wheels apart.

Toe-out The amount the front wheels are closer together at the rear than at the front. On front wheel drive vehicles, a slight amount of toe-out is usually specified.

Tools For full information on choosing and using tools, refer to the *Haynes Automotive Tools Manual*.

Tracer A stripe of a second colour applied to a wire insulator to distinguish that wire from another one with the same colour insulator.

Tune-up A process of accurate and careful adjustments and parts replacement to obtain the best possible engine performance.

Turbocharger A centrifugal device, driven by exhaust gases, that pressurises the intake air. Normally used to increase the power output from a given engine displacement, but can also be used primarily to reduce exhaust emissions (as on VW's "Umwelt" Diesel engine).

U

Universal joint or U-joint A double-pivoted connection for transmitting power from a driving to a driven shaft through an angle. A U-joint consists of two Y-shaped yokes and a cross-shaped member called the spider.

V

Valve A device through which the flow of liquid, gas, vacuum, or loose material in bulk may be started, stopped, or regulated by a movable part that opens, shuts, or partially obstructs one or more ports or passageways. A valve is also the movable part of such a device.

Valve clearance The clearance between the valve tip (the end of the valve stem) and the rocker arm or tappet. The valve clearance is measured when the valve is closed.

Vernier caliper A precision measuring instrument that measures inside and outside dimensions. Not quite as accurate as a micrometer, but more convenient.

Viscosity The thickness of a liquid or its resistance to flow.

Volt A unit for expressing electrical "pressure" in a circuit. One volt that will produce a current of one ampere through a resistance of one ohm.

W

Welding Various processes used to join metal items by heating the areas to be joined to a molten state and fusing them together. For more information refer to the *Haynes Automotive Welding Manual*.

Wiring diagram A drawing portraying the components and wires in a vehicle's electrical system, using standardised symbols. For more information refer to the *Haynes Automotive Electrical and Electronic Systems Manual*.

Chapter 1 Part A
Routine maintenance and servicing – petrol models

Contents

Degrees of difficulty

| Easy, suitable for novice with little experience | | Fairly easy, suitable for beginner with some experience | 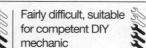 | Fairly difficult, suitable for competent DIY mechanic | | Difficult, suitable for experienced DIY mechanic | 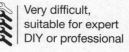 | Very difficult, suitable for expert DIY or professional | |

Specifications

Lubricants and fluids

Engine oil . . . . Genuine Nissan Motor Oil 5W-40 or ACEA A3/B4 equivelant (eg.
Castrol Magnatec SAE 10W-40 – part synthetic, to ACEA A3/B4)
Cooling system. . . . . Genuine long-life coolant or equivalent*
Manual transmission . . . . Nissan MT-XZ Gear Oil TL/JR Type or API GL-4, Viscosity SAE 75W-80
Braking system. . . . . Genuine Nissan brake fluid or equivalent hydraulic fluid to DOT 4*
*Refer to your Nissan dealer or specialist for brand name and latest type recommendations

Capacities

Engine oil (including oil filter) . . . . 4.6 litres
Cooling system (approximate) . . . . 6.4 litres
Transmission (manual) . . . . 2.0 litres
Washer fluid reservoir. . . . . 2.5 litres
Fuel tank . . . . 55.0 litres

Cooling system

Antifreeze mixture:
   50% antifreeze . . . . Protection down to -37°C
Note: *Refer to the antifreeze manufacturer for latest recommendations.*

Ignition system

Spark plugs (Platinum tipped):
   Type   . . . . NGK – ILKAR7F7G
   Gap   . . . . 0.65 mm (preset)

Brakes

Friction material minimum thickness:
   Front brake pads . . . . 1.5 mm
   Rear brake shoes . . . . 1.0 mm

Tyre pressures

Note: *Pressures given here are a guide only, and apply to original-equipment tyres – the recommended pressures may vary if any other make or type of tyre is fitted; check with the car handbook, or the tyre manufacturer or supplier for the latest recommendations. A tyre pressure label is fitted on the driver's door B-pillar, with readings for each specific vehicle (see illustration).*

Normal load (up to 3 people)

	Front	Rear
215/65R16 98H	2.6 bar (38 psi)	2.4 bar (35 psi)
215/60R17 96H	2.3 bar (33 psi)	2.1 bar (30 psi)
215/55R18 83T, 85T, 87T or 88T	2.3 bar (33 psi)	2.1 bar (30 psi)
225/45R19 92W or 95W.	2.3 bar (33 psi)	2.1 bar (30 psi)

Remote control battery

Type CR2032, 3V

Torque wrench settings

	Nm	lbf ft
Engine oil drain plug.	50	37
Ignition coils	10	7
Manual transmission drain plug	23	17
Roadwheel nuts	113	83
Spark plugs	24	18

1 Maintenance schedule

1 The maintenance intervals in this manual are provided with the assumption that you, not the dealer, will be carrying out the work. These are the minimum maintenance intervals based on the standard service schedule recommended by the manufacturer for vehicles driven daily. If you wish to keep your vehicle in peak condition at all times, you may wish to perform some of these procedures more often. We encourage frequent maintenance, because it enhances the efficiency, performance and resale value of your vehicle.

2 If the vehicle is driven in dusty areas, used to tow a trailer, or driven frequently at slow speeds (idling in traffic) or on short journeys, more frequent maintenance intervals are recommended.

3 When the vehicle is new, it should be serviced by a dealer service department (or other workshop recognised by the vehicle manufacturer as providing the same standard of service) in order to preserve the warranty. The vehicle manufacturer may reject warranty claims if you are unable to prove that servicing has been carried out as and when specified, using only original equipment parts or parts certified to be of equivalent quality.

Every 250 miles or weekly

- [ ] Check the engine oil level (Section 5)
- [ ] Check the coolant level (Section 6)
- [ ] Check the brake and clutch fluid level (Section 7)
- [ ] Screenwash fluid (Section 8)
- [ ] Tyre condition and pressure check (Section 9)
- [ ] Wiper blades check (Section 10)
- [ ] Battery check (Section 11)
- [ ] Check the electrical systems (Section 12)

Every 12 500 miles or 12 months, whichever comes first

In addition to the items listed above, carry out the following:

Note: *Nissan recommend that the engine oil and filter are changed every 12,500 miles or 12 months. However, oil and filter changes are good for the engine, and we recommend that the oil and filter are renewed more frequently, especially if the car is used on a lot of short journeys.*

- [ ] Renew the engine oil and filter (Section 13)
- [ ] Reset the service indicator (Section 14)
- [ ] Check all components, pipes and hoses for fluid leaks (Section 15)
- [ ] Check the condition of the auxiliary drivebelt (Section 17)
- [ ] Check the condition of the auxiliary drivebelt (Section 16)
- [ ] Check the condition and operation of the seat belts (Section 17)
- [ ] Check the brake pads and discs for wear (Section 18)
- [ ] Check the condition of the driveshaft gaiters (Section 19)
- [ ] Check the steering and suspension components for condition and security (Section 20).
- [ ] Check the condition of the exhaust system components (Section 21)
- [ ] Check the roadwheel nuts are tightened to the specified torque (Section 22)
- [ ] Lubricate all door, bonnet and tailgate hinges and locks (Section 23)
- [ ] Carry out a road test (Section 24)
- [ ] Check the coolant strength (Section 33)

Every 25 000 miles or 2 years, whichever comes first

In addition to the items listed above, carry out the following:

- [ ] Renew the pollen filter (Section 25)
- [ ] Renew the air filter (Section 26)
- [ ] Renew the brake fluid (Section 27)

Every 37 500 miles or 3 years, whichever comes first

In addition to the items listed above, carry out the following:

- [ ] Check the braking system rubber hoses (Section 28)
- [ ] Renew the auxiliary drivebelt and tensioner (Section 29)
- [ ] Renew the spark plugs Section 30
- [ ] Check the manual transmission oil level Section 31
- [ ] Renew the remote control battery (Section 32)
- [ ] Renew the coolant (Section 33)

Note: *Nissan state that, if their Nissan antifreeze is in the system from new, the coolant need only be changed every 5 years. If there is any doubt as to the type or quality of the antifreeze which has been used, we recommend this shorter interval be observed.*

2 Component locations

Underbonnet view of a 1.2 litre model

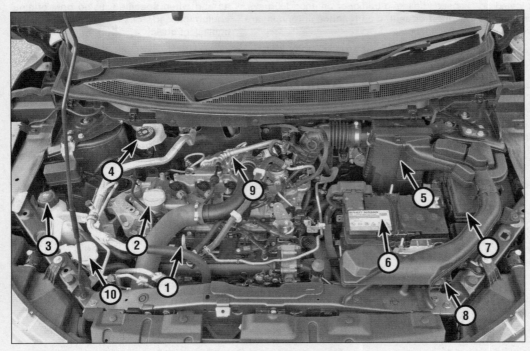

1 Engine oil level dipstick
2 Engine oil filler cap
3 Coolant reservoir (expansion tank)
4 Brake and clutch fluid reservoir
5 Air cleaner
6 Battery
7 Fuse/relay box
8 Engine management ECM
9 Turbocharger
10 Windscreen washer fluid filler cap

Front underbody view

1 Transmission drain plug
2 Exhaust front pipe
3 Rear engine/transmission mounting
4 Subframe
5 Suspension lower arm
6 Brake calipers
7 Track rod end
8 Engine oil drain plug
9 Engine oil filter

Rear underbody view

1 *Fuel tank*
2 *Rear brake calipers*
3 *Rear axle torsion beam*
4 *Exhaust rear silencer*
5 *Shock absorber*
6 *Rear coil springs*

3 General Information

1 This Chapter is designed to help the home mechanic maintain his/her car for safety, economy, long life and peak performance.
2 The Chapter contains a master maintenance schedule, followed by Sections dealing specifically with each task in the schedule. Visual checks, adjustments, component renewal and other helpful items are included. Refer to the accompanying illustrations of the engine compartment and the underside of the car for the locations of the various components.
3 Servicing your car in accordance with the mileage/time maintenance schedule and the following Sections will provide a planned maintenance programme, which should result in a long and reliable service life. This is a comprehensive plan, so maintaining some items but not others at the specified service intervals, will not produce the same results.
4 As you service your car, you will discover that many of the procedures can – and should – be grouped together, because of the particular procedure being performed, or because of the proximity of two otherwise-unrelated components to one another. For example, if the car is raised for any reason, the exhaust can be inspected at the same time as the suspension and steering components.
5 The first step in this maintenance programme is to prepare yourself before the actual work begins. Read through all the Sections relevant to the work to be carried out, then make a list and gather all the parts and tools required. If a problem is encountered, seek advice from a parts specialist, or a dealer service department.

4 Regular maintenance

1 If, from the time the car is new, the routine maintenance schedule is followed closely, and frequent checks are made of fluid levels and high-wear items, as suggested throughout this manual, the engine will be kept in relatively good running condition, and the need for additional work will be minimised.
2 It is possible that there will be times when the engine is running poorly due to the lack of regular maintenance. This is even more likely if a used car, which has not received regular and frequent maintenance checks, is purchased. In such cases, additional work may need to be carried out, outside of the regular maintenance intervals.
3 If engine wear is suspected, a compression test (refer to Chapter 2D Section 2) will provide valuable information regarding the overall performance of the main internal components. Such a test can be used as a basis to decide on the extent of the work to be carried out. If, for example, a compression test indicates serious internal engine wear, conventional maintenance as described in this Chapter will not greatly improve the performance of the engine, and may prove a waste of time and money, unless extensive overhaul work is carried out first.
4 The following series of operations are those most often required to improve the performance of a generally poor-running engine:

Primary operations

a) *Clean, inspect and test the battery (refer to Section 11).*
b) *Check all the engine-related fluids.*
c) *Check the condition of all hoses, and check for fluid leaks (Section 15).*
d) *Check the condition of the auxiliary drivebelt (Section 16).*
e) *Renew the spark plugs (Section 30).*
f) *Check the condition of the air filter, and renew if necessary (Section 26).*

5 If the above operations do not prove fully effective, carry out the following secondary operations:

Secondary operations

6 All items listed under Primary operations, plus the following:
a) *Check the charging system (Chapter 5 Section 5).*
b) *Check the ignition system (Chapter 6A Section 8).*
c) *Check the fuel system (Chapter 4A Section 1).*
d) *Check the engine control and emission systems (Chapter 6A Section 2).*

5.8 The dipstick is located at the front of the engine (see Underbonnet check points); the dipstick is often brightly coloured and/or has a picture of an oil-can on the top for identification. Withdraw the dipstick

5.9 Using a clean rag or paper towel, remove all oil from the dipstick. Insert the clean dipstick into the tube as far as it will go, then withdraw it again

may result if the engine is overfilled by adding too much oil.

8 Locate the engine oil level dipstick and pull it from place **(see illustration)**.

9 Wipe the dipstick clean, then fully insert it into the guide tube **(see illustration)**.

10 Withdraw the dipstick again and examine the oil level. It should be between the upper (MAX) and lower (MIN) marks **(see illustration)**. If it is near the lower mark, new engine oil needs to be added.

11 Rotate the engine oil filler cap anti-clockwise and remove it. Using a funnel, add new engine oil, a little at a time, to bring the level to the upper (MAX) mark on the dipstick **(see illustration)**. Add the oil slowly, frequently checking the level on the dipstick.

12 Securely refit the filler cap.

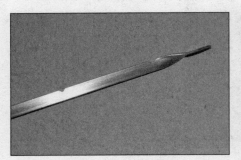

5.10 Note the oil level on the end of the dipstick, which should be between the upper mark and lower mark in the side of the dipstick. Approximately 1.0 litre of oil will raise the level from the lower mark to the upper mark

5.11 Oil is added through the filler cap aperture. Unscrew the cap and top-up the level; a funnel may help to reduce spillage. Add the oil slowly, checking the level on the dipstick often. Don't overfill

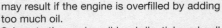

6 Coolant level check

> ⚠ **Warning: Do not attempt to remove the expansion tank pressure cap when the engine is hot, as there is a very great risk of scalding. Do not leave open containers of coolant about, as it is poisonous.**

1 With this type of cooling system (sealed), adding coolant should not be necessary on a regular basis. If frequent topping-up is required, it is likely there is a leak. Check the radiator, all hoses and joint faces for signs of staining or wetness, and rectify as necessary.

2 It is important that antifreeze is used in the cooling system all year round, not just during the winter months. Don't top up with water alone, as the antifreeze will become diluted. Refer to 'Specifications' at the beginning of this Chapter.

3 With the engine completely cold, the coolant level should be between the upper and lower marks on the side of the reservoir (expansion tank) **(see illustration)**.

4 If more coolant is required, rotate the filler cap anti-clockwise (see 'Warning', at the beginning of this Section) and then remove it **(see illustration)**.

5 Add new coolant to bring the level to the upper mark, then securely refit the cap **(see illustration)**.

5 Engine oil level check
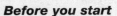

Before you start

1 Make sure that the car is on level ground.
2 The transmission must be in Neutral or Park, and the pedals not depressed.
3 The engine must be at normal operating temperature, and switched off.

The correct oil

4 Modern engines place great demands on

their oil. It is very important that the correct oil for your car is used (see 'Specifications' at the beginning of this Chapter).

Level check

5 If you have to add oil frequently, you should check whether you have any oil leaks. Place some clean paper under the car overnight, and check for stains in the morning. If there are no leaks, then the engine may be burning oil.

6 Always maintain the level between the upper and lower dipstick marks.

7 If the oil level is too low, severe engine damage may occur, and also, oil seal failure

6.3 The coolant level is indicated by the minimum and maximum marks visible on the side of the reservoir

6.4 Rotate the cap anti-clockwise and remove it

6.5 Add new coolant to bring the level to the upper mark

7   Brake and clutch fluid level check
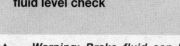

⚠️ **Warning: Brake fluid can harm your eyes and damage painted surfaces, so use extreme caution when handling and pouring it.**

⚠️ **Warning: Do not use fluid that has been standing open for some time, as it absorbs moisture from the air, which can cause a dangerous loss of braking effectiveness.**

1 The fluid level in the reservoir will drop slightly as the brake pads wear down, but the fluid level must never be allowed to drop below the MIN mark.

Before you start

2 Make sure that the car is on level ground.

Safety first!

3 If the reservoir requires repeated topping-up this is an indication of a fluid leak somewhere in the system, which should be investigated immediately.

4 If a leak is suspected, the car should not be driven until the braking system has been checked. Never take any risks where brakes are concerned

Level check

5 The fluid level is visible through the reservoir. The level must be kept between the MAX and MIN marks at all times **(see illustration)**.

6 If topping-up is necessary, first wipe clean the area around the filler cap to prevent dirt entering the hydraulic system **(see illustration)**.

7 Rotate the cap anti-clockwise and remove it **(see illustration)**. If the fluid is dirty, the hydraulic system should be drained and refilled as described later on in this Chapter.

8 Carefully add new fluid from a sealed container to bring the level to the upper mark **(see illustration)**. Use only the fluid specified (see 'Specifications' at the beginning of this Chapter); mixing different types can cause damage to the system. After topping-up to the correct level, securely refit the cap and wipe off any spilt fluid.

8   Screenwash fluid

1 Screenwash additives not only keep the windscreen clean during bad weather, they also prevent the washer system freezing in cold weather – which is when you are likely to need it most. Don't top-up using plain water, as the screenwash will become diluted, and will freeze during cold weather.

⚠️ **Warning: On no account use engine coolant antifreeze in the screen washer system – this may damage the paintwork.**

7.5 The MAX and MIN marks are indicated on the side of the reservoir. The fluid level must be kept between the marks at all times

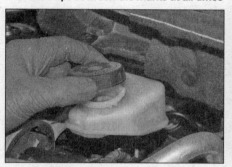
7.7 Unscrew the reservoir cap and carefully lift it out of position

2 The screen washer fluid reservoir filler cap is located at the front, right-hand side of the engine compartment **(see illustration)**. The headlight washers (where fitted), are supplied from the same reservoir.

3 Add screenwash as per the manufacturers instructions, written on the side of the bottle **(see illustration)**.

9   Tyre condition and pressure check

Tyre condition and pressure

1 It is very important that tyres are in good condition, and at the correct pressure – having a tyre failure at any speed is highly dangerous.

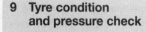

8.2 Lift the cap

7.6 Wipe the top of the reservoir

7.8 Carefully add fluid taking care not to spill it onto the surrounding components

2 Tyre wear is influenced by driving style – harsh braking and acceleration, or fast cornering, will all produce more rapid tyre wear. As a general rule, the front tyres wear out faster than the rears. Interchanging the tyres from front to rear ("rotating" the tyres) may result in more even wear. However, if this is completely effective, you may have the expense of replacing all four tyres at once!

3 Remove any nails or stones embedded in the tread before they penetrate the tyre to cause deflation. If removal of a nail does reveal that the tyre has been punctured, refit the nail so that its point of penetration is marked. Then immediately change the wheel, and have the tyre repaired by a tyre dealer.

4 Regularly check the tyres for damage in the form of cuts or bulges, especially in the sidewalls. Periodically remove the wheels,

8.3 When topping-up, add a screenwash additive in the quantities recommended by the manufacturer

9.6 The tyres may have tread wear safety bands (B), which will appear when the tread depth reaches approximately 1.6 mm. The band positions are indicated by a triangular mark on the tyre sidewall (A)

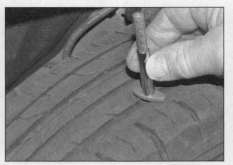

9.7 Tread wear can be monitored with a tread depth indicator gauge

9.8 Check the tyre pressures regularly with the tyres cold

Shoulder wear

Centre wear

Uneven wear

and clean any dirt or mud from the inside and outside surfaces. Examine the wheel rims for signs of rusting, corrosion or other damage. Light alloy wheels are easily damaged by "kerbing" whilst parking; steel wheels may also become dented or buckled. A new wheel is very often the only way to overcome severe damage.

5 New tyres should be balanced when they are fitted, but it may become necessary to re-balance them as they wear, or if the balance weights fitted to the wheel rim should fall off. Unbalanced tyres will wear more quickly, as will the steering and suspension components. Wheel imbalance is normally signified by vibration, particularly at a certain speed (typically around 50 mph). If this vibration is felt only through the steering, then it is likely that just the front wheels need balancing. If, however, the vibration is felt through the whole car, the rear wheels could be out of balance. Wheel balancing should be carried out by a tyre dealer or garage.

6 The tyres may have tread wear safety bands, which indicate when the tread depth reaches the legal limit **(see illustration)**.

7 Alternatively, monitor the tread wear with a simple, inexpensive device known as a tread depth indicator gauge **(see illustration)**.

8 Regularly check the pressures with a pressure gauge when the tyres are cold **(see illustration)**. Do not adjust the pressures immediately after the vehicle has been used, or an inaccurate setting will result.

Tyre tread wear patterns

Shoulder wear

Underinflation (wear on both sides)

Under-inflation will cause overheating of the tyre, because the tyre will flex too much, and the tread will not sit correctly on the road surface. This will cause a loss of grip and excessive wear, not to mention the danger of sudden tyre failure due to heat build-up.

Remedy: Check and adjust pressures.

Incorrect wheel camber (wear on one side)

Remedy: Repair or renew suspension parts

Hard cornering

Remedy: Reduce speed!

Centre wear

Overinflation

Over-inflation will cause rapid wear of the centre part of the tyre tread, coupled with reduced grip, harsher ride, and the danger of shock damage occurring in the tyre casing.

Remedy: Check and adjust pressures.

Note: *If you sometimes have to inflate your car's tyres to the higher pressures specified for maximum load or sustained high speed,* don't forget to reduce the pressures to normal afterwards.

Uneven wear

Front tyres may wear unevenly as a result of wheel misalignment. Most tyre dealers and garages can check and adjust the wheel alignment (or "tracking") for a modest charge.

Incorrect camber or castor

Remedy: Repair or renew suspension parts.

Malfunctioning suspension

Remedy: Repair or renew suspension parts.

Unbalanced wheel

Remedy: Have the wheels balanced.

Incorrect toe setting

Remedy: Adjust front wheel alignment (see Chapter 10 Section 17).

Note: *The feathered edge of the tread which typifies toe wear is best checked by feel.*

10 Wiper blades

1 Check the condition of the wiper blades; if they are cracked or show any signs of deterioration, or if the glass swept area is smeared, renew them **(see illustration)**. Wiper blades should be renewed annually.

2 To remove a front wiper blade, pull the arm away from the screen, turn the blade slightly and depress the clip, then slide the blade down the arm to release **(see illustrations)**. Take care not to allow the arm to spring back against the windscreen!

3 To remove a rear wiper blade, pull the arm away from the screen, squeeze together the clips, swing the blade out and remove it **(see illustration)**.

11   Battery check

Caution: Before carrying out any work on the vehicle battery, read the precautions given in 'Safety first!' at the start of this manual.

1 Make sure that the battery tray is in good condition, and that the clamp is tight. Corrosion on the tray, retaining clamp and the battery itself can be removed with a solution of water and baking soda. Thoroughly rinse all cleaned areas with water. Any metal parts damaged by corrosion should be covered with a zinc-based primer, then painted.

2 Periodically (approximately every three months), check the charge condition of the battery as described in Chapter 5 Section 3.

3 If the battery is flat, and you need to jump start your vehicle, see *Roadside Repairs*.

4 The battery is located on the left-hand-side of the engine compartment. where fitted, lift the cover to access the battery **(see illustrations)**.

Battery corrosion can be kept to a minimum by applying a layer of petroleum jelly to the clamps and terminals after they are reconnected.

12   Electrical systems check

1 Check all external lights and the horn. Refer to the appropriate Sections of the Wiring Diagrams, at the end of this manual, for details of any circuits that are found to be inoperative.

2 Visually check all accessible wiring connectors, harnesses and retaining clips for security, and for signs of chafing or damage.

If you need to check your brake lights and indicators unaided, back up to a wall or garage door and operate the lights. The reflected light should show if they are working properly.

3 If a single indicator light, stop-light or

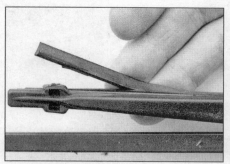

10.1 Check the condition of the wiper blades

10.2a Depress the clip. . .

10.2b . . . and slide the blade down to release from the arm

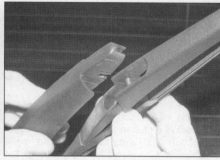

10.3 Pull the arm away from the screen, squeeze together the clips, swing the blade out, and remove it from the catch

11.4a Lift the plastic cover to gain access to the battery positive terminal. The exterior of the battery should be inspected periodically for damage such as a cracked case or cover.

11.4b Check the battery lead clamps for tightness to ensure good electrical connections, and check the leads for signs ofdamage.

11.4c If corrosion (white, fluffy deposits) is evident, remove the cables from the battery terminals, clean them with asmall wire brush, then refit them. Automotive stores sell a tool for cleaning the battery post. . .

11.4d . . . as well as the battery cable clamps.

12.3 If a single indicator light, stop-light or headlight has failed, it is likely that a bulb has blown

12.4 The fuses are located in the fuse-box under the passengers side of the facia.

12.5 Use fuse puller to remove the fuse

headlight has failed, it is likely that a bulb has blown and will need to be renewed **(see illustration)**. Refer to Chapter 12 Section 5 for details. If both stop-lights have failed, it is possible that the switch has failed (see Chapter 9 Section 16).

4 If more than one indicator light or tail light has failed, check that a fuse has not blown or that there is a fault in the circuit (see Chapter 12 Section 3). The fuses are located in the fuse-box under the passengers side of the facia **(see illustration)**. Slacken the screws, and fold down the fuseholder. The fuse allocations are given on a separate sheet.

5 To renew a blown fuse, simply pull it out and fit a new fuse of the correct rating (see Chapter 12 Section 3) **(see illustration)**. If the fuse blows again, it is important that you find out why.

13 Engine oil and filter renewal

1 Frequent oil and filter changes are the most important preventative maintenance procedures that can be undertaken by the DIY owner. As engine oil ages, it becomes diluted and contaminated, which leads to premature engine wear.

2 Before starting this procedure, gather together all the necessary tools and materials. Also make sure that you have plenty of clean rags and newspapers handy, to mop-up any spills. Ideally, the engine oil should be warm, as it will drain more easily, and more built-up sludge will be removed with it.

3 Take care not to touch the exhaust or any

other hot parts of the engine when working under the vehicle. To avoid any possibility of scalding, and to protect yourself from possible skin irritants and other harmful contaminants in used engine oils, it is advisable to wear gloves when carrying out this work.

4 Access to the underside of the vehicle will be greatly improved if it can be raised on a lift, driven onto ramps, or jacked up and supported on axle stands (see *Jacking and vehicle support*). Whichever method is chosen, make sure that the vehicle remains level, or if it is at an angle, that the drain plug is at the lowest point. The drain plug is located at the rear of the sump **(see illustration 13.8)**. Undo the retaining bolts and remove the engine undershield from under the front of the vehicle.

5 Remove the oil filler cap from the cylinder head camshaft cover at the timing chain end (twist it anti-clockwise and withdraw it) **(see illustration)**.

6 Using a spanner, or a suitable socket and bar, slacken the drain plug about half a turn. Position the draining container under the drain plug, and then remove the plug completely. If possible, try to keep the plug pressed into the sump while unscrewing it by hand the last couple of turns.

7 Allow some time for the oil to drain, noting that it may be necessary to reposition the container as the oil flow slows to a trickle.

8 After all the oil has drained; wipe the drain plug with a clean rag. Remove the old sealing washer from the drain plug and fit a new one. Clean the area around the drain plug opening, and refit the plug complete with the new sealing washer. Tighten the drain plug securely – preferably to the specified torque, using a torque wrench **(see illustration)**.

9 The oil filter is located in the lower part of the of the cylinder block, at the front – access is obtained from underneath the vehicle.

10 Move the container into position under the oil filter to catch the oil spillage.

11 The filter is a cartridge inside the oil filter housing. Using a bar and socket, unscrew the filter housing cap **(see illustration)**, and then withdraw the filter cartridge, draining the oil into the container.

12 Use a clean rag to remove any oil, dirt and sludge from up inside the oil filter housing in the cylinder block **(see illustration)**. Remove

13.5 Remove oil filler cap

13.8 Using a torque wrench to tighten the drain plug

13.11 Unscrew the oil filter housing cap

13.12 Clean out the filter housing

any old rubber seals from the oil filter housing and filter cap and fit the new seals, which should be supplied with the filter.

13 Apply a light coating of clean engine oil to the sealing rings, then insert the filter cartridge. Screw the filter cap into position on the engine. Tighten the filter cap firmly by hand at first, then to the specified torque, using a torque wrench **(see illustrations)**.

14 Remove the old oil and all tools from under the vehicle, and where applicable lower the vehicle to the ground.

15 Fill the engine through the oil filler hole in the cylinder head cover, using the correct grade and type of oil (see 'Specifications' at the beginning of this Chapter). Pour in half the specified quantity of oil first, and then wait a few minutes for the oil to drain into the sump. Continue to add oil, a small quantity at a time, until the level is up to the lower mark on the dipstick. Adding a further 0.5 litre will bring the level up to the upper mark on the dipstick. Refit the oil filler cap when correct level is achieved (see Section 5).

16 Start the engine and run it for a few minutes, while checking for leaks around the oil filter seal and the sump drain plug. Note that there may be a delay of a few seconds before the low oil pressure warning light goes out when the engine is first started, as the oil circulates through the new oil filter and the engine oil galleries before the pressure builds-up. Do not run the engine above idle speed while the warning light is on.

17 Stop the engine, and wait a few minutes for the oil to settle in the sump once more. With the new oil circulated and the filter now completely full, recheck the level on the dipstick, and add more oil as necessary. Where applicable, refit the engine undershield.

18 Dispose of the used engine oil and filter safely, referring to *General repair procedures*. Do not discard the old filter with domestic household waste. The facility for waste oil disposal provided by many local council refuse tips generally has a filter receptacle alongside.

14 Resetting the service indicator

1 The instrument cluster mileage recorder incorporates a service interval indicator. When the vehicle is started, the unit displays the mileage until the next service, or the mileage covered since the service was due. The service indicator is manually reset to zero after the vehicle has been serviced. The indicator can also be reset at any time using a suitable diagnostic tool.

2 If your ignition is on, turn it off and then back on. Press the left-hand steering wheel button until you reach the settings section on the instrument panel. Once you reach the settings section, keep the button pressed until a new menu appears. Scroll to the "maintenance"

13.13a Lubricate the new seal with clean engine oil

13.13b . . . fit new filter element to housing. . .

13.13c . . . then fit the filter housing cap. . .

13.13d . . . and tighten to the specified torque

category, then press the button, and scroll down to the "Service" category. Press the button again and scroll down to the "Reset" option. Once on the "Reset" option, press the button. Turn the ignition off, then on and your service indicator light should now be turned off.

3 Switch on the ignition – the distance remaining until (or covered since) the next service is due will flash in the display.

15 Hose and fluid leak check

General

1 Visually inspect the engine joint faces, gaskets and seals for any signs of water or oil leaks. Pay particular attention to the areas around the cylinder head cover, cylinder head, oil filter and sump joint faces. Bear in mind that, over a period of time, some very slight seepage from these areas is to be expected – what you are really looking for is any indication of a serious leak. Should a leak be found, renew the offending gasket or oil seal by referring to the appropriate Chapters in this manual.

2 High temperatures in the engine compartment can cause the deterioration of the rubber and plastic hoses used for engine, accessory and emission systems operation. Periodic inspection should be made for cracks, loose clamps, material hardening and leaks.

3 When checking the hoses, ensure that all the cable-ties or clips used to retain the hoses are in place, and in good condition. Clips which are broken or missing can lead to chafing of the hoses, pipes or wiring, which could cause more serious problems in the future.

4 Carefully check the large top and bottom radiator hoses, along with the other smaller-diameter cooling system hoses and metal pipes; do not forget the heater hoses/pipes which run from the engine to the bulkhead. Inspect each hose along its entire length, renewing any that is cracked, swollen or shows signs of deterioration. Cracks may become more apparent if the hose is squeezed, and may often be apparent at the hose ends.

5 Make sure that all hose connections are tight. If the large-diameter air hoses from the air cleaner are loose, they will leak air, and upset the engine idle quality. If the spring clamps that are used to secure some of the hoses appear to be slackening, they should be updated with worm-drive clips to prevent the possibility of leaks.

6 Some other hoses are secured to their fittings with clamps. Where clamps are used, check to be sure they haven't lost their tension, allowing the hose to leak. If clamps aren't used, make sure the hose has not expanded and/or hardened where it slips over the fitting, allowing it to leak.

7 Check all fluid reservoirs, filler caps, drain plugs and fittings, etc, looking for any signs of leakage of oil, transmission and/or brake

15.16 Check the security of the fuel hose where it joins the fuel pump

hydraulic fluid and coolant. Also check the clutch hydraulic fluid lines which lead from the fluid reservoir, master cylinder, and the slave cylinder, on the transmission (where applicable).

8 If the vehicle is regularly parked in the same place, close inspection of the ground underneath it will soon show any leaks; ignore the puddle of water which will be left if the air conditioning system is in use. Place a clean piece of cardboard below the engine, and examine it for signs of contamination after the vehicle has been parked over it overnight – be aware, however, of the fire risk inherent in placing combustible material below the catalytic converter.

9 Remember that some leaks will only occur with the engine running, or when the engine is hot or cold. With the handbrake firmly applied, start the engine from cold, and let the engine idle while you examine the underside of the engine compartment for signs of leakage.

10 If an unusual smell is noticed inside or around the car, especially when the engine is thoroughly hot, this may point to the presence of a leak.

11 As soon as a leak is detected, its source must be traced and rectified. Where oil has been leaking for some time, it is usually necessary to use a steam cleaner, pressure washer or similar, to clean away the accumulated dirt, so that the exact source of the leak can be identified.

Vacuum hoses

12 It's quite common for vacuum hoses, especially those in the emissions system,

16.4 Check for drive belt wear

to be colour-coded, or to be identified by coloured stripes moulded into them. Various systems require hoses with different wall thicknesses, collapse resistance and temperature resistance. When renewing hoses, be sure the new ones are made of the same material.

13 Often the only effective way to check a hose is to remove it completely from the vehicle. If more than one hose is removed, be sure to label the hoses and fittings to ensure correct installation.

14 When checking vacuum hoses, be sure to include any plastic T-fittings in the check. Inspect the fittings for cracks, and check the hose where it fits over the fitting for distortion, which could cause leakage.

15 A small piece of vacuum hose (approximately 6 mm inside diameter) can be used as a stethoscope to detect vacuum leaks. Hold one end of the hose to your ear, and probe around vacuum hoses and fittings, listening for the 'hissing' sound characteristic of a vacuum leak.

⚠ Warning: When probing with the vacuum hose stethoscope, be very careful not to come into contact with moving engine components such as the auxiliary drivebelt, radiator electric cooling fan, etc.

Fuel hoses

⚠ Warning: There are certain precautions which must be taken when inspecting or servicing fuel system components. Work in a well-ventilated area, and do not allow open flames (cigarettes, appliance pilot lights, etc) or bare light bulbs near the work area. Mop-up any spills immediately, and do not store fuel-soaked rags where they could ignite.

16 Check all fuel hoses for deterioration and chafing. Check especially for cracks in areas where the hose bends, and also just before fittings, such as where a hose attaches to the fuel rail (see illustration).

17 High-quality fuel line, usually identified by the word 'Fluoroelastomer' printed on the hose, should be used for fuel line renewal. Never, under any circumstances, use non-reinforced vacuum line, clear plastic tubing or water hose as a substitute for fuel lines.

18 Spring-type clamps may be used on fuel lines. These clamps often lose their tension over a period of time, and can be 'sprung' during removal. Renew all spring-type clamps with proper petrol pipe clips whenever a hose is renewed.

Metal pipes

19 Sections of metal piping are often used for fuel line between the fuel tank and the engine, and for most air conditioning applications. Check carefully to be sure the piping has not been bent or crimped, and that cracks have not started in the line; also check for signs of excessive corrosion.

20 If a section of metal fuel line must be renewed, only seamless steel piping should be used, since copper and aluminium piping don't have the strength necessary to withstand normal engine vibration.

21 Check the metal lines where they enter the brake master cylinder, ABS hydraulic unit or clutch master/slave cylinders (as applicable) for cracks in the lines or loose fittings. Any sign of brake fluid leakage calls for an immediate and thorough inspection.

Air conditioning refrigerant

⚠ Warning: Refer to the safety information given in 'Safety first!' and Chapter 3 Section 12, regarding the dangers of disturbing any of the air conditioning system components.

22 The air conditioning system is filled with a liquid refrigerant, which is retained under high pressure. If the air conditioning system is opened and depressurised without the aid of specialised equipment, the refrigerant will immediately turn into gas and escape into the atmosphere. If the liquid comes into contact with your skin, it can cause severe frostbite. In addition, the refrigerant contains substances which are environmentally damaging; for this reason, it should not be allowed to escape into the atmosphere.

23 Any suspected air conditioning system leaks should be immediately referred to a Nissan dealer or air conditioning specialist. Leakage will be shown up as a steady drop in the level of refrigerant in the system.

24 Note that water may drip from the condenser drain pipe, underneath the car, immediately after the air conditioning system has been in use. This is normal, and should not be cause for concern.

16 Auxiliary drivebelt check

1 A single auxiliary drivebelt is fitted at the right-hand side of the engine. The length of the drivebelt varies according to whether air conditioning is fitted.

2 Due to their function and material makeup, drivebelts are prone to failure after a long period of time, and should therefore be inspected regularly.

3 Since the drivebelt is located very close to the right-hand side of the engine compartment, it is possible to gain better access by raising the front of the car and removing the right-hand wheel and wheel arch inner liner.

4 With the engine stopped, inspect the full length of the drivebelt for cracks and separation of the belt plies. It will be necessary to turn the engine (using a spanner or socket and bar on the crankshaft pulley bolt) in order to move the belt from the pulleys so that the belt can be inspected thoroughly. Twist the belt between the pulleys so that both sides can be viewed (see illustration). Also check

for fraying, and glazing which gives the belt a shiny appearance. Check the pulleys for nicks, cracks, distortion and corrosion.

5 Small cracks in the belt ribs are not usually serious, but look closely to see whether the crack has extended into the belt plies. If the belt is in any way suspect, or is known to have seen long service, renew it as described in Section 29.

17 Seat belt check

1 All models are fitted with three-point diagonal inertia reel seat belts for all seats.
2 Check the seat belts for satisfactory operation and condition. Pull sharply on the belt to check that the locking mechanism engages correctly. Check that they retract smoothly and without binding into their reels.
3 Inspect the belts for signs of fraying or other damage and check the operation of the buckles. Ensure that all mounting bolts are securely tightened, noting that the bolts are shouldered so that the belt anchor points are free to rotate.
4 If there is any sign of damage, or any doubt about the condition of a belt, it must be renewed. If the vehicle has been involved in a collision, any belts in use at the time should be renewed as a matter of course, and all other belts should be checked carefully.
5 Use only warm water and non-detergent soap to clean the belts. Never use any chemical cleaners, strong detergents, dyes or bleaches. Keep the belts fully extended until they have dried naturally – do not apply heat to dry them.

18 Brake pad and disc wear check

1 Slacken the roadwheel nuts, apply the handbrake, then jack up the car and support it securely on axle stands (see *Jacking and vehicle support*). Remove the relevant roadwheel, depending on which brakes are to be checked.
2 The brake pad thickness, and the condition

18.2 With the wheel removed, the pad thickness can be seen through the front of the caliper

of the disc, can be assessed roughly with just the wheels removed (**see illustration**). For a comprehensive check, the brake pads should be removed and cleaned. The operation of the caliper can then also be checked, and the condition of the brake disc itself can be fully examined on both sides. Refer to Chapter 9, for further information.
3 On completion, refit the roadwheels and lower the car to the ground. Tighten the roadwheel nuts to their specified torque.

19 Driveshaft gaiter check

1 With the vehicle raised and securely supported on stands, turn the steering onto full lock, then slowly rotate the roadwheel. Inspect the condition of the outer constant velocity (CV) joint rubber gaiters while squeezing the gaiters to open out the folds. Check for signs of cracking, splits or deterioration of the rubber which may allow the grease to escape and lead to water and grit entry into the joint. Also check the security and condition of the retaining clips. Repeat these checks on the inner CV joints (**see illustration**). If any damage or deterioration is found, the gaiters should be renewed as described in Chapter 8 Section 9.
2 At the same time, check the general condition of the CV joints themselves by first holding the driveshaft and attempting to rotate the wheel. Repeat this check

19.1 Check the constant velocity (CV) joint gaiters – outer one shown

by holding the inner joint and attempting to rotate the driveshaft. Any appreciable movement indicates wear in the joints, wear in the driveshaft splines, or a loose driveshaft retaining nut.

20 Steering and suspension check

Front suspension and steering

1 Firmly apply the handbrake, and then jack up the front of the vehicle and support it securely on axle stands (see *Jacking and vehicle support*).
2 Visually inspect the balljoint dust covers and the steering rack and pinion gaiters for splits, chafing or deterioration (**see illustrations**). Any wear of these components will cause loss of lubricant, together with dirt and water entry, resulting in rapid deterioration of the balljoints or steering gear.
3 Grasp the roadwheel at the 12 o'clock and 6 o'clock positions, and try to rock it (**see illustration**). Very slight free play may be felt, but if the movement is appreciable, further investigation is necessary to determine the source. Continue rocking the wheel while an assistant depresses the footbrake. If the movement is now eliminated or significantly reduced, it is likely that the hub bearings are at fault. If the free play is still evident with the footbrake depressed, then there is wear in the suspension joints or mountings.

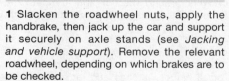

20.2a Check the ball joint dust covers. . .

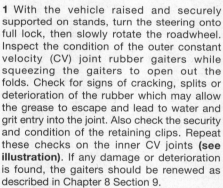

20.2b . . . the steering rack gaiters. . .

20.2c . . . and the anti-roll bar drop link ball joint dust covers

20.3 Check for wear in the hub bearings by grasping the wheel and trying to rock it

20.4 Check for wear in the steering rack or ball joints by grasping the wheel and trying to rock it

4 Now grasp the wheel at the 9 o'clock and 3 o'clock positions, and try to rock it as before **(see illustration)**. Any movement felt now may again be caused by wear in the hub bearings or the steering track rod balljoints. If the inner or outer balljoint is worn, the visual movement will be obvious.

5 Using a large screwdriver or flat bar, check for wear in the suspension mounting bushes by levering between the relevant suspension component and its attachment point. Some movement is to be expected as the mountings are made of rubber, but excessive wear should be obvious. Also check the condition of any visible rubber bushes, looking for splits, cracks or contamination of the rubber.

6 With the car standing on its wheels, have an assistant turn the steering wheel back-and-forth about an eighth of a turn each way. There should be very little, if any, lost movement between the steering wheel and roadwheels. If this is not the case, closely observe the joints and mountings previously described, but in addition check the steering column universal joints for wear, and also check the rack-and-pinion steering gear itself.

Rear suspension

7 Chock the front wheels, then jack up the rear of the vehicle and support securely on axle stands (see *Jacking and vehicle support*).

8 Working as described previously for the front suspension, check the rear hub bearings, the suspension bushes and the shock absorber mountings for wear.

21.2 Check the condition of the exhaust rubber mountings

Strut/shock absorber check

9 Check for any signs of fluid leakage around the suspension strut/shock absorber body, or from the rubber gaiter around the piston rod. Should any fluid be noticed, the suspension strut/shock absorber is defective internally, and should be renewed.

Note: *Suspension struts/shock absorbers should always be renewed in pairs on the same axle.*

10 The efficiency of the suspension strut/shock absorber may be checked by bouncing the vehicle at each corner. Generally speaking, the body will return to its normal position and stop after being depressed. If it rises and returns on a rebound, the suspension strut/shock absorber is probably suspect. Examine the suspension strut/shock absorber upper and lower mountings for any signs of wear.

21 Exhaust system check

1 With the engine cold (at least three hours after the vehicle has been driven), check the complete exhaust system, from its starting point at the engine to the end of the tailpipe. Ideally, this should be done on a hoist, where unrestricted access is available; if a hoist is not available, raise and support the vehicle on axle stands (see *Jacking and vehicle support*).

2 Make sure that all brackets and rubber mountings are in good condition, and tight; if any of the mountings are to be renewed, ensure that the new ones are of the correct type – in the case of the rubber mountings, their colour is a good guide. Those nearest to the catalytic converter are more heat-resistant than the others **(see illustration)**.

3 Check the pipes and connections for evidence of leaks, severe corrosion, or damage. One of the most common points for a leak to develop is around the welded joints between the pipes and silencers. Leakage at any of the joints or in other parts of the system will usually show up as a black sooty stain in the vicinity of the leak. **Note:** *Exhaust sealants should not be used on any part of the exhaust system upstream of the catalytic converter*

(between the converter and engine) – even if the sealant does not contain additives harmful to the converter, pieces of it may break off and foul the element, causing local overheating.

4 At the same time, inspect the underside of the body for holes, corrosion, open seams, etc, which may allow exhaust gases to enter the passenger compartment. Seal all body openings with silicone or body putty.

5 Rattles and other noises can often be traced to the exhaust system, especially the rubber mountings. Try to move the system, silencer(s), heat shields and catalytic converter. If any components can touch the body or suspension parts, secure the exhaust system with new mountings.

6 Check the running condition of the engine by inspecting inside the end of the tailpipe; the exhaust deposits here are an indication of the engine's state of tune. The inside of the tailpipe should be dry, and should vary in colour from dark grey to light grey/brown; if it is black and sooty, or coated with white deposits, this may indicate the need for a full fuel system inspection.

22 Roadwheel nut tightness check

1 Remove the wheel trims or alloy wheel centre covers where necessary, and slacken the roadwheel nuts slightly.

2 Securely tighten the wheel nuts in a diagonal sequence, then tighten the nuts to the specified torque, using a torque wrench. Refit the wheel trim/hub cap/wheel nut covers (as applicable).

23 Hinge and lock lubrication

1 Work around the car and lubricate the hinges of the bonnet, doors and tailgate with light oil.

2 Lightly lubricate the bonnet release mechanism with a smear of grease.

3 Check carefully the security and operation of all hinges, latches and locks, adjusting them where required. Check the operation of the central locking system.

4 Check the condition and operation of the tailgate struts, renewing them both if either is leaking or no longer able to support the tailgate securely when raised.

24 Road test

Instruments and electrical equipment

1 Check the operation of all instruments and electrical equipment.

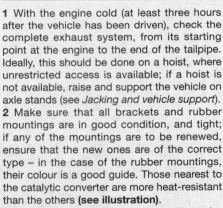

25.2a Unclip the filter cover...

25.2b ...and remove it from the heater housing

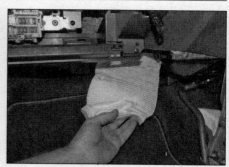
25.3 Withdraw the pollen filter from the housing

2 Make sure that all instruments read correctly, and switch on all electrical equipment in turn, to check that it functions properly.

Steering and suspension

3 Check for any abnormalities in the steering, suspension, handling or road 'feel'.
4 Drive the car, and check that there are no unusual vibrations or noises.
5 Check that the steering feels positive, with no excessive 'sloppiness', or roughness, and check for any suspension noises when cornering and driving over bumps.

Drivetrain

6 Check the performance of the engine, clutch, transmission and driveshafts.
7 Listen for any unusual noises from the engine, clutch and transmission.
8 Make sure that the engine runs smoothly when idling, and that there is no hesitation when accelerating.
9 Check that, where applicable, the clutch action is smooth and progressive, that the drive is taken up smoothly, and that the pedal travel is not excessive. Also listen for any noises when the clutch pedal is depressed.
10 Check that all gears can be engaged smoothly without noise, and that the gear lever action is smooth and not abnormally vague or 'notchy'.
11 Listen for a metallic clicking sound from the front of the car, as the car is driven slowly in a circle with the steering on full-lock. Carry out this check in both directions. If a

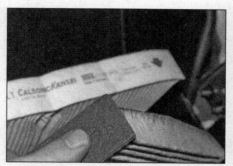
25.4 Note the direction arrow on the filter for refitting

25.5 Make sure the filter cover is secured

clicking noise is heard, this indicates wear in a driveshaft joint (see Chapter 8).

Braking system

12 Make sure that the car does not pull to one side when braking, and that the wheels do not lock when braking hard.
13 Check that there is no vibration through the steering when braking.
14 Check that the handbrake operates correctly, without excessive movement of the lever, and that it holds the car stationary on a slope.
15 Test the operation of the brake servo unit as follows. Depress the footbrake 4 or 5 times to exhaust the vacuum, then start the engine. As the engine starts, there should be a noticeable 'give' in the brake pedal as vacuum builds-up. Allow the engine to run for at least 2 minutes, and then switch it off.

If the brake pedal is now depressed again, it should be possible to detect a hiss from the servo as the pedal is depressed. After about 4 or 5 applications, no further hissing should be heard, and the pedal should feel considerably harder.

25 Pollen filter renewal

1 Remove the glovebox as described in Chapter 11 Section 25.
2 Release the securing clips and unclip the filter cover, from the rear of the heater housing unit **(see illustrations)**.
3 Collapse the pollen filter inside the housing and withdraw it, then wipe clean the area around the housing **(see illustration)**.

26.2a Remove the two retaining clips...

26.2b ...undo the bolt...

26.2c ...then release the clips and slide ducting from air cleaner housing

26.2d The clips at the centre are fragile and can break easily

26.3a Release the two securing clips (one at each side). . .

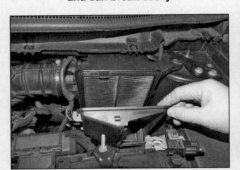

26.3b . . . then tilt the cover forwards. . .

26.3c . . . and withdraw the filter element

4 Fit the new filter to the housing, in the same way as it was removed, making sure it is fitted in the correct position, with the arrows facing towards the inside of the vehicle **(see illustration)**.

5 Refit the filter cover, making sure it is located correctly in the housing **(see illustration)**. Note if the securing clips have been damaged on removal, there are holes in the cover, so that screws can be used on refitting, if required.

6 Refit the glovebox back into the facia panel, as described in Chapter 11 Section 25.

26 Air filter element renewal

Caution: Never drive the vehicle with the air cleaner filter element removed. Excessive engine wear could result, and backfiring could even cause a fire under the bonnet.

1 The air filter element is located in the air cleaner assembly on the left-hand side rear of the engine compartment.

2 Release the two retaining clips on the front crossmember, undo the retaining bolt, then release the clips on the filter housing and slide the air intake resonator/inlet duct from the air cleaner housing **(see illustrations)**. The intake resonator and inlet duct to the front crossmember can be split, to remove, but the retaining clips at the centre can break easily, so we found removing the complete assembly as one is best.

3 Release the retaining clips and remove the front cover from the air cleaner housing, then

withdraw the filter element from the air cleaner housing **(see illustrations)**.

4 If carrying out a routine service, the element must be renewed regardless of its apparent condition.

5 If you are checking the element for any other reason, inspect its lower surface; if it is oily or very dirty, renew the element. If it is only moderately dusty, it can be re-used by blowing it clean from the upper to the lower surface with compressed air. Because it is a pleated-paper type filter, it cannot be washed or re-oiled. If it cannot be cleaned satisfactorily with compressed air, discard and renew it.

 Warning: Wear eye protection when using compressed air.

6 Position the new filter element in the housing, and secure the front cover in position with the retaining clips. Refit the air intake duct to the front of the air cleaner housing.

28.2 Rubber brake hose fitted to the front caliper

27 Brake fluid renewal

Caution: Brake hydraulic fluid can harm your eyes and damage painted surfaces, so use extreme caution when handling and pouring it. Do not use fluid that has been standing open for some time, as it absorbs moisture from the air. Excess moisture can cause a dangerous loss of braking effectiveness.

1 The procedure is similar to that for bleeding the hydraulic system as described in Chapter 9 Section 3, except that allowance should be made for the old fluid to be expelled when bleeding each section of the circuit.

2 Working as described in Chapter 9 Section 3, open the first bleed screw in the sequence, and pump the brake pedal gently until the level in the reservoir is approaching the MIN mark. Top-up to the MAX level with new fluid, and continue pumping until only new fluid remains in the reservoir, and new fluid can be seen emerging from the bleed screw. Tighten the screw, and top the reservoir level up to the MAX level line.

3 Work through all the remaining bleed screws in the sequence until new fluid can be seen at all of them. Be careful to keep the master cylinder reservoir topped-up above the MIN level at all times, or air may enter the system. If this happens, further bleeding will be required, to remove the air.

4 When the operation is complete, check that all bleed screws are securely tightened, and that their dust caps are refitted. Wash off all traces of spilt fluid, and recheck the master cylinder reservoir fluid level.

5 Check the operation of the brakes before taking the car on the road.

28 Braking system rubber hose check

1 Position the car over an inspection pit, on car ramps, or jack it up one wheel at a time (see *Jacking and vehicle support*).

2 Inspect the braking system rubber hoses fitted to each front caliper, and on each side of the rear axle **(see illustration)**. Look for perished, swollen or hardened rubber, and any signs of cracking, especially at the metal end fittings. If there's any doubt as to the condition of any hose, renew it as described in Chapter 9 Section 4.

29 Auxiliary drivebelt renewal

Removal

1 Slacken the right-hand roadwheel nuts, firmly apply the handbrake, then jack up the

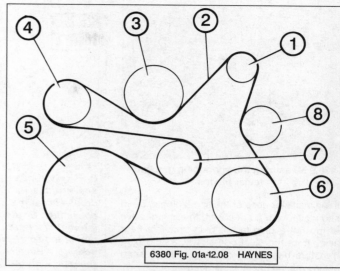

29.2 Turn the drivebelt tensioner (1) clockwise to release the tension on the belt

29.4 Auxilliary drivebelt routing (1.2 litre engines)

1	Alternator	5	Crankshaft pulley
2	Drivebelt	6	Air conditioning compressor
3	Coolant pump	7	Drivebelt tensioner
4	Idler roller	8	Idler roller

front of the vehicle and support it securely on axle stands (see *Jacking and vehicle support*). Remove the right-hand front wheel, and wheelarch liner.

2 Working under the right-hand front wheel arch, release the tension on the belt by turning the tensioner clockwise (as viewed from the right-hand side of the car) using a 16 mm spanner or socket **(see illustration)**.

3 Hold the tensioner in the released position, slip the belt off the pulleys, then release the tensioner. If the belt is to be re-used mark the direction of rotation on the belt.

Refitting

4 Fit the belt around the pulleys, then turn the tensioner clockwise again and slip the belt over the tensioner roller **(see illustration)**. Carefully release the pressure and the spring loaded tensioner will move anti-clockwise so the belt will automatically become tensioned.

5 Refit the wheelarch liner, then refit the roadwheel and lower the vehicle to the ground. Tighten the road wheels to the specified torque setting.

30 Spark plug renewal

1 The correct functioning of the spark plugs is vital for the correct running and efficiency of the engine. It is essential that the plugs fitted are appropriate for the engine (the suitable type is given in the Specifications at the beginning of this Chapter). If this type is used and the engine is in good condition, the spark plugs should not need attention between scheduled renewal intervals. Spark plug

cleaning is rarely necessary, and should not be attempted unless specialised equipment is available, as damage can easily be caused to the firing ends.

2 Disconnect the wiring connectors from the four ignition coils **(see illustration)**.

3 Undo the retaining bolts and withdraw the ignition coils from the top of the spark plugs **(see illustrations)**.

4 Unscrew the plugs using a deep spark plug socket and extension bar. Keep the socket aligned with the spark plug; otherwise if it is forcibly moved to one side, the ceramic insulator may be broken off. As each plug is removed **(see illustration)**, examine it as follows.

5 Examination of the spark plugs will give a good indication of the condition of the engine.

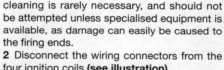

30.2 Disconnect the coil wiring connectors

30.3a Remove the retaining bolts. . .

30.3b . . .and withdraw the ignition coils

30.4 Using a length of rubber hose to remove the spark plugs

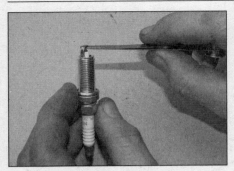

30.9 Measuring the spark plug gap with feeler blades

If the insulator nose of the spark plug is clean and white, with no deposits, this is indicative of too hot a plug (a hot plug transfers heat away from the electrode slowly, a cold plug transfers heat away quickly) or a possible engine management system fault.

6 If the tip and insulator nose are covered with hard black-looking deposits, then this is also indicative of a possible problem in the engine management system. Should the plug be black and oily, and then it is likely that the engine is fairly worn.

7 It is normal for the insulator nose to be covered with light tan to greyish-brown deposits, indicating that both the spark plug and the engine are in good condition.

8 The spark plug electrode gap is of considerable importance as, if it is too large or too small, the size of the spark and its efficiency will be seriously impaired. The gap should be set to the value given in the Specifications.

9 To set it, measure the gap with a feeler blade and then bend open, or closed, the outer plug electrode until the correct gap is achieved **(see illustration)**. The centre electrode should never be bent, as this may crack the insulator and cause plug failure, if nothing worse.

10 Special spark plug electrode gap adjusting tools are available from most motor accessory shops, or from some spark plug manufacturers.

11 Before fitting the spark plugs, check that the threaded connector sleeves (where fitted) are tight, and that the plug exterior surfaces and threads are clean. Insert each spark plug

It is very often difficult to insert spark plugs into their holes without cross-threading them. To avoid this possibility, fit a short length of 8 mm internal diameter rubber hose over the end of the spark plug. The flexible hose acts as a universal joint to help align the plug with the plug hole. Should the plug begin to cross-thread, the hose will slip on the spark plug, preventing thread damage to the cylinder head.

by hand, taking care to enter the plug threads correctly **(see Haynes Hint)**.

12 Tighten the plug to the specified torque using the spark plug socket and a torque wrench. Refit the remaining spark plugs in the same manner.

13 Refit the ignition coils to the top of the spark plugs and tighten the retaining bolts, ensuring the wiring connectors are fitted securely to the ignition coils.

31 Manual transmission oil level check

1 Park the car on a level surface. The oil level must be checked before the car is driven, or at least 5 minutes after the engine has been switched off. If the oil is checked immediately after driving the car, some of the oil will remain distributed around the transmission components, resulting in an inaccurate level reading. To improve access, position the car over an inspection pit, or raise the car off the ground and position it on axle stands, (see

Jacking and vehicle support) making sure the vehicle remains level to the ground.

2 Wipe clean the area around the filler/level plug, and unscrew it from the casing. The filler/level plug is situated on the left-hand rear of the transmission unit, behind the driveshaft **(see illustration)**.

3 The oil level should reach the lower edge of the filler/level hole. A certain amount of oil will have gathered behind the filler/level plug and will trickle out when it is removed; this does **not** necessarily indicate that the level is correct. To ensure that a true level is established, wait until the initial trickle has stopped, then add oil as necessary until a trickle of new oil can be seen emerging. The level will be correct when the flow ceases; use only good-quality oil of the specified type.

4 Remove the left-hand front road wheel for better access to the filler/level plug. Use a length of hose and a funnel to make topping up easier **(see illustrations)**.

5 Refilling the transmission is an extremely awkward operation; above all, allow plenty of time for the oil to settle properly before checking it. If a large amount had to be added to the transmission and a large amount flows out on checking the level, refit the filler/level plug, and take the vehicle on a short journey. This will allow the new oil to be distributed fully around the transmission components. On returning, recheck the level when the oil has settled again.

6 If the transmission has been overfilled so that oil flows out as soon as the filler/level plug is removed, check that the car is completely level (front-to-rear and side-to-side). If necessary, allow the surplus to drain off into a suitable container.

7 When the level is correct, refit the filler/level plug, tightening it to the specified torque wrench setting. Wash off any spilt oil.

32 Remote control battery renewal

Note: *All the remote control units described below are fitted with a type CR 2032, 3 volt battery.*

1 Although not in the Nissan maintenance schedule, we recommend that the battery is

31.2 Transmission oil filler/level plug

31.4a Using a funnel and hose. . .

31.4b . . . to fill up the transmission

32.2a Release the clip. . .

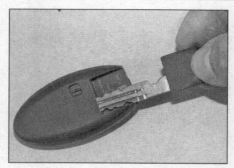

32.2b . . . and withdraw the key

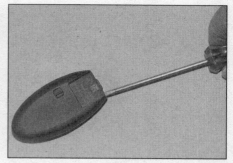

32.3a Twist a small screwdriver in the slot. . .

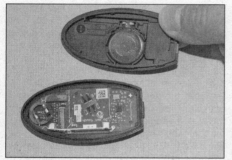

32.3b . . . and unclip one side of the transmitter

32.4 Unclip the battery from its location in the cover

32.5 Battery type (CR2032 – 3V)

changed every 2 years, regardless of the vehicle's mileage. However, if the door locks repeatedly fail to respond to signals from the remote control at the normal distance, change the battery in the remote control before attempting to troubleshoot any of the vehicle's other systems.

2 Release the securing clip and withdraw the key from the remote control body **(see illustrations)**.

3 Using a small screwdriver, carefully prise the two halves of the transmitter apart **(see illustrations)**.

4 Carefully unclip the battery from its position in the transmitter housing, noting its fitted position **(see illustration)**.

5 Fit the new battery **(see illustration)**, observing the correct polarity, and clip the transmitter housing back together.

33 Coolant strength check and renewal

⚠️ *Warning: Do not allow antifreeze to come in contact with your skin or painted surfaces of the vehicle. Flush contaminated areas immediately with plenty of water. Don't store new coolant, or leave old coolant lying around, where it's accessible to children or pets – they're attracted by its sweet smell. Ingestion of even a small amount of coolant can be fatal. Wipe up garage-floor and drip-pan spills immediately. Keep antifreeze containers covered, and repair cooling system leaks as soon as they're noticed.*

⚠️ *Warning: Never remove the expansion tank filler cap when the engine is running, or has just been switched off, as the cooling system will be hot, and the consequent escaping steam and scalding coolant could cause serious injury.*

⚠️ *Warning: Wait until the engine is cold before starting these procedures.*

Strength check

1 Use a hydrometer to check the strength of the antifreeze. Follow the instructions provided with your hydrometer. The antifreeze strength should be approximately 50%. If it is significantly less than this, drain a little coolant from the radiator (see this Section), add antifreeze to the coolant expansion tank, then recheck the strength.

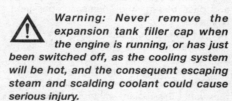

33.4 Coolant drain plug

Coolant draining

2 To drain the system, first remove the expansion tank filler cap.

3 Firmly apply the handbrake, then jack up the front of the vehicle and support it securely on axle stands (see *Jacking and vehicle support*). Where applicable, release the fasteners and remove the engine undershield.

4 Place a suitable container beneath the left-hand side of the radiator, then undo the drain plug **(see illustration)**, and drain the coolant into the container. If possible, place a funnel (or similar) to catch the coolant, as part of the front crossmember is below the radiator, so this will cause the coolant to splash in different directions.

5 To aid draining of the cooling system, release the retaining clamp and disconnect the bottom hose from the mounting bracket on the lower part of the fan cowling **(see illustration)**.

33.5 Release the clamp and disconnect the bottom hose

33.19 Disconnect the heater upper hose

33.20a Radiator upper bleed screw. . .

33.20b . . . and on coolant housing

Allow the coolant to drain into the container.

6 Once the coolant has stopped draining from the radiator, tighten the drain plug and then reconnect the bottom hose, securing it with the retaining clamp.

System flushing

7 With time, the cooling system may gradually lose its efficiency, as the radiator core becomes choked with rust, scale deposits from the water, and other sediment. To minimise this, as well as using only good-quality antifreeze and clean soft water, the system should be flushed as follows whenever any part of it is disturbed, and/or when the coolant is renewed.

8 With the coolant drained, refit the radiator bottom hose and refill the system with fresh water. Refit the expansion tank filler cap, start the engine and warm it up to normal operating temperature, then stop it and (after allowing it to cool down completely) drain the system again. Repeat as necessary until only clean water can be seen to emerge, then refill finally with the specified coolant mixture.

9 If only clean, soft water and good-quality antifreeze (even if not to Nissan's specification) has been used, and the coolant has been renewed at the suggested intervals, the above procedure will be sufficient to keep the system clean for a considerable length of time. If, however, the system has been neglected, a more thorough operation will be required, as follows.

10 First drain the coolant, then disconnect the radiator top hose. Insert a garden hose into the radiator top hose connection, and allow water to circulate through the radiator until it runs clean from the bottom outlet. DO NOT use pressurised water from the garden hose, just normal water flow.

11 To flush the engine, insert the garden hose into the radiator bottom hose, wrap a piece of rag around the garden hose to seal the connection, and allow water to circulate until it runs clear.

12 Try the effect of repeating this procedure in the top hose, although this may not be effective, since the thermostat will probably close and prevent the flow of water.

13 In severe cases of contamination, reverse-flushing of the radiator may be necessary. This may be achieved by inserting the garden hose into the bottom outlet, wrapping a piece of rag around the hose to seal the connection, then flushing the radiator until clear water emerges from the top hose outlet.

14 If the radiator is suspected of being severely choked, remove the radiator (Chapter 3 Section 5), turn it upside-down, and repeat the procedure described in paragraph 13.

15 Flushing the heater matrix can be achieved using a similar procedure to that described in paragraph 13, once the heater inlet and outlet hoses have been identified. These two hoses will be of the same diameter, and pass through the engine compartment bulkhead.

16 The use of chemical cleaners is not recommended, and should be necessary only as a last resort; the scouring action of some chemical cleaners may lead to other cooling system problems. Normally, regular renewal of the coolant will prevent excessive contamination of the system.

Coolant filling

17 Prepare a sufficient quantity of the specified coolant mixture; allow for a surplus, so as to have a reserve supply for topping-up.

18 Before attempting to fill the cooling system, make sure that all hoses and clips are in good condition, and that the clips are tight. Note that an antifreeze mixture must be used all year round, to prevent corrosion of the alloy engine components.

19 If not already done reconnect the radiator hoses, then disconnect the upper heater matrix hose from the rear of the bulkhead (see illustration). Raise the hose until it is above the 'MAX' line on the coolant expansion tank.

20 Unscrew the air bleed screw from the upper left-hand side of the radiator, and the one on the coolant housing on the left-hand end of the cylinder head (see illustrations).

21 Position containers under the radiator and under the disconnected heater matrix hose. Very slowly refill the cooling system through the expansion tank, until coolant runs from the radiator air bleed screw and the coolant housing bleed screw, then refit and tighten the tap/cap.

22 Continue to fill the system through the expansion tank until the coolant, free from air bubbles, emerges from the heater hose. Refit the heater hose back to the bulkhead heater connection, once the coolant escaping is free from air bubbles.

23 Continue to fill the expansion tank until the coolant level reaches the MAX mark.

24 Start the engine, and increase the engine speed to approx 1500 rpm for two to three minutes, keeping the coolant level at 'MAX', then refit the expansion tank cap.

25 Run the engine for approximately 10 minutes at 2500 rpm (until the thermostat operates). Check the coolant temperature gauge for signs of overheating.

26 Stop the engine; allow it to cool completely, and then check for leaks, particularly around the disturbed components. With the system cold (the system must be cold for an accurate coolant level indication), check the level in the expansion tank.

27 If necessary, top-up the coolant level in the expansion tank to the MAX level mark. Repeat the procedures contained in paragraphs 25 to 27 until the coolant level in the expansion tank no longer drops.

28 After refilling, always check carefully all components of the system (but especially any unions disturbed during draining and flushing) for signs of coolant leaks. Fresh antifreeze has a searching action, which will rapidly expose any weak points in the system.

Antifreeze type and mixture

Caution: Do not use engine antifreeze in the windscreen/tailgate washer system, as it will damage the vehicle's paintwork. A screenwash additive should be added to the washer system in its maker's recommended quantities.

29 If the vehicle's history (and therefore the quality of the antifreeze in it) is unknown, owners are advised to drain and thoroughly reverse-flush the system, before refilling with fresh coolant mixture.

30 If the antifreeze used is to Nissan's specification, the levels of protection it affords are indicated in the coolant packaging.

31 To give the recommended standard mixture ratio for antifreeze, 50% (by volume) of antifreeze must be mixed with 50% of clean, soft water; if you are using any other

type of antifreeze, follow its manufacturer's instructions to achieve the correct ratio.

32 You are unlikely to fully drain the system at any one time (unless the engine is being completely stripped), and the capacities quoted in the Specifications are therefore slightly academic for routine coolant renewal. As a guide, only two-thirds of the system's total capacity is likely to be needed for coolant renewal.

33 As the drained system will be partially filled with flushing water, in order to establish the recommended mixture ratio, measure out 50% of the system capacity in antifreeze and pour it into the hose/expansion tank as described above, then top-up with water. Any topping-up while refilling the system should be done with a suitable mixture.

34 Before adding antifreeze, the cooling system should be drained, preferably flushed, and all hoses checked for condition and security. As noted earlier, fresh antifreeze will rapidly find any weaknesses in the system.

35 After filling with antifreeze, a label should be attached to the expansion tank, stating the type and concentration of antifreeze used, and the date installed. Any subsequent topping-up should be made with the same type and concentration of antifreeze.

General cooling system checks

36 The engine should be cold for the cooling system checks, so perform the following procedure before driving the vehicle, or after it has been shut off for at least three hours.

37 Remove the expansion tank filler cap, and clean it thoroughly inside and out with a rag. Also clean the filler neck on the expansion tank. The presence of rust or corrosion in the filler neck indicates that the coolant should be changed. The coolant inside the expansion tank should be relatively clean and transparent. If it is rust-coloured, drain and flush the system, and refill with a fresh coolant mixture.

38 Carefully check the radiator hoses and heater hoses along their entire length; renew any hose which is cracked, swollen or deteriorated.

39 Inspect all other cooling system components (joint faces, etc) for leaks. A leak in the cooling system will usually show up as white- or antifreeze-coloured deposits on the area adjoining the leak. Where any problems of this nature are found on system components, renew the component or gasket with reference to Chapter 3.

Airlocks

40 If, after draining and refilling the system, symptoms of overheating are found which did not occur previously, then the fault is almost certainly due to trapped air at some point in the system, causing an airlock and restricting the flow of coolant; usually, the air is trapped because the system was refilled too quickly.

41 If an airlock is suspected, first try gently squeezing all visible coolant hoses. A coolant hose which is full of air feels quite different to one full of coolant when squeezed. After refilling the system, most airlocks will clear once the system has cooled, and been topped-up.

42 While the engine is running at operating temperature, switch on the heater and heater fan, and check for heat output. Provided there is sufficient coolant in the system, lack of heat output could be due to an airlock in the system.

43 Airlocks can have more serious effects than simply reducing heater output – a severe airlock could reduce coolant flow around the engine. Check that the radiator top hose is hot when the engine is at operating temperature – a top hose which stays cold could be the result of an airlock (or a non-opening thermostat).

44 If the problem persists, stop the engine and allow it to cool down completely, before unscrewing the expansion tank filler cap or loosening the hose clips and squeezing the hoses to bleed out the trapped air. In the worst case, the system will have to be at least partially drained (this time, the coolant can be saved for re-use) and flushed to clear the problem. If all else fails, have the system evacuated and vacuum filled by a suitably-equipped garage.

Expansion tank cap check

45 Wait until the engine is completely cold – perform this check before the engine is started for the first time in the day.

46 Place a wad of cloth over the expansion tank cap, then unscrew it slowly and remove it.

47 Examine the condition of the rubber seal on the underside of the cap. If the rubber appears to have hardened, or cracks are visible in the seal edges, a new cap should be fitted.

48 If the car is several years old, or has covered a large mileage, consider renewing the cap regardless of its apparent condition – they are not expensive. If the pressure relief valve built into the cap fails, excess pressure in the system will lead to puzzling failures of hoses and other cooling system components.

Notes

Chapter 1 Part B
Routine maintenance and servicing – diesel models

Contents

Degrees of difficulty

 Easy, suitable for novice with little experience

 Fairly easy, suitable for beginner with some experience

 Fairly difficult, suitable for competent DIY mechanic

 Difficult, suitable for experienced DIY mechanic

 Very difficult, suitable for expert DIY or professional

Specifications

Lubricants and fluids

Engine oil	Nissan Motor oil 5W30 DPF or SAE 5W30 low SAPS or ACEA C4.*
Cooling system	Genuine long-life coolant or equivalent*
Manual transmission	Nissan MT-XZ Gear Oil or API GL-4. Viscosity SAE 75W-80*
Braking system	Genuine Nissan brake fluid or equivalent hydraulic fluid to DOT 4*

Refer to your Nissan dealer or specialist for brand name and latest type recommendations

Capacities

Engine oil (including oil filter):	
K9K (1.5 litre) engine	4.6 litres
R9M (1.6 litre) engine	5.5 litres
Cooling system (approximate):	
K9K (1.5 litre) engine	6.3 litres
R9M (1.6 litre) engine	7.3 litres
Manual transmission:	
K9K (1.5 litre) engine – RS6F94R transmission	2.0 litres
R9M (1.6 litre) engine – RS6F95R transmission	1.7 litres
Washer fluid reservoir	2.5 litres
Fuel tank	55.0 litres

Cooling system

Antifreeze mixture:	
50% antifreeze	Protection down to -37°C

Note: *Refer to antifreeze manufacturer for latest recommendations.*

Brakes

Friction material minimum thickness:	
Front brake pads	1.5 mm
Rear brake shoes	1.0 mm

Tyre pressures

Note: *Pressures given here are a guide only, and apply to original-equipment tyres – the recommended pressures may vary if any other make or type of tyre is fitted; check with the car handbook, or the tyre manufacturer or supplier for the latest recommendations. A tyre pressure label is fitted on the driver's door pillar, with readings for each specific vehicle.*

Normal load (up to 3 people)	Front	Rear
215/65R16 98H	2.6 bar (38 psi)	2.4 bar (35 psi)
215/60R17 96H	2.3 bar (33 psi)	2.1 bar (30 psi)
215/55R18 83T (85T, 87T, 88T)	2.3 bar (33 psi)	2.1 bar (30 psi)
225/45R19 92W or 95W	2.3 bar (33 psi)	2.1 bar (30 psi)

Remote control battery

Type	CR2032, 3V

Torque wrench settings

	Nm	lbf ft
Engine oil drain plug (K9K – 1.5 litre engine)	20	15
Engine oil drain plug (R9M – 1.6 litre engine):		
Alloy sump	25	18
Steel plate sump	50	37
Engine oil filter (K9K – 1.5 litre engine)	14	10
Engine oil filter cover (R9M – 1.6 litre engine)	25	18
Manual transmission oil drain plug	23	17
Roadwheel nuts	113	83

1 Maintenance schedule

1 The maintenance intervals in this manual are provided with the assumption that you, not the dealer, will be carrying out the work. These are the minimum maintenance intervals based on the standard service schedule recommended by the manufacturer for vehicles driven daily. If you wish to keep your vehicle in peak condition at all times, you may wish to perform some of these procedures more often. We encourage frequent maintenance, because it enhances the efficiency, performance and resale value of your vehicle.

2 If the vehicle is driven in dusty areas, used to tow a trailer, or driven frequently at slow speeds (idling in traffic) or on short journeys, more frequent maintenance intervals are recommended.

3 When the vehicle is new, it should be serviced by a dealer service department (or other workshop recognised by the vehicle manufacturer as providing the same standard of service) in order to preserve the warranty. The vehicle manufacturer may reject warranty claims if you are unable to prove that servicing has been carried out as and when specified, using only original equipment parts or parts certified to be of equivalent quality.

Every 250 miles or weekly

- [ ] Check the engine oil level (Section 5)
- [ ] Check the coolant level (Section 6)
- [ ] Check the brake and clutch fluid level (Section 7)
- [ ] Screenwash fluid (Section 8)
- [ ] Tyre condition and pressure check (Section 9)
- [ ] Wiper blades check (Section 10)
- [ ] Battery check (Section 11)
- [ ] Check the electrical systems (Section 12)

Every 12 500 miles or 12 months, whichever comes first

In addition to the items listed above, carry out the following:
Note: *Nissan recommend that the engine oil and filter are changed every 18 000 miles or 12 months. However, oil and filter changes are good for the engine, and we recommend that the oil and filter are renewed more frequently, especially if the car is used on a lot of short journeys.*

- [ ] Renew the engine oil and filter (Section 13)
- [ ] Reset the service indicator (Section 14)
- [ ] Renew the pollen filter (Section 15
- [ ] Drain any water from the fuel filter (Section 16)
- [ ] Check all components, pipes and hoses for fluid leaks (Section 17)
- [ ] Check the condition of the auxiliary drivebelt (Section 33, 34)
- [ ] Check the condition and operation of the seat belts (Section 18)
- [ ] Check the brake pads and discs for wear (Section 19)
- [ ] Check the condition of the driveshaft gaiters (Section 20)
- [ ] Check the steering and suspension components for condition and security (Section 21)
- [ ] Check the condition of the exhaust system components (Section 22)
- [ ] Check the roadwheel nuts are tightened to the specified torque (Section 23)
- [ ] Lubricate all door, bonnet and tailgate hinges and locks (Section 24)
- [ ] Carry out a road test (Section 25)
- [ ] Check the coolant strength (Section 32)

Every 25 000 miles or 2 years, whichever comes first

In addition to the items listed above, carry out the following:
- [ ] Renew the fuel filter (Section 26)
- [ ] Renew the air filter (Section 27)
- [ ] Renew the brake fluid (Section 28)

Every 37 500 miles or 3 years, whichever comes first

In addition to the items listed above, carry out the following:
- [ ] Check the braking system rubber hoses (Section 29)
- [ ] Check the manual transmission oil level (Section 30)
- [ ] Renew the remote control battery (Chapter 11 Section 16)
- [ ] Renew the coolant (Section 32)

Note: *Nissan state that, if their Nissan antifreeze is in the system from new, the coolant need only be changed every 3 years. If there is any doubt as to the type or quality of the antifreeze which has been used, we recommend this shorter interval be observed.*

Every 75 000 miles or 4 years, whichever comes first

In addition to the items listed above, carry out the following:
- [ ] Renew the auxiliary drivebelt and tensioner (Section 33, 34)

Note: *Although the normal interval for timing belt renewal is 90 000 miles or 5 years, it is strongly recommended that the interval suggested is observed, especially on cars which are subjected to intensive use, ie, mainly short journeys or a lot of stop-start driving. The actual belt renewal interval is very much up to the individual owner, but bear in mind that severe engine damage will result if the belt breaks.*

- [ ] Renew the timing belt and tensioner – 1.5 litre engines (Section 35)

2 Component locations

Underbonnet view of a 1.6 litre model

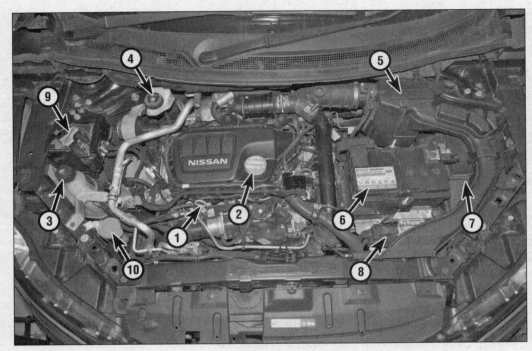

1 Engine oil level dipstick
2 Engine oil filler cap
3 Coolant reservoir (expansion tank)
4 Brake and clutch fluid reservoir
5 Air cleaner
6 Battery
7 Fuse/relay box
8 Engine management ECM
9 Fuel filter
10 Windscreen washer fluid filler cap

Front underbody view

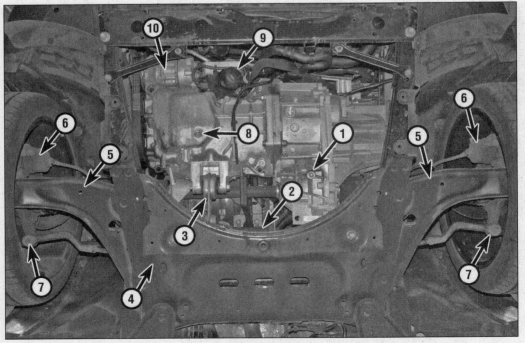

1 Transmission drain plug
2 Exhaust front pipe
3 Rear engine/transmission mounting
4 Subframe
5 Suspension lower arm
6 Brake calipers
7 Track rod end
8 Engine oil drain plug
9 Engine oil filter
10 Air conditioning compressor

Rear underbody view

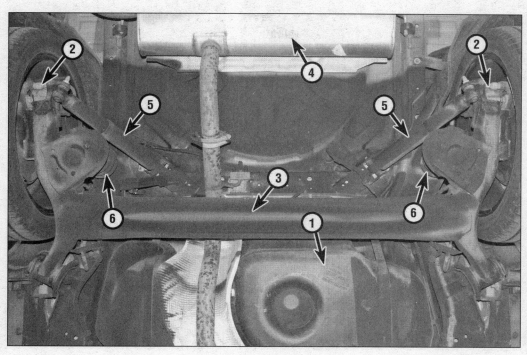

1 *Fuel tank*
2 *Rear brake calipers*
3 *Rear axle torsion beam*
4 *Exhaust rear silencer*
5 *Shock absorber*
6 *Rear coil springs*

3 General Information

1 This Chapter is designed to help the home mechanic maintain his/her car for safety, economy, long life and peak performance.

2 The Chapter contains a master maintenance schedule, followed by Sections dealing specifically with each task in the schedule. Visual checks, adjustments, component renewal and other helpful items are included. Refer to the accompanying illustrations of the engine compartment and the underside of the car for the locations of the various components.

3 Servicing your car in accordance with the mileage/time maintenance schedule and the following Sections will provide a planned maintenance programme, which should result in a long and reliable service life. This is a comprehensive plan, so maintaining some items but not others at the specified service intervals, will not produce the same results.

4 As you service your car, you will discover that many of the procedures can – and should – be grouped together, because of the particular procedure being performed, or because of the proximity of two otherwise-unrelated components to one another. For example, if the car is raised for any reason, the exhaust can be inspected at the same time as the suspension and steering components.

5 The first step in this maintenance programme is to prepare yourself before the actual work begins. Read through all the Sections relevant to the work to be carried out, then make a list and gather all the parts and tools required. If a problem is encountered, seek advice from a parts specialist, or a dealer service department.

4 Regular maintenance

1 If, from the time the car is new, the routine maintenance schedule is followed closely, and frequent checks are made of fluid levels and high-wear items, as suggested throughout this manual, the engine will be kept in relatively good running condition, and the need for additional work will be minimised.

2 It is possible that there will be times when the engine is running poorly due to the lack of regular maintenance. This is even more likely if a used car, which has not received regular and frequent maintenance checks, is purchased. In such cases, additional work may need to be carried out, outside of the regular maintenance intervals.

3 If engine wear is suspected, a compression test or leakdown test (refer to Chapter 2D Section 2), will provide valuable information regarding the overall performance of the main internal components. Such a test can be used as a basis to decide on the extent of the work to be carried out. If, for example, the test indicates serious internal engine wear, conventional maintenance as described in this Chapter will not greatly improve the performance of the engine, and may prove a waste of time and money, unless extensive overhaul work is carried out first.

4 The following series of operations are those most often required to improve the performance of a generally poor-running engine:

Primary operations

a) *Clean, inspect and test the battery (Chapter 5 Section 3).*
b) *Check all the engine-related fluids (Section 5, 6).*
c) *Check the condition of all hoses, and check for fluid leaks (Section 17).*
d) *Check the condition of the auxiliary drivebelt (Section 33, 34).*
e) *Renew the fuel filter (Section 26).*
f) *Check the condition of the air filter, and renew if necessary (Section 27).*

5 If the above operations do not prove fully effective, carry out the following secondary operations:

Secondary operations

6 All items listed under Primary operations, plus the following:

a) *Check the charging system (Chapter 5 Section 2).*
b) *Check the engine control and emissions systems (Chapter 6B).*
c) *Check the fuel system (Chapter) 4B.*

5.8a Withdraw the dipstick
(1.6 litre engine)...

5.8b ... it is part of the oil filler cap on
1.5 litre engines

5.9 Using a clean rag or paper towel,
remove all oil from the dipstick. Insert the
clean dipstick into the tube as far as it will
go, then withdraw it again

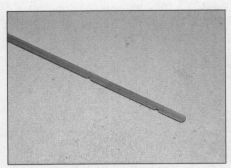

5.10 Note the oil level on the end of the
dipstick, which should be between the
upper and lower mark (1.6 litre shown).

5.11a Unscrew the oil filler cap
(1.6 litre engine)...

5.11b ... and top-up the level, add the oil
slowly, checking the level on the dipstick
often. Don't overfill

5 Engine oil level check

Before you start

1 Make sure that the car is on level ground.
2 The transmission must be in Neutral or Park, and the pedals not depressed.
3 The engine must be at normal operating temperature, and switched off.

The correct oil

4 Modern engines place great demands on their oil. It is very important that the correct oil for your car is used, see 'Lubricants and fluids' at the beginning of this Chapter.

6.3 The coolant level is indicated by the
minimum and maximum marks visible on
the side of the reservoir

Level check

5 If you have to add oil frequently, you should check whether you have any oil leaks. Place some clean paper under the car overnight, and check for stains in the morning. If there are no leaks, then the engine may be burning oil.
6 Always maintain the level between the upper and lower dipstick marks. If the level is too low severe engine damage may occur. Oil seal failure may result if the engine is overfilled by adding too much oil.
7 If the oil level is too low, severe engine damage may occur. Oil seal failure may result if the engine is overfilled by adding too much oil.
8 Locate the engine oil level dipstick and pull it from place **(see illustrations)**. The dipstick is located at the front of the engine; the dipstick is often brightly coloured and/or has a picture of an oil-can on the top for identification. On 1.5 litre diesel engines, the dipstick is part of the oil filler cap.
9 Wipe the dipstick clean, then fully insert it into the guide tube **(see illustration)**.
10 Withdraw the dipstick again and examine the oil level. It should be between the upper (MAX) and lower (MIN) marks **(see illustration)**. If it is near the lower mark, new engine oil needs to be added. Approximately 1.0 litre of oil will raise the level from the lower mark to the upper mark
11 On 1.6 litre engines, rotate the engine oil filler cap anti-clockwise and remove it. Add new engine oil (using a funnel if required), a

little at a time, to bring the level to the upper (MAX) mark on the dipstick **(see illustrations)**. Add the oil slowly, frequently checking the level on the dipstick.
12 Securely refit the filler cap on 1.6 litre engines, and refit the dipstick/filler cap on 1.5 litre engines.

6 Coolant level check

 Warning: Do not attempt to remove the expansion tank pressure cap when the engine is hot, as there is a very great risk of scalding. Do not leave open containers of coolant about, as it is poisonous.

1 With this type of cooling system (sealed), adding coolant should not be necessary on a regular basis. If frequent topping-up is required, it is likely there is a leak. Check the radiator, all hoses and joint faces for signs of staining or wetness, and rectify as necessary.
2 It is important that antifreeze is used in the cooling system all year round, not just during the winter months. Don't top up with water alone, as the antifreeze will become diluted. Refer to 'Specifications' at the beginning of this Chapter.
3 With the engine completely cold, the coolant level should be between the upper and lower marks on the side of the reservoir (expansion tank) **(see illustration)**.

4 If more coolant is required, rotate the filler cap anti-clockwise (see 'Warning') and then remove it **(see illustration)**.

5 Add new coolant to bring the level to the upper mark, then securely refit the cap **(see illustration)**.

7 Brake and clutch fluid level check

⚠️ **Warning: Brake fluid can harm your eyes and damage painted surfaces, so use extreme caution when handling and pouring it.**

⚠️ **Warning: Do not use fluid that has been standing open for some time, as it absorbs moisture from the air, which can cause a dangerous loss of braking effectiveness.**

1 The fluid level in the reservoir will drop slightly as the brake pads wear down, but the fluid level must never be allowed to drop below the MIN mark.

2 Make sure that the car is on level ground.

Safety first!

3 If the reservoir requires repeated topping-up this is an indication of a fluid leak somewhere in the system, which should be investigated immediately.

4 If a leak is suspected, the car should not be driven until the braking system has been checked. Never take any risks where brakes are concerned

Level check

5 The fluid level is visible through the reservoir. The level must be kept between the MAX and MIN marks at all times **(see illustration)**.

6 If topping-up is necessary, first wipe clean the area around the filler cap to prevent dirt entering the hydraulic system **(see illustration)**.

7 Rotate the cap anti-clockwise and remove it **(see illustration)**. If the fluid is dirty, the hydraulic system should be drained and refilled as described later on in this Chapter.

8 Carefully add new fluid from a sealed container to bring the level to the upper mark **(see illustration)**. Use only the fluid specified (see Specifications); mixing different types can cause damage to the system. After topping-up to the correct level, securely refit the cap and wipe off any spilt fluid.

8 Screenwash fluid

1 Screenwash additives not only keep the windscreen clean during bad weather, they also prevent the washer system freezing in cold weather – which is when you are likely to need it most. Don't top-up using plain water, as the screenwash will become diluted, and will freeze during cold weather.

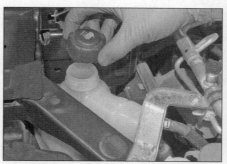

6.4 Rotate the cap anti-clockwise and remove it

7.5 The MAX and MIN marks are on the side of the reservoir. The fluid level must be kept between the marks at all times

7.7 Unscrew the reservoir cap and carefully lift it out of position

⚠️ **Warning: On no account use engine coolant antifreeze in the screen washer system – this may damage the paintwork.**

2 The screen washer fluid reservoir filler cap is located at the front, right-hand

8.2 Lift the cap

6.5 Add new coolant to bring the level to the upper mark

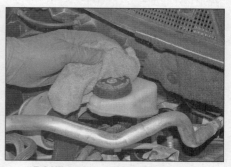

7.6 Wipe the top of the reservoir

7.8 Carefully add fluid taking care not to spill it onto the surrounding components

side of the engine compartment **(see illustration)**. The headlight washers (where fitted), are supplied from the same reservoir.

3 Add screenwash as per the manufacturers instructions **(see illustration)**.

8.3 When topping-up, add screenwash as recommended by the manufacturer

9.6 The tyres may have tread wear safety bands (B), which will appear when the tread depth reaches approximately 1.6 mm. The band positions are indicated by a triangular mark on the tyre sidewall (A)

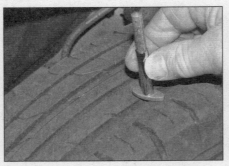

9.7 Tread wear can be monitored with a tread depth indicator gauge

9.8 Check the tyre pressures regularly with the tyres cold

Shoulder wear

Centre wear

Uneven wear

9 Tyre condition and pressure check

Tyre condition and pressure

1 It is very important that tyres are in good condition, and at the correct pressure – having a tyre failure at any speed is highly dangerous.
2 Tyre wear is influenced by driving style – harsh braking and acceleration, or fast cornering, will all produce more rapid tyre wear. As a general rule, the front tyres wear out faster than the rears. Interchanging the tyres from front to rear ("rotating" the tyres) may result in more even wear. However, if this is completely effective, you may have the expense of replacing all four tyres at once!
3 Remove any nails or stones embedded in the tread before they penetrate the tyre to cause deflation. If removal of a nail does reveal that the tyre has been punctured, refit the nail so that its point of penetration is marked. Then immediately change the wheel, and have the tyre repaired by a tyre dealer.
4 Regularly check the tyres for damage in the form of cuts or bulges, especially in the sidewalls. Periodically remove the wheels, and clean any dirt or mud from the inside and outside surfaces. Examine the wheel rims for signs of rusting, corrosion or other damage. Light alloy wheels are easily damaged by "kerbing" whilst parking; steel wheels may also become dented or buckled. A new wheel is very often the only way to overcome severe damage.
5 New tyres should be balanced when they are fitted, but it may become necessary to re-balance them as they wear, or if the balance weights fitted to the wheel rim should fall off. Unbalanced tyres will wear more quickly, as will the steering and suspension components. Wheel imbalance is normally signified by vibration, particularly at a certain speed (typically around 50 mph). If this vibration is felt only through the steering, then it is likely that just the front wheels need balancing. If, however, the vibration is felt through the whole car, the rear wheels could be out of balance. Wheel balancing should be carried out by a tyre dealer or garage.
6 The tyres may have tread wear safety bands, which indicate when the tread depth reaches the legal limit **(see illustration)**.
7 Alternatively, monitor the tread wear with a simple, inexpensive device known as a tread depth indicator gauge **(see illustration)**.
8 Regularly check the pressures with a pressure gauge when the tyres are cold **(see illustration)**. Do not adjust the pressures immediately after the vehicle has been used, or an inaccurate setting will result.

Tyre tread wear patterns

Shoulder wear

Underinflation (wear on both sides)

Under-inflation will cause overheating of the tyre, because the tyre will flex too much, and the tread will not sit correctly on the road surface. This will cause a loss of grip and excessive wear, not to mention the danger of sudden tyre failure due to heat build-up.
Remedy: Check and adjust pressures.

Incorrect wheel camber (wear on one side)

Remedy: Repair or renew suspension parts

Hard cornering

Remedy: Reduce speed!

Centre wear

Overinflation

Over-inflation will cause rapid wear of the centre part of the tyre tread, coupled with reduced grip, harsher ride, and the danger of shock damage occurring in the tyre casing.
Remedy: Check and adjust pressures.
Note: *If you sometimes have to inflate your car's tyres to the higher pressures for maximum load or sustained high speed, don't forget to reduce the pressures to normal afterwards.*

Uneven wear

Front tyres may wear unevenly as a result of wheel misalignment. Most tyre dealers and garages can check and adjust the wheel alignment (or "tracking") for a modest charge.

Incorrect camber or castor

Remedy: Repair or renew suspension parts.

Malfunctioning suspension

Remedy: Repair or renew suspension parts.

Unbalanced wheel

Remedy: Have the wheels balanced.

Incorrect toe setting

Remedy: Adjust front wheel alignment (see Chapter 10 Section 17).
Note: *The feathered edge of the tread which typifies toe wear is best checked by feel.*

10 Wiper blades

1 Check the condition of the wiper blades; if they are cracked or show any signs of deterioration, or if the glass swept area is smeared, renew them **(see illustration)**. Wiper blades should be renewed annually.
2 To remove a front wiper blade, pull the arm away from the screen, turn the blade slightly and depress the clip, then slide the blade down the arm to release **(see illustrations)**. Take care not to allow the arm to spring back against the windscreen!
3 To remove a rear wiper blade, pull the arm away from the screen, squeeze together the clips, swing the blade out and remove it **(see illustration)**.

11 Battery check

Caution: Before carrying out any work on the vehicle battery, read the precautions given in Safety first!' at the start of this manual.
1 Make sure that the battery tray is in good condition, and that the clamp is tight. Corrosion on the tray, retaining clamp and the battery itself can be removed with a solution of water and baking soda. Thoroughly rinse all cleaned areas with water. Any metal parts damaged by corrosion should be covered with a zinc-based primer, then painted.
2 Periodically (approximately every three months), check the charge condition of the battery as described in Chapter 5 Section 3.
3 If the battery is flat, and you need to jump start your vehicle, see *Roadside Repairs*.
4 The battery is located on the left-hand-side of the engine compartment. where fitted, lift the cover to access the battery **(see illustrations)**.

Battery corrosion can be kept to a minimum by applying a layer of petroleum jelly to the clamps and terminals after they are reconnected.

12 Electrical systems check

1 Check all external lights and the horn. Refer to the appropriate Sections of the Wiring Diagrams, at the end of this manual, for details of any circuits that are found to be inoperative.
2 Visually check all accessible wiring connectors, harnesses and retaining clips for security, and for signs of chafing or damage.

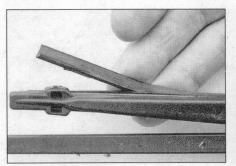
10.1 Check the condition of the wiper blades

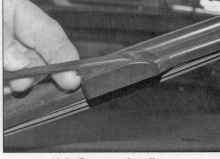
10.2a Depress the clip. . .

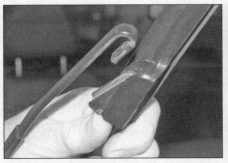
10.2b . . . and slide the blade down to release from the arm

10.3 Pull the arm away from the screen, squeeze together the catches, swing the blade out,and remove it from the catch

11.4a Lift the plastic cover to gain access to the battery positive terminal,. The exterior of the battery should be inspected periodically for damage such as a cracked case or cover.

11.4b Check the battery lead clamps for tightness to ensure good electrical connections, and check the leads for signs of damage.

11.4c If corrosion (white, fluffy deposits) is evident, remove the cables from the battery terminals, clean them with a small wire brush, then refit them. Automotive stores sell a tool for cleaning the battery post. . .

11.4d . . . as well as the battery cable clamps.

12.3 If a single indicator light, stop-light or headlight has failed, it is likely that a bulb has blown

12.4 The fuses are located in the fuse-box under the passengers side of the facia.

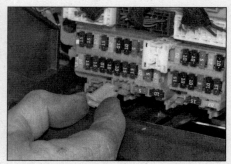

12.5 Use fuse puller to remove the fuse

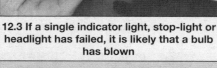

HAYNES HINT *If you need to check your brake lights and indicators unaided, back up to a wall or garage door and operate the lights. The reflected light should show if they are working properly.*

3 If a single indicator light, stop-light or headlight has failed, it is likely that a bulb has blown and will need to be renewed **(see illustration)**. Refer to Chapter 12 Section 5 for details. If both stop-lights have failed, it is possible that the switch has failed (see Chapter 9 Section 16).

4 If more than one indicator light or tail light has failed, check that a fuse has not blown or that there is a fault in the circuit (see Chapter 12 Section 3). The fuses are located in the fuse-box under the passengers side of the facia **(see illustration)**. Slacken the screws,

and fold down the fuseholder. The fuse allocations are given on a separate sheet.

5 To renew a blown fuse, simply pull it out and fit a new fuse of the correct rating (see Chapter 12 Section 3) **(see illustration)**. If the fuse blows again, it is important that you find out why.

13 Engine oil and filter renewal

1 Frequent oil and filter changes are the most important preventative maintenance procedures that can be undertaken by the DIY owner. As engine oil ages, it becomes diluted and contaminated, which leads to premature engine wear.

2 Before starting this procedure, gather together all the necessary tools and materials. Also make sure that you have plenty of clean

rags and newspapers handy, to mop-up any spills. Ideally, the engine oil should be warm, as it will drain more easily, and more built-up sludge will be removed with it.

3 Take care not to touch the exhaust or any other hot parts of the engine when working under the vehicle. To avoid any possibility of scalding, and to protect yourself from possible skin irritants and other harmful contaminants in used engine oils, it is advisable to wear gloves when carrying out this work.

4 Access to the underside of the vehicle will be greatly improved if it can be raised on a lift, driven onto ramps, or jacked up and supported on axle stands (see *Jacking and vehicle support*). Whichever method is chosen, make sure that the vehicle remains level, or if it is at an angle, that the drain plug is at the lowest point. The drain plug is located at the rear of the sump. Undo the retaining bolts and remove the engine undershield from under the front of the vehicle.

5 Remove the oil filler cap from the top of the engine camshaft cover on 1.6 litre engines and on 1.5 litre diesel engines, the dipstick is part of the oil filler cap **(see illustrations)**.

6 Slacken the drain plug about half a turn, position the draining container under the drain plug, and then remove the plug completely **(see illustrations)**. Note that on some engines an 8 mm square section drain plug key will be needed to unscrew the drain plug. If possible, try to keep the plug pressed into the sump while unscrewing it by hand the last couple of turns.

7 Allow some time for the oil to drain, noting that it may be necessary to reposition the container as the oil flow slows to a trickle.

8 After all the oil has drained; wipe the drain plug with a clean rag. Remove the old sealing washer from the drain plug and fit a new one. Clean the area around the drain plug opening, and refit the plug complete with the new sealing washer **(see illustration)**. Tighten the drain plug securely – preferably to the specified torque, using a torque wrench.

9 The oil filter is located at the front of the cylinder block – access is most easily obtained from underneath the vehicle on 1.6 litre engines, and from the top on 1.5 litre engines **(see illustrations)**.

10 Move the container into position under the oil filter, to catch any oil spillage.

13.5a Remove the oil filler cap (1.6 litre engine). . .

13.5b . . . and remove cap with dipstick on 1.5 litre engines

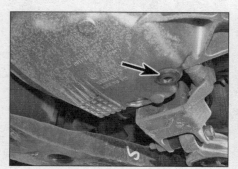

13.6a Engine oil drain plug – 1.5 litre engines

13.6b Engine oil drain plug – 1.6 litre engines

13.8 Fit a new sealing washer to the drain plug

**13.9a Oil filter location –
1.5 litre engines**

**13.9b Oil filter location –
1.6 litre engines**

1.5 litre engines

11 Use an oil filter removal tool to slacken the filter initially, then unscrew it by hand the rest of the way **(see illustration)**. Position it with its open end uppermost to prevent further spillage of oil, then empty the oil from the old filter into the container.

12 Use a clean rag to remove any oil, dirt and sludge from the filter sealing area on the engine. Check the old filter to make sure that the rubber sealing ring has not stuck to the engine. If it has, carefully remove it.

13 Apply a light coating of clean engine oil to the sealing ring on the new filter **(see illustration)**, then screw the filter into position on the engine. Lightly tighten the filter until its sealing ring contacts the block, and then tighten it through a further two-thirds of a turn. Tighten the filter firmly by hand only – **do not** use any tools.

1.6 litre engines

14 The filter is a cartridge inside the oil filter housing. Using a bar and socket, unscrew the filter housing cap and withdraw the filter cartridge, draining the oil into the container **(see illustration)**.

15 Use a clean rag to remove any oil, dirt and sludge from inside the oil filter housing. Remove any old rubber seals from the oil filter housing and filter cap and fit the new seals, which should be supplied with the filter **(see illustration)**.

16 Insert the new filter cartridge into the cap, then apply a light coating of clean engine oil to the sealing rings **(see illustration)**. Screw the filter cap/filter into position on the engine.

13.11 Slacken the oil filter with a removal tool

Tighten the filter cap firmly by hand at first, then tighten to the specified torque.

All models

17 Refit the undertray and securely tighten its retaining screws. Remove the old oil and all tools from under the vehicle then lower the vehicle to the ground.

18 Fill the engine through the filler hole in the cylinder head cover, using the correct grade and type of oil (refer to Section 5 for details of topping-up). Pour in half the specified quantity of oil first, and then wait a few minutes for the oil to drain into the sump. Continue to add oil, a small quantity at a time, until the level is up to the lower mark on the dipstick. Adding approximately a further 1.0 litre will bring the level up to the upper mark on the dipstick. Refit the oil filler cap when correct level is achieved.

19 Start the engine and run it for a few minutes, while checking for leaks around the

13.13 Apply clean oil to the seal on the oil filter

oil filter seal and the sump drain plug. Note that there may be a delay of a few seconds before the low oil pressure warning light goes out when the engine is first started, as the oil circulates through the new oil filter and the engine oil galleries before the pressure builds-up. Do not run the engine above idle speed while the warning light is on.

20 Stop the engine, and wait a few minutes for the oil to settle in the sump once more. With the new oil circulated and the filter now completely full, recheck the level on the dipstick, and add more oil as necessary.

21 Where applicable, refit the plastic engine cover(s).

22 Dispose of the used engine oil safely with reference to *General repair procedures*. Do not discard the old filter with domestic household waste. The facility for waste oil disposal provided by many local council refuse tips generally has a filter receptacle alongside.

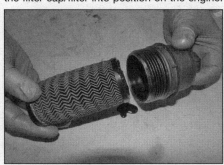

13.14 Withdraw the filter from the cap

13.15 Fit new seal to the filter cap

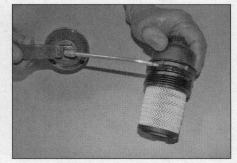

13.16 Lubricate the seal with clean engine oil

15.2a Unclip the filter cover. . .

15.2b . . . and remove it from the heater housing

15.3 Withdraw the pollen filter from the housing

15.4 Note the direction arrow on the filter for refitting

15.5 Make sure the filter cover is secured

14 Resetting the service indicator

1 The instrument cluster mileage recorder incorporates a service interval indicator. When the vehicle is started, the unit displays the mileage until the next service, or the mileage covered since the service was due. The service indicator is manually reset to zero after the vehicle has been serviced. The indicator can also be reset at any time using a suitable diagnostic tool.

2 If your ignition is on, turn it off and then back on. Press the left-hand steering wheel button until you reach the settings section on the instrument panel. Once you reach the settings section, keep the button pressed until a new menu appears. Scroll to the "maintenance" category, then press the button, and scroll down to the "Service" category. Press the button again and scroll down to the "Reset" option. Once on the "Reset" option, press the button. Turn the ignition off, then on and your service indicator light should now be turned off.

3 Switch on the ignition – the distance remaining until (or covered since) the next service is due will flash in the display.

15 Pollen filter renewal

1 Remove the glovebox as described in Chapter 11 Section 25.

2 Release the securing clips and unclip the filter cover, from the rear of the heater housing unit (see illustrations).

3 Collapse the pollen filter inside the housing and withdraw it, then wipe clean the area around the housing (see illustration).

4 Fit the new filter to the housing, in the same way as it was removed, making sure it is fitted in the correct position, with the arrows facing towards the inside of the vehicle (see illustration).

5 Refit the filter cover, making sure it is located correctly in the housing (see illustration). Note if the securing clips have been damaged on removal, there are holes in the cover, so that screws can be used on refitting, if required.

6 Refit the glovebox back into the facia panel, as described in Chapter 11 Section 25.

16 Fuel filter water draining

1 On most models a water drain screw is provided on the base of the fuel filter (see illustration).

2 To make access to the drain screw easier, undo the retaining bolt/nuts and remove the metal cage from around the fuel filter (see illustration).

3 Place a suitable container beneath the drain screw. To make draining easier, a suitable length of tubing can be attached to the outlet pipe at the centre of the screw to direct the fuel flow (see illustration) – on some models a drain tube is provided as standard.

Note: *If desired, access can be improved by unscrewing the nuts securing the filter*

16.1 Water drain screw fitted to base of filter

16.2 Remove the metal cage from around the filter

16.3 Fit length of tube to drain screw

head bracket to the body and by raising the complete filter assembly to a more convenient position – if this is done, take care not to strain the fuel hoses and electrical wiring.

4 Open the drain screw by turning it anti-clockwise and allow the fuel to flow through the filter until any water is dispersed.

5 Allow the entire contents of the filter to drain into the container, and then securely tighten the drain screw.

6 Prime and bleed the fuel system as described in Chapter 4B Section 6.

7 Dispose of the used fuel safely with reference to *General repair procedures*. Do not discard the fuel with domestic household waste. The facility for waste oil/fuel disposal provided by many local council refuse tips generally has a filter receptacle alongside.

17 Hose and fluid leak check

General

1 Visually inspect the engine joint faces, gaskets and seals for any signs of water or oil leaks. Pay particular attention to the areas around the cylinder head cover, cylinder head, oil filter and sump joint faces. Bear in mind that, over a period of time, some very slight seepage from these areas is to be expected – what you are really looking for is any indication of a serious leak. Should a leak be found, renew the offending gasket or oil seal by referring to the appropriate Chapters in this manual.

2 High temperatures in the engine compartment can cause the deterioration of the rubber and plastic hoses used for engine, accessory and emission systems operation. Periodic inspection should be made for cracks, loose clamps, material hardening and leaks.

3 When checking the hoses, ensure that all the cable-ties or clips used to retain the hoses are in place, and in good condition. Clips which are broken or missing can lead to chafing of the hoses, pipes or wiring, which could cause more serious problems in the future.

4 Carefully check the large top and bottom radiator hoses, along with the other smaller-diameter cooling system hoses and metal pipes; do not forget the heater hoses/pipes which run from the engine to the bulkhead. Inspect each hose along its entire length, renewing any that is cracked, swollen or shows signs of deterioration. Cracks may become more apparent if the hose is squeezed, and may often be apparent at the hose ends.

5 Make sure that all hose connections are tight. If the large-diameter air hoses from the air cleaner are loose, they will leak air, and upset the engine idle quality. If the spring clamps that are used to secure some of the

hoses appear to be slackening, they should be updated with worm-drive clips to prevent the possibility of leaks.

6 Some other hoses are secured to their fittings with clamps. Where clamps are used, check to be sure they haven't lost their tension, allowing the hose to leak. If clamps aren't used, make sure the hose has not expanded and/or hardened where it slips over the fitting, allowing it to leak.

7 Check all fluid reservoirs, filler caps, drain plugs and fittings, etc, looking for any signs of leakage of oil, transmission and/or brake hydraulic fluid and coolant. Also check the clutch hydraulic fluid lines which lead from the fluid reservoir, master cylinder, and the slave cylinder, on the transmission (where applicable).

8 If the vehicle is regularly parked in the same place, close inspection of the ground underneath it will soon show any leaks; ignore the puddle of water which will be left if the air conditioning system is in use. Place a clean piece of cardboard below the engine, and examine it for signs of contamination after the vehicle has been parked over it overnight – be aware, however, of the fire risk inherent in placing combustible material below the catalytic converter.

9 Remember that some leaks will only occur with the engine running, or when the engine is hot or cold. With the handbrake firmly applied, start the engine from cold, and let the engine idle while you examine the underside of the engine compartment for signs of leakage.

10 If an unusual smell is noticed inside or around the car, especially when the engine is thoroughly hot, this may point to the presence of a leak.

11 As soon as a leak is detected, its source must be traced and rectified. Where oil has been leaking for some time, it is usually necessary to use a steam cleaner, pressure washer or similar, to clean away the accumulated dirt, so that the exact source of the leak can be identified.

Vacuum hoses

12 It's quite common for vacuum hoses, especially those in the emissions system, to be colour-coded, or to be identified by coloured stripes moulded into them. Various systems require hoses with different wall thicknesses, collapse resistance and temperature resistance. When renewing hoses, be sure the new ones are made of the same material.

13 Often the only effective way to check a hose is to remove it completely from the vehicle. If more than one hose is removed, be sure to label the hoses and fittings to ensure correct installation.

14 When checking vacuum hoses, be sure to include any plastic T-fittings in the check. Inspect the fittings for cracks, and check the hose where it fits over the fitting for distortion, which could cause leakage.

15 A small piece of vacuum hose

(approximately 6 mm inside diameter) can be used as a stethoscope to detect vacuum leaks. Hold one end of the hose to your ear, and probe around vacuum hoses and fittings, listening for the 'hissing' sound characteristic of a vacuum leak.

 Warning: When probing with the vacuum hose stethoscope, be very careful not to come into contact with moving engine components such as the auxiliary drivebelt, radiator electric cooling fan, etc.

Fuel hoses

Warning: There are certain precautions which must be taken when inspecting or servicing fuel system components. Work in a well-ventilated area, and do not allow open flames (cigarettes, appliance pilot lights, etc) or bare light bulbs near the work area. Mop-up any spills immediately, and do not store fuel-soaked rags where they could ignite.

16 Check all fuel hoses for deterioration and chafing. Check especially for cracks in areas where the hose bends, and also just before fittings, such as where a hose attaches to the fuel rail.

17 High-quality fuel line, usually identified by the word 'Fluoroelastomer' printed on the hose, should be used for fuel line renewal. Never, under any circumstances, use non-reinforced vacuum line, clear plastic tubing or water hose as a substitute for fuel lines.

18 Spring-type clamps may be used on fuel lines. These clamps often lose their tension over a period of time, and can be 'sprung' during removal. Renew all spring-type clamps with proper petrol pipe clips whenever a hose is renewed.

Metal pipes

19 Sections of metal piping are often used for fuel line between the fuel tank and the engine, and for most air conditioning applications. Check carefully to be sure the piping has not been bent or crimped, and that cracks have not started in the line; also check for signs of excessive corrosion.

20 If a section of metal fuel line must be renewed, only seamless steel piping should be used, since copper and aluminium piping don't have the strength necessary to withstand normal engine vibration.

21 Check the metal lines where they enter the brake master cylinder, ABS hydraulic unit or clutch master/slave cylinders (as applicable) for cracks in the lines or loose fittings. Any sign of brake fluid leakage calls for an immediate and thorough inspection.

Air conditioning refrigerant

Warning: Refer to the safety information given in 'Safety first!' and Chapter 3 Section 12, regarding the dangers of disturbing any of the air conditioning system components.

19.2 With the wheel removed, the pad thickness can be seen through the front of the caliper

20.1 Check the constant velocity (CV) joint gaiters – outer gaiter shown

22 The air conditioning system is filled with a liquid refrigerant, which is retained under high pressure. If the air conditioning system is opened and depressurised without the aid of specialised equipment, the refrigerant will immediately turn into gas and escape into the atmosphere. If the liquid comes into contact with your skin, it can cause severe frostbite. In addition, the refrigerant contains substances which are environmentally damaging; for this reason, it should not be allowed to escape into the atmosphere.

23 Any suspected air conditioning system leaks should be immediately referred to a Nissan dealer or air conditioning specialist. Leakage will be shown up as a steady drop in the level of refrigerant in the system.

24 Note that water may drip from the condenser drain pipe, underneath the car, immediately after the air conditioning system has been in use. This is normal, and should not be cause for concern.

18 Seat belt check

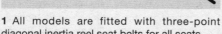

1 All models are fitted with three-point diagonal inertia reel seat belts for all seats.

2 Check the seat belts for satisfactory operation and condition. Pull sharply on the belt to check that the locking mechanism engages correctly. Check that they retract smoothly and without binding into their reels.

3 Inspect the belts for signs of fraying or

other damage and check the operation of the buckles. Ensure that all mounting bolts are securely tightened, noting that the bolts are shouldered so that the belt anchor points are free to rotate.

4 If there is any sign of damage, or any doubt about the condition of a belt, it must be renewed. If the vehicle has been involved in a collision, any belts in use at the time should be renewed as a matter of course, and all other belts should be checked carefully.

5 Use only warm water and non-detergent soap to clean the belts. Never use any chemical cleaners, strong detergents, dyes or bleaches. Keep the belts fully extended until they have dried naturally – do not apply heat to dry them.

19 Brake pad and disc wear check

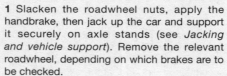

1 Slacken the roadwheel nuts, apply the handbrake, then jack up the car and support it securely on axle stands (see *Jacking and vehicle support*). Remove the relevant roadwheel, depending on which brakes are to be checked.

2 The brake pad thickness, and the condition of the disc, can be assessed roughly with just the wheels removed **(see illustration)**. For a comprehensive check, the brake pads should be removed and cleaned. The operation of the caliper can then also be checked, and the condition of the brake disc itself can be fully

examined on both sides. Refer to Chapter 9, for further information.

3 On completion, refit the roadwheels and lower the car to the ground. Tighten the roadwheel nuts to their specified torque.

20 Driveshaft gaiter check

1 With the vehicle raised and securely supported on stands, turn the steering onto full lock, then slowly rotate the roadwheel. Inspect the condition of the outer constant velocity (CV) joint rubber gaiters while squeezing the gaiters to open out the folds. Check for signs of cracking, splits or deterioration of the rubber which may allow the grease to escape and lead to water and grit entry into the joint. Also check the security and condition of the retaining clips. Repeat these checks on the inner CV joints **(see illustration)**. If any damage or deterioration is found, the gaiters should be renewed as described in Chapter 8 Section 9.

2 At the same time, check the general condition of the CV joints themselves by first holding the driveshaft and attempting to rotate the wheel. Repeat this check by holding the inner joint and attempting to rotate the driveshaft. Any appreciable movement indicates wear in the joints, wear in the driveshaft splines, or a loose driveshaft retaining nut.

21 Steering and suspension check

Front suspension and steering

1 Firmly apply the handbrake, and then jack up the front of the vehicle and support it securely on axle stands (see *Jacking and vehicle support*).

2 Visually inspect the balljoint dust covers and the steering rack and pinion gaiters for splits, chafing or deterioration **(see illustrations)**. Any wear of these components will cause loss of lubricant, together with dirt and water entry, resulting in rapid deterioration of the balljoints or steering gear.

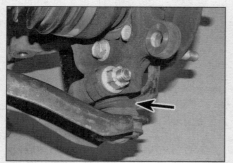

21.2a Check the ball joint dust covers. . .

21.2b . . . the steering rack gaiters. . .

21.2c . . . and the anti-roll bar drop link ball joint dust covers

3 Grasp the roadwheel at the 12 o'clock and 6 o'clock positions, and try to rock it **(see illustration)**. Very slight free play may be felt, but if the movement is appreciable, further investigation is necessary to determine the source. Continue rocking the wheel while an assistant depresses the footbrake. If the movement is now eliminated or significantly reduced, it is likely that the hub bearings are at fault. If the free play is still evident with the footbrake depressed, then there is wear in the suspension joints or mountings.

4 Now grasp the wheel at the 9 o'clock and 3 o'clock positions, and try to rock it as before **(see illustration)**. Any movement felt now may again be caused by wear in the hub bearings or the steering track rod balljoints. If the inner or outer balljoint is worn, the visual movement will be obvious.

5 Using a large screwdriver or flat bar, check for wear in the suspension mounting bushes by levering between the relevant suspension component and its attachment point. Some movement is to be expected as the mountings are made of rubber, but excessive wear should be obvious. Also check the condition of any visible rubber bushes, looking for splits, cracks or contamination of the rubber.

6 With the car standing on its wheels, have an assistant turn the steering wheel back-and-forth about an eighth of a turn each way. There should be very little, if any, lost movement between the steering wheel and roadwheels. If this is not the case, closely observe the joints and mountings previously described, but in addition check the steering column universal joints for wear, and also check the rack-and-pinion steering gear itself.

Rear suspension

7 Chock the front wheels, then jack up the rear of the vehicle and support securely on axle stands (see *Jacking and vehicle support*).

8 Working as described previously for the front suspension, check the rear hub bearings, the suspension bushes and the shock absorber mountings for wear.

Strut/shock absorber check

9 Check for any signs of fluid leakage around the suspension strut/shock absorber body, or from the rubber gaiter around the piston rod. Should any fluid be noticed, the suspension strut/shock absorber is defective internally, and should be renewed.

Note: *Suspension struts/shock absorbers should always be renewed in pairs on the same axle.*

10 The efficiency of the suspension strut/shock absorber may be checked by bouncing the vehicle at each corner. Generally speaking, the body will return to its normal position and stop after being depressed. If it rises and returns on a rebound, the suspension strut/shock absorber is probably suspect. Examine the suspension strut/shock absorber upper and lower mountings for any signs of wear.

21.3 Check for wear in the hub bearings by grasping the wheel and trying to rock it

22 Exhaust system check

1 With the engine cold (at least three hours after the vehicle has been driven), check the complete exhaust system, from its starting point at the engine to the end of the tailpipe. Ideally, this should be done on a hoist, where unrestricted access is available; if a hoist is not available, raise and support the vehicle on axle stands (see *Jacking and vehicle support*).

2 Make sure that all brackets and rubber mountings are in good condition, and tight; if any of the mountings are to be renewed, ensure that the new ones are of the correct type – in the case of the rubber mountings, their colour is a good guide. Those nearest to the catalytic converter are more heat-resistant than the others **(see illustration)**.

3 Check the pipes and connections for evidence of leaks, severe corrosion, or damage. One of the most common points for a leak to develop is around the welded joints between the pipes and silencers. Leakage at any of the joints or in other parts of the system will usually show up as a black sooty stain in the vicinity of the leak. **Note:** *Exhaust sealants should not be used on any part of the exhaust system upstream of the catalytic converter (between the converter and engine) – even if the sealant does not contain additives harmful to the converter, pieces of it may break off and foul the element, causing local overheating.*

4 At the same time, inspect the underside of the body for holes, corrosion, open seams,

22.2 Check the condition of the exhaust rubber mountings

21.4 Check for wear in the steering rack or ball joints by grasping the wheel and trying to rock it

etc, which may allow exhaust gases to enter the passenger compartment. Seal all body openings with silicone or body putty.

5 Rattles and other noises can often be traced to the exhaust system, especially the rubber mountings. Try to move the system, silencer(s), heat shields and catalytic converter. If any components can touch the body or suspension parts, secure the exhaust system with new mountings.

23 Roadwheel nut tightness check

1 Remove the wheel trims or alloy wheel centre covers where necessary, and slacken the roadwheel nuts slightly.

2 Securely tighten the wheel nuts in a diagonal sequence, then tighten the nuts to the specified torque, using a torque wrench. Refit the wheel trim/hub cap/wheel nut covers (as applicable).

24 Hinge and lock lubrication

1 Work around the car and lubricate the hinges of the bonnet, doors and tailgate with light oil.

2 Lightly lubricate the bonnet release mechanism with a smear of grease.

3 Check carefully the security and operation of all hinges, latches and locks, adjusting them where required. Check the operation of the central locking system.

4 Check the condition and operation of the tailgate struts, renewing them both if either is leaking or no longer able to support the tailgate securely when raised.

25 Road test

Instruments and electrical equipment

1 Check the operation of all instruments and electrical equipment.

26.2a Undo the bolt and nuts. . .

26.2b . . . and remove the metal cage

26.3 Disconnect the wiring plug

26.4 Remove the clamp bolt

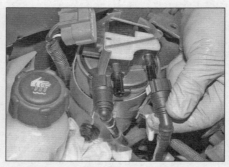
26.5 Depress the buttons and disconnect the pipes

26.6 Withdraw the fuel filter

2 Make sure that all instruments read correctly, and switch on all electrical equipment in turn, to check that it functions properly.

Steering and suspension

3 Check for any abnormalities in the steering, suspension, handling or road 'feel'.
4 Drive the car, and check that there are no unusual vibrations or noises.
5 Check that the steering feels positive, with no excessive 'sloppiness', or roughness, and check for any suspension noises when cornering and driving over bumps.

Drivetrain

6 Check the performance of the engine, clutch, transmission and driveshafts.
7 Listen for any unusual noises from the engine, clutch and transmission.
8 Make sure that the engine runs smoothly when idling, and that there is no hesitation when accelerating.
9 Check that the clutch action is smooth and progressive, that the drive is taken up smoothly, and that the pedal travel is not excessive. Also listen for any noises when the clutch pedal is depressed.
10 Check that all gears can be engaged smoothly without noise, and that the gear lever action is smooth and not abnormally vague or 'notchy'.
11 Listen for a metallic clicking sound from the front of the car, as the car is driven slowly in a circle with the steering on full-lock.

Carry out this check in both directions. If a clicking noise is heard, this indicates wear in a driveshaft joint (see Chapter 8).

Braking system

12 Make sure that the car does not pull to one side when braking, and that the wheels do not lock when braking hard.
13 Check that there is no vibration through the steering when braking.
14 Check that the handbrake operates correctly, without excessive movement of the lever, and that it holds the car stationary on a slope.
15 Test the operation of the brake servo unit as follows. Depress the footbrake 4 or 5 times to exhaust the vacuum, then start the engine. As the engine starts, there should be a noticeable 'give' in the brake pedal as vacuum builds-up. Allow the engine to run for at least 2 minutes, and then switch it off. If the brake pedal is now depressed again, it should be possible to detect a hiss from the servo as the pedal is depressed. After about 4 or 5 applications, no further hissing should be heard, and the pedal should feel considerably harder.

26 Fuel filter renewal

Note: *Various types of fuel filters are fitted to these engines depending on model year and*

territory. The following procedures depict a typical example.
1 The fuel filter is located at the right-hand side of the engine compartment.
2 Undo the bolt and two nuts, then remove metal cage from over the fuel filter (see illustrations).
3 Release the locking clip and and disconnect the wiring plug from the top of the filter (see illustration).
4 Slacken and remove the bolt from the clamp around the fuel filter (see illustration).
5 Position some rag around the base of the fuel filter to catch the spilt fuel, then depress the release buttons and disconnect the fuel pipes from the filter (see illustration). Plug the openings to prevent contamination.
6 Lift the filter from the mounting bracket (see illustration).
7 Locate the new fuel filter into the mounting bracket and tighten the clamp retaining bolt.
8 Reconnect the fuel pipes to their original locations, and reconnect the wiring plug.
9 Refit the metal cage over the filter and tighten the retaining bolt/nuts securely.
10 The remainder of refitting is a reversal of removal, noting the following points:
a) Ensure that the fuel hose connections are securely remade.
b) On completion, prime and bleed the fuel system as described in Chapter 4B Section 6.
c) When the engine is running, check for any sign of leakage from the disturbed pipes.

27 Air filter element renewal

Caution: Never drive the vehicle with the air cleaner filter element removed. Excessive engine wear could result, and backfiring could even cause a fire under the bonnet.

1 The air filter element is located in the air cleaner assembly on the left-hand side rear of the engine compartment.

2 Release the two retaining clips on the front crossmember, undo the retaining bolt, then release the clips on the filter housing and slide the air intake resonator/inlet duct from the air cleaner housing **(see illustrations)**. The intake resonator and inlet duct to the front crossmember can be split, to remove, but the retaining clips at the centre can break easily, so we found removing the complete assembly as one is best.

3 Release the retaining clips and remove the front cover from the air cleaner housing, then withdraw the filter element from the air cleaner housing **(see illustrations)**.

4 If carrying out a routine service, the element must be renewed regardless of its apparent condition.

5 If you are checking the element for any other reason, inspect its lower surface; if it is oily or very dirty, renew the element. If it is only moderately dusty, it can be re-used by blowing it clean from the upper to the lower surface with compressed air. Because it is a pleated-paper type filter, it cannot be washed or re-oiled. If it cannot be cleaned satisfactorily with compressed air, discard and renew it.

⚠️ **Warning: Wear eye protection when using compressed air.**

6 Position the new filter element in the housing, and secure the front cover in position with the retaining clips. Refit the air intake duct to the front of the air cleaner housing.

28 Brake fluid renewal

Caution: Brake hydraulic fluid can harm

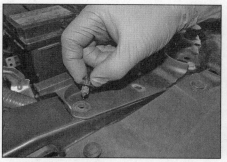
27.2a Remove the two retaining clips. . .

27.2b . . . undo the bolt. . .

27.2c . . .then release the clips and slide ducting from air cleaner housing

27.2d The clips at the centre are fragile and can break easily

your eyes and damage painted surfaces, so use extreme caution when handling and pouring it. Do not use fluid that has been standing open for some time, as it absorbs moisture from the air. Excess moisture can cause a dangerous loss of braking effectiveness.**

1 The procedure is similar to that for bleeding the hydraulic system as described in Chapter 9 Section 3, except that allowance should be made for the old fluid to be expelled when bleeding each section of the circuit.

2 Working as described in Chapter 9 Section 3, open the first bleed screw in the sequence, and pump the brake pedal gently until the level in the reservoir is approaching the MIN mark. Top-up to the MAX level with new fluid, and continue pumping until only new fluid

remains in the reservoir, and new fluid can be seen emerging from the bleed screw. Tighten the screw, and top the reservoir level up to the MAX level line.

3 Work through all the remaining bleed screws in the sequence until new fluid can be seen at all of them. Be careful to keep the master cylinder reservoir topped-up above the MIN level at all times, or air may enter the system. If this happens, further bleeding will be required, to remove the air.

4 When the operation is complete, check that all bleed screws are securely tightened, and that their dust caps are refitted. Wash off all traces of spilt fluid, and recheck the master cylinder reservoir fluid level.

5 Check the operation of the brakes before taking the car on the road.

27.3a Release the two securing clips (one at each side). . .

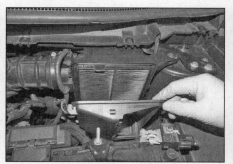
27.3b . . . then tilt the cover forwards. . .

27.3c . . . and withdraw the filter element

29 Braking system rubber hose check

1 Position the car over an inspection pit, on car ramps, or jack it up one wheel at a time (see *Jacking and vehicle support*).
2 Inspect the braking system rubber hoses fitted to each front caliper, and on each side of the rear axle **(see illustration)**. Look for perished, swollen or hardened rubber, and any signs of cracking, especially at the metal end fittings. If there's any doubt as to the condition of any hose, renew it as described in Chapter 9 Section 4.

30 Manual transmission oil level check

1 Park the car on a level surface. The oil level must be checked before the car is driven, or at least 5 minutes after the engine has been switched off. If the oil is checked immediately after driving the car, some of the oil will remain distributed around the transmission components, resulting in an inaccurate level reading. To improve access, position the car over an inspection pit, or raise the car off the ground and position it on axle stands, (see *Jacking and vehicle support*) making sure the vehicle remains level to the ground.
2 Wipe clean the area around the filler/level plug, and unscrew it from the casing. On 1.5 litre engines, the filler/level plug is situated on the left-hand rear of the transmission unit, behind

29.2 Rubber brake hose fitted to the front caliper

the driveshaft. On 1.6 litre engines, the filler/level plug is situated on the left-hand front of the transmission unit **(see illustrations)**.
3 The oil level should reach the lower edge of the filler/level hole. A certain amount of oil will have gathered behind the filler/level plug and will trickle out when it is removed; this does **not** necessarily indicate that the level is correct. To ensure that a true level is established, wait until the initial trickle has stopped, then add oil as necessary until a trickle of new oil can be seen emerging. The level will be correct when the flow ceases; use only good-quality oil of the specified type.
4 Remove the left-hand front road wheel for better access to the filler/level plug. Use a length of hose and a funnel to make topping up easier **(see illustrations)**.
5 Refilling the transmission is an extremely awkward operation; above all, allow plenty of time for the oil level to settle properly before

checking it. If a large amount had to be added to the transmission and a large amount flows out on checking the level, refit the filler/level plug, and take the vehicle on a short journey. This will allow the new oil to be distributed fully around the transmission components. On returning, recheck the level when the oil has settled again.
6 If the transmission has been overfilled so that oil flows out as soon as the filler/level plug is removed, check that the car is completely level (front-to-rear and side-to-side). If necessary, allow the surplus to drain off into a suitable container.
7 When the level is correct, refit the filler/level plug, tightening it to the specified torque wrench setting. Wash off any spilt oil.

31 Remote control battery renewal

Note: *All the remote control units described below are fitted with a CR 2032, 3 volt battery.*
1 Although not in the Nissan maintenance schedule, we recommend that the battery is changed every 2 years, regardless of the vehicle's mileage. However, if the door locks repeatedly fail to respond to signals from the remote control at the normal distance, change the battery in the remote control before attempting to troubleshoot any of the vehicle's other systems.
2 Release the securing clip and withdraw the key from the remote control body **(see illustrations)**.

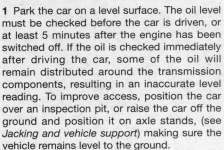

30.2a Transmission oil filler/level plug (1.5 litre engines)

30.2b Transmission oil filler/level plug (1.6 litre engines)

30.4a Using a funnel and hose. . .

30.4b . . . to fill up the transmission

31.2a Release the clip. . .

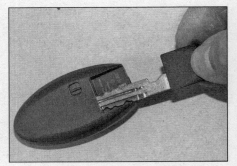

31.2b . . . and withdraw the key

3 Using a small screwdriver, carefully prise the two halves of the transmitter apart **(see illustrations)**.
4 Carefully unclip the battery from its position in the transmitter housing, noting its fitted position **(see illustration)**.
5 Fit the new battery **(see illustration)**, observing the correct polarity, and clip the transmitter housing back together.

32 Coolant strength check and renewal

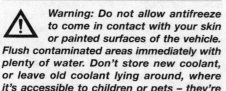

⚠️ **Warning: Do not allow antifreeze to come in contact with your skin or painted surfaces of the vehicle. Flush contaminated areas immediately with plenty of water. Don't store new coolant, or leave old coolant lying around, where it's accessible to children or pets – they're attracted by its sweet smell. Ingestion of even a small amount of coolant can be fatal. Wipe up garage-floor and drip-pan spills immediately. Keep antifreeze containers covered, and repair cooling system leaks as soon as they're noticed.**

⚠️ **Warning: Never remove the expansion tank filler cap when the engine is running, or has just been switched off, as the cooling system will be hot, and the consequent escaping steam and scalding coolant could cause serious injury.**

⚠️ **Warning: Wait until the engine is cold before starting these procedures.**

Strength check

1 Use a hydrometer to check the strength of the antifreeze. Follow the instructions provided with your hydrometer. The antifreeze strength should be approximately 50%. If it is significantly less than this, drain a little coolant from the radiator (see this Section), add antifreeze to the coolant expansion tank, then recheck the strength.

Coolant draining

2 To drain the system, first remove the expansion tank filler cap.
3 Firmly apply the handbrake, then jack up the front of the vehicle and support it securely on axle stands (see). Where applicable, release the fasteners and remove the engine undershield.
4 Place a suitable container beneath the left-hand side of the radiator, then undo the drain plug **(see illustration)**, and drain the coolant into the container. If possible, place a funnel (or similar) to catch the coolant, as part of the front crossmember is below the radiator, so this will cause the coolant to splash in different directions.
5 If required, to aid draining of the cooling system, release the retaining clamp and disconnect the bottom hose from the radiator

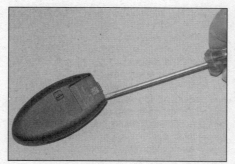
31.3a Twist a small screwdriver in the slot. . .

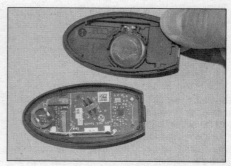
31.3b . . . and unclip one side of the transmitter

31.4 Unclip the battery from its location in the cover

31.5 Battery type (CR2032 – 3V)

(see illustration). Allow the coolant to drain into the container.
6 Once the coolant has stopped draining from the radiator, tighten the drain plug and then reconnect the bottom hose, securing it with the retaining clamp.

System flushing

7 With time, the cooling system may gradually lose its efficiency, as the radiator core becomes choked with rust, scale deposits from the water, and other sediment. To minimise this, as well as using only good-quality antifreeze and clean soft water, the system should be flushed as follows whenever any part of it is disturbed, and/or when the coolant is renewed.
8 With the coolant drained, refit the radiator bottom hose and refill the system with fresh water. Refit the expansion tank filler cap, start the engine and warm it up to normal operating

temperature, then stop it and (after allowing it to cool down completely) drain the system again. Repeat as necessary until only clean water can be seen to emerge, then refill finally with the specified coolant mixture.
9 If only clean, soft water and good-quality antifreeze (even if not to Nissan's specification) has been used, and the coolant has been renewed at the suggested intervals, the above procedure will be sufficient to keep the system clean for a considerable length of time. If, however, the system has been neglected, a more thorough operation will be required, as follows.
10 First drain the coolant, then disconnect the radiator top hose. Insert a garden hose into the radiator top hose connection, and allow water to circulate through the radiator until it runs clean from the bottom outlet. DO NOT use pressurised water from the garden hose, just normal water flow.

32.4 Coolant drain plug

32.5 Release the clamp and disconnect the bottom hose

11 To flush the engine, insert the garden hose into the radiator bottom hose, wrap a piece of rag around the garden hose to seal the connection, and allow water to circulate until it runs clear.

12 Try the effect of repeating this procedure in the top hose, although this may not be effective, since the thermostat will probably close and prevent the flow of water.

13 In severe cases of contamination, reverse-flushing of the radiator may be necessary. This may be achieved by inserting the garden hose into the bottom outlet, wrapping a piece of rag around the hose to seal the connection, then flushing the radiator until clear water emerges from the top hose outlet.

14 If the radiator is suspected of being severely choked, remove the radiator (Chapter 3 Section 5), turn it upside-down, and repeat the procedure described in paragraph 13.

15 Flushing the heater matrix can be achieved using a similar procedure to that described in paragraph 13, once the heater inlet and outlet hoses have been identified. These two hoses will be of the same diameter, and pass through the engine compartment bulkhead.

16 The use of chemical cleaners is not recommended, and should be necessary only as a last resort; the scouring action of some chemical cleaners may lead to other cooling system problems. Normally, regular renewal of the coolant will prevent excessive contamination of the system.

Coolant filling

17 With the cooling system drained and flushed, ensure that all disturbed hose unions are correctly secured. If it was raised, lower the vehicle to the ground.

18 Set the heater temperature control to maximum heat, but ensure the blower is turned off.

19 Prepare a sufficient quantity of the specified coolant mixture (see below); allow for a surplus, so as to have a reserve supply for topping-up.

20 Slowly fill the system through the expansion tank. Since the tank is the highest point in the system, all the air in the system should be displaced into the tank by the rising liquid. Slow pouring reduces the possibility of air being trapped and forming airlocks.

21 Continue filling until the coolant level reaches the expansion tank MAX level line (see Section 6), then refit the filler cap.

22 Start the engine and run it at 2500 rpm for 15 minutes. If the level in the expansion tank drops significantly, top-up to the MAX level line, to minimise the amount of air circulating in the system.

23 Increase the engine speed to 5000 rpm, then allow it to return to idle. Repeat this sequence 6 times.

24 Increase the engine speed to 4000 rpm, maintain this speed for 10 seconds, then reduce the engine speed to 2500 rpm and maintain this speed for 10 minutes.

25 Stop the engine, then leave the car to cool down completely (overnight, if possible).

26 With the system cool, open the expansion tank, and top-up the tank to the MAX level line. Refit the filler cap, tightening it securely, and clean up any spillage.

27 After refilling, always check carefully all components of the system (but especially any unions disturbed during draining and flushing) for signs of coolant leaks. Fresh antifreeze has a searching action, which will rapidly expose any weak points in the system.

Antifreeze type and mixture

Caution: Do not use engine antifreeze in the windscreen/tailgate washer system, as it will damage the vehicle's paintwork. A screenwash additive should be added to the washer system in its maker's recommended quantities.

28 If the vehicle's history (and therefore the quality of the antifreeze in it) is unknown, owners are advised to drain and thoroughly reverse-flush the system, before refilling with fresh coolant mixture.

29 If the antifreeze used is to Nissan's specification, the levels of protection it affords are indicated in the coolant packaging.

30 To give the recommended standard mixture ratio for antifreeze, 50% (by volume) of antifreeze must be mixed with 50% of clean, soft water; if you are using any other type of antifreeze, follow its manufacturer's instructions to achieve the correct ratio.

31 You are unlikely to fully drain the system at any one time (unless the engine is being completely stripped), and the capacities quoted in the Specifications are therefore slightly academic for routine coolant renewal. As a guide, only two-thirds of the system's total capacity is likely to be needed for coolant renewal.

32 As the drained system will be partially filled with flushing water, in order to establish the recommended mixture ratio, measure out 50% of the system capacity in antifreeze and pour it into the hose/expansion tank as described above, then top-up with water. Any topping-up while refilling the system should be done with a suitable mixture.

33 Before adding antifreeze, the cooling system should be drained, preferably flushed, and all hoses checked for condition and security. As noted earlier, fresh antifreeze will rapidly find any weaknesses in the system.

34 After filling with antifreeze, a label should be attached to the expansion tank, stating the type and concentration of antifreeze used, and the date installed. Any subsequent topping-up should be made with the same type and concentration of antifreeze.

General cooling system checks

35 The engine should be cold for the cooling system checks, so perform the following procedure before driving the vehicle, or after it has been shut off for at least three hours.

36 Remove the expansion tank filler cap, and clean it thoroughly inside and out with a rag.

Also clean the filler neck on the expansion tank. The presence of rust or corrosion in the filler neck indicates that the coolant should be changed. The coolant inside the expansion tank should be relatively clean and transparent. If it is rust-coloured, drain and flush the system, and refill with a fresh coolant mixture.

37 Carefully check the radiator hoses and heater hoses along their entire length; renew any hose which is cracked, swollen or deteriorated.

38 Inspect all other cooling system components (joint faces, etc) for leaks. A leak in the cooling system will usually show up as white- or antifreeze-coloured deposits on the area adjoining the leak. Where any problems of this nature are found on system components, renew the component or gasket with reference to Chapter 3.

Airlocks

39 If, after draining and refilling the system, symptoms of overheating are found which did not occur previously, then the fault is almost certainly due to trapped air at some point in the system, causing an airlock and restricting the flow of coolant; usually, the air is trapped because the system was refilled too quickly.

40 If an airlock is suspected, first try gently squeezing all visible coolant hoses. A coolant hose which is full of air feels quite different to one full of coolant when squeezed. After refilling the system, most airlocks will clear once the system has cooled, and been topped-up.

41 While the engine is running at operating temperature, switch on the heater and heater fan, and check for heat output. Provided there is sufficient coolant in the system, lack of heat output could be due to an airlock in the system.

42 Airlocks can have more serious effects than simply reducing heater output – a severe airlock could reduce coolant flow around the engine. Check that the radiator top hose is hot when the engine is at operating temperature – a top hose which stays cold could be the result of an airlock (or a non-opening thermostat).

43 If the problem persists, stop the engine and allow it to cool down completely, before unscrewing the expansion tank filler cap or loosening the hose clips and squeezing the hoses to bleed out the trapped air. In the worst case, the system will have to be at least partially drained (this time, the coolant can be saved for re-use) and flushed to clear the problem. If all else fails, have the system evacuated and vacuum filled by a suitably-equipped garage.

Expansion tank cap check

44 Wait until the engine is completely cold – perform this check before the engine is started for the first time in the day.

45 Place a wad of cloth over the expansion tank cap, then unscrew it slowly and remove it.

33.5 Check for drivebelt wear

33.6a Turning the spanner clockwise from under the vehicle. . .

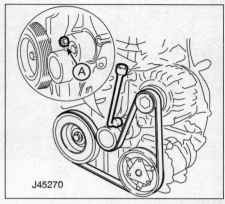

J45270

33.6b . . . or from above, using hexagon (A) on the tensioner pulley

46 Examine the condition of the rubber seal on the underside of the cap. If the rubber appears to have hardened, or cracks are visible in the seal edges, a new cap should be fitted.

47 If the car is several years old, or has covered a large mileage, consider renewing the cap regardless of its apparent condition – they are not expensive. If the pressure relief valve built into the cap fails, excess pressure in the system will lead to puzzling failures of hoses and other cooling system components.

33 Auxiliary drivebelt check and renewal – 1.5 litre diesel engine

Note: *Nissan recommend that the belt be always renewed if it is removed, along with the automatic tensioner. The belt and tensioner should be renewed every 72 000 miles or 5 years regardless of condition.*

Checking

1 The auxiliary drivebelt is located on the right-hand side of the engine.

2 Due to their function and material makeup, drivebelts are prone to failure after a period of time and should therefore be inspected, and if necessary adjusted periodically.

3 A basic check for obvious faults can be made from the engine compartment. However, because the belt runs very close to the right hand inner wing a through inspection can only be made from below.

4 Jack up the front of the car, and support it on axle stands (see *Jacking and vehicle support*). Remove the right-hand wheel and the inner wing panel.

5 With the engine stopped, inspect the full length of the drivebelt for cracks and separation of the belt plies **(see illustration)**. It will be necessary to turn the engine (using a spanner or socket and bar on the crankshaft pulley bolt) in order to move the belt from the pulleys so that the belt can be inspected thoroughly. Twist the belt between the pulleys so that both sides can be viewed. Also, check for fraying and glazing which gives the belt a shiny appearance. Check the pulleys for nicks, cracks, distortion and corrosion.

Renewal

Note: *Before removal of the belt, note the fitted position. On some models, the compressor pulley has six grooves and the belt has five. In this case the inner groove on the compressor pulley is left unused, so that the run of the belt is straight.*

6 Using a spanner on the outer nut on the tensioner, turn the tensioner clockwise to release the tension on the belt **(see illustrations)**, then lift the drivebelt from the pulleys, noting its fitted position on the pulleys.

7 If the belt is removed, it is recommended by Nissan that it must be renewed.

8 Unbolt the tensioner unit and fit a new one, tightening the retaining bolt to the specified torque.

9 Using the spanner on the outer nut on the tensioner, hold the tensioner clockwise, to allow the new belt to be fitted around the pulleys, making sure that it is correctly located in the grooves.

10 Fit a socket to the crankshaft pulley and rotate the engine several times to check the belt alignment.

11 Refit the wing liner and wheel, then lower the vehicle to the ground. Tighten the road wheels to the specified torque setting.

34 Auxiliary drivebelt check and renewal – 1.6 litre diesel engine

Note: *Nissan recommend that the belt be always renewed if it is removed, along with the automatic tensioner and idler pulley. These should be renewed every 72 000 miles or 5 years regardless of condition.*

Checking

1 The auxiliary drivebelt is located at the right-hand side of the engine.

2 Due to their function and material makeup, drivebelts are prone to failure after a period of time and should therefore be inspected, and if necessary adjusted periodically.

3 Since the drivebelt is located very close to the right-hand side of the engine compartment, it is possible to gain better access by raising the front of the vehicle and

removing the right-hand wheel, then removing the inner panel **(see illustration 33.4)**, from inside the wheel arch, and if required the engine undertray.

4 With the engine stopped, inspect the full length of the drivebelt for cracks and separation of the belt plies **(see illustration 33.5)**. It will be necessary to turn the engine (using a spanner or socket and bar on the crankshaft pulley bolt) in order to move the belt from the pulleys so that the belt can be inspected thoroughly. Twist the belt between the pulleys so that both sides can be viewed. Also check for fraying, and glazing which gives the belt a shiny appearance. Check the pulleys for nicks, cracks, distortion and corrosion.

5 A spring-loaded tensioner is fitted to automatically maintain the correct tension on the belt. If the line on the tensioner body is outside the indicator range, then the belt will need to be renewed **(see illustration)**. If problems with belt squeal or slip are encountered, the belt should be renewed. If the problem continues, it will be necessary to renew the tensioner assembly.

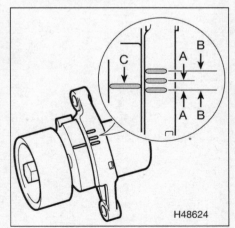

H48624

34.5 Tensioner indicator – 1.6 litre engines

A-A New drive belt range
B-B Used drive belt range
C Indicator marking on tensioner

34.6a Turn the tensioner...

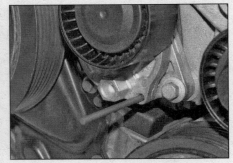

34.6b ...and insert the locking peg

Renewal

6 To remove the belt, use a socket on the hexagon provided to turn the tensioner anti-clockwise (as viewed from the right-hand side of the car). A 3.0mm Allen key or drill bit can be inserted into a hole in the tensioner body to hold it in the released position (see illustrations).

7 Note the routing of the belt, then slip the belt off the pulleys (see illustration).

8 Fit the new belt ensuring that it is routed correctly.

9 With the belt in position, use the socket to hold the tensioner in position while the 3.0mm Allen key is removed, then carefully release the tension clockwise so the belt will automatically become tensioned.

10 Fit a socket to the crankshaft pulley and rotate the engine several times to check the belt alignment. Check the position of the line on the tensioner body, to make sure it is between the two outer wear lines on the tensioner.

11 Refit the wing liner and wheel, then lower the vehicle to the ground. Tighten the road wheels to the specified torque setting.

35 Timing belt renewal

1 Refer to the procedures contained in Chapter 2B Section 5, for timing belt renewal for 1.5 litre diesel engines.

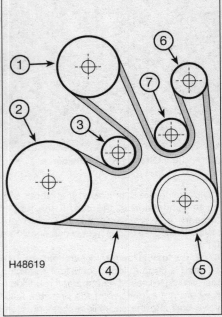

H48619

34.7 Auxilliary drivebelt configuration – 1.6 litre engines

1 Coolant pump
2 Crankshaft pulley
3 Drive belt tensioner
4 Drivebelt
5 Air-conditioning compressor
6 Alternator
7 Idler pulley

Chapter 2 Part A
1.2 litre petrol engine in-car repair procedures

Contents

Degrees of difficulty

Easy, suitable for novice with little experience 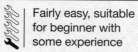 | Fairly easy, suitable for beginner with some experience | Fairly difficult, suitable for competent DIY mechanic | Difficult, suitable for experienced DIY mechanic | Very difficult, suitable for expert DIY or professional

Specifications

Engine (general)
Engine code HRA2DDT
Capacity . . . . 1197 cc
Bore . . . . 72.2 mm
Stroke . . . . 73.1 mm
Direction of crankshaft rotation . . . . Clockwise (viewed from right-hand side of vehicle)
No. 1 cylinder location . . . . At timing chain end of engine
Firing order. 1-3-4-2
Compression ratio . . . . 10 : 1

Valve clearances
Cold engine:
  Inlet . . . . 0.25 to 0.35 mm
  Exhaust. . . . . 0.46 to 0.54 mm

Lubrication system
Oil pump type. . . . . Rotor-type, driven off crankshaft right-hand end
Minimum oil pressure at normal operating temperature (approx. 80ºC):
  At Idle speed. . . . . 1.7 bars (minimum)
  At 4000 rpm . . . . 3.5 bars (minimum)

Torque wrench settings	Nm	lbf ft
Big-end bearing cap bolts: *		
Stage 1	25	18
Stage 2	Angle tighten a further 110°	
Camshaft bearing cap bolts:		
Stage 1	4	3
Stage 2	11	8
Camshaft sprocket retaining bolts	75	55
Crankshaft pulley bolt: *		
Stage 1	50	37
Stage 2	Angle-tighten a further 200°	
Cylinder head bolts: *		
Stage 1	25	18
Stage 2	Angle-tighten a further 270°	
Cylinder head closing plate bolts	25	18
Cylinder head cover bolts	10	8
Engine-to-transmission fixing bolts	62	46
Flywheel: *		
Stage 1	40	30
Stage 2	Angle-tighten a further 50°	
Left-hand transmission mounting:		
Through-bolt/stud nut	60	44
Through-bolt/stud-to-bracket	65	48
Mounting-to-bracket nuts	105	77
Mounting bracket-to-inner wing panel bolts	50	37
Mounting-to-transmission bolts	60	44
Main bearing cap bolts: *		
Stage 1	33	24
Stage 2	Angle-tighten a further 60°	
Main bearing cap support beam	25	18
Oil pump sprocket retaining nut	25	18
Rear engine/transmission torque/link arm mounting:		
Mounting-to-front subframe bolt	80	59
Mounting bracket-to-transmission bolt	80	59
Right-hand engine mounting:		
Bracket bolts to engine	60	44
Mounting bolts to inner wing	60	44
Sump oil drain plug	50	37
Lower sump oil pan bolts	10	7
Upper sump casing bolts to cylinder block	25	18
Timing chain cover bolts:		
Lower bolts x 8 (6mm)	25	18
Upper bolts x 6 (8mm)	55	41
Centre bolts x 3	10	7
Timing chain guide bolts	25	18
Timing chain tensioner bolts	10	7

Use new nuts/bolts

1 General Information

Using this Chapter

1 This part of Chapter 2 is devoted to in-car repair procedures for the 1.2 litre petrol engine. Similar information covering the other engine types can be found in Parts B and C. All procedures concerning engine removal and refitting, and engine block/cylinder head overhaul can be found in Part D of this Chapter.
2 Note that many operations that would normally be classed as in-car repair procedures and be covered in this Chapter, are actually covered in Part D. This is due to the design of the engine and the limited clearance in the engine compartment making it physically impossible to remove and refit many components and assemblies with the engine in the car.
3 In Parts A, B and C, the assumption is made that the engine is installed in the car, with all ancillaries connected. If the engine has been removed for overhaul, the preliminary dismantling information, which precedes each operation, may be ignored.

Engine description

4 The engine is of the sixteen-valve, in-line four-cylinder, double overhead camshaft (DOHC) type, mounted transversely at the front of the car with the transmission attached to the left-hand end.
5 The crankshaft runs in five main bearings. Thrustwashers are fitted to No 3 main bearing (upper half) to control crankshaft endfloat.
6 The connecting rods rotate on horizontally split bearing shells at their big ends. The pistons are attached to the connecting rods by gudgeon pins, which are a sliding fit in the small end of the connecting rod and retained in the pistons by circlips. The aluminium-alloy pistons are fitted with three piston rings – two compression rings and an oil control ring.
7 The cylinder block is made of aluminium alloy and the cylinder bores are an integral part of the block. On this type of engine the cylinder bores are sometimes referred to as having dry liners.
8 The inlet and exhaust valves are each closed by coil springs, and operate in guides pressed into the cylinder head; the valve seat inserts are also pressed into the cylinder head, and can be renewed separately if worn. Both camshafts have a variable valve timing sprocket at their right-hand end which is oil fed through a control solenoid valve.

2.2a Undo the two retaining nuts. . .

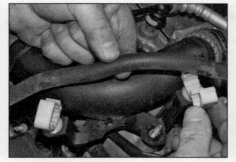

2.2b . . . unclip the hose. . .

2.2c . . . release the hose clip from the intercooler. . .

9 The camshaft is driven by a timing chain, and operates the sixteen valves via bucket-type followers. The followers are situated directly below the camshafts. Valve clearances are adjusted by replacing the relevant follower with a different thickness. The camshafts rotate directly in the cylinder head.

10 Lubrication is by means of an oil pump, which is driven off the right-hand end of the crankshaft. It draws oil through a strainer located in the sump, and then forces it through an externally mounted filter into galleries in the cylinder block/crankcase. From there, the oil is distributed to the crankshaft (main bearings) and camshaft. The big-end bearings are supplied with oil via internal drillings in the crankshaft, while the camshaft bearings also receive a pressurised supply. The camshaft lobes and valves are lubricated by splash, as are all other engine components.

Repairs with engine in car

11 The design of the engine and the limited working clearance within the engine compartment dictate that the engine/transmission assembly must be removed from the car to carry out many of the more involved repair operations. Refer to Chapter 2D, for procedures not contained in the following list.

12 The following work can be carried out with the engine in the car:

a) Compression pressure – testing.
b) Cylinder head cover – removal and refitting.
c) Valve clearances – checking.

2.2d . . . and the other end on the turbo

d) Sump oil pan – removal and refitting.
e) Crankshaft oil seals – renewal.
f) Engine/transmission mountings – inspection and renewal.
g) Flywheel – removal, inspection and refitting.

---

2 Cylinder head cover – removal and refitting

Removal

1 Disconnect the battery negative terminal (refer to *Disconnecting the battery* in Chapter 5 Section 4).

2 Undo the retaining nuts and release the hose from the retaining clips on the cylinder head cover. Release the retaining clips and disconnect the charge air cooler inlet hose

2.3 Disconnect the hose at the quick-release connector

from the intercooler and turbocharger **(see illustrations)**.

3 Release the securing clip and disconnect the evaporative emissions purge hose from the rear of the cylinder head cover **(see illustration)**. Release the EVAP hose from the clips and move it to one side.

4 Remove the upper oxygen sensor, as described in Chapter 6A Section 15.

5 With the upper oxygen sensor removed, unclip the wiring connectors from the retaining clips, then undo the three retaining screws, and remove the heat shield from the top of the cylinder head cover **(see illustrations)**.

6 Remove the ignition coils, as described in Chapter 6A Section 7.

7 Disconnect the crankcase ventilation hose from the front of the cylinder head cover **(see illustration)**.

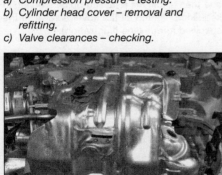

2.5a Undo the three retaining screws. . .

2.5b . . . and withdraw the heat shield

2.7 Disconnect the ventilation hose from the cover

2.8 Disconnecting the wiring from the inlet camshaft sensor

2.10a Remove the mounting bracket. . .

2.10b . . . and undo the fuel pipe mounting bracket bolt

2.11a Unclip the wiring. . .

2.11b . . . release the securing clips. . .

2.11c . . . and move the wiring loom to one side

8 Disconnect the wiring connectors from the inlet and exhaust camshaft sensors, on the transmission end of the cylinder head cover (see illustration).

9 Remove the high-pressure fuel pump as described in Chapter 4A Section 9.

10 Undo the retaining bolts and remove the mounting bracket from the front of the cylinder head, then undo the retaining bolt and disconnect the fuel pipe from the corner of the cylinder head cover (see illustrations).

11 Disconnect any remaining wiring connectors and move the wiring harness clear of the cylinder head cover (see illustrations).

12 Working in the **reverse** of the tightening sequence (see illustration 3.19), slacken and remove the cylinder head cover retaining bolts. Note that bolts 1, 2 and 3, down the centre of the cover (see illustration), are longer than the rest.

13 Lift off the cylinder head cover, and recover the rubber seal, which goes around the outer edge of the cover, and also around each of the spark plug holes.

14 Inspect the cover seals for signs of damage and deterioration, and renew as necessary. Nissan recommends that the cylinder head cover seal should always be renewed, if the cover is removed.

Refitting

15 Carefully clean the cylinder head and cover mating surfaces, and remove all traces of oil.

16 Apply a small amount of sealant to each side of the exhaust camshaft bearing cap at the transmission end (see illustration).

17 Fit the rubber seal to the cylinder head cover groove, ensuring that it is correctly located along its entire length, and around the four spark plug holes in the centre of the cover (see illustration).

18 Carefully lower the cylinder head cover onto the cylinder head, taking great care not to displace any of the rubber seal.

19 Make sure the cover is correctly seated, and then install the retaining bolts. Working in sequence, tighten all the cover screws to the specified torque (see illustration).

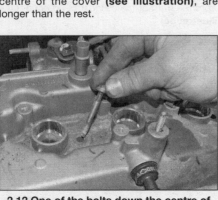
2.12 One of the bolts down the centre of the cover

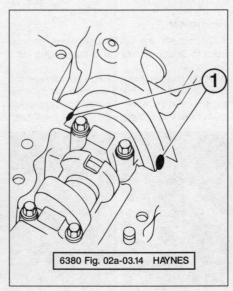
6380 Fig. 02a-03.14   HAYNES

2.16 Apply sealant to the position (1) on the camshaft bearing cap

2.17 Fit the new rubber gasket to the cylinder head cover

20 The remainder of refitting is a reversal of removal.

3 Crankshaft pulley – removal and refitting

Removal

1 Remove the auxiliary drivebelt as described in Chapter 1A Section 29.

2 To prevent crankshaft rotation while the pulley bolt is unscrewed, the pulley should be held by a suitable tool which locates in the slots in the pulley to prevent it from turning **(see illustration)**. If this is not available, select top gear and have an assistant apply the brakes firmly.

3 Unscrew the pulley bolt, along with its washer (where applicable), and remove the pulley from the crankshaft **(see illustration)**.

4 If the pulley is a tight fit on the end of the crankshaft, use a puller to withdraw the pulley from the end of the shaft. Refit the pulley bolt and screw it back into the end of the crankshaft, leaving it approx. 5 mm out from the pulley face. Fit the puller (this can be a homemade puller, using a piece of flat bar and three bols/nuts) to the pulley and tighten the centre bolt to withdraw the pulley from the end of the crankshaft **(see illustrations)**.

Refitting

5 Align the crankshaft pulley groove with the

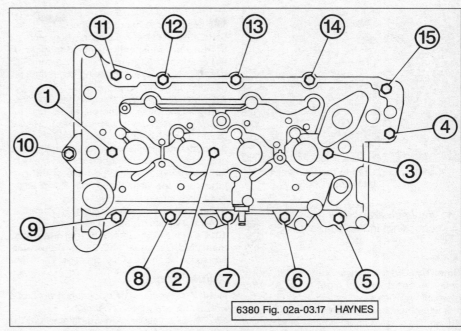

6380 Fig. 02a-03.17 HAYNES

2.19 Cylinder head cover bolt tightening sequence

key **(see illustration)**, then slide the sprocket onto the crankshaft.

6 Lubricate under the head of the bolt, also the bolt threads with clean engine oil **(see illustration)**, and then refit the retaining bolt/ washer.

7 Lock the crankshaft by the method used

on removal, and tighten the pulley retaining bolt to the specified Stage 1 torque setting. Using an angle tightening gauge, tighten the bolt through the specified Stage 2 angle.

8 Refit the auxiliary drivebelt and adjust it as described in Chapter 1A Section 29.

3.2 Using a homemade tool to hold the pulley

3.3 Remove the crankshaft pulley bolt

3.4a Remove the pulley using a puller. . .

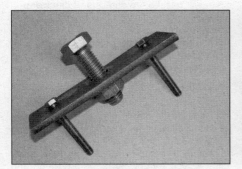

3.4b . . .which can be made out of a piece of flat metal bar

3.5 Align the slot in the pulley centre hub with the woodruff key

3.6 Apply a small amount of oil to the threads

4.11 Markings inside the follower for thickness

4 Valve clearances – checking and adjustment

Note: *This is not a routine operation. It should only be necessary at high mileage, after overhaul, or when investigating noise or power loss which may be attributable to the valve gear. Adjustment involves removing the camshaft and changing the cam followers (valve lifters) that are available in 31 different thicknesses (ranging from 2.96 mm to 3.56 mm, in steps of 0.02 mm).*
Note: *Checking of the valve clearances can be done with the engine in the car. If adjustment is necessary, the engine must be removed from the car to allow for camshaft removal.*

Checking

1 The importance of having the valve clearances correctly adjusted cannot be overstressed, as they vitally affect the performance of the engine. The clearances are checked as follows.
2 Draw the outline of the engine on a piece of paper, numbering the cylinders 1 to 4, with No 1 cylinder at the timing chain end of the engine. Show the position of each valve, together with the specified valve clearance. Above each valve, draw two lines for noting the actual clearance and the amount of adjustment required.
3 Remove the cylinder head cover as described in Section 2.
4 Apply the handbrake then jack up the front of the car and securely support it on axle

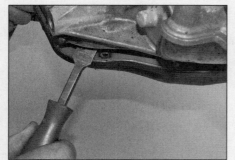

5.4 Using a flat ended scraper to prise the sump away

stands (see *Jacking and vehicle support*). Remove the right-hand roadwheel.
5 Remove the front right-hand wheel arch.
6 Turn the crankshaft, using a spanner on the crankshaft pulley bolt, until the camshaft lobes for No. 1 cylinder (timing chain end) are pointing upwards.
7 Using feeler gauges, measure the clearance between the base of the cam lobe and the follower of each of the valves of No.1 cylinder, recording each clearance on the paper.
8 Rotate the crankshaft until the next set of cam lobes are pointing upwards and measure the clearance between the base of the cam lobes and the associated follower. Record each clearance on the paper.
9 Repeat this procedure until the clearances for all the valves have been recorded.
10 Calculate the difference between each measured clearance and the desired value, and record it on the piece of paper.

Adjustment

Note: *A micrometer or dial gauge and probe will be required for this operation.*
11 Where a valve clearance differs from the specified value, then the cam follower (valve lifter) for that valve must be substituted with a thinner or thicker one accordingly. The cam followers have the thickness stamped on the bottom face of the follower; e.g. 302 indicates the follower is 3.02 mm thick at the top centre of the follower **(see illustration)**.
12 If required use a micrometer or dial gauge to measure the true thickness of any follower removed, as it may have been reduced by wear. **Note:** *Followers are available in thicknesses between 2.96 mm and 3.56 mm, in steps of 0.02 mm.*
13 To access the cam followers (valve lifters), first remove the camshafts as described in Chapter 2D. Note that it will be necessary to remove the engine to facilitate camshaft removal.
14 The size of follower required is calculated as follows. If the measured clearance is less than specified, subtract the measured clearance from the specified clearance, and deduct the result from the thickness of the existing follower. For example:

    Sample calculation – clearance too small
    Clearance measured (A) = 0.16 mm
    Desired clearance (B) = 0.30 mm
    Difference (B – A) = 0.14 mm
    Cam follower thickness fitted = 3.50 mm
    Cam follower thickness required =
    3.50 – 0.14 = 3.36 mm
15 If the measured clearance is greater than specified, subtract the specified clearance from the measured clearance, and add the result to the thickness of the existing follower. For example:

    Sample calculation – clearance too big
    Clearance measured (A) = 0.40 mm
    Desired clearance (B) = 0.30 mm
    Difference (A – B) = 0.10 mm
    Cam follower thickness fitted = 3.26 mm
    Cam follower thickness required =
    3.26 + 0.10 = 3.36 mm

16 Working on each separately, lift out the follower to be renewed, then oil the new one and carefully locate it in the cylinder head, on top of the valve.
17 Refit the camshafts with reference to Chapter 2D Section 10.
18 It will be helpful for future adjustment if a record is kept of the thickness of cam followers (valve lifters) fitted at each position. The cam followers required could be purchased in advance once the clearances and the existing follower thicknesses are known.
19 Once all valve clearances have been adjusted, rotate the crankshaft through at least four complete turns in the correct direction of rotation, to settle all disturbed followers, then recheck the clearances as described above.
20 With all valve clearances correctly adjusted, refit the cylinder head cover as described in Section 2, Then refit the engine to the car (Chapter 2D Section 4).

5 Sump – removal and refitting

Note: *The oil sump is made up of two parts; it has an upper alloy part and a lower steel oil pan. The following procedure is for the lower oil pan part. To remove the upper alloy part, the engine will need to be removed and the upper alloy sump then split from the cylinder block.*

Removal

1 Firmly apply the handbrake, and then jack up the front of the vehicle and support it securely on axle stands (see *Jacking and vehicle support*).
2 Drain the engine oil, then clean and refit the engine oil drain plug, fit a new sealing washer on refitting. And then tighten it to the specified torque. If the engine is nearing its service interval when the oil and filter are due for renewal, it is recommended that the filter is also removed, and a new one fitted. Refer to Chapter 1A Section 13 for further information.
3 Progressively slacken and remove all of the steel oil pan retaining bolts.
4 The lower steel oil pan is sealed to the upper alloy sump casing with strong liquid gasket sealer, which is very difficult to remove, however methodical use of a spatula or thin knife will release the sump **(see illustration)**. Take care not to distort or damage the mating surfaces of the lower oil pan and upper alloy sump. Take adequate precautions to catch any oil remaining inside the sump housing, as the oil pan is removed.

Refitting

5 Clean all traces of sealant from the mating surfaces of the upper alloy part of the sump and steel oil pan, then use a clean rag to wipe out the oil pan and the sump interior.
6 Ensure that the lower oil pan and upper alloy casing mating surfaces are clean and dry. Apply a continuous bead of suitable sealant to the mating surface of the oil pan.

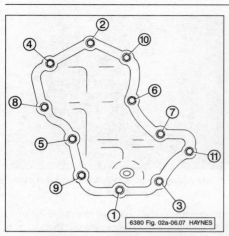

5.7 Tighten the bolts in the sequence shown

Apply a 4 mm to 5 mm diameter bead of sealant to the oil pan, going around the inner edge of each bolt hole.

7 Offer up the sump, locating it in the correct position, and refit its retaining bolts. Tighten the bolts evenly and progressively to the specified torque and in the correct sequence **(see illustration)**.

8 After reassembly, the engine can then be refilled with fresh engine oil. Refer to Chapter 1A Section 13, for further information.

9 Start the engine and warm it up to normal operating temperature, check for any leaks from the sump area.

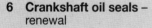

6   Crankshaft oil seals –
    renewal

Timing chain cover oil seal

1 Remove the crankshaft pulley as described in Section 3.

2 Carefully lever the oil seal out of position, using a large flat-bladed screwdriver, taking care not to damage the end of the crankshaft or timing cover **(see illustration)**.

3 Clean the seal housing, and polish off any burrs or raised edges, which may have caused the seal to fail in the first place.

4 Lubricate the lips of the new seal with a smear of clean oil and offer up the seal ensuring its sealing lip is facing inwards. Carefully ease the seal into position, taking care not to damage its sealing lip. Drive the seal into position until it seats flush with the face of the timing chain cover **(see illustrations)**. Take care not to damage the seal lips during fitting.

5 Wash off any traces of oil, then refit the crankshaft pulley as described in Section 3.

Flywheel oil seal

6 Remove the flywheel, as described in Section 7.

7 Note the fitted position of the old seal, then prise it out of the right-hand cover/housing

6.2 Carefully prise out the oil seal

6.4b . . .press the seal into position. . .

using a screwdriver or suitable hooked instrument, taking care not to damage the surface of the crankshaft. Alternatively, the oil seal can be removed by drilling a hole in the seal, and then inserting a self-tapping screw. A pair of grips/pliers can then be used to pull

6.7a Carefully drill a hole in the seal. . .

6.7c . . .and lever the seal out from the casing

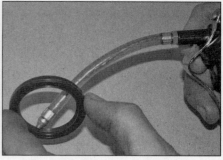

6.4a Lubricate the inner lip of the seal. . .

6.4c . . .carefully fit the seal into the cover

out the oil seal **(see illustrations)**. Take care when drilling the hole, to not drill into anything other than the seal.

8 Clean the seal housing, and polish off any burrs or raised edges, which may have caused the seal to fail in the first place **(see illustration)**.

6.7b . . .insert a self tapping screw. . .

6.8 Clean around the seal fitting surface area

6.9a Using clean oil to lubricate the inner lip of the seal. . .

6.9b . . .place the seal into position. . .

6.10a Apply some sealant around the outer edge of the seal. . .

6.10b . . .press the seal fully into position. . .

6.10c . . .then clean off the excess sealant from around the casing

9 Lubricate with clean oil the lips of the new seal and the crankshaft shoulder, then offer up the seal to the cylinder block/crankcase. Ease the sealing lip of the seal over the crankshaft shoulder by hand only, and press the seal evenly into its recess to make it square in the casing **(see illustrations)**.

10 With the seal still protruding out from the cylinder block, apply a coat of liquid gasket/sealant all the way around the outer edge of the seal. Carefully drive the seal into position until it seats flush with the face of the cylinder block, and then wipe off the excess liquid gasket/sealant from the casing **(see illustrations)**. Make sure the outer edge of the seal is sitting flush with the cylinder block casing.

11 Wash off any traces of oil or sealant, then refit the flywheel as described in Section 7.

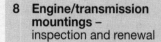

7 Flywheel –
removal, inspection and refitting

Removal

Note: *New flywheel retaining bolts will be required for refitting.*

1 Remove the transmission as described in Chapter 7 Section 6.

2 Remove the clutch assembly as described in Chapter 8 Section 6.

3 Prevent the flywheel from turning by locking the ring gear teeth **(see illustration)**. Alternatively, bolt a strap between the flywheel and the cylinder block.

4 Slacken and remove the retaining bolts **(see**

illustration), then remove the flywheel from the end of the crankshaft. Do not drop it, as it is very heavy.

Inspection

5 If the flywheel's clutch mating surface is deeply scored, cracked or otherwise damaged, the flywheel must be renewed. Seek the advice of a Nissan dealer or engine reconditioning specialist.

6 If the ring gear is badly worn or has missing teeth, it must be renewed. Check with your Nissan dealer or engine reconditioning specialist, to see if the flywheel can be repaired.

Refitting

7 Clean the mating surfaces of the flywheel and crankshaft.

8 Offer up the flywheel, and fit the new retaining bolts.

9 Lock the ring gear using the method employed on dismantling, and tighten the retaining bolts to the specified Stage 1 torque, then through the Stage 2 angle, using an angle tightening gauge.

10 Refit the clutch as described in Chapter 8 Section 6.

11 Remove the locking tool, and refit the transmission as described in Chapter 7 Section 6.

8 Engine/transmission mountings –
inspection and renewal

Inspection

1 If improved access is required, firmly apply the handbrake, and then jack up the front of the vehicle and support it securely on axle stands (see *Jacking and vehicle support*).

2 Check the mounting rubber to see if it is cracked, hardened or separated from the metal at any point; renew the mounting if any such damage or deterioration is evident.

3 Check that all the mounting's fasteners are securely tightened; use a torque wrench to check if possible.

4 Using a large screwdriver or a crowbar, check for wear in the mounting by carefully levering against it to check for free play.

7.3 Using a tool to prevent the flywheel from turning. . .

7.4 . . .when slackening the flywheel bolts

8.7 Remove the mounting bracket retaining bolts

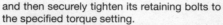

8.14 Undo the centre retaining nut

8.24 Rear lower mounting

Where this is not possible, enlist the aid of an assistant to move the engine/transmission back-and-forth, or from side-to-side, while you watch the mounting. While some free play is to be expected even from new components, excessive wear should be obvious. If excessive free play is found, check first that the fasteners are correctly secured, and then renew any worn components as described below.

Renewal

Right-hand mounting

5 Disconnect the battery negative terminal (refer to *Disconnecting the battery* in Chapter 5 Section 4).
6 Place a jack beneath the engine, with a block of wood on the jack head. Raise the jack until it is supporting the weight of the engine.
7 Slacken and remove the three retaining bolts from the inner wing panel, remove the three retaining bolts from the engine mounting bracket, and then withdraw the complete mounting from the engine compartment **(see illustration)**.
8 Check carefully for signs of wear or damage on all components, and renew them where necessary.
9 On refitting, fit the engine mounting and bracket to the inner wing panel and engine,

and then securely tighten its retaining bolts to the specified torque setting.
10 With the engine mounting back in position, lower the jack and remove it from underneath the engine.
11 Reconnect the battery negative terminal.

Left-hand mounting

12 Remove the battery and tray, as described in Chapter 5 Section 4.
13 Place a jack and block of wood beneath the transmission, and raise the jack to take the weight of the transmission.
14 Slacken and remove the bolts, then remove the mounting from the top of the transmission **(see illustration)**.
15 Slacken and remove the two outer retaining nuts, to remove the mounting from the mounting bracket.
16 Check carefully for signs of wear or damage on all components, and renew them where necessary.
17 On refitting, fit the upper and lower mounting brackets (where removed) and securely tighten the retaining bolts.
18 Align the left-hand rubber mounting with the bolt/stud on the lower mounting bracket and tighten its nut to the specified torque setting.
19 Refit the two outer retaining nuts, and tighten to the specified torque setting.

20 With the transmission mounting back in position, lower the jack and remove it from underneath the transmission.
21 Refit the battery and battery tray, with reference to Chapter 5 Section 4.

Rear lower mounting

22 If not already done, firmly apply the handbrake, and then jack up the front of the vehicle and support it securely on axle stands (see *Jacking and vehicle support*).
23 Slacken and remove the bolts securing the rear mounting bracket to the transmission, and then withdraw the bracket from transmission.
24 Slacken and remove the bolt securing the rear mounting link to the subframe, and then withdraw the mounting link from subframe **(see illustration)**.
25 Check carefully for signs of wear or damage on all components, and renew them where necessary.
26 On reassembly, fit the rear mounting to the subframe, and tighten the retaining bolt to the specified torque.
27 Refit the mounting bracket to the lower part of the transmission and tighten its retaining bolts to the specified torque.
28 With the transmission rear mounting link arm back in position, lower the vehicle to the ground.

Notes

Chapter 2 Part B
1.5 litre diesel engine in-car repair procedures

Contents

Degrees of difficulty

Easy, suitable for novice with little experience 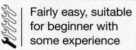	Fairly easy, suitable for beginner with some experience 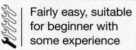	Fairly difficult, suitable for competent DIY mechanic 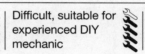	Difficult, suitable for experienced DIY mechanic 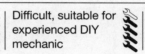	Very difficult, suitable for expert DIY or professional

Specifications

General

Type	Four cylinder, in-line, single overhead camshaft
Designation	K9K
Capacity	1461 cc
Bore	76.0 mm
Stroke	80.5 mm
Firing order	1-3-4-2 (No 1 cylinder at flywheel end)
Direction of crankshaft rotation	Clockwise viewed from timing belt end
Compression ratio	15.3 : 1

Compression pressures

Engine warm – approximately 80°C:	
Minimum pressure	18 bars
Maximum difference between cylinders	4 bars

Camshaft

Drive	Toothed belt
Number of bearings	6
Camshaft endfloat	0.080 o 0.178 mm

Valve clearances

Inlet	0.125 to 0.250 mm
Exhaust	0.325 to 0.450 mm

Lubrication system

System pressure (at 80°C):	
At idle	1.2 bars minimum
At 3000 rpm	3.5 bars minimum
Oil pump type	Gear-type, chain-driven off the crankshaft right-hand end
Oil level sensor resistance	6.0 to 20 ohms

Torque wrench settings

	Nm	lbf ft
Alternator	21	15
Big-end bearing caps:		
Stage 1	20	15
Stage 2	Angle-tighten a further 45° ± 6°	
Brake vacuum pump	21	15
Camshaft bearing caps	11	8
Camshaft sprocket:		
Stage 1	30	22
Stage 2	Angle-tighten a further 86°	
Clutch pressure plate	12	9
Crankshaft main bearing caps:		
Stage 1	25	18
Stage 2	Angle-tighten a further 47°	
Crankshaft pulley bolt:		
Stage 1	120	89
Stage 2	Angle-tighten a further 95°	
Crankshaft seal end cover	11	8
Cylinder block TDC blanking plug	20	15
Cylinder head bolts: *		
Stage 1	25	18
Stage 2	Angle-tighten a further 255°	
Cylinder head coolant outlet	10	7
Cylinder head cover bolts	12	9
Exhaust gas recirculation valve	21	15
Exhaust manifold	26	19
Flywheel*		
Stage 1	20	15
Stage 2	Angle-tighten a further 36°	
Glow plugs	15	11
High-pressure fuel pump bolts	21	15
High-pressure fuel pump sprocket	70	52
High-pressure pipe nuts	24	18
High-pressure rail nuts	28	21
Injector flange mounting bolts	30	22
Knock sensor	20	15
Left-hand transmission mounting:		
Through-bolt/stud nut	65	48
Through-bolt/stud-to-bracket	65	48
Mounting-to-bracket nuts	105	77
Mounting bracket-to-inner wing panel bolts	70	52
Mounting bracket-to-transmission bolts	45	33
Oil cooler – through bolt	45	33
Oil filter body – through bolt	45	33
Oil level sensor	22	16
Oil pressure sensor	35	26
Oil pump	25	18
Rear lower engine torque/link arm mounting:		
Torque link arm to front subframe bolt	110	81
Torque link arm to mounting bracket bolt	155	114
Mounting bracket-to-sump bolts	80	59
Right-hand engine mounting:		
Mounting bracket to cylinder head	25	18
Alloy mounting bracket to cylinder head mounting bracket	55	41
Mounting bracket bolts to inner wing	55	41
Mounting bolt to engine bracket (horizontal)	75	55
Torque arm mounting bolts	140	103
Sump (refer to sequence in text)	14	10
Timing belt tensioner	27	20
Turbocharger oil delivery pipe	23	17
Turbocharger oil return pipe	12	9
Turbocharger to exhaust manifold	26	19
Water pump	11	8
Water pump inlet pipe	20	15

* Use new bolts.

1 General Information

How to use this Chapter

1 This Part of Chapter 2 is devoted to in-car repair procedures for the 1.5 litre diesel engine. Similar information covering the other engine types can be found in Parts A and C. All procedures concerning engine removal and refitting, and engine block/cylinder head overhaul can be found in Part D of this Chapter.

2 Refer to *Vehicle identification numbers* in the beginning of this manual for details of engine code locations.

3 Most of the operations included in this Part are based on the assumption that the engine is still installed in the car. Therefore, if this information is being used during a complete engine overhaul, with the engine already removed, many of the steps included here will not apply.

Engine description

4 The engine is of four cylinder, in-line, single overhead camshaft type, mounted transversely at the front of the vehicle.

5 The cylinder block is of cast iron with conventional dry liners bored directly into the cylinder block. The crankshaft is supported in five shell-type main bearings. Thrustwashers are fitted to No 3 main bearing to control crankshaft endfloat.

6 The connecting rods are attached to the crankshaft by 'cracked' horizontally split shell-type big-end bearings and to the pistons by gudgeon pins. The gudgeon pins are fully-floating and are retained by circlips. The aluminium alloy pistons are fitted with three piston rings, comprising two compression rings and a scraper-type oil control ring.

7 The single overhead camshaft is mounted directly in the cylinder head, and is driven by the crankshaft via a toothed timing belt.

8 The camshaft operates the valves via inverted bucket type tappets (cam followers), which operate in bores machined directly in the cylinder head. The valve clearances are adjusted by changing the cam followers, which are available in 25 different thicknesses. The inlet and exhaust valves are mounted vertically in the cylinder head and are each closed by a single valve spring.

9 The high-pressure fuel injection pump is driven by the timing belt and is described in further detail in.

10 A semi-closed crankcase ventilation system is employed, and crankcase fumes are drawn from the cylinder block and passed via a hose to the inlet tract (see Section for further details).

11 Engine lubrication is by pressure feed from a gear type oil pump located beneath the crankshaft. Engine oil is fed through an externally mounted oil filter to the main oil gallery feeding the crankshaft, auxiliary shaft (where fitted) and camshaft. Oil spray jets are fitted to the cylinder block to supply oil to the underside of the pistons. An oil cooler is mounted between the oil filter and the cylinder block.

Operations with engine in place

12 The following operations can be carried out without having to remove the engine from the vehicle:
a) *Removal and refitting of the cylinder head.*
b) *Removal and refitting of the timing belt and sprockets*
c) *Renewal of the camshaft oil seals.*
d) *Removal and refitting of the camshaft*
e) *Removal and refitting of the sump.*
f) *Removal and refitting of the connecting rods and pistons**
g) *Removal and refitting of the oil pump.*
h) *Renewal of the crankshaft oil seals.*
i) *Renewal of the engine mountings.*
j) *Removal and refitting of the flywheel.*
* *Although the operation marked with an asterisk can be carried out with the engine in the car after removal of the sump, it is better for the engine to be removed in the interests of cleanliness and improved access. For this reason, the procedure is described in Chapter 2D.*

2 Top Dead Centre (TDC) for No 1 piston – locating

Note: *Special Nissan/Renault timing tools are required for this work, or tools obtained from an automotive accessory shop.*

1 Top Dead Centre (TDC) is the highest point in the cylinder that each piston reaches as the crankshaft turns. Each piston reaches TDC at the end of the compression stroke and again at the end of the exhaust stroke; however, for the purpose of timing the engine, TDC refers to the position of No 1 piston at the end of its compression stroke. No 1 piston is at the flywheel end of the engine.

2 When No 1 piston is at TDC, the timing hole in the camshaft sprocket will be aligned

2.12 Fitting the crankshaft TDC pin

with the hole in the cylinder head so that the timing pin can be inserted. Additionally, if the crankshaft timing pin is fully screwed into the cylinder block, it will just contact the timing flat on the crankshaft web.

3 Setting the TDC timing is necessary to ensure that the valve timing is maintained during operations that require removal and refitting of the timing belt. Note that the engine does not have a conventional diesel injection pump, however it is still necessary to align a mark on the pump sprocket with a bolt head on the cylinder head.

4 To set the engine at TDC, the right-hand engine mounting support and upper timing belt cover must be removed for access to the camshaft sprocket. First jack up the right-hand front of the car and support on axle stands (see *Jacking and vehicle support*). Remove the front right wheel, engine undertray and wheel arch liner.

5 Remove the auxiliary drivebelt with reference to Chapter 1B Section 33.

6 Support the right-hand end of the engine with a support bar across the engine compartment, with a hoist, or alternatively with a jack and block of wood beneath the sump. Unbolt the right-hand engine mounting from the engine and body.

7 Undo the retaining bolts and remove the engine mounting support bracket from the end of the cylinder head as described in Section 14. Then release the retaining clips and remove the upper timing belt cover.

8 Release the fasteners and remove the lower timing belt cover.

9 Unscrew and remove the plug from the TDC hole on the front (transmission end) of the cylinder block. If required, remove the starter motor as described in Chapter 5 Section 10, to make access to the TDC plug easier.

10 The crankshaft must now be turned using a spanner on the crankshaft pulley bolt. To enable the engine to be turned more easily, remove the glow plugs or the fuel injectors (Chapter 4B Section 10). Before removing the injectors, consider that Nissan stipulate the high-pressure fuel lines must be renewed after removing them. New high-pressure fuel lines are expensive.

11 Turn the crankshaft clockwise until the timing hole in the camshaft sprocket is approaching the hole in the cylinder head.

12 Insert and tighten the special TDC pin into the cylinder block timing hole **(see illustration)**.

Note: *If the pin is not available, an alternative method of determining the TDC position is to use a dial gauge on the top of piston No 1 after removing the fuel injector or glow plug.*

13 Slowly turn the crankshaft clockwise until its web contacts the timing pin. Now insert the remaining timing pin through the hole in the camshaft sprocket and into the cylinder head **(see illustrations)**. The engine is now positioned with No 1 piston at TDC on its compression stroke.

Caution: Do not attempt to rotate the

2.13a Fitting the camshaft TDC pin. . .

2.13b . . . or using a bolt to align the camsahft

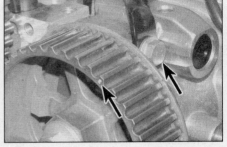

2.14 The mark on the high-pressure pump sprocket must be aligned with the bolt head on the cylinder head

engine whilst the crankshaft and camshaft timing pins are in position. If the engine is to be left in this state for a long period of time, it is a good idea to place suitable warning notices inside the vehicle, and *in the engine compartment. This will reduce the possibility of the engine being accidentally cranked on the starter motor, which would cause considerable damage.*

14 Check that the mark on the high-pressure injection pump sprocket is aligned with the bolt head on the cylinder head **(see illustration)**.

15 On completion, remove the timing pins and refit all removed components.

3 Cylinder head cover – removal and refitting

Removal

1 Disconnect the battery negative terminal (refer to *Disconnecting the battery* in Chapter 5 Section 4).

2 Where fitted, unclip the engine plastic cover from the top of the engine **(see illustration)**.

3 Release the retaining clip at the turbo end of the pipe and disconnect the intercooler pipe **(see illustrations)**.

4 Undo the retaining nut, then release the securing clip at the intercooler end of the hose, then remove it from across the top of the engine **(see illustrations)**.

5 Release the securing clip, and disconnect the air intake hose from the throttle valve housing **(see illustration)**.

6 Disconnect the wiring connectors and unclip the wiring loom from the end of the cylinder head plastic cover **(see illustration)**.

7 Undo the two retaining bolts at the rear of the cover, then release the two securing clips at the front and lift off the plastic shield/cover **(see illustrations)**.

8 Disconnect the wiring connector from the camshaft position sensor, undo the retaining

3.2 Unclip the upper trim cover

3.3a Release the retaining clip. . .

3.3b . . . and disconnect the intercooler rubber hose

3.4a Undo the retaining nut. . .

3.4b . . . and disconnect hose from intercooler

3.5 Disconnecting the intercooler rubber hose

3.6 Disconnect the wiring connector and unclip wiring loom

3.7a Undo the two retaining bolts at the rear. . .

3.7b . . . release the two securing clips at the front. . .

3.7c . . . then remove the plastic cover

3.8a Disconnect the wiring connector. . .

3.8b . . . and remove the camshaft sensor

3.9 Remove the mounting bracket

bolt and remove it from the cylinder head cover **(see illustrations)**.
Note: *Twist the sensor slightly to remove it completely from the cover, as it will catch on the lug on the alloy air intake housing.*
9 Undo the retaining bolts and remove the EGR control valve mounting bracket from the rear of the cylinder head cover **(see illustration)**.
10 Slacken the retaining clip and disconnect the breather hose from the rear of the cylinder head cover **(see illustration)**.
11 Using a jack support the engine, and then undo the retaining bolts and remove the right-hand engine mounting as described in Section 14 of this Chapter.
12 Release the retaining clip, and then remove the plastic upper timing belt cover **(see illustrations)**.
13 Disconnect the wiring connectors from the fuel injectors, then unclip the wiring and the fuel return lines from across the front of the cylinder head cover and move them to one side **(see illustration)**.
14 Working from the outer ends of the cover, spiraling inwards to the centre, slacken and remove the cylinder head cover retaining bolts.
15 Lift off the cylinder head cover, and recover the rubber seal, which goes around the outer edge of the cover.
16 Inspect the cover seal for signs of damage and deterioration, and renew as necessary. Nissan recommends that the cylinder head cover seal should always be renewed, if the cover is removed.

Refitting

17 Carefully clean the cylinder head and cover mating surfaces, and remove all traces of oil. Then apply four beads of sealant, 2.0

3.10 Disconnect the breather hose

3.12b . . . and remove the plastic upper timing cover

mm wide, to the camshaft end bearing caps (No's 1 and 6) **(see illustration)**.
18 Fit the rubber seal to the cylinder head cover groove, ensuring that it is correctly

3.12a Release the clips. . .

3.13 Disconnect the wiring connectors

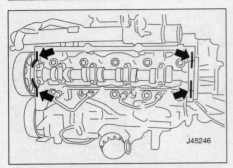

3.17 Apply 2.0 mm wide beads of sealant to the camshaft end bearing caps as shown

3.20a Check the retaining clips are secure

3.20b Check the retaining clip is located securely in the intake pipe

located along its entire length. Carefully lower the cylinder head cover onto the cylinder head, taking great care not to displace any of the rubber seal

19 Make sure the cover is correctly seated, and then install the retaining bolts. Working from the centre of the cover and spiraling outwards, tighten all the cover bolts to the specified torque.

20 The remainder of the refitting procedure is the reversal of removal, bearing in mind the following points.

a) *Make sure the two securing clips on the front of the plastic shield/cover are secure* **(see illustration).**

b) *Make sure the securing clip in the intercooler metal pipe is fitted correctly* **(see illustration).**

c) *Ensure that the engine mounting is fitted securely (see Section 14), before removing the jack from under the engine.*

d) *Check all wiring connectors and retaining clips are correctly fitted and routed, as noted on removal.*

e) *Tighten all the hose clips securely*

21 Reconnect the battery negative terminal. Run the engine and check for any oil leaks around the engine cylinder head cover.

---

4 Valve clearances – checking and adjustment

Note: *This operation is not part of the maintenance schedule. It should be undertaken if noise from the valve gear becomes evident,*

4.6 Using a feeler blade to check the valve clearances

or if loss of performance gives cause to suspect that the clearances may be incorrect. Adjustment involves removing the camshaft and changing the cam followers (valve lifters) that are available in 25 different thicknesses.

Checking

1 Remove the cylinder head cover as described in Section 3.

2 During the following procedure, the crankshaft must be turned using a spanner on the crankshaft pulley bolt. Improved access to the pulley bolt can be obtained by jacking up the front right-hand corner of the vehicle and removing the roadwheel and placing the vehicle on an axle stand (see *Jacking and vehicle support*). Remove the fasteners and withdraw the plastic inner wheel arch panel.

3 If desired, to enable the crankshaft to be turned more easily, remove the glow plugs or the fuel injectors (Chapter 4B Section 10). Before removing the injectors, consider that Nissan stipulate the high-pressure fuel lines must be renewed after removing them. New high-pressure fuel lines are expensive.

4 Draw the valve positions on a piece of paper, numbering them 1 to 8 from the flywheel end of the engine. Identify them as inlet or exhaust (i.e. 1E, 2I, 3E, 4I, 5E, 6I, 7E, 8I).

VALVES ROCKING ON CYLINDER	CHECK CLEARANCE ON CYLINDER
1	4
3	2
4	1
2	3

J45252

4.7 Valve clearance measurement

  X   *Clearance*
  Y   *Cam follower thickness*

5 Turn the crankshaft until the valves of No 1 cylinder (flywheel end) are 'rocking'. The exhaust valve will be closing and the inlet valve will be opening. The piston of No 4 cylinder will be at the top of its compression stroke, with both valves fully closed. The clearances for both valves of No 4 cylinder may be checked at the same time.

6 Insert a feeler blade of the correct thickness (see Specifications) between the cam lobe and the top of the cam follower (valve lifter), and check that it is a firm sliding fit **(see illustration)**. If it is not, use the feeler blades to ascertain the exact clearance, and record this for use when calculating the thickness of the new cam follower required. Note that the inlet and exhaust valve clearances are different (see Specificationsat the beginning of this Chapter).

7 With No 4 cylinder valve clearances checked, turn the engine through half a turn so that No 3 valves are 'rocking', then check the valve clearances of No 2 cylinder in the same way. Similarly check the remaining valve clearances in the sequence shown **(see illustration)**.

Adjustment

Note: *A micrometer or dial gauge and probe will be required for this operation.*

8 Where a valve clearance differs from the specified value, the cam follower for that valve must be changed with a thinner or thicker one accordingly. On new follower, the thickness is stamped on the bottom face of the tappet; however, the original followers may not have any thickness stamped on them. It is therefore

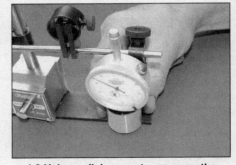

4.8 Using a dial gauge to measure the thickness of the removed cam follower

prudent to use a micrometer or dial gauge to measure the true thickness of any follower removed, as it may have been reduced by wear **(see illustration)**.

9 To access the cam followers, first remove the camshaft as described in Section 8. Remove and refit each follower separately, to avoid confusion **(see illustration)**.

10 The size of follower required is calculated as follows. If the measured clearance is less than specified, subtract the measured clearance from the specified clearance, and deduct the result from the thickness of the existing follower. For example:

Sample calculation – clearance too small
Clearance measured (A) = 0.15 mm
Desired clearance (B) = 0.20 mm
Difference (B – A) = 0.05 mm
Cam follower thickness fitted = 7.70 mm
Cam follower thickness required =
7.70 – 0.05 = 7.65 mm

11 If the measured clearance is greater than specified, subtract the specified clearance from the measured clearance, and add the result to the thickness of the existing follower. For example:

Sample calculation – clearance too big
Clearance measured (A) = 0.50 mm
Desired clearance (B) = 0.40 mm
Difference (A – B) = 0.10 mm
Cam follower thickness fitted = 7.55 mm
Cam follower thickness required =
7.55 + 0.10 = 7.65 mm

12 Working on each separately, lift out the follower to be renewed, then oil the new one and carefully locate it in the cylinder head **(see illustration)**.

25 Refit the camshaft with reference to Section 8.

26 Where removed, refit the glow plugs or the fuel injectors.

27 Remove the spanner from the crankshaft pulley bolt and refit the plastic inner wheel arch panel.

28 Refit the cylinder head cover as described in Section 3.

5 Timing belt – removal, inspection and refitting

Caution: If the timing belt breaks in service, extensive engine damage will result. Renew the belt at the intervals specified in Chapter 1B, or earlier if its condition is at all doubtful.

Removal

1 Disconnect the battery negative lead (refer to *Disconnecting the battery* in Chapter 5 Section 4).

2 Jack up the right-hand front of the car and support on axle stands (see *Jacking and vehicle support*). Remove the front right wheel, engine/radiator undertray and wheel arch liner. Also remove the engine top cover, where applicable **(see illustration)**.

4.9 Removing a cam follower

5.2 Remove the engine trim cover

5.9a Unscrew and remove the crankshaft pulley bolt. . .

4.12 Lubricate the cam follower before refitting it

5.6 Removing the right-hand engine mounting support bracket (note the bracket extension is fitted beneath the timing belt)

5.9b . . . and remove the pulley

3 Remove the auxiliary drivebelt with reference to Chapter 1B Section 33, and then unbolt and remove the drivebelt tensioner.

4 Remove the right-hand engine mounting, as described in Section 14.

5 Release the retaining clips and remove the upper timing belt cover from around the engine mounting support bracket.

6 Unbolt and remove the engine mounting support bracket **(see illustration)**.

7 The crankshaft must now be turned to the TDC position using a spanner on the crankshaft pulley bolt. Set the engine to Top Dead Centre (TDC), as described in Section 2.

8 Temporarily remove the timing pins while the crankshaft pulley bolt is being loosened. *Caution: Do not use the timing pins to lock the engine when removing the crankshaft pulley bolt, as the timing pins may break and cause damage to the engine.*

9 Before loosening the crankshaft pulley bolt, note that the crankshaft sprocket is not keyed to the crankshaft as is the normal arrangement, therefore if the crankshaft pulley is removed it is important to have an accurate method of determining the TDC position of No 1 piston. Although the sprocket is not keyed to the crankshaft, there is still a groove in the crankshaft nose, which is at the 12 o'clock position when piston No 1 is at TDC. Unscrew the crankshaft pulley bolt while holding the crankshaft stationary. Have an assistant engage 4th gear and firmly depress the brake pedal. Alternatively, remove the starter motor or where applicable remove the cover plate from the transmission bellhousing, and have an assistant insert a screwdriver or similar tool in the starter ring gear teeth. With the bolt removed, ease the pulley from the crankshaft **(see illustrations)**.

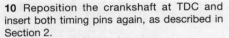

5.11 Loosen the tensioner locknut. . .

5.12. . . then release the timing belt

10 Reposition the crankshaft at TDC and insert both timing pins again, as described in Section 2.

11 Loosen the tensioner locknut, then turn the tensioner clockwise to release the tension. If necessary, use a 6.0 mm Allen key in the eccentric hub plate to move the tensioner **(see illustration)**.

12 If the original belt is to be re-used (contrary to Nissan's recommendation), check if the belt is marked with arrows to indicate its running direction, and if necessary mark it. Similarly, make accurate alignment marks on the belt, corresponding to the timing marks on the camshaft, high-pressure fuel injection pump and crankshaft sprockets. Check and make a note of the amount of teeth between the timing marks on the camshaft and injection pump sprockets, then release the timing belt from the camshaft sprocket, high-pressure injection pump, water pump pulley, crankshaft sprocket and tensioner **(see illustration)**.

13 Do not turn the camshaft or the crankshaft whilst the timing belt is removed, as there is a risk of piston-to-valve contact. If it is necessary to turn the camshaft for any reason, before doing so, turn the crankshaft anti-clockwise (viewed from the timing belt end of the engine) by a quarter turn to position all four pistons half-way down their bores. Leave the TDC pin tightened into the cylinder block.

14 Clean the sprockets, water pump pulley and tensioner and wipe them dry, although do not apply excessive amounts of solvent to the water pump and tensioner pulleys otherwise

the bearing lubricant may be contaminated. Also clean the rear timing belt cover, and the cylinder head and block.

Inspection

15 Examine the timing belt carefully for any signs of cracking, fraying or general wear, particularly at the roots of the teeth. Renew the belt if there is any sign of deterioration of this nature, or if there is any oil or grease contamination. The belt must, of course, be renewed if it has completed the maximum mileage given in the specifications in Chapter 1B.

16 It is recommended, that the timing belt should be renewed whenever it is disturbed. Due to the extent of damage that can be caused to the engine by belt failure, it is always best to renew the belt if it has been removed.

17 Thoroughly clean the nose of the crankshaft and the bore of the crankshaft sprocket, and also the contact surfaces of the sprocket and pulley. This is necessary to prevent the possibility of the sprocket slipping in use.

Refitting

18 Check that the crankshaft, camshaft and high-pressure fuel injection pump sprockets are still positioned at TDC, and that the groove in the crankshaft nose is pointing upwards. If the pistons have been positioned halfway down their bores, turn the crankshaft clockwise until the web contacts the TDC tool.

19 Check that the tensioner peg is correctly located in the groove in the cylinder head.

20 Align the timing marks on the belt with those on the camshaft and fuel injection pump sprockets **(see illustration)**, ensuring that the running direction arrows on the belt are pointing clockwise (viewed from the timing belt end of the engine). Note that the belt should be marked with lines across its width to act as timing marks. Fit the timing belt over the crankshaft sprocket first, followed by the water pump pulley, fuel injection pump sprocket, camshaft sprocket, and tensioner. Check the amount of teeth between the timing marks on the camshaft and injection pump sprockets, as noted on removal.

21 With the timing marks still aligned, use the 6.0 mm Allen key to pretension the belt by turning the tensioner anti-clockwise until the index pointer is positioned below the timing window **(see illustrations)**. Hold the tensioner stationary and tighten the locknut to the specified torque. This torque is critical, since if the nut were to come loose, considerable engine damage would result.

22 Remove the timing pins from the cylinder block and camshaft sprocket.

23 Refit the crankshaft pulley, then insert the bolt and tighten to the specified torque and angle.

24 Turn the crankshaft two complete turns in the normal direction of rotation, but just before the camshaft sprockets are aligned, refit and tighten the crankshaft timing pin. Slowly turn the crankshaft clockwise until its web is contacting the timing pin, and then check that it is possible to insert the remaining timing pin through the hole in the camshaft sprocket and into the cylinder head. If all is aligned, then the timing pins can be removed again.

25 Hold the tensioner with the Allen key, then loosen the locknut a maximum of one turn, and turn the tensioner clockwise until the index pointer is positioned in the middle of the timing window **(see illustration)**. Tighten the locknut to the specified torque.

26 Apply sealant to the threads, then refit the blanking plug to the cylinder block and tighten it to the specified torque.

27 Refit the engine mounting support bracket and tighten the bolts to the specified torque.

5.20 Align the timing marks on the belt with those on the camshaft and fuel injection pump sprockets

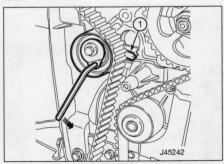

5.21a Pretension the timing belt by positioning the tensioner pointer (1) as shown

5.21b Pretensioning the timing belt

5.25 Position the pointer to its final setting in the middle of the timing window

28 Refit the lower timing cover and locate the fuel pipes in their clips (where applicable).
29 Clip the upper timing cover onto the lower cover, then refit the right-hand engine mounting to the engine and body and tighten the bolts to the specified torque (see Section 14).
30 Refit the auxiliary drivebelt with reference to Chapter 1B Section 33.
31 Refit the engine undertray and wheel arch liner.
32 Refit the front right wheel and lower the car to the ground. Tighten the wheel bolts to the specified torque.
33 Reconnect the battery negative lead (refer to *Disconnecting the battery* in Chapter 5 Section 4).

6 Timing belt sprockets, idler pulley and tensioner – removal and refitting

Crankshaft sprocket

Removal

1 Remove the timing belt as described in Section 5.
2 Slide the sprocket from the crankshaft; noting which way around it is fitted **(see illustration)**.

Refitting

3 Thoroughly clean the nose of the crankshaft and the bore of the crankshaft sprocket, and also the contact surfaces of the sprocket and pulley. This is necessary to prevent the possibility of the sprocket slipping in use.
4 Slide the sprocket onto the crankshaft the correct way around.
5 Refit the timing belt as described in Section 5.

High-pressure pump sprocket

Note: *A suitable puller will be required for this operation.*

Removal

6 The sprocket may be removed as follows, however, note that if it is being removed for pump renewal, a special Nissan tool is available to enable the pump to be removed without removing the timing belt. Check with your Nissan dealer for the availability of a sprocket support tool.

7 Remove the timing belt as described in Section 5.
8 Hold the sprocket stationary using a suitable gear holding tool. Alternatively, an old timing belt can be wrapped around the sprocket and held firmly with a pair of grips. Unscrew and remove the central securing nut.
9 Use a puller to release the sprocket from the taper on the pump shaft. Recover the Woodruff key from the groove in the pump shaft.

Refitting

10 Refitting is a reversal of removal, bearing in mind the following points.
a) Ensure that the Woodruff key is correctly engaged with the pump shaft and sprocket.
b) Tighten the sprocket securing nut to the specified torque.
c) Refit and tension the timing belt as described in Section 5. Make sure that the mark on the sprocket is aligned with the bolt on the cylinder head.

Camshaft sprocket

Removal

11 Remove the timing belt as described in Section 5.
12 Hold the sprocket stationary using a suitable gear holding tool. Alternatively, an old timing belt can be wrapped around the sprocket and held firmly with a pair of grips. Unscrew and remove the central securing nut.
13 Release the sprocket from the camshaft, noting the integral spline on the sprocket and

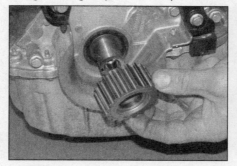

6.2 Removing the crankshaft sprocket

6.15 Angle-tightening the camshaft sprocket retaining bolt

the corresponding cut-out in the end of the camshaft **(see illustration)**.
14 Recover the Woodruff key from the end of the camshaft.

Refitting

15 Refit the camshaft sprocket, making sure that the integral spline locates in the camshaft cut-out. Insert the bolt and tighten it to the specified torque and angle, holding the sprocket stationary as during removal **(see illustration)**.
16 Refit and tension the timing belt as described in Section 5.

Tensioner

Removal

17 Remove the timing belt as described in Section 5.
18 Unscrew the securing nut and remove the washer and pivot bolt, then withdraw the tensioner assembly from the engine **(see illustration)**.

Refitting

19 Refitting is a reversal of removal. Refit and tension the timing belt as described in Section 5.

7 Camshaft oil seals – renewal

Timing belt end oil seal

1 Remove the camshaft sprocket as described in Section 6.

6.13 Removing the sprocket from the end of the camshaft – note the integral spline

6.18 Removing the timing belt tensioner

7.4a Screw the rod into the end of the camshaft. . .

7.4b . . . locate the new oil seal and protector onto the camshaft. . .

7.4c . . . then tighten the tool to press the seal into position

2 Note the fitted depth of the old oil seal. Using a small screwdriver, prise out the oil seal from the cylinder head taking care not to damage the sealing surface on the camshaft. Alternatively, the oil seal can be removed by drilling two small holes diagonally opposite each other and inserting self tapping screws in them. A pair of grips can then be used to pull out the oil seals, by pulling on each side in turn.

3 Inspect the seal rubbing surface on the camshaft. If it is grooved or rough in the area where the old seal was fitted, the new seal should be fitted slightly less deeply, so that it rubs on an unworn part of the surface.

4 Nissan technicians use a tool (Mot. 1632) to fit the oil seal. The tool consists of a threaded rod, metal tube and nut, and a machined shoulder to locate the protector/guide on. The rod is screwed into the end of the camshaft, and the protector/guide located on the shoulder. The metal tube is then fitted against the oil seal and the nut tightened to press the seal into the cylinder head/bearing cap (see illustrations). If the Nissan tool cannot be obtained, a similar tool can be made out of a threaded rod, metal tube, washer and nut.

5 Wipe clean the oil seal seating, then press the oil seal squarely into position. Note that the Nissan tool is designed to locate the seal at the original depth, however, if the camshaft sealing surface is excessively worn, position it less deeply so that it locates on the unworn surface.

6 After fitting the oil seal, remove the protector/guide and tool.

7 Wipe away any excess oil, then refit the camshaft sprocket as described in Section 6.

Flywheel end sealing

8 No oil seal is fitted to the flywheel end of the camshaft. The sealing is provided by a gasket between the cylinder head and the brake vacuum pump housing, and on certain models by an O-ring fitted between the vacuum pump and the housing. The gasket and the O-ring, where applicable, can be renewed after unbolting the vacuum pump from the cylinder head (see Chapter 9 Section 13).

8 Camshaft and followers – removal, inspection and refitting

Note: A new camshaft oil seal will be required, and suitable sealant will be required for the camshaft bearing caps and valve cover.

Removal

1 Removal of the camshaft will normally only be required for access to the cam followers (e.g. for valve clearance adjustment) or during cylinder head overhaul. For cylinder head overhaul, remove the head as described in Section 9.

2 Remove the cylinder head cover as described in Section 3.

3 Remove the camshaft sprocket as described in Section 6.

4 Disconnect the wiring connector, then remove the mounting bracket bolts, and

actuator retaining nuts then remove the throttle control actuator from the intake manifold as described in.

5 Remove the brake vacuum pump with reference to Chapter 9 Section 13. Note the position of the offset drive inside the pump, which engages the slot in the end of the camshaft (see illustrations).

6 Using a dial gauge, measure the camshaft endfloat, and compare with the value given in the Specifications. This will give an indication of the amount of wear present on the thrust surfaces.

7 If the original camshaft is to be refitted, it is advisable to measure the valve clearances at this stage as described in Section 4, so that any different thickness followers required can be obtained before the camshaft is refitted.

8 Check the camshaft bearing caps for identification marks, and if none are present, make identifying marks so that they can be refitted in their original positions and the same way round. Number the caps from the flywheel end of the engine (see illustration).

9 Progressively slacken the bearing cap bolts until the valve spring pressure is relieved. Remove the bolts and the bearing caps themselves.

10 Lift out the camshaft out from the top of the cylinder head, together with the oil seal.

11 Remove the cam followers, keeping each identified for position (see illustration). Place them in a compartmented box, or on a sheet of card marked into eight sections, so that they may be refitted to their original locations.

8.5a Removing the brake vacuum pump and gasket

8.5b Offset drive in the pump which engages the slot in the end of the camshaft

8.8 The camshaft bearing caps are numbered from the flywheel end of the engine

8.11 Removing the cam followers

8.17 Removing the camshaft from the cylinder head

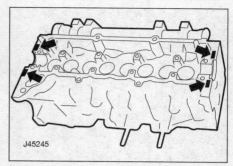

8.18a Apply 1.0 mm wide beads of sealant to the camshaft end bearing cap-to-cylinder head contact areas as shown

If any of the valve clearances measured in paragraph 7 is incorrect, use a micrometer to measure the thickness of the old follower from its upper surface to the inner surface, at the centre, which contacts the valve stem. Refer to Section 4 and obtain new followers of the correct thickness.

Inspection

12 Examine the camshaft bearing surfaces and cam lobes for wear ridges, pitting or scoring. Renew the camshaft if evident.
13 Renew the oil seal at the end of the camshaft as a matter of course. Lubricate the lips of the new seal before fitting, and store the camshaft so that its weight is not resting on the seal. Alternatively, the seal may be fitted after refitting the camshaft.
14 Examine the camshaft bearing surfaces in the cylinder head and bearing caps. Deep scoring or other damage means that the cylinder head must be renewed.
15 Inspect the cam followers for scoring, pitting and wear ridges. Renew as necessary.

Refitting

16 Oil the cam followers (inside and out) and fit them to the bores from which they were removed; where applicable, fit the new followers to their correct bores.
17 Oil the camshaft bearings. Place the camshaft without the oil seal onto the cylinder head **(see illustration)**.
18 Wipe clean the upper sealing edge of the cylinder head, then apply four beads of sealant, 1.0 mm wide, to the camshaft end bearing cap (Nos 1 and 6) contact areas as shown **(see illustrations)**.
19 Refit the camshaft bearing caps to their original locations, then insert the bearing cap bolts and progressively tighten them to the specified torque **(see illustration)**.
20 If a new camshaft has been fitted, measure the endfloat using a dial gauge, and check that it is within the specified limits.
21 Fit the new camshaft oil seal with reference to Section 7.
22 Refit the brake vacuum pump with reference to Chapter 9 Section 13.
23 Refit the throttle control actuator to the intake manifold, tighten the retaining bolts/nuts and reconnect the wiring connector.

8.18b Apply the beads of sealant. . .

24 Refit the camshaft sprocket as described in Section 6.
25 Refit the cylinder head cover as described in Section 3.

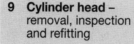
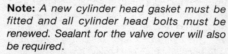

9 Cylinder head – removal, inspection and refitting

Note: *A new cylinder head gasket must be fitted and all cylinder head bolts must be renewed. Sealant for the valve cover will also be required.*
Note: *Before removing any of the high-pressure fuel pipes, consider that Nissan stipulate they must be renewed after removing them.*

Removal

1 Before starting work, allow the engine to

9.5a Release the breather hose. . .

8.19 . . . then refit the camshaft bearing caps

cool for as long as possible, to ensure the fuel pressure in the high-pressure lines, and the fuel temperature, are at a minimum.
2 Disconnect the battery negative lead (see *Disconnecting the battery* in Chapter 5 Section 4).
3 Drain the cooling system with reference to Chapter 1B Section 32. Refit and tighten the plug after draining.
4 Remove the cylinder head cover as described in Section 3.
5 Slacken the retaining clips and remove the air intake hose from the air flow meter to the turbocharger **(see illustrations)**.
6 Undo the retaining bolts and remove the bracket from the left-hand end of the cylinder head **(see illustration)**.
7 Disconnect the quick-release vacuum pipe from the brake vacuum pump on the left-hand end of the cylinder head **(see illustration)**.

9.5b . . . and remove the air intake hose

9.6 Remove the bracket from the end of the cylinder head

9.7 Disconnect the vacuum hose (arrowed)

9.8a Note the position of the coolant hoses on the left-hand end of the cylinder head

9.8b Disconnecting the wiring from the coolant temperature sensor

9.11 Removing the timing belt tensioner roller

8 Remove the hoses and coolant temperature sensor wiring connector, from the left-hand end of the cylinder head **(see illustrations)**.

9 Disconnect the wiring connector, then remove the mounting bracket bolts, and actuator retaining nuts then remove the throttle control actuator from the intake manifold **(see illustrations 9.4a, 9.4b & 9.4c)**

10 Remove the timing belt, as described in Section 5, and if necessary, the camshaft sprocket (in Section 6).

11 Unbolt and remove the timing belt tensioner roller from the cylinder head **(see illustration)**.

12 If required, unbolt and remove the auxiliary drivebelt tensioner from the cylinder block.

13 Unbolt and remove the inner timing cover from the cylinder block and head **(see illustration)**.

14 Remove the high-pressure fuel pump, as described in Chapter 4B Section 9.

15 If required, remove the fuel rail as described in Chapter 4B Section 11. If the removal of the cylinder head is just to renew the gasket, then it is possible to leave the injectors and fuel rail in position, together with the fuel pipes.

16 Remove the exhaust manifold, as described in Chapter 4B Section 13. Note the manifold does not have to be completely removed from the vehicle, once disconnected from the cylinder head the manifold can then be positioned to one side to allow the cylinder head to be removed.

17 The cylinder head assembly complete with ancillaries is very heavy. If required, seek the aid of an assistant to help lift the cylinder head from the vehicle.

18 Before removing the cylinder head, turn the crankshaft anti-clockwise (viewed from the timing belt end of the engine) by a quarter turn to position all four pistons halfway down their

bores. The TDC pin can remain in the cylinder block if necessary, however, remember that it is in position and do not turn the crankshaft further anti-clockwise.

19 Progressively slacken the cylinder head bolts in the **reverse** sequence to that shown **(see illustration 9.29)**. With all the bolts loose, remove them **(see illustration)**.

20 Lift the cylinder head upwards off the cylinder block. If it is stuck, tap it with a hammer and block of wood to release it. **Do not** try to turn the cylinder head (it is located by two dowels), nor attempt to prise it free using a screwdriver inserted between the block and head faces.

21 If necessary, remove the camshaft and followers, as described in Section 8.

Inspection

22 The mating faces of the cylinder head and block must be perfectly clean before refitting the head. Use a scraper to remove all traces of gasket and carbon, and also clean the tops of the pistons. Take particular care with the aluminium cylinder head, as the soft metal is damaged easily. Also, make sure that debris is not allowed to enter the oil and water channels – this is particularly important for the oil circuit, as carbon could block the oil supply to the camshaft or crankshaft bearings. Using adhesive tape and paper, seal the water, oil and bolt holes in the cylinder block. Clean the piston crowns in the same way.

23 Check the block and head for nicks, deep scratches and other damage. If slight, they may be removed carefully with a file. Machining of the cylinder head or cylinder block is not recommended by the manufacturers.

24 If warpage of the cylinder head is suspected, use a straight-edge to check it for distortion. If the warpage is more than 0.05 mm, the cylinder head must be renewed, as regrinding is not allowed.

25 Clean out the cylinder head bolt holes in the block using a pipe cleaner, or a rag and screwdriver. Make sure that all oil is removed, otherwise there is a possibility of the block being cracked by hydraulic pressure when the bolts are tightened. Examine the bolt threads in the cylinder block for damage, and if necessary, use the correct size tap to chase

9.13 Removing the inner timing cover

9.19 Removing the cylinder head bolts

9.27 Locate the new gasket on the cylinder block

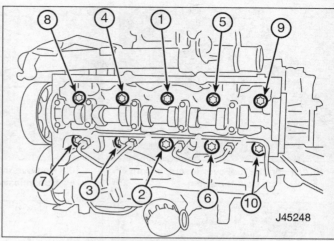

9.29 Cylinder head bolt tightening sequence

out the threads. The cylinder head bolts must be renewed each time they are removed, and must not be oiled before being fitted.

Refitting

26 Where removed, refit the cam followers, camshaft and camshaft sprocket with reference to Section 8 and Section 6. Turn the camshaft so that the sprocket is at its TDC position.

27 Ensure that the cylinder head locating dowels are fitted to the cylinder block, then fit the new gasket the right way round on the cylinder block **(see illustration)**.

28 Carefully lower the cylinder head onto the dowels and gasket, then insert the new bolts and hand-tighten. **Do not** oil the threads or heads of the new bolts.

29 Tighten the bolts in sequence, and in the stages given in the Specifications **(see illustration)**.

30 Turn the crankshaft clockwise by a quarter turn until the internal web contacts the TDC timing pin.

31 Refit the inner timing cover back to the cylinder block and head.

32 If removed, refit the auxiliary drivebelt tensioner to the cylinder block.

33 Refit the timing belt tensioner roller to the cylinder head.

34 Refit the timing belt, as described in Section 5.

35 Refit the exhaust manifold, as described in Chapter 4B Section 13.

36 If removed, refit the fuel rail as described in Chapter 4B Section 11.

37 Refit the high-pressure fuel pump, as described in Chapter 4B Section 9.

38 Refit the hoses and coolant temperature sensor wiring connector, to the housing on the left-hand end of the cylinder head.

39 Reconnect the quick-release vacuum pipe to the brake vacuum pump on the left-hand end of the cylinder head.

40 Refit the throttle control actuator to the intake manifold, tighten the retaining bolts/nuts and reconnect the wiring connector.

41 Refit the bracket to the left-hand end of the cylinder head.

42 Refit the air intake hose between the air flow meter and turbocharger, also connecting the breather pipe.

43 Refit the cylinder head cover as described in Section 3.

44 Reconnect the battery negative lead (refer to Chapter 5 Section 4).

45 Prime and bleed the fuel system as described in Chapter 4B Section 6.

46 Refill and bleed the cooling system as described in Chapter 1B Section 32.

10 Sump – removal and refitting

Removal

1 Disconnect the battery negative lead (see *Disconnecting the battery* in Chapter 5 Section 4).

2 Jack up the front of the vehicle and support on axle stands (see *Jacking and vehicle support*). Remove the engine compartment undertray and right-hand front road wheel.

3 Drain the engine oil referring to Chapter 1B Section 13, and then refit and tighten the drain plug, using a new washer.

4 Release the fasteners and remove the right-hand front wheel arch inner trim panel **(see illustrations)**.

5 Remove the rear lower engine mounting (torque link), and mounting bracket from the rear of the sump, as described in Section 14.

6 Disconnect the wiring connector and unscrew the oil level sensor from the front of the alloy sump housing **(see illustration)**. Also, if not already done, withdraw the oil level dipstick.

7 Unclip the fuel rail drain/overflow tube from

10.4a Release the retaining clips. . .

10.4b . . . and remove the inner wing panel

10.6 Oil level sensor

10.7 Unclip the fuel overflow pipe from below the sump

10.8 Remove the bolts through the transmission bell housing

10.12 Apply sealant where the right-hand cover meets the cylinder block. . .

10.13 . . . then locate a new gasket on the sump

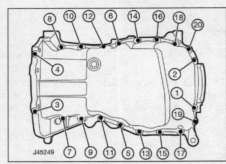

10.14 Sump bolt tightening sequence

the side and the lower part of the sump and move it to one side **(see illustration)**.

8 Slacken and remove the four bolts securing the sump to the lower part of the transmission housing **(see illustration)**.

9 Progressively slacken the bolts working in the **reverse** of the tightening sequence **(see illustration 10.14)** remove all the sump retaining bolts.

10 Tap the sump with a hide or plastic mallet to break the joint, and then remove the sump. Recover the gasket and discard it, as a new one must be used on refitting. There may be sealant at each end of the sump, use a spatula or thin knife to release the ends of the sump. Take care not to distort or damage the mating surfaces of the alloy sump or cylinder block. Take adequate precautions to catch any oil remaining inside the sump housing, as it is removed.

Refitting

11 Thoroughly clean the mating surfaces of the sump and cylinder block.

12 With the cylinder block lower surface clean and no traces of oil, apply four beads of sealant, 5.0 mm wide, to the crankshaft end bearing caps (No's 1 and 5), where they meet the cylinder block. Also apply a bead of sealant at the right-hand end of the cylinder block where the crankshaft oil seal housing is bolted **(see illustration)**.

13 Locate a new gasket on the sump, and then lift the sump into position on the cylinder block and use a straight-edge to align the flywheel end of the sump with the corresponding end face of the cylinder block **(see illustration)**.

14 Insert the bolts and working in the sequence shown **(see illustration)**, tighten

sump retaining bolts, to the torque setting given in the Specifications.

15 Refit the four remaining bolts from the sump to the lower part of the transmission and tighten them to the specified torque setting.

16 Refit the oil level sensor and clip the fuel drain/overflow pipe back in position under the sump.

17 Refit the engine rear lower mounting (torque link) and tighten the bolts to the specified torque.

18 Refit the right-hand front wheel arch liner panel.

19 Refit the engine compartment undertray and right-hand front road wheel, and then lower the car to the ground. Tighten the wheel bolts to the specified torque setting.

20 Reconnect the battery negative lead (refer to Chapter 5 Section 4).

21 Fill the engine with fresh engine oil, with reference to Chapter 1B Section 13.

Note: *Wait at least 30 mins, after the sump has been fitted, before refilling with engine oil.*

22 Start the engine and warm it up to normal operating temperature, check for any leaks from the sump area.

11 Oil pump and sprockets – removal, inspection and refitting

Removal

1 Remove the sump as described in Section 10.

2 Unscrew the two mounting bolts and withdraw the oil pump, tilting it to disengage its sprocket from the drive chain **(see illustrations)**. If the two locating dowels are displaced, refit them in their locations.

3 To remove the drive chain, first remove the crankshaft sprocket as described in Section 6, then unbolt the crankshaft seal end cover from the cylinder block. Where applicable, recover the gasket and discard, as a new one will be required on refitting.

4 Prise out the oil seal with a screwdriver, and discard it as a new one must be fitted on reassembly. If necessary, the new oil seal

11.2a Oil pump and mounting bolts

11.2b Removing the oil pump and drive chain

may be fitted with the right-hand cover on the bench **(see illustration)**.

5 Slide the oil pump drive sprocket and drive chain from the nose of the crankshaft. Note that the drive sprocket is not keyed to the crankshaft, but relies on the pulley bolt being tightened correctly to clamp the sprocket. It is most important that the pulley bolt is correctly tightened otherwise there is the possibility of the oil pump not functioning properly.

6 Unhook the drive chain from the drive sprocket.

Inspection

7 Clean the components and carefully examine the chain, sprockets and pump for any signs of excessive wear. If evident, it is recommended that all the components be renewed as a set.

8 Before refitting the oil pump, prime it by filling with clean engine oil whilst rotating the pump clockwise.

Refitting

9 Wipe clean the oil pump and cylinder block mating surfaces and check that the two locating dowels are fitted in the cylinder block.

10 Engage the drive chain with the drive sprocket, then slide the sprocket onto the nose of the crankshaft.

11 Fit new gasket to the end of the cylinder block and refit the crankshaft seal end cover, insert the bolts and tighten them to the specified torque setting. If a new oil seal has already been fitted to the cover, wrap tape around the nose of the crankshaft to protect the oil seal, and then remove it on completion. If there was no gasket fitted to the cover, apply a 2.0 mm wide bead of silicone sealant to the cover sealing face, making sure that the bead runs below the bolt holes **(see illustrations)**

12 Tilt the oil pump and engage the sprocket with the drive chain, then position it on the dowels and insert the two mounting bolts. Tighten the bolts to the specified torque.

13 Refit the sump with reference to Section 10.

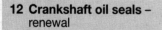

12 Crankshaft oil seals –
     renewal

Timing end cover oil seal

Note: *The new oil seal is extremely fragile and must only be handled by the protector.* **Do not** *touch the surface of the oil seal.*

1 Remove the crankshaft sprocket, as described in Section 6.

2 Note the fitted position of the old seal, then prise it out of the right-hand cover/housing using a screwdriver or suitable hooked instrument, taking care not to damage the surface of the crankshaft. Alternatively, the oil seal can be removed by drilling two small holes diagonally opposite each other and inserting self tapping screws in them. A pair of grips can then be used to pull out the oil seal,

11.4 Fitting a new oil seal to the right-hand cover

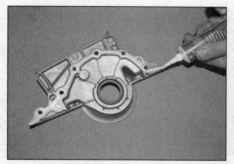

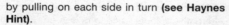

11.11b . . . apply sealant to the mating faces. . .

by pulling on each side in turn **(see Haynes Hint)**.

3 Inspect the seal rubbing surface on the crankshaft. If it is grooved or rough in the area where the old seal was fitted, the new seal should be fitted slightly less deeply, so that it rubs on an unworn part of the crankshaft surface.

4 Nissan technicians use a tool (drift set SST: KV113B0220 – Mot. 1586) to fit this oil seal. The tool consists of a threaded rod, metal tube and nut, and a machined shoulder to locate the protector/guide on. The rod is screwed into the end of the crankshaft, and the protector/guide located on the shoulder. The metal tube is then

Oil seals can be removed by drilling a small hole and inserting a self-tapping screw. A pair of grips can then be used to pull out the oil seal by pulling on the screw. If difficulty is experienced, insert two screws diagonally opposite each other.

11.11a Wrap some tape around the nose of the crankshaft. . .

11.11c . . . and fit the right-hand cover

fitted against the oil seal and the nut tightened to press the seal into the right-hand cover. If the Nissan tool cannot be obtained, a similar tool can be made out of a threaded rod, metal tube, washer and nut.

5 Wipe clean the oil seal seating, then press the oil seal squarely into position. Note that the Nissan tool is designed to locate the seal at the original depth, however, if the crankshaft sealing surface is excessively worn, position it less deeply so that it locates on the unworn surface.

6 After fitting the oil seal, remove the protector/guide and tool.

7 Refit the crankshaft sprocket as described in Section 6.

Flywheel end oil seal

8 Remove the flywheel as described in Section 13.

9 Renew the oil seal as described in paragraphs 2 to 6 inclusive **(see illustration)**.

12.9 Fitting a new oil seal to the flywheel end of the crankshaft

13.3a Using a home made tool to prevent the flywheel from turning. . .

13.8a Fit new flywheel bolts. . .

Nissan technicians use a tool (drift set SST: KV113B0210 – Mot. 1585) to fit the flywheel end oil seal.
10 Refit the flywheel with reference to Section 13.

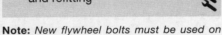

13 Flywheel –
removal, inspection and refitting

Note: *New flywheel bolts must be used on refitting.*

Removal

1 Remove the manual transmission as described in Chapter 7 Section 6.
2 Remove the clutch assembly as described in Chapter 8 Section 6.
3 Prevent the flywheel from turning by

14.6 Support the engine with a suitable jack

13.3b . . . or hold the flywheel stationary using a screwdriver in the starter ring gear

13.8b . . . and tighten in a diagonal sequence

locking the ring gear teeth with a special tool. Alternatively, locate a long bolt in one of the engine-to-gearbox mounting bolt holes and insert a wide-bladed screwdriver or similar into the starter ring gear **(see illustrations)**.
4 Unscrew the securing bolts and withdraw the flywheel from the crankshaft. Note that the flywheel bolt holes are offset so that the flywheel can only be fitted in one position. Discard the old bolts as new ones must be used on refitting.

Inspection

5 On manual transmission models, if the flywheel's clutch mating surface is deeply scored, cracked or otherwise damaged, the flywheel must be renewed. Seek the advice of a Nissan dealer or engine reconditioning specialist.
6 If the ring gear is badly worn or has missing

14.7 Remove the filter support bracket

teeth, it must be renewed. Check with your Nissan dealer or engine reconditioning specialist, to see if the flywheel can be repaired.

Refitting

7 Clean the flywheel and crankshaft faces, and then coat the locating face on the crankshaft with Loctite Autoform, or an equivalent compound.
8 Locate the flywheel on the crankshaft and insert the new securing bolts, then tighten them in a diagonal sequence to the specified torque. Hold the flywheel stationary as during removal **(see illustrations)**. **Do not** oil the new bolt threads as they are supplied with locking compound.
9 Refit the clutch assembly as described in Chapter 8 Section 6.
10 Remove the locking tool (where used), and refit the transmission as described in Chapter 7 Section 6.

14 Engine/transmission mountings –
inspection and renewal

Inspection

1 If improved access is required, firmly apply the handbrake, and then jack up the front of the vehicle and support it securely on axle stands (see *Jacking and vehicle support*).
2 Check the mounting rubber to see if it is cracked, hardened or separated from the metal at any point; renew the mounting if any such damage or deterioration is evident.
3 Check that all the mounting's fasteners are securely tightened; use a torque wrench to check if possible.
4 Using a large screwdriver or a crowbar, check for wear in the mounting by carefully levering against it to check for free play. Where this is not possible, enlist the aid of an assistant to move the engine/transmission back-and-forth, or from side-to-side, while you watch the mounting. While some free play is to be expected even from new components, excessive wear should be obvious. If excessive free play is found, check first that the fasteners are correctly secured, and then renew any worn components as described below.

Renewal

Right-hand mounting

5 Disconnect the battery negative lead (see *Disconnecting the battery* in Chapter 5 Section 4).
6 Place a jack beneath the engine, with a block of wood on the jack head. Raise the jack until it is supporting the weight of the engine **(see illustration)**.
7 If required, to make access easier, remove the fuel filter and support bracket **(see illustration)**.
8 Slacken and remove the retaining bolts from

the inner wing panel, remove the four retaining bolts from the engine mounting bracket, and then withdraw the complete mounting from the engine compartment (see illustration).

9 Check carefully for signs of wear or damage on all components, and renew them where necessary.

10 On refitting, fit the engine mounting and bracket to the inner wing panel and engine, and then securely tighten its retaining bolts to the specified torque setting.

11 Refit the torque link to the rear of the engine mounting and tighten the retaining bolts to the specified torque setting.

12 With the engine mounting back in position, refit the fuel filter and mounting bracket.

13 Lower the jack and remove it from underneath the engine.

14 Reconnect the earth cable and bracket to the top of the engine mounting and secure the fuel lines back in the clips, and then reconnect the battery negative terminal.

Left-hand mounting

15 Remove the battery and tray, as described in Chapter 5 Section 4.

16 Place a jack and block of wood beneath the transmission, and raise the jack to take the weight of the transmission (see illustration).

17 Slacken and remove the bolts, then remove the mounting from the top of the transmission (see illustration).

18 Slacken and remove the two outer retaining nuts, to remove the mounting from the mounting bracket.

19 Check carefully for signs of wear or damage on all components, and renew them where necessary.

20 On refitting, fit the upper and lower mounting brackets (where removed) and securely tighten the retaining bolts.

21 Align the left-hand rubber mounting with the bolt/stud on the lower mounting bracket and tighten its nut to the specified torque setting.

22 Refit the two outer retaining nuts, and tighten to the specified torque setting.

23 With the transmission mounting back in

14.8 Engine mounting bolts

14.16 Support the transmission with a trolley jack

14.17 Undo the centre retaining nut

14.26 Remove the torque link arm bolts

position, lower the jack and remove it from underneath the transmission.

24 Refit the battery and battery tray, with reference to Chapter 5 Section 4.

Rear lower mounting

25 If not already done, firmly apply the handbrake, and then jack up the front of the vehicle and support it securely on axle stands (see *Jacking and vehicle support*). Remove engine undertray.

26 Slacken and remove the bolts securing the rear mounting link to the subframe and the mounting bracket, and then withdraw the mounting link from under the vehicle (see illustration).

27 If required, slacken and remove the three bolts securing the rear mounting bracket to the sump, and then withdraw the bracket from under the vehicle.

28 Check carefully for signs of wear or damage on all components, and renew them where necessary.

29 Refit the mounting bracket to the rear of the sump housing and tighten its retaining bolts to the specified torque.

30 Fit the rear mounting link to the mounting bracket and subframe, and then tighten the retaining bolts to the specified torque.

31 With the transmission rear mounting link arm back in position, lower the vehicle to the ground.

Notes

Chapter 2 Part C
1.6 litre diesel engine in-car repair procedures

Contents

Degrees of difficulty

Easy, suitable for novice with little experience		Fairly easy, suitable for beginner with some experience		Fairly difficult, suitable for competent DIY mechanic		Difficult, suitable for experienced DIY mechanic		Very difficult, suitable for expert DIY or professional	

Specifications

Engine (general)

Capacity	1598 cc
Designation	R9M
Bore	80.0 mm
Stroke	79.5 mm
No.1 cylinder location.	At timing chain end of engine
Direction of crankshaft rotation	Clockwise (viewed from the right-hand side of vehicle)
Firing order	1-3-4-2
Compression ratio	15.4 : 1

Camshafts

Drive	Chain

Lubrication system

Oil pump type.	Chain-driven off the crankshaft
Minimum oil pressure at 80°C (with correct oil level):	
Idle speed.	0.7 bars
at 1750 rpm	1.5 bars
at 4000 rpm	3.6 bars

Torque wrench settings

	Nm	lbf ft
Auxiliary drivebelt tensioner bolts	25	18
Big-end bearing bolts: *		
Stage 1	25	18
Stage 2	Angle-tighten a further 110°	
Camshaft retaining cap bolts	10	7
Camshaft carrier-to-cylinder head:		
Stage 1	5	4
Stage 2	12	9
Camshaft sprocket bolts:		
Exhaust camshaft timing sprocket 3 bolts: *		
Stage 1	10	7
Stage 2	Angle-tighten a further 40°	
Intake camshaft timing gear bolt: *		
Stage 1	20	15
Stage 2	Angle-tighten a further 35°	
Exhaust camshaft fuel pump sprocket bolt*	30	22
Crankshaft pulley/vibration damper bolts: *		
Stage 1	50	37
Stage 2	Angle-tighten a further 150°	
Cylinder head bolts: *		
Stage 1	5	4
Stage 2	30	22
Stage 3	Angle-tighten a further 300°	
Crankshaft oil seals:		
Front oil seal	47	35
Rear oil seal housing bolts:		
Stage 1	5	4
Stage 2	12	9
Cylinder head cover bolts	10	7
Flywheel/driveplate retaining bolts: *		
Stage 1	40	30
Stage 2	Angle-tighten a further 50°	
High-pressure fuel pump sprocket retaining nut	90	66
Left-hand transmission mounting: *		
Mounting bracket-to-body bolts	75	55
Mounting bracket-to-transmission	75	55
Centre stud-to-transmission bracket	60	44
Rubber mounting centre nut	60	44
Rubber mounting two outer nuts	85	63
Main bearing bolts: *		
Stage 1	25	18
Stage 2	Angle-tighten a further 110°	
Oil filter cap	25	18
Oil level sensor nuts	8	6
Oil pressure warning switch	35	26
Oil pump-to-engine bolts:		
Stage 1	5	4
Stage 2	25	18
Oil pick-up strainer bolt	10	7
Rear lower engine/transmission mounting:		
Bracket to engine/transmission bolts	70	52
Torque arm mounting bolts	210	155
Right-hand upper engine mounting:		
Mounting-to-vehicle body and engine	60	44
Torque arm mounting bolts	120	89
Upper alloy sump-to-cylinder block bolts:		
Stage 1	10	7
Stage 2	25	18
Sump lower steel plate-to-upper sump housing:		
Stage 1	5	4
Stage 2	12	9
Sump drain plug:		
Alloy sump	25	18
Steel plate sump	50	35
Timing chain cover bolts: *		
Stage 1	5	4
Stage 2	15	12

Torque wrench settings (continued)

	Nm	lbf ft
Timing chain guides securing bolts	25	18
Timing chain tensioner-to-cylinder block bolts	10	7
Turbocharger oil feed pipe banjo-bolts	16	12
Turbocharger oil return pipe bolts	10	7

*Do not re-use

---

1   General Information

How to use this Chapter

1 This Part of Chapter 2 describes those repair procedures that can reasonably be carried out on the engine while it remains in the car. If the engine has been removed from the car and is being dismantled as described in Part D, any preliminary dismantling procedures can be ignored.

2 Note that many operations that would normally be classed as in-car repair procedures and be covered in this Chapter, are actually covered in Part D. This is due to the design of the engine and the limited clearance in the engine compartment making it physically impossible to remove and refit many components and assemblies with the engine in the car.

3 Part D describes the removal of the engine/transmission unit from the vehicle, and the full overhaul procedures that can then be carried out.

4 The engine is of in-line 4-cylinder, double-overhead camshaft, 16-valve type, mounted transversely at the front of the car. The clutch and transmission are attached to its left-hand end.

5 The cylinder block is of cast iron with conventional dry liners bored directly into the cylinder block.

6 The crankshaft runs in five main bearings. Thrustwashers are fitted to No 3 main bearing cap, to control crankshaft endfloat.

7 The connecting rods rotate on horizontally-split bearing shells at their big-ends. The pistons are attached to the connecting rods by gudgeon pins. The gudgeon pins are fully-floating and are retained by circlips. The aluminium alloy pistons are fitted with three piston rings, comprising two compression rings and a scraper-type oil control ring.

8 The camshafts operate 16 valves by rocker arms located beneath each cam lobe. The exhaust camshaft is driven by a chain, and the intake camshaft is gear-driven from the exhaust camshaft. The timing chain is located at the left-hand end of the engine. The valve clearances are self-adjusting by means of hydraulic followers in the cylinder head. The camshafts run in bearing locations at the top of the cylinder head. The inlet and exhaust valves are each closed by coil springs, and operate in guides pressed into the cylinder head.

9 The coolant pump is driven by the auxiliary belt and located in the right-hand end, at the front of the cylinder block.

10 Lubrication is by means of an oil pump, which is chain driven off the crankshaft. It draws oil through a strainer located in the sump, and then forces it through an externally-mounted filter and oil cooler, into galleries in the cylinder block/crankcase. From there, the oil is distributed to the crankshaft (main bearings) and camshaft. The big-end bearings are supplied with oil via internal drillings in the crankshaft; the camshaft bearings also receive a pressurised supply. The camshaft lobes and valves are lubricated by splash, as are all other engine components.

Operations with engine in the car

11 The following work can be carried out with the engine in the car:
a) Compression pressure – testing.
b) Cylinder head cover – removal and refitting.
c) Crankshaft pulley – removal and refitting.
d) Engine/transmission mountings – inspection and renewal.
e) Flywheel/driveplate – removal, inspection and refitting.

2   Top Dead Centre (TDC) for No 1 piston – locating

1 Top dead centre (TDC) is the highest point in the cylinder that each piston reaches as the crankshaft turns. Each piston reaches TDC at the end of the compression stroke and again at the end of the exhaust stroke. However, for the purpose of timing the engine, TDC refers to the position of No 1 piston at the end of its compression stroke.

2 Disconnect the battery negative terminal (refer to Chapter 5 Section 4).

3 Apply the handbrake, and then jack up the front of the car and support it on axle stands (see *Jacking and vehicle support*). Remove the right-hand roadwheel.

4 Remove the engine undertray and the right-hand wheel arch liner in order to gain access to the crankshaft pulley bolt.

5 Remove the starter motor, as described in Chapter 5 Section 10.

6 Unscrew the TDC plug from the front of the cylinder block and insert special tool (Nissan TDC tool Mot 1970), tightening it securely **(see illustrations)**.

7 Turn the crankshaft anti-clockwise until it just contacts the TDC tool.

8 The engine is now positioned with No 1 piston at TDC on its compression stroke. For further information on setting the timing up see timing chain removal and refitting in Chapter 2D Section 9.

Caution: Do not attempt to rotate the engine whilst the crankshaft timing pin is in position. If the engine is to be left in this state for a long period of time, it is a good idea to place suitable warning notices inside the vehicle, and in the engine compartment. This will reduce the possibility of the engine being accidentally cranked on the starter motor, which would cause considerable damage.

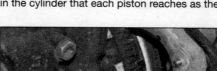

2.6a Unscrew the TDC plug. . .   2.6b . . . then insert the crankshaft TDC setting tool

3.1 Remove the engine oil filler cap

3.2a Unclip the wiring loom. . .

3.2b . . . from the engine cover

3.4a Release the securing clips. . .

3.4b . . . and remove the plastic cover

3.5 Disconnect the injector wiring connectors

3 Cylinder head cover and oil seperator – removal and refitting

Removal

1 Remove the engine oil filler cap from the top of the engine cover (see illustration).
2 Unclip the wiring loom from across the front of the cover, then release the two retaining clips and remove the upper cover (see illustrations).
3 Undo the two retaining bolts and nut from the rear of the engine cover.
4 Release the securing clips at the front and remove the plastic engine cover (see illustrations).
5 Note the routing of the wiring loom on the top of the engine. Disconnect the wiring plugs from the four fuel injectors, then lay the loom to one side (see illustration).
6 Disconnect the engine breather (PCV) hose from the rear of the oil seperator (see illustration).
7 Undo the eight retaining bolts, starting from the outer bolts and working to the inner bolts, then lift the oil separator from the cylinder head (see illustration). Discard the seals – new ones must be fitted.

Refitting

8 Thoroughly clean the gasket faces on the oil separator and the cylinder head, then renew the sealing gaskets and foam strip (see illustration).
9 Refit the oil separator, then tighten the bolts a couple of turns at a time, starting from the centre bolts and working outwards, to the specified torque.

10 The remainder of installation is the reverse of removal.

4 Crankshaft pulley/ vibration damper – removal and refitting

Removal

1 Slacken the right-hand front roadwheel bolts, raise the front of the vehicle and support it securely on axle stands (see *Jacking and vehicle support*). Remove the roadwheel, then undo the fasteners and remove the engine undershield.
2 Remove the auxiliary drivebelt as described in Chapter 1B Section 34.
3 To prevent crankshaft rotation, (the pulley retaining bolt is extremely tight) special Nissan

3.6 Disconnect the breather hose

3.7 Remove the oil separator

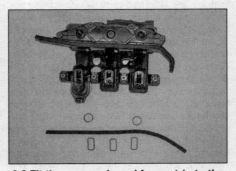

3.8 Fit the new seals and foam strip to the oil separator

tool No. MOT1770 is available. This tool fits on the crankshaft pulley centre spacer and is also available from automotive tool specialists. **(see illustration)**.

4 Slacken the crankshaft pulley retaining bolt, using the special tool that fits on the crankshaft pulley centre spacer **(see illustration)**. In the absence of the tool, remove the starter motor as described in Chapter 5 Section 10 to expose the flywheel ring gear, and have an assistant insert a wide blade screwdriver between the ring gear teeth and the transmission bellhousing whilst the pulley retaining bolts are slackened. If the engine is removed from the vehicle it will be necessary to lock the flywheel.

Caution: Do not attempt to lock the pulley by inserting a bolt/drill through the timing hole. If the locking pin is in position, temporarily remove it prior to slackening the pulley bolt, then refit it once the bolt has been slackened.

5 Undo the crankshaft pulley retaining bolt and remove the pulley from the centre hub on the end of the crankshaft, complete with spacer **(see illustrations)**.

Refitting

6 Locate the pulley on the hub on the end of the crankshaft, fit the bolt and spacer, then tighten it to the specified torque.

7 The remainder of refitting is a reversal of removal.

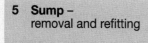

5 Sump – removal and refitting

Removal

1 Apply the handbrake, then jack up the front of the car and support it on axle stands (see *Jacking and vehicle support*). Undo the retaining screws and remove the plastic undertray from beneath the engine/transmission.

2 Drain the engine oil as described in Chapter 1B Section 13, and then refit and tighten the drain plug, using a new sealing washer. Ensure all the oil is completely drained.

3 Remove the engine oil level dipstick.

4 Working in an anti-clockwise direction, starting from the timing chain end, unscrew and remove the bolts securing the sump lower metal plate to the upper alloy sump housing.

5 The sump lower metal plate is sealed to the upper alloy sump housing with strong silicone adhesive/sealant that is very difficult to cut, however methodical use of a suitable spatula or thin knife will release the sump. A special Nissan tool No. SST: KV10111100 is available **(see illustration)**, this is used to slide between the sump and the upper alloy housing, and then tapped around to free the sealant.

6 Take care not to distort or damage the mating surfaces of the sump and baseplate,

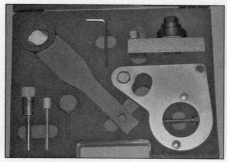

4.3 AST engine setting tool kit

4.4 Holding crankshaft with special tool

4.5a Remove the bolt, spacer. . .

4.5b . . . and crankshaft pulley

and take adequate precautions to catch any oil remaining in the sump.

Refitting

7 Thoroughly clean the mating surfaces of the sump and cylinder block baseplate, taking care not to damage their surfaces.

8 Apply a 5 ± 2 mm diameter bead of silicone adhesive/sealant to the sump as shown, working inside the bolt holes **(see illustration)**.

9 Lift the sump into position making sure it is correctly aligned with the holes in the baseplate, then insert the bolts and finger-tighten them.

10 Tighten the sump bolts to the Stage 1 torque given in Specifications. Working in a clockwise direction, starting from the timing chain end, tighten the bolts securing the sump

lower metal plate to the upper alloy sump housing.

11 Tighten the sump bolts to the Stage 2 torque using the same sequence.

12 Refit the undertray and lower the vehicle to the ground.

13 Fill the engine with fresh oil with reference to Chapter 1B Section 13.

6 Crankshaft oil seals – renewal

Timing chain cover oil seal

1 Remove the crankshaft pulley as described in Section 4.

2 Nissan supply a fitting tool with the new

5.5 Special tool to free sealant

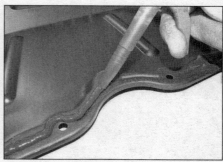

5.8 Applying silicone adhesive/sealant to the sump

6.2 Fit tool into seal and unscrew

6.4 Locate the seal into position over the crankshaft

6.5a Tighten the seal with the fitting tool. . .

6.5b . . .and remove the protector

oil seal, carefully remove the tool from the packaging, and using a socket unscrew the old oil seal from the timing chain cover **(see illustration)**.

3 Clean around the timing chain cover and check for any damage, which may cause the seal to leak.

4 Offer up the seal to the timing chain cover aligning the notches on the outer part of the seal with the notches in the timing chain cover. Carefully ease the seal into position, taking care not to damage its sealing lip and turn clockwise to locate in the cover **(see illustration)**.

5 Tighten the oil seal to the specified torque and then remove the protector from the end of the crankshaft **(see illustrations)**.

6 Wash off any traces of oil, then refit the crankshaft pulley as described in Section 4.

Transmission end oil seal

Note: *The transmission end oil seal is supplied together with the oil seal housing and cannot be renewed separately.*

7 Remove the flywheel as described in Section 7.

8 Unscrew the bolts and remove the oil seal housing from the cylinder block/baseplate **(see illustration)**.

9 Clean the contact faces of the cylinder block and baseplate. Do not remove the protector or touch the lip of the new oil seal during fitting as this will result in oil leakage.

10 Carefully locate the oil seal and housing onto the crankshaft and insert three long M6 studs loosely to act as guides **(see illustration)**. Do not press the housing into position at this stage.

11 Apply a 5 ± 2 mm diameter bead of silicone adhesive/sealant to the seal housing as shown, working inside the bolt holes **(see illustration)**.

12 Apply even pressure to the housing and press it into position until it contacts the cylinder block. Insert a couple of bolts, then remove the protector and the three guide studs **(see illustrations)**.

6.8 Removing the transmission end oil seal housing

6.10 Use 3 studs to act as guides when fitting the new oil seal housing

6.11 Apply sealant around the seal housing

6.12a Press the housing into position. . .

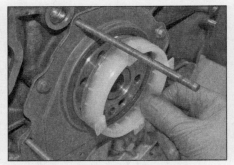

6.12b . . . remove the protector. . .

6.12c . . . and the locating studs

13 Insert the retaining bolts and finger-tighten, and then working in an anti-clockwise direction, starting from the upper bolts, tighten them to the initial torque given in the Specifications.

14 Tighten the bolts to their stage 2 and final torque using the same sequence.

15 Refit the flywheel as described in Section 7.

7 Flywheel –
removal, inspection and refitting

Note: *New flywheel bolts must be used on refitting.*

Removal

1 Remove the manual transmission as described in Chapter 7 Section 6.

2 Remove the clutch assembly as described in Chapter 8 Section 6.

3 Prevent the flywheel from turning by locking the ring gear teeth with a special tool. Alternatively, locate a long bolt in one of the engine-to-gearbox mounting bolt holes and insert a wide-bladed screwdriver or similar into the starter ring gear **(see illustrations)**.

4 Unscrew the securing bolts and withdraw the flywheel from the crankshaft. Note that the flywheel bolt holes are offset so that the flywheel can only be fitted in one position. Discard the old bolts as new ones must be used on refitting.

Inspection

5 On manual transmission models, if the flywheel's clutch mating surface is deeply scored, cracked or otherwise damaged, the flywheel must be renewed. Seek the advice of a Nissan dealer or engine reconditioning specialist.

6 If the ring gear is badly worn or has missing teeth, it must be renewed. Check with your Nissan dealer or engine reconditioning specialist, to see if the flywheel can be repaired.

Refitting

7 Clean the flywheel and crankshaft faces, and then coat the locating face on the crankshaft with Loctite Autoform, or an equivalent compound.

8 Locate the flywheel on the crankshaft and insert the new securing bolts, then tighten them in a diagonal sequence to the specified torque. Hold the flywheel stationary as during removal **(see illustrations)**. **Do not** oil the new bolt threads as they are supplied with locking compound.

9 Refit the clutch assembly as described in Chapter 8 Section 6.

10 Remove the locking tool (where used), and refit the transmission as described in Chapter 7 Section 6.

7.3a Using a home made tool to prevent the flywheel from turning. . .

7.3b . . . or hold the flywheel stationary using a screwdriver in the starter ring gear

7.8a Fit new flywheel bolts. . .

7.8b . . . and tighten in a diagonal sequence

8 Engine/transmission mountings –
inspection and renewal

Inspection

1 If improved access is required, firmly apply the handbrake, and then jack up the front of the vehicle and support it securely on axle stands (see *Jacking and vehicle support*).

2 Check the mounting rubber to see if it is cracked, hardened or separated from the metal at any point; renew the mounting if any such damage or deterioration is evident.

3 Check that all the mounting's fasteners are securely tightened; use a torque wrench to check if possible.

4 Using a large screwdriver or a crowbar, check for wear in the mounting by carefully levering against it to check for free play.

Where this is not possible, enlist the aid of an assistant to move the engine/transmission back-and-forth, or from side-to-side, while you watch the mounting. While some free play is to be expected even from new components, excessive wear should be obvious. If excessive free play is found, check first that the fasteners are correctly secured, and then renew any worn components as described below.

Renewal

Right-hand mounting

5 Disconnect the battery negative lead (see *Disconnecting the battery* in Chapter 5 Section 4).

6 Place a jack beneath the engine, with a block of wood on the jack head. Raise the jack until it is supporting the weight of the engine **(see illustration)**.

7 If required, to make access easier, remove the fuel filter and support bracket **(see illustration)**.

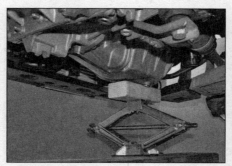

8.6 Support the engine with a suitable jack

8.7 Remove the filter support bracket

8.8 Remove the bolt from the torque link

8.9a Undo the retaining bolts. . .

8.9b . . . and withdraw the complete mounting

8 Slacken the retaining bolts and remove the torque link from the rear of the engine mounting (see illustration).

9 Slacken and remove the retaining bolts from the inner wing panel, remove the four retaining bolts from the engine mounting bracket, and then withdraw the complete mounting from the engine compartment (see illustrations).

10 Check carefully for signs of wear or damage on all components, and renew them where necessary.

11 On refitting, fit the engine mounting and bracket to the inner wing panel and engine, and then securely tighten its retaining bolts to the specified torque setting.

12 Refit the torque link to the rear of the engine mounting and tighten the retaining bolts to the specified torque setting.

13 With the engine mounting back in position, refit the fuel filter and mounting bracket.

14 Lower the jack and remove it from underneath the engine.

15 Reconnect the earth cable and bracket to the top of the engine mounting and secure the fuel lines back in the clips, and then reconnect the battery negative terminal.

Left-hand mounting

16 Remove the battery and tray, as described in Chapter 5 Section 4.

17 Place a jack and block of wood beneath the transmission, and raise the jack to take the weight of the transmission (see illustration).

18 Slacken and remove the upper retaining nuts, then remove the upper rubber mounting from the top of the mounting bracket (see illustration).

19 Slacken and remove the bolts, then remove the mounting bracket from the top of the transmission (see illustration).

20 Slacken and remove the two outer retaining nuts, to remove the mounting from the mounting bracket.

21 Check carefully for signs of wear or damage on all components, and renew them where necessary.

22 On refitting, fit the upper and lower mounting brackets (where removed) and securely tighten the retaining bolts.

23 Align the left-hand rubber mounting with the bolt/stud on the lower mounting bracket and tighten its nut to the specified torque setting.

24 Refit the two outer retaining nuts, and tighten to the specified torque setting.

25 With the transmission mounting back in position, lower the jack and remove it from underneath the transmission.

26 Refit the battery and battery tray, with reference to Chapter 5 Section 4.

Rear lower mounting

27 If not already done, firmly apply the handbrake, and then jack up the front of the vehicle and support it securely on axle stands (see Jacking and vehicle support). Remove engine undertray.

28 Slacken and remove the bolts securing the rear mounting link to the subframe and the mounting bracket, and then withdraw the mounting link from under the vehicle (see illustration).

29 If required, slacken and remove the three bolts securing the rear mounting bracket to the sump, and then withdraw the bracket from under the vehicle.

30 Check carefully for signs of wear or damage on all components, and renew them where necessary.

31 Refit the mounting bracket to the rear of the sump housing and tighten its retaining bolts to the specified torque.

32 Fit the rear mounting link to the mounting bracket and subframe, and then tighten the retaining bolts to the specified torque.

33 With the transmission rear mounting link arm back in position, lower the vehicle to the ground.

8.17 Support the transmission with a trolley jack

8.18 Remove the rubber mounting

8.19 Remove the mounting bracket

8.28 Remove the torque link arm bolts

9.1 Location of sensors- each side of the filter housing

9.6a Undo the retaining bolt. . .

9.6b . . . and remove the oil level sensor

9 Oil pressure sensor and level sensor – removal and refitting

1 The oil pressure sensor and oil level sensors are located on the front of the engine, each side of the oil filter housing **(see illustration)**.

Removal

2 Jack up the front of the vehicle and put it on axle stands (see *Jacking and vehicle support*), then remove the engine undertray to gain access to the sensors.

Oil pressure sensor

3 The sensor is fitted to the front of the engine, behind the oil cooler, next to the oil filter housing **(see illustration 9.1)**.

4 Disconnect the wiring plug, then unscrew the sensor. Recover the sealing washer. Be prepared for fluid spillage, and if the sensor is to be left removed from the engine for any length of time, plug the hole.

Oil level sensor

5 The oil level sensor is fitted to the front face of the engine sump.

6 Disconnect the wiring plug, undo the retaining bolt and remove the sensor **(see illustrations)**.

7 Recover the seal from the sensor – a new one must be fitted.

Refitting

Oil pressure sensor

8 Examine the sealing washer for signs of damage or deterioration and if necessary renew.

9 Refit the sensor, complete with washer, and tighten it to the specified torque. Reconnect the wiring connector.

10 The remainder of refitting is a reversal of removal. Top up the engine oil as described in Chapter 1B Section 5.

Oil level sensor

11 Ensure the sealing surfaces of the sensor and the sump are clean.

12 Renew the sensor O-ring seals.

13 Position the sensor in the sump, refit the retaining bolt and tight to the specified torque.

14 Reconnect the sensor wiring plug.

15 The remainder of refitting is a reversal of removal. Top up the engine oil as described in Chapter 1B Section 5.

Chapter 2 Part D
Engine removal and overhaul procedures

Contents

Degrees of difficulty

Easy, suitable for novice with little experience | Fairly easy, suitable for beginner with some experience | Fairly difficult, suitable for competent DIY mechanic 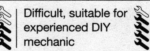 | Difficult, suitable for experienced DIY mechanic | Very difficult, suitable for expert DIY or professional

Specifications

General
Engine codes:
1.2 litre petrol engine	HRA2DDT
1.5 litre diesel engine	K9K
1.6 litre diesel engine	R9M

Cylinder head
Maximum gasket face distortion:
Petrol engines	0.10 mm
Diesel engines	0.05 mm

Cylinder head height:
1.2 litre petrol engines	124.8 mm
1.5 litre diesel engines	127.0 mm
1.6 litre diesel engines	131.5 mm

Camshaft and followers (1.2 litre petrol engines)

Drive	Chain
Number of bearings	6
Endfloat	0.203 to 0.239 mm
Camshaft lobe height:	
Inlet	44.322 to 44.522 mm
Exhaust	43.664 to 43.864 mm
Camshaft bearing journal outer diameter:	
No 1 bearing	27.934 to 28.0 mm
Nos 2 to 5 bearings	24.969 to 25.0 mm
Camshaft cylinder head bearing journal internal diameter:	
No 1 bearing	28.044 to 28.076 mm
Nos 2 to 6 bearings	25.040 to 25.060 mm
Camshaft journal-to-bearing clearance:	
No 1 bearing	0.044 to 0.142 mm
Nos 2 to 6 bearings	0.040 to 0.091 mm
Camshaft run-out	0.01 mm
Camshaft follower outer diameter	29.964 to 29.987 mm
Cylinder head hole diameter for follower	30.000 to 30.021 mm
Camshaft follower to cylinder head clearance	0.013 to 0.057 mm

Cylinder block

Maximum gasket face distortion:	
Petrol engines	0.10 mm
Diesel engines	0.05 mm

Valve springs

Spring free height:	
1.2 litre petrol engines:	
Inlet	45.0 to 47.0 mm
Exhaust	58.5 to 60.5 mm
1.5 litre diesel engines	43.31 mm
1.6 litre diesel engines	46.90 mm
Spring squareness:	
1.2 litre petrol engines:	
Inlet	less than 1.4 mm
Exhaust	less than 1.8 mm
1.5 litre diesel engines	less than 1.2 mm
1.6 litre diesel engines	less than 1.4 mm

Valves

	Inlet	Exhaust
Valve head diameter:		
1.2 litre petrol engines	26.48 to 26.72 mm	23.38 to 23.62 mm
1.5 litre diesel engines	33.38 to 33.62 mm	28.88 to 29.12 mm
1.6 litre diesel engines	23.38 to 23.62 mm	23.28 to 23.62 mm
Valve stem diameter:		
1.2 litre petrol engines	5.470 to 5.485 mm	5.455 to 5.470 mm
1.5 litre diesel engines	5.969 to 5.985 mm	5.955 to 5.971 mm
1.6 litre diesel engines	5.970 to 5.985 mm	5.955 to 5.970 mm
Overall length:		
1.2 litre petrol engines	100.84 mm	101.69 mm
1.5 litre diesel engines	100.74 to 101.16 mm	100.54 to 100.96 mm
1.6 litre diesel engines	104.17 mm	104.06 mm

Pistons

Piston skirt diameter:	
1.2 litre petrol engines	72.15 to 72.17 mm
1.5 litre diesel engines	75.938 to 75.952 mm
1.6 litre diesel engines	79.835 mm
Piston-to-bore clearance:	
1.2 litre engines	0.030 to 0.050 mm
1.6 litre diesel engines	0.192 to 0.236 mm
Piston protrusion:	
1.5 litre diesel engines	0.023 to 0.281 mm
1.6 litre diesel engines	0.387 to 0.551 mm

Piston rings

Ring-to-groove clearance:
  1.2 litre petrol engines:
    Top compression ring . . . . 0.030 to 0.070 mm
    Second compression ring . . . . 0.030 to 0.050 mm
    Oil control ring . . . . 0.030 mm
  1.5 litre diesel engines:
    Top compression ring . . . . 0.10 to 0.12 mm
    Second compression ring . . . . 0.08 to 0.10 mm
    Oil control ring . . . . 0.03 to 0.07 mm
  1.6 litre diesel engines:
    Top compression ring . . . . 0.09 to 0.13 mm
    Second compression ring . . . . 0.08 to 0.12 mm
    Oil control ring . . . . 0.05 mm
Ring end gaps (measured in cylinder):
  1.2 litre petrol engines:
    Top compression ring . . . . 0.15 to 0.30 mm
    Second compression ring . . . . 0.40 to 0.60 mm
    Oil control ring . . . . 0.20 to 0.90 mm
  Diesel engines:
    Top compression ring . . . . 0.20 to 0.35 mm
    Second compression ring . . . . 0.70 to 0.90 mm
    Oil control ring . . . . 0.25 to 0.50 mm

Crankshaft

Endfloat:
  1.2 litre petrol engines . . . . 0.098 to 0.260 mm
  1.5 litre diesel engines: . . . . 0.45 to 0.252 mm
  1.6 litre diesel engines: . . . . 0.112 to 0.438 mm
Main bearing running clearance:
  1.2 litre petrol engines . . . . 0.024 to 0.034 mm
  1.5 litre diesel engines . . . . 0.010 to 0.054 mm
  1.6 litre diesel engines . . . . 0.035 to 0.065 mm
Big-end bearing running clearance:
  1.2 litre petrol engines . . . . 0.020 to 0.030 mm
  1.5 litre diesel engines . . . . 0.010 to 0.064 mm
  1.6 litre diesel engines . . . . 0.053 to 0.093 mm

Torque wrench settings

Refer to the Specifications in Chapter 2A, Chapter 2B or Chapter 2C for the relevant engine.

1 General Information

1 Included in this Chapter are details of removing the engine/transmission from the vehicle, and general overhaul procedures for the cylinder head, cylinder block/crankcase and all other engine internal components.
2 The information given ranges from advice concerning preparation for an overhaul and the purchase of new parts, to detailed step-by-step procedures covering removal, inspection, renovation and refitting of engine internal components.
3 Note that many operations that would normally be classed as in-car repair procedures and be covered in previous Parts of this Chapter, are actually covered in this Part. This is due to the design of the engine and the limited clearance in the engine compartment making it physically impossible to remove and refit many components and assemblies with the engine in the car.
4 After Section 5, all instructions are based on the assumption that the engine has been removed from the vehicle. For information concerning in-car engine repair, as well as the removal and refitting of those external components necessary for full overhaul, refer to Part A, B or C of this Chapter and to Section 5. Ignore any preliminary dismantling operations described in Part A, B or C, that are no longer relevant once the engine has been removed.
5 Apart from torque wrench settings, which are given at the beginning of Part A, B or C, all specifications relating to engine overhaul are at the beginning of this Part of Chapter 2.

Engine overhaul

6 It is not always easy to determine when, or if, an engine should be completely overhauled, as a number of factors must be considered.
7 High mileage is not necessarily an indication that an overhaul is needed, while low mileage does not preclude the need for an overhaul. Frequency of servicing is probably the most important consideration. An engine, which has had regular and frequent oil and filter changes, as well as other required maintenance, should give many thousands of miles of reliable service. Conversely, a neglected engine may require an overhaul very early in its life.
8 Excessive oil consumption is an indication that piston rings, valve seals and/or valve guides are in need of attention. Make sure that oil leaks are not responsible before deciding that the rings and/or guides are worn. Perform a compression test to determine the likely cause of the problem.
9 Check the oil pressure with a gauge fitted in place of the oil pressure switch, and compare it with that specified in Part A, B or C of this Chapter. If it is extremely low, the main and big-end bearings, and/or the oil pump, are probably worn out.
10 Loss of power, rough running, knocking or metallic engine noises, excessive valve gear noise, and high fuel consumption may also point to the need for an overhaul, especially if they are all present at the same time. If a complete service does not remedy the situation, major mechanical work is the only solution.
11 An engine overhaul involves restoring all internal parts to the specification of a new engine. During an overhaul, the cylinder bores are rebored (where possible) and the pistons and piston rings are renewed. New main and big-end bearings are generally fitted; if

necessary, the crankshaft may be reground, to restore the journals. The valves are also serviced as well, since they are usually in less-than-perfect condition at this point. The end result should be an as-new engine that will give many trouble-free miles.

Note: *Critical cooling system components such as the hoses, thermostat and coolant pump should be renewed when an engine is overhauled. The radiator should be checked carefully, to ensure that it is not clogged or leaking. Also, it is a good idea to renew the oil pump whenever the engine is overhauled.*

12 Before beginning the engine overhaul, read through the entire procedure, to familiarise yourself with the scope and requirements of the job. Check on the availability of parts, and make sure that any necessary special tools and equipment are obtained in advance. Most work can be done with typical hand tools, although a number of precision measuring tools are required for inspecting parts to determine if they must be renewed.

13 The services provided by an engineering machine shop or engine reconditioning specialist will almost certainly be required, particularly if major repairs such as crankshaft regrinding or cylinder reboring are necessary. Apart from carrying out machining operations, these establishments will normally handle the inspection of parts; offer advice concerning reconditioning or renewal and supply new components such as pistons, piston rings and bearing shells. It is recommended that the establishment used is a member of the Federation of Engine Re-Manufacturers, or a similar society.

14 Always wait until the engine has been completely dismantled, and until all components (especially the cylinder block and the crankshaft) have been inspected, before deciding what service and repair operations must be performed by an automotive engineering works. The condition of these components will be the major factor to consider when determining whether to overhaul the original engine, or to buy a reconditioned unit. Do not, therefore, purchase parts or have overhaul work done on other components until they have been thoroughly inspected.

15 As a final note, to ensure maximum life and minimum trouble from a reconditioned engine, everything must be assembled with care, in a spotlessly-clean environment.

2 Compression and leakdown test – description and testing

1 When engine performance is down, or if misfiring occurs which cannot be attributed to the ignition or fuel systems, a compression test can provide diagnostic clues as to the engine's condition. If the test is performed regularly, it can give warning of trouble before any other symptoms become apparent.

2 The engine must be fully warmed-up to normal operating temperature, the battery must be fully charged, and the aid of an assistant will also be required.

3 Depressurise the fuel system by removing the fuel pump fuse from the fusebox – the fuses can usually be identified from the label inside the fusebox cover, or from the wiring diagrams at the end of this manual. With the fuse removed, start the engine, and allow it to run until it stalls. Try to start the engine at least twice more, to ensure that all residual pressure has been relieved.

Petrol engines

4 Remove the spark plugs as described in Chapter 1A Section 30.

5 Fit a compression tester to the No 1 cylinder spark plug hole – the type of tester which screws into the plug thread is to be preferred.

6 Have the assistant hold the throttle wide open, and crank the engine on the starter motor; after two or three revolutions, the compression pressure should build-up to a maximum figure, and then stabilise. Record the highest reading obtained.

7 Repeat the test on the remaining cylinders, recording the pressure in each.

8 All cylinders should produce very similar pressures in the order of 10 to 15 bars. Any one cylinder reading below 7 bars, or a difference of more than 3 bars between cylinders suggests a fault. Note that the compression should build-up quickly in a healthy engine; low compression on the first stroke, followed by gradually increasing pressure on successive strokes, indicates worn piston rings. A low compression reading on the first stroke, which does not build-up during successive strokes, indicates leaking valves or a blown head gasket (a cracked head could also be the cause). Deposits on the undersides of the valve heads can also cause low compression.

9 If the pressure in any cylinder is reduced to 10 bars or less, carry out the following test to isolate the cause. Introduce a teaspoonful of clean oil into that cylinder through its spark plug hole and repeat the test.

10 If the addition of oil temporarily improves the compression pressure, this indicates that bore or piston wear is responsible for the pressure loss. No improvement suggests that leaking or burnt valves, or a blown head gasket, may be to blame.

11 A low reading from two adjacent cylinders is almost certainly due to the head gasket having blown between them; the presence of coolant in the engine oil will confirm this.

12 If one cylinder is about 20 percent lower than the others and the engine has a slightly rough idle; a worn camshaft lobe could be the cause.

13 On completion of the test, refit the spark plugs and fuel pump fuse.

Diesel engines

Note: *A compression tester specifically designed for diesel engines must be used for this test.*

14 A compression tester is connected to an adaptor that screws into the glow plug hole. It is unlikely to be worthwhile buying such a tester for occasional use, but it may be possible to borrow or hire one – if not, have the test performed by a garage.

15 Unless specific instructions to the contrary are supplied with the tester, observe the following points:

a) *The battery must be in a good state of charge, the air filter must be clean and the engine should be at normal operating temperature.*

b) *All the glow plugs must be removed (see Chapter 6B Section 19) before starting the test and the wiring disconnected from the injectors.*

16 There is no need to hold the accelerator pedal down during the test because the diesel engine air inlet is not throttled.

17 The actual compression pressures measured are not so important as the balance between cylinders. Values are given in the Specifications.

18 The cause of poor compression is less easy to establish on a diesel engine than on a petrol one. The effect of introducing oil into the cylinders ('wet' testing) is not conclusive, because there is a risk that the oil will sit in the swirl chamber or in the recess on the piston crown instead of passing to the rings. However, the following can be used as a rough guide to diagnosis.

19 All cylinders should produce very similar pressures; any difference greater than that specified indicates the existence of a fault. Note that the compression should build-up quickly in a healthy engine; low compression on the first stroke, followed by gradually increasing pressure on successive strokes, indicates worn piston rings. A low compression reading on the first stroke, which does not build-up during successive strokes, indicates leaking valves or a blown head gasket (a cracked head could also be the cause).

20 A low reading from two adjacent cylinders is almost certainly due to the head gasket having blown between them.

Leakdown test

21 A leakdown test measures the rate at which compressed air fed into the cylinder is lost. It is an alternative to a compression test and in many ways it is better, since the escaping air provides easy identification of where pressure loss is occurring (piston rings, valves or head gasket).

22 The equipment needed for leakdown testing is unlikely to be available to the home mechanic. If poor compression is suspected, have the test performed by a suitably equipped garage.

3 Engine removal – methods and precautions

1 If you have decided that the engine must be removed for overhaul or major repair work, several preliminary steps should be taken.

2 Locating a suitable place to work is extremely important. Adequate workspace, along with storage space for the vehicle, will be needed. If a workshop or garage is not available, at the very least, a flat, level, clean work surface is required.

3 Cleaning the engine compartment and engine/transmission before beginning the removal procedure will help keep tools clean and organised.

4 An engine hoist will also be necessary. Make sure the equipment is rated in excess of the combined weight of the engine and transmission. Safety is of primary importance, considering the potential hazards involved in removing the engine/transmission from the vehicle.

5 The help of an assistant is essential. Apart from the safety aspects involved, there are many instances when one person cannot simultaneously perform all of the operations required during engine/transmission removal. Plan the operation ahead of time. Before starting work, arrange for the hire of, or obtain, all of the tools and equipment you will need. Some of the equipment necessary to perform engine/transmission removal and installation safely (in addition to an engine hoist) is as follows: a heavy-duty trolley jack, complete sets of spanners and sockets as described at the rear of this manual, wooden blocks, and plenty of rags and cleaning solvent for mopping-up spilled oil, coolant and fuel. If the hoist must be hired, make sure that you arrange for it in advance, and perform all of the operations possible without it beforehand. This will save you money and time.

7 Plan for the vehicle to be out of use for quite a while. An engineering machine shop or engine reconditioning specialist will be required to perform some of the work, which cannot be accomplished without special equipment. These places often have a busy schedule, so it would be a good idea to consult them before removing the engine, in order to accurately estimate the amount of time required to rebuild or repair components that may need work.

8 During the engine/transmission removal procedure, it is advisable to make notes of the locations of all brackets, cable ties, earthing points, etc, as well as how the wiring harnesses, hoses and electrical connections are attached and routed around the engine and engine compartment. An effective way of doing this is to take a series of photographs of the various components before they are disconnected or removed. The resulting photographs will prove invaluable when the engine is refitted.

9 Always be extremely careful when removing and refitting the engine/transmission. Serious injury can result from careless actions. Plan ahead and take your time, and a job of this nature, although major, can be accomplished successfully.

4 Engine and manual transmission – removal, separation, reconnection and refitting

Note: *The engine can be removed from the car only as a complete unit with the transmission; the two are then separated for overhaul. The engine/transmission unit is lowered out of position, and withdrawn from under the vehicle. Allow adequate clearance for the removal of the engine, between the front bumper and the ground when the vehicle is raised and supported. However, if preferred, the transmission can be removed from the engine first (as described in Chapter 7 Section 6) – this leaves the engine free to be either lifted out from above or lowered to the ground.*

Removal

1 On petrol engine models, release the pressure in the fuel system as described in Chapter 4A Section 4. On diesel engine models, release the fuel system residual pressure by unscrewing the fuel filler cap.

2 With reference to Chapter 5 Section 4 disconnect the battery negative terminal, then remove the battery and battery tray.

3 Firmly apply the handbrake, then jack up the front of the vehicle and support it securely on axle stands (see *Jacking and vehicle support*), bearing in mind the note at the start of this Section, about the height required. Remove both front roadwheels.

4 Remove the front wheel arch liner on the left-hand and right-hand side as described in Chapter 11 Section 20.

5 Drain the cooling system as described in Chapter 1A Section 33 for petrol engines, or Chapter 1B Section 32 for diesel engines. Save the coolant in a clean container, if it is fit for re-use.

6 Drain the transmission oil as described in Chapter 7 Section 2. Refit the drain and filler plugs using new sealing washers where required.

7 If the engine is to be dismantled, working as described in Chapter 1A Section 13, for petrol engines, or Chapter 1B Section 13 for diesel engines, drain the oil and if required remove the oil filter. Clean and refit the drain plug, tightening it to the specified torque, fit new sealing washers where required.

8 Remove both driveshafts as described in Chapter 8 Section 8.

9 Working around the engine, disconnect the wiring connectors from the alternator, starter motor, oil pressure switch, oil level switch, knock sensor, crankshaft sensor etc... depending on model. If necessary label the connectors as they are unplugged.

10 Similarly, working around the engine and engine compartment, disconnect all vacuum hoses likely to impede engine/transmission removal.

a) *Remove the air cleaner assembly and air inlet ducts.*

b) *Disconnect the fuel feed and return hoses from the fuel rail (plug all openings, to prevent loss of fuel and entry of dirt into the fuel system).*

c) *Disconnect the relevant electrical connectors from the throttle housing, inlet manifold and associated components. Free the wiring from the manifold, and position it clear of the cylinder head so that it does not hinder removal.*

d) *Disconnect the vacuum servo unit hose, coolant hose(s), and all the other relevant/ breather hoses from the manifold and associated valves.*

e) *On petrol engine models, remove the inlet manifold.*

f) *Disconnect or remove the exhaust front pipe.*

11 Slacken the retaining clips, and disconnect the heater hoses and all other relevant cooling system hoses from the engine, noting each hose's correct fitted location.

12 Remove the radiator assembly, as described in Chapter 3 Section 5.

13 Unbolt the air conditioning compressor and position it clear of the engine. Support the weight of the compressor by tying it to the vehicle body, to prevent any excess strain being placed on the compressor lines whilst the engine is removed. **Do not** disconnect the refrigerant lines from the compressor.

14 Be prepared for some fluid loss as the pipe is disconnected, place some cloth around the fitting. Depress the retaining spring clip and disconnect the clutch fluid hose from the slave cylinder connector pipe. Plug the ends of the slave cylinder pipe and clutch fluid hose to prevent fluid leakage and dirt ingress.

15 Working as described in Chapter 7 Section 3, disconnect the gear linkage cables from the operating levers on the transmission.

16 Note their fitted positions and harness routing, then disconnect all wiring plugs from the transmission. If necessary label the connectors as they are unplugged.

17 Manoeuvre the engine hoist into position, and attach it to the engine/transmission using suitable lifting brackets. Raise the hoist until it is supporting the weight of the engine/ transmission.

18 Mark the outline of the front engine/ transmission mounting bracket bolts to use as a guide on refitting. Slacken and remove the bolts/nut and remove both right- and left-hand side mountings from the inner wing panels, as described in Chapter 2A, Chapter 2B or Chapter 2C as applicable.

19 Make a final check that any components, which would prevent the removal of the engine/transmission from the car, have been removed or disconnected. Ensure that components such as the gearchange cables are secured so that they cannot be damaged on removal.

20 Manoeuvre the assembly out through the front of the vehicle, taking care not to damage any components.

Separation

21 Unscrew the retaining bolts, and remove the starter motor from the transmission.

22 Ensure that both engine and transmission are adequately supported, then slacken and remove the bolts securing the transmission housing to the engine. Note the correct fitted positions of each bolt (and, where fitted, the relevant brackets) as they are removed, to use as a reference on refitting.

23 Carefully withdraw the transmission from the engine, ensuring that the weight of the transmission is not allowed to hang on the input shaft while it is engaged with the clutch friction disc.

24 If they are loose, remove the locating dowels from the engine or transmission, and keep them in a safe place.

Reconnection

25 Apply a smear of high melting-point grease to the splines of the transmission input shaft. Do not apply too much; otherwise there is a possibility of the grease contaminating the clutch friction disc.

26 Carefully offer the transmission to the engine, until the locating dowels are engaged. Ensure that the weight of the transmission is not allowed to hang on the input shaft as it is engaged with the clutch friction disc.

27 Refit the transmission housing-to-engine bolts, ensuring that all the necessary brackets are correctly positioned, and tighten them to the specified torque setting.

28 Refit the starter motor and tighten the retaining bolts.

Refitting

29 Position the engine/transmission assembly under the vehicle, then reconnect the hoist and lifting tackle to the engine lifting brackets.

30 Lift the assembly up into the engine compartment; making sure that it clears the surrounding components.

31 Refit the left-hand engine/transmission mounting bracket, ensuring that it is correctly

6.4 Remove the coolant pump pulley

seated in position. Manoeuvre the mounting into position, then fit the bolts securing it to the transmission and tighten them to the specified torque setting. Insert the through-bolt and nut, tightening it by hand only at this stage.

32 Fit the right-hand body mounting bracket, ensuring that it is correctly seated in position. Refit the mounting to the top of its bracket, and tighten its retaining bolts to the specified torque setting.

33 The remainder of the refitting procedure is a direct reversal of the removal sequence, noting the following points:

a) Ensuring that the wiring harness is correctly routed and retained by all the relevant retaining clips, and all connectors are correctly and securely reconnected.

b) Prior to refitting the driveshafts to the transmission, renew the driveshaft oil seals as described in Chapter 8 Section 8.

c) Ensure that all coolant hoses are correctly reconnected and securely retained by their retaining clips.

d) Refill the engine and transmission unit with correct quantity and type of lubricant, as described in the relevant Sections of Chapter 1A or Chapter 1B.

e) Refill the cooling system as described in Chapter 1A Section 33 or Chapter 1B Section 32.

f) On diesel engine models, prime and bleed the fuel system as described in Chapter 4B Section 6.

g) On completion, start the engine and check for leaks.

5 Engine overhaul – dismantling sequence

1 It is preferable to dismantle and work on the engine with it mounted on a portable engine stand. These stands can often be hired from a tool hire shop. Before the engine is mounted on a stand, the flywheel should be removed, so that the stand bolts can be tightened into the end of the cylinder block/crankcase.

2 If a stand is not available, it is possible to dismantle the engine with it blocked up on a sturdy workbench, or on the floor. Be extra careful not to tip or drop the engine when working without a stand.

3 If a reconditioned engine is to be obtained, or if the original engine is to be overhauled, the external components in the following list must be removed first. These components can then be transferred to the reconditioned engine, or refitted to the existing engine after overhaul.

a) Alternator and air conditioning compressor mounting brackets (as applicable).

b) Coolant pump and thermostat/coolant outlet housings (Chapter 3).

c) Fuel system components (Chapter 4A or Chapter 4B).

d) All electrical switches and sensors, and the engine wiring harness.

e) Inlet and exhaust manifolds (Chapter 4A or Chapter 4B).

f) Engine mountings (Chapter 2A, Chapter 2B or Chapter 2C).

g) Flywheel (Chapter 2A, Chapter 2B or Chapter 2C).

Note: When removing the external components from the engine, pay close attention to details that may be helpful or important during refitting. Note the fitted position of gaskets, seals, spacers, pins, washers, bolts, and other small items.

4 If a 'short' engine is to be obtained (cylinder block, crankshaft, pistons and connecting rods all assembled), then the cylinder head, sump, oil pump, and timing chain/belt will have to be removed also.

5 If a complete overhaul of the existing engine is being undertaken, the engine can be dismantled, in the order given below, referring to Chapter 2A, Chapter 2B or Chapter 2C, unless otherwise stated.

a) Inlet and exhaust manifolds (Chapter 4A or Chapter 4B).

b) Timing chain/belt and sprockets (on 1.2 litre petrol engines, see Section 8 of this Chapter). (On 1.6 litre diesel engines, see Section 9 of this Chapter).

c) Cylinder head (on petrol engines and diesel engines, see Section 12 and Section 13 of this Chapter respectively).

d) Sump.

e) Oil pump (on 1.2 litre petrol engines, see Section 14 of this Chapter), (On 1.6 litre diesel engines, see Section 15 of this Chapter).

f) Flywheel.

g) Piston/connecting rod assemblies (see Section 16 of this Chapter).

h) Crankshaft (see Section 17 of this Chapter).

6 Before beginning the dismantling and overhaul procedures, make sure that you have all of the correct tools necessary. Refer to Tools and working facilities for further information.

6 Timing chain cover (1.2 litre petrol engines) – removal and refitting

Removal

1 With the engine removed from the car, drain the engine oil, then clean and refit the engine oil drain plug using a new sealing washer, tightening it to the specified torque. If the engine is nearing its service interval when the oil and filter are due for renewal, it is recommended that the filter is also removed, and a new one fitted. After reassembly, the engine can then be refilled with fresh oil. Refer to Chapter 1A Section 13 for further information.

2 Remove the cylinder head cover as described in Chapter 2A Section 2.

3 Remove the crankshaft pulley as described in Chapter 2A Section 3.

4 Undo the three retaining bolts and remove the coolant pump pulley (see illustration).

6.5 Remove the idler roller bolt

6.7 Removing the exhaust camshaft dephaser oil cover

6.12 Fit new seal/gasket

5 Remove the cap then undo the retaining bolt and remove the auxiliary drivebelt idler roller (see illustration).

6 Disconnect the wiring connector, then undo the retaining bolt and remove the inlet valve timing control solenoid from the front facing side of the timing cover. Remove the exhaust timing control solenoid from the rear facing side of the timing cover in the same way (see Chapter 4A Section 9).

7 Undo the bolts and remove the inlet and exhaust camshaft dephaser oil covers from the timing chain cover (see illustration). Recover the O-ring seals from the cover and discard, as new ones will be required on refitting.

8 Working in the **reverse** of the tightening sequence (see illustration 5.16), slacken and remove the timing chain cover retaining bolts. Note the correct fitted location of each bolt, as some of the bolts are different lengths and different diameters.

9 The timing chain cover has been fitted using a liquid gasket, and is bonded to the engine block/cylinder head. Taking care not to damage the timing chain cover work your way around the outside of the cover to release it from the engine.

Refitting

10 Prior to refitting the cover, it is recommended that the crankshaft oil seal should be renewed. Note the seals fitted position and the carefully lever the old seal out of the cover using a large flat-bladed screwdriver. Fit the new seal to the cover, making sure its sealing lip is facing inwards. Drive the seal into position until it seats squarely in the position noted on removal, for further information see Chapter 2A Section 6.

11 Ensure that the timing chain cover and engine cylinder block/cylinder head mating surfaces are clean/dry and free from any silicone sealer. Clean the steel dowels on the cylinder block, and apply a small amount of oil to aid fitting.

12 Fit the new cover rubber seal/gasket to the inside of the timing chain cover (see illustration).

13 Apply a thin bead of suitable sealant (3 mm to 4 mm diameter) to the timing chain cover surface, not forgetting to apply sealant

6.13 Apply a bead of sealant around the outside of the cover

to the area around the passages in the upper centre of the cover (see illustration).

14 Also apply a small amount of sealant to where the cylinder block joins the cylinder head, and where the cylinder block joins the upper sump housing (see illustration).

15 Manoeuvre the cover into position over

6.14 Apply sealant to the joints at both sides of the cylinder block

the end of the crankshaft, taking great care not to damage the oil seal lip.

16 Make sure the cover is correctly seated, and then install the retaining bolts. Working in sequence, tighten all the cover bolts to the specified torque (see illustration).

17 Refit the auxiliary drive belt idler pulley,

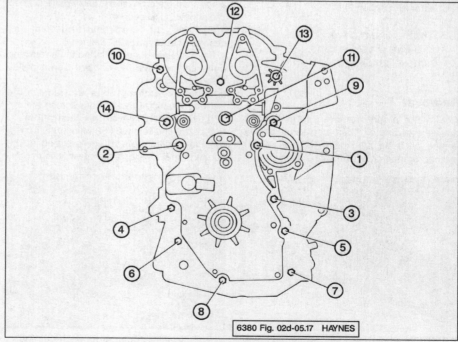
6.16 Tightening sequence for timing chain cover bolts

7.4 Remove the coolant pump pulley

7.5 Remove the engine mounting bracket

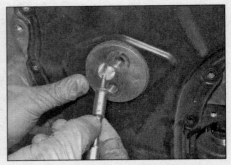

7.6 Remove the bolt from the alloy spacer

7.7a Tool for cutting sealant

7.7b Tapping tool to release the sealant

need to be removed **(see illustration)**. The alloy spacer will be removed with the timing chain cover.

7 The timing chain cover has been fitted using a liquid gasket, and is bonded to the engine block/cylinder head. Taking care not to damage the timing chain cover work your way around the outside of the cover to release it from the engine. Nissan tool KV10111100 is used to cut the sealant from around the cover, taking care not to damage or distort the timing chain cover **(see illustrations)**.

Refitting

8 Ensure that the timing chain cover and engine cylinder block/cylinder head mating surfaces are clean/dry and free from any silicone sealer. Clean the steel dowels on the cylinder block, and apply a small amount of oil to the dowels to aid fitting.

9 Apply a thin bead of suitable sealant (5 mm to 8 mm diameter) to the timing chain cover surface, not forgetting to apply sealant to the area around the centre of the cylinder head (2 mm to 3 mm diameter), where the alloy spacer fits **(see illustrations)**.

10 Also apply an extra small amount of sealant to where the cylinder block joins the cylinder head, and where the cylinder block joins the upper sump housing**(see illustration)**.

11 Insert two studs and manoeuvre the cover into position over the end of the crankshaft **(see illustrations)**.

12 Make sure the cover is correctly seated, and then install the retaining bolts. Working

tighten the retaining bolt and fit the plastic cap.

18 Refit the coolant pump pulley and tighten the three retaining bolts.

19 Refit the crankshaft pulley as described in Chapter 2A Section 3.

20 Refit the cylinder head cover as described in Chapter 2A Section 2.

7 Timing chain cover (1.6 litre diesel engines) – removal and refitting

Removal

1 With the engine removed from the car, drain the engine oil, then clean and refit the engine oil drain plug using a new sealing washer, tightening it to the specified torque.

If the engine is nearing its service interval when the oil and filter are due for renewal, it is recommended that the filter is also removed, and a new one fitted. After reassembly, the engine can then be refilled with fresh oil. Refer to Chapter 1B Section 13 for further information.

2 Remove the crankshaft pulley as described in Chapter 2C Section 4.

3 Remove the crankshaft oil seal, as described in Chapter 2C Section 6.

4 If not already done, undo the three retaining bolts and remove the coolant pump pulley **(see illustration)**.

5 Undo the retaining bolts and remove the engine mounting bracket from across the top of the timing chain cover **(see illustration)**.

6 Slacken and remove the timing chain cover retaining bolts. Note, there is a bolt at the centre of the cover in the alloy spacer, this will

7.9a Apply sealant around the timing cover

7.9b Sealant application for the timing cover

7.10 Apply a small amount of sealant (cylinder block to sump shown)

7.11a Manoeuvre the cover into position...

7.11b ... aligning the two dowels (one at each side)

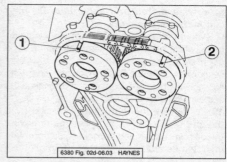

8.3 Position the timing marks (1 and 2) as shown

in an anti-clockwise direction, start from the lowest bolt and work your way around the timing chain cover to tighten all the cover bolts to the stage 1, specified torque (see specifications in Chapter 2C).

13 Following the previous sequence tighten all the cover bolts to the stage 2, specified torque.

14 Refit the engine mounting bracket and tighten the retaining bolts.

15 Refit the coolant pump pulley and tighten the three retaining bolts.

16 Refit the crankshaft oil seal, as described in Chapter 2C Section 6.

17 Refit the crankshaft pulley, as described in Chapter 2C Section 4.

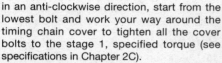

8 Timing chain, tensioner, guides and sprockets (1.2 litre petrol engines) – removal, inspection and refitting

Removal

1 Remove the cylinder head cover as described in Chapter 2A Section 2.

2 Remove the timing chain cover as described in Section 6 of this Chapter.

3 Set the engine at the TDC (Top Dead Centre) position for Nos 1 and 4 pistons as follows. Temporarily refit the crankshaft pulley to enable the engine to be turned. Using a socket or spanner on the crankshaft pulley bolt, turn the crankshaft until the timing marks (peripheral grooves) on the camshaft sprockets are positioned at 12 o'clock (exhaust camshaft) and 1 o'clock (inlet camshaft) **(see illustration)**. With the camshafts correctly positioned, remove the crankshaft pulley once more.

4 Whilst holding down the tensioner lever, push the tensioner plunger back into its body. With the plunger retracted, align the hole in the lever with the hole in the tensioner body and hold it in position by inserting a small-diameter rod through the plate hole and into the body of the tensioner **(see illustrations)**.

5 Undo the two retaining bolts, and remove the tensioner from the end of the cylinder block. Keep the rod inserted into the tensioner to prevent the plunger from springing out **(see illustrations)**.

6 Release the upper pivot point of the chain

tensioner guide, and remove it from the rear of the crankcase **(see illustration)**.

7 Unscrew the two mounting bolts, and remove the chain front guide from the crankcase.

8 Disengage the timing chain from the

8.4a Push the tensioner lever down...

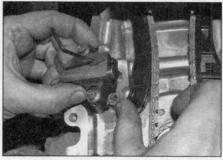

8.5a Undo the retaining bolts and remove the tensioner...

8.6 Release the upper pivot point and remove the tensioner guide

crankshaft sprocket, and manoeuvre it out from the engine **(see illustration)**.

⚠️ *Warning: Do not turn the crankshaft or camshafts while the timing chain is removed,*

8.4b ...and insert a locking pin through the tensioner

8.5b ...keeping the locking pin in place

8.8 Disengage the timing chain from the crankshaft sprocket

otherwise piston and valve contact may occur causing damage.

9 Slacken the camshaft sprocket retaining bolts, whilst retaining the camshaft with a large open-ended spanner fitted to the hexagonal section of each shaft. Remove the bolt along with its washer (where applicable), then disengage the sprocket from the end of its camshaft.

10 To remove the crankshaft sprocket from the end of the crankshaft, requires removing the oil pump chain and sprocket as a complete unit. See Section 14 for further information.

Inspection

11 Examine the teeth on the camshaft and crankshaft sprockets for any sign of wear or damage such as chipped, hooked or missing teeth. If there is any sign of wear or damage on either sprockets or timing chain then they should be renewed as a set.

12 Inspect the links of the timing chain for signs of wear or damage on the rollers. The extent of wear can be judged by checking the amount by which the chain can be bent sideways; a new chain will have very little sideways movement. If there is an excessive amount of side play in either timing chain, it must be renewed.

13 Note that it is a sensible precaution to renew the timing chain, regardless of apparent condition, if the engine has covered a high mileage, or if it has been noted that the chain has sounded noisy when the engine running.

Although not strictly necessary, it is always worth renewing the chain and sprockets as a matched set, since it is false economy to run a new chain on worn sprockets and *vice versa*. If there is any doubt about the condition of the timing chain and sprockets, seek the advice of a Nissan dealer service department, who will be able to advise you as to the best course of action.

14 Examine the chain guides for signs of wear or damage to their chain contact faces, renewing any which are badly marked.

15 Check the chain tensioner for signs of wear, and check that the plunger is free to slide freely in the tensioner body. The condition of the tensioner spring can only be judged in comparison to a new component. Renew the tensioner if it is worn or there is any doubt about the condition of its tensioning spring.

Refitting

16 Check the crankshaft is still positioned at TDC (the keyway will be in the 12 o'clock position, seen from the right-hand end of the engine).

17 Refit the sprockets to the camshafts engaging the lug on each sprocket with the slot on the camshaft. Refit the sprocket retaining bolts and tighten them to the specified torque. Retain the camshafts whilst tightening the bolts with a large open-ended spanner as used on removal.

18 Check that the camshafts are still in the TDC position **(see illustration 6.3)**.

19 Manoeuvre the chain into position, engaging it with the crankshaft sprocket so that its coloured link is aligned with the timing mark on the crankshaft sprocket. Engage the

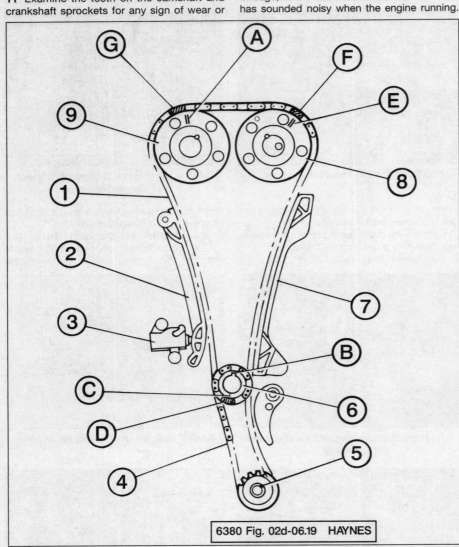

6380 Fig. 02d-06.19   HAYNES

8.19a Camshaft sprocket and timing chain timing mark relationship

1 Timing chain	*8 Inlet camshaft sprocket*	*C Crankshaft sprocket*
2 Chain tensioner guide	*9 Exhaust camshaft*	*timing mark*
3 Chain tensioner	*sprocket*	*D Coloured link*
4 Oil pump drive chain	*A Timing mark (peripheral*	*E Timing mark (peripheral*
5 Oil pump sprocket	*groove)*	*groove)*
6 Crankshaft sprocket	*B Crankshaft sprocket*	*F Coloured link*
7 Timing chain front guide	*keyway*	*G Coloured link*

8.19b Two coloured links lined up with grooves on camshaft sprockets. . .

8.19c . . . and coloured link lined up with arrow on crankshaft sprocket

chain with the camshaft sprockets, aligning the two dark chain links with the timing marks on the sprockets **(see illustrations)**.

20 Fit the chain front fixed guide to the cylinder block, and tighten its retaining bolts to the specified torque.

21 Fit the chain rear tensioner guide to the upper pivot point and locate it in position.

22 Fit the chain tensioner to the cylinder block, and tighten its retaining bolts to the specified torque. Whilst holding the guide against the tensioner plunger, withdraw the rod, and check that the tensioner plunger is forced out against the guide to take up the slack in the chain **(see illustration)**.

23 Check that all the timing marks are still correctly aligned with the chain links. If all timing marks are aligned, fit the crankshaft pulley and turn the engine two complete turns, and check the timing marks on the sprockets are all re-aligned.

Note: *The coloured links on the chain will not be re-aligned with the marks on the sprockets. The coloured links are just for the initial set up, and will take many turns before they will line up again, with the marks on the sprockets.*

24 Refit the timing chain cover as described in Section 6.

> **9 Timing chain, tensioner, guides and sprockets (1.6 litre diesel engines) –** removal, inspection and refitting

Note: *Removal of the engine from the car is necessary in order to carry out the*

8.22 Hold pressure against the tensioner and remove the locking pin

procedure in this Section. Also, special Nissan tool Mot. 1970 is required to set the engine to TDC, and tool Mot. 1969 to tighten the exhaust camshaft sprocket bolts. When renewing the timing chain, Nissan recommend renewal of the sprockets, guides and the hydraulic tensioner at the same time.

1 Specialist tools for this procedure are also available from automotive tool specialists **(see illustration)**.

Removal

2 Remove the timing chain cover as described in Section 7 of this Chapter.

3 Remove the starter motor, as described in Chapter 5 Section 10.

4 Unscrew the TDC plug/bolt from the front of the cylinder block and insert Nissan TDC tool Mot. 1970, tightening it securely **(see illustration)**.

9.1 AST engine setting locking kit

5 Turn the crankshaft **clockwise** until it just contacts the TDC tool. The engine is now set with No 1 piston at TDC on its compression stroke.

6 Make marks on the sprockets and cylinder head cover, the hole in the exhaust sprocket should be at 11 o'clock and the line on the inlet sprocket should be at 11 o'clock **(see illustration)**.

7 In this position the keyway slot in the crankshaft should be at 12 o'clock **(see illustration)**.

8 Slacken the three bolts in the exhaust camshaft sprocket **(see illustration)**.

9 Compress the timing chain hydraulic tensioner piston by pressing the guide, then lock it by inserting a 3.0 mm diameter Allen key or pin in the hole provided **(see illustration)**.

10 Unscrew the bolts and remove the tensioner **(see illustration)**.

9.4 Insert the TDC locking tool

9.6 Make alignment marks

9.7 Slot in crankshaft at 12 o'clock

9.8 Slacken the three sprocket bolts

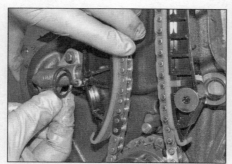

9.9 Locking the hydraulic tensioner piston in its retracted position with a 3.0 mm rod

9.10 Removing the hydraulic tensioner

9.11 Unscrew the bolt and remove the tensioner guide

9.12a Remove the bolts and special washer. . .

9.12b . . . and withdraw the sprocket and chain from the exhaust camshaft

9.13 Removing the timing chain sprocket from the nose of the crankshaft

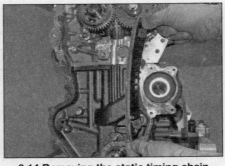

9.14 Removing the static timing chain guide

9.16 Locking the backlash mechanism in the inlet camshaft gear

11 Unscrew the single bolt at the top and remove the tensioner guide **(see illustration)**.
12 Completely remove the three exhaust camshaft sprocket bolts, remove the special washer and withdraw the sprocket and chain from the camshaft. Release the timing chain from the crankshaft sprocket as it is removed **(see illustrations)**.
13 Withdraw the sprocket from the nose of the crankshaft **(see illustration)**.
14 Unbolt and remove the static timing chain guide **(see illustration)**.
15 Unscrew and remove the TDC tool from the front of the cylinder block.
16 If required the exhaust and inlet camshaft gears can be removed from the ends of the camshafts, before they are removed the inlet camshaft gear will need to be locked in position as it has two rows of teeth to take up any backlash in the gears. Align the teeth

and insert a 4mm peg to lock the gears **(see illustration)**.
17 If the gears do not need to be removed, refit one of the bolts (with some washers), to the exhaust camshaft gear to prevent it coming off the camshaft and causing the inlet gear backlash mechanism to turn **(see illustration)**.

Inspection

18 Thoroughly clean then visually inspect all parts for wear and damage. Check the timing chain for loose pins, cracks, worn rollers and side plates. Check the sprockets for hook-shaped, chipped and broken teeth. Also check the timing chain for wear by extending it horizontally, holding each end and attempting to flex the chain. Renew the timing chain and sprockets as a set if the engine has high mileage or fails inspection.

Check the chain guides for excessive wear and scoring and renew them if necessary. Note that some scoring is normal but if they are deeply grooved they must be renewed.

Refitting

19 Carefully clean the surfaces of the timing cover, cylinder block and cylinder head, taking care not to damage the surfaces.
20 Check that the engine is still set to its TDC position as described in Chapter 2C Section 2 using the TDC setting tool Mot 1970.
21 The timing mark on the inlet camshaft timing gear should still be at 12 o'clock and the groove on the exhaust camshaft is horizontal with the larger offset uppermost.
22 Refit the static timing chain guide and tighten the bolts to the specified torque.
23 If removed, refit the crankshaft sprocket to the end of the crankshaft.
24 Locate the timing chain on the crankshaft sprocket so that the copper link is aligned with the timing mark. Raise the chain to keep it engaged with the crankshaft sprocket while locating the exhaust camshaft sprocket in the upper loop so that the two copper link aligns with the TDC hole in the sprocket **(see illustrations)**.
Note: *A new timing chain may be fitted either way round, however a re-used chain should be fitted in its original position as noted during removal.*
25 Fit the exhaust camshaft sprocket onto its timing gear, then locate the new special washer and bolts and finger-tighten the bolts at this stage. The sprocket must be free to rotate within the elongated holes **(see illustration)**.

9.17 Fit bolts with washers to secure gear

9.24a Align the copper link with the TDC mark on the crankshaft sprocket. . .

9.24b . . . then fit the exhaust camshaft sprocket with the copper link aligned with the TDC hole

9.25 Fit the bolts finger tight at this point

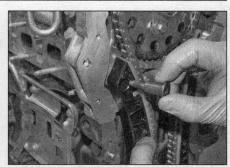

9.26 Apply thread lock to the guide bolt

26 Locate the tensioner guide in position and tighten the single bolt **(see illustration)**.

27 Refit the hydraulic tensioner together with locking pin, insert the bolts and tighten to the specified torque. Make sure the tensioner is in contact with the cylinder block before tightening the bolts **(see illustration)**.

28 Apply some pressure to the tensioner guide, then remove the locking pin to allow the tensioner piston to tension the timing chain **(see illustration)**.

29 At this stage Nissan tool Mot. 1969 is required to hold the gears and sprocket in position while the exhaust sprocket bolts are tightened. Engage the tool with the slot on the end of the exhaust camshaft then turn the tool until it is possible to locate the dowels in the inlet camshaft timing gear. Insert the bolt through the top of the tool and tighten into the hole in the camshaft housing **(see illustrations)**.

9.27 Fit the tensioner

30 Tighten the exhaust camshaft sprocket bolts in the two stages given in Specifications (see Chapter 2C). The special tool has a hole for access to one of the bolts **(see illustration)**.

9.28 Apply some pressure to the guide and remove the locking pin

31 Undo the retaining bolt and remove tool Mot. 1969 from the camshaft gears **(see illustration)**.

32 Remove TDC tool Mot. 1970 from the front of the cylinder block, then apply sealant

9.29a Align the dowels with the intake gear. . .

9.29b . . . with the slot in the exhaust gear. . .

9.29c . . . and fit upper bolt to hold in position

9.30 Access to camshaft sprocket bolts through tool

9.31 Remove special tool

9.32 Refitting the TDC hole plug

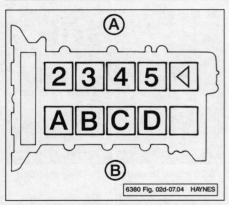

10.4 Camshaft bearing cap markings

A = Exhaust camshaft side
B = Inlet camshaft side

to the TDC hole plug and tighten it to the specified torque **(see illustration)**.

33 Refit the timing chain cover as described in Section 7.

34 Refit the crankshaft pulley as described in Chapter 2C Section 4.

35 Refit the engine and gearbox assembly as described in Section 4.

36 Refill the engine with oil as described in Chapter 1B Section 13.

10 Camshafts and followers (1.2 litre petrol engines) – removal, inspection and refitting

Removal

1 Remove the timing chain, tensioner, guides and sprockets as described in Section 8.

2 Undo the three retaining bolts and remove the closing plate from the left-hand end of the cylinder head on the inlet camshaft side. Use a screwdriver to carefully prise free the closing plate, taking great care not to damage the mating surfaces.

3 At the timing chain end of the camshafts, the bearing cap housing covers both of the camshafts. Undo the three retaining bolts and remove it from the cylinder head.

4 All remaining camshaft bearing caps, bar one, have identification markings stamped into their top surface; the exhaust camshaft

caps being marked 2 to 5 (with the cap at the left-hand end just having a triangular symbol) and the inlet camshaft caps being marked A to D (with the cap at the left-hand end having no marking). The No 2 and A caps are fitted nearest the timing chain end of the engine **(see illustration)**. Note the markings on the caps for refitting. If the caps are not marked, suitable identification marks should be made prior to removal. Using white paint or suitable marker pen, mark each cap in some way to indicate its correct fitted orientation and position. This will avoid the possibility of installing the caps in the wrong positions and/or the wrong way around on refitting.

5 Working in the **reverse** of the tightening sequence **(see illustration 7.20)**, evenly and progressively slacken the twenty remaining camshaft bearing cap retaining bolts by one turn at a time, to relieve the pressure of the valve springs on the bearing caps gradually and evenly. Once the valve spring pressure has been relieved, the bolts can be fully unscrewed and the caps removed.

6 With the bearing caps removed the inlet and exhaust camshafts can be simply lifted off the top of the cylinder head, noting their fitted position. Note that the exhaust camshaft is the longer of the two.

7 Obtain sixteen small, clean plastic containers, and number them 1 to 16. Alternatively, divide a larger container into sixteen compartments. Using a rubber sucker, withdraw each follower (valve lifter) in turn, and place it in its respective container **(see illustration)**. Do not interchange the cam followers, or the rate of wear will be increased.

8 If required, undo the retaining bolt and remove the inlet and exhaust camshaft variable valve timing control solenoids from the front of the cylinder head.

Inspection

9 Remove the plug from below each timing control solenoid and clean-out or renew the oil filter for the variable valve system.

10 Inspect the cam bearing surfaces of the head and the bearing caps. Look for score marks and deep scratches. Check the camshaft lobes for heat discoloration (blue appearance), score marks, chipped areas or flat spots.

11 Camshaft run-out can be checked by supporting each end of the camshaft on V-blocks, and measuring any run-out at the centre of the shaft using a dial gauge. If the run-out exceeds the specified limit, a new camshaft will be required.

12 Measure the height of each lobe with a micrometer **(see illustration)**, and compare the results to the figures given in the Specifications. If damage is noted or wear is excessive, new camshaft(s) must be fitted.

13 The camshaft bearing oil clearance should now be checked.

14 Fit the bearing caps to the cylinder head, using the identification markings or the marks made on removal to ensure that they are correctly positioned. Tighten the retaining bolts to the specified torque in sequence **(see illustration 7.20)**. Measure the diameter of each bearing cap journal, and compare the measurements obtained with the results given in the Specifications at the start of this Chapter. If any journal is worn beyond the service limit, the cylinder head must be renewed. The camshaft bearing oil clearance can then calculated by subtracting the camshaft bearing journal diameter from the bearing cap journal diameter.

15 Check the cam follower and cylinder head bearing surfaces for signs of wear or damage.

Refitting

16 Liberally oil the cylinder head cam follower bores and the followers. Carefully refit the followers to the cylinder head; ensuring that each follower is refitted to its original bore. Some care will be required to enter the followers squarely into their bores. Liberally oil the camshaft bearing and lobe contact surfaces.

17 Refit the inlet and exhaust camshaft to their correct locations in the cylinder head and position them so that the sprocket locating slot is at 12 o'clock for the exhaust camshaft and 1 o'clock for the inlet camshaft.

18 Ensure that the bearing cap and head mating surfaces are completely clean, unmarked and free from oil.

19 Refit the bearing caps, using the identification markings or the marks made on removal to ensure that each is installed the correct way round and in its original location.

20 Working in sequence, evenly and progressively tighten the camshaft bearing cap bolts by one turn at a time until the caps touch the cylinder head **(see illustration)**. Then go round again and tighten all the bolts to the specified torque setting. Work only as described, to impose the pressure of the valve springs gradually and evenly on the bearing caps.

21 Thoroughly clean the cylinder head closing plate and the mating surface on the cylinder head ensuring that all traces of old sealant are removed. Apply a 3 mm bead of sealant to the mating surface of the closing plate, then refit the plate to the cylinder head. Refit the retaining bolts and tighten them to the specified torque.

10.7 Remove the cam followers

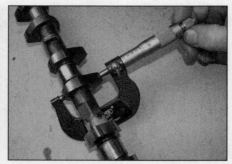

10.12 Checking the cam lobe height with a micrometer

22 Refit the timing chain, tensioner, guides and sprockets as described in Section 8.
23 If the cylinder head/camshafts have been overhauled, check the hydraulic tappets, as described in Section 13 before refitting the cylinder head cover.

11 Camshafts timing gears and followers (1.6 litre diesel engines) – removal, inspection and refitting

Note: *Removal of the engine from the car is necessary in order to carry out the procedure in this Section. Also, special Nissan tool Mot. 1969 is required to lock the camshaft gears, and tool Mot. 1773 to set the inlet camshaft timing gear automatic play compensator. The gear is in two parts, which are spring-loaded to keep the gear teeth accurately engaged.*

Removal

1 Remove the timing chain, tensioner, guides and sprockets as described in Section 9. This involves removal of the engine from the car.

Timing gears

Note: *If required, the camshaft gears can be left bolted to the ends of the camshafts.*
2 Fit tool Mot. 1969 to hold the inlet timing gear stationary, then loosen the bolt securing the timing gear to the inlet camshaft.
3 Remove the tool, then insert a screwdriver in the inlet timing gear special hole, and compress the wear compensation spring by lifting the screwdriver in order to release it from the exhaust timing gear.
4 Slide the exhaust timing gear from the exhaust camshaft extension and release the screwdriver from the inlet timing gear.
5 Completely unscrew the inlet timing gear bolt and remove the spacer followed by the timing gear.
6 Thoroughly clean then visually inspect the timing gears for wear and damage. Check for chipped and broken gear teeth and renew the gears if necessary.

Camshaft

7 If required, remove the timing gears from the end of the camshafts as described in paragraphs 2 to 6.

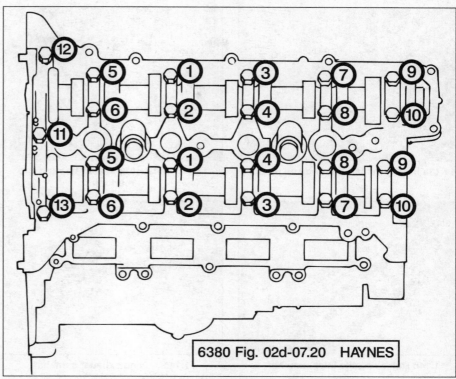

6380 Fig. 02d-07.20   HAYNES

10.20 Tighten the bearing caps in the sequence shown

A = Exhaust side   B = Inlet side

8 Remove the injector fuel return rail, the high-pressure pipes between the rail and injectors, then the injectors as described in Chapter 4B.
9 Remove the brake vacuum pump from the transmission end of the cylinder head, as described in Chapter 9 Section 13.
10 Remove the high pressure fuel pump from the transmission end of the cylinder head, as described in Chapter 4B Section 9.
11 Undo the retaining bolt and remove the camshaft position sensor from the top of the camshaft cover **(see illustration)**.
12 Progressively unscrew the camshaft housing retaining bolts in the reverse order of the tightening sequence **(see illustration 10.28)**, then carefully remove the housing complete with camshafts from the top of the

cylinder head **(see illustrations)**. If necessary, use a screwdriver and block of wood to lever the housing but take care not to damage the joint faces of the housing and cylinder head. There is no need to remove the camshaft followers and hydraulic tappets from the cylinder head.
13 With the housing upside down on the workbench, note the location of the inlet and exhaust camshafts, and the marks on the bearing caps to identify their position. The caps are marked ADM1 and ADM2 for the inlet camshaft, and ECH1 and ECH2 for the exhaust camshaft **(see illustrations)**.
14 Progressively unscrew the bolts, remove the bearing caps and lift the camshafts from the housing **(see illustrations)**.
15 If the exhaust camshaft is to be renewed,

11.11 Remove camshaft position sensor

11.12a Carefully lever...

11.12b ... the camshaft housing from the cylinder head

11.13a Inlet camshaft bearing cap marking

11.13b Exhaust camshaft bearing cap marking

11.14a Removing the camshaft bearing caps

11.14b Removing the inlet camshaft. . .

11.14c . . . and exhaust camshaft

11.15 High-pressure pump drivegear on the exhaust camshaft

remove the high-pressure pump drivegear from it as follows (see illustration). Grip the gear in a vice equipped with soft metal plates to protect the gear, then loosen the bolt, support the camshaft and fully unscrew the bolt.

Hydraulic followers

16 If required remove the hydraulic tappets and rockers from the cylinder head, have ready a container with 16 compartments and fill the container with engine oil to the depth of the tappets.
Note: *The tappets must remain immersed in oil during the period they are removed from the cylinder head to prevent air entering them.*
17 Remove each hydraulic tappet and follower assembly and place in the container

so that they can each be identified for location in the cylinder head. It is important they are each refitted to their correct bore on reassembly (see illustrations).

Inspection

18 Thoroughly clean all components taking care to remove all traces of sealant from the joint faces.
19 Examine the camshaft bearing surfaces and cam lobes for signs of wear ridges and scoring. Renew the camshaft if any of these conditions are apparent. Examine the condition of the bearing surfaces, both on the camshaft journals and in the cylinder head/bearing caps/housing. If the bearing surfaces are worn excessively, the cylinder head, camshafts and housing will need to be

renewed. Check the teeth of the high-pressure pump drivegear for wear and chipping, and if necessary renew the gear.

Refitting

20 If removed, refit the high-pressure pump drivegear by gripping it in the soft metal jawed vice, locating the camshaft from beneath, then screwing on the bolt. Tighten the bolt in the stages given in Specifications.
21 Lubricate the bearing surfaces with clean engine oil then locate the camshafts in the housing in their previously-noted positions (see illustration).
22 Refit the bearing caps, making sure they make contact with the housing before inserting the bolts finger-tight. Finally, tighten the bolts to their specified torque.

11.17a Hydraulic tappet and follower assembly in position

11.17b Removing the hydraulic tappet and follower assemblies

11.17c Keep the inlet and exhaust camshaft hydraulic tappet and follower assemblies identified for location and immersed in oil while removed from the cylinder head

11.21 Oil the bearing surfaces before fitting the camshafts

11.23 Camshafts set to their TDC positions

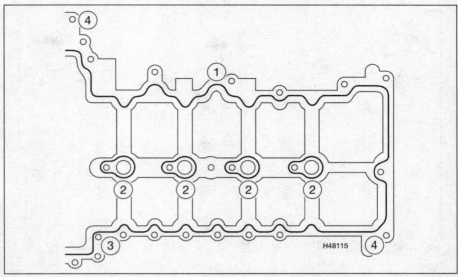

11.26a Silicone adhesive/sealant application to the cylinder head

1 Exhaust side bead
2 Central 'islands'
3 Inlet side bead
4 Locations for guide studs

23 The camshafts must now be set to their TDC positions. Temporarily place the housing on the bench in its normal position with the camshafts facing downward. Turn the exhaust camshaft as necessary so that the timing end grooves are horizontal with the larger offset uppermost. Turn the inlet camshaft as necessary so that the timing mark is at 12 o'clock and aligned with the boss on the camshaft housing **(see illustration)**.

24 If the hydraulic tappets and rockers have remained immersed in oil, no air will have entered them, however if there is any doubt, compress the piston head of the tappet and check that it does not move. If it does, the tappet may be reprimed by immersing it in clean diesel fuel. Also, check that the rocker-to-tappet clips are correctly in place.

25 Lubricate the tappet bores in the cylinder head with engine oil, then refit each hydraulic tappet and rocker assembly to its previously-noted location making sure that the rockers are correctly positioned on the valves.

26 Ensure the contact faces are clean, then apply a bead of silicone 1.5 ± 1.0 mm in diameter around the edges and central 'islands' of the cylinder head upper face. Make sure the bead runs on the inner side of the outer bolt holes **(see illustrations)**.

27 To assist in locating the camshaft housing correctly on the cylinder head, temporarily screw two M6 studs, 60 mm long in the diagonally opposite holes **(see illustration)**.

28 Set the crankshaft in its TDC position with pistons 1 and 4 at the top of their cylinders.

29 Carefully locate the camshaft housing

complete with camshafts onto the top of the cylinder head, making sure that the guide studs enter the correct holes before lowering it into position **(see illustration)**.

30 Referring to the diagram **(see illustration)** first insert then progressively tighten bolts 12, 15, 18 and 21 to the first stage, specified torque. Remove the two guide studs.

31 Insert the remaining retaining bolts and

tighten to the first stage, specified torque at this stage.

32 Completely loosen bolts 12, 15, 18 and 21, then tighten to the stage 1, specified torque.

33 Tighten the camshaft housing bolts to stage 2, specified torque in the sequence shown **(see illustration 10.28)**. Wipe away excess sealant from the outer joint face.

34 If removed, before the inlet timing gear

11.26b Apply sealant to the edges. . .

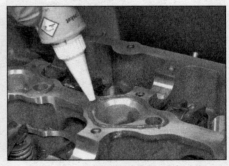

11.26c . . . and central 'islands' of the cylinder head upper face

11.27 Use two M6 studs as guides when refitting the camshaft housing

11.29 Locating the camshaft housing on the cylinder head

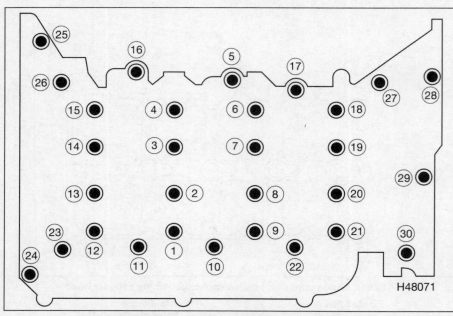

11.30 Camshaft housing bolt tightening sequence

can be refitted, the wear compensation spring must be compressed and a 4.0 mm diameter pin inserted in the special hole to lock it. Moderate force is necessary to compress the spring and it is recommended that Nissan bench tool Mot. 1773 be used to carry out the work safely, however a similar home-made tool may be used. Clamp the baseplate of the tool in a vice and locate the inlet timing gear on it making sure that the key is engaged to lock it. Now locate the tool lever on its pivot and tighten the wing nut. Engage the lever teeth with the lower wear compensation teeth and turn the lever anti-clockwise until the wear compensation teeth are aligned with the gear teeth. Lock the two gear sections in this position using a 4.0 mm diameter pin inserted in the special hole (see illustration).

Note: *New inlet timing gears are supplied with a plastic locking pin already fitted.*

35 Remove the inlet timing gear from the tool and locate it on the inlet camshaft (see illustration).

36 Refit the spacer and finger-tighten the bolt (see illustration).

37 Position the timing mark on the inlet camshaft timing gear at 12 o'clock and align it with the boss on the camshaft housing. Make sure that the groove on the exhaust camshaft is horizontal with the larger offset uppermost.

38 Offer the exhaust camshaft timing gear onto the camshaft so that the mounting holes are central within the gear elongated slots, then engage the gear teeth with the inlet timing gear and press it fully into position (see illustrations).

39 Check the alignment of the inlet timing gear with the boss, and the exhaust timing gear with the camshaft slots, then remove the locking pin from the inlet timing gear (see illustration).

40 The inlet timing gear bolt must now be tightened. Fit Nissan tool Mot. 1969 to hold the gear then tighten the bolt in the two stages given in Specifications. Remove the tool (see illustrations).

Refitting

41 Refit the injectors, high-pressure pipes and fuel return rail as described in Chapter 4B, and then refit the plastic cover to the top of the

11.34 Using the Nissan bench tool to set the wear compensator on the inlet timing gear

11.35 Locate the inlet timing gear on the inlet camshaft. . .

11.36 . . . and fit the spacer and bolt

11.38a Locate the exhaust timing gear on the exhaust camshaft. . .

11.38b . . . so that the mounting holes are central within the gear elongated slots

11.39 Removing the locking pin from the inlet timing gear

cylinder head, making sure that the leak-off pipes are correctly located.
42 Refit the high-pressure pump, as described in Chapter 4B Section 9.
43 Refit the brake vacuum pump as described in Chapter 9 Section 13.
44 Refit the camshaft gears, timing chain and sprockets as described in Section #9
45 On completion check the engine oil level as described in Chapter 1B Section 5. Start the engine and check for any noises.
Note: *Do not run the engine at high speeds until the correct oil pressure has been reached.*

12 Cylinder head (1.2 litre petrol engines) – removal and refitting

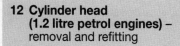

Removal

1 Remove the camshafts and followers as described in Section 10.
2 Remove the inlet manifold as described in Chapter 4A Section 11.
3 Remove the exhaust manifold as described in Chapter 4A Section 12.
4 Remove the fuel rail and injectors as described in Chapter 4A Section 9.
5 Remove the thermostat housing as described in Chapter 3 Section 6.
6 Working in the **reverse** of the tightening sequence **(see illustration 12.20)**, progressively slacken the ten main cylinder head bolts by half a turn at a time, until all bolts can be unscrewed by hand.
7 Lift out the cylinder head bolts and recover the washers, noting which way around they are fitted.
8 Lift the cylinder head off the top of the block. Remove the gasket, noting the locating dowels fitted to the top of the cylinder block. If they are a loose fit in the block, remove the locating dowels, noting which way round they are fitted, and store them with the head for safekeeping.
9 If the cylinder head is to be dismantled for overhaul, refer to.

Preparation for refitting

10 The mating faces of the cylinder head and cylinder block/crankcase must be perfectly clean before refitting the head. Use a hard plastic or wood scraper to remove all traces of gasket and carbon; also clean the piston crowns. Take particular care, as the surfaces are damaged easily. Also, make sure that the carbon is not allowed to enter the oil and water passages – this is particularly important for the lubrication system, as carbon could block the oil supply to any of the engine's components. Using adhesive tape and paper, seal the water, oil and bolt holes in the cylinder block/crankcase. To prevent carbon entering the gap between the pistons and bores, smear a little grease in the gap. After cleaning each piston, use a small brush to

11.40a Hold the gear with the special Nissan tool, then tighten the bolt to the specified torque. . .

remove all traces of grease and carbon from the gap, and then wipe away the remainder with a clean rag. Clean all the pistons in the same way.
11 Check the mating surfaces of the cylinder block/crankcase and the cylinder head for nicks, deep scratches and other damage. If slight, they may be removed carefully with a file, but if excessive, machining may be the only alternative to renewal.
12 Ensure that the cylinder head bolt holes in the crankcase are clean and free of oil. Syringe or soak up any oil left in the bolt holes. This is most important in order that the correct bolt tightening torque can be applied and to prevent the possibility of the block being cracked by hydraulic pressure when the bolts are tightened.
13 The cylinder head bolts must be discarded and renewed, regardless of their apparent condition.
14 If warpage of the cylinder head gasket surface is suspected, use a straight-edge to check it for distortion. If necessary, refer to.

Refitting

15 Wipe clean the mating surfaces of the cylinder head and cylinder block/crankcase. Check the locating dowels are in position at each end of the cylinder block/crankcase surface.
16 Fit a new gasket to the cylinder block/crankcase surface, aligning it with the locating dowels.
17 With the aid of an assistant, carefully refit the cylinder head assembly to the block, aligning it with the locating dowels.
18 Apply a smear of clean oil to the threads, and to the underside of the heads, of the new cylinder head bolts.
19 Fit the washer to each head bolt, then carefully enter each bolt into its relevant hole (do not drop them in). Screw them in, by hand only, until finger-tight.
20 Working progressively and in sequence, tighten the cylinder head bolts to their Stage 1 torque setting, using a torque wrench and suitable socket **(see illustration)**.
21 Go around in the specified sequence again and tighten the ten cylinder head bolts through the specified Stage 2 angle setting.

11.40b . . . and angle

22 Refit the thermostat housing as described in Chapter 3 Section 6.
23 Refit the fuel rail and injectors as described in Chapter 4A Section 9.
24 Refit the exhaust manifold as described in Chapter 4A Section 12.
25 Refit the inlet manifold as described in Chapter 4A Section 11.
26 Refit the camshafts and followers as described in Section 10.

13 Cylinder head (1.6 litre diesel engines) – removal and refitting

Removal

1 With the engine removed from the car, drain the engine oil, then clean and refit the engine oil drain plug using a new sealing washer, tightening it to the specified torque. If the engine is nearing its service interval when the oil and filter are due for renewal, it is recommended that the filter is also removed, and a new one fitted. After reassembly, the engine can then be refilled with fresh oil. Refer to Chapter 1B for further information.
2 Remove the camshaft and followers as described in Section 11.
3 Remove the exhaust manifold, as described in Chapter 4B Section 13.

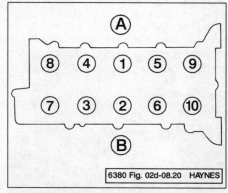

12.20 Cylinder head bolt tightening sequence

A = Inlet side   B = Exhaust side

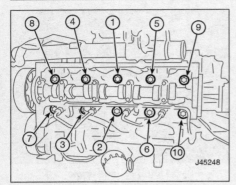

13.17 Cylinder head bolt tightening sequence

4 Remove the inlet manifold, as described in Chapter 4B Section 12.

5 Progressively slacken the cylinder head bolts in the **reverse** sequence to that shown **(see illustration 13.17)**. With all the bolts loose, remove them.

6 Lift the cylinder head upwards off the cylinder block. If it is stuck, tap it with a hammer and block of wood to release it. **Do not** try to turn the cylinder head (it is located by two dowels), nor attempt to prise it free using a screwdriver inserted between the block and head faces.

7 Remove the gasket, noting the locating dowels fitted to the top of the cylinder block. If they are a loose fit in the block, remove the locating dowels, noting which way round they are fitted, and store them with the head for safekeeping.

8 If the cylinder head is to be dismantled for overhaul, refer to.

Preparation for refitting

9 The mating faces of the cylinder head and block must be perfectly clean before refitting the head. Use a scraper to remove all traces of gasket and carbon, and also clean the tops of the pistons. Take particular care with the aluminium cylinder head, as the soft metal is damaged easily. Also, make sure that debris is not allowed to enter the oil and water channels – this is particularly important for the oil circuit, as carbon could block the oil supply to the camshaft or crankshaft bearings. Using adhesive tape and paper, seal the water, oil

and bolt holes in the cylinder block. Clean the piston crowns in the same way.

10 Check the block and head for nicks, deep scratches and other damage. If slight, they may be removed carefully with a file. Machining of the cylinder head or cylinder block is not recommended by the manufacturers.

11 If warpage of the cylinder head is suspected, use a straight-edge to check it for distortion. Refer to if necessary; if the warpage is more than the maximum, the cylinder head must be renewed, as regrinding is not allowed.

12 Clean out the cylinder head bolt holes in the block using a pipe cleaner, or a rag and screwdriver. Make sure that all oil is removed, otherwise there is a possibility of the block being cracked by hydraulic pressure when the bolts are tightened. Examine the bolt threads in the cylinder block for damage, and if necessary, use the correct size tap to chase out the threads. The cylinder head bolts must be renewed each time they are removed, and must not be oiled before being fitted.

Refitting

13 Wipe clean the mating surfaces of the cylinder head and cylinder block/crankcase. Check the locating dowels are in position at each end of the cylinder block/crankcase surface.

14 Fit a new gasket to the cylinder block/crankcase surface, aligning it with the locating dowels.

15 With the aid of an assistant, carefully refit the cylinder head assembly to the block, aligning it with the locating dowels.

16 Fit the washer to each new head bolt, then carefully enter each bolt into its relevant hole (do not drop them in). Screw them in, by hand only, until finger-tight.

17 Working progressively and in sequence, tighten the cylinder head bolts to their Stage 1 torque setting, using a torque wrench and suitable socket **(see illustration)**.

18 Go around in the specified sequence again and tighten the ten cylinder head bolts through the specified Stage 2 angle setting.

19 Refit the timing chain and sprockets, as described inr to the cylinder head and tighten the retaining bolt to the specified torque.

20 Refit the camshaft and followers as described in Section 11.

21 Refit the camshaft gears, timing chain and sprockets as described in Section 9

22 Refit the exhaust manifold, as described in Chapter 4B Section 13.

23 Refit the inlet manifold, as described in Chapter 4B Section 12.

24 On completion change the engine oil and filter as described in Chapter 1B Section 13. Start the engine and check for any noises.

Note: *Do not run the engine at high speeds until the correct oil pressure has been reached.*

14 Oil pump, drive chain and sprockets (1.2 litre petrol engines) – removal, inspection and refitting

Removal

1 Remove the timing chain as described in Section 8.

2 Remove the sump oil pan as described in Chapter 2A Section 5.

3 Disconnect the wiring plug from the oil pump solenoid valve, then extract the wire retaining clip and release the solenoid valve wiring connector from the upper sump housing **(see illustration)**.

4 Release the spring from the hole in the cylinder block and withdraw the chain tensioner from the pivot on the cylinder block **(see illustration)**.

5 Undo the retaining bolts from the oil pump strainer, oil pump bracket and oil pump, then withdraw the oil pump assembly out from the upper sump housing.

Inspection

6 Clean the components and carefully examine the chain, sprockets and pump for any signs of excessive wear. If evident, it is recommended that all the components are renewed as a set. Renew all disturbed O-ring seals as a matter of course.

7 Before refitting the oil pump, prime it by filling with clean engine oil whilst rotating the pump clockwise.

Refitting

8 Fit the oil pump components back in place in the sump upper housing and tighten the retaining bolts securely.

9 Make sure the chain is located around the

14.3 Release the solenoid wiring from the upper sump housing

14.4 Remove the tensioner from the cylinder block

14.9 Make sure the chain is located around the sprocket correctly

two sprockets correctly, and then refit them as a complete assembly to the oil pump drive shaft and crankshaft (see illustration).

10 Refit the chain tensioner to the pivot on the cylinder block, making sure the tensioner spring is located correctly in the cylinder block (see illustration).

11 Refit the solenoid valve wiring connector to the upper sump housing and secure with the wire retaining clip. Reconnect the wiring plug.

12 Refit the sump oil pan as described in Chapter 2A Section 5.

13 Refit the timing chain as described in Section 8.

14.10 Make sure the tensioner spring is located correctly

15.3 Remove the oil pump assembly

15 Oil pump, drive chain and sprockets (1.6 litre diesel engines) – removal, inspection and refitting

Removal

1 Remove the timing chain as described in Section 9.

2 Remove the sump oil pan as described in Chapter 2C Section 5.

3 Undo the retaining bolts from the oil pump strainer, oil pump bracket and oil pump, then withdraw the oil pump assembly, releasing the drive chain from the crankshaft sprocket (see illustration).

Inspection

4 Clean the components and carefully examine the chain, sprockets and pump for any signs of excessive wear. If evident, it is recommended that all the components are renewed as a set. Renew all disturbed O-ring seals as a matter of course.

5 Before refitting the oil pump, prime it by filling with clean engine oil whilst rotating the pump clockwise.

Refitting

6 Fit the oil pump components back in place in the sump upper housing and tighten the retaining bolts securely, making sure the chain is located around the two sprockets correctly.

7 Refit the sump oil pan as described in Chapter 2C Section 5.

8 Refit the timing chain as described in Section 9.

16 Piston/connecting rod assembly – removal

1 Remove the sump, timing chain/belt, oil pump and cylinder head as described in the relevant Sections of this Chapter or in Chapter 2A, Chapter 2B or Chapter 2C, as applicable.

2 On 1.2 litre petrol engines, remove the flywheel, then undo the retaining bolts and remove the upper alloy part of the sump from the bottom of the cylinder block.

3 On 1.2 litre petrol engines, undo the retaining bolts and remove the main bearing cap support beam.

4 If there is a pronounced wear ridge at the top of any bore, it may be necessary to remove it with a scraper or ridge reamer, to avoid piston damage during removal. Such a ridge indicates excessive wear of the cylinder bore.

5 Each connecting rod and bearing cap should be stamped with its respective cylinder number, No 1 cylinder being at the timing chain end of the engine (see illustration). If no markings are visible, using quick-drying paint or similar, mark each connecting rod and big-end bearing cap with its respective cylinder number on the flat machined surface provided.

6 Turn the crankshaft to bring pistons 1 and 4 to BDC (bottom dead centre).

7 Unscrew the bolts from No 1 piston big-end bearing cap. Take off the cap (see illustration), and recover the bottom half

bearing shell. If the bearing shells are to be re-used, tape the cap and the shell together.

8 Using a hammer handle, push the piston up through the bore, and remove it from the top of the cylinder block. Recover the bearing shell, and tape it to the connecting rod for safekeeping.

9 Loosely refit the big-end cap to the connecting rod, and secure with the bolts – this will help to keep the components in their correct order.

10 Remove No 4 piston assembly in the same way.

11 Turn the crankshaft through 180° to bring pistons 2 and 3 to BDC (bottom dead centre), and remove them in the same way.

17 Crankshaft – removal

1 Remove the pistons and connecting rods, as described in Section 16. If no work is to be done on the pistons and connecting rods, there is no need to remove the cylinder head, or to push the pistons out of the cylinder bores. The pistons should just be pushed far enough up the bores that they are positioned clear of the crankshaft journals.

2 Check the crankshaft endfloat as described in Section 20, then proceed as follows.

3 The main bearing caps should be numbered 1 to 5 from the timing chain end of the engine (petrol engines) or from the flywheel end of the engine (diesel engines) (see illustration). If not, using quick-drying paint or similar, mark

16.5 Big-end caps marked with a centre punch

16.7 Removing a big-end bearing cap

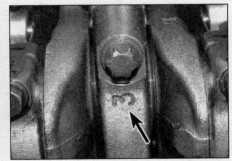

17.3 The main bearing caps are numbered for position

17.4 Removing a main bearing cap bolt

17.6 Lifting the crankshaft from the crankcase

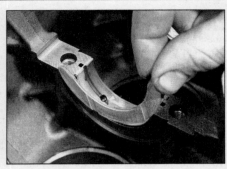

17.8 Removing the crankshaft thrustwashers

each cap so as to indicate its correct fitted orientation and position.

4 Working from the outer ends to the centre; progressively slacken the main bearing cap retaining bolts by a turn at a time. Once all bolts are loose, unscrew and remove them from the cylinder block **(see illustration)**.

5 Withdraw the bearing caps, and recover the lower main bearing shells. Tape each shell to its respective cap for safekeeping.

6 Carefully lift out the crankshaft, taking care not to displace the upper main bearing shells **(see illustration)**.

7 Recover the upper bearing shells from the cylinder block, and tape them to their respective caps for safekeeping.

8 Remove the thrustwasher halves from the side of No 3 main bearing **(see illustration)**, and store them with the bearing cap.

18 Cylinder block/crankcase – cleaning and inspection

Cleaning

1 Remove all external components and electrical switches/sensors from the block.

2 Scrape all traces of sealant from the cylinder block/crankcase, taking care not to damage the gasket sealing surfaces.

3 Where piston oil jet spray tubes are fitted, to the lower part of the cylinder, these should only be removed by a specialist, as damage may occur on removal

4 Remove all oil gallery plugs (where fitted).

19.2 Removing a piston ring with the aid of a feeler gauge

The plugs are usually very tight – they may have to be drilled out, and the holes retapped. Use new plugs when the engine is reassembled.

5 If any of the castings are extremely dirty, all should be steam-cleaned, or cleaned with a suitable degreasing agent.

6 After cleaning, clean all oil holes and oil galleries one more time. Flush all internal passages with warm water until the water runs clear. Dry thoroughly, and apply a light film of oil to the cylinder bores to prevent rusting. If possible, use compressed air to speed up the drying process, and to blow out all the oil holes and galleries.

 Warning: Wear eye protection when using compressed air.

7 If the castings are not very dirty, you can do an adequate cleaning job with very hot, soapy water and a stiff brush. Take plenty of time, and do a thorough job. Regardless of the cleaning method used, be sure to clean all oil holes and galleries very thoroughly, and to dry all components well. Protect the cylinder bores as described above, to prevent rusting.

8 All threaded holes must be clean, to ensure accurate torque readings during reassembly. To clean the threads, run the correct-size tap into each of the holes to remove rust, corrosion, thread sealant or sludge, and to restore damaged threads. If possible, use compressed air to clear the holes of debris produced by this operation.

9 Apply suitable sealant to the new oil gallery plugs, and insert them into the holes in the block. Tighten them securely.

10 If the engine is not going to be reassembled right away, cover it with a large plastic bag to keep it clean; protect all mating surfaces and the cylinder bores as described above, to prevent rusting.

Inspection

11 Visually check the casting for cracks and corrosion. Look for stripped threads in the threaded holes. If there has been any history of internal water leakage, it may be worthwhile having an engine reconditioning specialist check the cylinder block/crankcase with special equipment. If defects are found, have them repaired if possible, or obtain a new block.

12 Check each cylinder bore for scuffing and scoring. Check for signs of a wear ridge at the top of the cylinder, indicating that the bore is excessively worn.

13 Accurate measuring of the cylinder bores requires specialised equipment and experience. We recommend having the bores measured by an automotive engineering workshop, which will also be able to supply appropriate pistons should a rebore be necessary.

14 If the cylinder bores and pistons are in reasonably good condition, and not worn to the specified limits, and if the piston-to-bore clearances can be maintained properly, then it will only be necessary to renew the piston rings. If this is the case, the bores should be honed, to allow the new rings to bed in correctly and provide the best possible seal. An engine reconditioning specialist will carry out this work at moderate cost.

19 Piston/connecting rod assembly – inspection

1 Before the inspection process can begin, the piston/connecting rod assemblies must be cleaned, and the original piston rings removed from the pistons.

Note: *Always use new piston rings when the engine is reassembled.*

2 Carefully expand the old rings over the top of the pistons. The use of two or three old feeler blades will be helpful in preventing the rings dropping into empty grooves **(see illustration)**. Be careful not to scratch the piston with the ends of the ring. The rings are brittle, and will snap if they are spread too far. They're also very sharp – protect your hands and fingers.

3 Scrape away all traces of carbon from the top of the piston. A hand-held wire brush (or a piece of fine emery cloth) can be used, once the majority of the deposits have been scraped away.

4 Remove the carbon from the ring grooves in the piston, using an old ring. Break the ring in half to do this. Be careful to remove only the carbon deposits – do not remove any metal, and do not nick or scratch the sides of the ring grooves.

5 Once the deposits have been removed, clean the piston/connecting rod assembly with paraffin or a suitable solvent, and dry thoroughly. Make sure that the oil return holes in the ring grooves are clear.

6 If the pistons and cylinder bores are not damaged or worn excessively, and if the cylinder block does not need to be rebored, the original pistons can be refitted. Normal piston wear shows up as even vertical wear on the piston thrust surfaces, and slight looseness of the top ring in its groove. New piston rings, however, should always be used when the engine is reassembled.

7 Carefully inspect each piston for cracks around the skirt, around the gudgeon pin holes, and at the piston ring 'lands' (between the ring grooves).

8 Look for scoring and scuffing on the piston skirt, holes in the piston crown, and burned areas at the edge of the crown. If the skirt is scored or scuffed, the engine may have been suffering from overheating, and/or abnormal combustion, which caused excessively high operating temperatures. The cooling and lubrication systems should be checked thoroughly. Scorch marks on the sides of the pistons show that blow-by has occurred. A hole in the piston crown, or burned areas at the edge of the piston crown, indicates that abnormal combustion (pre-ignition, knocking, or detonation) has been occurring. If any of the above problems exist, the causes must be investigated and corrected, or the damage will occur again.

9 Corrosion of the piston, in the form of pitting, indicates that coolant has been leaking into the combustion chamber and/or the crankcase. Again, the cause must be corrected, or the problem may persist in the rebuilt engine.

10 Measure the piston ring-to-groove clearance by placing a new piston ring in each ring groove and measuring the clearance with a feeler blade. Check the clearance at three or four places around each groove. If the measured clearance is greater than specified, new pistons will be required.

11 Accurate measurement of the pistons requires specialised equipment and experience. We recommend having the piston measured by an automotive engineering workshop, which will also be able to supply appropriate pistons should a rebore be necessary.

12 Check the fit of the gudgeon pin by twisting the piston and connecting rod in opposite directions. Any noticeable play indicates excessive wear of the gudgeon pin, piston, or connecting rod small-end bearing.

13 If necessary, on models with circlips securing the gudgeon pin in place, the pistons and connecting rods can be separated and reassembled as follows. Before removing the piston from the connecting rod, mark both components to make sure they are fitted in the same position on reassembly.
Note: *On models with no circlips fitted,*

the gudgeon pin is a press fit in the top of the connecting rod. On these types, we recommend having the pistons removed by an automotive engineering workshop.

14 Using a small screwdriver, prise out the circlips, and push out the gudgeon pin. If necessary, support the piston, and tap the pin out using a suitable hammer and punch, taking great care not to mark the piston/connecting rod bores. Identify the piston, gudgeon pin and rod to ensure correct reassembly. Discard the circlips – new ones *must* be used on refitting.

15 Examine each connecting rod carefully for signs of damage, such as cracks around the big-end and small-end bearings. Check that the rod is not bent or distorted. Damage is highly unlikely, unless the engine has been seized or badly overheated. Detailed checking of the connecting rod assembly and any remedial action necessary can only be carried out by an engine reconditioning specialist with the necessary equipment.

16 To refit the pistons, position the piston on the connecting rod so that the markings noted on removal are positioned correctly in relation to both components.

17 Where applicable, apply a smear of clean engine oil to the gudgeon pin. Slide it into the piston and through the connecting rod small-end. If necessary, tap the pin into position using a hammer and suitable punch, whilst ensuring that the piston is securely supported. Check that the piston pivots freely on the rod, then secure the gudgeon pin in position with two new circlips. Ensure that each circlip is correctly located in its groove in the piston. **Note:** *Gudgeon pin installation will be greatly eased if the piston is first warmed.*

20 Crankshaft – inspection

Checking endfloat

1 If the crankshaft endfloat is to be checked, this must be done when the crankshaft is still installed in the cylinder block/crankcase, but is free to move (see Section 17).

2 Check the endfloat using a dial gauge in contact with the end of the crankshaft. Push the crankshaft fully one way, and then zero the gauge. Push the crankshaft fully the other way, and check the endfloat (see illustration). The result can be compared with the specified amount, and will give an indication as to whether new thrustwashers are required.

3 If a dial gauge is not available, feeler blades can be used. First push the crankshaft fully towards the flywheel/driveplate end of the engine, then use feeler blades to measure the gap between the No 4 crankpin web and No 3 main bearing thrustwasher.

Inspection

4 Clean the crankshaft using paraffin or a

suitable solvent, and dry it, preferably with compressed air if available. Be sure to clean the oil holes with a pipe cleaner or similar probe, to ensure that they are not obstructed.

> ⚠️ *Warning: Wear eye protection when using compressed air.*

5 Check the main and big-end bearing journals for uneven wear, scoring, pitting and cracking.

6 Big-end bearing wear is accompanied by distinct metallic knocking when the engine is running (particularly noticeable when the engine is pulling from low speed) and some loss of oil pressure.

7 Main bearing wear is accompanied by severe engine vibration and rumble – getting progressively worse as engine speed increases – and again by loss of oil pressure.

8 Check the bearing journal for roughness by running a finger lightly over the bearing surface. Any roughness (which will be accompanied by obvious bearing wear) indicates that the crankshaft requires regrinding (where possible) or renewal.

9 Check the oil seal contact surfaces at each end of the crankshaft for wear and damage. If the seal has worn a deep groove in the surface of the crankshaft, consult an engine overhaul specialist; repair may be possible, but otherwise a new crankshaft will be required.

10 Accurate measurement of the crankshaft requires specialised equipment and experience. We recommend having the crankshaft measured by an automotive engineering workshop, which will also be able to supply appropriate journal bearings should a regrind be necessary.

11 If the crankshaft has been reground, check for burrs around the crankshaft oil holes (the holes are usually chamfered, so burrs should not be a problem unless regrinding has been carried out carelessly). Remove any burrs with a fine file or scraper, and thoroughly clean the oil holes as described previously.

12 At the time of writing, it was not clear whether Nissan produce undersize bearing shells for all of these engines. On some engines, if the crankshaft journals have not already been reground, it may be possible to have the crankshaft reconditioned, and

20.2 Checking the crankshaft endfloat with a dial gauge

to fit undersize shells. If no undersize shells are available and the crankshaft has worn beyond the specified limits, it will have to be renewed. Consult your Nissan dealer or engine specialist for further information on parts availability.

21 Main and big-end bearings – inspection

1 Even though the main and big-end bearings should be renewed during the engine overhaul, the old bearings should be retained for close examination, as they may reveal valuable information about the condition of the engine. The bearing shells are graded by thickness, the grade of each shell being indicated by the colour code marked on it.

2 Bearing failure can occur due to lack of lubrication, the presence of dirt or other foreign particles, overloading the engine, or corrosion. Regardless of the cause of bearing failure, the cause must be corrected (where applicable) before the engine is reassembled, to prevent it from happening again **(see illustration)**.

3 When examining the bearing shells, remove them from the cylinder block/crankcase, the main bearing caps, the connecting rods and the connecting rod big-end bearing caps. Lay them out on a clean surface in the same general position as their location in the engine. This will enable you to match any bearing problems with the corresponding crankshaft journal. **Do not** touch any shell's bearing surface with your fingers while checking it, or the delicate surface may be scratched.

4 Dirt and other foreign matter get into the engine in a variety of ways. It may be left in

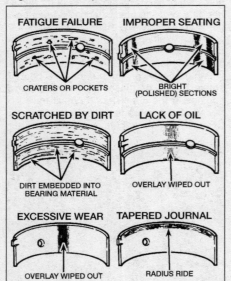

21.2 Typical bearing shell failures

the engine during assembly, or it may pass through filters or the crankcase ventilation system. It may get into the oil, and from there into the bearings. Metal chips from machining operations and normal engine wear are often present. Abrasives are sometimes left in engine components after reconditioning, especially when parts are not thoroughly cleaned using the proper cleaning methods. Whatever the source, these foreign objects often end up embedded in the soft bearing material, and are easily recognised. Large particles will not embed in the bearing, and will score or gouge the bearing and journal. The best prevention for this cause of bearing failure is to clean all parts thoroughly, and keep everything spotlessly clean during engine assembly. Frequent and regular engine oil and filter changes are also recommended.

5 Lack of lubrication (or lubrication breakdown) has a number of interrelated causes. Excessive heat (which thins the oil), overloading (which squeezes the oil from the bearing face) and oil leakage (from excessive bearing clearances, worn oil pump or high engine speeds) all contribute to lubrication breakdown. Blocked oil passages, which usually are the result of misaligned oil holes in a bearing shell, will also oil-starve a bearing, and destroy it. When lack of lubrication is the cause of bearing failure, the bearing material is wiped or extruded from the steel backing of the bearing. Temperatures may increase to the point where the steel backing turns blue from overheating.

6 Driving habits can have a definite effect on bearing life. Full-throttle, low-speed operation (labouring the engine) puts very high loads on bearings, tending to squeeze out the oil film. These loads cause the bearings to flex, which produces fine cracks in the bearing face (fatigue failure). Eventually, the bearing material will loosen in pieces, and tear away from the steel backing.

7 Short-distance driving leads to corrosion of bearings, because insufficient engine heat is produced to drive off the condensed water and corrosive gases. These products collect in the engine oil, forming acid and sludge. As the oil is carried to the engine bearings, the acid attacks and corrodes the bearing material.

8 Incorrect bearing installation during engine assembly will lead to bearing failure as well. Tight-fitting bearings leave insufficient bearing running clearance, and will result in oil starvation. Dirt or foreign particles trapped behind a bearing shell result in high spots on the bearing, which lead to failure.

9 **Do not** touch any shell's bearing surface with your fingers during reassembly; there is a risk of scratching the delicate surface, or of depositing particles of dirt on it.

10 As mentioned at the beginning of this Section, the bearing shells should be renewed as a matter of course during engine overhaul; to do otherwise is false economy. Refer to Section 24 and Section 25 for details of bearing shell selection.

22 Engine overhaul – reassembly sequence

1 Before reassembly begins, ensure that all new parts have been obtained, and that all necessary tools are available. Read through the entire procedure, to familiarise yourself with the work involved, and to ensure that all items necessary for reassembly of the engine are at hand. In addition to all normal tools and materials, thread–locking compound will be needed. A suitable tube of liquid sealant will also be required for the joint faces that are fitted without gaskets; it is recommended that Nissan's Genuine Liquid Gasket (available from your Nissan dealer) is used.

2 In order to save time and avoid problems, engine reassembly can be carried out in the following order:

a) *Crankshaft (see Section 24 of this Chapter).*
b) *Piston/connecting rod assemblies (see Section 25 of this Chapter).*
c) *Flywheel (see Chapter Chapter 2A, Chapter 2B or Chapter 2C).*
d) *Oil pump (see Chapter 2B Section 11or Section. On 1.2 litre petrol engines, see Section 14 of this Chapter).*
e) *Sump (see Chapter Chapter 2A, Chapter 2B or Chapter 2C).*
f) *Cylinder head (see Chapter 2B Section 9 or Section. On 1.2 litre petrol engines, see Section 12 of this Chapter).*
g) *Timing chain/belt and sprockets (see Chapter 2B Section 6 or Section. On 1.2 litre petrol engines, see Section 8 of this Chapter).*
h) *Inlet and exhaust manifolds (see Chapter 4A or Chapter 4B).*

3 At this stage, all engine components should be absolutely clean and dry, with all faults repaired. The components should be laid out (or in individual containers) on a completely clean work surface.

23 Piston rings – refitting

1 Before fitting new piston rings, the ring end gaps must be checked as follows.

2 Lay out the piston/connecting rod assemblies and the new piston ring sets, so that the ring sets will be matched with the same piston and cylinder during the end gap measurement and subsequent engine reassembly.

3 Insert the top ring into the first cylinder, and push it down the bore using the top of the piston **(see illustration)**. This will ensure that the ring remains square with the cylinder walls. Push the ring down into the bore until the piston skirt is level with the block mating surface, then withdraw the piston.

4 Measure the end gap using feeler gauges,

and compare the measurements with the figures given in the Specifications **(see illustration)**.

5 If the gap is too small (unlikely if reputable parts are used), it must be enlarged, or the ring ends may contact each other during engine operation, causing serious damage. Ideally, new piston rings providing the correct end gap should be fitted. As a last resort, the end gap can be increased by carefully filing the ring ends with a fine file. Mount the file in a vice with soft jaws, slip the ring over the file with the ends contacting the file face, and slowly move the ring to remove material from the ends. Take care, as piston rings are sharp, and are easily broken.

6 With new piston rings, it is unlikely that the end gap will be too large. If the gaps are too large, check that you have the correct rings for the engine and for the particular cylinder bore size.

7 Repeat the checking procedure for each ring in the first cylinder, and then for the rings in the remaining cylinders. Remember to keep rings, pistons and cylinders matched up.

8 Once the ring end gaps have been checked and if necessary corrected, the rings can be fitted to the pistons.

Note: *Always follow any instructions supplied with the new piston ring sets – different manufacturers may specify different procedures. Do not mix up the top and second compression rings, as they have different cross-sections.*

9 The oil control ring (lowest on the piston) is installed first. It is composed of three separate components. Slip the expander into the groove, then install the upper side rail into the groove between the expander and the ring land, and then install the lower side rail in the same manner **(see illustrations)**.

10 Install the second ring next. Note that the second ring and top ring are different, and can be identified by their cross-sections. Making sure the ring is the correct way up, fit the ring into the middle groove on the piston, taking care not to expand the ring any more than is necessary **(see illustration)**.

11 Install the top ring in the same way; making sure the ring is the correct way up. Where the ring is symmetrical, fit it with its identification marking facing upwards.

12 With all the rings in position on the piston, space the ring end gaps correctly **(see illustration)**.

13 Repeat the above procedure for the remaining pistons and rings.

24 Crankshaft –
bearing selection and refitting

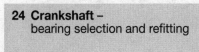

Bearing selection

1 Main bearings for the engines described in this Chapter are available in standard sizes and a range of undersizes to suit reground

23.3 Use the piston to push the rings into the cylinder bores. . .

23.4 . . .then measure the ring end gaps

23.9a Fit the oil control ring expander. . .

23.9b . . .followed by the ring

crankshafts. Refer to your Nissan dealer or automotive engineering workshop for details.

Refitting

2 Clean the backs of the bearing shells, and the bearing locations in both the cylinder block and the main bearing caps.

3 Press the bearing shells into their locations in the cylinder block and main bearing caps. As there are no locating tabs on the bearing shells, visually centralise each shell in its

location. Take care not to touch any shell's bearing surface with your fingers. Note that all the upper bearing shells have oil holes in them; and are sometimes grooved, the lower shells are plain.

4 Wipe dry the shells with a lint-free cloth. Liberally lubricate each bearing shell in the cylinder block/crankcase with clean engine oil.

5 Using a little grease, stick the upper thrustwashers to each side of the No 3 main

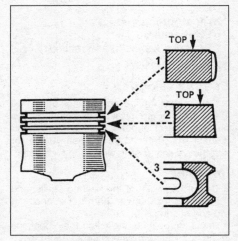

23.10 Piston ring profiles

1 *Top compression ring*
2 *Lower compression ring*
3 *Oil control ring*
Position the TOP markings as shown

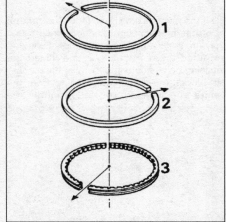

23.12 Position the piston ring end gaps 120° apart

1 *Top compression ring*
2 *Lower compression ring*
3 *Oil control ring*

24.5a Smear a little grease on the crankshaft thrustwashers. . .

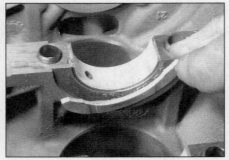

24.5b . . .and stick them to the centre main bearing

24.6 Lay the crankshaft in position in the crankcase

24.9 Fitting No 5 main bearing cap – diesel engine

24.10a Tighten the main bearing cap bolts to the specified torque. . .

24.10b . . .then through the specified angle

bearing upper location; ensure that the oilway grooves on each thrustwasher face outwards (away from the cylinder block) **(see illustrations)**.

6 Lower the crankshaft into position **(see illustration)**, and check the crankshaft endfloat as described in Section 20.

7 Thoroughly degrease the mating surfaces of the cylinder block and the main bearing caps.

8 Lubricate the lower bearing shells in the main bearing caps with clean engine oil. Make sure that the bearing shell is still centralised in the cap.

9 Fit the main bearing caps **(see illustration)**, using the identification marks to ensure that they are installed in the correct locations and are fitted the correct way round. Insert the retaining bolts, tightening them by hand only.

10 Working in sequence, starting from the centre and working outwards, tighten the

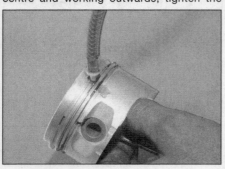

25.6 Lubricating the piston rings

bearing cap retaining bolts to the specified Stage 1 torque setting. Go around in the same sequence and tighten the bolts through the specified Stage 2 angle, using an angle tightening gauge **(see illustrations)**. Check that the crankshaft rotates freely before proceeding any further.

11 Fit the piston/connecting rod assemblies as described in Section 25.

12 On diesel engines, fit a new crankshaft left-hand oil seal as described in Chapter 2B Section 12 or Chapter 2C Section 6.

25 Piston/connecting rod assembly – bearing selection and refitting

Bearing selection

1 Big-end bearings for the engines described in this Chapter are available in standard sizes and a range of undersizes to suit reground crankshafts. Refer to your Nissan dealer or automotive engineering workshop for details.

Refitting

2 Clean the backs of the bearing shells, and the bearing locations in both the connecting rod and bearing cap.

3 Press the bearing shells into their locations in the connecting rods and caps. As there are no locating tabs on the bearing shells, visually centralise each shell in its location. Take care not to touch any shell's bearing surface with your fingers, and ensure that the shells are correctly installed so that the upper shell oil

hole is correctly aligned with the connecting rod oil hole.

4 Note that the following procedure assumes that the crankshaft and main bearing caps are in place (see Section 24).

5 Wipe dry the shells and connecting rods with a lint-free cloth.

6 Lubricate the cylinder bores, the pistons, and piston rings **(see illustration)**, then lay out each piston/connecting rod assembly in its respective position.

7 Start with assembly No 1. Make sure that the piston rings are still spaced as described in Section 23, and then clamp them in position with a piston ring compressor.

8 Insert the piston/connecting rod assembly into the top of cylinder No 1. Ensure that the piston marking (in the form of either an arrow, letter or a dot) on the piston crown is on the correct side of the bore, as noted on removal. Using a block of wood or hammer handle

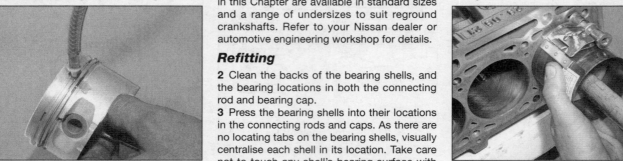

25.8 Using the wooden handle of a hammer to drive the piston into the bore

against the piston crown, tap the assembly into the cylinder until the piston crown is flush with the top of the cylinder **(see illustration)**.

9 Ensure that the bearing shell is still correctly installed. Liberally lubricate the crankpin and both bearing shells. Taking care not to mark the cylinder bores, tap the piston/connecting rod assembly down the bore and onto the crankpin. Refit the big-end bearing cap **(see illustration)**, tightening its retaining bolts finger-tight at first. Note that the faces with the identification marks must match.

10 Tighten the bearing cap retaining bolts to the specified torque, then through the specified angle in the Stages given in the Specifications.

11 Rotate the crankshaft. Check that it turns freely; some stiffness is to be expected if new components have been fitted, but there should be no signs of binding or tight spots.

12 Refit the three remaining piston/connecting rod assemblies in the same way.

13 On 1.2 litre petrol engines, refit the main bearing cap support beam and progressively tighten the retaining bolts to the specified torque.

14 On 1.2 litre petrol engines, apply a bead of sealant to the mating face and refit the upper alloy part of the sump to the bottom of the cylinder block. Tighten all retaining bolts to the specified torque. With the upper alloy part of the sump in place, fit a new crankshaft left-hand oil seal, then refit the flywheel, referring to Chapter 2A Section 6.

15 Refit the cylinder head, oil pump, timing chain/belt and sump.

26 Engine – initial start-up after overhaul

1 With the engine refitted in the vehicle, double-check the engine oil and coolant levels. Make a final check that everything has been reconnected, and that there are no tools or rags left in the engine compartment.

2 On diesel engine models, prime and bleed the fuel system as described in. Turn the ignition on and wait for the preheating warning light to go out.

3 Start the engine, noting that this may take a little longer than usual, due to the fuel system components having been disturbed.

4 Once started, keep the engine running at a fast tickover. Check that the oil pressure warning light goes out, then check that there are no leaks of oil, fuel and coolant. Don't be alarmed if there are some odd smells and smoke from parts getting hot and burning off oil deposits.

5 Assuming all is well; keep the engine idling

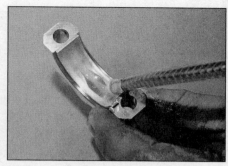

25.9 Lubricate the big-end cap bearing shell then refit the cap

until hot water is felt circulating through the top hose, then switch off the engine.

6 After a few minutes recheck the oil and coolant levels as described in Chapter 1A or Chapter 1B, and top-up as necessary.

7 Note that there is no need to retighten the cylinder head bolts once the engine has first run after reassembly.

8 If new pistons, rings or crankshaft bearings have been fitted, the engine must be treated as new, and run-in for the first 500 miles. Do not operate the engine at full-throttle, or allow it to labour at low engine speeds in any gear. It is recommended that the oil and filter be changed at the end of this period.

Notes

Chapter 3
Cooling, heating and ventilation systems

Contents

Degrees of difficulty

Easy, suitable for novice with little experience		Fairly easy, suitable for beginner with some experience		Fairly difficult, suitable for competent DIY mechanic		Difficult, suitable for experienced DIY mechanic		Very difficult, suitable for expert DIY or professional	

Specifications

General

Cooling system type....................................	Pressurised sealed system, with front mounted radiator and electric cooling fan(s)
Cooling system pressure:	
Brown cap	1.2 bar
Black cap with yellow hand mark.........................	1.4 bar
Reservoir capacity	0.8 litres
Engine capacity:	
1.2 litre (HRA2DDT) petrol engine......................	6.5 litres
1.5 litre (K9K) diesel engine	6.3 litres
1.6 litre (R9M) diesel engine	7.3 litres

Thermostat

Opening temperatures:	
1.2 litre (HRA2DDT) petrol engine......................	77 to 80°C (fully open at 90°C)
1.5 litre (K9K) diesel engine	Starts opening 83°C
1.6 litre (R9M) diesel engine.........................	80 to 92°C

Engine coolant temperature sensor

Resistance at approx:	
At 25°C	2252 ± 112.16 ohms
At 50°C	810 ± 39 ohms
At 80°C	283 ± 8 ohms

Air conditioning

Compressor model.....................................	Denso 6SBH14
Compressor type	Swash plate
Disc to pulley clearance	0.21 to 0.55 mm
Compressor oil:	
Quantity	110 ml
Type	ND-OIL12
Refrigerant:	
Quantity	500 ± 25 g
Type	HFO-1234yf (R-1234yf)

Torque wrench settings

	Nm	lbf ft
Petrol engines:		
Coolant pump pulley securing bolts	8	7
Coolant pump securing bolts	25	18
Cylinder block drain plug	10	7
Thermostat cover securing bolts	21	15
Coolant housing (end of cylinder head) bolts	25	18
Air-conditioning compressor mounting bolts	25	18
Refrigerant pressure sensor	11	8
Diesel engines:		
Coolant pump pulley securing bolts (1.6 litre engine)	15	11
Coolant pump securing bolts:		
1.5 litre engine	11	8
1.6 litre engine	10	7
Thermostat housing assembly bolts:		
1.5 litre engine (end of cylinder head)	11	8
1.6 litre engine (front of cylinder block)	10	7
Air-conditioning compressor mounting bolts	25	18
Refrigerant pressure sensor	11	8

1 General information and precautions

General information

1 The cooling system is of pressurised type, comprising a coolant pump, crossflow radiator, coolant expansion tank, electric cooling fan(s), thermostat, heater matrix, and all associated hoses and switches. The coolant pump is driven by the auxiliary drivebelt on 1.2 litre petrol engines and 1.6 litre diesel engines. On 1.5 litre diesel engines the timing belt (cambelt) is used to drive the coolant pump.

2 The system functions as follows. The coolant pump pumps cold coolant around the cylinder block and head passages, and through the inlet manifold, heater and throttle housing to the thermostat housing.

3 When the engine is cold, the coolant is returned from the thermostat housing to the coolant pump. When the coolant reaches a predetermined temperature, the thermostat opens, and the coolant passes through the top hose to the radiator. As the coolant circulates through the radiator, it is cooled by the inrush of air when the car is in forward motion. The airflow is supplemented by the action of the electric cooling fan(s) when necessary. Upon reaching the bottom of the radiator, the coolant has now cooled, and the cycle is repeated.

4 When the engine is at normal operating temperature, the coolant expands, and some of it is released through the valve in the radiator pressure cap into the expansion tank. Coolant collects in the tank, and is returned to the radiator when the system cools.

5 A single or twin electric cooling fan arrangement is used according to model and equipment fitted. The fan assembly is mounted behind the radiator and controlled by the engine management electronic control unit in conjunction with the engine coolant temperature sensor.

Precautions

⚠️ *Warning: Do not attempt to remove the radiator pressure cap, or to disturb any part of the cooling system, while the engine is hot, as there is a high risk of scalding. If the radiator pressure cap must be removed before the engine and radiator have fully cooled (even though this is not recommended), the pressure in the cooling system must first be relieved. Cover the cap with a thick layer of cloth, to avoid scalding, and slowly unscrew the pressure cap until a hissing sound is heard. When the hissing has stopped, indicating that the pressure has reduced, slowly unscrew the pressure cap until it can be removed; if more hissing sounds are heard, wait until they have stopped before unscrewing the cap completely. At all times, keep your face well away from the pressure cap opening, and protect your hands.*

⚠️ *Warning: Do not allow antifreeze to come into contact with your skin, or with the painted surfaces of the vehicle. Rinse off spills immediately, with plenty of water. Never leave antifreeze lying around in an open container, or in a puddle in the driveway or on the garage floor. Children and pets are attracted by its sweet smell, but antifreeze can be fatal if ingested.*

⚠️ *Warning: If the engine is hot, the electric cooling fan may start rotating even if the engine is not running. Be careful to keep your hands, hair, and any loose clothing well clear when working in the engine compartment.*

⚠️ *Warning: Refer to Section 12 for precautions to be observed when working on models equipped with air conditioning.*

2 Troubleshooting

Coolant leaks

1 A coolant leak can develop anywhere in the cooling system, but the most common causes are:
a) A loose or weak hose clamp
b) A defective hose
c) A faulty pressure cap
d) A damaged radiator
e) A defective heater core
f) A faulty coolant pump
g) A leaking gasket at any joint that carries coolant

2 Coolant leaks aren't always easy to find. Sometimes they can only be detected when the cooling system is under pressure. Which is why a coolant system pressure tester is useful. After the engine has cooled completely, the tester is attached in place of the pressure cap, then pumped up to the pressure value equal to that of the pressure cap rating. Now, leaks that only exist when the engine is fully warmed up will become apparent. The tester can be left connected to locate a persistent slow leak.

Coolant level drops, but no external leaks

3 If you find it necessary to keep adding coolant, but there are no external leaks, the probable causes include:
a) A leaking head gasket
b) A leaking intake manifold gasket (only on engines that have coolant passages in the manifold), or a cracked cylinder head or cylinder block

4 Any of the above problems will also usually result in contamination of the engine oil, which will cause it to take on a milkshake-like appearance. A leaking head gasket or cracked head or block can also result in engine oil contaminating the cooling system.

5 Combustion leak detectors (also known as block testers) are available at most auto parts stores. These work by detecting exhaust gases in the cooling system, which indicates a compression leak from a cylinder into the coolant. The tester consists of a large bulb-type syringe and bottle of test fluid. A measured amount of the fluid is added to the syringe. The syringe is placed over the cooling system filler neck and, with the engine running, the bulb is squeezed and a sample of the gases present in the cooling system are drawn up through the test fluid. If any combustion gases are present in the sample taken, the test fluid will change color.

6 If the test indicates combustion gas is present in the cooling system, you can be sure that the engine has a leaking head gasket or a crack in the cylinder head or block, and will require disassembly to repair.

Pressure cap

 Warning: Wait until the engine is completely cool before beginning this check.

7 The cooling system is sealed by a spring-loaded cap, which raises the boiling point of the coolant. If the cap's seal or spring are worn out, the coolant can boil and escape past the cap. With the engine completely cool, remove the cap and check the seal; if it's cracked, hardened or deteriorated in any way, replace it with a new one.

8 Even if the seal is good, the spring might not be; this can be checked with a cooling system pressure tester. If the cap can't hold a pressure within approximately 0.13 bar of its rated pressure (which is marked on the cap), replace it with a new one.

9 The cap is also equipped with a vacuum relief spring. When the engine cools off, a vacuum is created in the cooling system. The vacuum relief spring allows air back into the system, which will equalise the pressure and prevent damage to the radiator (the radiator tanks could collapse if the vacuum is great enough). If, after turning the engine off and allowing it to cool down you notice any of the cooling system hoses collapsing, replace the pressure cap with a new one.

Thermostat

10 Before assuming the thermostat is responsible for a cooling system problem, check the coolant level, and temperature gauge (or light) operation.

11 If the engine takes a long time to warm up (as indicated by the temperature gauge or heater operation), the thermostat is probably stuck open. Replace the thermostat with a new one.

12 If the engine runs hot or overheats, a thorough test of the thermostat should be performed.

Note: *The following test only applicable to vehicles with a separate thermostat. Most*

modern engines are now equipped with a thermostat that is integral with it's housing. In this case, no testing of the thermostat is possible, and the complete assembly may need to be replaced.

13 Definitive testing of the thermostat can only be made when it is removed from the vehicle. If the thermostat is stuck in the open position at room temperature, it is faulty and must be replaced.

Caution: Do not drive the vehicle without a thermostat. The engine management ECM may stay in open loop and emissions and fuel economy will suffer.

14 To test a thermostat, suspend the (closed) thermostat on a length of string or wire in a pot of cold water.

15 Heat the water while observing the thermostat. The thermostat should fully open before the water boils.

16 If the thermostat doesn't open and close as specified, or sticks in any position, replace it.

Cooling fan

17 If the engine is overheating and the cooling fan is not coming on when the engine temperature rises to an excessive level, unplug the fan motor wiring plugs(s) and connect the motor directly to the battery with fused bridging wires. If the fan motor doesn't come on, replace the motor.

18 If the radiator fan motor is okay, but it isn't coming on when the engine gets hot, the fan relay might be defective. A relay is used to control a circuit by turning it on and off in response to a control decision by the engine management Electronic Control Module (ECM). These control circuits are fairly complex, and checking them should be left to a qualified automotive technician. Sometimes, the control system can be fixed by simply identifying and replacing a faulty relay.

19 Locate the fan relays in the engine compartment fuse/relay box and test the relay.

20 If the relay is okay, check all wiring and connections to the fan motor. Refer to the wiring diagrams in Chapter 12. If no obvious problems are found, the problem could be the Engine Coolant Temperature (ECT) sensor or the engine management Electronic Control Module (ECM). Have the cooling fan system and circuit diagnosed by a dealer service department or suitably equipped repairer.

Coolant pump

21 A failure in the coolant pump can cause serious engine damage due to overheating.

Auxiliary drivebelt-driven coolant pump

22 There are two ways to check the operation of the coolant pump while it's installed on the engine. If the pump is found to be defective, it should be replaced with a new or rebuilt unit.

23 Coolant pumps are normally equipped with weep (or vent) hole in the housing. If a

failure occurs in the pump seal, coolant will leak from the hole.

24 If the coolant pump shaft bearings fail, there may be a howling sound at the pump while it's running. Shaft wear can be felt with the drivebelt removed if the coolant pump pulley is rocked up and down (with the engine off). Don't mistake drivebelt slippage, which causes a squealing sound, for coolant pump bearing failure.

Timing chain or timing belt-driven coolant pump

25 Coolant pumps driven by the timing chain or timing belt are located underneath the timing chain or timing belt cover.

26 Checking the coolant pump is limited because of where it is located. However, some basic checks can be made before deciding to remove the coolant pump. If the pump is found to be defective, it should be replaced with a new or rebuilt unit.

27 One sign that the coolant pump may be failing is that the heater (climate control) may not work well. Warm the engine to normal operating temperature, confirm that the coolant level is correct, then run the heater and check for hot air coming from the ducts.

28 Check for noises coming from the coolant pump area. If the coolant pump impeller shaft or bearings are failing, there may be a howling sound at the pump while the engine is running.

Note: *Be careful not to mistake drivebelt noise (squealing) for coolant pump bearing or shaft failure.*

29 It you suspect coolant pump failure due to noise, wear can be confirmed by feeling for play at the pump shaft. This can be done by rocking the drive sprocket on the pump shaft up and down. To do this you will need to remove the tension on the timing chain or belt as well as access the coolant pump.

All coolant pumps

30 Finding coolant in the engine oil could indicate other serious issues besides a failed coolant pump, such as a leaking head gasket or a cracked cylinder head or block.

31 Even a pump that exhibits no outward signs of a problem, such as noise or leakage, can still be due for replacement. Removal for close examination is the only sure way to tell. Sometimes the fins on the back of the impeller can corrode to the point that cooling efficiency is diminished significantly.

Heater system

32 If the fan motor will run at all speeds, the electrical part of the system is okay. The three basic heater problems fall into the following general categories:

a) *Not enough heat*
b) *Heat all the time*
c) *No heat*

33 If there's not enough heat, the control valve or flap is stuck in a partially open position, the coolant coming from the engine isn't hot enough, or the heater matrix is restricted. If the coolant isn't hot enough, the thermostat in the engine cooling system is stuck open, allowing coolant to pass through the engine so rapidly that it doesn't heat up quickly enough. If the vehicle is equipped with a temperature gauge instead of a warning light, watch to see if the engine temperature rises to the normal operating range after driving for a reasonable distance.

34 If there's heat all the time, the control valve or the flap is stuck wide open.

35 If there's no heat, coolant is probably not reaching the heater matrix, or the heater matrix core is blocked. The likely cause is a collapsed or blocked hose, matrix, or a seized heater control valve. If the heater is the type that flows coolant all the time, the cause is a stuck flap or a broken or kinked control cable.

Air conditioning system

36 If the cool air output is inadequate:
a) Inspect the condenser coils and fins to make sure they're clear
b) Check the compressor clutch for slippage
c) Check the blower motor for proper operation
d) Inspect the blower discharge passage for obstructions
e) Check the system air intake filter for clogging

37 If the system provides intermittent cooling air:
a) Check the fuse, blower switch and blower motor for a malfunction
b) Make sure the compressor clutch isn't slipping
c) Inspect the plenum flap to make sure it's operating properly
d) Inspect the evaporator to make sure it isn't blocked
e) If the unit is icing up, it may be caused by excessive moisture in the system, defective evaporator temperature sensor, control unit

38 If the system provides no cooling air:
a) Inspect the compressor drivebelt; make sure it isn't loose or broken
b) Make sure the compressor clutch engages; if it doesn't, check for a blown fuse
c) Inspect the wire harness for broken or disconnected wires

d) If the compressor clutch doesn't engage, bridge the terminals of the AC pressure switch(es) with a jumper wire; if the clutch now engages, and the system is properly charged, the pressure switch is bad
e) Make sure the blower motor is not disconnected or burned out
f) Make sure the compressor isn't partially or completely seized
g) Inspect the refrigerant pipes for leaks
h) Check the components for leaks
i) Inspect the receiver-drier/accumulator or expansion valve/tube for blocked screens

39 If the system is noisy:
a) Look for loose panels in the passenger compartment
b) Inspect the compressor drivebelt; it may be loose or worn
c) Check the security of the compressor mounting bolts
d) Listen carefully to the compressor; it may be worn out
e) Listen to the idler pulley and bearing, and the clutch; either may be defective
f) The winding in the compressor clutch coil or solenoid may be defective
g) The compressor oil level may be low
h) The blower motor fan bushing or the motor itself may be worn out
i) If there is an excessive charge in the system, you'll hear a rumbling noise in the high pressure pipe, or a thumping noise in the compressor
j) If there is a low charge in the system, you might hear hissing in the evaporator case at the expansion valve

3 Cooling system hoses – disconnection and renewal

1 The number, routing and pattern of hoses will vary according to model, but the same basic procedure applies. Before commencing work, make sure that the new hoses are to hand, along with new hose clips if needed. It is good practice to renew the hose clips at the same time as the hoses.
2 Drain the cooling system, as described in Chapter 1A Section 33 or Chapter 1B Section 32, saving the coolant if it is fit for

re-use. Squirt a little penetrating oil onto the hose clips if they are corroded.
3 Release the hose clips from the hose concerned. Three types of clip are used; worm-drive, spring and 'sardine-can'. The worm-drive clip is released by turning its screw anti-clockwise. The spring clip is released by squeezing its tangs together with pliers, at the same time working the clip away from the hose stub. The 'sardine-can' clip is not re-usable, and is best cut off with snips or side-cutters.
4 Unclip any wires, cables or other hoses, which may be attached to the hose being removed. Make notes for reference when reassembling if necessary.
5 Release the hose from its stubs with a twisting motion. Be careful not to damage the stubs on delicate components such as the radiator. If the hose is stuck fast, the best course is often to cut it off using a sharp knife, but again be careful not to damage the stubs.
6 Before fitting the new hose, smear the stubs with washing-up liquid or a suitable rubber lubricant to aid fitting. Do not use oil or grease, which may attack the rubber.
7 Fit the hose clips over the ends of the hose, and then fit the hose over its stubs. Work the hose into position. When satisfied, locate and tighten the hose clips.
8 Refill the cooling system as described in Chapter 1A Section 33 for petrol engines, or Chapter 1B Section 32 for diesel engines. Run the engine, and check that there are no leaks.
9 Recheck the tightness of the hose clips on any new hoses after a few hundred miles.
10 Top-up the coolant level if necessary.

4 Coolant expansion tank – removal and refitting

Removal

1 Drain the cooling system sufficiently to empty the expansion tank. Do not drain any more coolant than is necessary.
2 Disconnect the 2 hoses, from the expansion tank **(see illustrations)**.
3 Undo the mounting bolt, securing the expansion tank to the inner wing panel **(see illustration)**.

4.2a Disconnect the upper hose. . .

4.2b . . . and the lower hose

4.3 Undo the mounting bolt

4 Lift the coolant expansion tank to release it from the inner wing panel, then manoeuvre it from place.

Refitting

5 Refitting is the reverse of removal, ensuring the hoses are securely reconnected. On completion, top-up the coolant level as described in Chapter 1A Section 6 or Chapter 1B Section 6.

5 Radiator – removal, inspection and refitting

Note: *If leakage is the reason for removing the radiator, bear in mind that minor leaks can often be cured using a radiator sealant with the radiator left in position.*

Removal

1 Drain the cooling system (see Chapter 1A Section 33 for petrol engines, or Chapter 1B Section 32 for diesel engines).
2 Remove the front bumper as described in Chapter 11 Section 5.
3 Remove the intercooler (charge air cooler), as described in Chapter 4A Section 14 on petrol engines, or for diesel engines.
4 Unclip the air-conditioning condenser from the front of the radiator and secure it in position, taking care not to damage the refrigerant pipes. Note, secure the condenser in position to prevent any strain on the air conditioning pipes.
5 Disconnect the remaining coolant hose(s) from the rear of the radiator (**see illustrations**).
6 Reaching down the back of the radiator, disconnect the wiring connector(s) from the cooling fan and resistor, then unclip the wiring from the cooling fan cowling (**see illustration**).
7 Lift the radiator out from the engine compartment complete with fan cowling assembly; recover the lower mounting rubbers as the radiator is withdrawn (**see illustration**).

Inspection

8 If the radiator has been removed due to suspected blockage, reverse-flush it as described in Chapter 1A Section 33, or Chapter 1B Section 32. Clean dirt and debris from the radiator fins, using an airline (in which case, wear eye protection) or a soft brush. Be careful, as the fins are sharp, and easily damaged.
9 If necessary, a radiator specialist can perform a 'flow test' on the radiator, to establish whether an internal blockage exists.
10 A leaking radiator must be referred to a specialist for permanent repair. Do not attempt to weld or solder a leaking radiator, as damage to the plastic components may result.
11 Inspect the condition of the radiator mounting rubbers, and renew them if necessary.

Refitting

12 Refitting is a reversal of removal, bearing in mind the following points:

5.5a Disconnect the upper hose. . .

5.5b . . . and lower hose from the radiator

5.6 Disconnect the wiring connectors from the fan/resistor

a) *Ensure that the radiator lower lugs engage correctly with the lower mounting rubbers.*
b) *On completion, refill the cooling system (see Chapter 1A Section 33 for petrol engines, or Chapter 1B Section 32 for diesel engines).*

6 Thermostat – removal, testing and refitting

Note: *A new seal will be required when refitting the thermostat housing.*

Removal

1.2 litre petrol engines

1 The thermostat is located in a housing bolted to the front facing side of the cylinder block..

6.4 Disconnect the hoses from the housing

5.7 Radiator and fan cowling assembly

2 Drain the cooling system as described in Chapter 1A Section 33.
3 Remove the inlet manifold as described in Chapter 4A Section 11.
4 Noting their fitted position slacken the retaining clips and disconnect the cooling system hoses from the thermostat housing (**see illustration**).
5 Disconnect the wiring connector and release the wiring securing clips from the housing (**see illustration**).
6 Place a suitable container beneath the thermostat housing and be prepared for coolant spillage.
7 Undo the two bolts and remove the thermostat housing from the cylinder block. Recover the sealing ring (**see illustration**). Note that the thermostat is integral with the housing and cannot be separated.

6.5 Release the wiring from the housing

6.7 Fit a new sealing ring

6.12 Disconnect the wiring connector from the temperature sensor

6.14a Undo the coolant housing upper bolts. . .

6.14b . . .and lower bolt

6.16 Coolant control valve and thermostat housing

1.5 litre diesel engines

8 The thermostat is located in a housing bolted to the left-hand side of the cylinder head, at the transmission end of the engine.
9 Remove the battery (see Chapter 5 Section 4).

10 Remove the brake vacuum pump, as described in Chapter 9 Section 13.
11 Drain the cooling system as described in Chapter 1B Section 32.
12 Disconnect the wiring connector from the

temperature sensor in the coolant housing **(see illustration)**.
13 Noting their fitted position slacken the retaining clips and disconnect the cooling system hoses from the coolant housing.
14 Unscrew the securing bolts, and remove the coolant housing from the cylinder head **(see illustrations)**. Note the fitted position of the support bracket also secured by the housing bolts.
15 Lift the thermostat, O-ring and seal from the housing, noting the fitted position of the thermostat.

1.6 litre diesel engines

16 The thermostat is located in a housing bolted to the front facing side of the cylinder block, along with the coolant control valve **(see illustration)**.
17 Drain the cooling system as described in Chapter 1B Section 32.
18 Remove the inlet manifold as described in Chapter 4B Section 12.
19 Place a suitable container beneath the thermostat housing and be prepared for coolant spillage, that may be trapped in the hoses and housing.
20 Slacken the retaining clips and disconnect the hoses from the thermostat housing **(see illustrations)**.
21 Undo the bolts and remove the thermostat housing from the cylinder block **(see illustrations)**.
22 If required, slacken the retaining clips and disconnect the hoses from the coolant control valve housing **(see illustration)**.
23 Undo the bolts and remove the coolant

6.20a Disconnect the hoses. . .

6.20b . . . from the thermostat housing

6.21a Undo the mounting bolts. . .

6.21b . . . and remove the thermostat housing

6.22 Disconnect the hoses

6.23a Undo the mounting bolts. . .

6.23b . . . and remove the coolant control valve housing

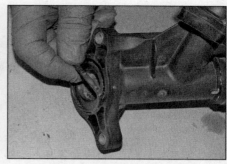

6.29 Fit a new gasket to the housing (1.6 litre diesel shown)

control valve housing from the cylinder block **(see illustrations)**.

Testing

Note: *If there is any question about the operation of the thermostat, it's best to renew it – they are not usually expensive items. Testing involves heating in, or over, an open pan of boiling water, which carries with it the risk of scalding. A thermostat that has seen more than five years' service may well be past its best already.*

24 A rough test of the thermostat may be made by suspending it with a piece of string in a container full of water. Heat the water to bring it to the boil – the thermostat must open by the time the water boils. If not, renew it.
25 If a thermometer is available, the precise opening temperature of the thermostat may be determined; compare with the figures given in the Specifications. The opening temperature may also be marked on the thermostat.
26 A thermostat, which fails to close as the water cools down, must also be renewed.

Refitting

27 Commence refitting by thoroughly cleaning the mating faces of the cover and the housing.
28 Refit the thermostat and new seal to the housing, making sure it is fitted in the position noted on removal.
29 Fit the thermostat housing and gasket **(see illustration)**, refit the securing bolts and tighten to the specified torque.
30 Refit the coolant hoses to the housing in the positions noted on removal.
31 Where applicable, reconnect the wiring

plug to the temperature sensor on the coolant housing.
32 On completion, refill the cooling system as described in Chapter 1A, or Chapter 1B.

7 Electric cooling fan and resistor – removal and refitting

1 Disconnect the battery negative terminal (refer Chapter 5 Section 4).
2 Release the two retaining clips, undo the mounting bolts and remove the air intake ducting from the front of the engine **(see illustration)**.

Cooling fan

3 Reaching down the back of the radiator, release the securing clips, then disconnect the wiring plug connectors from the fan resistor and the cooling fan motor **(see illustration)**.

7.2 Remove the air intake ducting – 1.2 litre petrol engine shown

7.4 Undo the fan cowling lower securing bolts

7.5 Withdraw the fan cowling upwards

Release the wiring loom retaining clips from the fan cowling.
4 Slacken and remove the retaining bolts (one at each side) from the lower part of the fan cowling **(see illustration)**.
5 Release the retaining clips, then carefully withdraw the cooling fan and cowling upward out from the engine compartment **(see illustration)**. Take care not to damage the radiator fins as the fan cowling is withdrawn.
6 Refitting is a reversal of removal.

Cooling fan resistor

7 The cooling fan resistor is fitted to the top left-hand side of the fan cowling.
8 Remove the fan cowling as described in paragraphs 3 to 6.
9 Undo the retaining bolt, release the locating clips and then slide the resistor out from the fan cowling **(see illustration)**.
10 Refitting is a reversal of removal.

7.3 Disconnect the wiring connector from the resistor and the fan

7.9 Remove the resistor from the cowling

8.9 Disconnect the wiring connector – 1.2 litre petrol model shown

8.10a Withdraw the retaining clip. . .

8.10b . . . and remove the sensor and seal – 1.2 litre petrol model shown

8 Cooling system electrical sensors – testing, removal and refitting

Coolant temperature sensor

Testing

1 The coolant temperature sensor is fitted to the coolant/thermostat housing on the left-hand end of the cylinder head, on 1.2 litre petrol engines and 1.5 litre diesel engines. On 1.6 litre diesel engines, the sensor is located in the front of the cylinder block above the coolant control valve (see illustration 6.22).

2 The coolant temperature gauge and the cooling fan are all operated by the engine management ECM using the signal supplied by this sensor.

3 The unit contains a thermistor – an electronic component whose electrical resistance decreases at a predetermined rate as its temperature rises.

4 The engine management ECM supplies the sensor with a set voltage and then, by measuring the current flowing in the sensor circuit, it determines the engine temperature. This information is then used, in conjunction with other inputs, to control the engine management system and associated components.

5 If the sensor circuit should fail to provide plausible information, the ECM back-up facility will override the sensor signal. In this event, the ECM assumes a predetermined setting which will allow the engine

management system to operate, albeit at reduced efficiency. When this occurs, the engine warning light on the instrument panel will come on, and the advice of a Nissan dealer should be sought. The sensor itself can be tested by removing it, and checking the resistances at various temperatures using an ohmmeter (heat the sensor in a container of water, and monitor the temperature with a thermometer). The resistance values are given in the Specifications. **Do not** attempt to test the circuit with the sensor fitted to the engine, and the wiring connector fitted, as there is a high risk of damaging the ECM.

Removal

6 To make access easier, remove the battery, as described in Chapter 5 Section 4.

7 Partially drain the cooling system to just below the level of the sensor (see Chapter 1A Section 33 for petrol engines, or Chapter 1B Section 32 for diesel engines). Alternatively, have ready a suitable bung to plug the aperture in the housing when the sensor is removed.

8 On 1.6 diesel engines, it may be necessary to remove the inlet manifold (see Chapter 4B Section 12), to access the temperature sensor.

9 Disconnect the wiring connector from the sensor (see illustration).

10 The sensor is clipped in place; prise out the sensor retaining circlip then remove the sensor and sealing ring from the housing (see illustrations). If the system has not been drained, plug the sensor aperture to prevent further coolant loss.

11 On 1.6 litre diesel engines, disconnect the

wiring connector and carefully unscrew the sensor from the front of the cylinder block (see illustration) and recover the sealing ring. If the system has not been drained, plug the sensor aperture to prevent further coolant loss.

Refitting

12 Check the condition of the sealing ring and renew it if necessary.

13 Refitting is a reversal of removal, but refill (or top-up) the cooling system as described in Chapter 1A Section 33 for petrol engines, or Chapter 1B Section 32 for diesel engines.

14 On completion, start the engine and run it until it reaches normal operating temperature. Continue to run the engine until the cooling fan cuts in and out correctly.

Air conditioning temperature sensor

15 The sensor is located inside the heater/air conditioning unit behind the facia. Remove the centre console left-hand side front trim panel and disconnect the temperature sensor wiring connector (see illustration).

16 Twist the temperature sensor and withdraw it from the left-hand side of the heater housing (see illustration).

17 Refitting is a reversal of removal.

9 Coolant pump – removal, inspection and refitting

Note: *A new gasket will be required when refitting the coolant pump.*

8.11 Coolant temperature sensor – 1.6 litre diesel engines

8.15 Disconnect the wiring connector to evaporator sensor

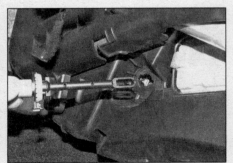

8.16 Withdraw the temperature sensor

9.5 Remove the coolant pump pulley

9.6a Undo the bolts. . .

9.6b . . . remove the coolant pump. . .

Removal

1 Drain the cooling system (see Chapter 1A Section 33 for petrol engines, or Chapter 1B Section 32 for diesel engines).
2 Remove the auxiliary drivebelts (see Chapter 1A Section 29 for petrol engines, or Chapter 1B Section 33, 34 for diesel engines).
3 On 1.2 litre petrol engines and 1.6 litre diesel engines, there is not much room between the coolant pump pulley and the chassis leg. It will be necessary to slacken the engine mounting bolts and move the engine over slightly to be able to withdraw the coolant pulley from the coolant pump.
4 Remove the battery and tray to access the transmission engine mounting, as described in Chapter 5 Section 4.

1.2 litre petrol engine

5 Unscrew the three retaining bolts, and remove the pulley from the coolant pump (see illustration). If required, counterhold the pulley in order to unscrew the bolts. This is most easily achieved by wrapping an old drivebelt tightly around the pulley to act in a similar manner to a strap wrench.
6 Unscrew the retaining bolts, and withdraw the coolant pump from the cylinder block (see illustrations). Remove the gasket and discard, as a new one will be required for refitting.

1.5 litre diesel engine

7 Remove the timing belt as described in Chapter 2B Section 5.
8 Undo the retaining bolts and remove the rear timing belt cover from the cylinder block (see illustration).
9 Unscrew the retaining bolts, and remove the coolant pump from the cylinder block (see illustrations). Remove the gasket and discard, as a new one will be required for refitting.

1.6 litre diesel engine

10 Unscrew the three retaining bolts, and remove the pulley from the coolant pump (see illustration). If required, counterhold the pulley in order to unscrew the bolts. This is most easily achieved by wrapping an old drivebelt tightly around the pulley to act in a similar manner to a strap wrench.
11 Unscrew the retaining bolts, and withdraw

9.6c . . . and renew the gasket

the coolant pump from the cylinder block (see illustrations). Prise out the O-ring seal from the groove in the pump body, discard, as a new one will be required for refitting.

9.9a Undo the pump retaining bolts (arrowed)

9.10 Undo the three retaining bolts

9.8 Unscrew the securing bolts (arrowed)

Inspection

12 Check the pump body and impeller for signs of excessive corrosion. Turn the impeller,

9.9b Fit a new gasket to the coolant pump

9.11a Undo the retaining bolts. . .

9.11b . . . and remove the coolant pump

9.15 Fit new O-ring seal to the coolant pump – 1.6 diesel engine shown

and check for stiffness due to corrosion, or roughness due to excessive endplay.

13 No spare parts are available for the pump, and if faulty, worn or corroded, a new pump should be fitted.

Refitting

14 Commence refitting by thoroughly cleaning all traces of gasket/sealant from the mating faces of the pump and cylinder block.

15 Where applicable, fit new gasket/seal to the coolant pump (see illustration).

16 Place the pump in position in the cylinder block, refit the bolts to their correct locations and tighten to the specified torque.

17 On 1.2 litre petrol engines and 1.6 litre diesel engines, refit the pump pulley and tighten to the specified torque. Counterhold the pulley using an old drivebelt as during removal.

18 On 1.5 litre diesel engines refit the timing belt as described in Chapter 2B Section 5.

19 Refit and tension the auxiliary drivebelts (see Chapter 1A Section 29 for petrol engines, or Chapter 1B Section 33, 34 for diesel engines).

20 Refill the cooling system as described in Chapter 1A Section 33 for petrol engines, or Chapter 1B Section 32 for diesel engines.

21 If slackened, tighten the engine mounting bolts to the specified torque setting. Refit the battery as described in Chapter 5 Section 4.

10 Heater/ventilation system – general information

Note: Refer to Section 12 for information on the air conditioning side of the system.

Manually-controlled system

1 The heating/ventilation system consists of a variable-speed blower motor (housed behind the facia), face level vents in the centre and at each end of the facia, and air ducts to the front footwells.

2 The control unit is located in the facia, and the controls operate flap valves to deflect and mix the air flowing through the various parts of the heating/ventilation system. The flap valves are contained in the air distribution housing, which acts as a central distribution unit, passing air to the various ducts and vents.

3 Cold air enters the system through the grille in the scuttle. If required, the airflow is boosted by the blower, and then flows through the various ducts, according to the settings of the controls. Stale air is expelled through ducts at the rear of the vehicle. If warm air is required, the cold air is passed over the heater matrix, which is heated by the engine coolant.

4 A recirculation button enables the outside air supply to be closed off, while the air inside the vehicle is recirculated. This can be useful to prevent unpleasant odours entering from outside the vehicle, but should only be used

briefly, as the recirculated air inside the vehicle will soon become stale.

5 On some diesel engine models an electric heater is fitted into the heater housing. When the coolant temperature is cold, the heater warms the air before it enters the heater matrix. This quickly increases the temperature of the heater matrix on cold starts, resulting in warm air being available to heat the vehicle interior soon after start-up.

Automatic climate control

6 A fully automatic electronic climate control system is fitted to some models. The main components of the system are exactly the same as those described for the manual system, the only major difference being that the temperature and distribution flaps in the heating/ventilation housing are operated by electric motors rather than cables.

7 The operation of the system is controlled by the electronic control module (which is incorporated in the blower motor assembly) along with the following sensors.

a) The passenger compartment sensor – informs the control module of the temperature of the air inside the passenger compartment.

b) Evaporator temperature sensor – informs the control module of the evaporator temperature.

c) Heater matrix temperature sensor – informs the control module of the heater matrix temperature.

8 Using the information from the above sensors, the control module determines the appropriate settings for the heating/ventilation system housing flaps to maintain the passenger compartment at the desired setting on the control panel.

9 If the system develops a fault, the vehicle should be taken to a Nissan dealer. A complete test of the system can then be carried out, using a special electronic diagnostic test unit, which is simply plugged into the system's diagnostic connector. This is located inside the passenger compartment, on the drivers side of the facia panel (see illustration).

11 Heater/ventilation components – removal and refitting

1 Disconnect the battery negative terminal (refer to Disconnecting the battery in Chapter 5 Section 4).

Heater blower motor

2 Remove the clutch pedal assembly, as described in Chapter 8 Section 5.

3 Reaching up around the rear of the heater housing, disconnect the wiring connector from the top of the blower motor (see illustration).

4 Undo the retaining screw, then turn the blower motor clockwise and withdraw it

10.9 Vehicle diagnostic plug location

11.3 Disconnect the wiring connector

11.4a Remove the retaining screw (arrowed) – where fitted

11.4b Rotate the motor anti-clockwise...

11.4c ... and remove it from the heater housing

11.8 Disconnect the wiring connectors

11.9a Remove the lower retaining screw...

11.9b ... and withdraw it from the heater housing

from the rear of the heater housing (see illustrations).

5 Refitting is a reversal of removal.

Heater blower motor resistor

6 Remove the glovebox as described in Chapter 11 Section 25.

7 The resistor is located below the blower motor, in the left-hand side of the heater housing.

8 Disconnect the wiring connectors from the blower motor resistor (see illustration).

9 Undo the retaining screw and withdraw the resistor, releasing the upper part of the resistor from the heater housing (see illustrations).

10 Refitting is a reversal of removal.

Heater control panel

11 Unclip the heater control panel from the facia by carefully levering out the bottom of the control panel, to release the securing clips (see illustrations).

12 As the control panel is withdrawn disconnect the wiring connectors from the rear of the panel (see illustration).

13 Refitting is the reverse of removal.

Heater air flap motors

14 Depending on model, there is a number of air flap motors located on each side of the heater/blower motor housing.

15 To access the motors on the left-hand side of the heater housing, remove the glovebox assembly, as described in Chapter 11 Section 25.

16 To access the air mix door motor on the

right-hand side of the heater housing, release the retaining clips and remove the trim panel from the lower part of the facia, as described in Chapter 11 Section 25.

17 Disconnect the motor wiring connector,

11.11a Unclip the control panel...

11.12 Disconnect the wiring connectors as it is removed

then unscrew the retaining bolts and withdraw the motor (see illustrations). Note, as the motor is withdrawn from the flap spindle, depending on the position of the flap, it may rotate in the heater housing.

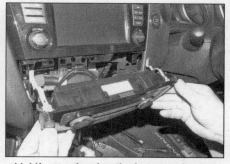

11.11b ... releasing the lower and upper securing clips

11.17a Disconnect the wiring connector, undo the retaining screws...

11.17b . . . and remove the motor from the housing

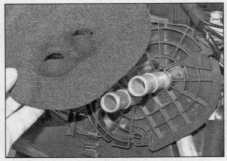

11.22 Remove the sealing foam from around the heater matrix pipes

11.23a Undo the retaining screws. . .

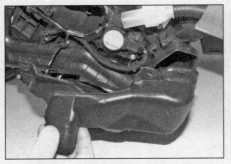

11.23b . . . and remove the air intake ducting

11.24a Undo the retaining screws. . .

11.24b . . . and remove the trim cover

18 Refitting is a reversal of removal, making sure the motors are located correctly on the housing. Before refitting the trim panels, check the operation of the motors, as they may need to be turned on the spindles to operate correctly.

Pollen filter

19 Remove and refit the pollen filter, as described in Chapter 1A Section 25.

Heater matrix

Note: *Check for the availability of parts with your local Nissan dealer, before commencing any work.*

20 Check the coolant pipe connections on the heater matrix. If the pipes are fixed to the heater matrix, carry out the following procedure. As the coolant pipes go up through the bulkhead, if the pipes are part of the heater matrix assembly.

21 This work entails removal of the centre console, complete facia assembly, wiring loom, facia support braces and metal crossmember, as described in Chapter 11 Section 25.

22 With the heater assembly removed from the vehicle, remove the sealing foam from around the coolant pipes **(see illustration)**.

23 Undo the retaining screws, and remove the air intake ducting from the left-hand side of the heater assembly **(see illustrations)**.

24 Undo the retaining screws, unclip the wiring and remove the plastic trim cover from over the coolant pipes **(see illustrations)**.

25 Disconnect the wiring connector from the sensor **(see illustration)**.

26 Undo the retaining screw and unclip the plastic mounting bracket from around the coolant pipes **(see illustrations)**.

27 Slide the matrix out from the heater housing, keeping the coolant pipes uppermost to prevent any coolant spillage **(see illustration)**.

11.25 Disconnect the wiring connector

11.26a Undo the retaining screw (arrowed). . .

11.26b . . . and unclip the plastic bracket

11.27 Slide the heater matrix out from the side of the housing

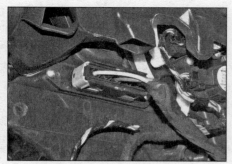

11.29 Location of the additional heater

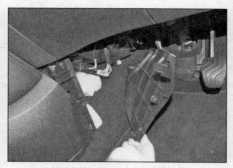

11.30 Unclip the trim panel

11.32a Undo the retaining screws. . .

11.32b . . . and remove the heater element

11.34 Location of the ambient temperature sensor

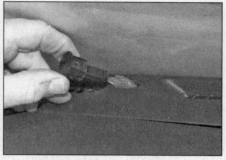

11.39 Unclip the sunlight sensor

28 Refitting is a reversal of removal, making sure the foam seal around the heater matrix is located correctly, before sliding it back into the housing.

Additional heater

29 Depending on model, there may be an additional heater fitted, to the right-hand side of the heater housing (see illustration).
30 Remove the trim panel above the pedals, release the two fasteners and remove the trim panel at the front of the centre console, adjacent to the pedals (see illustration).
31 Release the wiring securing clip and disconnect the wiring plug connectors for the heater element.
32 Undo the two retaining screws, and slide the heater element out from the housing. (see illustrations).
33 Refitting is the reverse of removal.

Ambient temperature sensor

34 The ambient temperature sensor is located, at the front of the vehicle, behind the front bumper just below the front crossmember (see illustration).
35 To remove the sensor, it will be necessary to remove the front bumper as described in Chapter 11 Section 5.
36 Disconnect the wiring connector from the sensor, and then unclip the sensor from the front crossmember.
37 Refitting is the reverse of removal.

Sunlight sensor

38 The sunlight sensor is fitted on the top of the facia panel, at the centre, nearest to the windscreen.
39 Carefully unclip the sensor from the grill panel, and then disconnect the wiring connector (see illustration).
40 Refitting is the reverse of removal.

12 Air conditioning system – general information and precautions

General information

1 An air conditioning system is available on all models. It enables the temperature of incoming air to be lowered, and also dehumidifies the air, which makes for rapid demisting and increased comfort.
2 The cooling side of the system works in the same way as a domestic refrigerator.

12.5 Automatic air-conditioning control unit

Refrigerant gas is drawn into a belt-driven compressor, and passes into a condenser mounted on the front of the radiator, where it loses heat and becomes liquid. The liquid passes through an expansion valve to an evaporator, where it changes from liquid under high pressure to gas under low pressure. This change is accompanied by a drop in temperature, which cools the evaporator. The refrigerant returns to the compressor, and the cycle begins again.
3 Air blown through the evaporator passes to the heating/ventilation housing, where it is mixed with hot air blown through the heater matrix to achieve the desired temperature in the passenger compartment.
4 The heating side of the system works in the same way as on models without air conditioning (see Section 11).
5 The operation of the system is controlled electronically by the ECM, which is located at the rear lower part of the heater assembly (see illustration). Any problems with the system should be referred to a Nissan dealer, or suitably-equipped specialist.

Precautions

6 When an air conditioning system is fitted, it is necessary to observe special precautions whenever dealing with any part of the system, or its associated components. The refrigerant is potentially dangerous, and should only be handled by qualified persons. Uncontrolled discharging of the refrigerant is dangerous and damaging to the environment for the following reasons.

13.3a Undo the bolts securing the refrigerant pipes to the compressor...

13.3b ... then plug the compressor and pipes to prevent contamination

13.4 Disconnect the compressor wiring connector

a) *If it is splashed onto the skin, it can cause frostbite.*

b) *The refrigerant is heavier then air and so displaces oxygen. In a confined space, which is not adequately ventilated, this could lead to a risk of suffocation. The gas is odourless and colourless so there is no warning of its presence in the atmosphere.*

c) *Although not poisonous, in the presence of a naked flame (including a cigarette) it forms a noxious gas that causes headaches, nausea, etc.*

⚠️ **Warning: Never attempt to open any air conditioning system refrigerant pipe/hose union without first having the system fully discharged by an air conditioning specialist. On completion of work, have the system recharged with the correct type and amount of fresh refrigerant.**

⚠️ **Warning: Always seal disconnected refrigerant pipe/ hose unions as soon as they are disconnected. Failure to form an airtight seal on any union will result in the dehydrator reservoir become saturated, necessitating its renewal. Also renew all sealing rings disturbed.**

Caution: Do not operate the air conditioning system if it is known to be short of refrigerant as this could damage the compressor.

13 Air conditioning system components – removal and refitting

⚠️ **Warning: Refer to the precautions given in Section 12 and have the system discharged by an air conditioning specialist before carrying out any work on the air conditioning system.**

Note: *If necessary for access to other components, the compressor can be unbolted and moved aside, without disconnecting its flexible hoses, after removing the auxiliary drivebelt.*

Compressor

1 Have the air conditioning system fully

discharged and evacuated by an air conditioning specialist.

2 Remove the auxiliary drivebelt (see Chapter 1A Section 29 for petrol engines, or Chapter 1B Section 33, 34 for diesel engines).

3 Unscrew the bolts securing the refrigerant pipe retaining plates to the compressor **(see illustrations)**. Separate the pipes from the compressor and quickly seal the pipe and compressor unions to prevent the entry of moisture into the refrigerant circuit. Discard the sealing rings, new ones must be used on refitting.

⚠️ **Warning: Failure to seal the refrigerant pipe unions will result in the dehydrator reservoir become saturated, necessitating its renewal.**

4 Disconnect the compressor wiring connector(s), and unclip the wiring harness from the retaining clips **(see illustration)**.

5 Unscrew the compressor mounting nut and bolts, then free the compressor from its mounting bracket and remove it from the engine **(see illustration)**. Where applicable, take care not to lose any spacers from the compressor mountings.

6 If the compressor is to be renewed, drain the refrigerant oil from the old compressor. The specialist who recharges the refrigerant system will need to add this amount of oil to the system.

7 If a new compressor is being fitted, drain the refrigerant oil.

8 Where fitted, ensure any spacers are correctly fitted to the mounting bolts, then manoeuvre the compressor into position and

13.5 Remove the compressor mounting nut and bolts

fit the bolts. Tighten the compressor front (drivebelt pulley end) mounting bolts to the specified torque first then tighten the rear bolts.

9 Lubricate the new refrigerant pipe sealing rings with compressor oil. Remove the plugs and install the sealing rings then quickly fit the refrigerant pipes to the compressor. Ensure the refrigerant pipes are correctly joined then refit the retaining bolt, tighten it securely.

10 Reconnect the wiring connector then refit the auxiliary drivebelt, (see Chapter 1A Section 29 for petrol engines, or Chapter 1B Section 33, 34 for diesel engines).

11 Have the air conditioning system recharged with the correct type and amount of refrigerant by a specialist before using the system. Remember to inform the specialist which components have been renewed, so they can add the correct amount of oil.

Condenser and receiver/dryer

12 Have the air conditioning system fully discharged by an air conditioning specialist.

13 Remove the front bumper as described in Chapter 11 Section 5.

14 Undo the retaining bolts and disconnect the refrigerant pipes from the right-hand side of the condenser. Recover the O-ring seals. Separate the pipes from the condenser and quickly seal the pipe and condenser unions to prevent the entry of moisture into the refrigerant circuit. Discard the sealing rings, new ones must be used on refitting.

⚠️ **Warning: Failure to seal the refrigerant pipe unions will result in the dehydrator reservoir become saturated, necessitating its renewal.**

15 Unclip the air-conditioning condenser from the front of the radiator, taking care not to damage the refrigerant pipes.

16 Refitting is a reversal of removal. Noting the following points:

a) *Ensure the condenser is seated in the locating clips on the radiator securely.*

b) *Lubricate the sealing rings with compressor oil. Remove the plugs and install the sealing rings then quickly fit the refrigerant pipes to the condenser. Securely tighten the dehydrator pipe union bolt/nut and ensure the compressor pipe is correctly joined.*

c) Have the air conditioning system recharged with the correct type and amount of refrigerant by a specialist before using the system.

Pressure switch

17 Have the air conditioning system fully discharged by an air conditioning specialist.
18 Remove the front bumper as described in Chapter 11 Section 5.
19 The switch is located in the refrigerant pipe to the right-hand side of the condenser/radiator (see illustration).
20 Disconnect the wiring connector and unscrew the sensor from the refrigerant pipe. Seal the refrigerant pipe, once the sensor has been removed.

⚠️ **Warning: Failure to seal the refrigerant pipe unions will result in the dehydrator reservoir become saturated, necessitating its renewal.**

21 Refitting is a reversal of removal noting the following points:
a) Lubricate the switch seal with compressor oil.
b) Have the air conditioning system recharged with the correct type and amount of refrigerant by a specialist prior to using the system.

Evaporator

22 Have the air conditioning system fully discharged and evacuated by an air conditioning specialist.
23 Remove the heating/ventilation housing as described in Section 11, and remove the heater matrix.
24 Release the securing clip and remove the pollen filter (noting its fitted position), from the rear of the heater housing (see illustrations).
25 With the heater assembly removed from the vehicle, remove the sealing foam from around the refrigerant expansion valve connection (see illustration).
26 Working your way around the heater housing, undo the retaining screws and strip down the heater housing (see illustrations).
27 Slide the plastic trim panel from in front of the evaporator, then withdraw the evaporator from the heater housing (see illustrations).

28 Refitting is a reversal of removal but have the air conditioning system recharged with the correct type and amount of refrigerant by a specialist prior to using the system.

Air intake temperature sensor

29 The air temperature sensor is located in the lower part of the heater housing, on the

13.19 Pressure switch location in refrigerant pipe

13.24a Unclip the cover. . .

13.24b . . . and withdraw the pollen filter

13.25 Remove the sealing foam from the expansion valve

13.26a Remove the upper part. . .

13.26b . . . followed by the air intake ducting. . .

13.26c . . . then split the heater housing. . .

13.26d . . . noting that some screws are inside the housing

13.27a Slide out the plastic panel. . .

13.27b . . . and withdraw the evaporator

13.29 Air temperature sensor location

13.31 Disconnect the wiring connector

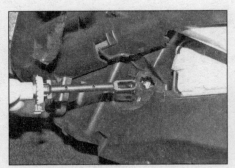

13.32 Turn the sensor anti-clockwise to remove

13.35 Pull back the sound proofing. . .

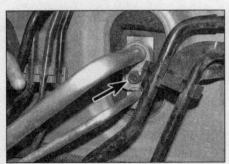

13.36a . . . to access the refrigerant pipe retaining bolt. . .

13.36b . . . undo bolt and disconnect the refrigerant pipes

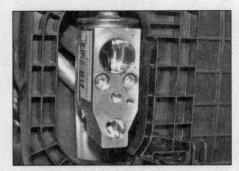

13.38 Undo the two bolts to remove the expansion valve

13.39 Fit new O-ring seals on re-assembly

left-hand side, in front of the heater matrix **(see illustration)**.

30 To make access easier, remove the glovebox, as described in Chapter 11 Section 25.

31 Working in the passenger side footwell, reach up and disconnect the wiring connector from the temperature sensor **(see illustration)**.

32 Turn the sensor a quarter of a turn anti-clockwise and withdraw from the heater housing **(see illustration)**.

33 Refitting is a reversal of removal

Expansion valve

34 Have the air conditioning system fully discharged and evacuated by an air conditioning specialist.

35 Release the fasteners and remove the sound insulation material from the engine compartment bulkhead **(see illustration)**.

36 Undo the retaining bolt and withdraw the refrigerant pipes from the connection at the engine compartment bulkhead **(see illustrations)**.

37 Plug/cover the openings in the refrigerant pipes and the expansion valve to prevent contamination/saturation.

⚠ *Warning: Failure to seal the refrigerant pipe unions will result in the receiver/dryer becoming saturated, necessitating its renewal*

38 Pull the rubber seal from around the pipes connection at the bulkhead, and then undo the two bolts from the centre of the expansion valve **(see illustration)**, and remove it from the bulkhead.

39 Recover and discard the O-ring seals from the refrigerant pipes and expansion valve – new ones must be fitted **(see illustration)**.

40 Refitting is a reversal of removal but have the air conditioning system recharged with the correct type and amount of refrigerant by a specialist prior to using the system.

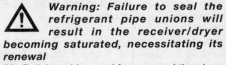

Chapter 4 Part A
Fuel and exhaust systems – petrol models

Contents

Degrees of difficulty

Easy, suitable for novice with little experience	Fairly easy, suitable for beginner with some experience	Fairly difficult, suitable for competent DIY mechanic	Difficult, suitable for experienced DIY mechanic	Very difficult, suitable for expert DIY or professional

Specifications

General

Engine identification	Engine code
Designation:	
1.2 litre engine	HRA2DDT

System type

Fuel system type	Hitachi Electronic Concentrated Control System (ECCS) 2, high-pressure direct fuel injection with turbocharger

Fuel system data

Fuel pump type	Electric, immersed in tank, and engine driven high-pressure pump
High-pressure fuel pump	Mechanical – driven by exhaust camshaft
Specified idle speed	750 ± 50 rpm (not adjustable – controlled by ECU)
Idle mixture CO content	Less than 1% (not adjustable – controlled by ECU)

Recommended fuel

Minimum octane rating	95 RON unleaded (UK unleaded premium). Leaded/lead replacement fuel (LRP) must not be used
Fuel tank capacity	55 litres

Torque wrench settings

	Nm	lbf ft
Camshaft position sensor	10	7
Coolant feed-to-turbocharger banjo bolts	25	18
Exhaust manifold nuts-to-cylinder head	30	22
Fuel pipe:		
To-fuel rail	22	16
To-high pressure fuel pump	30	22
Fuel rail mounting bolts	12	9
Fuel rail pressure sensor	35	26
High-pressure fuel pump bolts	25	18
Inlet manifold	10	7
Intercooler bolts	8	6
Oil feed-to-turbocharger banjo bolt	12	9
Oil drain-to-turbocharger bolts	10	7
Oil drain-to-cylinder block banjo bolt	40	30
Throttle body bolts	8	6

1 General information and precautions

1 The fuel supply system consists of a fuel tank, which is mounted under the rear of the car, with an electric fuel pump immersed in it, a fuel filter (depending on model), fuel feed and return pipes. All petrol models are equipped with a direct injection system, where the tank-immersed electric pump supplies fuel to an engine-driven high-pressure pump. This pump supplies fuel to a common fuel rail, where it is distributed under high-pressure to the injectors. Fuel is then injected directly into the combustion chambers, resulting in lower emissions, higher engine output, for reduced consumption.

2 Refer to Chapter 6A for further information on the operation of the engine management system.

⚠ *Warning: Many of the procedures in this Chapter require the removal of fuel pipes and connections, which may result in some fuel spillage. Before carrying out any operation on the fuel system, refer to the precautions given in 'Safety first!' at the beginning of this manual, and follow them implicitly. Petrol is a highly dangerous and volatile liquid, and the precautions necessary when handling it cannot be overstressed.*

Note: *Residual pressure may remain in the fuel pipes long after the vehicle was last used. When disconnecting any fuel line, first depressurise the fuel system as described in Section 4.*

2 Troubleshooting

Low pressure fuel pump

1 The lower pressure fuel pump is located inside the fuel tank. Sit inside the vehicle with the windows closed, turn the ignition key to ON (not START) and listen for the sound of the fuel pump as it's briefly activated. You will only hear the sound for a second or two, but

3.1 Remove the air resonator ducting

that sound indicates that the pump is working. Alternatively, have an assistant listen at the fuel filler cap.

2 If the pump does not come on, check the relevant fuses and relays as described in Chapter 12 Section 3.

3 If the fuses and relays are okay, check the wiring back to the fuel pump. If the wiring is okay, the fuel pump control module may be defective. If the pump runs continuously with the ignition key in the ON position, engine management ECU may be defective. Have the circuit checked by a dealer or suitably equipped repairer.

Fuel injection system

Note: *The following procedure is based on the assumption that the fuel pump is working and the fuel pressure is adequate.*

4 Check all electrical connectors that are related to the system. Check the earth wire connections for tightness (see Chapter 12 Section 2).

5 Verify that the battery is fully charged (see Chapter 5 Section 2).

6 Inspect the air filter element (see Chapter 1A Section 26).

7 Check all fuses related to the fuel system (see Chapter 12 Section 3).

8 Check the air intake system between the throttle body and the intake manifold for leaks. Also inspect the condition of all vacuum hoses connected to the intake manifold and to the throttle body.

9 Remove the air intake duct from the throttle body and look for dirt, carbon, varnish, or

other residue in the throttle body, particularly around the throttle plate. If it's dirty, clean it with carburettor cleaner, a toothbrush and a clean rag.

10 With the engine running, place an automotive stethoscope against each injector, one at a time, and listen for a clicking sound that indicates operation.

⚠ *Warning: Stay clear of the drivebelt and any rotating or hot components.*

11 If you can hear the injectors operating, but the engine is misfiring, the electrical circuits are functioning correctly, but the injectors might be dirty or blocked. Try a commercial injector cleaning product (available at auto parts suppliers). If cleaning the injectors doesn't help, the injectors may need to be replaced.

12 If an injector is not operating (it makes no sound), disconnect the injector electrical plug and measure the resistance across the injector terminals with an ohmmeter. Compare this measurement to the other injectors. If the resistance of the non-operational injector is quite different from the other injectors, replace it.

13 If the injector is not operating, but the resistance reading is within the range of resistance of the other injectors, the ECU or the circuit between the ECU and the injector might be faulty.

3 Air cleaner assembly – removal and refitting

Removal

1 Release the retaining clips and slide the air intake resonator from the air cleaner housing, and from the air intake duct, which is secured to the front crossmember **(see illustration)**. Note, the retaining clips on the intake duct are fragile and could break easily, if the bolt and two retaining clips at the front of the duct are removed, the complete air intake duct can be removed in one piece.

2 Release the two retaining clips, undo the mounting bolt and remove the air intake duct from the front of the engine compartment **(see illustrations)**.

3.2a Release the two retaining clips. . .

3.2b . . . undo the retaining bolt. . .

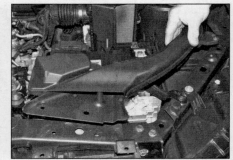
3.2c . . . and remove the front air intake duct

3.3 Slacken the air intake rubber hose retaining clip

3.4a Undo the upper mounting bolt. . .

3.4b . . . and remove the air cleaner housing

3 Slacken the retaining clip and disconnect the rubber air intake hose from the side of the air cleaner housing **(see illustration)**.
4 Undo the upper mounting bolt, then pull the air cleaner housing upwards to release it from the rubber mountings and remove the complete assembly from the rear of the engine compartment **(see illustrations)**.

Refitting

5 Refitting is a reversal of the removal procedure, ensuring that all hoses and ducts are properly reconnected and correctly seated and, where necessary, securely held by their retaining clips. Do not use any grease or lubricant when refitting the air hoses/ducts.

4 Fuel system – depressurisation

Note: *Refer to the precautions given in Section 1 before proceeding.*

⚠️ *Warning: The following procedure will merely relieve the pressure in the fuel system – remember that fuel will still be present in the system components, and take precautions accordingly before disconnecting any of them. Use clean rags wrapped around the connections to catch escaping fuel, and dispose of any fuel-soaked rags with care. Plug or tape over any open fuel lines, to prevent further loss of fuel or ingress of dirt.*
1 The fuel system referred to in this Section is defined as the tank-mounted fuel pump, the high-pressure fuel pump, the fuel rail and injectors, the pressure regulator, and the metal pipes and flexible hoses of the fuel lines between these components. All these contain fuel, which will be under pressure while the engine is running and/or while the ignition is switched on. The pressure will remain for some time after the ignition has been switched off, and must be relieved before any of these components are disturbed for servicing work.
2 Identify and remove the fuel pump fuse (see wiring diagram in Chapter 12 Section 3) from the fusebox in the left-hand side of the engine compartment – the fuses can also be identified from the label inside the fusebox cover.

3 Start the engine, and allow it to run until it runs out of fuel in the injection system, and the engine stalls.
4 Try to start the engine at least twice more, to ensure that all residual pressure has been relieved.
5 Disconnect the battery negative terminal (refer to Chapter 5 Section 4).
6 For safety, the fuel pump fuse should not be refitted until all work on the fuel system has been completed. If you refit the fuse now, **do not** switch on the ignition until completion of the work.

5 Fuel pipes and fittings – general information and disconnection

1 Disconnect the battery negative lead as described in Chapter 5 Section 4.
2 The fuel supply pipe connects the fuel pump in the fuel tank to the fuel rail on the engine.
3 Whenever you're working under the vehicle, be sure to inspect all fuel and evaporative emission pipes for leaks, kinks, dents and other damage. Always replace a damaged fuel pipe immediately.
4 If you find signs of dirt in the pipes during disassembly, disconnect all pipes and blow them out with compressed air. Inspect the fuel strainer on the fuel pump pick-up unit for damage and deterioration.

Steel tubing

5 It is critical that the fuel pipes be

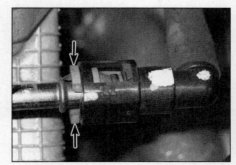

5.10a Two-tab type fitting; depress both tabs with your fingers, then pull the fuel pipe and the fitting apart

replaced with pipes of equivalent type and specification.
6 Some steel fuel pipes have threaded fittings. When loosening these fittings, hold the stationary fitting with a spanner while turning the union nut.

Plastic tubing

⚠️ *Warning: When removing or installing plastic fuel tubing, be careful not to bend or twist it too much, which can damage it. Also, plastic fuel tubing is NOT heat resistant, so keep it away from excessive heat.*
7 When replacing fuel system plastic tubing, use only original equipment replacement plastic tubing.

Flexible hoses

8 When replacing fuel system flexible hoses, use original equipment replacements, or hose to the same specification.
9 Don't route fuel hoses (or metal pipes) within 100 mm of the exhaust system or within 280 mm of the catalytic converter. Make sure that no rubber hoses are installed directly against the vehicle, particularly in places where there is any vibration. If allowed to touch some vibrating part of the vehicle, a hose can easily become chafed and it might start leaking. A good rule of thumb is to maintain a minimum of 8.0 mm clearance around a hose (or metal pipe) to prevent contact with the vehicle underbody.

Disconnecting Fuel pipe Fittings

10 Typical fuel pipe fittings:

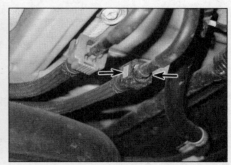

5.10b On this type of fitting, depress the two buttons on opposite sides of the fitting, then pull it off the fuel pipe

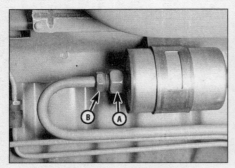

5.10c Threaded fuel pipe fitting; hold the stationary portion of the pipe or component (A) while loosening the union nut (B) with a flare-nut spanner

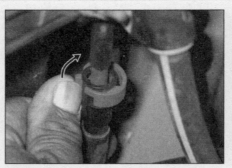

5.10d Plastic collar-type fitting; rotate the outer part of the fitting

5.10e Metal collar quick-connect fitting; pull the end of the retainer off the fuel pipe and disengage the other end from the female side of the fitting. . .

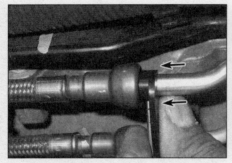

5.10f . . . insert a fuel pipe separator tool into the female side of the fitting, push it into the fitting and pull the fuel pipe off the pipe

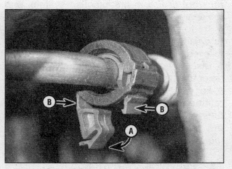

5.10g Some fittings are secured by lock tabs. Release the lock tab (A) and rotate it to the fully-opened position, squeeze the two smaller lock tabs (B). . .

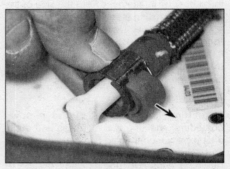

5.10h . . . then push the retainer out and pull the fuel pipe off the pipe

5.10i Spring-lock coupling; remove the safety cover, install a coupling release tool and close the tool around the coupling. . .

5.10j . . . push the tool into the fitting, then pull the two pipes apart

5.10k Hairpin clip type fitting: push the legs of the retainer clip together, then push the clip down all the way until it stops and pull the fuel pipe off the pipe

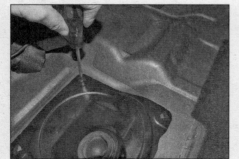

6.4a Turn the four retaining clips. . .

6 Fuel pump and fuel gauge sender unit – removal and refitting

 Warning: Refer to the warning note in Section 1 before proceeding.

Removal

1 Depressurise the fuel system as described in Section 4.
2 Disconnect the battery negative terminal (refer to *Disconnecting the battery* in Chapter 5 Section 4).

3 To gain access to the sender unit, lift out the rear seat cushion, as described in Chapter 11 Section 21.
4 Turn the retaining clips through 90° anti-clockwise, and lift up the access cover to expose the sender unit **(see illustrations)**.
5 Brush away any accumulated dust or dirt around the top of the sender unit so it does not drop into the fuel tank when the unit is removed.
6 Disconnect the wiring connector from the top of the sender unit **(see illustration)**.
7 Release the retaining clip and disconnect the fuel hose from the top of the unit **(see illustration)**. Plug the hose end to prevent dirt ingress.

6.4b . . . and remove the access cover

6.6 Disconnect the pump wiring plug

6.7 Depress the release button and disconnect the fuel pipe

6.9a Using a home-made tool. . .

6.9b . . . slacken the locking ring. . .

6.9c . . . and remove it from the fuel pump

8 Note the fitted position of the sender unit and if necessary make an alignment mark on the sender unit and fuel tank to ensure correct refitting.

9 Twist the locking ring from the top of the fuel tank and carefully lift the sender unit out, taking care not to damage the sender unit or spill fuel onto the interior of the vehicle **(see illustrations)**.

10 Remove the sealing ring from the top of the fuel tank and discard; as a new one will be required for refitting **(see illustration)**.

Refitting

11 Refitting is a reversal of the removal procedure, noting the following points:

a) Fit a new sealing ring to the top of the fuel tank.

b) Align the marks made on the sender unit and fuel tank during removal, the two locating tabs facing to the front **(see illustration)**.

c) Secure the unit with the locking ring, making sure the locking ring raised locking tabs are centralised **(see illustration)**.

d) Ensure that the fuel hose and the wiring connector are securely reconnected to the sender unit.

e) Prior to refitting the access cover, reconnect the battery, then start the engine and check the fuel hose(s) for signs of leaks.

6.9d . . . then withdraw the fuel pump, taking care not to damage the float arm

6.10 Fit a new sealing ring to the top of the tank

6.11a Position the two tabs at the front

6.11b Centralise the locking ring raised tabs

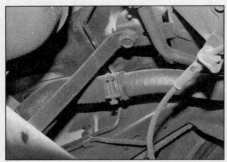

7.6 Undo the fuel filler neck retaining clip

7.9a Undo the fuel tank retaining strap front bolts (one side shown). . .

7.9b . . . and retaining strap rear bolt (one side shown)

7 Fuel tank – removal and refitting

⚠ *Warning: Refer to the warning note in Section 1 before proceeding.*

Removal

1 Before removing the fuel tank, all fuel must be drained from the tank. Since a fuel tank drain plug is not provided, it is therefore preferable to carry out the removal operation when the tank is nearly empty.

2 Depressurise the fuel system as described in Section 4.

3 Disconnect the battery negative terminal (refer to Chapter 5 Section 4), then syphon or hand-pump the remaining fuel from the tank.

4 Remove the relevant sections of the exhaust system from below the fuel tank, as described in Section 15. If required, release the fasteners and remove the heatshield from below the fuel tank.

5 Disconnect the wiring connector(s) and fuel hose(s) from the fuel pump/gauge sender unit, as described in Section 6.

6 Working at the right-hand side rear of the fuel tank, release the retaining clip and disconnect the filler neck hose from the fuel tank **(see illustration)**.

7 Working at the rear of the fuel tank, release the retaining clip and disconnect the fuel vent pipe hose from the fuel tank.

8 Place a trolley jack with an interposed block of wood beneath the tank, then raise the jack until it is supporting the weight of the tank.

9 Slacken and remove the bolts securing the two fuel tank retaining straps to the vehicle body **(see illustrations)**.

10 Slowly lower the fuel tank out of position and remove the tank from underneath the vehicle. Note, depending on model, it may be necessary to disconnect any other relevant vent/EVAP pipes as they become accessible.

11 If the tank is contaminated with sediment or water, remove the sender unit/fuel pump (Section 6) and swill the tank out with clean fuel. If any damage is evident, the tank should be renewed.

Refitting

12 Refitting is the reverse of the removal procedure, noting the following points:

a) *When lifting the tank back into position, reconnect all the relevant breather hoses, and take great care to ensure that none of the hoses become trapped between the tank and vehicle body. Tighten the fuel tank mounting bolts to the specified torque setting.*

b) *Ensure that all pipes and hoses are correctly routed, and securely held in position with their retaining clips.*

c) *On completion, refill the tank with fuel, and check for signs of leakage prior to taking the vehicle on the road.*

8 Throttle housing – removal and refitting

Note: *The throttle potentiometer is mounted on the rear of the throttle housing and can only be renewed as a complete unit – Check with your local Nissan dealer for the availability of parts.*

Removal

1 Disconnect the battery negative terminal (refer to Chapter 5 Section 4).

2 Undo the retaining bolts and remove the air inlet tube away from the throttle housing **(see illustration)**.

3 Disconnect the wiring connector from the throttle housing **(see illustration)**.

4 Slacken and remove the bolts securing the throttle housing assembly to the inlet manifold (working diagonally), and remove it from the engine compartment. Remove the O-ring seal/gasket and discard it; a new one must be used on refitting. Plug the inlet manifold port with a wad of clean cloth, to prevent the possible entry of foreign matter.

Refitting

5 Refitting is a reverse of the removal procedure, bearing in mind the following:

a) *Ensure that the mating surfaces of the manifold and throttle housing are clean and dry, and fit a new O-ring seal/gasket to the manifold. Fit the throttle housing then, working in a diagonal sequence, tighten the retaining bolts to the specified torque setting.*

9 Fuel injection system components – removal and refitting

Fuel rail and injectors

Note: *Refer to the warning note in Section 1 before proceeding.*

Note: *If a faulty injector is suspected, before condemning the injector it is worth trying the effect of one of the proprietary injector-cleaning treatments.*

8.2 Disconnect the air inlet tube

8.3 Disconnect the wiring connector

9.4 Renew the fuel pipe on refitting

9.5 Disconnect the wiring connector

9.6 Unclip the wiring harness from the rail

9.7a Undo the mounting bolts. . .

9.7b . . . and withdraw the fuel rail complete with injectors

9.9 Pull the injector from the fuel rail

Note: *Renewal of the Teflon sealing ring at the base of each injector entails the use of Nissan special tools. Have this work carried out by a Nissan dealer or fuel injection specialist. Note also that Nissan state that the fuel rail and fuel pipe must always be renewed after removal.*

1 Depressurise the fuel system as described in Section 4.

2 Disconnect the battery negative terminal (refer to *Disconnecting the battery* in Chapter 5 Section 4).

3 Remove the inlet manifold as described in Section 11. Using duct tape (or similar), cover the intake ducts in the cylinder head to prevent anything being dropped down into the cylinders.

4 Thoroughly clean the high-pressure fuel pipe unions on the fuel rail and high-pressure fuel pump. Unscrew the union nuts, undo the support clip retaining bolt and withdraw the pipe **(see illustration)**. Plug or cover the open unions to prevent dirt entry.

5 Disconnect the wiring connector from the fuel pressure sensor on the fuel rail **(see illustration)**.

6 Unclip the wiring harness from the fuel rail, then disconnect the wiring connectors from the four fuel injectors **(see illustration)**.

7 Undo the four retaining bolts and carefully ease the fuel rail and injectors from their location in the cylinder head **(see illustrations)**.

8 Using duct tape (or similar), cover the injector recesses in the cylinder head to prevent anything being dropped down inside them.

9 Pull the injector to remove it from its location in the fuel rail, noting the locating peg on the top of the injector **(see illustration)**. Recover the sealing rings, then repeat the procedure to remove any of the other injectors.

10 Discard the seals, sealing rings, fuel pipe and fuel rail; new components must be used on refitting.

11 Refitting is a reversal of the removal procedure, noting the following points:
a) *Fit new O-rings to all disturbed injectors and have new Teflon seals fitted by a Nissan dealer or specialist.*
b) *Apply a smear of engine oil to the O-rings to aid installation, and then ease the injectors into the new fuel rail.*
c) *Make sure the injectors are located correctly in the fuel rail.*

d) *On completion, start the engine and check for fuel leaks.*

Valve timing control solenoids

12 The valve timing control solenoids are fitted to each side of the timing chain cover, one solenoid serves the inlet camshaft and one serves the exhaust camshaft **(see illustration)**.

13 Disconnect the wiring connector from the relevant solenoid **(see illustration)**.

14 Undo the retaining bolt and withdraw the relevant solenoid from the timing chain cover **(see illustrations)**. Be prepared for some oil spillage, and have some cloth ready to catch it.

15 Refitting is the reverse of removal.

9.12 Valve timing solenoids at each side

9.13 Disconnect the wiring connector – inlet side shown

9.14a Undo the retaining bolt. . .

9.14b . . . and withdraw the solenoid – inlet side shown

9.16 High-pressure fuel pump location

9.20a Release the locking clip. . .

9.20b . . . and disconnect the fuel pipe

9.21 Disconnect the wiring connector

High-pressure fuel pump

Note: *Refer to the warning note in Section 1 before proceeding.*
Note: *Nissan recommend that the fuel pipe is renewed, once it has been removed.*

16 The high-pressure fuel pump is mounted on the cylinder head cover and is operated by the exhaust camshaft, via a lifter **(see illustration)**.
17 Depressurise the fuel system as described in Section 4.

18 Disconnect the battery negative terminal (refer to *Disconnecting the battery* in Chapter 5 Section 4).
19 Remove the hoses and and wiring from across the top of the fuel pump.
20 Release the coloured tab of the quick-release fitting and disconnect the fuel supply hose from the fuel pump **(see illustrations)**. Suitably cover the hose union and the fitting on the pump to prevent dirt ingress.
21 Disconnect the wiring connector from the fuel pump **(see illustration)**.
22 Remove the inlet manifold, as described in Section 11. This will need to be removed to access the fuel pipe from the fuel pump to the fuel rail, as Nissan recommend that this is renewed on refitting.
23 Thoroughly clean the high-pressure fuel pipe unions on the fuel rail and high-pressure fuel pump. Unscrew the union nuts, undo the support clip retaining bolt and withdraw the pipe **(see illustration 9.4)**. Plug or cover the open unions to prevent dirt entry. Note that a new fuel pipe will be required for refitting.
24 Undo the fuel pump retaining bolts and remove the fuel pump from the cylinder head cover, recover the O-ring, then remove the pump lifter **(see illustrations)**. Remove the bolts evenly, turning them the same amount of turns at a time, until the pump is removed.
25 Commence refitting by placing a new O-ring on the pump body. Apply a smear of engine oil to the O-ring to aid installation.
26 Place the pump lifter in position in the cylinder head cover, making sure the peg on the side aligns with the groove in the cylinder head cover **(see illustration)**. If the lifter is not

9.24a Undo the mounting bolts. . .

9.24b . . . withdraw the fuel pump. . .

9.24c . . . and the lifter

9.26 Align with the groove inside the cover

in its lowest position, turn the crankshaft by means of the crankshaft pulley bolt until the lifter camshaft lobe points downward.

27 Refit the pump, screw in the retaining bolts and progressively tighten them to the specified torque.

28 Fit the new fuel pipe to the pump and fuel rail and tighten the pipe unions securely. Refit and tighten the support clip retaining bolt.

29 Reconnect the pump wiring connector and the fuel supply hose.

30 Refit the inlet manifold as described in Section 11.

31 On completion, start the engine and check for fuel leaks.

10 Fuel pressure sensor – removal and refitting

Removal

1 Remove the inlet manifold, as described in Section 11.

2 Release the locking clip and disconnect the wiring plug from the sensor, which is screwed into the underside of the fuel rail **(see illustration)**.

3 Unscrew the sensor from the fuel rail and recover the teflon sealing washer. Discard the sealing washer, as a new one will be required for refitting. Be prepared for fluid spillage and plug the openings to prevent contamination.

10.2 Fuel pressure sensor location

Refitting

4 Fit the sealing washer, then screw the sensor back into the fuel rail, and tighten it to the specified torque.

5 The remainder of refitting is a reversal of removal.

11 Inlet manifold – removal and refitting

Removal

1 Disconnect the battery negative terminal (refer to *Disconnecting the battery* in Chapter 5 Section 4).

11.2a Undo the two retaining nuts. . .

2 Undo the retaining nuts and release the hose from the retaining clips on the cylinder head cover. Release the retaining clips and disconnect the charge air cooler inlet hose from the intercooler and turbocharger **(see illustrations)**.

3 Remove the throttle housing from the inlet manifold, as described in Section 8.

4 Disconnect the following hoses from the inlet manifold **(see illustrations)** :
a) EVAP Charcoal canister purge hose.
b) PCV Crankcase ventilation hose.
c) Brake servo vacuum hose.

5 Disconnect the wiring connectors at the inlet manifold pressure sensor**(see illustration)**.

6 Undo the retaining bolt and unclip the

11.2b . . . unclip the hose. . .

11.2c . . . release the clips from the intercooler. . .

11.2d . . . and the other end on the turbo

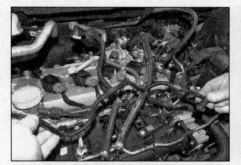
11.4a Disconnect the charcoal canister purge hose. . .

11.4b . . . the crankcase ventilation hose. . .

11.4c . . . and the brake servo vacuum hose

11.5 Disconnect the wiring connector

11.6a Remove the wiring loom bracket. . .

11.6b . . . and unclip the wiring loom

11.7 Unclip the pipe from the top of the manifold

11.9 Remove the inlet manifold

11.10 Ensure new manifold seals are fitted

wiring loom from across the front of the inlet manifold **(see illustrations)**. Withdraw the oil level dipstick to make access to the manifold centre bolts easier.

7 Unclip the metal pipe from across the top of the inlet manifold and move it to one side **(see illustration)**.

8 Make a final check that all the necessary vacuum/breather hoses and wiring have been disconnected from the manifold then, working from the outside to the centre, slacken and remove the manifold retaining bolts.

9 Manoeuvre the manifold away from the cylinder head, and out of the engine compartment **(see illustration)**. Remove the manifold rubber gasket and discard it, a new one will be required for refitting.

Refitting

10 Refitting is the reverse of the removal procedure, noting the following points:

13.5 Disconnect the vacuum pipe

a) *Ensure that the manifold and cylinder head mating surfaces are clean and dry, and fit the new rubber gasket to the manifold **(see illustration)**.*
b) *Install the manifold, and tighten its retaining bolts to the specified torque, starting at the centre and working outwards.*
c) *Ensure that all relevant hoses are reconnected to their original positions, and are securely held (where necessary) by their retaining clips.*

12 Exhaust manifold –
removal and refitting

1 The exhaust manifold is integral with the turbocharger. Refer to Section 13.

13.6 Disconnect the wiring connector

13 Turbocharger –
removal and refitting

Note: *This Section describes removal and refitting of the turbocharger, together with the exhaust manifold. The turbocharger cannot be separately removed from the exhaust manifold.*

Removal

1 Raise the front of the vehicle and support it securely on axle stands (see *Jacking and vehicle support*). Remove the right-hand side front wheel, then release the fasteners and remove the wheelarch liner.

2 Undo the retaining nuts and release the hose from the retaining clips on the cylinder head cover. Release the retaining clips and disconnect the charge air cooler inlet hose from the intercooler and turbocharger **(see illustrations 11.2a, 11.2b, 11.2c and 11.2d)**.

3 Drain the coolant as described in Chapter 1A Section 33.

4 Remove the catalytic converter, as describe in Chapter 6A Section 18.

5 Release the securing clip and disconnect the vacuum pipe from the turbocharger **(see illustration)**.

6 Release the securing clip and disconnect the wiring connector from the turbocharger **(see illustration)**.

7 Release the securing clips and remove the air intake hose from between the turbocharger and air cleaner housing **(see illustration)**.

13.7 Remove the air intake hose

13.8a Undo the banjo bolts. . .

13.8b . . . remove the bolt securing the bracket. . .

8 Undo the retaining bolt from the coolant pipe retaining bracket, then undo the two banjo bolts and disconnect the two coolant pipes from the rear of the turbocharger **(see illustrations)**. Nissan recommend that the metal pipes be renewed when refitting, as the sealing rings/ washers are part of the end fittings. If the turbocharger is not being renewed and is being refitted back to the vehicle, then disconnect the two rubber coolant hoses from the metal pipes and do not disturb the banjo bolts, this will prevent having to renew the metal pipes.
9 Undo the banjo bolt and disconnect the oil feed pipe from the top of the turbocharger **(see illustration)**. Nissan recommend that the metal pipes be renewed when refitting, as the sealing rings/washers are part of the end fittings.
10 Undo the two bolts and remove the oil return pipe from the underside of the turbocharger to the cylinder block **(see illustrations)**. Nissan recommends that the

13.8c . . .and disconnect the coolant pipes

oil return pipe be renewed when refitting, as the sealing rings/washers are part of the end fittings. Be prepared for oil spillage.
11 Undo the three retaining bolts and remove the heat shield from the lower part of the exhaust manifold **(see illustrations)**.

13.9 Disconnect the oil feed pipe

12 Unscrew the mounting nuts, then remove the turbocharger/exhaust manifold from the cylinder head **(see illustrations)**. Do not attempt to separate the inlet and exhaust sections of the turbocharger.
13 Remove the gasket noting its fitted

13.10a Undo the two bolts. . .

13.10b . . . and disconnect the oil return pipe

13.11a Undo the three bolts. . .

13.11b . . . and remove the heat shield

13.12a Undo the mounting nuts. . .

13.12b . . . and remove the exhaust manifold/turbocharger

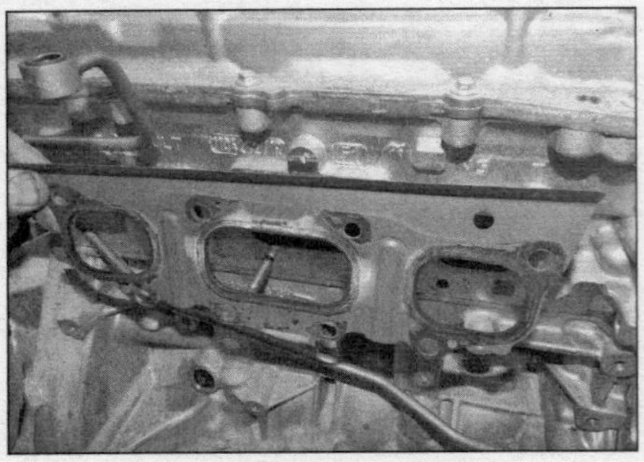

13.13 Renew the gasket

position, and discard, as a new one will be required for refitting **(see illustration)**.

Refitting

14 Refitting is a reversal of removal, using a new manifold gasket. Renew any damaged hose clamps, and tighten the manifold nuts to the specified torque. Fit new oil supply pipe O-rings and copper seals, then apply Loctite Frenetanch (or similar sealant) to the union threads before refitting the pipe and tightening the union nuts to the specified torque. Fit a new gasket to the top of the oil return pipe, and new O-ring seals to the grooves in the bottom of the pipe.

15 On completion refill the cooling system as described in Chapter 1A Section 33.

14 Intercooler – removal and refitting

Removal

1 The intercooler is located behind the front bumper, to the right-hand side of the radiator and air conditioning condenser.

2 Remove the front bumper as described in Chapter 11 Section 5.

3 Undo the retaining nuts and release the hose from the retaining clips on the cylinder head cover. Release the retaining clips and disconnect the charge air cooler upper hose from the intercooler and turbocharger **(see illustrations)**.

4 Slacken the retaining clip and release the intercooler lower air intake pipe from the bottom of the intercooler, then undo the mounting bracket bolts and the bolts in the throttle housing, then remove the air intake pipe **(see illustrations)**. Disconnect the wiring connector from the turbocharger boost pressure sensor in the air intake pipe.

5 Release the wiring loom and connectors from across the reinforcement crossmember, then undo the retaining nuts and remove the crossmember from the front of the vehicle **(see illustration)**.

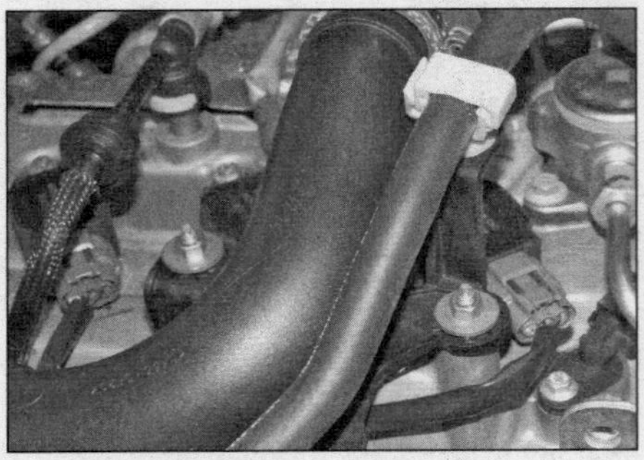

14.3a Undo the two retaining nuts. . .

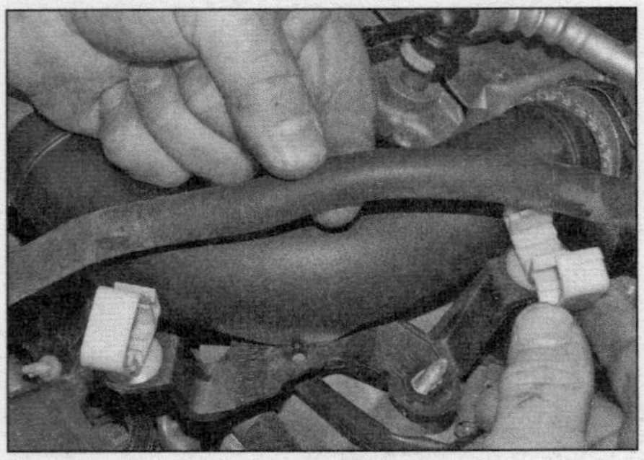

14.3b . . . unclip the hose. . .

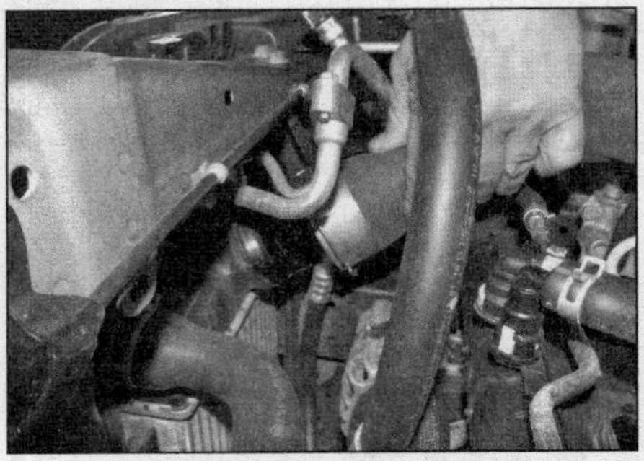

14.3c . . . release the hose clip from the intercooler. . .

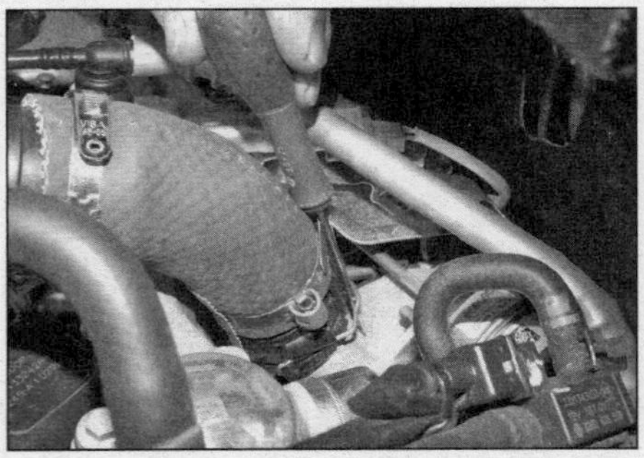

14.3d . . . and the other end on the turbo

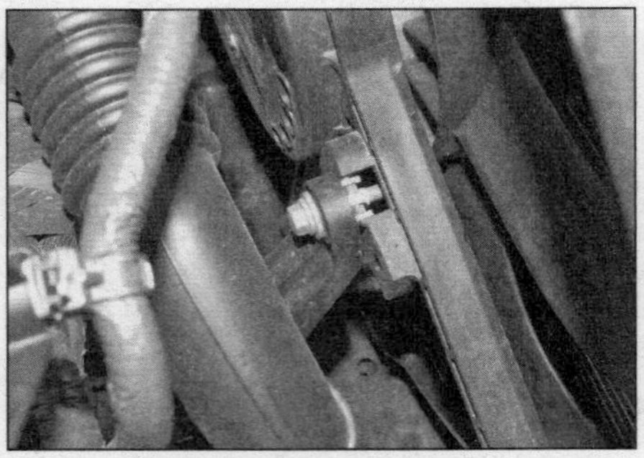

14.4a Undo the bolts. . .

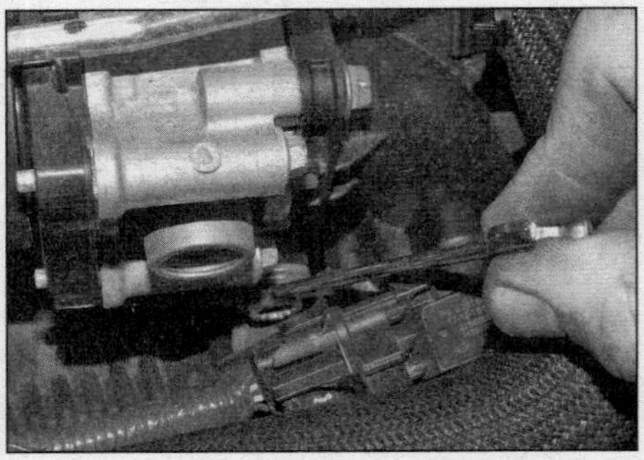

14.4b . . . from the mounting brackets. . .

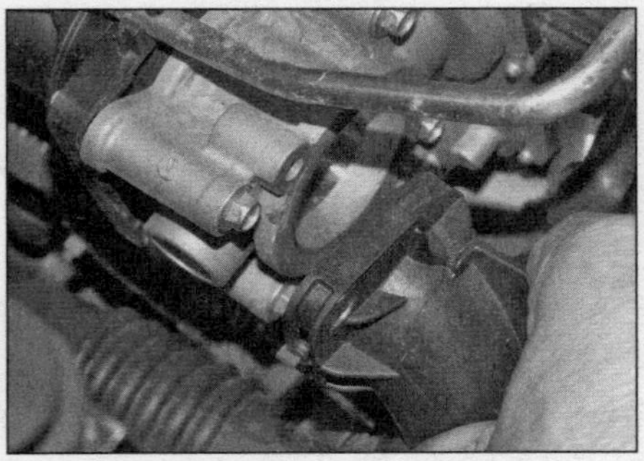

14.4c . . . and the throttle housing. . .

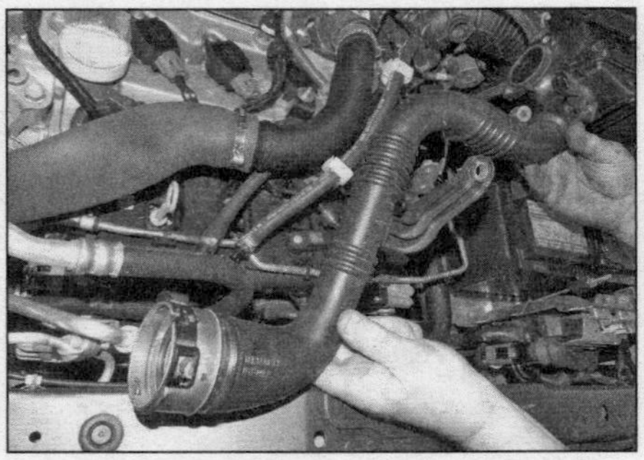

14.4d . . . and remove the air intake pipe

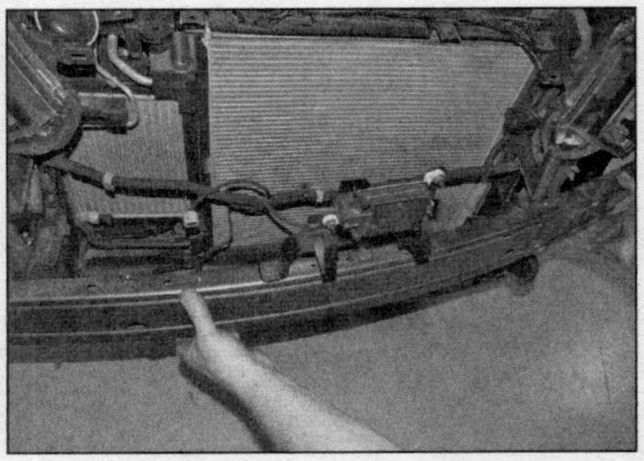

14.5 Remove the front crossmember

6 Release the retaining clips and remove the plastic trim from the front of the intercooler **(see illustration)**.

7 Undo the retaining bolts and move the upper crossmember from across the top of the radiator **(see illustration)**. Place the crossmember across the top of the engine, taking care not to place it on the battery terminals.

8 Undo the retaining bolts and remove the crossmember mounting bracket from the right-hand side of the vehicle **(see illustration)**.

9 Unclip the lower part of the condenser from the radiator, then unhook the intercooler from the bottom of the radiator. Rotate the intercooler and pull it upwards to release it from the radiator, then remove it from the front of the vehicle **(see illustrations)**.

Refitting

10 Refitting is a reversal of removal, making sure all the connections are securely fitted.

---

15 Exhaust system –
general information and component renewal

General information

Note: *Allow exhaust system components to cool before inspection or repair. Also, when working under the vehicle, make sure it is securely supported on axle stands (see 'Jacking and vehicle support').*

1 The exhaust system consists of the exhaust manifold/turbocharger, catalytic converter, front flexible pipe, centre silencer/pipe, rear silencer/tailpipe, and all flanges and clamps. The exhaust system is isolated from the vehicle body and from chassis components by a series of rubber hangers. Periodically inspect these hangers for cracks or other signs of deterioration, replacing them as necessary.

2 Conduct regular inspections of the exhaust system to keep it safe and quiet. Look for any damaged or bent parts, open seams, holes, loose connections, excessive corrosion or other defects which could allow exhaust fumes to enter the vehicle. Do not repair deteriorated exhaust system components; replace them with new parts.

3 If the exhaust system components are extremely corroded, or rusted together, a cutting torch is the most convenient tool for removal. Consult a properly-equipped repairer. If a cutting torch is not available, you can use a hacksaw, or if you have compressed air, there are special pneumatic cutting chisels that can also be used. Wear safety goggles to

14.6 Remove the plastic trim

14.7 Remove the upper crossmember

14.8 Remove the mounting bracket

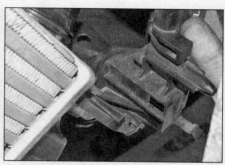
14.9a Release the intercooler from the radiator. . .

14.9b . . . and rotate it. . .

14.9c . . . to remove it from the vehicle

protect your eyes from metal chips and wear work gloves to protect your hands.

4 Here are some simple guidelines to follow when repairing the exhaust system:

a) *Work from the back to the front when removing exhaust system components.*

b) *Apply penetrating oil to the exhaust system component fasteners to make them easier to remove.*

c) *Use new gaskets, hangers and clamps.*

d) *Apply anti-seize compound to the threads of all exhaust system fasteners during reassembly.*

e) *Be sure to allow sufficient clearance between newly installed parts and all points on the underbody to avoid overheating the floor pan and possibly damaging the interior carpet and insulation. Pay particularly close attention to the catalytic converter and heat shield.*

Catalytic converter renewal

5 Renewal of the catalytic converter is described in Chapter 6A Section 18.

Notes

Chapter 4 Part B
Fuel and exhaust systems – diesel models

Contents

Degrees of difficulty

Easy, suitable for novice with little experience	Fairly easy, suitable for beginner with some experience	Fairly difficult, suitable for competent DIY mechanic	Difficult, suitable for experienced DIY mechanic	Very difficult, suitable for expert DIY or professional

Specifications

General

System type	Rear-mounted fuel tank, high-pressure pump with common-rail, direct injection, turbocharger

Type:

1.5 litre engine (K9K)	Siemens
1.6 litre engine (R9M)	Bosch EDC16

Fuel system data

1.5 litre engines

Firing order	1-3-4-2 (number 1 at flywheel end)
Idle speed	850 ± 50 rpm
Maximum no-load speed	4500 ± 150 rpm
Maximum under-load speed	5000 ± 150 rpm

High-pressure fuel pump:

Type	Delphi
Direction of rotation	Clockwise viewed from sprocket end

Injectors:

Type	Delphi solenoid injector
Maximum pressure	1400 bars
Resistance	Not-measurable

Turbocharger:

Type	Garrett
Boost pressure	1300 ± 2 mbars

1.6 litre engines

Firing order	1-3-4-2 (number 1 at flywheel end)
Idle speed	850 ± 100 rpm

High-pressure fuel pump:

Type	Bosch
Operating pressure	300 to 1350 bar
Direction of rotation	Clockwise viewed from sprocket end

Injectors:

Type	Bosch solenoid injector
Solenoid resistance	< 0.2 ohms
Operating pressure	1350 bar
Maximum pressure	1525 bar

Turbocharger:

Operating vacuum	0.5 bar
Valve rod movement	1.7mm
Glow plug resistance at 20° C – (connector removed)	less than 2.0 ohms

Sensor resistances

Coolant temperature sensor resistances (terminals 1 and 2):	
At 25°C	2.252 ± 112 ohms
At 50°C	810 ± 39 ohms
At 80°C	283 ± 8 ohms
Crankshaft position sensor resistance:	
Terminals 1 and 2	612 to 748 ohms
EGR volume control valve motor resistance:	
Terminals 2 and 6	2.3 ohms
Fuel pump temperature sensor resistances (terminals 1 and 2):	
At 25°C	2.051 ± 123 ohms
At 50°C	811 ± 47 ohms
At 80°C	309 ± 17 ohms
Fuel injector resistance at 20°C:	
Terminals 1 and 2	15.0 to 25.0 ohms
Fuel pump resistance at 25°C:	
Terminals 1 and 3	0.2 to 5.0 ohms
Fuel volumetric control valve (on pump):	
Terminals 1 and 2	1.5 to 15.0 ohms
High pressure fuel pump pressure control valve:	
Terminals 3 and 5	1.5 to 15 ohms
Intake air temperature sensor (terminals 1 and 2):	
At 10° C	3.714 ± 161 ohms
At 20° C	2.448 ± 95 ohms
At 30° C	1.671 ± 58 ohms
Throttle pedal position sensor resistances:	
Terminals 2 and 4	1.70 ohms
Terminals 1 and 5	2.85 ohms
Turbocharger boost control valve (at 23°C):	
Terminals 1 and 2	19.9 to 23.1 ohms

Fuel tank

Capacity	55 litres

Torque wrench settings

	Nm	lbf ft
1.5 litre engines		
Catalytic converter:		
Rear mounting	21	15
To side mounting strut	25	18
To turbocharger	26	19
Strut to engine	44	32
EGR valve	21	15
EGR valve heat shield	12	9
Engine lifting eye	21	15
Exhaust manifold	26	19
Exhaust pipe clamp	21	15
Flow actuator	6	4
Fuel gauge sender unit	65	48
Fuel injectors to cylinder head	28	21
Fuel tank	21	15
Fuel temperature sensor (on high-pressure pump)	15	11
High-pressure fuel rail	28	21
High-pressure pipe union nuts	24	18
High-pressure pump	21	15
High-pressure pump sprocket nut	55	41
High-pressure pump venturi	6	4
Turbocharger oil supply pipe:		
On cylinder head	23	17
On turbocharger	12	9
Turbocharger to exhaust manifold	26	19
1.6 litre engines		
Catalytic converter-to-turbocharger nuts	21	15
Throttle/damper unit:		
Mounting bracket to unit	12	9
Mounting bracket to inlet manifold	12	9
Turbocharger pressure sensor mounting nut	8	6
Turbocharger oil pipe bolts on turbocharger	10	7

Torque wrench settings (continued)

1.6 litre engines (continued)

	Nm	lbf ft
Turbocharger oil pipe union bolt on the cylinder block	16	12
Turbocharger oil pipe support bolt.	25	18
Turbocharger air outlet pipe.	8	6
Fuel rail mounting bolts	25	18
Fuel pipe mounting on valve cover	10	7
High-pressure pipe union nuts.	32	24
High-pressure pump pinion	90	66
High-pressure pump mounting	25	18
Injector clamp bolt	35	26
Inlet manifold	25	18
Exhaust manifold:		
Studs	9	7
Mounting nuts:		
Stage 1	18	13
Stage 2	30	22
EGR rigid pipe:		
To cooler.	35	26
To exhaust manifold	35	26
EGR rigid pipe on cylinder head.	10	7
EGR rigid pipe heatshield.	10	7

1 General information and precautions

General information

1 The fuel system consists of a rear-mounted fuel tank, a fuel filter, a high-pressure pump with common rail injection system, electronic injectors and associated components.

2 The main components of the system are as follows:
a) Priming bulb on the low-pressure circuit.
b) Fuel filter.
c) High-pressure fuel pump.
d) Injector rail.
e) Pressure sensor located on the injector rail.
f) Four electronic solenoid injectors.
g) Fuel temperature sensor.
h) Coolant temperature sensor.
i) Air temperature sensor.
j) Cylinder reference sensor.
k) Engine speed sensor.
l) Turbocharging pressure sensor.
m) EGR solenoid valve.
n) Accelerator pedal potentiometer.
o) Atmospheric pressure sensor.
p) Engine Control Module (ECM).

3 The common rail injection system operates as follows. Fuel is drawn from the fuel tank to the high-pressure pump by a low-pressure transfer pump integrated in the high-pressure pump. Before reaching the high-pressure pump, the fuel passes through a fuel filter, where foreign matter and water are removed. As the fuel passes through the filter, it is heated by an electric heater. On reaching the high-pressure pump, the fuel is pressurised according to demand, and accumulates in the injection common-rail. The pressure in the rail is accurately maintained using a pressure sensor in the rail and a pressure

regulator under the control of the engine management ECM. This arrangement keeps heat generation to a minimum, and improves engine output. The rail pressure is also maintained by the injectors themselves; short electrical pulses which are not long enough to open the injector allow fuel into the return (leak-off) circuit, and also the normal pulses which open the injectors cause a reduction in pressure. The ECM determines the exact timing and duration of the injection period according to engine operating conditions.

4 The four fuel injectors inject a homogeneous spray of fuel into the combustion chambers located in the cylinder head. The injectors operate sequentially according to the firing order of the cylinders, and each injector needle is lubricated by fuel, which accumulates in the spring chamber. Each injector has its own unique flow characteristics, which are used by the system ECM to calculate the exact quantity of fuel to inject.

5 In terms of the sensors used by the ECM to control a modern common-rail diesel system, these engines are very similar to their petrol equivalents. The ECM determines engine speed and position from a TDC sensor fitted to the transmission bellhousing, which detects a reference tooth on the flywheel ring gear, and signals the ECM. A similar sensor is fitted to monitor the camshaft, to give a reference for No 1 cylinder. Further sensors are used to monitor airflow into the engine, air temperature, and turbocharging pressure. On the fuel side, fuel pressure, temperature and flow rate are all monitored, according to model, via sensors on the high-pressure pump and/or the fuel rail. As with the petrol-engine models, an 'electronic' throttle is fitted, with an accelerator position sensor instead of the mechanical cable previously used.

6 Provided that the specified maintenance is carried out, the fuel injection equipment will give long and trouble-free service. The

main potential cause of damage to the high-pressure pump and injectors is dirt or water in the fuel. It is highly recommended that a set of fuel line plugs is obtained – these are available from motor accessory shops and better motor factors.

7 Servicing of the high-pressure pump, injectors, and electronic equipment and sensors is very limited for the home mechanic, and any dismantling or adjustment other than that described in this Chapter must be entrusted to a Nissan dealer or a diesel fuel injection specialist.

8 If a fault appears in the injection system, first ensure that all the system wiring connectors are securely connected and free of corrosion. Should the fault persist, the vehicle should be taken to a Nissan dealer or specialist who can test the system on a diagnostic tester (see illustration). The tester will locate the fault quickly and simply, alleviating the need to test all the system components individually, which is a time-consuming operation that carries a risk of damaging the ECM. It is advisable to have any faulty components renewed by the dealer as in many instances the tester is required to reprogramme the ECM in the event of component or sensor renewal.

1.8 Vehicle diagnostic connector

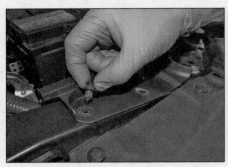

3.1a Remove the two retaining clips. . .

3.1b . . . undo the bolt. . .

3.1c . . .then release the clips and slide ducting from air cleaner housing

3.1d The clips at the centre are fragile and can break easily

Precautions

⚠ **Warning: It is necessary to take certain precautions when working on the fuel system components, particularly the fuel injectors and high-pressure pump. Before carrying out any operations on the fuel system, refer to the precautions given in 'Safety first!' at the beginning of this manual, and to any additional warning notes at the start of the relevant Sections. Allow the engine to cool for 5 to 10 minutes to ensure the fuel pressure and temperatures are at a minimum.**

⚠ **Warning: Exercise extreme caution when working on the high-pressure fuel system. Do not attempt to test the fuel injectors or disconnect the high-pressure lines with the engine running. Never expose the hands or any part of the body to injector spray, as the high working pressure can cause the fuel to penetrate the skin, with possibly fatal results. You are strongly advised to have any work that involves testing the injectors under pressure carried out by a dealer or fuel injection specialist.**

2 Troubleshooting

Fuel pump

1 The fuel pump is located inside the fuel

tank. Sit inside the vehicle with the windows closed, turn the ignition key to ON (not START) and listen for the sound of the fuel pump as it's briefly activated. You will only hear the sound for a second or two, but that sound indicates that the pump is working. Alternatively, have an assistant listen at the fuel filler cap.
2 If the pump does not operate, check all of the fuses and relays (see Chapter 12 Section 3).
3 If the fuses are okay, check the wiring back to the fuel pump. If the wiring is okay, the fuel pump control module may be defective. If the pump runs continuously with the ignition key in the ON position, the ECU may be defective. Have the circuit checked by a dealer or suitably equipped repairer.

Fuel injection system

Note: *The following procedure is based on the assumption that the fuel pump is working and the fuel pressure is adequate.*

3.2 Disconnect the wiring connector

4 Check all electrical wiring plugs that are related to the system. Check the earth wire connections for tightness.
5 Check that the battery is fully charged.
6 Inspect the air filter element (see Chapter 1B Section 27).
7 Check all fuses and relays related to the fuel system.
8 Check the air intake system between the throttle body and the intake manifold for air leaks. Also inspect the condition of all vacuum hoses connected to the intake manifold and to the throttle body.
9 Remove the air intake duct from the throttle body and look for dirt, carbon, varnish, or other residue in the throttle body, particularly around the throttle plate. If it's dirty, clean it with carburettor cleaner, a toothbrush and a clean rag.
10 With the engine running, place an automotive stethoscope against each injector, one at a time, and listen for a clicking sound that indicates operation.

⚠ **Warning: Stay clear of the drivebelt and any rotating or hot components.**

11 If you can hear the injectors operating, but the engine is misfiring, the electrical circuits are functioning correctly, but the injectors might be dirty or blocked. Try a commercial injector cleaning product (available at auto parts suppliers). If cleaning the injectors doesn't help, they may need replacing.
12 If the injector is not operating, the circuit between the ECU and the injector might be faulty.

3 Air cleaner assembly – removal and refitting

Removal

1 Release the two retaining clips on the front crossmember, undo the retaining bolt, then release the clips on the filter housing and slide the air intake resonator/inlet duct from the air cleaner housing **(see illustrations)**. The intake resonator and inlet duct to the front crossmember can be split, to remove, but the retaining clips at the centre can break easily, so we found removing the complete assembly as one is best.
2 Disconnect the wiring connector from the air flow sensor, and release the wiring loom retaining clip from the housing **(see illustration)**.
3 Slacken the retaining clip and disconnect the rubber air intake hose from the side of the air cleaner housing **(see illustration)**.
4 Undo the upper mounting bolt, then pull the air cleaner housing upwards to release it from the rubber mountings and remove the complete assembly from the rear of the engine compartment **(see illustrations)**.

3.3 Slacken the air intake rubber hose retaining clip

3.4a Undo the upper mounting bolt. . .

3.4b . . . and remove the air cleaner housing

Refitting

5 Refitting is a reversal of the removal procedure, ensuring that all hoses and ducts are properly reconnected and correctly seated and, where necessary, securely held by their retaining clips. Do not use any grease or lubricant when refitting the air hoses/ducts.

4 Fuel pump and fuel gauge sender unit – removal and refitting

1 The diesel engine fuel pump/gauge sender unit has the same removal procedure as the petrol engines. Remove the fuel pump/gauge sender unit, as described in Chapter 4A Section 6.

5 Fuel tank – removal and refitting

1 The diesel engine fuel tank has the same removal procedure as the petrol engines. Remove the fuel tank, as described in Chapter 4A Section 7.

6 Fuel system – priming and bleeding

⚠ **Warning: Refer to the precautions in Section 1 before proceeding. Do not attempt to bleed the**

system by loosening any of the unions on the high-pressure circuit.
Note: *Priming of the fuel system after filter renewal will be improved if the filter is filled with clean diesel fuel before securing it to the filter head. To avoid spillages of fuel, keep the filter upright during refitting.*

1 After disconnecting part of the fuel supply system or running out of fuel, it is necessary to prime the system and bleed off any air that may have entered the system components.
2 Attempt to start the engine normally, however, do not operate the starter motor for more than 5 seconds at a time. If necessary, operate the starter motor in 4 to 5 second bursts followed by pauses of 8 to 10 seconds. As soon as the engine starts, let it run at fast idle speed until a regular idle speed is reached.

7 Idle speed – general

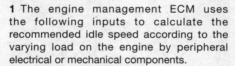

1 The engine management ECM uses the following inputs to calculate the recommended idle speed according to the varying load on the engine by peripheral electrical or mechanical components.
a) Engine coolant temperature.
b) Battery voltage.
c) The gear selected.
d) Electrical consumers (heater fan, climate control system, etc).
2 At normal engine temperature with no

electrical consumers switched on and neutral selected, the engine idle speed will be 700 to 900 rpm, depending on engine type.
3 If the accelerator pedal potentiometer internal tracks are faulty, the ECM will override the idle speed to approx. 1200 rpm, and the injection warning light will be illuminated on the instrument panel. If the brake pedal is depressed, the idle speed will revert to its normal level.
4 If there is an injector fault, the idle speed will be set to 1200 rpm and the warning light will be illuminated.
5 Should the idle speed be repeatedly incorrect, the car should be taken to a Nissan dealer who will have the necessary diagnostic equipment to pinpoint the faulty component responsible.

8 Throttle valve housing – removal and refitting

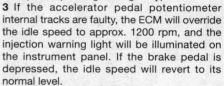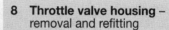

1.5 litre engines

1 Release the retaining clip and disconnect the air intake pipe from the throttle/damper unit (see illustrations). Move the hose to one side.
2 Disconnect the wiring from the throttle/damper unit (see illustration).
3 Unscrew the bolts from the mounting bracket and also the nuts from the intake manifold, and remove the unit from the engine. Remove and discard the gasket/seal (see illustrations).

8.1a Release the retaining clip. . .

8.1b . . . and remove the air intake pipe

8.2 Disconnect the wiring connector

8.3a Undo the retaining bolt (arrowed). . .

8.3b . . . and the securing nuts to the manifold

8.6 Disconnect the air inlet hose from the throttle valve housing

8.7 Unclip the coolant pipe

8.8 Disconnect the wiring connector

8.9 Undo the bolt from the mounting bracket

4 Refitting is a reversal of removal, using a new gasket/seal and tightening to the specified torque.

1.6 litre engines

5 Disconnect the wiring connector from the

turbocharger pressure sensor and the EGR solenoid valve.

6 Slacken the retaining clip and disconnect the air intake hose from the throttle/damper unit **(see illustration)**, then move the hose to one side.

7 Unclip the coolant pipe from the mounting bracket at the front of the throttle housing **(see illustration)**.

8 Disconnect the wiring from the throttle/damper unit **(see illustration)**.

9 Undo the retaining bolt from the mounting bracket, at the front of the throttle housing **(see illustration)**.

10 Disconnect the wiring from the air inlet pressure and temperature sensors on top of the throttle housing **(see illustration)**.

11 Unscrew the bolts from the intake manifold, and remove the unit from the engine. Remove and discard the gasket/seal **(see illustrations)**.

12 Refitting is a reversal of removal, using a new gasket/seal and tightening to the specified torque **(see illustration)**.

8.10 Disconnect the wiring connectors from the sensors

8.11a Undo the mounting bolts. . .

9 High-pressure pump – removal and refitting

⚠️ **Warning: Refer to the warning note in Section 1 before proceeding.**
Caution: Before starting work, allow the engine to cool for 5 to 10 minutes, to ensure the fuel pressure and temperature are at a minimum.
Note: On 1.5 litre engines, the high-pressure pump is removed after first removing the timing belt as described in Chapter 2B Section 5.
Note: Nissan recommend that all high-pressure pipes that are removed, must be renewed as a matter of course.

8.11b . . . the remove the throttle valve housing

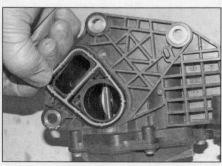

8.12 Fit a new gasket

9.2 Remove the upper trim panel

9.3 Disconnect the intake hose

9.4a Undo the retaining bolt. . .

9.4b . . . and remove the air intake pipe

9.5a undo the nut and bolt. . .

9.5b . . .release the securing clips. . .

Note: *Cleanliness is of critical importance when working on the fuel system of any modern diesel engine. The smallest speck of grit or dirt can cause extensive damage to the pump and injectors. Always clean thoroughly the pump and injector unions before dismantling. Immediately plug and seal all pipes and components. Components that are removed from the engine should immediately be placed in clean plastic bags.*

Removal

1.5 litre engine

1 Disconnect the battery negative lead (refer to Chapter 5 Section 4).
2 Remove the plastic trim cover from the top of the engine **(see illustration)**.
3 Slacken the retaining clip and disconnect the intercooler pipe rubber hose **(see illustration)**.
4 Undo the retaining bolt, then release the securing clip at the turbo end of the pipe and pull the pipe upwards to remove it from across the top of the engine **(see illustrations)**.
5 Undo the upper bolt and retaining nut, release the two lower securing clips and remove the upper protective cover **(see illustrations)**.

6 Undo the bolt and retaining nut and remove the bracket from the front of the fuel pump **(see illustrations)**.
7 Undo the two retaining bolts and pull back the dipstick bracket from the front of the cylinder head **(see illustrations)**.

9.5c . . . unclip the wiring clip. . .

9.5d . . . and remove the upper plastic cover

9.6a Undo the bolt and nut. . .

9.6b . . . and remove the bracket from the fuel pump

9.7a Undo the two bolts. . .

9.7b . . . and pull back the dipstick bracket

9.8 Disconnect the pressure sensor wiring connector

9.9 Unclip the wiring loom from the plastic cover

9.10a Unclip the drain tube. . .

9.10b . . . undo the retaining nuts. . .

9.10c . . . and remove the lower plastic cover

8 Disconnect the wiring connector from the pressure switch on the bottom of the fuel rail **(see illustration)**.

9 Release the securing clip and remove the wiring loom from the top of the lower cover **(see illustration)**.

9.14a Disconnect the wiring connectors. . .

9.14b . . . from the fuel pump sensors

10 Release the drain tube from the bottom of the cover, undo the two retaining nuts and remove the lower protective cover **(see illustrations)**.

11 Jack up the right-hand front of the car and support on axle stands. Remove the front

9.15a Remove the fuel pipe. . .

9.15b . . . and hoses from the pump

right wheel, engine undertray and wheel arch liner.

12 Remove the auxiliary drivebelt with reference to Chapter 1B Section 33.

13 Loosen the alternator lower bolt and remove the top bolt. Tip the alternator away from the engine.

14 Disconnect the three wiring connectors from the fuel pump **(see illustrations)**.

15 Place a clean rag over the alternator and then remove the fuel pipe/hoses from the pump **(see illustrations)**. As a precaution against remaining pressure in the pipes, first wrap them loosely in cloth/rag. The high-pressure pipe will need to be renewed. Seal the pump and pipe/hoses immediately. Do not allow fuel to contaminate the alternator.

16 Remove the timing belt as described in Chapter 2B Section 5. Note it would be a sensible precaution to renew the timing belt anyway.

17 Unbolt and remove the fuel pump, and then place the pump in a vice to remove the sprocket. Use a strap wrench and a ring spanner to do this. A puller will then be required to remove the sprocket from the pump.

1.6 litre engines

18 To make access easier, remove the air cleaner assembly, as described in Section 3.

19 Disconnect the wiring connector from the rear of the fuel pump **(see illustration)**.

20 Remove the cylinder head cover, then unscrew the union nut and disconnect the high-pressure pipe from the fuel rail to the fuel

9.19 Disconnect the wiring connector

9.20a Remove the plastic cover. . .

9.20b . . . remove the pipe retaining bolt. . .

pump **(see illustrations)**, refer to Section 11, to gain access to the fuel rail. As a precaution against remaining pressure in the pipes, first wrap them loosely in cloth/rag. Cap or plug the open connections to reduce fuel loss and prevent entry of dirt.
21 Disconnect the quick-release fuel supply and return hoses from the high-pressure pump and plug the openings **(see illustration)**.
22 Progressively unscrew the mounting bolts then withdraw the high-pressure pump from the cylinder head. Remove the O-ring seal from the groove, a new one will be required for refitting **(see illustrations)**.
23 If necessary, the pinion may be removed from the high-pressure pump drive shaft **(see illustration)**. To do this, first lock the pinion in a soft-jawed vice and unscrew the retaining nut. A puller will now be required to remove the pinion from the drive shaft.

Refitting

Note: *The manufacturers stipulate that the high-pressure pipe is renewed whenever it is removed.*
24 Refitting is a reversal of removal, but take care not to place the new high-pressure pipe under any stress. If fitting a new pump, it is highly recommended that the pump is primed with diesel on the bench before fitting.
25 On 1.6 litre engines, fit a new O-ring seal to the pump and new retaining bolts.
26 New high-pressure pipes are supplied with a lubricant for the threads on the pipe. If no lubricant is supplied the pipes are self-lubricating and lubricant should not be applied.
27 Tighten all nuts and bolts to the specified torque and angle as applicable.
28 Prime and bleed the fuel system as described in Section 6.
29 Before restarting the engine, it may be necessary to use a diagnostic tool to clear any faults that may be stored in the engine control module (ECM).

10 Fuel injectors –
testing, removal and refitting

⚠️ *Warning: Exercise extreme caution when working on the high-pressure fuel system. Do*

9.20c . . . then using two spanners disconnect the fuel pipe from the fuel pump

9.21 Disconnect the fuel supply hose

not attempt to test the fuel injectors or disconnect the high-pressure lines with the engine running. Never expose the hands or any part of the body to injector spray, as the high working pressure can cause

the fuel to penetrate the skin, with possibly fatal results. You are strongly advised to have any work that involves testing the injectors under pressure carried out by a dealer or fuel injection specialist. Refer to

9.22a Unscrew the mounting bolts. . .

9.22b . . .withdraw the pump from the cylinder head. . .

9.22c. . . and remove the O-ring seal

9.23 High-pressure pump pinion

10.5 Disconnect the injector wiring connectors

10.6a Unscrew the fuel injector pipe union nuts. . .

10.6b . . . and also at the fuel rail

10.7 Release the leak-off pipe retaining clips

10.8 Injector plate retaining bolts

the precautions given in Section 1 of this Chapter before proceeding. After switching off the engine, allow the engine to cool for 5 to 10 minutes to allow the fuel pressure to drop before disconnecting any of the high-pressure fuel pipes.

Note: *Each new injector is supplied with a unique code, which specifies its flow characteristics. This code must be programmed into the engine management ECM with a special diagnostic tool; therefore this work should be entrusted to a Nissan dealer or suitably equipped garage.*

Note: *Nissan recommend that all high-pressure pipes that are removed, must be renewed as a matter of course.*

Testing

1 It is not possible to test the fuel injectors without specialist equipment, therefore, if they are thought to be faulty, consult a Nissan dealer or diesel specialist.

Removal

Note: *Take care not to allow dirt into the injectors or fuel pipes during this procedure; clean around the area before commencing work. Note that all high-pressure pipes removed must be renewed as a matter of course. The injector flame shield washers must also be renewed.*

2 Disconnect the battery negative lead (refer to Chapter 5 Section 4).

1.5 litre engine

3 Remove the upper protective cover from the top of the cylinder head as described in Section 9, paragraphs 2 to 5.

4 Before removal thoroughly clean the area around the fuel injectors.

5 Disconnect the wiring connector from the top of the fuel injector **(see illustration)**.

6 While holding the injector central unions with one spanner, unscrew the high-pressure

pipe union nuts with a further spanner. Use some cloth around the pipe unions to soak up the spilt fuel, and then loosen them. Similarly, unscrew the union nuts from the fuel rail, and then remove the pipes **(see illustrations)**. As a precaution against remaining pressure in the pipes, first wrap them loosely in cloth/rag. Discard the fuel pipe, as a new one will be required for refitting. Plug all fuel apertures to prevent entry of dust and dirt.

7 Using a thin screwdriver, release the securing clip and disconnect the fuel leak-off pipe from the side of the injector **(see illustration)**. Tape over or plug all fuel apertures to prevent entry of dust and dirt.

8 Unscrew the bolt securing each injector clamp plate to the cylinder head **(see illustration)**. Lift off the clamp plates and remove the injectors then recover the flame shield washers between the injectors and the cylinder head.

1.6 litre engines

9 Remove the cylinder head cover and oil separator from the top of the engine with reference to Chapter 2C Section 3.

10 Carefully clean around the fuel injectors and injector pipe union nuts.

11 Note the fitted position of the leak-off pipes, then remove the securing clips and disconnect them from the top of the fuel injectors **(see illustrations)**.

12 Unscrew the union nuts securing the injector pipes to the fuel rail whilst being prepared for some fuel spillage, then unscrew the union nuts and disconnect the pipes from the injectors. Where necessary, undo the pipe support clamp bolts **(see illustrations)**. As a precaution against remaining pressure in the pipes, first wrap them loosely in cloth/rag. Plug all fuel apertures to prevent entry of dust and dirt. Note, Nissan recommend that all high-pressure pipes that are removed, must be renewed as a matter of course.

13 Using a felt-tipped pen, mark each injector for its position (No 1 cylinder at the timing chain end). This is important because the engine management ECM recognises each injector by the cylinder it is located in. If new injectors are obtained, the code on each injector must be noted and programmed into the ECM.

10.11a Remove the securing clips. . .

10.11b . . . and remove the leak-off pipes from the injectors

10.12a Unscrew the union nuts. . .

10.12b . . . and disconnect the pipes from the injectors and fuel rail

10.14a Unscrew the retaining bolts. . .

10.14b . . . remove the clamp plates. . .

10.14c . . . then withdraw the injector. . .

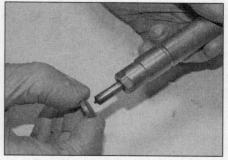

10.18 Fit new sealing washer to injector

14 Unscrew the bolt securing each injector clamp plate, lift off the clamp plates and withdraw the injectors. Recover the copper washer between the injectors and the cylinder head (see illustrations).

Refitting

15 Take care not to drop the injectors or allow the needles at their tips to become damaged. The injectors are precision-made to fine limits and must not be handled roughly. In particular, do not mount them in a bench vice. It is recommended that the injectors are stored vertically at all times.

16 Clean the cylinder head, taking care to prevent foreign matter entering the fuel apertures. The injectors can be cleaned with a lint-free cloth soaked in brake cleaning fluid or fresh diesel. Do not clean them with a wire brush or emery cloth.

17 Obtain new injector sealing washers and new fuel pipes for refitting.

18 Fit new sealing washer to the injectors (see illustration), then insert the injectors and fit the clamp plates. Tighten the clamp plate bolts to the specified torque.

19 Fit new injector pipes, and tighten the union nuts on the injectors and the fuel rail by hand at first. Make sure the pipe clamps are in their previously noted positions. Bearing in mind the high vibration levels with a diesel engine, if the clamps are wrongly positioned or missing, problems may be experienced with pipes breaking or splitting. With all the pipes in place tighten them to the specified torque setting.

20 Renew the injector leak-off pipes, and refit in the position noted on removal.

21 Refit the engine cylinder cover and oil separator, with reference to Chapter 2C Section 3.

22 Reconnect the battery negative lead (refer to Chapter 5 Section 4).

23 If new injectors have been fitted, have the code programmed into the engine management ECM by a Nissan dealer.

24 Start the engine. If difficulty is experienced, bleed the fuel system as described in Section 6.

11 Injector rail (common rail) – removal and refitting

⚠️ Warning: Refer to the warning note in Section 1 before proceeding. After switching off the engine, allow several minutes for the fuel pressure so subside before disconnecting any of the high-pressure fuel pipes.

Note: Take care not to allow dirt into the fuel pipes during this procedure, clean around the area before commencing work. Note that all high-pressure pipes removed must be renewed as a matter of course.

Note: Nissan recommend that all high-pressure pipes that are removed, must be renewed as a matter of course.

Removal

1 Disconnect the battery negative lead (refer to Chapter 5 Section 4).

2 Remove the plastic engine cover (where fitted) from the top of the engine.

1.5 litre engine

3 Remove the upper and lower protective covers from around the fuel rail, as described in Section 9, paragraphs 2 to 10.

4 Disconnect the wiring connectors from the heater (glow) plugs and move the wiring loom to one side (see illustration).

5 Undo the union nuts and remove the high-pressure fuel pipe from the fuel pump to the fuel rail (see illustration). As a precaution against remaining pressure in the pipes, first wrap them loosely in cloth/rag. Discard the fuel pipe, as a new one will be required for refitting. Plug all fuel apertures to prevent entry of dust and dirt.

6 While holding the injector central unions with one spanner, unscrew the high-pressure pipe union nuts with a further spanner. As a precaution against remaining pressure in the

11.4 Disconnect the heater plug wiring connector

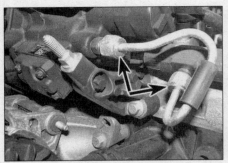

11.5 Remove the high pressure fuel pipe

11.7 Undo the fuel rail mounting nuts

11.9 Disconnect the pressure sensor wiring connector

11.11a Undo the fuel pipe union nut. . .

11.11b . . . and release the pipe from the clamp

11.12 Remove the four injector-to-fuel rail pipes

pipes, first wrap them loosely in cloth/rag. Similarly, unscrew the union nuts from the fuel rail, and then remove the pipes. Discard the fuel pipes, as new ones will be required for refitting. Plug all fuel apertures to prevent entry of dust and dirt.

7 Unbolt and remove the fuel rail from the front of the cylinder head **(see illustration)**.

1.6 litre engine

8 Remove the cylinder head cover and oil separator from the top of the engine with reference to Chapter 2C Section 3.

9 Disconnect the wiring connector from the fuel rail pressure switch, at the end of the fuel rail **(see illustration)**.

10 Unclip the plastic cover, then unscrew the union nut and disconnect the high-pressure pipe from the fuel pump, see Section 9. As a precaution against remaining pressure in the pipes, first wrap them loosely in cloth/rag.

11 Unscrew the union nut and disconnect the high-pressure pipe from the fuel rail, undo the pipe securing clamp bolt and remove the pipe from the engine **(see illustrations)**. Discard the fuel pipes, as new ones will be required for refitting.

12 With reference to Section 10, unscrew the union nuts and disconnect the fuel supply pipes from the injectors and fuel rail, new ones will be required for refitting **(see illustration)**. Release the fuel pipes and unclip from any retaining clips, note their position for refitting. Discard the fuel pipes, as new ones will be required for refitting.

13 Cover or plug all fuel apertures to prevent entry of dust and dirt into the fuel system.

14 Unbolt and remove the fuel rail from the front of the cylinder head **(see illustration)**.

Refitting

15 Refitting is a reversal of removal, but

take care not to place the new high-pressure pipe under any stress. Before fitting the new pipe, lubricate the threads of the union nuts with oil from the sachet provided, and finger-tighten the nuts before tightening them to the specified torque. When tightening the pipe union nuts onto the injectors, counter-hold the injectors with a further spanner.

16 On completion, prime and bleed the fuel system as described in Section 6. Run the engine, and check for fuel leaks.

12 Inlet manifold – removal and refitting

1.5 litre engines

1 The inlet manifold on 1.5 litre diesel engines is incorporated into the cylinder head and therefore cannot be removed separately.

1.6 litre engines

2 Drain the cooling system sufficiently for the coolant level to be lower than the height of the inlet manifold (see Chapter 1B Section 32).

3 The inlet manifold is located on the front of the cylinder head. First, remove the throttle valve assembly, as described in Section 8.

4 Unclip the coolant hose from the bracket on the front of the manifold**(see illustration)**.

5 Disconnect the wiring connector from the coolant outlet unit regulation solenoid valve, and release the wiring loom securing clip **(see illustration)**.

6 Disconnect the vacuum pipe, then undo the

11.14 Undo the mounting bolts and remove the fuel rail

12.4 Release the coolant hose retaining clip

12.5 Disconnect the wiring connector from the solenoid valve

12.6 Remove the solenoid valve, complete with mounting bracket

12.7 Disconnect the coolant pipe

12.8a Unclip the wiring connector, undo the bolt. . .

12.8b . . . and remove the dipstick tube

12.9 Release the wiring loom from the lower part of the manifold

retaining bolts and remove the coolant outlet unit regulation solenoid valve from the front of the inlet manifold **(see illustration)**.

7 Disconnect the coolant pipe from the front of the inlet manifold **(see illustration)**.

8 Unclip the wiring connector, undo the retaining bolt and remove the oil level dipstick tube from the front of the manifold **(see illustrations)**.

9 Undo the retaining bolt and nut, then release the wiring loom plastic cover from the lower part of the inlet manifold **(see illustration)**.

10 Unclip the vacuum pipe from the top of the manifold and move it to one side **(see illustration)**.

11 Undo the retaining nut and remove the bracket from the end of the manifold **(see illustration)**.

12 Disconnect the wiring connectors from the EGR volume control valve **(see illustration)**.

13 Undo the retaining bolt and disconnect the wiring loom mounting bracket from the transmission end of the manifold **(see illustration)**.

14 Starting from the outer nuts and working to the centre, unscrew and remove the

mounting nuts, then withdraw the inlet manifold (complete with EGR volume control valve) from the cylinder head. Recover the gasket and discard it as a new gasket must be used on refitting **(see illustrations)**. Also

12.10 Unclip the vacuum pipe from the top of the manifold

12.11 Remove the mounting bracket

12.12 Disconnect the wiring connector

12.13 Undo the mounting bracket securing bolt

12.14a Remove the inlet manifold. . .

12.14b . . . and renew the gasket

obtain a new gasket for the EGR control valve, if removed from the manifold.

15 Refitting is the reverse of removal using new gaskets, and tightening the manifold retaining bolts to the specified torque. Start

13.7a Remove the exhaust manifold. . .

13.13a Undo the bolts. . .

13.14 Remove the heat shield

from the centre nuts, then spiraling outwards to the outer nuts, to tighten.

13 Exhaust manifold – removal and refitting

Removal

1 The exhaust manifold is located on the rear of the cylinder head. Remove the engine top cover, and then disconnect the battery negative terminal.

2 Apply the handbrake, and then jack up the front of the vehicle and support it on axle stands (see *Jacking and vehicle support*).

1.5 litre engines

3 Disconnect the exhaust front pipe/ particle filter (where fitted), with reference to Section 17.

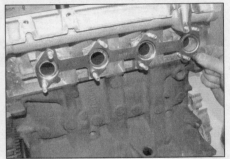

13.7b . . . and recover the gasket

13.13b . . . and remove the mounting bracket

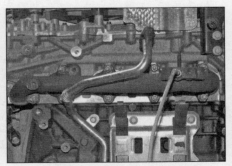

13.15a Unscrew the manifold nuts and. . .

4 Remove the turbocharger as described in Section 15. If the reason for removing the manifold is simply to renew the gasket, the turbocharger can remain attached to the manifold.

5 Loosen the two clamps, then remove the EGR metal tube between the inlet and exhaust manifolds. The manufacturers recommend that the metal tube and clamps are renewed as a matter of course.

6 Unscrew the mounting bolts and remove the EGR unit from the inlet manifold.

7 Progressively unscrew the mounting nuts and remove the exhaust manifold from the studs on the cylinder head. Recover the metal gasket (see illustrations).

8 Clean the surfaces of the cylinder head and exhaust manifold, then locate a new gasket on the cylinder head studs.

1.6 litre engines

9 Drain the cooling system (see Chapter 1B Section 32).

10 Remove the air cleaner assembly, as described in Section 3.

11 Remove the turbocharger, as described in Section 15.

12 Remove the EGR cooler and low pressure volume control valve, as described in Chapter 6B Section 21.

13 Unbolt the EGR cooler/valve mounting bracket from the rear of the engine (see illustrations).

14 Undo the two bolts and remove the heat shield from the top of the exhaust manifold (see illustration).

15 Starting from the outer nuts and working to the centre, unscrew and remove the nuts and withdraw the exhaust manifold from the cylinder head. Recover the manifold gasket and discard it as a new gasket must be used on refitting (see illustrations). Nissan state that the manifold nuts must also be renewed.

16 Check the condition of the exhaust manifold studs and renew them if necessary. Tighten into the cylinder head to the specified torque.

Refitting

17 Refitting is the reverse of removal using a new gasket and seals, and tightening the manifold retaining nuts to the specified torque. Start from the centre nuts, then spiraling outwards to the outer nuts, to tighten.

13.15b . . . and recover the gasket

14 Turbocharger – description and precautions

1 A turbocharger increases engine efficiency by raising the pressure in the inlet manifold above atmospheric pressure. Instead of the air simply being sucked into the cylinders, it is forced in. Additional fuel is supplied in proportion to the increased air intake.

2 Energy for the operation of the turbocharger comes from the exhaust gas. The gas flows through a specially shaped housing (the turbine housing) and in so doing, spins the turbine wheel. The turbine wheel is attached to a shaft, at the end of which is another vaned wheel known as the compressor wheel. The compressor wheel spins in its own housing and compresses the inducted air on the way to the inlet manifold.

3 Between the turbocharger and the inlet manifold, the compressed air passes through an intercooler. This is an air-to-air heat exchanger, mounted behind the front bumper, in front of the air conditioning condenser and the coolant radiator. The purpose of the intercooler is to remove some of the heat gained in being compressed from the inducted air. Because cooler air is denser, removal of this heat further increases engine efficiency.

4 Boost pressure (the pressure in the inlet manifold) is limited by a wastegate, which diverts the exhaust gas away from the turbine wheel in response to a pressure-sensitive actuator. Turbocharging pressure is controlled by a pressure sensor located in the air intake **(see illustrations)**. The boost pressure sensor also measures the intake air temperature (IAT).

5 The boost control solenoid valve is located at the left-hand rear of the engine compartment by the air cleaner housing **(see illustrations)**.

6 The turbo shaft is pressure-lubricated by an oil feed pipe from the main oil gallery. The shaft 'floats' on a cushion of oil. A drain pipe returns the oil to the sump.

Precautions

The turbocharger operates at extremely high speeds and temperatures. Certain precautions must be observed to avoid premature failure of the turbo or injury to the operator.

a) *Do not race the engine immediately after start-up, especially if it is cold. Give the oil a few seconds to circulate.*

b) *Always allow the engine to return to idle speed before switching it off – do not blip the throttle and switch off, as this will leave the turbo spinning without lubrication.*

c) *Allow the engine to idle for several minutes before switching off after a high speed run.*

d) *Observe the recommended intervals for oil and filter changing, and use a reputable oil of the specified quality. Neglect of oil changing, or use of inferior oil, can cause*

14.4a Turbo pressure sensor location – 1.5 litre engine

14.5a Disconnecting the wiring connector from the boost control valve – 1.5 litre engine

14.4b Turbo pressure sensor location – 1.6 litre engine

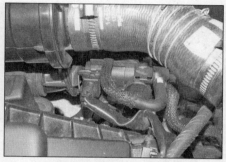

14.5b Boost control valve location – 1.6 litre engine

carbon formation on the turbo shaft and subsequent failure.

⚠ **Warning: Do not operate the turbo with any parts exposed. Foreign objects falling onto the rotating vanes could cause damage and (if ejected) personal injury.**

15 Turbocharger – removal and refitting

Note: *New turbocharger-to-exhaust manifold nuts must be used on refitting.*

Note: *New oil supply pipe O-rings and copper washers must be used on refitting.*

1 Apply the handbrake, then jack up the front of the vehicle, and support securely on axle stands

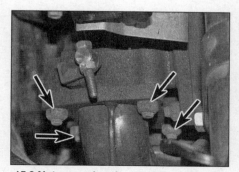

15.9 Nuts securing the catalytic converter to the turbocharger

(see *Jacking and vehicle support*). Remove the right-hand front roadwheel.

2 Disconnect the battery negative lead (refer to Chapter 5 Section 4).

3 Remove the cylinder head cover and oil separator from the top of the engine with reference to Chapter 2C Section 3.

4 Remove the air cleaner assembly, as described in Section 3.

Removal

1.5 litre engines

5 At the rear of the engine, disconnect the wiring from the downstream air temperature sensor and EGR solenoid valve.

6 Disconnect the tube from the turbocharger pressure adjustment valve on the air duct, then loosen the clips and disconnect the air ducts from between the EGR unit and turbocharger.

7 Unbolt and remove the engine lifting eye from the right-hand rear of the cylinder head.

8 Unscrew the bolt and remove the air inlet metal tube.

9 Unscrew the four nuts securing the catalytic converter to the turbocharger **(see illustration)**.

10 Working under the front of the car, unscrew the nuts and disconnect the intermediate pipe flexible flange from the catalytic converter. Also, unbolt the strut from the side of the catalytic converter and block **(see illustration)**.

11 Unbolt the catalytic converter and lower it as far as possible **(see illustration)** or remove it completely.

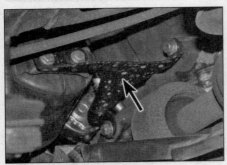

15.10 Unbolt the strut from the side of the catalytic converter

15.11 View of the turbocharger wastegate (upper) and vanes (lower) with the catalytic converter removed

15.13a Removing the oil supply pipe and copper sealing rings from the turbocharger

15.13b Removing the oil supply pipe from the cylinder head

15.14a Oil return pipe flange bolts on the bottom of the turbocharger

15.14b Removing the oil return pipe

12 In the engine compartment, unbolt the heat shield from the EGR solenoid valve.
13 Unscrew the union and disconnect the oil supply pipe from the turbocharger, collect the copper sealing rings, then unscrew the union nut and disconnect the pipe from the cylinder head (see illustrations).
14 Unscrew the bolts and detach the oil return pipe from the bottom of the turbocharger – if necessary, remove the pipe from the cylinder block (see illustrations).
15 Unscrew the turbocharger upper and lower mounting nuts (see illustrations), then remove the turbocharger together with the oil return pipe from the exhaust manifold. With the assembly on the bench, remove the oil return pipe. Do not attempt to separate the inlet and exhaust sections of the turbocharger.

1.6 litre engines

16 Remove the exhaust particle filter (refer to Section 17).
17 Remove the catalytic converter as described in Section 17.
18 Release the securing clip, undo the mounting bolts and remove the air duct from the turbocharger (see illustrations).
19 Undo the mounting nuts and remove the

15.15a Turbocharger upper mounting nuts. . .

15.15b . . . and lower mounting nut

15.18a Release the securing clip. . .

15.18b . . . and remove the air intake ducting

15.19a Remove the boost control valve. . .

15.19b . . . and mounting bracket

15.20 Remove the wiring bracket from the turbo

15.21 Disconnect the vacuum pipe

15.22a Remove the bolt from the cylinder head. . .

15.22b . . . the bolt from the turbocharger. . .

15.22c . . . and remove the air intake housing

turbocharger boost control solenoid valve, then undo the bolts and remove the mounting bracket **(see illustrations)**.

20 Disconnect the wiring connectors, then undo the bolts and remove the mounting bracket from the rear of the turbocharger **(see illustration)**.

21 Unclip the vacuum pipe and disconnect it from the turbocharger wastegate actuator **(see illustration)**.

22 Undo the mounting bolts, disconnect the hoses and remove the plastic air intake housing from the turbocharger **(see illustrations)**.

23 Undo the two flange bolts and disconnect the oil return pipe from under the turbocharger. Unscrew the support bolt and remove the pipe from the cylinder block **(see illustrations)**. Renew the O-ring oil seal in the cylinder block and the gasket between the flange and the turbocharger on refitting.

24 Unscrew the union bolt and disconnect the oil supply pipe from the top of the turbocharger. Unscrew the support bolt, then undo the union bolt and disconnect the lower end of the pipe from the cylinder block and

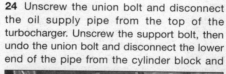

15.23a Undo the two flange bolts. . .

remove the pipes from the cylinder block **(see illustrations)**. Renew the oil supply pipe on refitting, as the sealing washers are built into the ends of the supply pipe.

25 If not already removed, withdraw the heat

15.23b . . . and the oil tube support bolt

15.24a Undo the turbocharger union bolt. . .

15.24b . . . and the union bolt in the cylinder block. . .

15.24c . . . then the support bracket bolt and remove pipe

15.25 Remove heatshield/gasket

15.26a Undo the upper mounting nut. . .

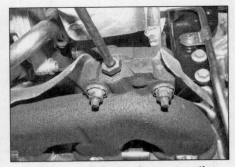

15.26b . . . and the two lower mounting nuts. . .

15.26c . . . then remove the turbocharger

15.27 Renew the heatshield/gasket

15.28a Fit a new gasket to the top of the oil return pipe. . .

shield/gasket from the turbocharger **(see illustration)**.

26 Unscrew the nuts/bolts and remove the turbocharger and mounting bracket from the exhaust manifold **(see illustrations)**.

27 Undo the mounting bolts and remove the heatshield/gasket from the top of the exhaust manifold **(see illustration)**. Discard and renew on refitting

Refitting

28 Refitting is a reversal of removal, but renew any damaged hose clamps, and use new turbocharger-to-exhaust manifold nuts which should be tightened to the specified torque. Fit new oil supply pipe, O-rings and copper seals (where applicable), then apply Loctite Frenetanch (or similar sealant) to the union threads (1.5 litre engines), before refitting the pipe and tightening the union nuts

to the specified torque. Fit a new gasket to the top of the oil return pipe, and new O-ring seal(s) to the groove(s) in the bottom of the pipe **(see illustrations)**. On completion, the following procedure must be observed before starting the engine in order to establish initial oil pressure in the turbocharger.

a) *Disconnect the wiring from the fuel injectors.*
b) *Crank the engine on the starter motor until the instrument panel oil pressure warning light goes out (this may take several seconds).*
c) *Reconnect the wiring to the injectors, then start the engine using the normal procedure.*
d) *Run the engine at idle speed, and check the turbocharger oil unions for leakage.*
e) *After the engine has been run, check the engine oil level, and top–up if necessary.*

16 Intercooler – removal and refitting

Removal

1 The intercooler is located behind the front bumper, to the right-hand side of the radiator and air conditioning condenser.

2 Remove the front bumper as described in Chapter 11 Section 5.

3 Release the retaining clips and disconnect the charge air cooler upper hose from the intercooler and turbocharger **(see illustrations)**.

4 Undo the mounting bolt then release the retaining clip and disconnect the air intake pipe from the throttle housing. Undo the mounting bolt from the lower support

15.28b . . . fit new O-ring seals to the grooves in the bottom of the pipe – 1.5 litre engine

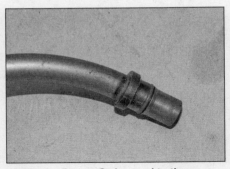

15.28c . . . fit new O-ring seal to the groove in the bottom of the pipe – 1.6 litre engine

16.3a Release the securing clips. . .

16.3b . . . and remove the upper intercooler hose

16.4a Disconnect from the throttle housing. . .

16.4b . . . and from the intercooler

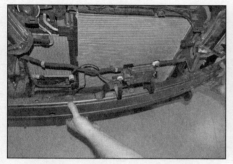

16.5 Remove the front crossmember

16.6 Remove the plastic trim

16.7 Remove the upper crossmember

bracket, then release the retaining clip and release the intercooler lower air intake pipe from the bottom of the intercooler (see illustrations).

5 Release the wiring loom and connectors

16.8 Remove the mounting bracket

16.9b . . . and rotate it. . .

from across the reinforcement crossmember, then undo the retaining nuts and remove the crossmember from the front of the vehicle (see illustration).

6 Release the retaining clips and remove the

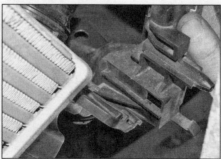

16.9a Release the intercooler from the radiator. . .

16.9c . . . to remove it from the vehicle

plastic trim from the front of the intercooler (see illustration).

7 Undo the retaining bolts and move the upper crossmember from across the top of the radiator (see illustration). Place the crossmember across the top of the engine, taking care not to place it on the battery terminals.

8 Undo the retaining bolts and remove the crossmember mounting bracket from the right-hand side of the vehicle (see illustration).

9 Unclip the lower part of the condenser from the radiator, then unhook the intercooler from the bottom of the radiator. Rotate the intercooler and pull it upwards to release it from the radiator, then remove it from the front of the vehicle (see illustrations).

Refitting

10 Refitting is a reversal of removal, making sure all the connections are securely fitted.

17 Exhaust system –
general information and component renewal

General information

1 The exhaust system consists of the exhaust manifold (see Section 13), the turbocharger (see Section 14), the catalytic converter, the front pipe/particle filter (depending on model) and the remaining exhaust section consisting of the intermediate pipe/tailpipe and silencer.

17.2 Front exhaust flexible joint

17.3a Exhaust rubber mounting. . .

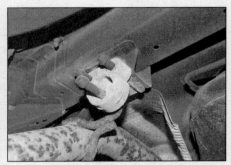

17.3b . . . along the length. . .

17.3c . . . of the exhaust system

17.5 Undo the front pipe-to-catalytic converter bolts/nuts

17.6 Undo the front pipe to intermediate pipe bolts

2 The front pipe is connected by a flexible flange joint (see illustration).

3 The system is suspended throughout its entire length by rubber mountings (see illustrations), and all exhaust sections are joined by flanged joints, which are then secured together by nuts and/or bolts.

4 To remove the system or part of the system, firmly apply the handbrake, and then jack up the vehicle and support it securely on axle stands (see Jacking and vehicle support). Alternatively, position the car over an inspection pit, or on car ramps. Where fitted, remove the engine compartment undertray.

Front pipe (models without DPF)

5 Undo the nuts securing the front pipe to the catalytic converter (see illustration). With the nuts removed retrieve the washers and springs, and then separate the front pipe from the catalytic converter/manifold.

6 Slacken and remove the two bolts securing the front pipe/silencer flange joint to the intermediate pipe. Withdraw the front pipe from underneath the vehicle, and recover the gasket from the joint (see illustration).

Front pipe/particle filter (models with DPF) – 1.5 litre engines

7 Unscrew the pressure take-off unions from the side and base of the assembly (see illustrations). Undo the retaining nuts and disconnect any securing clamps from the pipes.

8 Disconnect the sensor wiring plug on the side of the exhaust system (see illustration).

9 Slacken the retaining nuts securing the front pipe/particle filter to the catalytic converter (see illustration 17.2b). Take care not to damage the flexible section of the front exhaust pipe.

10 Slacken and remove the two bolts securing the front pipe/particle filter flange joint to the intermediate pipe. Withdraw the front pipe/particle filter from underneath the vehicle, and recover the gasket from the joint (see illustration).

17.7a Front pressure take off pipe connection. . .

17.7b . . . and rear pressure take-off pipe connection

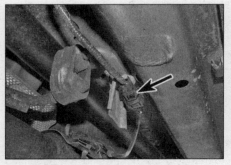

17.8 Disconnect the sensor wiring connector

17.10 Undo the front pipe/particle filter to intermediate pipe bolts/nuts

17.13 Remove the pressure take off pipe connections

17.14 Remove the rear heatshield

17.15a Remove the heat shield. . .

17.15b . . . and undo the two retaining bolts

17.16 Disconnect the oxygen sensor wiring connector

17.17 Undo the two retaining nuts

Front pipe/particle filter (models with DPF) – 1.6 litre engines

11 Remove the front subframe as described in Chapter 10 Section 12.

12 Remove the right-hand side driveshaft, as described in Chapter 8 Section 8.

13 Unscrew the pressure take-off unions from the rear of the assembly **(see illustration)**. Undo the retaining nuts and disconnect any securing clamps from the pipes.

14 Undo the four retaining bolts and removed the heatshield from the rear of the particle filter **(see illustration)**.

15 Undo the retaining bolts and removed the heatshield, then undo the two bolts from the left-hand side of the particle filter **(see illustrations)**.

16 Disconnect the oxygen sensor wiring plug at the right-hand rear corner of the cylinder head **(see illustration)**.

17 Remove the retaining nuts and disconnect the front pipe from the particle filter **(see illustration)**. Take care not to damage the flexible section of the front exhaust pipe.

18 Undo the retaining bolts and remove the support bracket from under the particle filter **(see illustrations)**.

19 Slacken the union in the rear of the manifold, then undo the bolt from the mounting bracket and remove the exhaust gas pressure sensor from the left-hand rear of the cylinder head **(see illustration)**.

20 Slacken and remove the three nuts securing the particle filter flange joint to the turbocharger, and recover the gasket/heat shield from the joint **(see illustration)**.

21 If not already done, undo the retaining bolts and remove the driveshaft support bracket from the rear of the cylinder block **(see illustration)**.

22 Support the particle filter, then undo the two retaining bolts and remove the support straps from around the particle filter, lower the particle filter down to remove **(see illustrations)**.

17.18a Undo the mounting bolts. . .

17.18b . . . and remove the support bracket

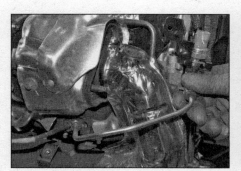

17.19 Remove the gas pressure sensor

17.20 Undo the securing nuts

17.21 Remove the driveshaft support bracket

17.22a Undo the two bolts from the straps. . .

17.22b . . . and remove the particle filter

17.25a Undo the retaining clips. . .

17.25b . . . and remove the heat shield

17.26a Where applicable, fit new sealing rings. . .

17.26b . . . and the exhaust front pipe

Intermediate pipe/silencer/tailpipe

23 Slacken and remove the two bolts securing the front pipe flange joint to the intermediate pipe and seperate. Support the disconnected front pipe so as not to place undue strain on the front part of the exhaust system.

24 With the aid of an assistant, working along the underside of the vehicle, unhook the intermediate pipe/silencer/tailpipe from its mounting rubbers, and then manoeuvre the pipe out from underneath the vehicle.

Heat shield(s)

25 The heat shields are secured in position by a mixture of fasteners. Some heatshields are fitted to the underside of the vehicle. And also some are fitted to parts of the exhaust system. When an exhaust section is renewed, transfer any relevant heat shields from the original over to the new section before installing the exhaust section on the vehicle **(see illustrations)**.

Refitting

26 Each section is refitted by a reverse of the removal sequence, noting the following points:

a) *Ensure that all traces of corrosion have been removed from the flanges, and renew all necessary gaskets***(see illustrations)**.

b) *Inspect the rubber mountings for signs of damage or deterioration, and renew as necessary.*

c) *Prior to tightening the exhaust system fasteners, ensure that all rubber mountings are correctly located, and that there is adequate clearance between the exhaust system and vehicle underbody/suspension components, etc.*

Chapter 5
Starting and charging systems

Contents

Degrees of difficulty

Easy, suitable for novice with little experience	Fairly easy, suitable for beginner with some experience	Fairly difficult, suitable for competent DIY mechanic	Difficult, suitable for experienced DIY mechanic	Very difficult, suitable for expert DIY or professional

Specifications

General

System type . . . . 12 volt, negative earth

Battery

Type . . . . Low-maintenance or maintenance-free (depending on model)
Rating . . . . 60 – 70 Ah (depending on model)
Charge condition:
  Poor . . . . 12.5 volts
  Normal . . . . 12.6 volts
  Good . . . . 12.7 volts

Alternator

Make . . . . Bosch or Valeo
Type:
  HRA2DDT:
    Bosch . . . . F 000 BL0 814
    Valeo. TG12C164
  K9K . . . . Bosch F 000 BL0 825
  R9M . . . . Bosch F 000 BL0 814
Output rating:
  Bosch . . . . 150 amp
  Valeo . . . . 120 amp
Regulated output voltage. . . . . 14.1 to 14.5 Volts

Starter motor

Make . . . . Mitsubishi or Bosch
Type:
  HRA2DDT. . . . . Mitsubishi M000TD0371, M000TD0375 or M000T46571
  K9K . . . . Bosch 0 001 170 605
  R9M . . . . Bosch 0 001 170 607

Torque wrench settings

	Nm	lbf ft
Alternator mounting bolts:		
HRA2DDT and R9M	25	18
K9K	21	15
Oil pressure switch:		
HRA2DDT	15	11
K9K	25	18
R9M	35	26
Oil level sensor:		
HRA2DDT	10	7
K9K and R9M	25	18
Starter motor mounting bolts (all models)	44	32

1 General information and precautions

General information

1 The engine electrical system consists mainly of the charging and starting systems. Because of their engine-related functions, these components are covered separately from the body electrical devices such as the lights, instruments, etc (which are covered in Chapter 12).

2 The electrical system is of the 12-volt negative earth type.

3 The battery is of the low-maintenance or 'maintenance-free' (sealed for life) type, and is charged by the alternator, which is belt-driven from the crankshaft pulley.

4 The starter motor is of the pre-engaged, reduction gear type, incorporating an integral solenoid. On starting, the solenoid moves the drive pinion into engagement with the flywheel ring gear before the starter motor is energised. Once the engine has started, a one-way clutch prevents the motor armature being driven by the engine until the pinion disengages from the flywheel.

Precautions

5 Further details of the various systems are given in the relevant Sections of this Chapter. While some repair procedures are given, the usual course of action is to renew the component concerned. The owner whose interest extends beyond mere component renewal should obtain a copy of The Haynes Car Electrical Systems Manual, available from the publishers of this manual.

6 It is necessary to take extra care when working on the electrical system, to avoid damage to semi-conductor devices (diodes and transistors), and to avoid the risk of personal injury. In addition to the precautions given in Safety first! at the beginning of this manual, observe the following when working on the system:

7 Always remove rings, watches, etc, before working on the electrical system. Even with the battery disconnected, capacitive discharge could occur if a component's live terminal is earthed through a metal object. This could cause a shock or nasty burn.

8 Do not reverse the battery connections. Components such as the alternator, ECCS control unit, or any other components having semi-conductor circuitry could be irreparably damaged.

9 If the engine is being started using jump leads and a slave battery, connect the batteries positive-to-positive and negative-to-negative (see Jump starting). This also applies when connecting a battery charger.

10 Never disconnect the battery terminals, the alternator, any electrical wiring, or any test instruments, when the engine is running.

11 Do not allow the engine to turn the alternator when the alternator is not connected.

12 Never 'test' for alternator output by 'flashing' the output lead to earth.

13 Never use an ohmmeter of the type incorporating a hand-cranked generator for circuit or continuity testing.

14 Always ensure that the battery negative terminal is disconnected when working on the electrical system.

15 Before using electric-arc welding equipment on the car, disconnect the battery, alternator and components such as electronic control units, to protect them from the risk of damage.

16 Several systems fitted to the vehicle require battery power to be available at all times, either to ensure their continued operation (such as the clock) or to maintain security codes which would be wiped if the battery were to be disconnected. To ensure that there are no unforeseen consequences of this action, refer to Disconnecting the battery later in this Chapter for further information.

2 Troubleshooting

Battery

Note: The following is intended as a guide only. Always refer to the manufacturer's recommendations (often printed on a label attached to the battery) before charging a battery.

1 General electrical fault finding is described in Chapter 12 Section 2.

2 All models are fitted with a maintenance-free battery in production, which should require no maintenance under normal operating conditions.

3 In all cases, a 'sealed for life' maintenance-free battery is fitted, and topping-up and testing of the electrolyte in each cell is not possible. The condition of the battery can therefore only be tested using a battery condition indicator or a voltmeter.

4 If testing the battery using a voltmeter, connect the voltmeter across the battery and compare the result with those given in the Specifications under 'charge condition'. The test is only accurate if the battery has not been subjected to any kind of charge for the previous six hours. If this is not the case, switch on the headlights for 30 seconds, then wait four to five minutes before testing the battery after switching off the headlights. All other electrical circuits must be switched off, so check that the doors and tailgate are fully shut when making the test.

5 Generally speaking, if the voltage reading is less than 12.2 volts, then the battery is discharged, whilst a reading of 12.2 to 12.4 volts indicates a partially discharged condition.

Charging system

Note: Refer to the warnings given in 'Safety first!' and in Section 1 of this Chapter before starting work.

6 If the ignition warning light fails to illuminate when the ignition is switched on, first check the alternator wiring connections for security. If satisfactory, check that the warning light bulb (where applicable) has not blown, and that the bulbholder is secure in its location in the instrument panel. If the light still fails to illuminate, check the continuity of the warning light feed wire from the alternator to the bulbholder. On most vehicles, the warning light is an LED integral with the instrument cluster, and no repair is possible. Any malfunction of the instrument panel should generate an error code. The systems self-diagnosis facility can be interrogated using suitable diagnostic equipment connected via the vehicles 16-pin diagnostic plug located under the drivers side of the facia. If all is satisfactory, the alternator may be at fault and should be renewed or taken to an auto-electrician for testing and repair.

7 If the ignition warning light illuminates when the engine is running, stop the engine and check that the drivebelt is correctly fitted and tensioned, also that the alternator connections are secure. If all is so far satisfactory, have the alternator checked by an auto-electrician for testing and repair.

8 If the alternator output is suspect even though the warning light functions correctly, the regulated voltage may be checked as follows.

9 Connect a voltmeter across the battery terminals and start the engine.

10 Increase the engine speed until the voltmeter reading remains steady; the reading should be approximately 12 to 13 volts, and no more than 15 volts.

11 Switch on as many electrical accessories (eg, the headlights, heated rear window and heater blower) as possible, and check that the alternator maintains the regulated voltage of around 13 to 14 volts.

12 If the regulated voltage is not as stated, the fault may be due to worn brushes, weak brush springs, a faulty voltage regulator, a faulty diode, a severed phase winding or worn or damaged slip-rings. The alternator should be renewed or taken to an auto-electrician for testing and repair.

Starting system

The starter motor rotates, but the engine doesn't

13 Remove the starter motor (see Section 10). Have the starter motor checked by a automotive electrician or suitably equipped repairer.

14 Check the flywheel/driveplate ring gear for missing teeth and other damage. With the ignition turned off, rotate the flywheel/driveplate so you can check the entire ring gear.

The starter motor is noisy

15 If the solenoid is making a chattering noise, first check the battery as described previously in this Section. If the battery is okay, check the cables and connections.

16 If you hear a grinding, crashing metallic sound when you turn the key to Start, check for loose starter mounting bolts. If they're tight, remove the starter and inspect the teeth on the starter pinion gear and flywheel ring gear. Look for missing or damaged teeth.

17 If the starter sounds fine when you first turn the key to Start, but then stops rotating the engine and emits a zinging sound, the problem may be a defective starter motor drive pinion. Remove the starter motor (see Section 10), check the pinion gear teeth and the flywheel/driveplate ring gear teeth. Replace as necessary.

The starter motor rotates slowly

18 Check the battery as previously described in this Section.

19 If the battery is okay, verify all connections (at the battery, the starter solenoid and motor) are clean, corrosion-free and secure. Make sure the cables aren't frayed or damaged.

20 Check that the starter mounting bolts are secure so it earths properly. Also check the pinion gear and flywheel/driveplate ring gear for evidence of mechanical damage (galling, deformed gear teeth or other damage).

The starter motor does not rotate at all

21 Check the battery as previously described in this Section.

22 If the battery is okay, verify all connections (at the battery, the starter solenoid and motor) are clean, corrosion-free and secure. Make sure the cables aren't frayed or damaged.

23 Check all of the fuses in the fuse/relay box.

24 Check that the starter mounting bolts are secure so it earths properly.

25 Check for voltage at the starter solenoid "S" terminal when the ignition key is turned to the start position. If voltage is present, replace the starter/solenoid assembly. If no voltage is present, the problem could be the starter relay, the ignition/starter switch, the inhibitor/gear position switch (automatic transmission models), or with an electrical connector somewhere in the circuit (see the wiring diagrams in Chapter 12). Also, on many modern vehicles, the engine management ECU and/or Body Control Module (BCM) control the voltage signal to the starter solenoid; on such vehicles a special scan tool is required for diagnosis.

---

3 Battery – testing and charging

Note: *The following is intended as a guide only. Always refer to the manufacturer's recommendations (often printed on a label attached to the battery) before charging a battery.*

1 All models are fitted with a maintenance-free battery in production, which should require no maintenance under normal operating conditions.

4.4 Slacken the earth clamp

2 In all cases, a 'sealed for life' maintenance-free battery is fitted, and topping-up and testing of the electrolyte in each cell is not possible. The condition of the battery can therefore only be tested using a battery condition indicator or a voltmeter.

3 If testing the battery using a voltmeter, connect the voltmeter across the battery and compare the result with those given in the Specifications under 'charge condition'. The test is only accurate if the battery has not been subjected to any kind of charge for the previous six hours. If this is not the case, switch on the headlights for 30 seconds, then wait four to five minutes before testing the battery after switching off the headlights. All other electrical circuits must be switched off, so check that the doors and tailgate are fully shut when making the test.

4 Generally speaking, if the voltage reading is less than 12.2 volts, then the battery is discharged, whilst a reading of 12.2 to 12.4 volts indicates a partially discharged condition.

---

4 Battery and tray – disconnection, removal and refitting

Disconnection

1 Open the drivers side door, and pull the bonnet release catch.

⚠ *Warning: Make sure the keys are not left in the car, in case of the vehicle locking system activating and locking all the doors.*

4.8a Slacken the clamp nut. . .

2 Close the drivers door and open the bonnet, with the engine off and not operating any of the vehicles electrics (including open and closing doors), wait at least 4 minutes for all power to the electrical components to clear.

⚠ *Warning: Power is supplied to certain electrical components (including ECUs), for a length of time, after the ignition switch has been switched off. If the battery is disconnected to early, then damage to the electrical component may occur.*

3 The battery is located on the left-hand side of the engine compartment.

4 Slacken the negative (earth) lead clamp nut, and disconnect the connector from the battery **(see illustration)**. The following guidelines should be adhered to:

a) *Do not attach any additional connections to the negative terminal.*
b) *Do not modify the earth lead.*
c) *Do not use force when disconnecting the earth terminal.*
d) *Do not pull on the earth cable.*

5 Pull up the negative (earth) lead clamp from the battery terminal with a twisting motion. Position the lead clamp to one side and cover it to prevent accidental re-connection.

Removal

6 Disconnect the battery negative terminal, as described previously in this Section.

7 Remove the air cleaner housing air intake ducts from across the top of the battery, as described in Chapter 4A Section 3, for petrol engines, or Chapter 4B Section 3 for diesel engines.

8 Remove the insulation cover (where fitted) and disconnect the positive clamp in the same way **(see illustrations)**.

9 Slacken the two securing nuts, unhook the threaded retaining rods, then remove the battery retaining clamp bracket from over the top of the battery **(see illustration)**.

10 Make sure everything is clear, then lift the battery out of the engine compartment.

11 If necessary, the battery tray/mounting bracket can also be unbolted and removed from the engine compartment. First undo the retaining bolts and remove the engine management ECU from the front of the battery

4.8b . . . and disconnect the positive terminal

4.9 Slacken the two retaining nuts and remove the battery retaining clamp

4.12 Undo the two bolts and move restart relay from tray

4.13 Unclip the wiring loom retaining clips

4.14a Undo the three mounting bolts. . .

4.14b . . . and remove the battery tray

mounting bracket as described in Chapter 6A Section 6, for petrol engines, or Chapter 6B Section 6 for diesel engines.

12 Undo the two retaining bolts and remove the engine restart relay from the rear of the battery tray **(see illustration)**.

13 Depending on model, it will be necessary to disconnect wiring loom retaining clips and various brackets from the battery tray **(see illustration)**.

14 Undo the mounting bolts and remove the battery tray from the engine compartment **(see illustrations)**.

Refitting

15 Refitting is a reversal of removal, but smear petroleum jelly on the terminals after reconnecting the leads, and always reconnect the positive lead first, and the negative lead last.

5 Charging system – testing

Note: *Refer to the warnings given in 'Safety first!' and in Section 1 of this Chapter before starting work.*

1 If the ignition/no-charge warning light fails to come on when the ignition is switched on, first check the alternator wiring connections for security. If satisfactory, check that the warning light bulb has not blown, and that the bulbholder is secure in its location in the instrument panel. If the light still fails to come on, check the continuity of the warning light

feed wire from the alternator to the bulbholder. If all is satisfactory, the alternator is at fault, and should be taken to an auto-electrician for testing and repair.

2 If the ignition warning light comes on when the engine is running, stop the engine as soon as possible. Check that the drivebelt is correctly tensioned (see Chapter 1A Section 16 for petrol engines or Chapter 1B Section 33, 34 for diesel engines), that the drivebelt is not contaminated (with oil or water, for example), and that the alternator connections are secure. If all is so far satisfactory, the alternator should be renewed or taken to an auto-electrician for testing and repair.

3 If the alternator output is suspect, even though the warning light functions correctly, the regulated voltage may be checked as follows.

4 Connect a voltmeter across the battery terminals, and start the engine.

7.3 Remove the belt from around the pulley

5 Increase the engine speed until the voltmeter reading remains steady; the reading should be approximately 12 to 13 volts, and no more than 14 volts.

6 Switch on as many electrical accessories (e.g. the headlights, heated rear window and heater blower) as possible, and check that the alternator maintains the regulated voltage at around 13 to 14 volts.

7 If the regulated voltage is not as stated, the fault may be due to worn brushes, weak brush springs, a faulty voltage regulator, a faulty diode, a severed phase winding, or worn or damaged slip-rings. The alternator should be taken to an auto-electrician for testing and repair.

6 Alternator drivebelt – removal, refitting and tensioning

1 Refer to the procedure given for the auxiliary drivebelt in Chapter 1A Section 29 for petrol engines, or Section for diesel engines.

7 Alternator – removal and refitting

Removal

Petrol engines

1 Disconnect the battery negative terminal (refer to Section 4).

2 Remove the inlet manifold, as described in Chapter 4A Section 11.

3 Remove the auxiliary drivebelts (see Chapter 1A Section 29), then disengage it from the alternator pulley **(see illustration)**.

4 Release the locking clip and disconnect the wiring plug connector from the rear of the alternator **(see illustration)**.

5 Remove the rubber cover (where fitted) from the alternator terminal, then unscrew the retaining nut and disconnect the wiring cable from the rear of the alternator **(see illustration)**.

6 Unscrew the alternator upper and lower mounting bolts, and then manoeuvre the

7.4 Disconnect the wiring connector. . .

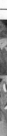

7.5 . . . and battery cable from the alternator

7.6a Undo the upper bolt. . .

7.6b . . . and lower bolt. . .

7.6c . . . then carefully lever the alternator from the bracket. . .

7.6d . . . complete with lower bolt. . .

alternator away from its mounting bracket and out of position **(see illustrations)**. The lower mounting bolt cannot be removed completely, as it contacts the body side member. The mounting bracket has a cut out to allow the alternator to be withdrawn with the bolt still in place.

Diesel engines

7 Jack up the front of the vehicle and support it on axle stands (see *Jacking and vehicle support*), then remove the drivers side front wheel and wheel arch liner. Remove the engine undershield.
8 Slacken the auxiliary drivebelt, (see Chapter 1B Section 33, 34,), then disengage it from the alternator pulley.
9 Slacken the retaining clips and remove the intercooler air intake hose from above the alternator, as described in Chapter 4B Section 16.
Caution: Cover the open ends of the intercooler and hoses to prevent anything being dropped inside them.
10 Unclip the coolant hose from the top of the alternator and move it to one side.
11 Remove the rubber covers (where fitted) from the alternator terminals, then unscrew the retaining nut(s) and disconnect the terminal and wiring plug connector from the rear of the alternator **(see illustrations)**.
12 Where applicable, release the retaining clip and disconnect the wiring loom cable clip from the rear of the alternator.
13 Unscrew the alternator upper mounting bracket and lower mounting bolt and washers, and then manoeuvre the alternator away from

its mounting brackets and out of position **(see illustrations)**.
14 The lower mounting bolt cannot be removed completely, as it contacts the body side member. The mounting bracket has a cut

out to allow the alternator to be withdrawn with the bolt still in place.

Refitting

15 Refitting is a reversal of removal,

7.6e . . . and remove the alternator from the engine compartment

7.11b . . . and disconnect the the wiring plug

7.11a Undo the retaining nut, disconnect the terminal. . .

7.13a Undo the two alternator mounting bolts. . .

7.13b . . . and withdraw the alternator – 1.6 litre shown

7.16a Use bolt and socket to withdraw. . .

7.16b . . . the pull back into place with bolt

tensioning the auxiliary drivebelt as described in Chapter 1A Section 29 for petrol engines, or for diesel engines, ensuring that the alternator mountings are tightened to the specified torque. Tighten the upper bolt first, then the lower bolt.
Caution: Take care when removing the spacers, as the alloy brackets of the alternator may get damaged. DO NOT hammer the spacers out.
16 Before refitting the alternator, make sure the spacers in the mounting brackets are free to slide. Carefully use a bolt and socket to withdraw the spacers if they are a tight fit **(see illustrations)**. Clean the spacers and then refit. Take care when removing the spacers, as the alloy brackets of the alternator may get damaged. DO NOT hammer the spacers out.

8 Alternator – testing and overhaul

1 If the alternator is thought to be suspect, it should be removed from the vehicle and taken to an auto-electrician for testing. Most auto-electricians will be able to supply fit new parts at reasonable cost. However, check on the cost of repairs before proceeding, as it may prove more economical to obtain a new or exchange alternator.

9 Starting system – testing

Note: *Refer to the precautions given in 'Safety first!' and in Section 1 of this Chapter before starting work.*
1 If the starter motor fails to operate when the ignition key is turned to the appropriate position, the following may be to blame:
a) *The battery is faulty.*
b) *The electrical connections between the switch, solenoid, battery and starter motor are somewhere failing to pass the necessary current from the battery through the starter to earth.*
c) *The solenoid is faulty.*
d) *The starter motor is mechanically or electrically defective.*

2 To check the battery, switch on the headlights. If they dim after a few seconds, this indicates that the battery is discharged – recharge or renew the battery. If the headlights glow brightly, operate the ignition switch and observe the lights. If they dim, then this indicates that current is reaching the starter motor; therefore the fault must lie in the starter motor. If the lights continue to glow brightly (and no clicking sound can be heard from the starter motor solenoid), this indicates that there is a fault in the circuit or solenoid – see following paragraphs. If the starter motor turns slowly when operated, but the battery is in good condition, then this indicates that either the starter motor is faulty, or there is considerable resistance somewhere in the circuit.
3 If a fault in the circuit is suspected, disconnect the battery leads (including the earth connection to the body), the starter/solenoid wiring and the engine/transmission earth strap (refer to *Disconnecting the battery* in Section 4). Thoroughly clean the connections, reconnect the leads and wiring, then use a voltmeter or test light to check that full battery voltage is available at the battery positive lead connection to the solenoid, and that the earth is sound. Smear petroleum jelly around the battery terminals to prevent corrosion – corroded connections are amongst the most frequent causes of electrical system faults.
4 If the battery and all connections are in good condition, check the circuit by disconnecting the wire from the solenoid blade terminal. Connect a voltmeter or test light between the wire end and a good earth (such as the battery

10.4 Disconnect the coolant hose

negative terminal), and check that the wire is live when the ignition switch is turned to the 'start' position. If it is, then the circuit is sound – if not, the circuit wiring can be checked as described in Chapter 12 Section 2.
5 The solenoid contacts can be checked by connecting a voltmeter or test light between the battery positive feed connection on the starter side of the solenoid, and earth. When the ignition switch is turned to the 'start' position, there should be a reading or lighted bulb, as applicable. If there is no reading or lighted bulb, the solenoid is faulty and should be renewed.
6 If the circuit and solenoid are proved sound, the fault must lie in the starter motor. In this event, it may be possible to have the starter motor overhauled by a specialist, but check on the availability and cost of spares before proceeding, as it may prove more economical to obtain a new or exchange motor.

10 Starter motor – removal and refitting

Removal

Petrol engines

1 Disconnect the battery negative terminal (refer to Section 4).
2 Drain the engine coolant, as described in Chapter 1A Section 33.
3 Remove the inlet manifold, as described in Chapter 4A Section 11.
4 Slacken the retaining clip and disconnect the coolant hose from the thermostat housing on the front of the cylinder block **(see illustration)**.
5 Remove the rubber cover(s) from the starter solenoid terminals, then unscrew the two retaining nuts and disconnect the wiring cable connectors, from the starter solenoid **(see illustrations)**.
6 Unclip the wiring loom from the retaining clip on the transmission bell housing **(see illustration)**, to access the starter motor mounting bolts.
7 Unscrew the starter upper and lower mounting bolts, and then manoeuvre the starter out from the transmission bell housing **(see illustrations)**.

10.5a Pull back the rubber cover, undo the nut. . .

10.5b . . . and disconnect the upper cable. . .

10.5c . . . then undo the securing nut. . .

Diesel engines

8 Disconnect the battery negative terminal (refer to Section 4).

9 On turbo-diesel models, slacken the retaining clips and remove the intercooler air intake hose (see Chapter 4B Section 16), from above the starter motor.

Caution: Cover the open ends of the intercooler and hoses to prevent anything being dropped inside them.

10 Working down the front of the engine compartment, move the wiring loom and hoses to one side to access the starter motor, which is located at the front of the cylinder block, bolted to the transmission bell housing.

11 Pull back the rubber cover, and then slacken and remove the two retaining nuts. Disconnect the main battery cable, and the small solenoid wiring from the starter motor solenoid **(see illustrations)**.

12 Unscrew the starter motor mounting bolts **(see illustration)**, supporting the motor as the bolts are withdrawn, and manoeuvre the starter motor out from its location.

Refitting

13 Refitting is a reversal of removal.

10.5d . . . and disconnect the smaller cable

10.6 Unclip the wiring loom

taken to an auto-electrician for testing. Most auto-electricians will be able to supply fit new parts at reasonable cost. However, check on the cost of repairs before proceeding, as it may prove more economical to obtain a new or exchange motor.

11 Starter motor – testing and overhaul

1 If the starter motor is thought to be suspect, it should be removed from the vehicle and

10.7a Undo the mounting bolts. . .

10.7b . . . and remove the starter from the engine

10.11a Undo the retaining nuts. . .

10.11b . . . and disconnect the starter wiring cables

10.12 Remove the starter motor from the transmission housing

13.2 Location of oil pressure switch

13.4 Disconnect the wiring connector (1.2 litre petrol shown)

13.10 Disconnect the wiring connector

13.11 Oil pressure switch behind oil filter – 1.6 litre shown

12 Ignition stop/start switch –
removal and refitting

1 The ignition stop/start switch is located n the facia panel, to left-hand side the steering wheel, and can be removed as described in Chapter 12 Section 4.

13 Oil pressure switch –
removal and refitting

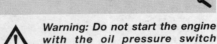

⚠ *Warning: Do not start the engine with the oil pressure switch removed.*

Petrol engines

1 Access to the switch is improved if the

14.9 Disconnect the level sensor wiring connector

vehicle is jacked up and supported on axle stands (see *Jacking and vehicle support*), so that the switch can be reached from underneath. Remove the engine undershield.
2 The switch is located at the front of the cylinder block, below the thermostat housing **(see illustration)**.
3 Disconnect the battery negative terminal (refer to Section 4).
4 Disconnect the wiring connector from the oil pressure switch **(see illustration)**.
5 Unscrew the switch and recover the sealing washer (where fitted). Be prepared for oil spillage. If the switch is to be left removed from the engine for any length of time, plug the hole to prevent excessive oil loss.
6 Where the switch was fitted with a sealing washer, examine the sealing washer for signs of damage or deterioration, and if necessary renew it. Where no sealing washer was fitted, clean the switch and apply a smear of sealant to its threads.
7 Refit the switch, tightening it securely, and reconnect the wiring connector.
8 Where applicable refit the engine undershield and lower the vehicle to the ground.
9 Check and if necessary, top-up the engine oil as described in Chapter 1A Section 5.

Diesel engines

10 On 1.5 litre engines, the switch is fitted to the front of the engine in the cylinder block, above the oil filter housing **(see illustration)**.
11 On 1.6 litre engines, the switch is fitted to the front of the engine, behind the oil cooler, next to the oil filter housing **(see illustration)**.

12 Disconnect the wiring plug, then unscrew the switch. Recover the sealing washer. Be prepared for fluid spillage, and if the switch is to be left removed from the engine for any length of time, plug the hole.
13 Examine the sealing washer for signs of damage or deterioration and if necessary renew.
14 Refit the switch, complete with washer, and tighten it to the specified torque. Reconnect the wiring connector.
15 The remainder of refitting is a reversal of removal. Top up the engine oil as described in Chapter 1B Section 5.

14 Oil level sensor –
removal and refitting

⚠ *Warning: Do not start the engine with the oil level sensor removed.*

1 Access to the switch is improved if the vehicle is jacked up and supported on axle stands (see *Jacking and vehicle support*). Remove the engine undershield, so that the switch can be reached from underneath.
2 The sensors are located as follows:
a) *1.2 litre petrol engine (where fitted) – At the front of the engine and screwed into the upper alloy sump housing, next to the oil filter.*
b) *1.5 litre diesel engine – At the front of the engine and screwed into the top of the alloy sump housing, at the transmission end.*
c) *1.6 litre diesel engine – At the front of the engine, bolted to the alloy sump housing.*
3 Disconnect the battery negative terminal (refer to Section 4).

Petrol engines

4 Disconnect the wiring from the oil level sensor.
5 Undo the retaining bolt and withdraw the sensor from the front of the alloy upper sump. Be prepared for oil spillage. If the sensor is to be left removed from the engine for any length of time, plug the hole to prevent excessive oil loss.
6 Where the sensor was fitted with a sealing washer, examine the sealing washer for signs of damage or deterioration, and if necessary renew it. Where no sealing washer was fitted, clean the sensor and apply a smear of sealant to its threads.
7 Refit the sensor, tightening to the torque setting specified, and reconnect the wiring connector.
8 Lower the vehicle to the ground, then check and if necessary, top-up the engine oil.

Diesel engines

1.5 litre engines

9 Disconnect the wiring plug, then unscrew the switch and recover the sealing washer **(see illustration)**. If the sensor is to be left removed from the engine for any length of time, plug the hole to prevent excessive oil loss.

10 Recover the seal from the sensor – a new one must be fitted.

11 Ensure the sealing surfaces of the sensor and the sump are clean.

12 Where applicable, renew the sensor O-ring seals.

13 Screw the sensor and tighten to the specified torque.

14 Reconnect the sensor wiring plug.

15 The remainder of refitting is a reversal of removal. Top up the engine oil as described in Chapter 1B Section 5.

1.6 litre engines

16 Disconnect the wiring plug, undo the retaining bolt and remove the sensor **(see illustrations)**.

17 Recover the seal from the sensor – a new one must be fitted.

14.16a Undo the retaining bolt. . .

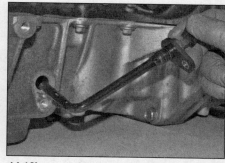

14.16b . . . and remove the oil level sensor-
1.6 litre shown

18 Ensure the sealing surfaces of the sensor and the sump are clean.

19 Renew the sensor O-ring seals.

20 Position the sensor in the sump, refit the retaining bolt and tighten to the specified torque.

21 Reconnect the sensor wiring plug.

22 The remainder of refitting is a reversal of removal. Top up the engine oil as described in Chapter 1B Section 5.

Chapter 6 Part A
Engine and emission control systems – petrol models

Contents

Degrees of difficulty

Easy, suitable for novice with little experience	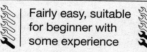	Fairly easy, suitable for beginner with some experience		Fairly difficult, suitable for competent DIY mechanic		Difficult, suitable for experienced DIY mechanic		Very difficult, suitable for expert DIY or professional	

Specifications

Ignition system

Type	Distributorless ignition system controlled by engine management ECU, 1 coil per spark plug

Spark plugs:
Type	NGK – ILKAR7F7G
Gap	0.65 mm (preset)
Ignition timing	Controlled by engine management ECU

Engine management system

Petrol engines	MED17UDS multipoint sequential direct fuel injection with turbocharger

Torque wrench settings

	Nm	lbf ft
Camshaft position sensors	10	7
Catalytic converter:		
To-turbocharger nuts	20	15
Mounting bracket:		
To-cylinder block	25	18
To-catalytic converter	20	15
Common fuel rail pressure sensor	32	24
Crankshaft position sensor	7	6
Ignition coil retaining bolt	8	6
Knock sensor retaining bolt	23	17
Oxygen sensors	44	32

1 Engine management system

Electronic control system

1 The fuel injection and ignition functions are combined into a single engine management system. The system incorporates a closed-loop catalytic converter and an evaporative emission control system, and complies with the latest emission control standards. The fuel side of the system operates as follows.

2 The fuel pump, which is situated in the fuel tank, supplies fuel from the tank to the high-pressure fuel pump. The pump motor is permanently immersed in fuel, to keep it cool. The fuel rail is mounted directly above the fuel injectors and acts as a fuel reservoir.

3 Fuel rail supply pressure is controlled by the pressure regulator, also located in the fuel tank. The regulator contains a spring-loaded valve, which lifts to allow excess fuel to recirculate within the tank when the optimum operating pressure of the fuel system is exceeded (eg, during low speed, light load cruising).

4 The fuel injectors are electromagnetic valves, which spray atomised fuel into the combustion chambers under the control of the engine management system ECU. There is one injector per cylinder, mounted in the cylinder head. The fuel is injected directly in the top of the combustion chambers. The ECU controls the volume of fuel injected by varying the length of time for which each injector is held open. The fuel injection systems are of the sequential type, whereby each injector operates individually in cylinder sequence.

5 The electrical control system consists of the ECU, along with the following sensors:
a) *Coolant temperature sensor – informs the ECU of engine temperature.*
b) *Inlet air temperature sensor – informs the ECU of the temperature of the air passing through the throttle housing.*
c) *Oxygen sensors – inform the ECU of the oxygen content of the exhaust gases.*

1.9 Diagnostic connector location

d) *Charge/Manifold pressure sensor – informs the ECU of the charge pressure in the intake manifold.*
e) *Charge pressure sensor (upstream of the throttle valve) – informs the ECU of the charge pressure from the turbocharger.*
f) *Crankshaft position sensor – informs the ECU of engine speed and crankshaft angular position.*
g) *Knock sensor – informs the ECU of pre-ignition (detonation) within the cylinders.*
h) *Camshaft sensors – informs the ECU on the camshaft positions.*
i) *Accelerator pedal position sensor – informs the ECU of the pedal position and rate of change.*
j) *Clutch and brake pedal position sensor – informs the ECU of the pedal positions (not all models).*

6 Signals from each of the sensors are compared by the ECU and, based on this information, the ECU selects the response appropriate to those values, and controls the fuel injectors (varying the pulse width – the length of time the injectors are held open – to provide a richer or weaker air/fuel mixture, as appropriate). The air/fuel mixture is constantly varied by the ECU, to provide the best settings for cranking, starting (with either a hot or cold engine) and engine warm-up, idle, cruising and acceleration.

7 The ECU also has full control over the engine idle speed, via the motorised throttle body. A sensor informs the ECU of the position, and rate of change, of the accelerator pedal. The ECU then controls the throttle body – no accelerator cable is fitted. The ECU also carries out 'fine tuning' of the idle speed by varying the ignition timing to increase or reduce the torque of the engine as it is idling. This helps to stabilise the idle speed when electrical or mechanical loads (such as headlights, air conditioning, etc) are switched on and off.

8 If there is any abnormality in any of the readings obtained from the coolant temperature sensor, the inlet air temperature sensor or the oxygen sensor, the ECU enters its 'back-up' mode. If this happens, the erroneous sensor signal is overridden, and the ECU assumes a pre-programmed 'back-up' value, which will allow the engine to continue running, albeit at reduced efficiency. If the ECU enters this mode, the warning lamp on the instrument panel will be illuminated, and the relevant fault code will be stored in the ECU memory.

9 If the warning light illuminates, the vehicle should be taken to a Nissan dealer or specialist at the earliest opportunity. Once there, a complete test of the engine management system can be carried out, using a special electronic diagnostic test unit, which is plugged into the system's diagnostic connector, located under the drivers side of the facia **(see illustration)**.

Ignition system

10 The ignition system is integrated with the fuel injection system to form a combined engine management system under the control of one ECU. The ignition side of the system is of the static (distributorless) type, consisting of the ignition coils and spark plugs. Each ignition coil is mounted directly above the spark plugs. The coils are integral with the spark plug caps and are pushed directly onto the spark plugs, one for each plug. This removes the need for any HT leads connecting the coils to the plugs.

11 The ECU uses its inputs from the various sensors to calculate the required ignition advance setting and coil charging time, depending on engine temperature, load and speed. At idle speeds, the ECU varies the ignition timing to alter the torque characteristic of the engine, enabling the idle speed to be controlled.

12 A knock sensor is also incorporated into the ignition system. Mounted onto the cylinder block, the sensor detects the high-frequency vibrations caused when the engine starts to pre-ignite, or 'pink'. Under these conditions, the knock sensor sends an electrical signal to the ECU, which in turn retards the ignition advance setting in small steps until the 'pinking' ceases.

2 Emissions systems – general information

1 All petrol engines use unleaded petrol and also have various other features built into the fuel system to help minimise harmful emissions. In addition, all engines are equipped with the crankcase emission control system described below. All engines are also equipped with a catalytic converter and an evaporative emission control system.

2 The emission control systems function as follows.

Crankcase emission control

3 To reduce the emission of unburned hydrocarbons from the crankcase into the atmosphere, the engine is sealed and the blow-by gases and oil vapour are drawn from inside the crankcase, through a wire mesh oil separator, into the inlet tract to be burned by the engine during normal combustion.

4 Under all conditions the gases are forced out of the crankcase by the (relatively) higher crankcase pressure; if the engine is worn, the raised crankcase pressure (due to increased blow-by) will cause some of the flow to return under all manifold conditions.

Exhaust emission control

5 To minimise the amount of pollutants which escape into the atmosphere, a catalytic converter is fitted in the exhaust system. On all models where a catalytic converter is fitted, the system is of the closed-loop type, in

which oxygen (lambda) sensors in the exhaust system provides the fuel injection/ignition system ECU with constant feedback, enabling the ECU to adjust the mixture to provide the best possible conditions for the converter to operate.

6 The oxygen sensors have a heating element built-in that is controlled by the ECU through the oxygen sensor relay to quickly bring the sensor's tip to an efficient operating temperature. The sensor's tip is sensitive to oxygen and sends the ECU a varying voltage depending on the amount of oxygen in the exhaust gases; if the inlet air/fuel mixture is too rich, the exhaust gases are low in oxygen so the sensor sends a low-voltage signal, the voltage rising as the mixture weakens and the amount of oxygen rises in the exhaust gases. Peak conversion efficiency of all major pollutants occurs if the inlet air/fuel mixture is maintained at the chemically correct ratio for the complete combustion of petrol of 14.7 parts (by weight) of air to 1 part of fuel (the 'stoichiometric' ratio). The sensor output voltage alters in a large step at this point, the ECU using the signal change as a reference point and correcting the inlet air/fuel mixture accordingly by altering the fuel injector pulse width.

Evaporative emission control

7 To minimise the escape into the atmosphere of unburned hydrocarbons, an evaporative emission control system is fitted to all models. The fuel tank filler cap is sealed and a charcoal canister is mounted underneath the fuel tank to collect the petrol vapours generated in the tank when the car is parked. It stores them until they can be cleared from the canister (under the control of the fuel injection/ignition system ECU) via the purge valve into the inlet tract to be burned by the engine during normal combustion.

8 To ensure that the engine runs correctly when it is cold and/or idling and to protect the catalytic converter from the effects of an over-rich mixture, the purge control valve is not opened by the ECU until the engine has warmed-up, and the engine is under load; the valve solenoid is then modulated on and off to allow the stored vapour to pass into the inlet tract.

3 European On Board Diagnosis (EOBD) system

General description

1 All models are equipped with the European On-Board Diagnosis (EOBD) system. This system consists of an on-board computer known as the ECU (Electronic Control Unit), Electronic Control Module (ECM) or Powertrain Control Module (PCM), and information sensors, which monitor various functions of the engine and send data to the

ECU/ECM/PCM. This system incorporates a series of diagnostic monitors that detect and identify fuel injection and emissions control system faults and store the information in the computer memory. This system also tests sensors and output actuators, diagnoses drive cycles, freezes data and clears codes.

2 The ECU/ECM/PCM is the brain of the electronically controlled fuel and emissions system. It receives data from a number of sensors and other electronic components (switches, relays, etc.). Based on the information it receives, the ECU/ECM/PCM generates output signals to control various relays, solenoids (fuel injectors) and other actuators. The ECU/ECM/PCM is specifically calibrated to optimise the emissions, fuel economy and driveability of the vehicle.

3 Whilst the vehicle is within the manufactures warranty, have any faults diagnosed and rectified by the dealer service department.

Scan tool information

4 As extracting the Diagnostic Trouble Codes (DTCs) from an engine management system is now the first step in troubleshooting many computer-controlled systems and components, a code reader, at the very least, will be required. More powerful scan tools can also perform many of the diagnostics once associated with expensive factory scan tools **(see illustration)**. If you're planning to obtain a generic scan tool for your vehicle, make sure that it's compatible with EOBD systems. If you don't plan to purchase a code reader or scan tool and don't have access to one, you can have the codes extracted by a dealer service department or a suitably equipped repairer.

4 Obtaining and clearing Diagnostic Trouble Codes (DTCs)

1 All models covered by this manual are equipped with on-board diagnostics. When the ECU/ECM/PCM recognises a malfunction in a monitored emission or engine control system, component or circuit, it turns on the Malfunction Indicator Light (MIL) on the dash. The ECU/ECM/PCM will continue to display the MIL until the problem is fixed and the Diagnostic Trouble Code (DTC) is cleared from the ECU/ECM/PCM's memory. You'll need a scan tool to access any DTCs stored in the ECU/ECM/PCM.

2 Before outputting any DTCs stored in the ECU/ECM/PCM, thoroughly inspect ALL electrical connectors and hoses. Make sure that all electrical connections are secure, clean and free of corrosion. And make sure that all hoses are correctly connected, fit securely and are in good condition.

Accessing the DTCs

3 The Diagnostic Trouble Codes (DTCs) can only be accessed with a code reader or scan tool. Professional scan tools are expensive,

3.4 Hand-held scan tools like these can extract computer codes and also perform diagnostics

but relatively inexpensive generic code readers or scan tools **(see illustration 3.4)** are available at most auto parts stores. Simply plug the connector of the scan tool into the diagnostic connector **(see illustration)**. Then follow the instructions included with the scan tool to extract the DTCs.

4 Once you have outputted all of the stored DTCs, look them up on the accompanying DTC chart.

5 After troubleshooting the source of each DTC, make any necessary repairs or replace the defective component(s).

Clearing the DTCs

6 Clear the DTCs with the code reader or scan tool in accordance with the instructions provided by the tool's manufacturer.

Diagnostic Trouble Codes

7 The accompanying tables (overleaf) are a sample list of the Diagnostic Trouble Codes (DTCs) that can be accessed by a do-it-yourselfer working at home (there are many, many more DTCs available to professional mechanics with proprietary scan tools and software, but those codes cannot be accessed by a generic scan tool). If, after you have checked and repaired the connectors, wire harness and vacuum hoses (if applicable) for an emission-related system, component or circuit, the problem persists, have the vehicle checked by a dealer service department or suitably equipped repairer.

4.3 The 16-pin Data Link Connector (DLC) is located under the right-hand side of the facia

EOBD trouble codes

Code	Probable cause
P000A	Camshaft 1 position, (bank no.1), slow response
P000B	Camshaft 2 position, (bank no.1), slow response
P0010	Camshaft 1 position, (bank no.1), actuator circuit open
P0013	Camshaft 2 position, (bank no.1), actuator circuit open
P0016	Crankshaft/camshaft timing (bank no.1. sensor no.1) misalignment
P0017	Crankshaft/camshaft timing (bank no.1. sensor no.2) misalignment
P0031	Upstream oxygen sensor (cylinder bank no. 1), heater circuit low voltage
P0032	Upstream oxygen sensor heater (cylinder bank no. 1), heater circuit high voltage
P0037	Downstream oxygen sensor (cylinder bank no. 1), heater circuit low voltage
P0038	Downstream oxygen sensor (cylinder bank no. 1), heater circuit high voltage
P0068	Manifold pressure/throttle position correlation – high-flow/vacuum leak
P0070	Ambient temperature sensor stuck
P0071	Ambient temperature sensor performance
P0072	Ambient temperature sensor, low voltage
P0073	Ambient temperature sensor, high voltage
P0107	Manifold Absolute Pressure (MAP) sensor, low voltage
P0108	Manifold Absolute Pressure (MAP) sensor, high voltage
P0110	Intake Air Temperature (IAT) sensor, stuck
P0111	Intake Air Temperature (IAT) sensor performance
P0112	Intake Air Temperature (IAT) sensor, low voltage
P0113	Intake Air Temperature (IAT) sensor, high voltage
P0116	Engine Coolant Temperature (ECT) sensor performance
P0117	Engine Coolant Temperature (ECT) sensor, low voltage
P0118	Engine Coolant Temperature (ECT) sensor, high voltage
P0121	Throttle Position (TP) sensor performance
P0122	Throttle Position (TP) sensor, low voltage
P0123	Throttle Position (TP) sensor, high voltage
P0125	Insufficient coolant temperature for closed-loop control; closed-loop temperature not reached
P0128	Thermostat rationality
P0129	Barometric pressure out-of-range (low)
P0131	Upstream oxygen sensor (cylinder bank no. 1), low voltage or shorted to ground
P0132	Upstream oxygen sensor (cylinder bank no. 1), high voltage or shorted to voltage
P0133	Upstream oxygen sensor (cylinder bank no. 1), slow response
P0134	Upstream oxygen sensor (cylinder bank no. 1), sensor remains at center (not switching)
P0135	Upstream oxygen sensor (cylinder bank no. 1), heater failure
P0137	Downstream oxygen sensor (cylinder bank no. 1), low voltage or shorted to ground
P0138	Downstream oxygen sensor (cylinder bank no. 1), high voltage or shorted to voltage
P0139	Downstream oxygen sensor (cylinder bank no. 1), slow response
P0140	Downstream oxygen sensor (cylinder bank no. 1), sensor remains at center (not switching)
P0141	Downstream oxygen sensor (cylinder bank no. 1), heater failure
P0171	Fuel control system too lean (cylinder bank no. 1)
P0172	Fuel control system too rich (cylinder bank no. 1)
P0201	Injector circuit malfunction – cylinder no. 1
P0202	Injector circuit malfunction – cylinder no. 2
P0203	Injector circuit malfunction – cylinder no. 3
P0204	Injector circuit malfunction – cylinder no. 4
P0300	Multiple cylinder misfire detected
P0301	Cylinder no. 1 misfire detected
P0302	Cylinder no. 2 misfire detected
P0303	Cylinder no. 3 misfire detected
P0304	Cylinder no. 4 misfire detected
P0315	No crank sensor learned
P0320	No crankshaft reference signal at Powertrain Control Module (PCM)
P0325	Knock sensor circuit malfunction
P0335	Crankshaft Position (CKP) sensor circuit
P0339	Crankshaft Position (CKP) sensor intermittent
P0340	Camshaft Position (CMP) sensor circuit
P0344	Camshaft Position (CMP) sensor intermittent
P0351	Ignition coil no. 1, primary circuit
P0352	Ignition coil no. 2, primary circuit
P0353	Ignition coil no. 3, primary circuit
P0354	Ignition coil no. 4, primary circuit
P0365	Camshaft Position (CMP) sensor circuit (bank no.1. sensor no.2)
P0369	Camshaft Position (CMP) sensor intermittent (bank no.1. sensor no.2)
P0440	General Evaporative Emission Control (EVAP) system failure
P0441	Evaporative Emission Control (EVAP) system, incorrect purge flow
P0442	Evaporative Emission Control (EVAP) system, medium leak (0.040-inch) detected
P0443	Evaporative Emission Control (EVAP) system, purge solenoid circuit malfunction
P0452	Natural Vacuum Leak Detector (NVLD) pressure sensor circuit, low voltage
P0453	Natural Vacuum Leak Detector (NVLD) pressure sensor circuit, high input
P0455	Evaporative Emission Control (EVAP) system, large leak detected
P0456	Evaporative Emission Control (EVAP) system, small leak (0.020-inch) detected
P0460	Fuel level sending unit, no change as vehicle is operated
P0461	Fuel level sensor circuit, range or performance problem
P0462	Fuel level sending unit or sensor circuit, low voltage
P0463	Fuel level sending unit or sensor circuit, high voltage
P0480	Low-speed fan control relay circuit malfunction
P0498	Natural Vacuum Leak Detector (NVLD) canister vent valve solenoid circuit, low voltage
P0499	Natural Vacuum Leak Detector (NVLD) canister vent valve solenoid circuit, high voltage
P0500	No vehicle speed signal (four-speed automatic transaxles)
P0501	Vehicle speed sensor, range or performance problem
P0503	Vehicle speed sensor 1, erratic
P0506	Idle speed control system, rpm lower than expected
P0507	Idle speed control system, rpm higher than expected
P0508	Idle Air Control (IAC) valve circuit, low voltage
P0509	Idle Air Control (IAC) valve circuit, high voltage
P0513	Invalid SKIM key (engine immobilizer problem)
P0516	Battery temperature sensor, low voltage
P0517	Battery temperature sensor, high voltage
P0519	Idle speed performance
P0522	Engine oil pressure sensor/switch circuit, low voltage
P0532	Air conditioning refrigerant pressure sensor, low voltage
P0533	Air conditioning refrigerant pressure sensor, high voltage
P0551	Power Steering Pressure (PSP) switch circuit, range or performance problem
P0562	Battery voltage low
P0563	Battery voltage high
P0579	Speed control switch circuit, range or performance problem
P0580	Speed control switch circuit, low voltage

Code	Probable cause	Code	Probable cause
P0581	Speed control switch circuit, high voltage	P0632	Odometer not programmed in Powertrain Control Module (PCM)
P0582	Speed control vacuum solenoid circuit		
P0858	Speed control switch 1/2 correlation	P0633	SKIM key not programmed in Powertrain Control Module (PCM)
P0586	Speed control vent solenoid circuit		
P0591	Speed control switch 2 circuit, performance problem	P0642	Sensor reference voltage 2 circuit, low voltage
P0592	Speed control switch 2 circuit, low voltage	P0643	Sensor reference voltage 2 circuit, high voltage
P0593	Speed control switch circuit 2, high voltage	P0645	Air conditioning clutch relay circuit
P0594	Speed control servo power circuit	P0685	Automatic Shutdown (ASD) relay control circuit
P0600	Serial communication link malfunction	P0688	Automatic Shutdown (ASD) relay sense circuit, low voltage
P0601	Powertrain Control Module (PCM), internal controller failure	P0700	Electronic Automatic Transaxle (EATX) control system malfunction or DTC present
P0622	Alternator field control circuit malfunction or field not switching correctly		
		P0703	Brake switch circuit malfunction
P0627	Fuel pump relay circuit	P0833	Clutch released switch circuit
P0630	Vehicle Identification Number (VIN) not programmed in Powertrain Control Module (PCM)	P0850	Park/Neutral switch malfunction
		P0856	Traction control torque request circuit

5 Accelerator pedal – removal and refitting

1 Remove the trim panel from the lower part of the facia on the drivers side, as described in Chapter 11 Section 25.

2 Reaching up behind the facia, disconnect the wiring connector from the top of the accelerator pedal assembly (see illustration).

3 Undo the two mounting bolts, then twist the pedal to release it from the mounting bracket, and pull it away to release it from the locating peg (see illustrations).

4 Refitting is a reversal of the removal procedure.

6 Electronic Control Unit (ECU) – removal and refitting

Removal

Note: *Disconnecting the battery will erase any fault codes stored in the ECU. It is strongly recommended that the fault code memory of the unit is interrogated using a code reader or scanner prior to battery disconnection.*

1 The ECU is located on a mounting bracket at the front of the battery, on the left-hand side of the engine compartment.

2 Disconnect the battery as described in Chapter 5 Section 4.

3 Remove the air cleaner housing air intake ducts from across the top of the ECU, as described in Chapter 4A Section 3.

4 Release the locking clips and disconnect the wiring connectors from the ECU (see illustrations).

5 Undo the retaining nuts and remove the ECU from the mounting bracket.

6 If required the mounting bracket can be unbolted from the battery tray, first remove the battery, as described in Chapter 5 Section 4.

Refitting

7 Refitting is a reversal of removal. After re-connection, the vehicle must be driven for several miles so that the ECU can re-learn its basic settings. If the engine still runs

5.2 Disconnect the wiring connector

5.3a Undo the two mounting bolts. . .

5.3b . . . release the pedal from the locating peg. . .

5.3c . . . and withdraw it from the mounting bracket

6.4a Release the locking clips. . .

6.4b . . . and disconnect the wing connectors

7.1 Disconnect the wiring connector

7.2a Undo the retaining bolt. . .

7.2b . . . and withdraw the coil from the sparkplug

erratically, the basic setting may be reinstated by a Nissan dealer or suitably equipped repairer. **Note:** *If a new ECU has been fitted, it will need to be coded using Nissan diagnostic equipment. Entrust this task to a Nissan dealer or suitably equipped repairer.*

7 Ignition coils – removal and refitting

Removal

1 Release the locking clip and disconnect the wiring connector from the top of the ignition coil **(see illustration).**
2 Undo the retaining bolt, and gently pull the coil upwards, off the spark plug **(see illustrations).**
3 Repeat this procedure on the remaining ignition coils.

Testing

4 The circuitry arrangement of the ignition coil unit on these engines is such that testing of an individual coil in isolation from the remainder of the engine management system is unlikely to prove effective in diagnosing a particular fault. Should there be any reason to suspect a faulty individual coil, the engine management system self-diagnosis system should be interrogated as described in, Section 4.

Refitting

5 Refitting is a reversal of the relevant removal

procedure ensuring the wiring connectors are securely reconnected, and the coil retaining bolts are tightened to their specified torque.

8 Ignition timing – checking and adjustment

1 There are no timing marks on the flywheel or crankshaft pulley. The timing is constantly being monitored and adjusted by the engine management ECU, and nominal values cannot be given. Therefore, it is not possible for the home mechanic to check the ignition timing.
2 The only way in which the ignition timing can be checked is using special electronic test equipment, connected to the engine management system diagnostic connector; see Section 4 for further information.

9 Knock sensor – removal and refitting

Removal

1 The knock sensor(s) is screwed into the front of the cylinder block, below the intake manifold. Remove the intake manifold as described in Chapter 4A Section 11.
2 Disconnect the wiring plug, undo the retaining bolt and remove the sensor **(see illustrations).** Note the position of the knock sensor on the cylinder block for refitting.

Refitting

3 Ensure the mating surfaces of the cylinder block and knock sensor are clean.
4 Position the sensor on the cylinder block, as noted on removal, then insert the retaining bolt and tighten it to the specified torque.
Note: *It's essential for the correct functioning of the knock sensor that the retaining bolt is tightened to the specified torque.*
5 Refitting is a reversal of the removal procedure.

10 Coolant temperature sensor – removal and refitting

Removal

1 Partially drain the cooling system to just below the level of the sensor (as described in Chapter 1A Section 33). Alternatively, have ready a suitable bung to plug the sensor aperture whilst the sensor is removed. If this method is used, take great care not to damage the switch aperture or use anything which will allow foreign matter to enter the cooling system.
2 Remove the air cleaner housing air intake ducts from across the top of the coolant housing, on the left-hand side of the cylinder head, as described in Chapter 4A Section 3.
3 Disconnect the wiring plug, prise out the retaining clip, then pull the sensor from the coolant housing **(see illustrations).** If the system has not been drained, plug the sensor aperture to prevent further coolant loss.

9.2a Disconnect the wiring connector. . .

9.2b . . . and undo the retaining bolt

10.3a Disconnect the wiring connector. . .

10.3b . . . release the retaining clip. . .

10.3c . . . and remove the temperature sensor

11.3 Crankshaft position sensor

Refitting

4 Check the condition of the O-ring seal, then fit the temperature sensor, and secure in place with retaining clip.
5 Reconnect the wiring plug.
6 The remainder of refitting is a reversal of removal. Top-up the cooling system as described in Chapter 1A Section 33.

11 Crankshaft position sensor – removal and refitting

Removal

1 Remove the air cleaner housing and air intake ducts from the engine compartemnt, as described in Chapter 4A Section 3.
2 The sensor is located at the rear of the transmission bell housing, release the securing clip and disconnect the sensor wiring plug.
3 Undo the retaining bolt, remove the bracket and withdraw the sensor (see illustration).

Refitting

4 Refitting is reverse of the removal procedure. Tighten the sensor retaining bolt to the specified torque.

12 Vehicle speed sensor

1 The engine management ECU receives

vehicle speed data from the wheel speed sensors, via the ABS ECU.

13 Camshaft position sensors – removal and refitting

Removal

1 There are two camshaft sensors fitted to the left-hand end of the cylinder head cover (see illustration), one for the intake camshaft and one for the exhaust camshaft.
2 When removing the camshaft position sensors, it may be necessary to move any wiring or breather pipes to one side.
3 Disconnect the wiring plug, then undo the bolt and remove the relevant sensor from the cylinder head cover (see illustration).

Refitting

4 Refitting is the reverse of removal ensuring the sensor seal is in good condition. Tighten the sensor retaining bolt to the specified torque.

14 Accelerator pedal position sensor

1 The sensor is integral with the accelerator pedal assembly – see Section 5.

15 Oxygen sensors – removal and refitting

Removal

⚠ **Warning: Ensure the exhaust system/turbocharger is completely cool before proceeding.**
Note: The oxygen sensors are delicate and will not work if dropped or knocked, if its power supply is disrupted, or if any cleaning materials are used on it.
Note: There are two oxygen sensors – one at the inlet, and one at the outlet sides of the catalytic converter.
1 Firmly apply the handbrake then jack up the front of the vehicle and support it on axle stands (see Jacking and vehicle support). Remove the engine undershield, to access the lower sensor.
2 Trace the wiring back from the oxygen sensor and disconnect its wiring connector, freeing the wiring from any relevant retaining clips or ties (see illustrations).
3 Using a special socket, unscrew the sensor and remove it from the exhaust catalytic converter (see illustrations). Access to the lower oxygen sensor will be easier from under the vehicle.

Refitting

4 Refitting is a reverse of the removal procedure. Prior to installing the sensor apply a

13.1 Location of the two camshaft sensors

13.3 Disconnect the wiring connector

15.2a Upper oxygen sensor wiring connector

15.2b Disconnect the lower oxygen sensor wiring connector

15.3a Using a special socket. . .

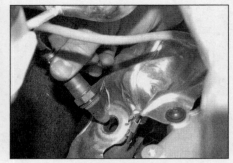

15.3b . . . unscrew the oxygen sensor (upper one shown)

smear of high temperature grease to the sensor threads. Ensure that the sensor is tightened to the specified torque, and that the wiring is correctly routed and in no danger of contacting either the exhaust system or engine.

16 Manifold pressure sensor

1 The sensor is located on the top of the inlet manifold.
2 Disconnect the wiring connector from the sensor (see illustration).
3 Undo the retaining bolt and remove the sensor from the manifold.
4 Discard the O-ring seal; a new one must be used on refitting.
5 Refitting is a reversal of the removal procedure, noting the following points:

16.2 Disconnect the wiring connector

a) Fit a new O-ring seal to the sensor.
b) Apply a smear of engine oil to the O-ring to aid installation, and then ease the sensor into position.

17 Inlet air temperature (IAT) sensor

1 The inlet air temperature sensor is integral with the inlet manifold pressure sensor, see Section 16.

18 Emission control systems – testing and component renewal

Crankcase emission control

1 The components of this system require no

18.4a Release the retaining clip. . .

attention other than to check that the hose(s) are clear and undamaged at regular intervals.

Evaporative emission control

2 If the system is thought to be faulty, disconnect the hoses from the charcoal canister and purge control valve and check that they are clear by blowing through them. If the purge control valve or charcoal canister is thought to be faulty, they must be renewed.

Charcoal (fuel vapour) canister renewal

3 The charcoal canister is located inside the engine compartment behind the right-hand headlamp unit, between the windscreen washer bottle and the chassis leg.
4 Using a thin screwdriver release the retaining clip and slide the canister upwards to remove it from the chassis leg (see illustrations).
5 Note the fitted position and disconnect the hoses from the top of the canister (see illustration).
6 Refitting is a reverse of the removal procedure, ensuring that the hoses are correctly reconnected.

Purge control solenoid valve renewal

7 The purge valve is mounted onto the right-hand side inner wing panel (see illustration).
8 To renew the purge valve, disconnect the battery negative terminal then depress the retaining clip and disconnect the wiring connector from the valve.

18.4b . . . and slide the canister from the securing clip

18.5 Note the markings on the side of the canister

18.7 Location of the purge valve

18.15a Undo the three retaining screws. . .

18.15b . . . and withdraw the heat shield

18.17a Undo the mounting bolts. . .

18.17b . . . and remove the right-hand side mounting bracket

18.18a Undo the two bolts on the left-hand side. . .

18.18b . . . the two on the right. . .

9 Disconnect the hose from the valve, then release the solenoid valve from the mounting bracket.

10 Refitting is a reversal of the removal procedure, ensuring that a new o-ring seal is fitted to the valve, before refitting to the manifold.

Exhaust emission control

11 The performance of the catalytic converter can be checked only by measuring the exhaust gases using a good-quality, carefully-calibrated exhaust gas analyser.

12 If the CO level at the tailpipe is too high, the vehicle should be taken to a Nissan dealer or specialist so that the complete fuel injection and ignition systems, including the oxygen sensor, can be thoroughly checked using the special diagnostic equipment.

Catalytic converter renewal

13 Raise the front of the vehicle and support it securely on axle stands (see *Jacking and vehicle support*). Release the fasteners and remove the engine undershield.

14 Remove the oxygen sensors as described in Section 15. If required, the lower oxygen sensor can be left in place in the catalytic converter. The upper oxygen sensor will need to be removed, as this will allow the upper heat shield to be removed.

15 With the upper oxygen sensor removed, unclip the wiring connectors from the retaining clips, then undo the three retaining screws, and remove the heat shield from the top of the cylinder head cover **(see illustrations)**.

16 Working under the front of the vehicle, remove the front section of the exhaust system, as described in Chapter 4A Section 15.

17 Undo the five retaining bolts and remove the mounting bracket from the right-hand

side of the catalytic converter **(see illustrations)**.

18 Undo the six retaining bolts and remove the lower mounting bracket from the bottom of the catalytic converter **(see illustrations)**.

18.18c . . . and the two at the rear of the outlet pipe. . .

18.18d . . . then withdraw lower mounting bracket from the cylinder block

18.19a Disconnect the catalytic converter upper pipe. . .

18.19b . . . and remove the gasket

19 Undo the 3 nuts securing the top of the catalytic converter to the turbocharger, then lower it from place and manoeuvre it out from the rear of the engine compartment **(see illustrations)**. Remove the gasket and discard, as a new one will be required for refitting.

20 Prior to refitting position the new gasket on the manifold/turbo flange.

21 Manoeuvre the catalytic converter upwards into position against the turbocharger flange (ensure the new gasket remains in place), then refit and finger-tighten the three nuts, securing the catalytic converter to the manifold/turbo.

22 Fit the catalytic converter lower mounting brackets, then when they are all in place, tighten the bolts to the specified torque.

23 The remainder of refitting is a reversal of removal.

Chapter 6 Part B
Engine and emission control systems – diesel models

Contents

Degrees of difficulty

| Easy, suitable for novice with little experience | | Fairly easy, suitable for beginner with some experience | | Fairly difficult, suitable for competent DIY mechanic | | Difficult, suitable for experienced DIY mechanic | 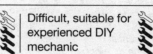 | Very difficult, suitable for expert DIY or professional | |

Specifications

Engine management system

Diesel engines . . . . DDE High-pressure direct injection with full electronic control, intercooler and turbocharger

Torque wrench settings

	Nm	lbf ft
Camshaft position sensors.	4	3
Common fuel rail pressure sensor	70	52
Common fuel rail pressure control valve:		
Stage 1.	60	44
Stage 2.	Angle-tighten a further 90°	
Stage 3.	85	63
Crankshaft position sensor	5	4
Exhaust gas/particulate filter temperature sensor	30	20
Glow plugs.	10	7
Oxygen sensors	50	37
Particulate filter-to-turbocharger clamp*	15	10

*Do not re-use

1 Engine management system

Electronic control system

1 The electronic control system consists of the following components:

a) Electronic control unit (ECU).

b) Crankshaft speed/position sensor – informs the ECU of the engine speed and crankshaft angular position.

c) Camshaft position sensor – informs the ECU of the camshafts' positions.

d) Accelerator pedal position sensor – informs the ECU of the pedal position and rate of change.

e) Coolant temperature sensor – informs the ECU of the engine coolant temperature.

f) Fuel temperature sensor – informs the ECU of the fuel temperature.

g) Air mass meter – informs the ECU of the intake air quantity.

h) Fuel pressure sensor – informs the ECU of the fuel pressure within the accumulator (common) rail.

i) Fuel injectors.

j) Fuel pressure control valve – allows the ECU to control the pressure of the fuel in the accumulator (common) rail.

k) Preheating control unit – controls the voltage and duty-cycle of the glow plugs.

l) EGR solenoid valve – allows the ECU to control the flow of exhaust gasses recirculated in to the intake system.

m) Charge air temperature/pressure sensor – informs the ECU of the pressure and temperature of the intake air.

n) Charge pressure sensor – informs the ECU of the air pressure in the intake manifold.

o) Exhaust gas temperature sensor – informs the ECU of the temperature of the exhaust gasses.

p) Particulate filter pressure differential sensor – informs the ECU of the difference in pressure between gasses entering and leaving the particulate filter.

2 The information from the various sensors is passed to the ECU, which evaluates the signals. The ECU contains electronic 'maps' which enable it to calculate the optimum

1.10 Diagnostic plug connector

quantity of fuel to inject, the appropriate start of injection, and even pre- and post-injection fuel quantities, for each individual engine cylinder under any given condition of engine operation.

3 Additionally, the ECU carries out monitoring and self-diagnostic functions. Any faults in the system are stored in the ECU memory, which enables quick and accurate fault diagnosis using appropriate diagnostic equipment (such as a suitable fault code reader/scan tool).

Pre/post-heating system

4 To assist cold starting, diesel engines are fitted with a preheating system, which consists of three glow plugs (one per cylinder), a glow plug relay unit, a facia-mounted warning lamp, the engine management ECU, and the associated electrical wiring.

5 The glow plugs are miniature electric heating elements, encapsulated in a ceramic case with a probe at one end and electrical connection at the other. Each combustion chamber has one glow plug threaded into it, with the tip of the glow plug probe positioned directly in line with incoming spray of fuel from the injectors. When the glow plug is energised, it heats up rapidly, causing the fuel passing over the glow plug probe to be heated to its optimum temperature, ready for combustion. In addition, some of the fuel passing over the glow plugs is ignited and this helps to trigger the combustion process.

6 The preheating system begins to operate as soon as the ignition key is switched to the second position. A facia-mounted warning lamp informs the driver that preheating is taking place. The lamp extinguishes when sufficient preheating has taken place to allow the engine to be started, but power will still be supplied to the glow plugs for a further period until the engine is started. If no attempt is made to start the engine, the power supply to the glow plugs is switched off after 10 seconds to prevent battery drain and glow plug burnout.

7 With the electronically-controlled diesel injection systems fitted to models in this manual, the glow plug relay unit is controlled by the engine management system ECU, which determines the necessary preheating time based on inputs from the various system sensors. The system monitors the temperature of the inlet air, and then alters the preheating time (the length for which the glow plugs are supplied with current) to suit the conditions.

8 Post-heating takes place after the ignition key has been released from the 'start' position. The glow plugs continue to operate for a maximum of 60 seconds, helping to improve fuel combustion whilst the engine is warming-up, resulting in quieter, smoother running and reduced exhaust emissions.

9 The glow plug for cylinder No.2 incorporates a pressure sensor to monitor the combustion chamber pressure. This steel cased glow plug element incorporates a strain gauge. The deformation of the strain gauge is

converted into a voltage signal, and is used by the engine management ECU to determine fuel quality, and engine condition.

Testing

10 The glow plugs are not supplied with battery voltage in order to operate. They are provided with a voltage of between 5 and 7 volts, but the pulse-width of the voltage is modulate. This makes it impossible to test the plugs using traditional methods. If a fault is suspected, have the engine management self-diagnosis system interrogated using diagnostic equipment connected to the 16-pin diagnostic plug located under the drivers side of the facia (see illustration).

2 Emissions systems – general information

1 All petrol engines use unleaded petrol and also have various other features built into the fuel system to help minimise harmful emissions. In addition, all engines are equipped with the crankcase emission control system described below. All engines are also equipped with a catalytic converter and an evaporative emission control system.

2 All diesel engines are also designed to meet the strict emission requirements and are equipped with a crankcase emission control system and a catalytic converter/particulate filter. To further reduce exhaust emissions, all diesel engines are also fitted with an exhaust gas recirculation (EGR) system. The particulate uses porous silicon carbide substrate to trap particulates of carbon as the exhaust gases pass through.

3 The emission control systems function as follows.

Crankcase emission control

4 Refer to the description for petrol engines.

Exhaust emission control

5 To minimise the level of exhaust pollutants released into the atmosphere, a catalytic converter/particulate filter is fitted in the exhaust system of all models.

6 The catalytic converter consists of a canister containing a fine mesh impregnated with a catalyst material, over which the hot exhaust gases pass. The catalyst speeds up the oxidation of harmful carbon monoxide, un-burnt hydrocarbons and soot, effectively reducing the quantity of harmful products released into the atmosphere via the exhaust gases.

Exhaust gas recirculation system

7 This system is designed to recirculate small quantities of exhaust gas into the inlet tract, and therefore into the combustion process. This process reduces the level of oxides of nitrogen present in the final exhaust gas, which is released into the atmosphere.

3.4 Hand-held scan tools like these can extract computer codes and also perform diagnostics

4.3 The 16-pin Data Link Connector (DLC) is located under the right-hand side of the facia

8 The volume of exhaust gas recirculated is controlled by the system electronic control unit.

9 A vacuum-operated valve is fitted to the manifold, to regulate the quantity of exhaust gas recirculated. The valve is operated by the vacuum supplied by the solenoid valve, or electrically powered solenoid.

Particulate filter system

10 The particulate filter is combined with the catalytic converter in the exhaust system, and its purpose it to trap particulates of carbon (soot) as the exhaust gases pass through, in order to comply with latest emission regulations.

11 The filter can be automatically regenerated (cleaned) by the system's ECU on-board the vehicle. The engine's high-pressure injection system is utilised to inject fuel into the exhaust gases during the post-injection period; this causes the filter temperature to increase sufficiently to oxidise the particulates, leaving an ash residue. The regeneration period is automatically controlled by the on-board ECU.

3 European On Board Diagnosis (EOBD) system

General description

1 All models are equipped with the European On-Board Diagnosis (EOBD) system. This system consists of an on-board computer known as the ECU (Electronic Control Unit), Electronic Control Module (ECM) or Powertrain Control Module (PCM), and information sensors, which monitor various functions of the engine and send data to the ECU/ECM/PCM. This system incorporates a series of diagnostic monitors that detect and identify fuel injection and emissions control system faults and store the information in the computer memory. This system also tests sensors and output actuators, diagnoses

drive cycles, freezes data and clears codes.

2 The ECU/ECM/PCM is the brain of the electronically controlled fuel and emissions system. It receives data from a number of sensors and other electronic components (switches, relays, etc.). Based on the information it receives, the ECU/ECM/PCM generates output signals to control various relays, solenoids (fuel injectors) and other actuators. The ECU/ECM/PCM is specifically calibrated to optimise the emissions, fuel economy and driveability of the vehicle.

3 Whilst the vehicle is within the manufactures warranty, have any faults diagnosed and rectified by the dealer service department.

Scan tool information

4 As extracting the Diagnostic Trouble Codes (DTCs) from an engine management system is now the first step in troubleshooting many computer-controlled systems and components, a code reader, at the very least, will be required. More powerful scan tools can also perform many of the diagnostics once associated with expensive factory scan tools (see illustration). If you're planning to obtain a generic scan tool for your vehicle, make sure that it's compatible with EOBD systems. If you don't plan to purchase a code reader or scan tool and don't have access to one, you can have the codes extracted by a dealer service department or a suitably equipped repairer.

4 Obtaining and clearing Diagnostic Trouble Codes (DTCs)

1 All models covered by this manual are equipped with on-board diagnostics. When the ECU/ECM/PCM recognises a malfunction in a monitored emission or engine control system, component or circuit, it turns on the Malfunction Indicator Light (MIL) on the dash. The ECU/ECM/PCM will continue to display the MIL until the problem is fixed and the Diagnostic Trouble Code (DTC) is cleared from the ECU/ECM/PCM's memory. You'll need a

scan tool to access any DTCs stored in the ECU/ECM/PCM.

2 Before outputting any DTCs stored in the ECU/ECM/PCM, thoroughly inspect ALL electrical connectors and hoses. Make sure that all electrical connections are secure, clean and free of corrosion. And make sure that all hoses are correctly connected, fit securely and are in good condition.

Accessing the DTCs

3 The Diagnostic Trouble Codes (DTCs) can only be accessed with a code reader or scan tool. Professional scan tools are expensive, but relatively inexpensive generic code readers or scan tools (see illustration 3.4) are available at most auto parts stores. Simply plug the connector of the scan tool into the diagnostic connector (see illustration). Then follow the instructions included with the scan tool to extract the DTCs.

4 Once you have outputted all of the stored DTCs, look them up on the accompanying DTC chart.

5 After troubleshooting the source of each DTC, make any necessary repairs or replace the defective component(s).

Clearing the DTCs

6 Clear the DTCs with the code reader or scan tool in accordance with the instructions provided by the tool's manufacturer.

Diagnostic Trouble Codes

7 The accompanying tables (overleaf) are a sample list of the Diagnostic Trouble Codes (DTCs) that can be accessed by a do-it-yourselfer working at home (there are many, many more DTCs available to professional mechanics with proprietary scan tools and software, but those codes cannot be accessed by a generic scan tool). If, after you have checked and repaired the connectors, wire harness and vacuum hoses (if applicable) for an emission-related system, component or circuit, the problem persists, have the vehicle checked by a dealer service department or suitably equipped repairer.

EOBD trouble codes

Code	Probable cause
P000A	Camshaft 1 position, (bank no.1), slow response
P000B	Camshaft 2 position, (bank no.1), slow response
P0010	Camshaft 1 position, (bank no.1), actuator circuit open
P0013	Camshaft 2 position, (bank no.1), actuator circuit open
P0016	Crankshaft/camshaft timing (bank no.1. sensor no.1) misalignment
P0017	Crankshaft/camshaft timing (bank no.1. sensor no.2) misalignment
P0031	Upstream oxygen sensor (cylinder bank no. 1), heater circuit low voltage
P0032	Upstream oxygen sensor heater (cylinder bank no. 1), heater circuit high voltage
P0037	Downstream oxygen sensor (cylinder bank no. 1), heater circuit low voltage
P0038	Downstream oxygen sensor (cylinder bank no. 1), heater circuit high voltage
P0068	Manifold pressure/throttle position correlation – high-flow/vacuum leak
P0070	Ambient temperature sensor stuck
P0071	Ambient temperature sensor performance
P0072	Ambient temperature sensor, low voltage
P0073	Ambient temperature sensor, high voltage
P0107	Manifold Absolute Pressure (MAP) sensor, low voltage
P0108	Manifold Absolute Pressure (MAP) sensor, high voltage
P0110	Intake Air Temperature (IAT) sensor, stuck
P0111	Intake Air Temperature (IAT) sensor performance
P0112	Intake Air Temperature (IAT) sensor, low voltage
P0113	Intake Air Temperature (IAT) sensor, high voltage
P0116	Engine Coolant Temperature (ECT) sensor performance
P0117	Engine Coolant Temperature (ECT) sensor, low voltage
P0118	Engine Coolant Temperature (ECT) sensor, high voltage
P0121	Throttle Position (TP) sensor performance
P0122	Throttle Position (TP) sensor, low voltage
P0123	Throttle Position (TP) sensor, high voltage
P0125	Insufficient coolant temperature for closed-loop control; closed-loop temperature not reached
P0128	Thermostat rationality
P0129	Barometric pressure out-of-range (low)
P0131	Upstream oxygen sensor (cylinder bank no. 1), low voltage or shorted to ground
P0132	Upstream oxygen sensor (cylinder bank no. 1), high voltage or shorted to voltage
P0133	Upstream oxygen sensor (cylinder bank no. 1), slow response
P0134	Upstream oxygen sensor (cylinder bank no. 1), sensor remains at center (not switching)
P0135	Upstream oxygen sensor (cylinder bank no. 1), heater failure
P0137	Downstream oxygen sensor (cylinder bank no. 1), low voltage or shorted to ground
P0138	Downstream oxygen sensor (cylinder bank no. 1), high voltage or shorted to voltage
P0139	Downstream oxygen sensor (cylinder bank no. 1), slow response
P0140	Downstream oxygen sensor (cylinder bank no. 1), sensor remains at center (not switching)
P0141	Downstream oxygen sensor (cylinder bank no. 1), heater failure
P0171	Fuel control system too lean (cylinder bank no. 1)
P0172	Fuel control system too rich (cylinder bank no. 1)
P0201	Injector circuit malfunction – cylinder no. 1
P0202	Injector circuit malfunction – cylinder no. 2
P0203	Injector circuit malfunction – cylinder no. 3
P0204	Injector circuit malfunction – cylinder no. 4
P0300	Multiple cylinder misfire detected
P0301	Cylinder no. 1 misfire detected
P0302	Cylinder no. 2 misfire detected
P0303	Cylinder no. 3 misfire detected
P0304	Cylinder no. 4 misfire detected
P0315	No crank sensor learned
P0320	No crankshaft reference signal at Powertrain Control Module (PCM)
P0325	Knock sensor circuit malfunction
P0335	Crankshaft Position (CKP) sensor circuit
P0339	Crankshaft Position (CKP) sensor intermittent
P0340	Camshaft Position (CMP) sensor circuit
P0344	Camshaft Position (CMP) sensor intermittent
P0351	Ignition coil no. 1, primary circuit
P0352	Ignition coil no. 2, primary circuit
P0353	Ignition coil no. 3, primary circuit
P0354	Ignition coil no. 4, primary circuit
P0365	Camshaft Position (CMP) sensor circuit (bank no.1. sensor no.2)
P0369	Camshaft Position (CMP) sensor intermittent (bank no.1. sensor no.2)
P0440	General Evaporative Emission Control (EVAP) system failure
P0441	Evaporative Emission Control (EVAP) system, incorrect purge flow
P0442	Evaporative Emission Control (EVAP) system, medium leak (0.040-inch) detected
P0443	Evaporative Emission Control (EVAP) system, purge solenoid circuit malfunction
P0452	Natural Vacuum Leak Detector (NVLD) pressure sensor circuit, low voltage
P0453	Natural Vacuum Leak Detector (NVLD) pressure sensor circuit, high input
P0455	Evaporative Emission Control (EVAP) system, large leak detected
P0456	Evaporative Emission Control (EVAP) system, small leak (0.020-inch) detected
P0460	Fuel level sending unit, no change as vehicle is operated
P0461	Fuel level sensor circuit, range or performance problem
P0462	Fuel level sending unit or sensor circuit, low voltage
P0463	Fuel level sending unit or sensor circuit, high voltage
P0480	Low-speed fan control relay circuit malfunction
P0498	Natural Vacuum Leak Detector (NVLD) canister vent valve solenoid circuit, low voltage
P0499	Natural Vacuum Leak Detector (NVLD) canister vent valve solenoid circuit, high voltage
P0500	No vehicle speed signal (four-speed automatic transaxles)
P0501	Vehicle speed sensor, range or performance problem
P0503	Vehicle speed sensor 1, erratic
P0506	Idle speed control system, rpm lower than expected
P0507	Idle speed control system, rpm higher than expected
P0508	Idle Air Control (IAC) valve circuit, low voltage
P0509	Idle Air Control (IAC) valve circuit, high voltage
P0513	Invalid SKIM key (engine immobilizer problem)
P0516	Battery temperature sensor, low voltage
P0517	Battery temperature sensor, high voltage
P0519	Idle speed performance
P0522	Engine oil pressure sensor/switch circuit, low voltage
P0532	Air conditioning refrigerant pressure sensor, low voltage
P0533	Air conditioning refrigerant pressure sensor, high voltage
P0551	Power Steering Pressure (PSP) switch circuit, range or performance problem
P0562	Battery voltage low
P0563	Battery voltage high
P0579	Speed control switch circuit, range or performance problem

Code	Probable cause	Code	Probable cause
P0580	Speed control switch circuit, low voltage	P0632	Odometer not programmed in Powertrain Control Module (PCM)
P0581	Speed control switch circuit, high voltage		
P0582	Speed control vacuum solenoid circuit	P0633	SKIM key not programmed in Powertrain Control Module (PCM)
P0858	Speed control switch 1/2 correlation		
P0586	Speed control vent solenoid circuit	P0642	Sensor reference voltage 2 circuit, low voltage
P0591	Speed control switch 2 circuit, performance problem	P0643	Sensor reference voltage 2 circuit, high voltage
P0592	Speed control switch 2 circuit, low voltage	P0645	Air conditioning clutch relay circuit
P0593	Speed control switch circuit 2, high voltage	P0685	Automatic Shutdown (ASD) relay control circuit
P0594	Speed control servo power circuit	P0688	Automatic Shutdown (ASD) relay sense circuit, low voltage
P0600	Serial communication link malfunction	P0700	Electronic Automatic Transaxle (EATX) control system malfunction or DTC present
P0601	Powertrain Control Module (PCM), internal controller failure		
P0622	Alternator field control circuit malfunction or field not switching correctly	P0703	Brake switch circuit malfunction
		P0833	Clutch released switch circuit
P0627	Fuel pump relay circuit	P0850	Park/Neutral switch malfunction
P0630	Vehicle Identification Number (VIN) not programmed in Powertrain Control Module (PCM)	P0856	Traction control torque request circuit

5 Accelerator pedal – removal and refitting

1 The diesel accelerator pedal has the same removal procedure as the petrol engines. Remove the accelerator pedal, as described in Chapter 6A Section 5.

6 Electronic Control Unit (ECU) – removal and refitting

1 The diesel electronic control unit (ECU) has the same removal procedure as the petrol engines. Remove the ECU, as described in Chapter 6A Section 6.

7 Charge air pressure sensor – removal and refitting

Note: *The charge air temperature sensor is part of the air pressure sensor.*

Removal

1 The pressure sensor is located in the top of the throttle control unit assembly **(see illustrations)**.

2 Disconnect the wiring connector, then undo the bolt and pull the sensor from the throttle body.

Refitting

3 Check the condition of the sensor O-ring seal, and renew if necessary.
4 Apply a thin smear of grease to the O-ring seal, then press the sensor firmly into position in the throttle body.
5 Tighten the sensor retaining bolt and refit the wiring connector.

8 Charge air temperature sensor – removal and refitting

1 The charge air temperature sensor is part of the charge air pressure sensor, fitted to the top of the throttle assembly, see Section 7.

9 Coolant temperature sensor – removal and refitting

Removal

1 To make access easier, remove the battery, as described in Chapter 5 Section 4.
2 Partially drain the cooling system to just below the level of the sensor (see Chapter 1B Section 32). Alternatively, have ready a suitable bung to plug the aperture in the housing when the sensor is removed.
3 On 1.6 diesel engines, it may be necessary to remove the inlet manifold (see Chapter 4B Section 12), to access the temperature sensor.
4 Disconnect the wiring connector from the sensor **(see illustration)**.
5 On 1.5 litre engines, the sensor is clipped in place; prise out the sensor retaining circlip then remove the sensor and sealing ring from the housing **(see illustrations)**. If the system has not been drained, plug the sensor aperture to prevent further coolant loss.

7.1a Location of sensor – 1.5 litre engines

7.1b Location of sensor – 1.6 litre engines

9.4 Disconnect the wiring connector

9.5a Withdraw the retaining clip. . .

9.5b . . . and remove the sensor and seal

9.6 Coolant temperature sensor – 1.6 litre diesel engines

9 The remainder of refitting is a reversal of removal. Top-up the cooling system as described in Chapter 1B Section 32.

10 Crankshaft position sensor – removal and refitting

Removal

1 Remove the air cleaner housing and air intake ducts from the engine compartemnt, as described in Chapter 4A Section 3.
2 The sensor is located at the rear of the transmission bell housing, release the securing clip and disconnect the sensor wiring plug.
3 Undo the retaining bolt, remove the bracket and withdraw the sensor **(see illustrations)**.

10.3a Undo the retaining bolt. . .

10.3b . . . and remove the crankshaft position sensor

Refitting

4 Refitting is reverse of the removal procedure. Tighten the sensor retaining bolt to the specified torque.

11 Vehicle speed sensor

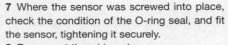

1 The engine management ECU receives vehicle speed data from the wheel speed sensors, via the ABS ECU.

Refitting

7 Where the sensor was screwed into place, check the condition of the O-ring seal, and fit the sensor, tightening it securely.
8 Reconnect the wiring plug.

6 On 1.6 litre engines, disconnect the wiring connector and carefully unscrew the sensor from the front of the cylinder block **(see illustration)** and recover the sealing ring. If the system has not been drained, plug the sensor aperture to prevent further coolant loss.

12 Camshaft position sensor(s) – removal and refitting

Removal

1 The camshaft position sensor is fitted to the transmission end of the cylinder head cover **(see illustrations)**.
2 If required, to make access easier, undo the retaining bolts and remove the air intake pipe from across the top of the cylinder head.
3 Disconnect the wiring connector from the camshaft position sensor **(see illustrations)**.
4 Undo the retaining bolt and withdraw the sensor from the cover **(see illustrations)**.
5 Discard the O-ring seal; a new one must be used on refitting.

12.1a Location of camshaft sensor – 1.5 litre engine

12.1b Location of camshaft sensor – 1.6 litre engine

12.3a Disconnect the wiring connector – 1.5 litre engine

12.3b Disconnect the wiring connector – 1.6 litre engine

12.4a Undo the bolt and remove the sensor – 1.5 litre engines

12.4b Undo the bolt and remove the sensor – 1.6 litre engines

14.2 Disconnect the wiring connector

14.3 Undo the sensor retaining screws

6 Refitting is a reversal of the removal procedure, noting the following points:
a) *Fit a new O-ring seal to the sensor.*
b) *Apply a smear of engine oil to the O-ring to aid installation, and then ease the sensor into position.*

Refitting

7 Apply a thin coat of clean engine oil to the sensor sealing ring, install it in the cylinder head, and tighten the bolt to the specified torque.
8 The remainder of refitting is a reversal of removal.

13 Accelerator pedal position sensor

1 The sensor is integral with the accelerator pedal assembly – see Chapter 6A Section 5.

14 Mass airflow (MAF) sensor – removal and refitting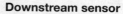

Removal

1 The airflow sensor is mounted in the air cleaner housing, at the outlet end of the intake hose to the throttle housing. The inlet air temperature sensor is combined with the mass airflow sensor. Prior to removal, disconnect the battery negative terminal (refer to Chapter 5 Section 4).
2 Disconnect the wiring connector from the airflow sensor **(see illustration)**.
3 Undo the retaining bolts, and then remove the sensor from the air cleaner housing **(see illustration)**. Recover its sealing ring and renew.

Refitting

4 Refitting is the reverse of removal, using a new sealing ring (where applicable) and tightening its retaining screws securely. If a new meter has been fitted, the adaption values stored in the engine management ECU may need to be reset using diagnostic equipment. Entrust this task to a Nissan dealer or suitably equipped repairer.

15 Oxygen sensors – removal and refitting

Removal

Upstream sensor

1 On 1.5 litre engines, pull the plastic cover on the top of the engine upwards from its' mountings.
2 Disconnect the breather hose, undo the retaining screw, release the clamps and remove the air intake pipe behind the cylinder head.
3 Trace the sensor wiring back to the wiring plug and disconnect it.
4 Using a crows foot or a split-type socket

15.4a Using a crows foot spanner. . .

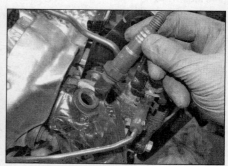

15.4b . . . to remove the sensor

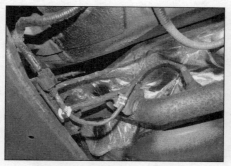

15.6 Location of oxygen sensor

15.7 Using a split-type socket

unscrew and remove the sensor **(see illustrations)**.

Downstream sensor

5 Raise the front of the vehicle and support it securely on axle stands (see *Jacking and vehicle support*). Release the fasteners and remove the engine undershield.
6 Trace the wiring back from the sensor. Disconnect the wiring plug and unclip it from the bracket **(see illustration)**.
7 Using a split-type socket, unscrew the sensor and remove it **(see illustration)**.

Refitting

8 Refitting is a reversal of removal. New sensors have their threads pre-coated with anti-seize compound. If a sensor is being refitted, apply a little anti-seize compound to the threads. Tighten it to the specified torque.

16.3 Location of pressure sensor – 1.6 litre engine

16 Exhaust gas pressure sensor – removal and refitting

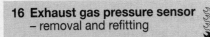

Removal

1 On 1.5 litre engines, pull the plastic cover on the top of the engine upwards from its' mountings.

2 If required, to give better access, release the clamps and remove the air intake pipe from the rear of the cylinder head.

3 The sensor is located at the rear of the engine, on a mounting bracket **(see illustration)**.

4 If removing the sensor complete with pipe, slacken the union in the rear of the manifold, then undo the bolt from the mounting bracket and remove the exhaust gas pressure sensor from the left-hand rear of the cylinder head **(see illustration)**.

17.2 Location of upper temperature sensor – 1.6 litre engine shown

18.2 Location of fuel pressure sensor – 1.6 litre engine shown

16.4 Remove the pressure sensor – 1.6 litre shown

5 If required, disconnect the hose from the lower part of the sensor.

Refitting

6 Refitting is a reversal of removal, noting the following points:

a) Check the pressure hose – replace if hardened.

b) Install the hose without any kinks.

c) If the original hose is being refitted, secure it with a screw-type clamp.

17 Exhaust gas temperature sensor(s) – removal and refitting

Removal

1 On 1.5 litre engines, pull the plastic cover

17.5 Location of lower temperature sensor – 1.6 litre engine shown

18.3 Disconnect the wiring connector – 1.6 litre engine

on the top of the engine upwards from its' mountings.

Particulate filter upstream sensor

2 Trace the wiring back to the wiring plug, and disconnect it **(see illustration)**.

3 Unscrew the sensor from the rear of the exhaust manifold

Particulate filter downstream sensor

4 Raise the front of the vehicle and support it securely on axle stands (see *Jacking and vehicle support*). Release the fasteners and remove the engine undershield.

5 Trace the wiring back to the wiring plug, and disconnect it **(see illustration)**.

6 Working underneath the vehicle, unscrew and remove the sensor.

Refitting

7 Refitting is a reversal of removal. Check the tip of the sensor is not damaged, and tighten it to the specified torque.

18 Fuel pressure sensor – removal and refitting

Removal

1 Remove the cylinder head cover from the top of the engine with reference to Chapter 2C Section 3.

2 The fuel pressure sensor is located in the end of the fuel supply rail **(see illustration)**.

3 Disconnect the wiring plug connector from the fuel pressure sensor **(see illustration)**.

4 On 1.5 litre engines, the sensor appears to be integral with the fuel supply pipe. Check with a Nissan dealer or part specialist. Unclip and remove the pipe along with the sensor.

5 On 1.6 litre engines, unscrew the sensor from the end of the fuel rail.

Refitting

6 Refitting is a reversal of removal.

19 Glow plugs – removal, inspection and refitting

Caution: If the preheating system has just been energised, or if the engine has been running, the glow plugs may be very hot.

Removal

1 Disconnect the battery negative (earth) lead and position it away from the terminal (refer to Chapter 5 Section 4).

1.5 litre engine

2 Where fitted, remove the plastic trim cover from the top of the engine.

3 Slacken the retaining clip and disconnect the intercooler pipe rubber hose **(see illustration)**.

4 Undo the retaining bolt, then release the securing clip at the turbo end of the pipe and

19.3 Disconnect the intercooler hose

19.4a Undo the retaining bolt. . .

19.4b . . . and release the securing clip
(arrowed) to remove the pipe

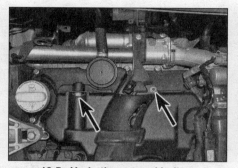

19.5a Undo the nut and bolt. . .

19.5b . . .release the securing clips. . .

19.5c . . . unclip the wiring clip. . .

pull the pipe upwards to remove it from across the top of the engine (see illustrations).

5 Undo the upper bolt and retaining nut, release the two lower securing clips and remove the upper protective cover (see illustrations).

6 Pull the plastic leg to disconnect the wiring plugs from the glow plugs (see illustration).

7 Clean the surrounding area, then unscrew and remove the glow plugs from the cylinder head (see illustration).

1.6 litre engine

8 Remove the throttle valve housing from the top of the inlet manifold, as described in Chapter 4B Section 8.

9 Pull the plastic leg to disconnect the wiring plugs from the glow plugs (see illustrations).

10 Clean the surrounding area, then unscrew and remove the glow plugs from the cylinder head.

Inspection

11 Inspect the glow plugs for physical damage. Burnt or eroded glow plug tips can be caused by a bad injector spray pattern. Have the injectors checked if this sort of damage is found.

12 If the glow plugs are in good physical condition, check them electrically using a 12-volt test lamp or continuity tester with reference to the previous Section.

13 The glow plugs can be energised by

19.5d . . . and remove the upper plastic cover

19.6 Disconnect the wiring connector –
1.5 litre engine

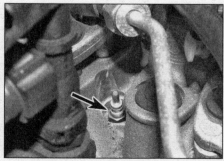

19.7 Unscrew the glow plug from the cylinder head

19.9a Disconnect the wiring connectors. . .

19.9b . . . from the glow plugs –
1.6 litre engine

19.15 Tighten the glow plugs to the correct torque

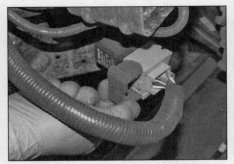

20.3 Release the wiring connector

20.4 Undo the mounting bolt

applying 12-volts to them, this will verify that they heat up evenly and in the required time. Observe the following precautions:

a) *Support the glow plug by clamping it carefully in a vice or self-locking pliers. Remember it will become red-hot.*

b) *Make sure that the power supply or test lead incorporates a fuse or overload trip to protect against damage from a short-circuit.*

c) *After testing, allow the glow plug to cool for several minutes before attempting to handle it.*

14 A glow plug in good condition will start to glow red at the tip after drawing current for 5 seconds or so. Any plug that takes much longer to start glowing, or which starts glowing in the middle instead of at the tip, is defective.

Refitting

15 Refit by reversing the removal operations. Apply a smear of copper based anti-seize compound to the plug threads and tighten the glow plugs to the specified torque **(see illustration)**. Do not overtighten, as this can damage the glow plug element.

---

20 Pre/post-heating system control unit – removal and refitting

Removal

1 The pre/post-heating control unit is located on a bracket below the left-hand headlight

21.8 Location of the EGR valve

unit. Before proceeding, make sure that the ignition is switched off.

2 Working under the left-hand front wing panel, remove the retaining clips and remove the inner wheel arch liner. If required, to gain better access remove the front bumper, as described in Chapter 11 Section 5.

3 Slide the securing clip to disconnect the wiring connector from the control unit **(see illustration)**.

4 Unscrew the mounting nuts/bolts and remove the control unit from the mounting bracket **(see illustration)**.

Refitting

5 Refitting is a reversal of removal.

---

21 Emission control systems – testing and component renewal

Crankcase emission control

1 The components of this system require no attention other than to check that the hose(s) are clear and undamaged at regular intervals.

2 If the system is thought to be faulty, first check that the hoses are unobstructed and not damaged.

3 On high-mileage cars, particularly when regularly used for short journeys, a sludge-like deposit may be evident inside the system hoses and oil separators. If excessive deposits are present, the relevant component(s) should be removed and cleaned.

4 Periodically inspect the system components

21.10 Disconnect the EGR valve wiring connector

for security and damage, and renew them as necessary.

Exhaust emission control

Testing

5 The performance of the catalytic converter can be checked by measuring the exhaust gases using an exhaust gas analyser, which is suitable for diesel engines.

Catalytic converter renewal

6 Refer to Chapter 4A Section 15.

Exhaust gas recirculation system

Testing

7 Testing of the system should be entrusted to a Nissan dealer, who will have the specialist diagnostic equipment to carry out any tests.

EGR valve renewal – 1.5 litre engine

8 The EGR valve is mounted on the inlet manifold at the rear of the cylinder head **(see illustration)**.

9 Disconnect the battery negative lead (refer to *Disconnecting the battery* in Chapter 5 Section 4).

10 Remove the plastic engine cover and disconnect the wiring from the EGR solenoid valve **(see illustration)**.

11 Unbolt and remove the EGR valve **(see illustrations)**. Recover the gasket.

12 Thoroughly clean and inspect the EGR valve. Ensure the valve seats correctly **(see illustration)**.

13 Refitting is a reversal of removal, but a new gasket should be fitted.

21.11a Undo the mounting bolts. . .

21.11b . . . and remove the EGR valve

21.12 Clean and inspect the valve seat

21.15 Remove the mounting bracket

21.16 Disconnect the EGR valve wiring connector

21.17a Undo the two mounting screws

21.17b Insert bolt to carefully lift the EGR valve. . .

EGR volume control valve renewal – 1.6 litre engines

14 The EGR solenoid valve is located on the front of the intake manifold on the front of the engine. First disconnect the wiring from the unit.

15 Remove the mounting bracket from the inlet manifold **(see illustration)**.

16 Disconnect the wiring from the EGR solenoid valve **(see illustration)**.

17 Undo the screws and lift the solenoid valve from the throttle valve housing **(see illustrations)**. If the EGR valve is a tight fit and cannot easily be removed from the top of the manifold, use a bolt in the threaded hole provided to carefully tighten the bolt and get the EGR valve to lift from the manifold. Recover the gasket and renew on refitting.

18 Refitting is a reversal of removal, using a new gasket and ensuring that the valve and housing surfaces are clean and the bolts are securely tightened.

EGR pipework – 1.5 litre engine

19 If required, the pipework between the valve housing and exhaust manifold can be removed for cleaning and inspection.

20 Disconnect the hose from the turbocharger pressure adjustment valve on the air duct **(see illustration)**.

21 Loosen the clips and remove the air duct from between the EGR unit and turbocharger **(see illustration)**.

22 Unbolt and remove the right-hand rear engine lifting eye.

23 Unscrew the bolt and remove the air inlet metallic tube **(see illustration)**.

24 Where fitted, remove the heat shield from over the EGR solenoid valve.

25 Loosen both clamps and remove the EGR convoluted metal tube from the EGR valve and exhaust manifold **(see illustrations)**.

21.17c . . . then remove the EGR valve

26 Unscrew the mounting bolts and remove the EGR valve unit from its location on the inlet manifold. Note that the solenoid valve is not available separately.

27 Refitting is a reversal of removal, but

21.20 Disconnect the wastegate valve hose

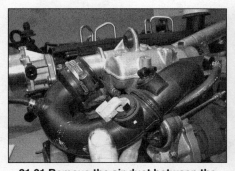

21.21 Remove the air duct between the EGR valve and the turbo

21.23 Remove the inlet pipe

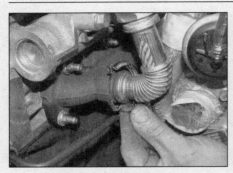

21.25a Release the clamps. . .

21.25b . . . and remove the EGR convoluted metal tube

21.27 Use pincer type pliers to tighten the clamp

21.30 Remove air cleaner housing and intake hose

21.31a Disconnect the intake air ducting. . .

21.31b . . . and remove it from the engine

renew the air inlet duct O-rings. Check the condition of the convoluted metal tube retaining clamps and if necessary, renew them

– if the special tool is not available, use a pair of pincers to tighten the clamps until the clip is engaged **(see illustration)**.

EGR cooler and EGR low pressure volume control valve renewal – 1.6 litre engine

28 The EGR cooler and EGR low pressure volume control valve are located on the rear of the engine. First drain the cooling system as described in Chapter 1B Section 32.
29 Remove the battery, as described in Chapter 5 Section 4.
30 Remove the air cleaner assembly, as described in Chapter 4B Section 3. Remove the air cleaner housing, complete with rubber intake hose **(see illustration)**.
31 Release the retaining clip, undo the mounting nuts and remove the intake air ducting and intercooler inlet pipe **(see illustrations)**.
32 Undo the retaining bolts and remove the heat shield from over the EGR cooler pipe **(see illustration)**.
33 Undo the retaining bolts to disconnect the EGR cooler from the particle filter (DPF) **(see illustration)**.
34 Disconnect the wiring connectors from the EGR valve **(see illustration)**.
35 Disconnect the two coolant hoses from the side of the EGR cooler **(see illustration)**.
36 Unbolt the EGR cooler from the rear of the cylinder block **(see illustrations)**.
37 Refitting is a reversal of removal, but tighten the bolts to the specified torque.

Particulate filter system

Particulate filter renewal

38 The particle filter is part of the exhaust

21.32 Remove the heat shield

21.33 Undo the two mounting bolts

21.34 Disconnect the wiring connectors

21.35 Disconnect the two coolant hoses

21.36a Undo the mounting bolts. . .

21.36b . . . then remove the EGR are cooler and valve

21.36c Renew the gaskets on refitting

front section. Remove the front pipe/particle filter, as described in Chapter 4B Section 17.

Temperature sensors renewal

39 The temperature sensors monitor the exhaust gas temperature both upstream and downstream of the particulate filter during regeneration **(see illustrations)**. To remove the sensors, disconnect the wiring at the connector, unbolt the wiring support and unscrew the sensor from the exhaust.

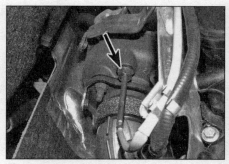

21.39a Particulate filter upper temperature sensor. . .

21.39b . . . and lower temperature sensor

Notes

Chapter 7
Manual transmission

Contents

Degrees of difficulty

Easy, suitable for novice with little experience	Fairly easy, suitable for beginner with some experience	Fairly difficult, suitable for competent DIY mechanic	Difficult, suitable for experienced DIY mechanic	Very difficult, suitable for expert DIY or professional

Specifications

General

Type	Manual six forward speeds and reverse. Synchromesh on all forward speeds

Designation:
1.2 litre (HRA2DDT) petrol engines	RS6F94R – (6 speed)
1.5 litre (K9K) diesel engine	RS6F94R – (6 speed)
1.6 litre litre (R9M) diesel engine.	RS6F95R – (6 speed)

Models code:
1.2 litre (HRA2DDT) petrol engines	1KG0B (TL4 137)
1.5 litre (K9K) diesel engine	JD50D (TL4 126)
1.6 litre litre (R9M) diesel engine.	4EA2A

Gear Ratio:
1.2 litre (HRA2DDT) petrol engines:
1st Gear	3.727 : 1
2nd Gear	1.947 : 1
3rd Gear	1.322 : 1
4th Gear	0.975 : 1
5th Gear	0.763 : 1
6th Gear	0.638 : 1
Reverse Gear	3.686 : 1
Final drive gears (12/59)	4.214 : 1

1.5 litre (K9K) diesel engine:
1st Gear	3.727 : 1
2nd Gear	1.947 : 1
3rd Gear	1.225 : 1
4th Gear	0.837 : 1
5th Gear	0.652 : 1
6th Gear	0.560 : 1
Reverse Gear	3.686 : 1
Final drive gears (16/66)	4.125 : 1

1.6 litre litre (R9M) diesel engine:
1st Gear	3.727 : 1
2nd Gear	2.043 : 1
3rd Gear	1.323 : 1
4th Gear	0.947 : 1
5th Gear	0.723 : 1
6th Gear	0.596 : 1
Reverse Gear	3.641 : 1
Final drive gears (15/62)	4.133 : 1

Lubrication
Oil capacities:
RS6F94R – 6-speed transmissions	2.0 litres
RS6F95R – 6-speed transmissions	1.8 litres

Torque wrench settings

	Nm	lbf ft
Engine-to-transmission fixing bolts/nuts:		
HRA2DDT	48	35
K9K	48	35
R9M	44	32
Gear change cable mounting bracket bolts*	35	26
Oil drain plug	23	17
Oil filler/level plug (plastic plug)	3	2
Reversing light switch	23	17

Use new nuts/bolts

1 General Information

1 The transmission is contained in a cast-aluminium alloy casing bolted to the left-hand end of the engine, and consists of the gearbox and final drive differential, often called a transaxle.

2 Drive is transmitted from the crankshaft via the clutch to the input shaft, which has a splined extension to accept the clutch friction disc, and rotates in sealed ball-bearings. From the input shaft, drive is transmitted to the output shaft, which rotates in a roller bearing at its right-hand end, and a sealed ball-bearing at its left-hand end. From the output shaft, the drive is transmitted to the differential crownwheel, which rotates with the differential case and planetary gears, thus driving the sun gears and driveshafts. The rotation of the planetary gears on their shaft allows the inner roadwheel to rotate at a slower speed than the outer roadwheel when the car is cornering.

3 The input and output shafts are arranged side-by-side, parallel to the crankshaft and driveshafts, so that their gear pinion teeth are in constant mesh. In the neutral position, the output shaft gear pinions rotate freely, so that drive cannot be transmitted to the crownwheel.

4 Gear selection is via a floor-mounted lever and dual cable arrangement. The selector cables cause the appropriate selector fork to move its respective synchro-sleeve along the shaft, to lock the gear pinion to the synchro-hub. Since the synchro-hubs are splined to the output shaft, this locks the pinion to the shaft so that drive can be transmitted. To ensure that gearchanging can be made quickly and quietly, a synchromesh system is fitted to all forward gears, consisting of baulk rings and spring-loaded fingers, as well as the gear pinions and synchro-hubs; the synchromesh cones are formed on the mating faces of the baulk rings and gear pinions.

2.4a Oil filler/level plug – 1.2 litre petrol and 1.5 litre diesel engines

2.4b Oil filler/level plug – 1.6 litre diesel

2.6 Oil drain plug

2.7 Drain the transmission oil

2 Transmission – draining and refilling

1 This operation is much quicker and more efficient if the car is first taken on a journey of sufficient length to warm the engine/transmission up to normal operating temperature.

2 Park the car on level ground, switch off the ignition and apply the handbrake firmly. For improved access, jack up the front of the car and support it securely on axle stands (see *Jacking and vehicle support*). Note that the car must be lowered to the ground and be level to ensure accuracy when refilling and checking the oil level.

3 Undo the retaining bolts and remove the plastic undershield from below the engine/transmission.

4 Wipe clean the area around the filler/level plug, and unscrew it from the casing. On 1.2 litre petrol engines and 1.5 litre diesel engines, the filler/level plug is situated on the left-hand rear of the transmission unit, behind the driveshaft. On 1.6 litre diesel engines, the filler/level plug is situated on the left-hand front of the transmission unit **(see illustrations)**.

5 Remove the oil filler/level plug, be prepared for some oil spillage as the plug is removed.

6 Position a suitable container under the drain plug, which is situated at the lower rear of the transmission differential housing **(see illustration)**.

7 Remove the drain plug and allow the oil to drain completely into the container **(see illustration)**. If the oil is hot, take precautions against scalding. Clean both the filler/level and the drain plug, discard the sealing washers, as new ones will be required on refitting.

8 When the oil has finished draining, clean the drain plug threads and those of the transmission casing, then fit the new sealing washer and refit the drain plug **(see illustration)**, tightening it to the specified torque wrench setting. If the car was raised for the draining operation, lower it to the ground, to make sure it is level.

9 Refilling the transmission is an awkward operation. Above all, allow plenty of time for the oil level to settle properly before checking it. Note that the car must be parked on flat level ground when checking the oil level.

10 Refill the transmission with the exact amount of the specified type of oil, then check the oil level as described in Chapter 1A Section 31, or Chapter 1B Section 30 ; if the correct amount was poured into the transmission, and a large amount flows out on checking the level, refit the filler/level plug and take the car on a short journey so that the new oil is distributed fully around the transmission components, then check the level again on your return.

11 When the level is correct, refit the filler/level plug **(see illustration)**, tightening it to the specified torque wrench setting. Wash off any spilt oil.

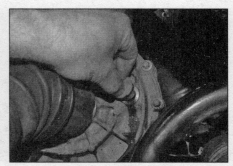
2.8 Use a new sealing washer when refitting the drain plug

2.11 Refit the filler/level plug when fluid is correct

3 Gearchange linkage – removal and refitting

3.2a Release the locking clips. . .

3.2b . . . and disconnect the cables from the ball joint

Removal

Gear lever assembly

1 Remove the centre console as described in Chapter 11 Section 24.
2 Release the white securing clips and disconnect the two cables from the ball joints on the gear change selector levers **(see illustrations)**.
3 Release the locating peg and withdraw the two outer cables from the gear change housing **(see illustrations)**.
4 With the cables disconnected, undo the four mounting bolts from the bottom of the gear change housing, and manoeuvre the gear lever assembly out of position.

Gear change cables

5 Release the cables from the gear lever assembly, as described in paragraphs 1 to 3.
6 Remove the battery (see Chapter 5 Section 4.

7 Also to make access to the cables on top of the transmission housing easier, remove the air cleaner housing, as described in Chapter 4A Section 3, or Chapter 4B Section 3.
8 Prise the ends of the two cables from the

ball joints, to release them from the gear change selector levers **(see illustrations)**.
9 Squeeze the locking clips and withdraw the two outer cables from the transmission mounting bracket **(see illustrations)**.

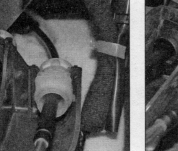
3.3a Unclip the outer cables. . .

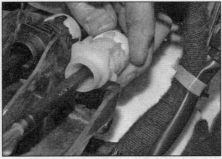
3.3b . . . from the gear lever bracket

3.8a Prise the ends of the cables. . .

3.8b . . . from the ball joints on the levers

3.9a Squeeze the locking clips. . .

3.9b . . . and unclip the outer cables from the transmission bracket

3.11a Undo the retaining clips. . .

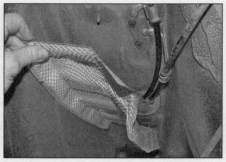

3.11b . . . and remove the heatshield

3.12a Release the cables from the retaining bracket. . .

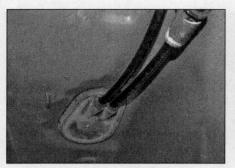

3.12b . . . and remove the rubber grommet from the floor panel

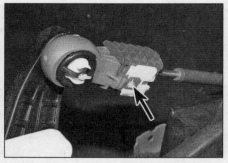

3.15 Release the locking clip to adjust the cable

3.18 Insert pin through slot in the gear lever

10 Firmly apply the handbrake, and then jack up the front of the vehicle and support it securely on axle stands (see *Jacking and vehicle support*).

11 From underneath the vehicle, release the fasteners and remove the heat shield from under the centre tunnel of the vehicle **(see illustrations)**. Note depending on model, it may be necessary to remove the exhaust front pipe to give better access to the heat shield.

12 Unclip the outer cables from the mounting bracket on the underside of the vehicle, and then release the rubber grommet from the floor panel and withdraw the cables from under the vehicle **(see illustrations)**.

13 Inspect all the gear linkage components for signs of wear or damage, paying particular attention to the cables, renew worn components as necessary.

Refitting

14 Refitting is a reversal of the removal procedure, applying a smear of multipurpose grease to the gear lever pivot ball and bushes.

Adjustment

15 Adjustment is made from inside the vehicle, on the gear lever end of the left-hand selector cable **(see illustration)**.

16 Remove the centre console as described in Chapter 11 Section 24.

17 Slide the centre clip and withdraw the locking clip from the end of the gear change cable; this will disengage the inner cable.

18 Position the gear lever so that the slot in the lever aligns with the hole in the gear lever

housing **(see illustration)**, and then insert a 3mm locating pin (drill bit) to lock the gear lever in position.

19 With the gear lever in position, slide the centre locking clip back into position, securing the cable in position.

20 When completed remove the 3mm locating pin and move the gear lever through all gears to check smooth operation.

21 Refitting is a reversal of the removal procedure.

4   Oil seals –
renewal

Driveshaft oil seal

1 Firmly apply the handbrake, and then jack up the front of the vehicle and support

4.4 Using a vernier gauge to measure the seal depth

it securely on axle stands (see *Jacking and vehicle support*). Remove the appropriate front roadwheel.

2 Drain the transmission oil as described in Section 2.

3 Working as described in Chapter 8 Section 8, free the inner end of the driveshaft from the transmission, and place it clear of the seal, noting that there is no need to completely remove the driveshaft; the driveshaft can be left secured to the hub. Support the driveshaft, to avoid placing any strain on the driveshaft joints or gaiters.

4 Before removing the seal, use a vernier gauge to check the seal depth in the transmission casing **(see illustration)**. This will give you the position of the seal in the transmission casing for refitting, see following measurements:

a) On 6-speed (RS6F94R) transmissions: The depth of the left-hand side seal should be 1.2 to 1.8 mm and the right-hand side seal should be 2.7 to 3.3 mm.

b) On 6-speed (RS6F95R) transmissions: The left and right-hand side seals should be flush with casing.

5 Carefully prise the oil seal out of the transmission using a large flat-bladed screwdriver **(see illustration)**. Take care not to damage the transmission casing as the seal is removed.

6 Remove all traces of dirt from the area around the oil seal aperture, then apply a smear of oil to the lip of the new oil seal, and locate it in its aperture **(see illustration)**.

7 Drive the seal squarely into position, using a

4.5 Use a large flat-bladed screwdriver to prise out the driveshaft oil seals

4.6 Fit the new seal squarely to the transmission. . .

4.7 . . . and tap it into position using a tubular drift/socket

suitable tubular drift (such as a socket), which bears only on the hard outer edge of the seal **(see illustration)**. Drive the seal into position until it is at the depth noted on removal.

8 Refit the driveshaft as described in Chapter 8 Section 8.

9 Refill the transmission with the specified quantity of oil, as described in the specifications at the beginning of this Chapter. Refer to the specifications at the beginning of Chapter 1A, or Chapter 1B for the specified type of oil used.

Input shaft oil seal

10 To renew the input shaft seal, the transmission must be dismantled. This task should therefore be entrusted to a Nissan dealer.

5 Reversing light switch – testing, removal and refitting

Testing

1 The reversing light circuit is controlled by a plunger-type switch that is screwed into the front, upper part of the transmission housing **(see illustration)**.

2 If a fault develops in the circuit, first ensure that the circuit fuse has not blown (see Chapter 12 Section 3).

3 To test the switch, disconnect the wiring connector, and use a multi-meter (set to the resistance function) or a battery-and-bulb test circuit to check that there is continuity between the switch terminals only when

reverse gear is selected. If this is not the case, and there are no obvious breaks or other damage to the wires, the switch is faulty and must be renewed.

Removal

4 Firmly apply the handbrake, and then jack up the front of the vehicle and support it securely on axle stands (see *Jacking and vehicle support*).

5 Disconnect the wiring connector from the reversing light switch **(see illustration)**.

6 Unscrew the switch from the transmission, and remove it.

Refitting

7 Fit a new sealing washer to the switch, and then screw it back into the transmission housing.

8 Tighten the switch to the specified torque, then reconnect the wiring connector and check the operation of the circuit.

9 Lower the vehicle to the ground, and top-up/refill the transmission oil (as applicable) as described in Section 2.

6 Manual transmission – removal and refitting

Note: *This Section describes the removal of the transmission leaving the engine in position in the car. Alternatively the engine and transmission can be removed together, as described in Chapter 2D Section 4, and then separated on the bench.*

Note: *Transmission model code number is on a label on the top of the transmission housing (see illustration); see specifications at the beginning of this Chapter.*

Removal

1 Firmly apply the handbrake, and then jack up the front of the vehicle and support it securely on axle stands (see *Jacking and vehicle support*). Remove both front roadwheels. Undo the retaining screws, and remove the plastic undershields from beneath the engine/transmission, and the covers from underneath both wheel arches.

2 Drain the transmission oil as described in Section 2, then refit the drain and filler/level plugs and tighten them to their specified torque settings.

3 Remove the battery as described in Chapter 5 Section 4.

4 Remove the front subframe as described in Chapter 10 Section 12.

5 Remove the starter motor as described in Chapter 5 Section 10.

6 Remove the air cleaner assembly as described in Chapter 4A Section 3 or Chapter 4B Section 3.

7 Remove the exhaust system front pipe as described in Chapter 4A Section 15 or Chapter 4B Section 17.

8 Release the gearchange cables from the transmission as described in Section 3.

9 Working as described in Chapter 8 Section 8, remove the two front driveshafts from the transmission.

10 Undo the retaining bolt and disconnect

5.1 Location of reversing light switch

5.5 Disconnect the switch wiring connector

6.0 Label with transmission model code

6.10 Undo the earth cable retaining bolt

6.12a Release the locking clip. . .

6.12b . . . and disconnect the clutch fluid hose

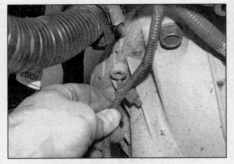

6.13a Release the wiring loom. . .

6.13b . . . retaining clips from the transmission

(see illustrations). Plug the ends of the slave cylinder pipe and clutch fluid hose to prevent fluid leakage and dirt ingress.

13 Work around the transmission and free the wiring loom from any relevant retaining clips (see illustrations), and position the wiring clear of the transmission.

14 Make sure the breather pipe on top of the transmission housing is not secured to any other components. This does not have to be completely removed and left across the top of the transmission.

15 Place a jack with interposed block of wood beneath the engine, to take the weight of the engine (see illustration). Alternatively, attach a hoist or support bar to the engine and take the weight of the engine.

16 Also place a jack and block of wood beneath the transmission, and raise the jack to take the weight of the transmission.

17 Slacken and remove the nut from the centre stud on the left-hand engine/transmission mounting. Undo the two bolts securing the mounting to the bracket, and remove the rubber mounting (see illustration). For further information on engine/transmission mounting removal, see the relevant part of Chapter 2A, B, C or D.

18 Unclip the clutch fluid pipe from the clip on the mounting bracket, and then undo the bolts and remove the mounting from the top of the transmission (see illustration).

19 With the jack positioned beneath the transmission taking the weight, slacken and remove the remaining bolts securing the transmission housing to the engine (see illustrations). Note the correct fitted positions

the earth cable from the left-hand end of the transmission (see illustration).

11 Disconnect the wiring connector from the reversing light switch, see Section 5 for reversing light switch location.

12 Be prepared for some fluid loss as the pipe is disconnected, place some cloth around the fitting. Release the retaining spring clip and disconnect the clutch fluid hose from the slave cylinder connector pipe

6.15 Support the transmission with a trolley jack

6.18 Undo the mounting bracket retaining bolts

6.17 Remove the transmission mounting – 1.2 litre petrol shown

6.19a Remove the upper mounting nuts. . .

6.19b . . . rear mounting bolts. . .

6.19c . . . lower mounting bolts. . .

6.19d . . . and front mounting bolt –
1.6 litre diesel shown

6.22 Lower the transmission from under
the vehicle

of each bolt (and the relevant brackets) as they are removed, to use as a reference on refitting – the bolts are of different lengths. Note that it may be necessary to raise the transmission slightly to gain access to the lower bolts.

20 Make a final check that all necessary components have been disconnected, and are positioned clear of the transmission so that they will not hinder the removal procedure.

21 Move the trolley jack and transmission to the left to free it from its locating dowels. Keep the transmission fully supported until the input shaft is free of the engine.

22 Once the transmission is free, lower the jack and manoeuvre the unit out from under the car **(see illustration)**. If they are loose, remove the locating dowels from the transmission or engine, and keep them in a safe place.

Refitting

23 The transmission is refitted by a reversal of the removal procedure, bearing in mind the following points:

a) *Apply a little high melting-point grease to the splines of the transmission input shaft. Do not apply too much; otherwise there is a possibility of the grease contaminating the clutch friction disc.*

b) *Ensure that the locating dowels are correctly positioned prior to installation.*

c) *Insert the transmission-to-engine bolts into their original locations, as noted on removal. Tighten all nuts and bolts to the specified torque (where given).*

d) *Refit the driveshafts as described in Chapter 8 Section 8. If required renew the driveshaft oil seals using the information given in Section 4.*

e) *Bleed the clutch system as described in Chapter 8 Section 2.*

f) *Refit the gearchange cables as described in Section 3, and check operation.*

g) *On completion, refill the transmission with the specified type and quantity of lubricant as described in Section 2.*

7 Manual transmission overhaul – general information

1 Overhauling a manual transmission is a difficult and involved job for the DIY home mechanic. In addition to dismantling and reassembling many small parts, clearances must be precisely measured and, if necessary, changed by selecting shims and spacers.

Internal transmission components are also often difficult to obtain, and in many instances, extremely expensive. Because of this, if the transmission develops a fault or becomes noisy, the best course of action is to have the unit overhauled by a specialist repairer, or to obtain an exchange reconditioned unit.

2 Nevertheless, it is not impossible for the more experienced mechanic to overhaul the transmission, if the special tools are available, and the job is done in a deliberate step-by-step manner so that nothing is overlooked.

3 The tools necessary for an overhaul include internal and external circlip pliers, bearing pullers, a slide hammer, a set of pin punches, a dial test indicator, and possibly a hydraulic press. In addition, a large, sturdy workbench and a vice will be required.

4 During dismantling of the transmission, make careful notes of how each component is fitted, to make reassembly easier and accurate.

5 Before dismantling the transmission, it will help if you have some idea which area is malfunctioning. Certain problems can be closely related to specific areas in the transmission, which can make component examination and renewal easier. Refer to the *Fault finding* Section in the beginning of this manual for more information.

Notes

Chapter 8
Clutch and driveshafts

Contents

Degrees of difficulty

Easy, suitable for novice with little experience	Fairly easy, suitable for beginner with some experience	Fairly difficult, suitable for competent DIY mechanic 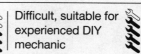	Difficult, suitable for experienced DIY mechanic	Very difficult, suitable for expert DIY or professional

Specifications

General

Clutch type	Single dry plate with diaphragm spring. Hydraulic with master cylinder and operating (slave) cylinder
Driveshaft type	Unequal length, solid steel shafts, splined to inner and outer constant velocity joints

Friction disc

Outer diameter:	
HRA2DDT	225 mm
K9K	225 mm
R9M	240 mm
Inner diameter (of friction materiel):	
HRA2DDT	150 mm
K9K	150 mm
R9M	170 mm
Friction material thickness (new):	
HRA2DDT	2.9 mm
K9K	2.9 mm
R9M	3.45 mm
Maximum friction disc run-out	1.0 mm

Driveshaft overhaul

Lubricant type	Nissan grease supplied with manufacturer gaiter repair kit

Lubricant quantity:
  HRA2DDT:
    Wheel end. . . . .   100 to 120g
    Transmission end . . . .   155 to 175g
  K9K:
    Wheel end. . . . .   115 to 135g
    Transmission end . . . .   215 to 235g
  R9M:
    Wheel end. . . . .   175 to 205g
    Transmission end . . . .   165 to 175g
Driveshaft boot installed length:
  HRA2DDT:
    Wheel end. . . . .   131.0 mm
    Transmission end:
      Left driveshaft. . . . .   180.4 mm
      Right driveshaft. . . . .   172.4 mm
  K9K:
    Wheel end. . . . .   133.5 mm
    Transmission end:
      Left driveshaft. . . . .   186.3 mm
      Right driveshaft. . . . .   173.1 mm
  R9M:
    Wheel end. . . . .   163.4 mm
    Transmission end:
      Left driveshaft. . . . .   173.1 mm
      Right driveshaft. . . . .   181.1 mm
Dynamic damper fitted position from wheel end bearing face:
  HRA2DDT . . . .   287 to 291 mm
  K9K . . . .   281 to 285 mm
  R9M . . . .   229.5 to 235.5 mm

Torque wrench settings

	Nm	lbf ft
Clutch pedal bracket nuts	14	10
Concentric slave cylinder (CSC) retaining bolts.	21	15
Pressure plate (clutch cover) retaining bolts:		
HRA2DDT		
Stage 1	6	5
Stage 2	15	11
K9K	12	9
R9M	15	11
Driveshaft front hub nut	255	188
Right-hand front driveshaft retaining plate bolts	25	18
Right-hand front driveshaft centre bearing housing bolts:		
HRA2DDT and R9M	48	35
K9K	44	32
Roadwheel nuts	113	83

* New nut(s) must be used.

1 General Information

Clutch

1 The clutch consists of a friction disc, a pressure plate assembly, a release bearing and the release mechanism. All of these components are contained in the large cast-aluminium alloy bellhousing, and sandwiched between the engine and the transmission. The release mechanism is hydraulic, operated by a master cylinder and a slave cylinder, which is part of the release bearing. The hydraulic master cylinder is located in the pedal bracket on the bulkhead, and the clutch fluid reservoir is shared with the brake fluid reservoir on the top of the brake master cylinder. Inside the reservoir each circuit has its own compartment, so that in the event of fluid loss in the clutch circuit, the brake circuit remains fully operational.

2 The friction disc/plate is fitted between the engine flywheel and the clutch pressure plate, and is allowed to slide on the transmission input shaft splines. It consists of two circular facings of friction material to provide the clutch bearing surface, and a spring-cushioned hub to damp out transmission shocks.

3 The pressure plate assembly is bolted to the engine flywheel, and is located by dowel pins. When the engine is running, drive is transmitted from the crankshaft via the flywheel to the friction disc (these components being clamped securely together by the pressure plate assembly), and from the friction disc to the transmission input shaft.

4 To interrupt the drive, the spring pressure must be relaxed. This is achieved by a sealed release bearing fitted concentrically around the transmission input shaft; when the driver depresses the clutch pedal, the release bearing is pressed against the fingers at the centre of the diaphragm spring. The pressure at its centre causes the springs to deform, so that it flattens and thus releases the clamping force it exerts at its periphery on the pressure plate.

5 When the pedal is released, the diaphragm spring forces the pressure plate into contact with the friction linings on the friction plate. The disc is now firmly sandwiched between the pressure plate and the flywheel, thus transmitting engine power to the transmission.

6 Wear of the friction material on the friction plate is automatically compensated for by the operation of the hydraulic system. As the friction material on the friction plate wears, the pressure plate moves towards the flywheel causing the clutch diaphragm spring inner fingers to move outwards. When the clutch pedal is released, excess fluid is expelled through the master cylinder into the fluid reservoir. There is a pulsation damper fitted in the hydraulic hose from the master cylinder to the (concentric) slave cylinder. It is located in the left-hand rear corner of the engine compartment below the air cleaner assembly (see illustration).

⚠ *Warning: Hydraulic fluid is poisonous, thoroughly wash off spills from bare skin without delay. Seek immediate medical advice if any fluid is swallowed or gets into the eyes. Certain types of hydraulic fluid are inflammable and may ignite when brought into contact with hot components. Hydraulic fluid is also an effective paint stripper. If spillage occurs onto painted bodywork or fittings, it should be washed off immediately, using copious quantities of cold water. It is also hygroscopic (i.e. it can absorb moisture from the air) which then renders it useless. Old fluid may have suffered contamination, and should never be re-used.*

Driveshafts

7 Drive is transmitted from the transmission differential to the front wheels by means of two driveshafts of unequal length. The right-hand driveshaft is longer and has a support bearing at the rear of the cylinder block.

8 Each driveshaft consists of three main components: the sliding (tripod type) inner joint, the driveshaft itself, and the outer CV (constant velocity) joint. The inner end of the tripod joint is splined and secured in the differential side gear by the engagement of a circlip. The right-hand driveshaft passes through the support housing/bearing, which is bolted to the rear of the cylinder block. The outer CV joint on both driveshafts is of ball-bearing type, and is secured in the front hub by the driveshaft nut and split pin.

9 Constant velocity (CV) joints are fitted to each end of the driveshafts, to ensure the smooth and efficient transmission of power at all suspension and steering angles. The outer constant velocity joints are of the ball-and-cage type, and the inner joints are of the tripod type.

1.6 Pulsation damper location

2 Clutch hydraulic system – bleeding

Note: *Refer to the warning in Section 1, regarding the hazards of working with hydraulic fluid.*

1 If any part of the hydraulic system is dismantled, or if air has accidentally entered the system, the system will need to be bled. The presence of air is characterised by the pedal having a spongy feel and it results in difficulty in changing gear.

2 Obtain a clean container, a suitable length of rubber or clear plastic tubing that is a tight fit over the bleed screw on the clutch slave cylinder, and a container of the specified hydraulic fluid. The help of an assistant will also be required. (If a one-man do-it-yourself bleeding kit for bleeding the brake hydraulic system is available, this can be used quite satisfactorily for the clutch also. Full information on the use of these kits may be found in Chapter 9 Section 3).

3 Remove the air cleaner inlet ducting from the front left-hand side of the engine compartment (see Chapter 4A Section 3 or Chapter 4B Section 3), to access the clutch bleed screw.

4 Remove the filler cap from the brake master cylinder reservoir, and if necessary top-up the fluid. Keep the reservoir topped-up during subsequent operations.

5 Remove the dust cap from the bleed screw at the hydraulic connection, located on the

2.6 Air bleed bottle connected to bleed screw

2.5 Remove the dust cap from the bleed screw

lower front facing side of the transmission (see illustration).

6 Connect one end of the bleed tube to the bleed screw, and insert the other end of the tube in the container with sufficient clean hydraulic fluid to keep the end of the tube submerged (see illustration).

7 With the tube on the bleed screw, press down on the hose retaining clip (see illustration), and then carefully pull the clutch fluid hose outwards from the bell housing, by 5mm on 5-speed transmissions, and 10mm on 6-speed transmissions. Be careful not to pull the clutch fluid hose completely out from the connection.

8 Have your assistant depress the clutch pedal and then slowly release it. Continue this procedure until clean hydraulic fluid, free from air bubbles, emerges from the tube. At the end of a downstroke, push the clutch fluid hose back into position, making sure the retaining clip secures the hose in place.

9 Make sure that the brake master cylinder reservoir is checked frequently to ensure that the level does not drop too far, allowing air into the system.

10 Check the operation of the clutch pedal. After a few strokes it should feel normal. Any sponginess would indicate air still present in the system; if so carry out the procedure once again.

11 On completion remove the bleed tube and refit the dust cover. Top-up the master cylinder reservoir if necessary and refit the cap. Fluid expelled from the hydraulic system should now be discarded, as it will be contaminated with moisture, air and dirt, making it unsuitable for further use.

2.7 Release the retaining clip

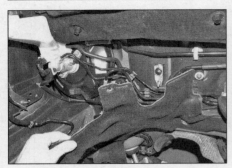

3.3 Unclip the bulkhead soundproofing

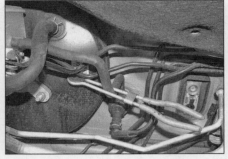

3.5 Clamp the fluid pipe from the reservoir

3.6 Disconnect the fluid pipes from the master cylinder

3 Clutch master cylinder – removal and refitting

Note: *Refer to the warning in Section 1, regarding the hazards of working with hydraulic fluid.*

Removal

1 Working inside the driver's footwell, release the securing clips, and then prise the master cylinder pushrod end from the pedal pin **(see illustration 5.5)**. Press on the securing clips to free the pushrod from the pedal.

2 To minimise hydraulic fluid loss, remove the brake master cylinder reservoir filler cap then tighten it down onto a piece of polythene to obtain an airtight seal.

3 Working inside the rear of the engine compartment, undo the fasteners and pull back the sound proofing protector from the bulkhead **(see illustration)**.

4 Place absorbent rags under the clutch master cylinder pipe connections in the engine compartment and be prepared for some hydraulic fluid loss.

5 Clamp the upper hydraulic fluid supply hose leading from the brake fluid reservoir to the clutch master cylinder using a brake hose clamp **(see illustration)**.

6 Release the master cylinder hydraulic pressure pipe from the retaining clip on the engine compartment bulkhead. Be prepared for some hydraulic fluid loss, then prise out the retaining wire clip and disconnect the pipe from the master cylinder **(see illustration)**. Suitably plug or cap the pipe end to prevent further fluid loss and dirt entry.

7 Be prepared for some hydraulic fluid loss and disconnect the fluid supply hose from the top of the master cylinder. Suitably plug or cap the pipe end to prevent further fluid loss and dirt entry.

8 Rotate the master cylinder 45 degrees clockwise, and remove it from the bulkhead.

Refitting

9 Refitting the master cylinder is the reverse sequence to removal, bearing in mind the following points.
a) *Ensure that the pedal-to-master cylinder pushrod is correctly fitted.*
b) *Ensure all retaining clips are correctly refitted.*
c) *Remove the piece of polythene from the top of the reservoir.*
d) *On completion, bleed the clutch hydraulic system as described in Section 2.*

4 Clutch concentric slave cylinder (CSC) – removal and refitting

1 The clutch slave cylinder (Concentric Slave Cylinder) is part of the release bearing assembly; refer to Section 7, for the removal and refitting procedure.

5 Clutch pedal – removal and refitting

Removal

1 Disconnect the battery negative (earth) lead and position it away from the terminal (refer to *Disconnecting the battery* in Chapter 5 Section 4).

2 Working inside the vehicle in the driver's side footwell, unclip the lower trim panel from the facia, as described in Chapter 11 Section 25.

3 Disconnect the wiring connector from the clutch pedal switch, and unclip the wiring loom securing clips from the pedal mounting bracket **(see illustrations)**.

4 Release the securing clips, and then using a flat bladed screwdriver, prise the master cylinder pushrod end from the pedal pin **(see illustration)**.

5 Hold the clutch pedal down and remove the return spring from the locating pegs on the mounting bracket and pedal **(see illustration)**.

5.3a Disconnect the switch wiring connector. . .

5.3b . . . and unclip the wiring loom retaining clip

5.4 Release the end of the pushrod from the pedal

5.5 Unclip the return spring from the pedal and mounting bracket

6 Slacken and remove the clutch pedal mounting bracket retaining nuts, then withdraw the pedal and mounting bracket out from under the facia (see illustration).

7 Check the condition of the pedal, pivot bush and return spring assembly and renew any components as necessary.

Refitting

8 Lubricate the pedal pivot bolt with multipurpose grease, then manoeuvre and locate the pedal and mounting bracket on the bulkhead. Refit the retaining nuts and tighten securely.

9 Reconnect the return spring to the pedal and pedal bracket; making sure it locates correctly (see illustration).

10 Reconnect the clutch master cylinder pushrod to the clutch pedal.

11 Depress the pedal two or three times and check the operation of the clutch release mechanism.

12 Reconnect the wiring connector to the clutch switch, and then secure the wiring loom back into position with the retaining clips on the pedal mounting bracket.

13 Refit the heater ducting back across the top of the pedal assembly and then refit the facia lower trim panels.

14 Reconnect the battery negative (earth) lead (refer to Chapter 5 Section 4).

<table>
<tr><td>6</td><td>Clutch assembly –
removal, inspection
and refitting</td></tr>
</table>

⚠️ **Warning: Dust created by clutch wear and deposited on the clutch components may contain harmful particles, which may be a health hazard. DO NOT blow it out with compressed air, or inhale any of it. DO NOT use petrol or petroleum-based solvents to clean off the dust. Brake system cleaner or methylated spirit should be used to flush the dust into a suitable receptacle. After the clutch components are wiped clean with rags, dispose of the contaminated rags and cleaner in a sealed, marked container.**

Removal

1 Unless the complete engine/transmission is to be removed from the car, and separated for major overhaul, the clutch can be reached by removing the transmission as described in Chapter 7 Section 6.

2 Before disturbing the clutch, use a dab of quick-drying paint or a marker pen to mark the relationship of the pressure plate assembly to the flywheel (see illustration).

3 Working in a diagonal sequence, slacken the pressure plate bolts by half a turn at a time, until the spring pressure is released and the bolts can be unscrewed by hand (see illustrations). If required lock the flywheel to prevent it from turning, by locking the ring gear teeth.

4 Prise the pressure plate assembly off its

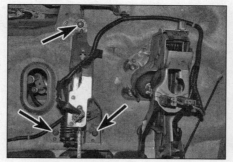

5.6 Clutch pedal mounting bracket nuts

locating dowels, and collect the friction disc, noting which way round the friction disc is fitted (see illustration).

Inspection

Note: *Due to the amount of work necessary to remove and refit clutch components, it is usually considered good practice to renew the clutch friction disc, pressure plate assembly and release bearing as a matched set, even if only one of these is actually worn enough to require renewal. It is worth considering the renewal of the clutch components on a preventative basis if the engine and/or transmission have been removed for some other reason.*

5 When cleaning clutch components, first read the warning at the beginning of this Section. Remove the dust only as described – working with dampened cloths will help to keep dust levels to a minimum. Wherever possible, work in a well-ventilated atmosphere.

6.2 Mark the position of the pressure plate on the flywheel

6.3b . . . using a homemade tool to prevent the flywheel from turning

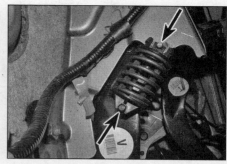

5.9 Make sure the return spring is located on the pegs correctly

6 Check the friction disc facings for signs of wear, damage or oil contamination. If the friction material is cracked, burnt, scored or damaged, or if it is contaminated with oil or grease (shown by shiny black patches), the friction disc must be renewed.

7 If the friction material is still serviceable, check that the centre boss splines are unworn, that the torsion springs are in good condition and securely fastened, and that all the rivets are tightly fastened. If excessive wear or damage is found, the friction disc must be renewed.

8 If the friction material is fouled with oil, this must be due to an oil leak from the crankshaft left-hand oil seal, from the sump-to-cylinder block joint, or from the transmission input shaft. Renew the seal or repair the joint, as appropriate, as described in Chapter 2A, Chapter 2B or Chapter 2C, before installing the new friction disc, or the new disc will quickly go the same way.

6.3a Undo the pressure plate bolts. . .

6.4 Remove the pressure plate complete with friction disc

6.13 Markings on friction disc – P.P.SIDE (pressure plate side)

6.16a Using a special tool to centralise the friction disc. . .

6.16b . . . on the pressure plate

6.17a Align the pressure plate on the dowels on the flywheel

6.17b Tighten the bolts to the correct torque setting

9 Check the pressure plate assembly for obvious signs of wear or damage; shake it to check for loose rivets, or worn or damaged fulcrum rings. Check that the drive straps securing the pressure plate to the cover do not show signs (such as a deep yellow or blue discoloration) of overheating. If the diaphragm spring is worn or damaged, or if its pressure is in any way suspect, the pressure plate assembly should be renewed.

10 Examine the machined bearing surfaces of the pressure plate and of the flywheel; they should be clean, completely flat, and free from scratches or scoring. If either is discoloured from excessive heat, or shows signs of cracks, it should be renewed; however, minor damage of this nature can sometimes be polished away using emery paper.

11 Check that the release bearing contact surface rotates smoothly and easily, with no sign of noise or roughness, and that the surface itself is smooth and unworn, with no signs of cracks, pitting or scoring. If there is any doubt about its condition, the bearing must be renewed

Refitting

12 On reassembly, ensure that the bearing surfaces of the flywheel and pressure plate are completely clean, smooth, and free from oil or grease. Use solvent to remove any protective grease from new components.

13 Fit the friction disc/plate so that its spring hub assembly faces away from the flywheel; there may also be a marking showing which way round the plate is to be refitted (see illustration).

14 Refit the pressure plate assembly, aligning the marks made on dismantling (if the original pressure plate is re-used), and locating the pressure plate on its locating dowels. Fit the pressure plate bolts, but tighten them only finger-tight so that the friction disc can still be moved.

15 The friction disc must now be centralised, so that when the transmission is refitted, its input shaft will pass through the splines at the centre of the friction disc.

16 Centralisation can be achieved by passing a screwdriver or other long bar through the friction disc, and into the hole in the crankshaft. The friction disc can then be moved around until it is centred on the crankshaft hole. Alternatively, a clutch-aligning tool can be used to eliminate the guesswork; these can be obtained from most accessory shops (see illustrations).

17 When the friction disc is centralised, tighten the pressure plate bolts evenly and in

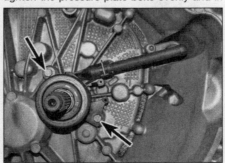

7.2 Undo the concentric slave cylinder (CSC) mounting bolts

a diagonal sequence to the specified torque setting (see illustrations). Lock the ring gear to prevent the flywheel from turning, using the method employed when dismantling.

18 Apply a thin smear of high melting-point grease to the splines of the friction disc and the transmission input shaft.

19 Refit the transmission as described in Chapter 7 Section 6.

---

7 Clutch release mechanism
– removal, inspection and refitting

Warning: Dust created by clutch wear and deposited on the clutch components may contain harmful particles, which may be a health hazard. DO NOT blow it out with compressed air, or inhale any of it. DO NOT use petrol or petroleum-based solvents to clean off the dust. Brake system cleaner or methylated spirit should be used to flush the dust into a suitable receptacle. After the clutch components are wiped clean with rags, dispose of the contaminated rags and cleaner in a sealed, marked container.

Removal

1 Unless the complete engine/transmission is to be removed from the car, and separated for major overhaul, the clutch release mechanism can be reached by removing the transmission as described in Chapter 7 Section 6.

2 With the transmission removed, undo the two mounting bolts from inside the bellhousing (see illustration).

3 Withdraw the concentric slave cylinder/ release bearing by sliding it over the transmission input shaft. Withdraw it complete with plastic fluid pipe out from the bellhousing.

4 If required, withdraw the securing clip from the plastic fluid pipe (see illustration), to disconnect it from the clutch slave cylinder/ release bearing.

Inspection

5 Check the release mechanism, renewing any component, which is worn or damaged. Carefully check all bearing surfaces and points of contact.

6 When checking the release bearing itself, note that it is often considered worthwhile to renew it as a matter of course, given that a significant amount of work is required to gain access to it. Check that the contact surface rotates smoothly and easily, with no sign of noise or roughness. Also check that the surface itself is smooth and unworn, with no signs of cracks, pitting or scoring. If there is any doubt about its condition, the bearing must be renewed.

Refitting

7 Slide the concentric slave cylinder/release bearing over the transmission input shaft and tighten the retaining bolts to the specified torque setting.
8 Refit the transmission as described in Chapter 7 Section 6.

8 Driveshafts – removal and refitting

Note: *A new split-pin and driveshaft inner joint circlip must be used on refitting.*

Removal

1 Firmly apply the handbrake, and then jack up the front of the vehicle and support it securely on axle stands (see *Jacking and vehicle support*). Remove the appropriate roadwheel(s).
2 To reduce spillage when the inner end of the driveshaft is withdrawn from the transmission, drain the transmission oil/fluid, as described in Chapter 7 Section 2.
3 Remove the split-pin from the outer end of the driveshaft, and remove the locking cap. Discard the split-pin – a new one must be used on refitting **(see illustrations)**.
4 The front hub must now be held stationary in order to loosen the driveshaft nut. Ideally, the hub should be held by a suitable tool bolted into place using two of the roadwheel nuts **(see illustration)**. Using a socket and extension bar, slacken and remove the driveshaft retaining nut.
5 Undo the retaining nut and disconnect the track rod end from the hub carrier **(see illustration)**. Refer to Chapter 10 Section 16, for further information.
6 Undo the retaining nut and disconnect the

upper drop link ball joint from the front strut **(see illustration)**. Refer to Chapter 10 Section 6, for further information.
7 Undo the retaining nut and withdraw the bolt from the lower ball joint. Using a wedge

shaped tool/chisel tap it into the slot in the hub assembly to release the lower ball joint. Use a length of bar, chain to lever the lower arm downwards and disconnect the lower ball joint from the hub carrier **(see illustrations)**.

7.4 Retaining clip securing plastic pipe to the slave cylinder

8.3a Remove the split pin. . .

8.3b . . .and remove the locking cap

8.4 Using fabricated tool to hold the front hub stationary

8.5 Disconnect the track rod end

8.6 Disconnect the drop link upper ball joint

8.7a Remove the lower ball joint retaining bolt. . .

8.7b . . . insert chisel to release ball joint. . .

8.7c . . . and lever the lower arm away from the hub

8.8 Tap the end of the driveshaft to release it from hub

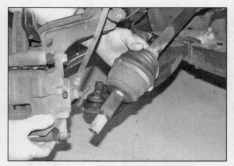

8.9 Withdraw the driveshaft from the hub

8.12a Lever the driveshaft to release the spring clip. . .

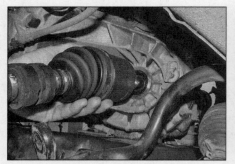

8.12b . . . and remove the driveshaft from the transmission

8.14a Undo the two retaining bolts. . .

8.14b . . . and remove the retaining plate

8 If the shaft is a tight fit in the splines in the hub, temporarily refit the driveshaft nut to the end of the driveshaft, to prevent damage to the driveshaft threads. Using a soft-faced mallet, or a piece of wood, then carefully tap the driveshaft to free it from the hub carrier **(see illustration)**. If required, a suitable puller can be used to force the end of the shaft from the hub.

9 Once the driveshaft is free, remove the driveshaft nut, turn the hub carrier outwards, and fully withdraw the outer end of the driveshaft from the hub **(see illustration)**. On models with ABS, take care not to strain the ABS wheel sensor wiring during this operation.

10 Proceed as follows, according to type.

Left-hand driveshaft

11 If the transmission oil has not been drained (see paragraph 2), have a clean container ready to catch the transmission oil/fluid as the driveshaft is withdrawn.

12 The driveshaft is held into the transmission by a spring circlip, which can take some effort to release. Using a suitable lever, on the shoulder of the driveshaft inner joint, prise it out from the transmission, and then remove the driveshaft **(see illustrations)**.

Right-hand driveshaft

13 If the transmission oil has not been drained (see paragraph 2), have a clean container ready to catch the transmission oil/fluid as the driveshaft is withdrawn.

14 There is a support bearing, which is bolted to the rear of the cylinder block. Undo the two bolts and remove the retaining plate from the bearing housing **(see illustrations)**. Note its fitted position for refitting, as there is a cut away in the retaining plate.

Note: *Nissan recommends that this retaining plate be renewed each time it is removed.*

15 Using a suitable drift, on the shoulder of

the driveshaft inner joint, carefully tap it out from the transmission, and then remove the driveshaft **(see illustration)**.

16 If the bearing is a tight fit in the housing, undo the retaining bolts and remove the bearing housing from the rear of the cylinder block, and remove the driveshaft complete with bearing housing from under the vehicle **(see illustrations)**.

Refitting

17 Before installing a driveshaft, examine the driveshaft oil seal in the transmission for signs of damage or deterioration and, if necessary, renew it, referring to Chapter 7 Section 4 for further information (it is advisable to renew the seal as a matter of course).

18 Thoroughly clean the driveshaft splines, and the apertures in the transmission and hub assembly. Apply a thin film of grease to the oil seal lips, and to the driveshaft splines

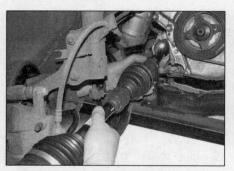

8.15 Withdraw the right-hand driveshaft from the vehicle

8.16a Undo the bearing housing mounting bolts. . .

8.16b . . . and remove it with the driveshaft

8.20 Apply a small amount of oil to the end of the driveshaft

8.25 Reconnect the lower arm ball joint to the hub

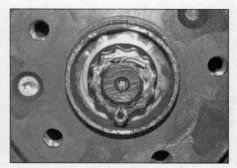

8.31 Fit a new split pin to the end of the driveshaft

and shoulders. Check that all driveshaft gaiter clips are securely fastened.

19 Note that the circlip at the inner end of the driveshaft **must** be renewed on refitting.

20 When refitting a driveshaft, great care must be taken to prevent damage to the driveshaft oil seals. Nissan specify the use of special tools, which guide the shafts through the seal lips on refitting. Provided that the seal lips and the shaft ends are lightly greased/oiled **(see illustration)**, and that care is taken on refitting, these tools should not be necessary.

21 Insert the inner end of the driveshaft into the transmission, taking care not to damage the oil seal.

22 Grasp the inner joint body firmly, and check that the circlip is correctly engaged by attempting to pull the driveshaft from the transmission.

23 Apply a thin film of grease to the outer driveshaft joint splines, then engage the outer end of the driveshaft with the hub, ensuring that the splines engage correctly.

24 Refit the new driveshaft nut, but do not tighten the nut fully at this stage.

25 Reconnect the lower ball joint to the bottom of the hub carrier **(see illustration)**. If required, use a length of bar, chain and a block of wood to lever the lower arm downwards, as described on removal. Fit new bolt and nut to the lower ball joint and tighten to the specified torque setting.

26 On right-hand driveshafts secure the support bearing back into position, on the rear of the cylinder block and tighten the bolts to the specified torque setting, where given.

Make sure the retaining plate is positioned back into place on the housing, as noted on removal.

27 Reconnect the lower drop link ball joint to the anti-roll bar and tighten the retaining nut. Refer to Chapter 10 Section 6, for further information.

28 Reconnect the track rod end to the hub carrier and tighten the retaining nut. Refer to Chapter 10 Section 16, for further information.

29 If removed, refit the ABS wheel sensor and tighten its retaining bolt securely.

30 Hold the front hub stationary as during removal, then tighten the new driveshaft nut to the specified torque.

31 Fit a new split-pin and bend over the split-pin legs **(see illustration)**.

32 Refit the roadwheel(s), and lower the vehicle to the ground.

33 Refill the transmission with oil/fluid as described in Chapter 7 Section 2.

9.2a Remove the outer. . .

9.2b . . . and inner retaining clips

9 Driveshaft rubber gaiters – renewal

Outer joint

1 Remove the driveshaft (see Section 8.

2 Release the rubber gaiter retaining clips **(see illustrations)**. If required, cut through them using a junior hacksaw. Spread the clips and remove them from the gaiter.

3 Pull the gaiter back to expose the outer constant velocity joint then scoop out the excess grease **(see illustration)**.

4 If the original joint is to be re-used, make alignment marks between the joint and the driveshaft, so that it is refitted in the same position.

5 Using a brass drift and hammer, sharply strike the centre part of the outer joint to drive it off the end of the shaft **(see illustrations)**. The joint

9.3 Pull back the gaiter and clean out the old grease

9.5a Using a soft metal drift. . .

9.5b . . . to release the outer joint

9.6a Remove the old spring clip. . .

9.6b . . . and slide the old gaiter off the shaft

9.10 Driveshaft joint and gaiter kit

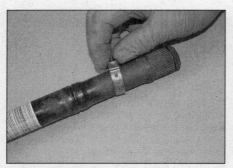

9.11a Fit the new inner retaining clip on the shaft. . .

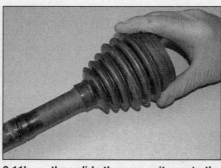

9.11b . . . then slide the new gaiter onto the shaft

9.12 Fit the new spring clip to its groove in the driveshaft splines

9.13 Squeeze some of the grease inside the joint

9.14a Locate the outer joint on the splines, and slide it into position. . .

9.14b . . . making sure the spring clip is located correctly

9.15 Tap the joint into place, check that the joint is secured by the spring clip

is retained on the driveshaft by a circlip, and striking the joint in this manner forces the circlip into its groove, so allowing the joint to slide off.
6 Remove the circlip from the groove in the driveshaft splines, and discard it, then slide the old gaiter from the end of the shaft **(see illustrations)**. A new circlip must be fitted on reassembly.
7 With the constant velocity joint removed from the driveshaft, thoroughly clean the joint using paraffin, or a suitable solvent, and dry it thoroughly. Carry out a visual inspection of the joint.
8 Move the inner splined driving member from side-to-side, to expose each ball in turn at the top of its track. Examine the balls for cracks, flat spots, or signs of surface pitting.
9 Inspect the ball tracks on the inner and outer members. If the tracks have widened, the balls will no longer be a tight fit. At the same time, check the ball cage windows for wear or cracking between the windows.
10 If any of the constant velocity joint components are found to be worn or damaged, it will be necessary to renew the complete joint assembly, as the internal parts are not available separately. If the joint is in satisfactory condition, obtain a repair kit consisting of a new gaiter, circlips, retaining clips **(see illustration)**, and use the correct type of grease.
11 Commence reassembly by sliding the smaller gaiter securing clip onto the driveshaft, followed by the gaiter **(see illustrations)**.
12 Fit a new joint retaining circlip to the groove in the end of the shaft **(see illustration)**.
13 Before fitting the outer joint, squeeze half of the grease supplied with the kit into the outer joint **(see illustration)**.
14 Fit the outer joint to the shaft, and engage it with the shaft splines **(see illustrations)**. If the original joint is re-used, align the previously made marks on the joint and the end of the driveshaft.
15 Take care not to damage the joint threaded end, and use a copper mallet to tap the joint onto the shaft until the circlip engages correctly behind the joint cage **(see illustration)**.

9.16 Pack the joint with grease, working it into the ball tracks while twisting the joint

9.17 Slide the gaiter into position over the outer joint

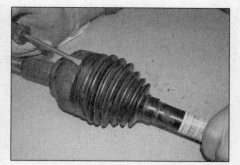

9.18a Using a screwdriver to displace the air inside the gaiter. . .

9.18b . . . measure the fitted position of the gaiter – see specifications

9.19a Slide the inner retaining clip into position. . .

9.19b . . .and secure the retaining clip with crimping pliers

16 Use the remainder of the grease to pack the joint with the correct amount of the specified grease (supplied with the gaiter kit), then twist the joint to ensure that all the recesses are filled **(see illustration)**.

17 Check that the smaller end of the gaiter is located in the driveshaft groove, and then slide the gaiter onto the outer joint **(see illustration)**.

18 Check that the gaiter does not swell or deform when fitted. Use a screwdriver to get rid of the air inside the gaiter, and then position the gaiter at the setting dimension given in the specifications **(see illustrations)**.

19 Slide the smaller securing clip over the gaiter, and secure it in place **(see illustrations)**.

20 Fit the new outer gaiter large securing clip, and secure it in place **(see illustration)**.

21 Refit the driveshaft (see Section 8).

Inner joint

22 Remove the driveshaft (see Section 8).

23 Release the rubber gaiter retaining clips **(see illustrations)**. If required, cut through them using a junior hacksaw. Slide the gaiter off the joint towards the middle of the driveshaft.

9.20 Secure the outer retaining clip with crimping pliers

24 If the original joint is to be re-used, make alignment marks between the joint body and the driveshaft **(see illustrations)**.

25 Withdraw the gaiter from the joint outer body and release the retaining clip from inside

9.23a Release the retaining clips from the gaiter. . .

9.23b . . . using a screwdriver to prise up the ends

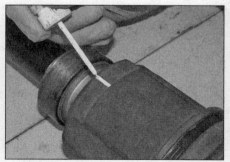

9.24a Mark the position of the inner joint. . .

9.24b . . . on the driveshaft

9.25a Pull back the gaiter and use a thin screwdriver. . .

9.25b . . . to remove the joint retaining clip

9.26a Make alignment marks on the tripod for refitting. . .

9.26b . . . then remove the circlip from the end of the shaft

9.27a Using a punch to. . .

9.27b . . . remove the tripod from the shaft. . .

the tripod joint. Wipe off the excess grease from the joint and slide the tripod joint out from the outer body (see illustrations).

26 If the original tripod joint is to be re-used, mark the relationship of the tripod joint and the driveshaft, then using circlip pliers, remove the circlip securing the tripod joint to the end of the shaft (see illustrations). Discard the circlip – a new one should be used on refitting.

27 Withdraw the tripod joint and the gaiter from the end of the shaft (see illustrations).
28 Thoroughly clean the constant velocity joint components and the end of the driveshaft using paraffin, or a suitable solvent, and dry thoroughly. Carry out a visual inspection of the joint. If any of the joint components are worn, the tripod joint assembly or the joint body can be renewed separately as complete units, but no other spare parts are available. If the joint is in satisfactory condition, obtain a repair kit consisting of a new gaiter, circlips, retaining clips (see illustration), and use the correct type of grease.
29 Commence reassembly by sliding the smaller gaiter securing clip onto the driveshaft, followed by the gaiter (see illustrations).
30 Refit the tripod joint, aligning the marks made previously if the original one is being used (see illustration).
31 Fit a new circlip to secure the tripod joint to the driveshaft (see illustration).

9.27c . . . then withdraw the old gaiter from the shaft

9.28 Driveshaft joint and gaiter kit

9.29a Fit the new inner retaining clip on the shaft. . .

9.29b . . . then slide the new gaiter onto the shaft

9.30 Using a soft metal drift to refit the tripod joint, noting the alignment marks

9.31 Fit the new circlip to the groove in the end of the shaft

9.32 Fit the new retaining clip around the shaft

9.34 Slide the joint back into position, noting the alignment marks

9.35a Fit the retaining clip back into the body. . .

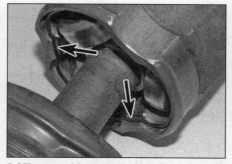

9.35b . . . making sure it locates securely in the groove

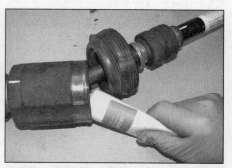

9.36 Pack the joint with grease, working it into the joint while twisting the shaft

32 Peel back the rubber gaiter and fit the new tripod joint retaining clip around the shaft **(see illustration)**.

33 Before fitting the tripod joint into the outer body, squeeze half of the grease supplied with the kit into the outer body.

34 Fit the joint body over the tripod joint. If the original body is being refitted, align the marks made between the body and the driveshaft before removal **(see illustration)**.

35 Slide the tripod joint into the outer body and fit the new securing clip into the grooves on the inner side of the outer body **(see illustrations)**.

36 Use the remainder of the grease to pack the joint with the correct amount of the specified grease (supplied with the gaiter kit), and then twist the joint to ensure that all the recesses are filled **(see illustration)**.

37 Check that the smaller end of the gaiter is located in the driveshaft groove, and then

slide the gaiter onto the outer body **(see illustration)**.

38 Check that the gaiter does not swell or deform when fitted. Use a screwdriver to get rid of the air inside the gaiter, and then

9.37 Peel the gaiter back into position over the outer body

position the joint at the setting dimension given in the specifications **(see illustrations)**.

39 Fit the new gaiter large securing clip, and tighten it in place **(see illustrations)**.

40 Locate the smaller gaiter securing clip

9.38a Using a screwdriver to displace the air inside the gaiter. . .

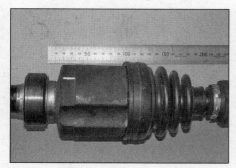

9.38b . . . measure the fitted position of the gaiter – see specifications

9.39a Slide the retaining clips into position. . .

9.39b . . .and secure them into position

on the end of the gaiter, and secure it as described previously **(see illustration)**.
41 Refit the driveshaft (see Section 8).

10 Driveshaft – inspection and overhaul

1 If any of the checks described in Chapter 1A Section 19 reveals wear in any driveshaft joint, first remove the roadwheel trim or centre cap (as appropriate).
2 Check that the driveshaft nut is correctly tightened; if in doubt, remove the split-pin. Check that the nut is tightened to the specified torque, and then refit a new split-pin. Refit the roadwheel trim or centre cap (as applicable), and repeat the check on the remaining driveshaft nut.
3 Road test the vehicle, and listen for a metallic clicking from the front as the vehicle

9.40 Make sure the gaiter clips are secure

is driven slowly in a circle on full-lock. If a clicking noise is heard, this indicates wear in the outer constant velocity joint.
4 If vibration, consistent with roadspeed, is felt through the car when accelerating, there

is a possibility of wear in the inner constant velocity joints.
5 To check the joints for wear, remove the driveshafts, then dismantle them as described in Section 9. If any wear or free play is found, the relevant joint, or joint components must be renewed.

Right-hand front driveshaft bearing

6 Remove the right-hand front driveshaft as described in Section 8.
7 If the bearing housing was removed with the driveshaft, the shaft will need to be carefully pressed from the housing **(see illustration)**.
8 Note the fitted position of the metal dust cap, and then remove it from the inner end of the driveshaft **(see illustration)**.
9 Remove the metal shield from the bearing, and then using circlip pliers, remove the circlip from the driveshaft **(see illustrations)**.
10 Using a long puller withdraw the bearing from the driveshaft **(see illustration)**.
11 Fit the new bearing onto the driveshaft and carefully tap it into position on the shaft.
12 Fit the new circlip making sure it is located in the groove in the shaft **(see illustration)**.
13 Fit the new metal shield onto the driveshaft and carefully tap it into position on the shaft **(see illustration)**.
14 Fit the new metal dust cap onto the driveshaft and carefully tap it into the position noted on removal **(see illustration)**.
15 Where applicable bolt the bearing housing to the rear of the cylinder block, then refit the driveshaft as described in Section 8.

10.7 Using a press to remove the bearing housing

10.8 Remove the dust cap, noting its fitted position

10.9a Remove the metal shield. . .

10.9b . . . then remove the circlip

10.10 Using a long puller to remove the bearing from the shaft

10.12 Fit a new circlip to secure the bearing

10.13 Refit the bearing shield

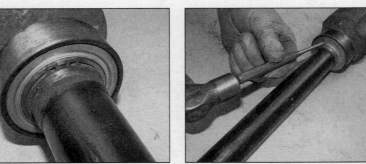
10.14 Refit the dust cap to the position noted on removal

Chapter 9
Braking system

Contents

Degrees of difficulty

Easy, suitable for novice with little experience	Fairly easy, suitable for beginner with some experience	Fairly difficult, suitable for competent DIY mechanic	Difficult, suitable for experienced DIY mechanic	Very difficult, suitable for expert DIY or professional

Specifications

General

System type . . . . Dual hydraulic circuit with Anti-lock braking system (ABS) fitted. Front ventilated disc brakes on all models. Solid rear disc brakes, with electric handbrake mechanism. Vacuum servo-assistance on all models.

Front brakes

Type . . . . Ventilated disc, with single-piston sliding caliper
Disc diameter . . . . 296 mm
Front brake disc:
   Standard thickness of brake disc . . . . 26.00 mm
   Wear limit thickness of brake disc . . . . 24.00 mm
Maximum disc run-out . . . . 0.035 mm
Minimum pad friction material thickness . . . . 2.0 mm

Rear disc brakes

Type . . . . Solid disc with single-piston sliding caliper
Disc diameter . . . . 292 mm
Rear brake disc:
   Standard thickness of brake disc . . . . 16.00 mm
   Wear limit thickness of brake disc . . . . 14.00 mm
Maximum disc run-out . . . . 0.070 mm
Minimum pad friction material thickness . . . . 1.5 mm

Brake pedal

Free height . . . . 175.9 to 185.9 mm

Pedal switch

Clearance (between pedal bracket and threads of switch) . . . . 0.20 to 1.96 mm

Brake master cylinder

Cylinder bore diameter . . . . 23.8 mm

Vacuum servo

Servo diameter . . . . 275 mm
Output rod length . . . . 30.5 mm
Input rod length . . . . 150.7 to 157.7 mm

Torque wrench settings

	Nm	lbf ft
ABS wheel sensor securing bolts	10	7
Brake bleed screw	8	6
Brake fluid hose union banjo bolts	18	13
Brake servo/pedal bracket securing nuts	15	11
Front brake caliper guide pin bolts	34	25
Front brake caliper mounting bracket bolts	150	112
Master cylinder securing nuts	15	11
Rear brake caliper guide pin bolts	35	26
Rear brake caliper mounting bracket bolts	84	62

1 General Information

1 The braking system is of the servo-assisted, dual-circuit hydraulic type. The arrangement of the hydraulic system is such that each circuit operates one front and one rear brake from a tandem master cylinder. Under normal circumstances, both circuits operate in unison. However, in the event of hydraulic failure in one circuit, full braking force will still be available at two diagonally opposite wheels.

2 All models are fitted with front and rear disc brakes. The front disc brakes are actuated by single-piston sliding type calipers, which ensure that equal pressure is applied to each disc pad. The rear disc brakes are also actuated by single-piston sliding type caliper, which incorporates the actuator for the electric handbrake.

3 To prevent the possibility of the rear wheels locking before the front wheels under heavy braking, pressure-regulating valves are incorporated in the hydraulic circuit to the rear brakes. All models have ABS fitted, there are valves located in a separate unit mounted in the left-hand rear corner of the engine compartment behind the air cleaner housing.

Note: *When servicing any part of the system, work carefully and methodically; also observe scrupulous cleanliness when overhauling any part of the hydraulic system. Always renew components (in axle sets, where applicable) if in doubt about their condition, and use only genuine Nissan parts, or at least those of known good quality. Note the warnings given in 'Safety first!' and at relevant points in this Chapter concerning the dangers of asbestos dust and hydraulic fluid.*

2 Troubleshooting

Probable cause	Corrective action
No brakes – pedal travels to floor	
1 Low fluid level	1 and 2 Low fluid level and air in the system are symptoms of another problem – a leak somewhere in the hydraulic system. Locate and repair the leak
2 Air in system	
3 Defective seals in master cylinder	3 Replace master cylinder
4 Fluid overheated and vaporised due to heavy braking	4 Bleed hydraulic system (temporary fix). Replace brake fluid (proper fix)
Brake pedal slowly travels to floor under braking or at a stop	
1 Defective seals in master cylinder	1 Replace master cylinder
2 Leak in a hose, line, caliper or wheel cylinder	2 Locate and repair leak
3 Air in hydraulic system	3 Bleed the system, inspect system for a leak
Brake pedal feels spongy when depressed	
1 Air in hydraulic system	1 Bleed the system, inspect system for a leak
2 Master cylinder or power booster loose	2 Tighten fasteners
3 Brake fluid overheated (beginning to boil)	3 Bleed the system (temporary fix). Replace the brake fluid (proper fix)
4 Deteriorated brake hoses (ballooning under pressure)	4 Inspect hoses, replace as necessary (it's a good idea to replace all of them if one hose shows signs of deterioration)

Probable cause	Corrective action
Brake pedal feels hard when depressed and/or excessive effort required to stop vehicle	
1 Servo unit faulty	1 Replace servo unit
2 Engine not producing sufficient vacuum, or hose to servo clogged, collapsed or cracked	2 Check vacuum to servo with a vacuum gauge. Replace hose if cracked or clogged, repair engine if vacuum is extremely low
3 Brake linings contaminated by grease or brake fluid	3 Locate and repair source of contamination, replace brake pads or shoes
4 Brake linings glazed	4 Replace brake pads or shoes, check discs and drums for glazing, service as necessary
5 Caliper piston(s) or wheel cylinder(s) binding or seized	5 Replace calipers or wheel cylinders
6 Brakes wet	6 Apply pedal to boil-off water (this should only be a momentary problem)
7 Kinked, clogged or internally split brake hose or line	7 Inspect lines and hoses, replace as necessary
Excessive brake pedal travel (but will pump up)	
1 Drum brakes out of adjustment	1 Adjust brakes
2 Air in hydraulic system	2 Bleed system, inspect system for a leak
Excessive brake pedal travel (but will not pump up)	
1 Master cylinder pushrod misadjusted	1 Adjust pushrod
2 Master cylinder seals defective	2 Replace master cylinder
3 Brake linings worn out	3 Inspect brakes, replace pads and/or shoes
4 Hydraulic system leak	4 Locate and repair leak

Probable cause	Corrective action
Brake pedal doesn't return	
1 Brake pedal binding	1 Inspect pivot bushing and pushrod, repair or lubricate
2 Defective master cylinder	2 Replace master cylinder
Brake pedal pulsates during brake application	
1 Brake drums out-of-round	1 Have drums machined by an automotive machine shop
2 Excessive brake disc runout or disc surfaces out-of-parallel	2 Have discs machined by an automotive machine shop
3 Loose or worn wheel bearings	3 Adjust or replace wheel bearings
4 Loose wheel nuts	4 Tighten wheel nuts
Brakes slow to release	
1 Malfunctioning servo unit	1 Replace servo unit
2 Pedal linkage binding	2 Inspect pedal pivot bushing and pushrod, repair/lubricate
3 Malfunctioning proportioning valve	3 Replace proportioning valve
4 Sticking caliper or wheel cylinder	4 Repair or replace calipers or wheel cylinders
5 Kinked or internally split brake hose	5 Locate and replace faulty brake hose
Brakes grab (one or more wheels)	
1 Grease or brake fluid on brake lining	1 Locate and repair cause of contamination, replace lining
2 Brake lining glazed	2 Replace lining, deglaze disc or drum
Vehicle pulls to one side during braking	
1 Grease or brake fluid on brake lining	1 Locate and repair cause of contamination, replace lining
2 Brake lining glazed	2 Deglaze or replace lining, deglaze disc or drum
3 Restricted brake line or hose	3 Repair line or replace hose
4 Tyre pressures incorrect	4 Adjust tyre pressures
5 Caliper or wheel cylinder sticking	5 Repair or replace calipers or wheel cylinders
6 Wheels out of alignment	6 Have wheels aligned
7 Weak suspension spring	7 Replace springs
8 Weak or broken shock absorber	8 Replace shock absorbers
Brakes drag (indicated by sluggish engine performance or wheels being very hot after driving)	
1 Brake pedal pushrod incorrectly adjusted	1 Adjust pushrod
2 Master cylinder pushrod (between servo and master cylinder) incorrectly adjusted	2 Adjust pushrod
3 Obstructed compensating port in master cylinder	3 Replace master cylinder
4 Master cylinder piston seized in bore	4 Replace master cylinder
5 Contaminated fluid causing swollen seals throughout system	5 Flush system, replace all hydraulic components
6 Clogged brake lines or internally split brake hose(s)	6 Flush hydraulic system, replace defective hose(s)
7 Sticking caliper(s) or wheel cylinder(s)	7 Replace calipers or wheel cylinders
8 Parking brake not releasing	8 Inspect parking brake linkage and parking brake mechanism, repair as required
9 Improper shoe-to-drum clearance	9 Adjust brake shoes
10 Faulty proportioning valve	10 Replace proportioning valve

Probable cause	Corrective action
Brakes fade (due to excessive heat)	
1 Brake linings excessively worn or glazed	1 Deglaze or replace brake pads and/or shoes
2 Excessive use of brakes	2 Downshift into a lower gear, maintain a constant slower speed (going down hills)
3 Vehicle overloaded	3 Reduce load
4 Brake drums or discs worn too thin	4 Measure drum diameter and disc thickness, replace drums or discs as required
5 Contaminated brake fluid	5 Flush system, replace fluid
6 Brakes drag	6 Repair cause of dragging brakes
7 Driver resting foot on brake pedal	7 Don't ride the brakes
Brakes noisy (high-pitched squeal)	
1 Glazed lining	1 Deglaze or replace lining
2 Contaminated lining (brake fluid, grease, etc.)	2 Repair source of contamination, replace linings
3 Weak or broken brake shoe hold-down or return spring	3 Replace springs
4 Rivets securing lining to shoe or backing plate loose	4 Replace shoes or pads
5 Excessive dust buildup on brake linings	5 Wash brakes off with brake system cleaner
6 Brake drums worn too thin	6 Measure diameter of drums, replace if necessary
7 Wear indicator on disc brake pads contacting disc	7 Replace brake pads
8 Anti-squeal shims missing or installed improperly	8 Install shims correctly
Brakes noisy (scraping sound)	
1 Brake pads or shoes worn out; rivets, backing plate or brake	1 Replace linings, have discs and/or drums machined (or replace) shoe metal contacting disc or drum
Brakes chatter	
1 Worn brake lining	1 Inspect brakes, replace shoes or pads as necessary
2 Glazed or scored discs or drums	2 Deglaze discs or drums with sandpaper (if glazing is severe, machining will be required)
3 Drums or discs heat checked	3 Check discs and/or drums for hard spots, heat checking, etc. Have discs/drums machined or replace them
4 Disc runout or drum out-of-round excessive	4 Measure disc runout and/or drum out-of-round, have discs or drums machined or replace them
5 Loose or worn wheel bearings	5 Adjust or replace wheel bearings
6 Loose or bent brake backing plate (drum brakes)	6 Tighten or replace backing plate
7 Grooves worn in discs or drums	7 Have discs or drums machined, if within limits (if not, replace them)
8 Brake linings contaminated (brake fluid, grease, etc.)	8 Locate and repair source of contamination, replace pads or shoes
9 Excessive dust buildup on linings	9 Wash brakes with brake system cleaner
10 Surface finish on discs or drums too rough after machining	10 Have discs or drums properly machined (especially on vehicles with sliding calipers)
11 Brake pads or shoes glazed	11 Deglaze or replace brake pads or shoes

Probable cause	Corrective action	Probable cause	Corrective action
Brake pads or shoes click		**Brake warning light on instrument panel comes on (or stays on)**	
1 Shoe support pads on brake backing plate grooved or	1 Replace brake backing plate excessively worn	1 Low fluid level in master cylinder reservoir (reservoirs with fluid level sensor)	1 Add fluid, inspect system for leak, check the thickness of the brake pads and shoes
2 Brake pads loose in caliper	2 Loose pad retainers or anti-rattle clips	2 Failure in one half of the hydraulic system	2 Inspect hydraulic system for a leak
3 Also see items listed under Brakes chatter		3 Piston in pressure differential warning valve not centered	3 Center piston by bleeding one circuit or the other (close bleeder valve as soon as the light goes out)
Brakes make groaning noise at end of stop		4 Defective pressure differential valve or warning switch	4 Replace valve or switch
1 Brake pads and/or shoes worn out	1 Replace pads and/or shoes	5 Air in the hydraulic system	5 Bleed the system, check for leaks
2 Brake linings contaminated (brake fluid, grease, etc.)	2 Locate and repair cause of contamination, replace brake pads or shoes	6 Brake pads worn out (vehicles with electric wear sensors – small	6 Replace brake pads (and sensors) probes that fit into the brake pads and ground out on the disc when the pads get thin)
3 Brake linings glazed	3 Deglaze or replace brake pads or shoes	**Brakes do not self adjust**	
4 Excessive dust buildup on linings	4 Wash brakes with brake system cleaner	1 Defective caliper piston seals	1 Replace calipers. Also, possible contaminated fluid causing soft or swollen seals (flush system and fill with new fluid if in doubt)
5 Scored or heat-checked discs or drums	5 Inspect discs/drums, have machined if within limits (if not, replace discs or drums)	2 Corroded caliper piston(s)	2 Same as above
6 Broken or missing brake shoe attaching hardware	6 Inspect drum brakes, replace missing hardware	3 Adjuster screw frozen	3 Remove adjuster, disassemble, clean and lubricate with high-temperature grease
Rear brakes lock up under light brake application		4 Adjuster lever does not contact star wheel or is binding	4 Inspect drum brakes, assemble correctly or clean or replace parts as required
1 Tyre pressures too high	1 Adjust tyre pressures	5 Adjusters mixed up (installed on wrong wheels after brake job)	5 Reassemble correctly
2 Tyres excessively worn	2 Replace tyres	6 Adjuster cable broken or installed incorrectly (cable-type adjusters	6 Install new cable or assemble correctly
3 Defective proportioning valve	3 Replace proportioning valve		
Rapid brake lining wear			
1 Driver resting foot on brake pedal	1 Don't ride the brakes		
2 Surface finish on discs or drums too rough	2 Have discs or drums properly machined		
3 Also see Brakes drag			

3 Hydraulic system – bleeding

![warning triangle] **Warning: Brake hydraulic fluid is poisonous; wash off immediately and thoroughly in the case of skin contact, and seek immediate medical advice if any fluid is swallowed, or gets into the eyes. Certain types of hydraulic fluid are inflammable, and may ignite when allowed into contact with hot components. When servicing any hydraulic system, it is safest to assume that the fluid IS inflammable, and to take precautions against the risk of fire as though it is petrol that is being handled. Hydraulic fluid is also an effective paint stripper, and will attack plastics; if any is spilt, it should be washed off immediately, using copious quantities of fresh water. Finally, it is hygroscopic (it absorbs moisture from the air) – old fluid may be contaminated and unfit for further use. When topping-up or renewing the fluid, always use the recommended type, and ensure that it comes from a freshly opened sealed container.**

General

1 The correct operation of any hydraulic system is only possible after removing all air from the components and circuit; and this is achieved by bleeding the system.
2 During the bleeding procedure, add only clean, unused brake hydraulic fluid of the recommended type; never re-use fluid that has already been bled from the system. Ensure that sufficient fluid is available before starting work.
3 If there is any possibility of incorrect fluid being already in the system, the brake components and circuit must be flushed completely with uncontaminated, correct fluid, and new seals should be fitted throughout the system.
4 If hydraulic fluid has been lost from the system, or air has entered because of a leak, ensure that the fault is cured before proceeding further.
5 Park the vehicle on level ground, switch off the engine and select first or reverse gear (or P), then chock the wheels and release the handbrake.
6 Check that all pipes and hoses are secure, unions tight and bleed screws closed.

Remove the dust caps (where applicable), and clean any dirt from around the bleed screws.
7 Unscrew the master cylinder reservoir cap, and top the master cylinder reservoir up to the MAX level line; refit the cap loosely. Remember to maintain the fluid level at least above the MIN level line throughout the procedure; otherwise there is a risk of further air entering the system.
8 There is a number of one-man, do-it-yourself brake bleeding kits currently available from motor accessory shops. It is recommended that one of these kits is used whenever possible, as they greatly simplify the bleeding operation, and also reduce the risk of expelled air and fluid being drawn back into the system. If such a kit is not available, the basic (two-man) method must be used, which is described in detail below.
9 If a kit is to be used, prepare the vehicle as described previously, and follow the kit manufacturer's instructions, as the procedure may vary slightly according to the type being used; generally, they are as outlined below in the relevant sub-section.
10 Whichever method is used, the same

sequence must be followed (paragraphs 11 and 12) to ensure that the removal of all air from the system.

Bleeding sequence

11 If the system has been only partially disconnected, and suitable precautions were taken to minimise fluid loss, it should be necessary to bleed only that part of the system (i.e. the primary or secondary circuit).

12 If the complete system is to be bled, then it should be done working in the following sequence:
a) *Left-hand rear wheel.*
b) *Right-hand rear wheel.*
c) *Left-hand front wheel.*
d) *Right-hand front wheel.*

Bleeding

Caution: On models equipped with ABS, switch off the ignition and disconnect the battery negative terminal (refer to 'Disconnecting the battery' in Chapter 5 Section 4), before carrying out the bleeding procedure.

Basic (two-man) method

13 Collect a clean glass jar, a suitable length of plastic or rubber tubing which is a tight fit over the bleed screw, and a ring spanner to fit the screw. The help of an assistant will also be required.

14 Remove the dust cap from the first screw in the sequence. Fit a suitable spanner and tube to the screw, place the other end of the tube in the jar, and pour in sufficient fluid to cover the end of the tube **(see illustrations)**.

15 Ensure that the master cylinder reservoir fluid level is maintained at least above the MIN level line throughout the procedure.

16 Have the assistant fully depress the brake pedal several times to build-up pressure, and then maintain it on the final down stroke.

17 While pedal pressure is maintained, unscrew the bleed screw (approximately one turn) and allow the compressed fluid and air to flow into the jar. The assistant should maintain pedal pressure, following the pedal down to the floor, and should not release the pedal until instructed to do so. When the flow stops, tighten the bleed screw again, have the assistant release the pedal slowly, and recheck the reservoir fluid level.

18 Repeat the steps given in paragraphs 16 and 17 until the fluid emerging from the bleed screw is free from air bubbles. If the master cylinder has been drained and refilled, and air is being bled from the first screw in the sequence, allow approximately five seconds between cycles for the master cylinder passages to refill.

19 When no more air bubbles appear, tighten the bleed screw securely, remove the tube and spanner, and refit the dust cap. Do not over tighten the bleed screw.

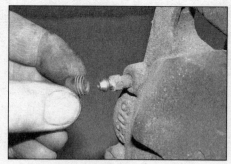

3.14a Remove the dust cap

3.14b Connect the bleed kit to the bleed screw

20 Repeat the procedure on the remaining screws in the sequence, until all air is removed from the system, and the brake pedal feels firm again.

Using a one-way valve kit

21 As their name implies, these kits consist of a length of tubing with a one-way valve fitted, to prevent expelled air and fluid being drawn back into the system; some kits include a translucent container, which can be positioned so that the air bubbles can be more easily seen flowing from the end of the tube.

22 The kit is connected to the bleed screw, which is then opened. The user returns to the driver's seat, depresses the brake pedal with a smooth, steady stroke, and slowly releases it; this is repeated until the expelled fluid is clear of air bubbles.

23 Note that these kits simplify work so much that it is easy to forget the master cylinder reservoir fluid level; ensure that this is maintained at least above the MIN level line at all times.

Using a pressure-bleeding kit

24 These kits are usually operated by the reservoir of pressurised air contained in the spare tyre. However, note that it will probably be necessary to reduce the pressure to a lower level than normal; refer to the instructions supplied with the kit.

25 By connecting a pressurised, fluid-filled container to the master cylinder reservoir, bleeding can be carried out simply by opening each screw in turn (in the specified

4.1 Using a brake hose clamp

sequence), and allowing the fluid to flow out until no more air bubbles can be seen in the expelled fluid.

26 This method has the advantage that the large reservoir of fluid provides an additional safeguard against air being drawn into the system during bleeding.

27 Pressure-bleeding is particularly effective when bleeding 'difficult' systems, or when bleeding the complete system at the time of routine fluid renewal.

All methods

28 When bleeding is complete, and firm pedal feel is restored, wash off any spilt fluid, tighten the bleed screws securely, and refit their dust caps.

29 Check the hydraulic fluid level in the master cylinder reservoir, and top up if necessary.

30 Discard any hydraulic fluid that has been bled from the system; it will not be fit for re-use.

31 Check the feel of the brake pedal. If it feels at all spongy, air must still be present in the system, and further bleeding is required. Failure to bleed satisfactorily after a reasonable repetition of the bleeding procedure may be due to worn master cylinder seals.

4 Hydraulic pipes and hoses – renewal

Note: *Before starting work, refer to the note at the beginning of Section 3 concerning the dangers of hydraulic fluid.*

1 If any pipe or hose is to be renewed, minimise fluid loss by first removing the master cylinder reservoir cap, then tighten the cap down onto a piece of polythene to obtain an airtight seal. Alternatively, flexible hoses can be sealed, if required, using a proprietary brake hose clamp **(see illustration)** ; metal brake pipe unions should be plugged (if care is taken not to allow dirt into the system) or capped immediately they are disconnected. Place a wad of rag under any union that is to be disconnected, to catch any spilt fluid.

2 If a flexible hose is to be disconnected, unscrew the brake pipe union nut before

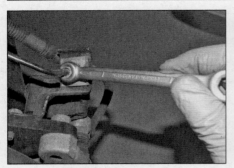

4.2a Slacken the union nut. . .

4.2b . . . and then remove the spring clip

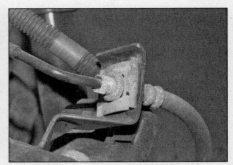

4.6 Make sure the spring clips are secure

removing the spring clip, which secures the hose to its mounting bracket **(see illustrations)**.

3 To unscrew the union nuts, it is preferable to obtain a brake pipe spanner of the correct size; these are available from most large motor accessory shops. Failing this, a close-fitting open-ended spanner will be required, though if the nuts are tight or corroded their flats may be rounded-off if the spanner slips. In such a case, a self-locking wrench is often the only way to unscrew a stubborn union, but it follows that the pipe and the damaged nuts must be renewed on reassembly. Always clean a union and surrounding area before disconnecting it. If disconnecting a component with more than one union, make a careful note of the connections before disturbing any of them.

4 If a brake pipe is to be renewed, it can be obtained, cut to length and with the union nuts and end flares in place, from Nissan dealers. All that is then necessary is to bend it to shape, following the line of the original, before fitting it to the vehicle. Alternatively, most motor accessory shops can make up brake pipes from kits, but this requires very careful measurement of the original, to ensure that the new one is of the correct length. The safest answer is usually to take the original to the shop as a pattern.

5 On refitting, do not over tighten the union nuts. It is not necessary to exercise brute force to obtain a sound joint.

6 Ensure that the pipes and hoses are correctly routed, with no kinks, and that they are secured in the clips or brackets provided **(see illustration)**. After fitting, remove the polythene from the reservoir, and bleed the hydraulic system as described in Section 3. When completed, wash off any spilt fluid, and then check carefully for any fluid leaks.

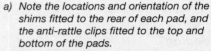

5 Front brake pads – renewal

 Warning: Renew BOTH sets of front brake pads at the same time – NEVER renew the pads on only one wheel, as uneven braking may result.

 Warning: Note that the dust created by wear of the pads contain materials, that may be a health hazard. Never blow it out with compressed air, and don't inhale any of it. An approved filtering mask should be worn when working on the brakes. DO NOT use petrol or petroleum-based solvents to clean brake parts; use brake cleaner or methylated spirit only.

1 Firmly apply the handbrake, and then jack up the front of the vehicle and support it securely on axle stands (see *Jacking and vehicle support*). Remove the front roadwheels.

2 Follow the accompanying photos **(see illustrations 5.2a to 5.2w)** for the actual pad replacement procedure. Be sure to stay in order and read the caption under each illustration, and note the following points:

a) *Note the locations and orientation of the shims fitted to the rear of each pad, and the anti-rattle clips fitted to the top and bottom of the pads.*

b) ***Do not*** *depress the brake pedal until the caliper is refitted and take care not to strain the brake fluid hose.*

c) *Working on one side of the vehicle, push the caliper piston into its bore slightly, by pulling the caliper outwards and then do the same on the other side.*

d) *When pushing the caliper piston back to accommodate new pads, keep a close eye on the fluid level in the reservoir.*

e) *Thoroughly clean the caliper guide surfaces, and apply a little brake assembly grease, where the ends of the pads contact.*

3 Check that the caliper body slides smoothly on the guide pins.

4 Repeat the procedure on the remaining front caliper.

5 With both sets of front brake pads refitted, depress the brake pedal repeatedly until the pads are pressed into firm contact with the brake disc, and normal pedal pressure is restored.

6 Refit the roadwheels, and lower the vehicle to the ground. Tighten the wheel bolts to the specified torque setting.

7 Finally, check the brake hydraulic fluid level as described in Chapter 1A Section 7.

Caution: Note that new pads will not give full braking efficiency until they have bedded-in. Be prepared for this, and avoid hard braking as far as possible for the first hundred miles or so after pad renewal.

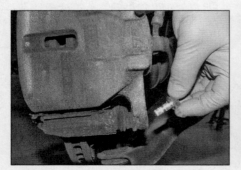

5.2a Remove the caliper lower guide pin bolt. . .

5.2b . . . then pivot the caliper upwards and away from the brake pads. . .

5.2c . . . and secure it to the suspension strut

5.2d Withdraw the inner. . .

5.2e . . . and outer brake pad from the caliper mounting bracket. . .

5.2f . . . then remove the lower. . .

5.2g . . . and upper anti-rattle shims, if required

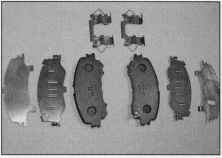

5.2h Remove the shim (where fitted) from the brake pad – noting their fitted position

5.2i Measure the thickness of the pads friction material – if friction material is less than 2mm, they will need to be renewed

5.2j Wire brush. . .

5.2k . . . and clean the caliper mounting bracket

5.2l Check the condition of the guide pins and gaiters

5.2m If new pads are to be fitted, use a retraction tool to push the piston back into the caliper. Keep an eye on the fluid level in the master cylinder reservoir!

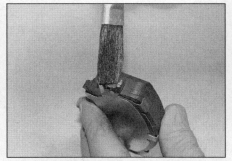

5.2n Use the special grease to lubricate the ends of the brake pads

5.2o Ensure the anti-rattle shims at the top. . .

5.2p . . . and bottom of the caliper mounting bracket are correctly fitted

5.2q Refit the inner. . .

5.2r . . . and outer brake pads with the friction material against the brake disc

5.2s Make sure the springs. . .

5.2t . . . are located in the shims correctly

5.2u Pivot the caliper down and over the pads. . .

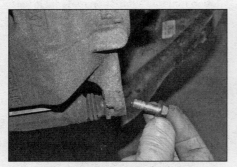
5.2v . . . refit the guide pin bolt. . .

5.2w . . . and tighten to the specified torque

6 Rear brake pads – renewal

Warning: Renew BOTH sets of rear brake pads at the same time – NEVER renew the pads on only one wheel, as uneven braking may result.

Warning: Before starting work, refer to the warning given at the beginning of Section 5, concerning the dangers of brake dust.

Warning: The handbrake on the rear wheels is electrically operated, before any work is carried out on the rear brakes the electric handbrake has to be immobilised by using diagnostic equipment (see illustration).

This will prevent the handbrake operating whilst working on the rear brakes. Never operate the handbrake switch or depress the brake pedal, whilst working on the rear brakes.

6.0 Disarm the electric handbrake before work commences on the rear brakes

1 Chock the front wheels, then jack up the rear of the car and support it on axle stands (see *Jacking and vehicle support*). Remove the rear roadwheels, and make sure the electric handbrake has been immobilised by using diagnostic equipment **(see illustration 6.0)**.

2 Follow the accompanying photos **(see illustrations 6.2a to 6.2p)** for the actual pad replacement procedure. Be sure to stay in order and read the caption under each illustration, and note the following points:

a) *Note the locations and orientation of the shims fitted to the rear of each pad, and the anti-rattle clips fitted to the top and bottom of the pads.*
b) **Do not** *depress the brake pedal until the caliper is refitted and take care not to strain the brake fluid hose.*
c) *Working on one side of the vehicle, push the caliper piston into its bore slightly, by pulling the caliper outwards and then do the same on the other side.*
d) *When pushing the caliper piston back to accommodate new pads, keep a close eye on the fluid level in the reservoir.*
e) *Thoroughly clean the caliper guide surfaces, and apply a little brake assembly grease, where the ends of the pads contact.*

3 Check that the caliper body slides smoothly on the guide pins.
4 Repeat the procedure on the remaining rear caliper.
5 With both sets of brake pads refitted and the calipers tightened in place, depress the

brake pedal repeatedly until the pads are pressed into firm contact with the brake disc, and normal pedal pressure is restored. Using the diagnostic equipment, as used before removal, the electric handbrake can now be reset **(see illustration 6.0)**.

6 Refit the roadwheels, and lower the vehicle to the ground.

7 Finally, check the brake hydraulic fluid level. *Caution: Note that new pads will not give full braking efficiency until they have bedded-in. Be prepared for this, and avoid hard braking as far as possible for the first hundred miles or so after pad renewal.*

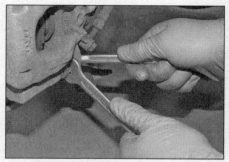
6.2a Remove the caliper lower guide pin bolt – using two spanners

6.2b Pivot the caliper upwards and secure it to the suspension

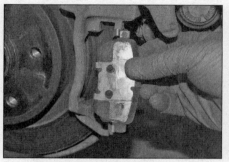
6.2c Withdraw the outer...

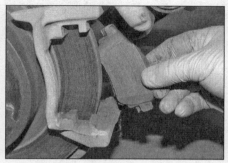
6.2d ...and inner brake pad from the caliper mounting bracket

6.2e Measure the thickness of the pads friction material – if friction material is less than 2mm, they will need to be renewed

6.2f Wire brush...

6.2g ...and clean the mounting bracket

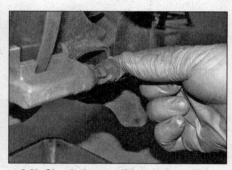
6.2h Check the condition of the rubber gaiters...

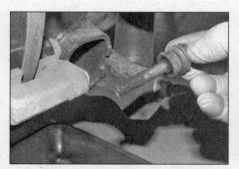
6.2i ...and the guide pins slide freely

6.2j If new pads are to be fitted, use a retraction tool to push the piston back into the caliper. Keep an eye on the fluid level in the master cylinder reservoir!

6.2k Apply a little brake grease to the mounting bracket...

6.2l . . . and to the ends of the pads

6.2m Refit the shims to the rear of the brake pads, as noted on removal

6.2n Pivot the caliper down and over the pads

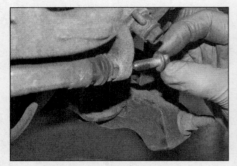

6.2o Using thread lock on the bolts. . .

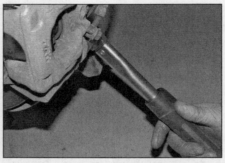

6.2p . . . tighten to the specified torque

7 Front brake disc –
inspection, removal and refitting

⚠️ **Warning: Before starting work, refer to the warning at the beginning of Section 5 concerning the dangers of asbestos dust.**

Note: *If either disc requires renewal, BOTH should be renewed at the same time, to ensure even and consistent braking. New brake pads should also be fitted.*

Inspection

1 Firmly apply the handbrake, and then jack up the front of the vehicle and support it securely on axle stands (see *Jacking and vehicle support*). Remove the appropriate front roadwheel.

2 Slowly rotate the brake disc so that the full area of both sides can be checked; remove the brake pads (see Section 5) if better access is required to the inboard surface. Light scoring is normal in the area swept by the brake pads, but if heavy scoring or cracks are found, the disc must be renewed.

3 It is normal to find a lip of rust and brake dust around the disc's perimeter; this can be scraped off if required. If, however, a lip has formed due to excessive wear of the brake pad swept area, then the disc's thickness must be measured using a micrometer **(see illustration)**. Take measurements at several places around the disc, at the inside and outside of the pad swept area; if the disc has worn at any point to the specified minimum thickness or less, the disc must be renewed.

4 If the disc is thought to be warped, it can be checked for run-out. Either use a dial gauge mounted on any convenient fixed point, while the disc is slowly rotated **(see illustration)**, or use feeler blades to measure (at several points all around the disc) the clearance between the disc and a fixed point, such as the caliper mounting bracket. If the measurements obtained are at the specified maximum or beyond, the disc is excessively warped, and must be renewed; however, it is worth checking first that the hub bearing is in good condition (Chapter 10 Section 2). Also try the effect of removing the disc and turning it through 180º, to reposition it on the hub; if the run-out is still excessive, the disc must be renewed.

5 Check the disc for cracks, especially around the wheel stud holes, and any other wear or damage, and renew if necessary.

Removal

6 If not already done, firmly apply the handbrake, and then jack up the front of the vehicle and support it securely on axle stands (see *Jacking and vehicle support*). Remove the appropriate front roadwheel.

7 Unscrew the two bolts securing the caliper mounting bracket to the hub carrier, then withdraw the caliper assembly, and suspend it using wire or cable tie **(see illustrations)**. Take care not to strain the brake fluid hose – if necessary release the hose from the securing clip(s).

8 If the original disc is to be refitted, mark the relationship between the disc and the hub, then undo the retaining screw and pull the disc from the hub assembly **(see illustrations)**.

7.3 Checking the thickness of the brake disc with a micrometer

7.4 Check the run out of the disc with a DTI gauge

7.7a Slacken the two caliper mounting bracket bolts. . .

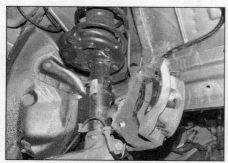

7.7b . . . and secure the assembly to the strut/spring assembly

7.8a undo the retaining screw. . .

7.8b . . .and remove the brake disc from the hub

Refitting

9 Ensure that the mating faces of the disc and the hub are clean and flat. If necessary, wipe the mating surfaces clean.

10 If the original disc is being refitted, align the marks made on the disc and hub before removal, then refit the disc and tighten the retaining screw.

11 If a new disc has been fitted, use a suitable solvent to wipe any preservative coating from the disc.

12 Refit the caliper, ensuring that the pads locate correctly over the disc. Then tighten the caliper mounting bracket securing bolts to the specified torque. Where applicable, refit the brake fluid hose to the clip(s).

13 Depress the brake pedal repeatedly until the pads are pressed into firm contact with the brake disc, and normal pedal pressure is restored.

14 Repeat the above procedure on the remaining brake, if a new disc was fitted.

15 Refit the roadwheel, and lower the vehicle to the ground. Tighten the wheel bolts to the specified torque setting.

8 Rear brake disc – inspection, removal and refitting

⚠ **Warning: Before starting work, refer to the warning at the beginning of Section 5 concerning the dangers of asbestos dust.**

Note: *If either disc requires renewal, BOTH should be renewed at the same time, to ensure even and consistent braking. New brake pads should also be fitted.*

⚠ **Warning: The handbrake on the rear wheels is electrically operated, before any work is carried out on the rear brakes the electric handbrake has to be immobilised by using diagnostic equipment (see illustration 6.0). This will prevent the handbrake operating whilst working on the rear brakes. Never operate the handbrake switch or depress the brake pedal, whilst working on the rear brakes.**

Inspection

1 Chock the front wheels then jack up the

rear of the vehicle and support it securely on axle stands (see *Jacking and vehicle support*). Remove the appropriate rear roadwheel.

2 Immobilise the electric handbrake, by using diagnostic equipment.

3 Proceed as described for the front disc in Section 7, but refer to Section 6 if the brake pads are to be removed.

Removal

4 If not already done, Chock the front wheels then jack up the rear of the vehicle and support it securely on axle stands (see *Jacking and vehicle support*). Remove the appropriate rear roadwheel and release the handbrake.

5 Unscrew the two bolts securing the caliper mounting bracket to the hub carrier **(see illustration)**. Withdraw the caliper assembly, and suspend it using wire or string. Take care not to strain the brake fluid hose – if necessary release the hose from the securing clip(s).

6 If the original disc is to be refitted, mark the relationship between the disc and the hub, then undo the retaining screw and pull the disc from the roadwheel studs **(see illustration)**.

Refitting

7 Ensure that the mating faces of the disc and the hub are clean and flat. If necessary, wipe the mating surfaces clean.

8 If the original disc is being refitted, align the marks made on the disc and hub before removal, then refit the disc.

9 If a new disc has been fitted, use a suitable solvent to wipe any preservative coating from the disc.

10 Refit the caliper, ensuring that the pads

8.5 Slacken the two caliper mounting bracket bolts

locate correctly over the disc. Then tighten the caliper mounting bracket securing bolts to the specified torque. Where applicable, refit the brake fluid hose to the clip(s).

11 Depress the brake pedal repeatedly until the pads are pressed into firm contact with the brake disc, and normal pedal pressure is restored. Using the diagnostic equipment, as used before removal, the electric handbrake can now be reset **(see illustration 6.0)**.

12 Repeat the above procedure on the remaining brake, if a new disc was fitted.

13 Refit the roadwheel, and lower the vehicle to the ground.

9 Front brake caliper – removal, overhaul and refitting

⚠ **Warning: Before starting work, refer to the note at the beginning of Section 3 concerning the dangers of hydraulic fluid, and to the warning at the beginning of Section 5 concerning the dangers of asbestos dust.**

Removal

1 Firmly apply the handbrake, and then jack up the front of the vehicle and support it securely on axle stands (see *Jacking and vehicle support*). Remove the appropriate front roadwheel.

2 To minimise fluid loss during the following operations, remove the master cylinder reservoir cap, then tighten it down onto a piece of polythene to obtain an airtight seal.

8.6 Undo the retaining screw

9.3 Unscrew the brake hose union bolt

9.6 Caliper mounting bracket bolts

Alternatively, use a brake hose clamp, a G-clamp or a similar tool to clamp the flexible hose running to the caliper **(see illustration 3.1)**.

3 Clean the area around the fluid hose union on the caliper, and then unscrew the hose union banjo bolt **(see illustration)**. Recover the two sealing washers noting that new washers will be required for refitting. Cover the open ends of the banjo and the caliper, to prevent dirt ingress.

4 Remove the brake pads as described in Section 5.

5 Unscrew the caliper upper guide pin bolt and withdraw the caliper from the mounting bracket.

6 If desired, the caliper mounting bracket can be unbolted from the hub carrier **(see illustration)**.

Overhaul

Note: *Before commencing work, check with your local dealer for the availability of parts, and ensure that the appropriate caliper overhaul kit is obtained.*

7 With the caliper on the bench, wipe away all traces of dust and dirt, but avoid inhaling the dust, as it is a health hazard.

8 Extract the caliper guide pins, if necessary by screwing the bolts into the pins, and pulling on the bolts to withdraw the pins. Peel off the rubber dust cover from each guide pin.

9 Place a small block of wood between the caliper body and the piston. Remove the piston, including the dust seal, by applying a jet of low-pressure compressed air, such as that from a tyre pump, to the fluid inlet port. *Caution: The piston may be ejected with some force. Only low pressure should be required, such as is generated by a foot pump.*

10 Peel the dust seal off the piston, and use a blunt instrument, such as a knitting needle, to extract the piston seal from the caliper cylinder bore.

11 Thoroughly clean all components, using only methylated spirit or clean hydraulic fluid. Never use mineral-based solvents such as petrol or paraffin, which will attack the hydraulic system rubber components.

12 The caliper piston seal and the dust seal, the guide pin dust covers, and the bleed

nipple dust cap, are only available as part of a seal kit. Since the manufacturers recommend that the piston seal and dust seal are renewed whenever they are disturbed, all of these components should be discarded, and new ones fitted on reassembly as a matter of course.

13 Carefully examine all parts of the caliper assembly, looking for signs of wear or damage. In particular, the cylinder bore and piston must be free from any signs of scratches, corrosion or wear. If there is any doubt about the condition of any part of the caliper, the relevant part should be renewed; note that if the caliper body or the mounting bracket are to be renewed, they are available only as part of the complete assembly.

14 The manufacturers recommend that minor scratches, rust, etc, may be polished away from the cylinder bore using fine emery paper, but the piston must be renewed to cure such defects. The piston surface is plated, and **must not** be polished with emery or similar abrasives.

15 Check that the threads in the caliper body and the mounting bracket are in good condition. Check that both guide pins are undamaged, and (when cleaned) a reasonably tight sliding fit in the mounting bracket bores.

16 Use compressed air to blow clear the fluid passages.

⚠️ *Warning: Wear eye protection when using compressed air.*

17 Before commencing reassembly, ensure that all components are spotlessly clean and dry.

18 Soak the new piston seal in clean hydraulic fluid, and fit it to the groove in the cylinder bore, using your fingers only (no tools) to manipulate it into place.

19 Fit the new dust seal inner lip to the cylinder groove, smear clean hydraulic fluid over the piston and caliper cylinder bore, and twist the piston into the dust seal. Press the piston squarely into the cylinder, then slide the dust seal outer lip into the groove in the piston.

20 Fit a new rubber dust cover to each guide pin, and apply a smear of brake grease to the guide pins before refitting them to their bores **(see illustration 5.10)**.

Refitting

21 Where applicable, refit the caliper mounting bracket to the hub carrier, and tighten the mounting bolts to the specified torque.

22 Place the caliper in position, refit the upper guide pin bolt, and tighten it to the specified torque.

23 Refit the brake pads as described in Section 5.

24 Check that the caliper slides smoothly on the mounting bracket.

25 Check that the hydraulic fluid hose is correctly routed, without being twisted, and then reconnect the union to the caliper, using two new sealing washers. Refit the union banjo bolt, and tighten to the specified torque.

26 Remove the polythene from the master cylinder reservoir cap, or remove the clamp from the fluid hose, as applicable.

27 Bleed the hydraulic fluid circuit as described in Section 3. Note that if no other part of the system has been disturbed, it should only be necessary to bleed the relevant front circuit.

28 Depress the brake pedal repeatedly to bring the pads into contact with the brake disc, and ensure that normal pedal pressure is restored.

29 Refit the roadwheel, and lower the vehicle to the ground. Tighten the wheel bolts to the specified torque setting.

10 Rear brake caliper – removal and refitting

⚠️ *Warning: Before starting work, refer to the note at the beginning of Section 3 concerning the dangers of hydraulic fluid, and to the warning at the beginning of Section 5 concerning the dangers materials.*

⚠️ *Warning: The handbrake on the rear wheels is electrically operated, before any work is carried out on the rear brakes the electric handbrake has to be immobilised by using diagnostic equipment (see illustration 6.0). This will prevent the handbrake operating whilst working on the rear brakes. Never operate the handbrake switch or depress the brake pedal, whilst working on the rear brakes.*

Removal

1 Chock the front wheels then jack up the rear of the vehicle and support it securely on axle stands (see *Jacking and vehicle support*). Remove the appropriate rear roadwheel.

2 To minimise fluid loss during the following operations, remove the master cylinder reservoir cap, then tighten it down onto a piece of polythene to obtain an airtight seal. Alternatively, use a brake hose clamp, a G-clamp or a similar tool to clamp the flexible hose running to the caliper **(see illustration)**.

10

10

10.2 To minimise fluid loss, fit a brake hose clamp to the flexible hose

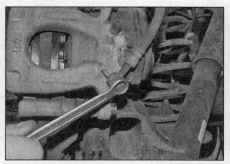
10.3 Unscrew the brake hose union bolt

10.5 Disconnect the wiring connector

3 Clean the area around the fluid hose union on the caliper, and then unscrew the hose union banjo bolt **(see illustration)**. Recover the two sealing washers noting that new washers will be required for refitting. Cover the open ends of the banjo and the caliper, to prevent dirt ingress.
4 Remove the brake pads as described in Section 6.
5 Disconnect the handbrake wiring connector from the top of the brake caliper **(see illustration)**.
6 Using two spanners to prevent the guide pin from turning, unscrew the upper guide pin bolt and remove the caliper from the mounting bracket **(see illustration)**.
7 If desired, the caliper mounting bracket can be unbolted from the hub carrier **(see illustration)**.

Refitting

8 Where applicable, refit the caliper mounting bracket to the hub carrier, and tighten the mounting bolts to the specified torque.
9 Place the caliper in position, refit the caliper upper guide pin bolt and tighten it to the specified torque.
10 Refit the brake pads as described in Section 6.
11 Check that the caliper slides smoothly on the mounting bracket.
12 Check that the brake fluid hose is correctly routed, without being twisted, and then reconnect the union to the caliper. Refit the union banjo bolt, using two new sealing washers, and then tighten to the specified torque.
13 Remove the polythene from the master cylinder reservoir cap, or remove the clamp from the fluid hose, as applicable.
14 Bleed the hydraulic fluid circuit as described in Section 3. Note that if no other part of the system has been disturbed, it should only be necessary to bleed the relevant rear circuit.
15 Depress the brake pedal repeatedly to bring the pads into contact with the brake disc, and ensure that normal pedal pressure is restored.
16 Refit the roadwheel, and lower the vehicle to the ground.

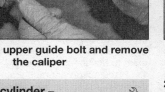
10.6 Undo the upper guide bolt and remove the caliper

10.7 Caliper mounting bracket bolts

11 Master cylinder – removal and refitting

Caution: Make sure the ignition switch is in the OFF position before disconnecting any braking system hydraulic union and do not switch it on until after the hydraulic system has been bled. Failure to do this could lead to air entering the ABS modulator unit. If air enters the modulator pump, it will prove very difficult to bleed the unit.
Note: *Before starting work, refer to the warning at the beginning of Section 3 concerning the dangers of hydraulic fluid.*

Removal

1 Disconnect the battery negative terminal (refer to *Disconnecting the battery* in Chapter 5 Section 4).

11.3 Disconnect the level sensor wiring plug

2 Remove the master cylinder fluid reservoir cap, and syphon the hydraulic fluid from the reservoir. Alternatively, open two bleed screws in the system (one in each of the dual circuit), and gently pump the brake pedal to expel the fluid through a tube connected to the bleed screws (see Section 3).

⚠️ *Warning: Do not syphon the fluid by mouth, as it is poisonous; use a syringe or an old antifreeze tester.*
3 Disconnect the wiring connector from the brake fluid level sender unit on the front of the reservoir **(see illustration)**. Unclip the wiring loom retaining clip from the lower front part of the reservoir.
4 On models with manual transmission, use a brake hose clamp, a G-clamp or a similar tool, to clamp the supply hose to the clutch master cylinder, and then disconnect the hose from the rear of the reservoir **(see illustrations)**. Plug or tape over the pipe end and reservoir

11.4a Fit a brake hose clamp to the clutch supply hose. . .

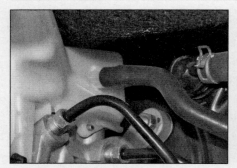
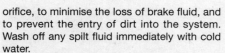

11.4b . . . and then disconnect the hose from the reservoir

11.5 Slacken the two brake fluid pipes

11.6 Remove the two nuts securing the master cylinder

orifice, to minimise the loss of brake fluid, and to prevent the entry of dirt into the system. Wash off any spilt fluid immediately with cold water.

5 Wipe clean the area around the brake pipe unions on the side of the master cylinder, and place absorbent rags beneath the pipe unions to catch any surplus fluid. Make a note of the correct fitted positions of the unions, then unscrew the union nuts and carefully withdraw the pipes **(see illustration)**. Plug or tape over the pipe ends and master cylinder orifices, to minimise the loss of brake fluid, and to prevent the entry of dirt into the system. Wash off any spilt fluid immediately with cold water.

6 Slacken and remove the two nuts securing the master cylinder to the vacuum servo unit **(see illustration)**, and then withdraw the master cylinder complete with reservoir from the engine compartment.

7 If required, remove the fixing at the lower

part of the reservoir, and then pull the reservoir upwards to release it from the master cylinder.

Refitting

8 Remove all traces of dirt from the master cylinder and servo unit mating surfaces.

9 If removed, refit the reservoir to the top of the master cylinder making sure the rubber seals are fitted correctly, and tighten the reservoir retaining screw.

10 Fit the master cylinder to the servo unit, ensuring that the servo unit pushrod enters the master cylinder bore centrally. Refit the master cylinder mounting nuts, and tighten them to the specified torque.

11 Place absorbent rags around and beneath the master cylinder, and then fill the reservoir with fresh hydraulic fluid.

12 Have an assistant slowly depress the brake pedal fully, and then hold it in the fully depressed position. Cover the outlet ports

on the master cylinder body with your fingers then have the assistant slowly release the brake pedal. Continue this procedure until the fluid emerging from the master cylinder is free from air bubbles. Take care to collect the expelled fluid in the rags and wash off any spilt fluid immediately with cold water.

13 When all air has been bled from the master cylinder, wipe clean the brake pipe unions, then refit them to the correct master cylinder ports, as noted before removal, and tighten the union nuts securely.

14 On manual transmission models, refit the clutch supply hose to the reservoir and remove the hose clamp. There should be no need to bleed the clutch system, but if required the clutch can be bled, as described in Chapter 8 Section 2.

15 Reconnect the wiring connector to the brake fluid level sender unit on the front of the reservoir, clip the wiring loom retaining clip back into position.

16 On completion, bleed the complete hydraulic system as described in Section 3.

12 Brake pedal –
removal, refitting
and adjustment

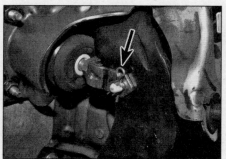

12.2a Remove the R-clip. . .

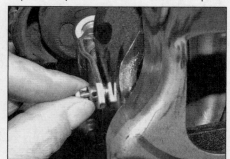

12.2b . . . squeeze the clips together. . .

Removal

1 To improve access, if not already done, remove the driver's side lower facia panel as described in Chapter 11 Section 25.

2 Working in the driver's foot well, remove the R clip from the end of the servo pushrod clevis pin, and then withdraw the clevis pin **(see illustrations)**.

3 Disconnect the wiring plug(s) from the stop-light switch(es) **(see illustration)**.

4 Disconnect the wiring plug from the accelerator pedal unit **(see illustration)**.

5 Unscrew the nuts securing the pedal bracket to the bulkhead (note that these nuts also secure the vacuum servo).

6 Withdraw the pedal/bracket assembly from the bulkhead and out through the footwell.

7 The brake pedal is integral with the bracket assembly, and cannot be renewed individually.

Refitting

8 Refitting is a reversal of removal (on

12.2c . . . and remove the clevis pin

12.3 Disconnect the switch wiring connector(s)

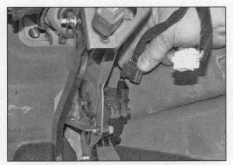

12.4 Disconnect the accelerator pedal wiring connector

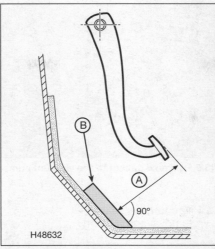

12.11 Check the height of the brake pedal (A) from the accelerator stopper plate (B)

13.1 Remove the engine upper trim cover – 1.5 litre engines

completion, check the pedal height as described later in this Section).

Adjustment

9 The pedal free height should be measured from the top face of the pedal to the floor reinforcement panel.
10 If desired, to improve access, remove the driver's side lower facia panel, as described in Chapter 11 Section 25. Lift the carpet to give the correct measurement.
11 Measure the pedal free height **(see illustration)**. Check the measured height against the value given in the Specifications.
12 If the height of the pedal requires adjustment, proceed as follows.
13 Loosen the locknut on the servo pushrod, and turn the pushrod as required until the specified height is achieved **(see illustration 14.8)**. Retighten the locknut on completion.

14 Check that the stop-lights go out when the pedal is released. If not, adjust the switch as described in Section 16.
15 On completion, refit the trim panel.

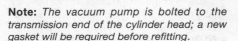

13 Vacuum pump (diesel engines) – removal, refitting and testing

Note: *The vacuum pump is bolted to the transmission end of the cylinder head; a new gasket will be required before refitting.*

Removal

1 On 1.5 litre diesel engines, remove the plastic trim cover from the top of the engine **(see illustration)**.
2 If required to give better access to the vacuum pump, remove the air intake hose and brackets **(see illustration)**.
3 Release the retaining clip and disconnect the vacuum hoses from the pump **(see illustrations)**.
4 Slacken and remove the mounting bolts securing the pump to the end of the cylinder head, then remove the pump **(see illustrations)**. Recover the gasket and discard, as a new one will be required for refitting.

Refitting

5 Ensure that the pump and cylinder head

13.2 Remove the air intake ducting – 1.6 litre engine shown

13.3a Disconnect the vacuum hose – 1.5 litre engine

13.3b Disconnect the small vacuum pipe. . .

13.3c . . . and the vacuum hose – 1.6 litre engine

13.4a Undo the two retaining bolts – 1.5 litre engine

13.4b Undo the three retaining bolts. . .

13.4c . . . and remove the vacuum pump –
1.6 litre engine

13.5 Fit a new gasket to the vacuum pump

13.6 Align the drive gear with the slot in the
camshaft

mating surfaces are clean and dry, and then fit the new gasket **(see illustration)**.

6 Manoeuvre the pump into position, aligning the drive gear with the slot in the end of the camshaft **(see illustration)**. Refit the pump mounting bolts and tighten securely.

7 Reconnect the vacuum hoses to the pump, making sure that the hoses are clipped into their relevant retaining clips.

8 If removed refit the air intake hoses and brackets, then refit the engine trim cover.

9 On completion, test the operation of the brakes as follows.

Testing

10 The operation of the braking system can be checked using a vacuum gauge.

11 Disconnect the vacuum hoes from the pump and connect the gauge to the pump using a length of hose.

12 Start the engine and allow it to idle, and then measure the vacuum created by the pump. As a guide after one minute, a minimum of approx. 500 mm Hg should be recorded.

13 If the vacuum registered is significantly less than this, it is likely that the pump is faulty. However seek the advice of a specialist, before condemning the pump.

14 Overhaul of the vacuum pump may not be possible; check the availability of spares.

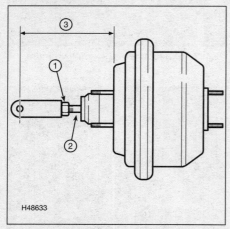

14.8 Servo input rod adjustment

1 Lock nut   3 Length of input
2 Input rod   rod

14 Vacuum servo unit – removal and refitting

Removal

1 Disconnect the battery negative terminal (refer to *Disconnecting the battery* in Chapter 5 Section 4).

2 Remove the brake master cylinder, with reference to Section 11.

3 Disconnect the vacuum hose from the top of the servo unit.

4 Remove the driver's side lower facia panel, as described in Chapter 11 Section 25.

5 Working in the driver's footwell, remove the spring clip from the end of the servo pushrod clevis pin, and then withdraw the clevis pin **(see illustrations 12.2a, 12.2b and 12.2c)**.

6 Again working in the driver's footwell, unscrew the four nuts securing the brake pedal mounting bracket to the servo studs.

7 Working in the engine compartment, withdraw the servo.

Refitting

8 Refitting is a reversal of removal, bearing in mind the following points:

a) *Before refitting the servo, check that the length of the pushrod is as specified (see Specifications), and adjust if necessary by loosening the locknut and turning the pushrod (see illustration).*

b) *Where applicable, tighten all fixings to the specified torque.*

c) *Refit the master cylinder as described in Section 11.*

d) *On completion, check the brake pedal height as described in Section 12.*

15 Vacuum servo unit check valve – removal, testing and refitting

Removal

1 The valve is located in the vacuum hose leading to the servo, and is secured to the body panel by a clip.

2 Release the valve from the securing clip. Take note of the direction of the arrow on the

valve body, which should point in the direction of the hose connected to the engine.

3 Release the retaining clips (where fitted), and disconnect the vacuum hoses from the valve, then withdraw the valve.

Testing

4 Examine the check valve for signs of damage, and renew if necessary. The valve may be tested by blowing through it in both directions. Air should flow through the valve in one direction only – when blown through from the servo unit end of the valve. Renew the valve if this is not the case.

Refitting

5 Refitting is a reversal of removal, ensuring that the arrow on the valve body and hoses, points towards the engine.

6 On completion, start the engine and check the hose connections to the valve for air leaks.

16 Stop-light switch – removal, adjustment and refitting

Removal

1 Remove the driver's side lower facia panel, as described in Chapter 11 Section 25.

2 Disconnect the switch wiring connector from the switch **(see illustration 12.3)**. Note on some models, there are two switches fitted to the brake pedal mounting bracket. One of the switches is to give information to the ECM for the cruise control.

16.3 Rotate the switch and remove it from
the mounting bracket

3 Twist the switch body and withdraw it from the pedal bracket **(see illustration)**.
4 When refitting the switch, hold the pedal upwards, and then push the switch back into the mounting bracket until the plunger on the end of the switch is fully pressed back into the switch **(see illustration)**. Once in place, turn the switch clockwise to lock it back in position in the mounting bracket.
5 Measure the pedal to switch clearance **(see illustration)**. Check the measurement against the value given in the Specifications.
6 Re-connect the wiring connector(s), and then check that the stop-lights are extinguished when the brake pedal is released, and illuminated within the first few millimeters of brake pedal travel.
7 If adjustment is required, remove the switch as described previously, and then when refitting the switch, fit it further inwards or outwards on the mounting bracket, until the pedal to switch clearance is correct and the lights operate correctly.
8 When completed, refit the driver's side lower facia panel, as described in Chapter 11 Section 25.

17 Anti-lock braking system (ABS) – general information and component renewal

General information

1 Anti-lock braking is available as standard equipment on the models covered by this manual. The system is fail-safe, and is fitted in addition to the conventional braking system, meaning that the vehicle retains conventional braking in the event of an ABS failure.
2 To prevent wheel locking, the system provides a means of modulating (varying) the hydraulic pressure in the braking circuits, to control the amount of braking effort at each wheel. To achieve this, sensors mounted at all four wheels monitor the rotational speeds of the wheels, and are thus able to detect when there is a risk of wheel locking (low rotational speed, relative to vehicle speed). Solenoid valves are positioned in the brake circuits to each wheel, and

16.4 Press the pedal down and fit the switch

the solenoid valves are incorporated in a modulator assembly, which is controlled by an electronic control unit. The electronic control unit controls the braking effort applied to each wheel, according to the information supplied by the wheel sensors.
3 Should an ABS fault develop, the system can only be satisfactorily tested using specialist diagnostic equipment available to a Nissan dealer. For safety reasons, owners are strongly advised against attempting to diagnose complex problems with the ABS using standard workshop equipment.

Component renewal
Wheel speed sensors

4 Jack up the front or rear of the vehicle (as applicable), and support it securely using axle stands (see *Jacking and vehicle support*). Remove the relevant roadwheel.

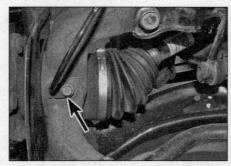
17.5a Location of front wheel speed sensor

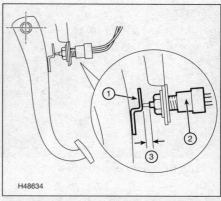

16.5 Check the pedal to switch clearance

1 Brake Pedal 3 Clearance
2 Switch

5 The front speed sensors are located on the rear side of each wheel hub carrier, whilst the rear sensors are located on the inner face of the stub axle assembly **(see illustrations)**.
6 For access to the front wheel sensor connector, release the retaining clips and remove the plastic inner trim from inside the wheel arch.
7 Trace the sensor wiring back to the connector, and separate the two halves of the wiring plug. Release the wiring from any retaining brackets/clips **(see illustrations)**.
8 Undo the retaining bolt and pull the sensor from the hub carrier/stub axle assembly

17.5b Location of rear wheel speed sensor

17.7a Disconnect the front sensor wiring connector...

17.7b ...and release the wiring from the support bracket

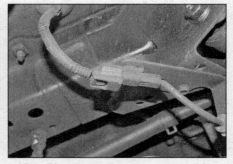
17.7c Disconnect the rear sensor wiring connector

17.8a Remove the front wheel sensor

17.8b Remove the rear wheel sensor

17.10 Location of ABS actuator

17.13 Release the wiring plug locking lever

17.14 Mark the location of the various brake pipes before disconnecting them from the actuator

17.15 Undo the actuator mounting nuts

(see illustrations). If the sensor is reluctant to move, apply releasing/penetrating fluid to the assembly, and leave it to soak for a few minutes before trying again. If the sensor still will not move, the hub carrier or rear brake disc must be removed, and the sensor driven from place.

9 Refitting is the reversal of removal, noting the following points:

a) Ensure the mating faces of the hub carrier/ stub axle assembly and sensor are clean and free from corrosion.

b) Apply a thin smear of anti-seize compound to mounting surfaces of the sensor and hub carrier/stub axle assembly.

c) Tighten the sensor retaining bolt to the specified torque.

Actuator (Modulator)

10 The actuator is located in the left-hand rear corner of the engine compartment (see illustration). Disconnect the battery negative lead (refer to *Disconnecting the battery* in Chapter 5 Section 4).

11 Open two bleed screws in the system (one in each of the dual circuit), and gently pump the brake pedal to expel the fluid through a tube connected to the bleed screws (see Section 3). Alternatively, have some caps handy to plug the open ends of the brake pipes once they are disconnected from the actuator.

12 Remove the air cleaner assembly as described in Chapter 4A Section 3 (petrol engines) or Chapter 4B Section 3 (diesel engines).

13 Release the locking clip, and then disconnect the wiring plug from the side of the actuator (see illustration).

14 Note their fitted locations, then undo the union nuts and disconnect the brake pipes from the ABS actuator (see illustration). If the system has not been drained, be prepared for fluid spillage. Plug the end of the pipes to prevent dirt ingress.

15 Undo the actuator mounting nuts (see illustration), and manoeuvre the actuator from the mounting bracket.

16 To refit the actuator, align the locating lug at the bottom of the unit with the corresponding hole in the mounting bracket, and then tighten the mounting nuts securely.

17 The remainder of refitting is a reversal of removal, bleeding the brake system as described in Section 3.

Chapter 10
Suspension and steering

Contents

Degrees of difficulty

Easy, suitable for novice with little experience	Fairly easy, suitable for beginner with some experience	Fairly difficult, suitable for competent DIY mechanic	Difficult, suitable for experienced DIY mechanic	Very difficult, suitable for expert DIY or professional 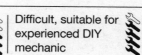

Specifications

Front suspension
Type . . . . Independent by MacPherson struts, with coil springs and integral shock absorbers, and lower arms. Anti-roll bar fitted to all models

Rear suspension
Type . . . . Rear suspension beam with coil springs and shock absorbers

Steering
Type . . . . Rack-and-pinion, electrically power-assisted.

Wheel bearings
Maximum endfloat at hub (front and rear) . . . . 0.00 mm

Roadwheels and tyres
See Chapter 1A or Chapter 1B.

Front wheel alignment
Front wheel toe setting . . . . 3.0 mm ± 1.0 mm toe-in

Torque wrench settings

	Nm	lbf ft
Front suspension		
Anti-roll bar drop link-to-anti-roll bar nuts	75	55
Anti-roll bar drop link-to-strut nuts	75	55
Anti-roll bar mounting bracket bolts	60	44
Subframe mounting bolts:		
Front bolts	160	119
Rear bolts	97	72
Hub carrier-to-suspension strut retaining bolt nut*	168	124
Lower arm balljoint-to-hub carrier bolt/nut*	92	68
Front hub nut (renew split pin)	255	188
Front wheel bearing hub assembly bolts	88	65
Lower arm front mounting-to-subframe bolts	138	102
Lower arm rear mounting-to-subframe bolt/nut*	97	72
Suspension strut damper rod top nut*	62	46
Suspension strut upper mounting bolts	16	11

*Use new nuts

Torque wrench settings (continued)

	Nm	lbf ft
Rear suspension		
Rear wheel bearing hub assembly bolts	88	65
Suspension damper upper mounting bolt/nut*	93	69
Suspension damper lower mounting bolt/nut*	98	72
Trailing arm-to-front mounting bracket bolt/nut*	184	136
Trailing arm front mounting bracket-to-body bolts	130	96
*Use new nuts		
Steering		
Steering column securing nuts.	17	13
Steering column upper universal joint clamp bolt	31	23
Steering column lower universal joint clamp bolt.	50	37
Steering gear mounting bracket bolts/nuts	147	109
Steering wheel securing bolt	44	32
Track rod end locknut.	88	65
Track rod end-to-steering arm/hub carrier nut.	34	25
Roadwheels		
Roadwheel nuts	113	83

1 General Information

Front suspension

1 The independent front suspension is of the MacPherson strut type, incorporating coil springs and integral telescopic shock absorbers. The upper ends of the MacPherson struts are connected to the bodyshell front suspension turrets; the lower ends are bolted to the hub carriers, which carry the wheel bearings, brake calipers and hub/disc assemblies. The hub carriers are located at their lower ends by transverse lower arms. A front anti-roll bar is fitted to all models.

Rear suspension

2 The rear suspension is of the semi-independent type, consisting of a torsion beam axle and trailing arms with coil springs and telescopic shock absorbers. The rear coil springs sit on top of the trailing arms and the shock absorbers are connected to the rear of the trailing arms.

Steering

3 The steering column has a universal joint fitted at its lower end, which is clamped to both the steering column shaft and the steering gear pinion by means of clamp bolts.
4 The steering gear is mounted on the rear of the engine/transmission subframe, and is connected to the steering arms projecting rearwards from the hub carriers. The track rods are fitted with balljoints at their inner and outer ends, to allow for suspension movement, and are threaded to facilitate adjustment.
5 Electric power steering is fitted as standard on all models. The electric motor is part of the steering column assembly inside the passenger compartment.

2 Front hub bearings – renewal

Note: *The bearing is part of the centre hub assembly and can only be replaced as a complete assembly.*

Removal

1 Firmly apply the handbrake, and then jack up the front of the vehicle and support it securely on axle stands (see *Jacking and vehicle support*). Remove the appropriate roadwheel.
2 Remove the brake disc, as described in Chapter 9 Section 7.
3 If required, to avoid the possibility of damage, unbolt the ABS wheel sensor, as described in Chapter 9 Section 17. Suspend the sensor away safely, from the working area.
4 Disconnect the outer end of the driveshaft from the hub carrier **(see illustration)**, as described in Chapter 8 Section 8. Note that there is no need to drain the transmission oil/fluid, or disconnect the inner end of the driveshaft from the transmission. **Do not** allow the end of the driveshaft to hang down under its own weight – support the end of the driveshaft using wire/string or axle stand.
5 Slacken the four hub/bearing retaining bolts **(see illustration)**. Remove two of the bolts completely, and then leave the other two bolts screwed most of the way into the rear of the hub/bearing.
6 Using a copper hammer, hit the heads of the two bolts that remain in the rear of the hub/bearing, whilst holding the strut assembly

2.4 Disconnect the driveshaft from the hub

2.5 Hub/bearing assembly mounting bolts

2.6a Using a copper hammer to free the bearing assembly. . .

2.6b . . . then withdraw it from the hub/ steering knuckle

2.7 Remove the brake disc back plate

securely. If the hub/bearing assembly is reluctant to move, remove the bolt securing the upper part of the hub to the base of the strut, then remove the complete hub assembly from the vehicle. Apply releasing/ penetrating fluid to the assembly, and leave it to soak for a few minutes before trying again **(see illustrations)**.

7 If required, the brake disc back plate can be removed from the hub carrier, noting its fitted position **(see illustration)**.

Refitting

8 If removed, fit the brake disc back plate into position (as noted on removal), and then fit the hub/bearing unit to the hub carrier and tighten the retaining bolts. Tighten the retaining bolts to the specified torque setting.

9 If removed completely from the vehicle, refit the hub/bearing carrier back to the lower part of the strut and fit the retaining bolt and new nut, in the position noted on removal. Tighten the retaining bolt to the specified torque setting.

10 Refit the outer end of the driveshaft back into the hub, as described in Chapter 8 Section 8.

11 Refit the wheel speed sensor back into the rear of the hub carrier, as described in Chapter 9 Section 17.

12 Refit the front brake disc, as described in Chapter 9 Section 7.

13 If removed, refit the brake caliper, as described in Chapter 9 Section 9.

14 On completion, refit the roadwheel and lower the vehicle to the ground. Tighten the wheel bolts to the specified torque setting.

3 Front suspension strut – removal, overhaul and refitting

Note: *New hub carrier-to-suspension strut retaining nuts must be used on refitting.*

Removal

1 Firmly apply the handbrake, and then jack up the front of the vehicle and support it securely on axle stands (see *Jacking and vehicle support*). Remove the appropriate roadwheel.

2 Extract the retaining clip and release the brake hydraulic hose from the support bracket on the suspension strut **(see illustration)**.

3 Unclip the ABS wiring loom from the support bracket on the lower part of the suspension strut, then trace the wiring and disconnect the wiring connector on the inner wing panel **(see illustrations)**.

4 Undo the mounting bolts and remove the brake caliper and carrier from the front hub assembly, as described in Chapter 9 Section 9. **Do not** allow the brake caliper to hang on the brake hose – support the caliper using wire/string or axle stand.

5 Disconnect the outer end of the driveshaft from the hub carrier **(see illustration)**, as described in Chapter 8 Section 8. Note that there is no need to drain the transmission oil/fluid, or disconnect the inner end of the driveshaft from the transmission. **Do not** allow the end of the driveshaft to hang down under its own weight – support the end of the driveshaft using wire/string or axle stand.

6 Open the bonnet, and remove the plastic grommet from the end of the scuttle panel **(see illustration)**, to access the rear bolt securing the top of the strut to the suspension turret.

7 Undo the bolts and nuts, then remove

3.2 Release the brake pipe securing clip

3.3a Unclip the wheel sensor wiring from the support bracket. . .

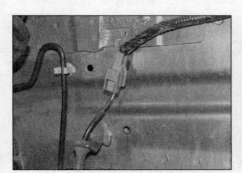

3.3b . . . and disconnect it on the inner wing panel

3.5 Remove outer end of driveshaft from hub

3.6 Remove the scuttle grill panel

3.7 Remove the mounting bracket

3.8a Undo the rear mounting bolt. . .

3.8b . . . and withdraw from scuttle with magnet

3.9a Undo the upper mounting bolts. . .

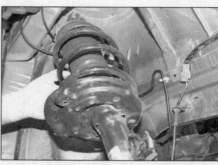

3.9b . . . and withdraw the front strut

Warning: Do not unscrew the centre damper rod nut at this stage.

10 If required, the hub assembly can be removed from the lower part of the strut. Undo the nut and withdraw the bolt securing the suspension strut to the hub carrier. Discard the nut, as a new one must be used on refitting.

Overhaul

Note: *Coil spring compressor tools will be required for this operation, and a new damper rod top nut must be used on reassembly.*

11 Fit the spring compressors to the spring, without tightening up fully, then using an Allen key to hold the damper centre rod, slacken the strut upper mounting nut **(see illustration)**. **Do not** remove the nut; only slacken to the top of the threads, so the nut is still fully on the threads.

12 Tighten the spring compressors to compress the spring sufficiently to enable the upper spring seat to be turned by hand **(see illustration)**.

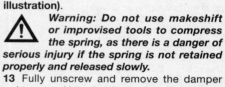

Warning: Do not use makeshift or improvised tools to compress the spring, as there is a danger of serious injury if the spring is not retained properly and released slowly.

13 Fully unscrew and remove the damper rod top nut. Note that it may be necessary to counterhold the damper rod, using an Allen key, as the nut is unscrewed **(see illustration)**. Discard the nut – a new one must be used on reassembly.

14 Withdraw the upper mounting plate, upper mounting insulator/bearing and upper spring seat/gaiter from the damper **(see illustrations)**.

the mounting bracket from the top of the suspension turret **(see illustration)**.

8 Undo the rear bolt from the top of the strut, then use a magnet to withdraw the bolt from inside the scuttle panel **(see illustrations)**.

9 Have an assistant support the strut assembly from underneath the wheel arch then, working in the engine compartment, unscrew the remaining two bolts securing the top of the strut to the suspension turret **(see illustrations)**. Mark the position of the bolts on the top of the suspension turret before removal, to aid refitting.

3.11 Place the spring compressors into position on the spring

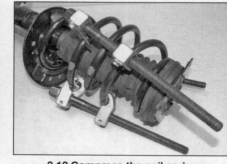

3.12 Compress the coil spring

3.13 The damper rod nut can now be completely removed

3.14a Remove the upper mounting plate. . .

3.14b . . . the insulator/bearing and gaiter. . .

3.14c . . . unclipping the lower part of the
gaiter from the strut

3.15a Withdraw the bump stop. . .

3.15b . . . the gaiter lower retaining cap. . .

15 Withdraw the spring, complete with the
compressors, then withdraw the rubber bump
stop, the gaiter lower plastic retaining cap,
and the lower spring seat rubber, noting there
fitted position **(see illustrations)**.
16 With the strut assembly now dismantled,
examine all the components for wear,
damage or deformation. Check the rubber
components for deterioration. Renew any
of the components as necessary. Remove
the bearing race, and check that it rotates
smoothly **(see illustration)**.
17 Examine the damper for signs of fluid
leakage. Check the damper rod for signs of pitting
along its entire length, and check the strut body
for signs of damage. While holding it in an upright
position, test the operation of the strut by moving
the damper rod through a full stroke, and then
through short strokes of 50 to 100 mm. In both
cases, the resistance felt should be smooth and
continuous. If the resistance is jerky, or uneven,
or if there is any visible sign of wear or damage
to the strut, renewal is necessary. Note that the
damper cannot be renewed independently, and if
leakage or damage is evident, the complete strut/
damper assembly must be renewed (in which
case, the spring, upper mounting components,
bushes, and associated components can be
transferred to the new strut).
18 If any doubt exists about the condition
of the coil spring, carefully remove the spring
compressors, and check the spring for
distortion and signs of cracking. Renew the
spring if it is damaged or distorted, or if there
is any doubt as to its condition.
19 Commence reassembly by refitting the
lower spring seat rubber, the gaiter lower
retaining cap and the bump stop, ensuring
that they are correctly located on the strut, as
noted on removal.
20 Ensure that the coil spring is compressed
sufficiently to enable the upper mounting
components to be fitted, and then locate the
spring on the strut, ensuring that the lower
end of the spring is correctly located on the
lower spring seat rubber **(see illustration)**.
21 If previously separated, refit the upper
mounting insulator/bearing and gaiter/upper
spring seat, fit the assembly to the top of the
spring, ensuring that the lower part of the
gaiter is fully engaged on the plastic retaining
cap on the strut.

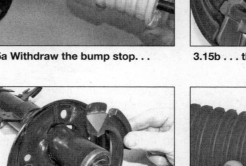

3.15c . . . and then remove the lower
rubber spring seat

22 Refit the upper mounting plate to the
damper, and fit a new damper rod top nut,
then tighten the top nut to the specified torque
(see illustration), counterholding the damper
rod as during dismantling.

3.20 Locate the spring in the lower seat
rubber

3.23a Align the upper end of the spring. . .

3.16 Unclip the gaiter from the upper
mounting bearing

23 Check that the spring ends are correctly
located in the upper and lower spring seats
(see illustrations), and then remove the
spring compressors.

3.22 Using a crows foot to torque upper
nut

3.23b . . . and the lower end of the spring

4.2a Remove the ball joint retaining nut and bolt. . .

4.2c . . . then lever the lower arm down to release the ball joint

Refitting

24 Manoeuvre the strut assembly into position under the wheel arch and up into the suspension turret. Make sure the upper mounting is in the correct position, as it is fitted inside the inner wheel arch, as noted on removal. Fit the upper mounting bolts, and tighten them to the specified torque.

25 Engage the lower end of the strut with the hub carrier and refit the securing bolt with the bolt head towards the front of the vehicle. Fit the new nut to the bolt, and tighten to the specified torque.

26 Refit the outer end of the driveshaft to the hub, as described in Chapter 8 Section 8.

27 Refit the brake caliper, as described in Chapter 9 Section 9.

28 Refit the drop link upper ball joint to the suspension strut, and then tighten the retaining nut to the specified torque.

4.3 Remove the lower arm rear mounting bolt and nut

4.2b . . . insert a chisel/wedge to release balljoint. . .

29 Locate the brake hydraulic hose and ABS wiring loom back in the support bracket on the suspension strut. Securing the brake hose with the retaining clip.

30 Refit the rubber grommet to the scuttle panel and the mounting bracket to the top of the suspension turret.

31 On completion, refit the roadwheel and lower the vehicle to the ground. Tighten the wheel bolts to the specified torque setting.

---

4 Front suspension lower arm – removal, inspection and refitting

Note: *The lower arm balljoint retaining nut must be renewed on refitting.*

Removal

1 Firmly apply the handbrake, and then jack up the front of the vehicle and support it securely on axle stands (see *Jacking and vehicle support*). Remove the appropriate roadwheel.

2 Undo the retaining nut and withdraw the bolt from the lower ball joint. Using a wedge shaped tool/chisel tap it into the slot in the hub assembly to release the lower ball joint. Use a length of bar, chain to lever the lower arm downwards and disconnect the lower ball joint from the hub carrier **(see illustrations)**. Discard the nut – a new one must be used on refitting.

3 Undo the bolt and nut securing the lower arm rear mounting to the subframe **(see**

4.4 Remove the lower arm front mounting bolt and nut

illustration). Discard the nut – a new one must be used on refitting.

4 Unscrew the lower arm front mounting bolt and nut, then withdraw the lower arm from the subframe **(see illustration)**.

Inspection

5 With the lower arm removed; examine the lower arm itself, and the mounting bushes for wear, cracks or damage.

6 Check the balljoint for wear, excessive play, or stiffness. Also check the balljoint dust boot for cracks or damage.

Refitting

7 Slide the rear of the lower arm into position in the subframe, and then the front into position, refit the bolts and nuts to secure the lower arm in position on the subframe. Tighten the bolts to the specified torque.

8 Reconnect the lower ball joint to the bottom of the hub carrier. If required, use a length of bar, chain and a block of wood to lever the lower arm downwards, as described on removal. Fit the retaining bolt and new nut to the lower ball joint, and then tighten to the specified torque setting.

9 Refit the roadwheel and lower the vehicle to the ground. Tighten the wheel bolts to the specified torque setting.

10 On completion the front wheel alignment should be checked, with reference to Section 17.

---

5 Front suspension lower arm balljoint – renewal

1 At the time of writing the lower arm balljoint was not available separately and is integral with the suspension lower arm. If the balljoint is worn or damaged, the complete lower arm must be renewed as described in Section 4.

---

6 Front suspension anti-roll bar – removal and refitting

Anti-roll bar

Removal

1 To remove the anti-roll bar it will be necessary to remove the front subframe, as described in Section 12. It may be possible to just lower the subframe slightly to get access and withdraw the anti-roll bar from its position on the upper side of the subframe.

2 If not already done, use an open ended spanner to counterhold the drop link ball joint, then unscrew the nut securing the end of the anti-roll bar to the drop link **(see illustration)**.

3 Repeat the operation on the other side of the anti-roll bar.

4 Unscrew the bolts, and withdraw the clamps securing the anti-roll bar to the top of the front subframe **(see illustration)**.
5 Manipulate the anti-roll bar out from between the subframe and the body.

Refitting

6 Inspect the mounting clamp rubbers for cracks or deterioration. If renewal is necessary, slide the old rubbers from the bar, and fit the new rubbers. Note that the rubbers should be positioned with the paint marks on the bar against their inner edges.
7 Refitting is a reversal of removal.

Drop link

Removal

8 To improve access, firmly apply the handbrake, and then jack up the front of the vehicle and support it securely on axle stands (see *Jacking and vehicle support*). Remove the relevant front roadwheel.
9 Counterhold the drop link ball joint with a Torx bit socket in the end of the threaded part of the ball joint, then using a spanner, unscrew the nut securing the drop link upper ball joint to the suspension strut **(see illustrations)**.
10 Again, counterhold the drop link lower ball joint, and then unscrew the nut securing the end of the anti-roll bar to the drop link **(see illustration 6.2)**.
11 With both upper and lower ball joints disconnected, withdraw the drop link from under the wheel arch.

Refitting

12 Check the condition of the drop link ball joints, if any wear or dust cap split, renew the complete drop link.
13 Refitting is a reversal of removal, making sure that drop link securing nuts are tightened to the specified torque.

7 Rear hub bearings – renewal

1 The rear hub bearings are integral with the rear hubs, and cannot be renewed independently. If the bearings require renewal, the complete hub assembly must be renewed as follows.
2 Chock the front wheels then jack up the rear of the vehicle and support it securely on axle stands (see *Jacking and vehicle support*). Remove the appropriate rear roadwheel and release the handbrake fully.
3 Remove the wheel speed sensor from the rear of the hub, as described in Chapter 9 Section 17.
4 Working at the rear of the hub assembly undo the four mounting bolts, and then withdraw the hub complete with back plate from the trailing arm **(see illustration)**.
5 Remove the back plate from the rear of the old hub/bearing and fit to the new one.
6 Thoroughly clean the back plate and trailing

6.2 Disconnect the drop link from the anti-roll bar

6.4 Undo the anti-roll bar clamp bolts

6.9a Using a Torx socket and spanner to undo the ball joint nut. . .

6.9b . . . and then disconnect the drop link from the strut

arm, and then slide the new hub assembly and back plate into position.
7 Fit the hub assembly to the trailing arm and then tighten the four retaining bolts to the specified torque.
8 Check that the hub spins freely, and then refit the brake disc, as described in Chapter 9 Section 8.
9 Refit the ABS wheel speed sensor and tighten its retaining bolt to the specified torque (see Chapter 9 Section 17).
10 Refit the roadwheel(s), lower the vehicle to the ground and tighten to the specified torque setting.

8 Rear shock absorber (damper) – removal, testing and refitting

Note: *New damper upper and lower securing nuts must be used on refitting. Also it is advisable to always renew dampers in pairs on the same axle.*

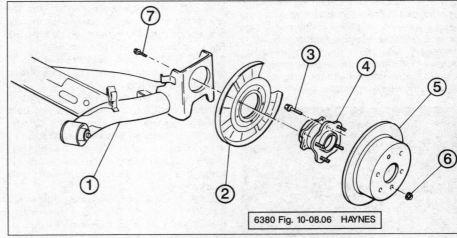
7.4 Rear wheel hub arrangement

1 Trailing arm
2 Brake backplate
3 Wheel stud - (early models)
4 Wheel hub assembly
5 Rear brake disc
6 Plug/screw
7 Hub bolt

8.2 Use a trolley jack to support the trailing arm

8.3 Undo the lower retaining bolt/nut

8.4 Damper upper securing bolt

Removal

1 Chock the front wheels then jack up the rear of the vehicle and support it securely on axle stands (see *Jacking and vehicle support*). For better access remove the appropriate rear roadwheel.

2 Using a trolley jack, raise the rear trailing arm, until the damper is slightly compressed **(see illustration)**.

3 Slacken the damper lower mounting bolt retaining nut, and then withdraw the bolt, disengaging the lower part of the damper from the trailing arm **(see illustration)**.

4 Slacken the damper upper mounting bolt, and then withdraw the bolt and disengage the top of the damper from the upper mounting bracket **(see illustration)**.

5 Withdraw the damper from under the rear of the vehicle.

Testing

6 Examine the damper for signs of fluid leakage. Check the damper rod for signs of pitting along its entire length, and check the body for signs of damage. While holding it in an upright position, test the operation by moving the damper rod through a full stroke, and then through short strokes of 50 to 100 mm. In both cases, the resistance felt should be smooth and continuous. If the resistance is jerky, or uneven, or if there is any visible sign of wear or damage to the damper, renewal is necessary. Also check the rubber mounting bushes for damage or deterioration, and inspect the mounting bolts for signs of wear or damage; renew if necessary.

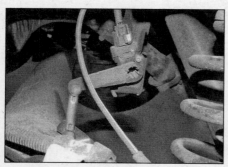

9.4 Disconnect the level sensor

Refitting

7 Offer up the top of the damper into its mounting bracket, then refit it's mounting bolt, fit the new retaining nut and tighten by hand at this stage.

8 Align the damper lower mounting with the trailing arm and refit the lower mounting bolt. Fit the new nut, also tightening it by hand at this stage.

9 Refit the rear roadwheel then lower the vehicle to the ground and tighten the wheel bolts to the specified torque.

10 With the vehicle down on its wheels, in the normal ride height position; tighten the upper and lower damper mounting bolts/nuts to the specified torque.

9 Rear coil spring – removal and refitting

Note: *It is advisable to always renew coil springs in pairs on the same axle. New suspension securing nuts must be used on refitting.*

Removal

1 Chock the front wheels then jack up the rear of the vehicle and support it securely on axle stands (see *Jacking and vehicle support*). Remove the appropriate rear roadwheel.

2 Using a trolley jack, raise the rear trailing arm, until the damper is slightly compressed **(see illustration 8.2)**.

3 Slacken the damper lower mounting bolt retaining nut, and then withdraw the bolt, disengaging the lower part of the damper from the trailing arm **(see illustration 8.3)**.

4 On models with Xenon headlights, disconnect the level sensor linkage bracket from the lower suspension arm **(see illustration)**.

5 Carefully lower the trailing arm on the trolley jack, taking care not to put any strain on the brake hose or wheel speed sensor wiring.

6 Withdraw the coil spring complete with upper rubber mounting from under the rear of the vehicle.

7 If required, unclip the spring lower rubber mounting from the trailing arm.

Refitting

8 Refit the coil spring back into position between the underbody and the trailing arm, making sure the upper and lower rubber mountings.

9 Carefully raise the trolley jack; aligning the damper lower mounting with the trailing arm and refit the lower mounting bolt. Fit the new nut, also tightening it by hand at this stage.

10 On models with Xenon headlights, reconnect the level sensor linkage bracket to the lower suspension arm.

11 Refit the rear roadwheel then lower the vehicle to the ground and tighten the wheel bolts to the specified torque.

12 With the vehicle down on its wheels, in the normal ride height position; tighten the lower damper mounting bolt to the specified torque.

10 Rear axle – removal and refitting

Removal

1 Chock the front wheels then jack up the rear of the car and support it on axle stands (see *Jacking and vehicle support*). Remove both rear roadwheels.

2 Unscrew the brake master cylinder fluid reservoir cap and screw it down onto a piece of polythene to minimise fluid loss during the following procedure.

3 Undo the bolt securing the ABS wheel speed sensor to the hub/stub axle assembly on each side **(see illustration)**. Withdraw the

10.3 Rear wheel speed sensor retaining bolt

sensors from the stub axles and unclip the sensor wiring from the rear axle.

4 Remove the rear brake discs as described in Chapter 9 Section 8.

5 Slacken the union nuts, and disconnect the brake pipes from the flexible hose unions on the rear axle **(see illustration)**. Plug the pipe and hose ends to minimise fluid loss and prevent the entry of dirt into the hydraulic system. Remove the retaining clips, and release the two flexible hoses from their mounting brackets.

6 Remove the rear coil springs as described in Section 9.

7 Support the weight of the axle assembly using two trolley jacks. Alternatively, one trolley jack and a length of wood may be used, but the help of an assistant will be required.

8 Undo the bolt at each side securing the axle front mounting to the underbody mounting bracket **(see illustration)**.

9 Make a final check that all necessary components have been disconnected and positioned so that they will not hinder the removal procedure. Carefully lower the axle assembly out of position, and remove it from underneath the vehicle.

10 The brake components can be removed from the axle, referring to the relevant Sections of Chapter 9. The hub bearing units can be removed with reference to Section 7.

11 Note that new through-bolt retaining nuts will be required for reassembly.

Refitting

12 Refit any components that were removed from the axle, referring to the relevant Sections of this Chapter and Chapter 9, as applicable. If the front mounting brackets were removed, refit the brackets, but only tighten the new through-bolt nuts lightly at this stage.

13 Support the axle on the trolley jacks, and position the assembly under the rear of the vehicle.

14 Raise the jacks, then refit and lightly tighten the front mounting bracket retaining bolts. With all the bolts in place, work progressively in a diagonal sequence, and tighten all the bolts to the specified torque.

15 Refit the rear coil springs as described in Section 9.

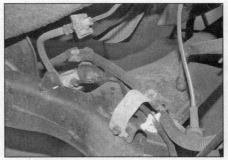
10.5 Disconnect the brake pipes from the flexible hose unions

16 Refit the brake hydraulic pipes and flexible hoses together with the retaining clips and tighten the union nuts securely.

17 Refit the ABS wheel speed sensors, tightening the retaining bolts to the specified torque.

18 Bleed the complete brake hydraulic system, as described in Chapter 9 Section 3.

19 Refit the roadwheels and lower the vehicle to the ground.

20 With the vehicle on its wheels, in the normal ride height position; where applicable, tighten the new front mounting bracket through-bolt nuts to the specified torque.

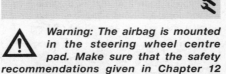

11 Steering wheel – removal and refitting

⚠️ **Warning: The airbag is mounted in the steering wheel centre pad. Make sure that the safety recommendations given in Chapter 12 Section 19, are followed to prevent personal injury.**

Note: There are two types of steering wheel fitted to this model. The type shown in the following section is of the later type, removal and refitting of the earlier type is similar.

Removal

1 Ensure that the ignition is switched off, and then disconnect the battery negative terminal (refer to Disconnecting the battery

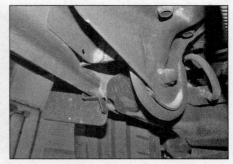
10.8 Rear axle front mounting retaining bolt

in Chapter 5 Section 4). Wait for at least ten minutes before carrying out any further work.

2 Remove the airbag unit from the centre of the steering wheel, as described in Chapter 12 Section 20.

3 Where applicable, release the steering lock by inserting the ignition key and set the front wheels in the straight-ahead position.

4 Counterhold the steering wheel and slacken the steering wheel retaining bolt **(see illustration)**.

5 The steering wheel should only fit in one position, as there is a master spline, which will need to be lined up for refitting. Check for alignment marks between the steering wheel and the end of the steering column shaft for refitting. Make your own alignment marks, if required.

6 Leave the bolt in a couple of threads, then pull on the steering wheel, to release it from the splines on the steering column **(see illustration)**.

7 Remove bolt completely, then disconnect the wiring connectors, inside the steering wheel **(see illustration)**. Withdraw the wheel from the top of the steering column shaft, feeding the wiring through the steering wheel, as it is withdrawn.

8 With the steering wheel removed, check the position of the rotary/spiral switch, tape in position to prevent it from moving, if required **(see illustration)**. Note the window on the upper right-hand side should show the colour yellow.

11.4 Undo the steering wheel retaining bolt

11.6 Release the steering wheel from the splines

11.7 Disconnect the wiring connectors

11.8 Make sure the rotary switch is not turned while wheel is removed

Refitting

9 Refitting is a reversal of removal, bearing in mind the following points:

a) Ensure that the front wheels are in the straight-ahead position.

b) Remove the tape (where fitted) from the rotary/spiral unit, making sure it is in the correct position.

c) Ensure that the direction indicator switch is in the central (cancelled/off) position, otherwise the switch may be damaged as the wheel is refitted.

d) Make sure all the wiring connectors are secure and clipped into position.

e) Where applicable, align the marks on the wheel and the steering column shaft, which where made before removal, and align the steering wheel with the rotary switch.

f) Tighten the steering wheel securing bolt to the specified torque.

12.2a Remove the plastic cover to access the lower steering column joint. . .

12.2c . . . disconnect the joint from the pinion shaft

g) Refit the airbag unit to the steering wheel as described in Chapter 12 Section 20.

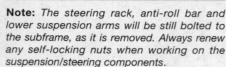
12 Front suspension subframe – removal and refitting

Note: The steering rack, anti-roll bar and lower suspension arms will be still bolted to the subframe, as it is removed. Always renew any self-locking nuts when working on the suspension/steering components.

Removal

1 Chock the rear wheels, firmly apply the handbrake, slacken the front roadwheel bolts, and then jack up the front of the vehicle and support it on axle stands (see Jacking and vehicle support). Remove both front roadwheels.

2 Working inside the drivers footwell, remove the plastic cover, then note the position of the steering column lower joint on the steering rack pinion shaft. Undo the retaining bolt and disconnect the steering column joint from the steering rack pinion shaft (see illustrations).

3 Working under the vehicle, slacken and remove the engine/transmission rear lower mounting bolt and nut, then undo the nut and bolt securing the link rod to the subframe and remove the link (see illustration).

4 Slacken and remove both front lower ball joint retaining nut and bolts and free the ball joint shank from the front hub carriers (see illustrations 4.2a and 4.2b). Discard the nuts, as new ones will be required for refitting.

12.2b . . . note the position and undo the retaining bolt. . .

12.3 Remove the rear lower mounting from the subframe

5 Counterhold the drop link lower ball joint, and then unscrew the nut securing the end of the anti-roll bar to the drop link (see illustrations 6.2a and 6.2b).

6 Undo the retaining nut and disconnect the track rod end from the hub carrier (see illustration). Refer to Section 16, for further information.

7 Make a final check that all cables/hoses that are attached to the subframe have been released and positioned clear so that they will not hinder the removal procedure.

8 Place a jack and a suitable block of wood under the subframe to support the subframe as it is lowered.

9 Slacken and remove the subframe rear mounting bolts and remove the support bracket from the rear of the subframe.

10 Slacken and remove the subframe front mounting bolts then carefully lower the subframe assembly out of position and remove it from underneath the vehicle, taking great care to ensure that the subframe assembly does not catch anything as it is lowered out of position.

Refitting

11 Refitting is a reversal of the removal procedure, noting the following points:

a) Use new lower ball joint, and steering track rod end nuts.

b) Use a new bolt for the steering column lower joint, making sure the captivated nut is fitted correctly.

c) Tighten all nuts and bolts to the specified torque settings (where given).

d) On completion check and, if necessary, adjust the front wheel alignment.

13 Steering column/motor – removal and refitting

⚠ **Warning: All models are equipped with an airbag system. Ensure that the safety recommendations given in Chapter 12 Section 19, are followed to prevent personal injury.**

Note: The steering column comprises the electric power steering (EPS) motor, the electronic control unit and the steering

12.6 Disconnect the track rod ends

13.6a Remove the plastic shield. . .

13.6b . . . to access the lower joint bolt

13.8 Unclip the wiring loom and retaining clips along the column

column itself. All these components form one assembly and cannot be individually separated or dismantled.

Removal

1 Disconnect the battery negative terminal (refer to *Disconnecting the battery* in Chapter 5 Section 4).

2 Remove the steering wheel as described in Section 11.

3 Remove the steering column stalk switches with reference to Chapter 12 Section 4.

4 To improve access remove the driver's side lower facia panel, as described in Chapter 11 Section 25.

5 Temporarily refit the steering wheel, and turn the steering column shaft as necessary for access to the universal joint clamp bolt.

6 Remove the plastic cover, then note the position of the steering column lower joint on the steering rack pinion shaft. Undo the retaining bolt and disconnect the steering column joint from the pinion shaft (see illustrations).

7 Fasten a cable tie around the lower end of the steering column, to prevent it from extending as the steering column is removed.

8 Check along the steering column and, free the wiring loom from the retaining clips along the column (see illustration). Note its fitted position, and position it clear so that it does not hinder column removal.

9 The steering column/motor assembly is very heavy, it will be necessary to have the aid of an assistant or have something inside the footwell of the vehicle, to support the steering column/motor as it is removed.

10 Slacken and remove the four mounting nuts from the top of the column (see illustration). Slide the column assembly upwards, and free the upper locating plate from the metal crossbeam.

11 Carefully lower the steering column and support it while disconnecting the wiring connectors from the top of the steering column motor (see illustration).

12 When the steering column/motor is free from any wiring, withdraw it from inside the vehicle.

Refitting

13 Refitting is a reversal of removal, bearing in mind the following points:

13.10 Undo the column mounting nuts (two upper ones shown)

a) Use new steering column bolts/nuts.
b) Tighten all bolts to their specified torque setting, where given.
c) Refit the steering column switches, as described in Chapter 12 Section 4.
d) Refit the steering wheel, as described in Section 11.
e) Refit the steering column lower facia panel, as described in Chapter 11 Section 25.

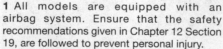

14 Steering gear assembly – removal, inspection and refitting

1 All models are equipped with an airbag system. Ensure that the safety recommendations given in Chapter 12 Section 19, are followed to prevent personal injury.
Note: *A balljoint separator tool may be required for this operation. New track rod end retaining nuts must be used on refitting.*

Removal

2 Firmly apply the handbrake, and then jack up the front of the vehicle and support it securely on axle stands (see *Jacking and vehicle support*). Remove the front roadwheels.

3 Remove the front subframe as described in Section 12. It may be possible to lower the subframe and not completely remove it, to allow for enough room for the steering gear assembly to be withdrawn from between the underbody and the subframe.

4 Unscrew the bolts securing the steering gear to the top of the subframe and then

13.11 Disconnect the wiring connectors from the motor

withdraw the steering gear out through the side of the vehicle (see illustration).

Inspection

5 Examine the assembly for obvious signs of wear or damage.

6 Check the rack for smooth operation through its full stroke of movement, and check that there is no binding or free play.

7 Check the track rods for deformation and cracks.

8 Check the condition of the steering gear rubber gaiters, and renew if necessary with reference to Section 15.

9 Examine the track rod ends for wear or damage, and renew if necessary with reference to Section 16.

10 Apart from renewal of the track rod ends and steering gear rubber gaiters, any further overhaul necessary should be entrusted to a Nissan dealer or specialist.

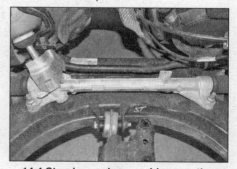

14.4 Steering rack assembly mounting bolts/nuts

15.3 Steering rack gaiter securing clips

Refitting

11 Refitting is a reversal of removal, bearing in mind the following points:
a) *Use new lower balljoint and steering track rod end nuts.*
b) *Use a new bolt for the steering column lower joint, making sure the captive nut is fitted correctly.*
c) *Tighten all nuts and bolts to the specified torque settings (where given).*

15 Steering gear rubber gaiters – renewal

Note: *New gaiter retaining clips should be used on refitting.*
1 Remove the relevant track rod end as described in Section 16.
2 If not already done, unscrew the track rod end locknut from the end of the track rod, noting how many turns to remove the nut, to aid refitting.

16.2 Using a Torx socket to prevent the ball joint from turning

16.3b . . . to release the tapered shank

3 Mark the correct fitted position of the gaiter on the track rod, then release the gaiter securing clips **(see illustration)**. Slide the gaiter from the steering gear, and off the end of the track rod.
4 Thoroughly clean the track rod and the steering gear housing, using fine abrasive paper to polish off any corrosion, burrs or sharp edges that might damage the new gaiter sealing lips on installation. Scrape off all the grease from the old gaiter, and apply it to the track rod inner balljoint. (This assumes that grease has not been lost or contaminated as a result of damage to the old gaiter. Use fresh grease if in doubt.)
5 Carefully slide the new gaiter onto the track rod, and locate it on the steering gear housing. Align the outer edge of the gaiter with the mark made on the track rod prior to removal, and then secure it in position with new retaining clips.
6 Screw the track rod end locknut onto the end of the track rod.
7 Refit the track rod end as described in Section 16.

16 Track rod end – removal and refitting

Note: *A balljoint separator tool will be required for this operation. A new track rod end retaining nut must be used on refitting.*

Removal

1 Firmly apply the handbrake, and then jack up the front of the vehicle and support it securely

16.3a Use a balljoint separator. . .

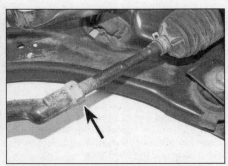

16.4 Slacken the track rod end locknut

on axle stands (see *Jacking and vehicle support*). Remove the relevant front roadwheel.
2 Using a Torx key to prevent the ball joint from turning, slacken the nut securing the track rod end to the steering arm **(see illustration)**.
3 Using a balljoint separator tool, separate the track rod end from the steering arm **(see illustrations)**. Remove the nut and discard, as a new one must be used on refitting.
4 Clean the threads on the track rod arm with a wire brush and lubricate. Counterhold the track rod arm using the flats provided, and then slacken the track rod end **(see illustration)**.
5 Counting the exact number of turns required to remove the track rod end, unscrew it from the track rod arm.

Refitting

6 Carefully clean the track rod end and the track rod threads.
7 Renew the track rod end if the rubber dust cover is cracked, split or perished, or if the movement of the balljoint is either sloppy or too stiff. Also check for other signs of damage such as worn threads.
8 Screw the track rod end onto the track rod by the number of turns noted before removal.
9 Counterhold the track rod arm using the flats provided, and then securely tighten the track rod lock nut.
10 Ensure that the balljoint taper is clean, and then engage the taper with the steering arm on the hub carrier.
11 Refit a new nut to the track rod end, and tighten to the specified torque.
12 Refit the roadwheel, and lower the vehicle to the ground.
13 Check the front wheel alignment and adjust, as required.

17 Wheel alignment check

Definitions

1 A vehicle's steering and suspension geometry is defined in four basic settings – all angles are expressed in degrees (toe settings are also expressed as a measurement); the relevant settings are camber, castor, steering axis inclination and toe setting. Some of these settings are adjustable, and in all cases special equipment is necessary to check them. Note that front wheel toe setting is often referred to as 'tracking' or 'front wheel alignment'.

Checking

2 Due to the special measuring equipment necessary to check the wheel alignment, and the skill required to use it properly, the checking and adjustment of these settings is best left to a Nissan dealer or similar expert. Note that most tyre-fitting shops now possess sophisticated checking equipment.

Chapter 11
Bodywork and fittings

Contents

Degrees of difficulty

Easy, suitable for novice with little experience	Fairly easy, suitable for beginner with some experience	Fairly difficult, suitable for competent DIY mechanic	Difficult, suitable for experienced DIY mechanic	Very difficult, suitable for expert DIY or professional

Specifications

Torque wrench settings	Nm	lbf ft
Door hinge bolts	23	17
Door lock striker bolts	15	11
Front seat belt mounting bolts:		
Lower sill anchorage	49	36
Seat belt inertia reel bolt	40	30
Pre-tensioner-to-sill bolt	50	37
Buckle-to-seat frame	49	36
Front seat securing bolts	40	30
Rear seat belt mounting bolts (all bolts)	49	36
Rear seat securing bolts:		
2 nuts securing bracket-to-body	28	21
1 bolt securing bracket-to-seat	44	32

1 General Information

1 The bodyshell is made of pressed-steel sections, most components are welded together, but some use is made of structural adhesives and some body components are bolted on.

2 Nissan vehicles have been designed with a rigid passenger safety compartment with reinforced pillars and sills, including safety 'waist' beams inside the doors. The use of high-strength steel in structural areas of the body enhances the rigidity of the structure.

3 Extensive use is made of plastic materials, mainly in the interior, but also in exterior components. The outer sections of the front and rear bumpers are injection-moulded from a synthetic material, which is very strong, and yet light. Plastic components such as wheel arch liners are fitted to the underside of the vehicle, to improve the body's resistance to corrosion.

2 Maintenance – bodywork and underframe
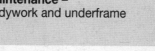

1 The general condition of a vehicle's bodywork is the one thing that significantly affects its value. Maintenance is easy, but needs to be regular. Neglect, particularly after minor damage, can lead quickly to further deterioration and costly repair bills. It is important also to keep watch on those parts of the vehicle not immediately visible, for instance the underside, inside all the wheel arches, and the lower part of the engine compartment.

2 The basic maintenance routine for the bodywork is washing – preferably with a lot of water, from a hose. This will remove all the loose solids, which may have stuck to the vehicle. It is important to flush these off in such a way as to prevent grit from scratching the finish. The wheel arches and underframe need washing in the same way, to remove any accumulated mud, which will retain moisture and tend to encourage rust. Paradoxically enough, the best time to clean the underframe and wheel arches is in wet weather, when the mud is thoroughly wet and soft. In very wet weather, the underframe is usually cleaned of large accumulations automatically, and this is a good time for inspection.

3 Periodically, except on vehicles with a wax-based underbody protective coating,

5.3 Undo the lower screw from the wheel arch trim

5.4 Unclip the wheel arch trim from the front bumper

it is a good idea to have the whole of the underframe of the vehicle steam-cleaned, engine compartment included, so that a thorough inspection can be carried out to see what minor repairs and renovations are necessary. Steam cleaning is available at many garages, and is necessary for the removal of the accumulation of oily grime, which sometimes is allowed to become thick in certain areas. If steam-cleaning facilities are not available, there are some excellent grease solvents available which can be brush-applied; the dirt can then be simply hosed off. Note that these methods should not be used on vehicles with wax-based underbody protective coating, or the coating will be removed. Such vehicles should be inspected annually, preferably just prior to winter, when the underbody should be washed down, and any damage to the wax coating repaired. Ideally, a completely fresh coat should be applied. It would also be worth considering the use of such wax-based protection for injection into door panels, sills, box sections, etc, as an additional safeguard against rust damage, where such protection is not provided by the vehicle manufacturer.

4 After washing paintwork, wipe off with a chamois leather to give an unspotted clear finish. A coat of clear protective wax polish will give added protection against chemical pollutants in the air. If the paintwork sheen has dulled or oxidised, use a cleaner/polisher combination to restore the brilliance of the shine. This requires a little effort, but such dulling is usually caused because regular

washing has been neglected. Care needs to be taken with metallic paintwork, as special non-abrasive cleaner/polisher is required to avoid damage to the finish. Always check that the door and ventilator opening drain holes and pipes are completely clear, so that water can be drained out. Brightwork should be treated in the same way as paintwork. Windscreens and windows can be kept clear of the smeary film, which often appears, by the use of proprietary glass cleaner. Never use any form of wax or other body or chromium polish on glass.

3 Maintenance – upholstery and carpets

1 Mats and carpets should be brushed or vacuum-cleaned regularly, to keep them free of grit. If they are badly stained, remove them from the vehicle for scrubbing or sponging, and make quite sure they are dry before refitting. Seats and interior trim panels can be kept clean by wiping with a damp cloth. If they do become stained (which can be more apparent on light-coloured upholstery), use a little liquid detergent and a soft nail brush to scour the grime out of the grain of the material. Do not forget to keep the headlining clean in the same way as the upholstery. When using liquid cleaners inside the vehicle, do not over-wet the surfaces being cleaned. Excessive damp could get into the seams and padded interior, causing stains, offensive odours or even rot.

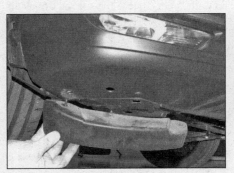

5.5 Remove the plastic shield (where fitted)

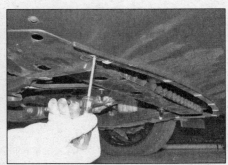

5.6a Undo the two remaining screws. . .

4 Body damage – general information

General information

1 In order to successfully repair damage to the vehicle bodywork, tools, skills and experience are required that are not normally possessed by the occasional DIY'er.
2 Whilst rectifying superficial scratches to the vehicle paintwork can be carried out using touch-up pens etc., it is difficult to achieve repairs of acceptable standard to more serious damage without access to professional equipment, and the necessary skills.
3 Consequently, we recommend that repairs are entrusted to suitably equipped professionals.
4 For minor repairs (scratch/dent removal) it may be worth trying one of the many companies that offer mobile 'smart' repairs. They can offer a convenient service, often with a guaranteed high-level of repair quality.
5 Major bodywork repairs should be carried out by fully equipped automotive bodywork specialist.

5 Front bumper – removal and refitting

Removal

1 Firmly apply the handbrake, and then jack up the front of the vehicle and support it securely on axle stands (see *Jacking and vehicle support*). To make access inside the wheel arch easier, remove the front roadwheels.
2 Working under the front of the vehicle, undo the retaining screws securing the engine undershield to the lower edge of the bumper.
3 Still working under the front of the vehicle, unscrew the lower securing screws at each end of the bumper wheel arch trims **(see illustration)**.
4 Carefully lever the wheel arch trim to release the retaining clips from the ends of the bumper **(see illustration)**.
Note: *The wheel arch trims do not have to be completely removed from the front wing panels, they just need to be released from the ends of the bumper. Take care not to damage them as the bumper is removed.*
5 Release the fasteners and remove the plastic shields (where fitted) from under each end of the bumper **(see illustration)**.
6 Undo the remaining two screws under the front edge of the bumper **(see illustrations)**.
7 Remove the securing clips from inside the wheel arch liner, then ease the liner away and undo the bolt securing the upper corner of the bumper to the front wing **(see illustration)**. Repeat the procedure on the other side of the vehicle.

5.6b . . . from under the bumper

5.7 Undo the bolt securing the upper part of the bumper

5.8a Undo the screws and release the retaining clips. . .

5.8b . . . then withdraw the upper plastic trim panel

5.9a Release the upper right-hand side. . .

5.9b . . . and left-hand side of the grille

8 Undo the eight screws and four retaining clips from the top of the front grille, and remove the plastic trim panel **(see illustrations)**.
9 Pull the upper part of the grille away at each end, to release it from the retaining clips on the inner part of the headlights **(see illustrations)**. Once the upper part is released, lift the grille upwards and release it from the front bumper. Where applicable, disconnect the wiring connector from the camera at the lower part of the grille.
10 Working inside the grille aperture, release the four retaining clips from the upper part of the bumper **(see illustrations)**.
11 Have an assistant support one end of the bumper, and then unclip the outer ends of the bumper from the front wing panels **(see illustration)**. If not completely removed, take care not to damage the wheel arch trims, as the bumper is removed.
12 Where fitted, disconnect the parking

sensor wiring connector, front fog lights and headlight washer pipes, as the front bumper is withdrawn from the vehicle.
13 Check that there is nothing still connected to the bumper, and then with the aid of an

assistant, draw the bumper forwards and remove it from the vehicle.

Refitting
14 Refitting is a reversal of removal.

5.9c Disconnect the wiring connector from the camera – where fitted

5.10a Remove the upper. . .

5.10b . . . and lower retaining clips. . .

5.10c . . . from inside the grille aperture

5.11 Release the bumper at each side, noting the locating slots

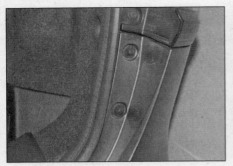

6.1 Undo the retaining bolts – one side shown

6.2 Remove the two centre securing clips

6.3 Undo the fasteners – one side shown

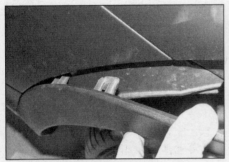

6.4a Release the retaining clips. . .

6.4b . . . and remove the wheel arch plastic trims

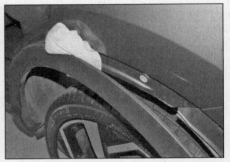

6.4c Place a cloth under the trim, if leaving in place

6.5a Pull back the inner trim panel. . .

6.5b . . . and undo the bolt securing the upper part of the bumper

6.6 Release the bumper at each side of the wing panel

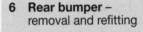

6.7 Release the three retaining clips

6 Rear bumper – removal and refitting

Removal

1 Open the tailgate, and undo the four mounting bolts (two at each side), from the upper part of the the rear bumper trim panel (see illustration).

2 Working under the rear of the vehicle, at the centre, release the two retaining clips securing the lower edge of the bumper (see illustration).

3 Working under each end of the bumper, undo the retaining screws and release the retaining clip (see illustration).

4 Carefully lever the wheel arch trim to release the retaining clips from the ends of the bumper (see illustrations). The wheel arch trims do not have to be completely removed from the rear wing panels, they just need to be released to access the ends of the bumper. Take care not to damage them as the bumper is removed.

5 Pull back the inner wheel arch liner and unscrew the two bolts (one each side) securing the upper corners of the bumper to the rear wing and body brackets (see illustrations).

6 Have an assistant support one end of the bumper, and then unclip the outer ends of the bumper from the rear wing panels (see illustration).

7 With the aid of an assistant, working at the top of the bumper, release the bumper from the three retaining clips, by carefully pulling back and withdrawing the bumper from the rear of the vehicle (see illustration). If not completely

removed, take care not to damage the wheel arch trims, as the bumper is removed.
8 On models with rear parking sensors, disconnect the wiring connectors as the bumper is removed **(see illustration)**.

Refitting
9 Refitting is a reversal of removal.

7 Bonnet – removal, refitting and adjustment

Removal
1 Open the bonnet and have an assistant support it. Using a pencil or felt tip pen, mark the outline of each bonnet hinge relative to the bonnet, to use as a guide on refitting.
2 With the help of an assistant to support one side of the bonnet, unscrew the nuts securing the hinges to the bonnet **(see illustration)**. Carefully lift the bonnet clear of the vehicle and store it out of the way in a safe place.
3 Inspect the bonnet hinges for signs of wear and free play at the pivots, and if necessary renew. Each hinge is secured to the body by bolts.

Refitting
4 With the aid of an assistant, offer up the bonnet, and loosely fit the retaining nuts. Align the hinges with the marks made on removal, and then tighten the retaining nuts securely.
5 Adjust the alignment of the bonnet as follows.

Adjustment
6 Close the bonnet, and check for alignment with the adjacent panels. If necessary, slacken the hinge nuts/bolts and re-align the bonnet to suit. Once the bonnet is correctly aligned, tighten the relevant hinge bolts securely.
7 Once the bonnet is correctly aligned, check that the bonnet fastens and releases in a satisfactory manner. If adjustment is necessary, slacken the bonnet lock retaining bolts **(see illustration 10.2)**, and adjust the position of the lock to suit. Once the lock is operating correctly, securely tighten its retaining bolts.
8 If necessary, align the front edge of the bonnet with the wing panels by turning the rubbers screwed into the body front panel, to raise or lower the front edge as required.

8 Bonnet release cable – removal and refitting

Removal
1 Open and support the bonnet.
2 Remove the bonnet lock from the front panel, as described in Section 9.
3 The bonnet release cable travels from the bonnet lock, along the front panel, and then under the right-hand headlight unit.
4 To make access easier, remove the front bumper as described in Section 5.

6.8 Disconnect the wiring connector

5 Working along the length of the cable, release it from any securing clips to the vehicle body.
6 Working in the driver's footwell, undo the two retaining bolts and unclip the bonnet release lever mounting bracket from the facia **(see illustrations)**.
7 Unclip the outer cable from the bracket, and then unhook the end of the bonnet release cable from the bonnet release lever **(see illustration)**.
8 Note the routing of the cable, and release it from any clips in the engine compartment, then feed the cable through the bulkhead grommet into the passenger compartment. It is advisable to tie a length of string to the end of the cable before removal, to aid refitting. Pull the cable through into the passenger compartment, then untie the string and leave it place until the new cable is to be refitted.

8.6a Undo the two retaining bolts. . .

8.7 Unhook the cable from the release lever

7.2 Bonnet hinge retaining nuts

Refitting
9 Refitting is a reversal of removal, but use the string to pull the cable into position, and ensure that the bulkhead grommet is securely located. Make sure that the cable is routed as noted before removal, and reposition the cable in its securing clips in the engine compartment. Check the bonnet release mechanism for correct operation on completion.

9 Bonnet lock – removal and refitting

Removal
1 Open and support the bonnet.
2 Undo the two securing nuts from inside the holes in the front crossmember and the one bolt from the rear of the crossmsmber, then

8.6b . . . and unclip the release levers from the facia

9.2a Undo the two nuts inside the front crossmember. . .

9.2b . . . the one bolt at the rear. . .

9.2c . . . then remove the lock assembly

10.2a Unclip the gaiter from the door pillar. . .

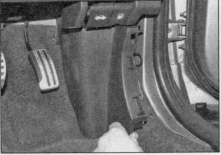

10.2b . . . and disconnect the wiring block connector

withdraw the lock assembly from the body panel (see illustrations).

3 Unclip the outer cable from the bracket, and then unhook the end of the bonnet release cable from the lock lever.

4 The bonnet lock assembly can then be removed from the vehicle.

Refitting

5 Refitting is a reversal of removal. If

necessary see adjustment, as described in Section 7.

10 Door – removal, refitting and adjustment

Removal

1 Disconnect the battery negative terminal (refer to Disconnecting the battery in Chapter 5 Section 4).

2 On rear doors, open the door and unclip the rubber gaiter from the door pillar, withdraw the wiring block connector from within the door pillar and disconnect (see illustrations).

3 On front doors, open the door and unclip the sill trim panel, then undo the retaining nut and remove the kick panel from inside the front door pillar. Disconnect the wiring connector and withdraw it through the door pillar (see illustrations).

4 Undo the bolt securing the door check strap to the body panel (see illustration).

5 Mark the positions of the hinges on the door, to aid alignment of the door on refitting.

6 Have an assistant support the door, then unscrew the nuts securing the door hinges to the door, and lift the door from the vehicle (see illustrations).

7 Examine the hinges for wear and damage. If necessary, the hinges can be unbolted from the body and renewed.

Refitting

8 Refitting is a reversal of removal, but align the

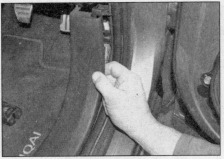

10.3a Unclip the sill trim panel. . .

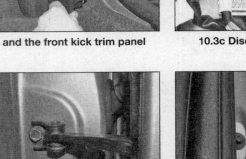

10.3b . . . and the front kick trim panel

10.3c Disconnect the wiring block connector. . .

10.3d . . . and pull the door wiring out from the front pillar

10.4 Undo the door check strap bolt

10.6a Undo the upper hinge retaining nuts. . .

hinges with the marks made on the body before removal, and before finally tightening the hinge securing bolts, check the door adjustment as described in the following paragraphs.

Adjustment

9 Close the door (**carefully**, in case the alignment is incorrect, which may cause scratching on the door or the body as the door is closed), and check the fit of the door with the surrounding panels.

10 If adjustment is required, loosen the hinge securing bolts (the hinge-to-door and the hinge-to-body bolt holes are elongated), and move the hinges as required to achieve satisfactory alignment. Tighten the securing bolts to the specified torque when the alignment is satisfactory.

11 Check the operation of the door lock. If necessary, slacken the securing bolts, and adjust the position of the lock striker on the body pillar to achieve satisfactory alignment (**see illustration**).

---

11 Door inner trim panel –
removal and refitting

Front door trim panel

1 Disconnect the battery negative terminal (refer to *Disconnecting the battery* in Chapter 5 Section 4).

2 Using a plastic trim tool carefully unclip the trim panel from around the inner door release handle (**see illustrations**).

3 Carefully unclip the grab handle trim panel, along with the side mirror switch assembly from the door panel and disconnect the wiring connector (**see illustrations**).

4 Undo the three mounting bolts and remove

the grab handle metal frame from the door panel (**see illustrations**).

5 Carefully unclip the switch panel from the top of the armrest, unhooking it from the front of the door trim panel, then disconnect the wiring connectors (**see illustrations**).

10.6b . . . and lower hinge retaining nuts

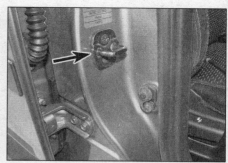
10.11 Door lock striker plate

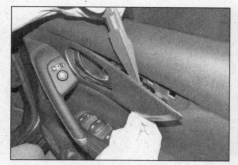
11.2a Using a trim tool. . .

11.2b . . . to remove the trim panel from the inner handle

11.3a Unclip the trim panel. . .

11.3b . . . and disconnect the wiring connector

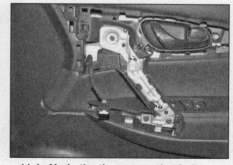
11.4a Undo the three mounting bolts. . .

11.4b . . . and remove the grab handle metal frame

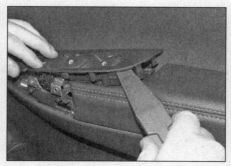
11.5a Unclip the switch panel. . .

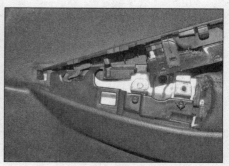
11.5b . . . unhooking it at the front. . .

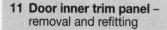

11.5c . . . then disconnect the wiring connectors

11.6a Undo the retaining bolt. . .

11.6b . . . release the retaining clips. . .

11.6c . . . then lift and remove the trim panel from the door

11.10a Unclip the switch panel. . .

11.10b . . . from the door trim panel

6 Undo the retaining bolt from inside the armrest aperture, then working your way around the edge of the panel, release the retaining clips securing the trim panel to the door. Using a forked trim tool, release the internal securing clips around the edge of the trim panel, then lift the panel upwards to release it from the door frame **(see illustrations)**.

7 If work is to be carried out on the door internal components, it will be necessary to remove the weather sealing sheet, as described later in this section.

8 Refitting is a reversal of removal, bearing in mind the following points:

a) *Make sure that the trim panel securing clips engage correctly with the door panel. Renew any broken clips.*

b) *Check the upper weatherstrip engages correctly with the door trim panel as the panel is refitted.*

Rear door trim panel

9 Disconnect the battery negative terminal (refer to *Disconnecting the battery* in Chapter 5 Section 4).

10 Carefully unclip the grab handle/ switch panel from the top of the armrest and disconnect the wiring connector **(see illustrations)**.

11 Using a plastic trim tool carefully unclip the trim panel from around the inner door release handle **(see illustrations)**.

12 Undo the retaining bolt from inside the armrest/grab handle aperture **(see illustration)**.

13 Working your way around the edge of the panel, release the retaining clips securing the trim panel to the door. Using a forked trim tool, release the internal securing clips around the edge of the trim panel, then lift the panel upwards to release it from the door frame **(see illustration)**.

14 If work is to be carried out on the door internal components, it will be necessary to remove the weather sealing sheet, as described later in this section.

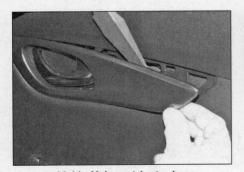

11.11a Using a trim tool. . .

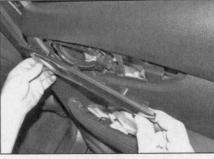

11.11b . . . to remove the trim panel from the inner handle

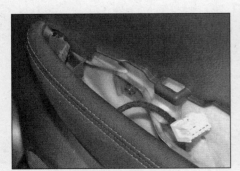

11.12 Undo the retaining bolt

11.13 Remove the trim panel from the door

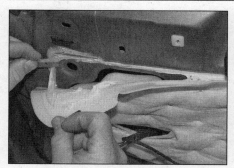

11.16a Using a sharp knife to cut the sealant. . .

11.16b . . . remove the weather sealing sheet

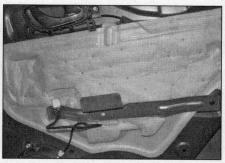

11.16c On rear doors, undo the bolts and remove the support bracket first

15 Refitting is a reversal of removal, bearing in mind the following points:
a) Ensure that the sealing sheet is correctly refitted, and sealed around its edge. It should be possible to use the original mastic sealant, but if necessary, new sealant can be obtained from a Nissan dealer.
b) Make sure that the trim panel securing clips engage correctly with the door panel. Renew any broken clips.
c) Check the upper weatherstrip engages correctly with the door trim panel as the panel is refitted.

Weather sealing sheet

16 Using a sharp knife, carefully release the sealant bead and pull the weather sealing sheet from the door (see illustrations). Try to keep the sealant intact as far as possible, to ease refitting.

12 Door handles and lock components – removal and refitting

Interior door release handle/lever

1 Remove the door inner trim panel and weather sealing sheet, as described in Section 11.
2 Undo the securing bolt and slide the release lever to the rear of the door to withdraw it from the door panel (see illustrations).
3 Unclip the operating cable outer sleeve from the release lever bracket, and then unclip the inner part of the operating cable from the lever (see illustration).
4 Refitting is a reversal of removal, bearing in mind the following points:
a) Ensure that the lock operating cables are routed as noted before removal.

b) Check the operation of the release lever/ lock mechanism before refitting the door inner trim panel.
c) Refit the door inner trim panel with reference to Section 11.

Exterior door handle (front doors)

5 Open the door and remove the plastic plug/grommet from the rear of the door, to access the door lock retaining screw (see illustration).
6 Remove the door inner trim panel and weather sealing sheet, as described in Section 11.
7 Working inside the rear of the door panel, undo the retaining bolt and remove the retaining clip, then remove the security shield from over the door lock mechanism (see illustrations).
8 Reaching inside the rear of the door pane at the rear of the door lock, use a thin

12.2a Undo the retaining bolt. . .

12.2b . . . then slide the release lever bracket from the door

12.3 Release the outer cable and disconnect the inner operating cable

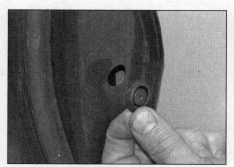

12.5 Remove the plastic plug/grommet

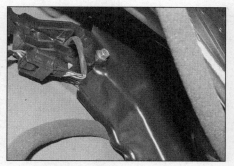

12.7a Undo the retaining bolt. . .

12.7b . . . release the retaining clip. . .

12.7c . . . and remove the security shield

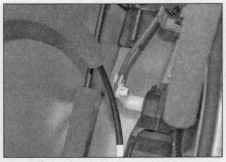

12.8 Release the plastic clip from the lock operating rod

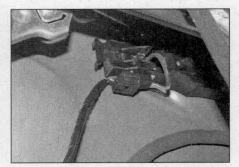

12.9a Release the wiring from the handle mounting bracket. . .

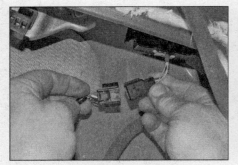

12.9b . . . and disconnect the wiring connector

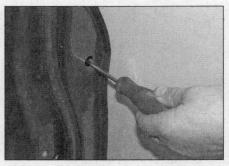

12.10a Slacken the retaining screw. . .

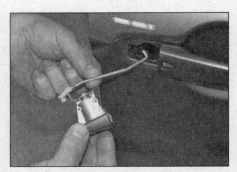

12.10b . . . and withdraw the door lock cylinder/push button

screwdriver to unclip the plastic retaining clip from the lower part of the door lock operating rod **(see illustration)**.

9 Release the wiring connector from the

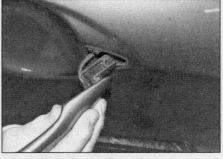

12.11a Slide the handle to the rear and pull it out to disengage it from the door

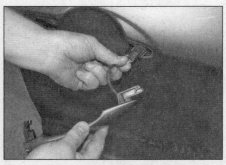

12.11b On models with intelligent key system, withdraw the wiring out from the door panel

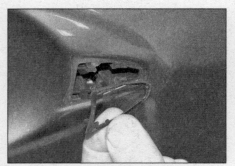

12.12a Unclip the seals. . .

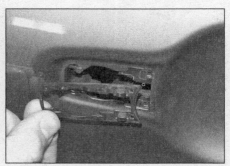

12.12b . . . from the door handle recess

front of the door handle mounting bracket and disconnect the wiring connector **(see illustrations)**.

10 Slacken the retaining screw, until it cannot

be turned any further and comes to a stop (DO NOT force the screw when it reaches the stop). The screw does not come completely out from the door panel. Carefully withdraw the push button/lock cylinder out from the door handle assembly, complete with operating rod **(see illustrations)**. Take care not to damage the paintwork as it is removed.

11 Detach the handle by sliding it to the rear of the door, and then pulling it out from the handle recess. On models with intelligent key system, withdraw the wiring cables out through the handle recess **(see illustrations)**.

12 If required unclip the rubber seals from around the handle recess in the door panel **(see illustrations)**.

13 Refitting is a reversal of removal, bearing in mind the following points:
a) Ensure that the lock operating cable/rods are routed as noted before removal.
b) Check the operation of the release lever/ lock mechanism before refitting the door inner trim panel.
c) Refit the door inner trim panel with reference to Section 11.

Exterior door handle (rear doors)

14 Open the door and remove the plastic cover/grommet from the rear of the door, to access the door lock retaining screw **(see illustration)**.

15 Slacken the retaining screw, until it cannot be turned any further and comes to a stop (DO NOT force the screw when it reaches the stop). The screw does not come completely out from the door panel. Carefully withdraw

12.14 Remove the plastic grommet from the access hole

12.15a Slacken the retaining screw. . .

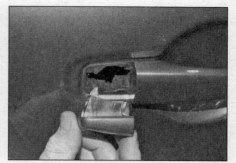

12.15b . . . and withdraw the door push button

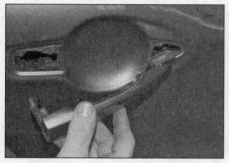

12.16 Slide the handle to the rear and pull it out to disengage it from the door

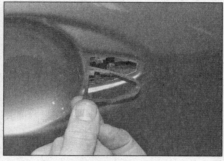

12.17a Unclip the seals. . .

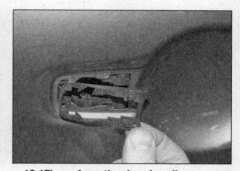

12.17b . . . from the door handle recess

the push button out from the door handle assembly **(see illustrations)**. Take care not to damage the paintwork as it is removed.

16 Detach the handle by sliding it to the rear of the door, and then pulling it out from the handle recess **(see illustration)**.

17 If required unclip the rubber seals from around the handle recess in the door panel **(see illustrations)**.

18 Refitting is a reversal of removal, but ensure that the handle locates securely inside the door lock housing. When fitting the rear of the door handle, make sure the leg on the rear of the handle is positioned behind the lever on the support bracket inside the door panel, before refitting the push button.

Front door lock

19 With the window glass in the fully raised position, remove the door inner trim panel and weather sealing sheet, as described in Section 11.

20 If required, remove the interior door release lever, as described in paragraphs 1 to 4.

21 Remove the exterior door handle, as described in paragraphs 5 to 12.

22 Undo the retaining bolt and then unclip the upper part of the window guide channel from the rear of the door frame **(see illustrations)**, to access the door lock assembly.

23 Unclip the door handle operating cable from the retaining clip on the door frame panel **(see illustration)**.

24 Working at the rear edge of the door, unscrew the three lock securing screws, then

release the outer handle support bracket, by sliding it to the rear of the door. Withdraw the the lock assembly from the inside of the door panel, and out through the door aperture **(see illustrations)**. Disconnect the wiring

connector from the door lock assembly as it is removed.

25 If required, unclip the operating cable outer sleeve from the exterior handle mounting bracket, and then unclip the inner

12.22a Undo the retaining bolt. . .

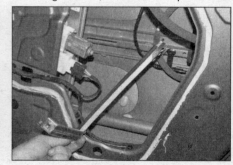

12.22b . . . and withdraw the window guide channel

12.23 Unclip the operating cable

12.24a Undo the three screws securing the lock. . .

12.24b . . . release the handle support from the handle recess. . .

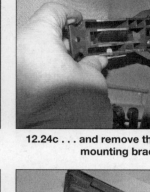

12.24c . . . and remove the outer handle mounting bracket

c) Refit the door inner trim panel with reference to Section 11.

Rear door lock

27 With the window glass in the fully raised position, remove door inner trim panel, weather sealing sheet and support bracket, as described in Section 11.

28 Remove the interior door release lever, as described in paragraphs 1 to 4.

29 Remove the exterior door handle, as described in paragraphs 14 to 18.

30 Undo the retaining bolt and the two upper retaining screws and remove the window guide channel from the rear of the door **(see illustrations)**, to access the door lock assembly.

31 Unclip the door handle operating cable from the retaining clip on the door frame panel **(see illustration)**.

12.24d . . . then withdraw the assembly from inside the door

12.25 Release the outer cable and disconnect the inner operating cable

part of the operating cable from the lever **(see illustration)**.

26 Refitting is a reversal of removal, bearing in mind the following points:

a) Ensure that the lock operating cable/rods

are correctly reconnected and routed, as noted before removal.

b) Check the operation of the release lever/ lock mechanism before refitting the door inner trim panel.

32 Working at the rear edge of the door, unscrew the three lock securing screws, then release the outer handle support bracket, by sliding it to the rear of the door. Withdraw the the lock assembly from the inside of the door panel, and out through the door aperture **(see illustration)**.

33 Disconnect the wiring connector from the door lock assembly as it is removed **(see illustration)**.

34 Refitting is a reversal of removal, bearing in mind the following points:

a) Ensure that the lock operating cables are correctly reconnected and routed, as noted before removal.

b) Check the operation of the mechanism before refitting the door inner trim panel.

c) Refit the door inner trim panel as described in Section 11.

12.30a Undo the retaining bolt. . .

12.30b . . . and the two retaining screws. . .

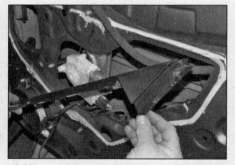

12.30c . . . then withdraw the window guide channel

12.31 Unclip the operating cable

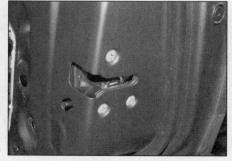

12.32 Undo the three screws securing the lock in position

12.33 Disconnect the wiring connector as it is removed

13.2 Undo the two window glass securing bolts

13.4a Release the glass from the regulator...

13.4b ... then withdraw the window glass from the door

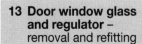

13 Door window glass and regulator – removal and refitting

Front window glass

1 Remove the door inner trim panel and weather sealing sheet, as described in Section 11.

2 Temporarily reconnect the electric window switch (and the battery negative terminal, if removed), and lower or raise the window until the two bolts securing the lower edge of the window glass to the regulator mechanism are accessible through the holes in the door panel. Support the glass, and then undo the two bolts **(see illustration)**.

3 To make removal of the glass easier, carefully ease the inner sealing weather strip from the top of the door frame.

4 Disengage the lower part of the window glass from the regulator, raise the glass at the rear, and then withdraw it from the door frame **(see illustrations)**.

5 Refitting is a reversal of removal, bearing in mind the following points:
a) Take care not to damage the weather strips when fitting the glass.
b) Check the operation of the window mechanism before refitting the door inner trim panel.
c) Refit the door inner trim panel with reference to Section 11.

Front window regulator

6 Remove the door inner trim panel and weather sealing sheet, as described in Section 11.

7 Disengage the window glass from the regulator and slide it to the top of the window frame and tape it in position. If required the window glass can be completely removed, as described in paragraphs 2 to 4.

8 Disconnect the wiring connector from the window regulator motor **(see illustration)**. If required, release the wiring loom from the retaining clips.

9 Undo the window regulator assembly securing bolts, then manipulate the complete motor/regulator assembly out through the aperture in the door **(see illustration)**.

13.8 Disconnect the motor wiring connector

10 Refitting is a reversal of removal, bearing in mind the following points:
a) Refit the front window glass with reference to paragraph 5.
b) Check the operation of the window mechanism before refitting the door inner trim panel.

Rear window glass

11 Remove the door inner trim panel and weather sealing sheet, as described in Section 11.

12 If not already done, temporarily reconnect the electric window switch (and the battery negative terminal, if removed), and fully close the window. Undo the retaining bolt and the two upper retaining screws and remove the window guide channel from the rear of the door **(see illustrations 12.30a, 12.30b & 12.30c)**.

13 Lower the window until the two bolts

13.13 Undo the two window glass securing bolts

13.9 Remove the window motor/regulator assembly from the door

securing the lower edge of the window glass to the regulator mechanism are accessible through the aperture in the door panel. Support the glass, and then undo the two bolts **(see illustration)**.

14 To make removal of the glass easier, carefully ease the inner sealing weather strip from the top of the door frame **(see illustration)**.

15 Disengage the lower part of the window glass from the regulator, raise the glass, and then withdraw it from the outside of the door frame **(see illustration)**.

16 Refitting is a reversal of removal, bearing in mind the following points:
a) When fitting the rear window guide, make sure the upper part is located correctly in the door frame.
b) Take care not to damage the weather strips when fitting the glass.

13.14 Unclip the weather strip from the door frame

13.15 Withdraw the window glass out from the door

13.20 Disconnect the motor wiring connector

13.21 Remove the window motor/regulator from the door

c) *Check the operation of the window mechanism before refitting the door inner trim panel.*

d) *Refit the door inner trim panel with reference to Section 11.*

Rear window regulator

17 Remove the door inner trim panel and weather sealing sheet, as described in Section 11.

18 Temporarily reconnect the electric window switch (and the battery negative terminal, if removed), and lower or raise the window until the two bolts securing the lower edge of the window glass to the regulator mechanism are accessible through the holes in the window regulator assembly. Support the glass, and then undo the two bolts **(see illustration 13.12)**.

19 Disengage the window glass from the regulator and slide it to the top of the window frame and tape it in position. If required the window glass can be completely removed, as described in paragraphs 12 to 15.

20 Disconnect the wiring connector from the window regulator motor **(see illustration)**.

21 Undo the window regulator and motor securing bolts, and then manipulate the complete motor/regulator assembly out through the aperture in the door **(see illustration)**.

22 Refitting is a reversal of removal, bearing in mind the following points:

a) *Refit the window glass and tighten the retaining bolts.*

b) *Check the operation of the window mechanism before refitting the door inner trim panel.*

c) *Refit the door inner trim panel with reference to Section 11.*

14 Tailgate and support struts
– removal, refitting and adjustment

Tailgate

Removal

1 Disconnect the battery negative terminal (refer to *Disconnecting the battery* in Chapter 5 Section 4).

2 Remove the tailgate interior trim panels as described in Section 23.

3 Working inside the tailgate, disconnect the wiring plugs to the wiper motor, the heated rear window element, the rear number plate lights, the rear light clusters, and the high-level stop-light. Also unbolt any earth lead(s). Check for any other wiring connectors, which must be disconnected to facilitate tailgate removal, and then release the harness securing cable ties **(see illustration)**.

4 Remove the tailgate high level brake light, as described in Chapter 12 Section 7, and disconnect the washer fluid hose.

5 Tie a length of string to the wiring harness and washer hose, then prise the wiring harness grommets from the both corners of the tailgate **(see illustrations)**. Feed the wiring harness through the aperture in the tailgate on the left-hand side and the washer fluid hose on the right-hand side. Untie the string from the wiring harness, and leave the string in place in the tailgate, to aid refitting.

6 Have an assistant support the tailgate in the open position.

7 Remove the securing clips and release both support struts from their upper mounting point on the tailgate **(see illustrations 15.16a and 15.16b)**.

8 Using a pencil or felt tip pen, mark the outline of each hinge relative to the tailgate, to use as a guide on refitting. Unscrew the nuts securing the hinges to the tailgate **(see illustration)**, and then lift the tailgate from the vehicle.

Refitting

9 Refitting is a reversal of removal, bearing in mind the following points.

10 Tie the string to the wiring harness and washer fluid hose, and use the string to pull

14.3 Disconnect the wiring connectors and earth cables inside the tailgate

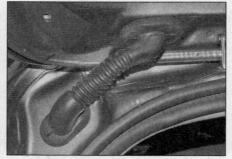

14.5a Unclip the wiring gaiters. . .

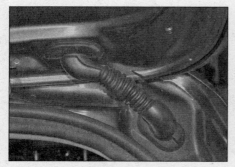

14.5b . . . from both sides of the vehicle

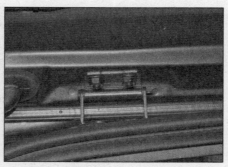

14.8 Undo the hinge retaining nuts

them back through the aperture and into the tailgate.

11 Do not fully tighten the hinge securing nuts until the tailgate adjustment has been checked, as described in the following paragraphs.

Adjustment

12 Close the tailgate (**carefully**, in case the alignment is incorrect, which may cause scratching on the tailgate or the body as the tailgate is closed), and check for alignment with the adjacent panels.

13 If adjustment is required, it will be necessary to slacken the hinge retaining nuts and re-align the tailgate to suit. Once the tailgate is correctly aligned, tighten the hinge retaining nuts fully.

14 Once the tailgate is correctly aligned, check that the tailgate fastens and releases in a satisfactory manner. If adjustment is necessary, slacken the tailgate lock striker retaining screws, and adjust the position of the catch, as described in Section 15. Once the tailgate lock is operating correctly, securely tighten the retaining screws.

Support struts

15 Before removing any of the struts, first ensure that the tailgate is adequately supported.

16 Remove the securing clips, and then release both support struts from their upper and lower mounting points (**see illustrations**).

17 Refitting is a reversal of removal.

---

15 Tailgate lock components – removal and refitting

Tailgate lock

1 Disconnect the battery negative terminal (refer to *Disconnecting the battery* in Chapter 5 Section 4).

2 Remove the tailgate inner trim panel as described in Section 23.

3 Reaching inside the tailgate, disconnect the wiring connector from the lock assembly (**see illustration**).

4 Unscrew the two lock securing bolts from the edge of the tailgate, then manipulate the

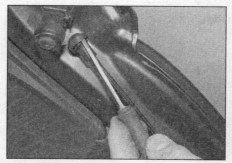
14.16a Prise out the upper securing clip. . .

14.16b . . . and lower securing clip to release the balljoints

lock out through the aperture in the tailgate (**see illustration**).

5 Refitting is a reversal of removal, but before refitting the trim panel, check that the tailgate fastens and releases in a satisfactory manner. If adjustment is necessary, slacken the tailgate lock retaining bolts, and adjust the position of the lock to suit. Once the lock is operating correctly, securely tighten its retaining bolts.

Tailgate lock striker

6 Unclip the trim panel from the rear of the luggage compartment, as described in Section 23.

7 Note the position of the striker plate, then unscrew the two securing screws, and withdraw the lock striker from the rear panel (**see illustration**).

8 Refitting is a reversal of removal, but check the operation of the tailgate release mechanism.

9 Check that the tailgate fastens and releases in a satisfactory manner. If adjustment is necessary, slacken the striker retaining screws, and adjust the position of the striker to suit. Once the lock is operating correctly, securely tighten the striker retaining screws.

Tailgate exterior switch

10 Remove the tailgate inner trim panel as described in Section 23.

11 Reach inside the tailgate and disconnect the wiring connector(s) for the tailgate switch and number plate lights (**see illustration**).

12 Undo the retaining nuts, securing the switch/light trim panel to the tailgate, working inside the tailgate undo the nuts and withdraw the trim panel from the tailgate. Release the rubber grommet and withdraw the wiring through the tailgate panel, as it is removed (**see illustrations**).

13 To remove the switch, disconnect the

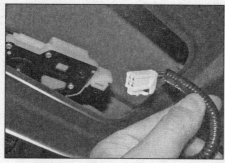
15.3 Disconnect the lock wiring plug connector

15.4 Undo the two bolts from the edge of the tailgate

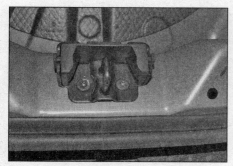
15.7 Undo the two screws to remove the lock striker

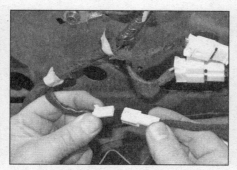
15.11 Disconnect the wiring plug connector

15.12a Unclip the wiring rubber grommet. . .

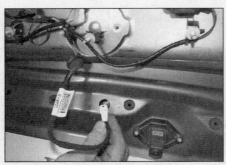

15.12b . . . and remove the tailgate trim panel with wiring

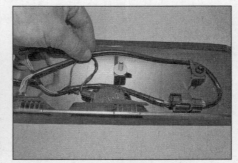

15.13a Disconnect and unclip the wiring. . .

15.13b . . . then release the switch from the trim panel

wiring connector, release the securing clips and withdraw the switch from the trim panel **(see illustrations)**.

14 Refitting is a reversal of removal.

16 Central locking system components – removal and refitting

Body Control Module (BCM)

Removal

1 The electronic body control unit is located behind the glovebox, on the left-hand side of the facia next to the fusebox **(see illustration)**.

2 Disconnect the battery negative terminal (refer to *Disconnecting the battery* in Chapter 5 Section 4).

3 Remove the glovebox as described in Section 25.

4 Note the location of the wiring block connectors, then disconnect them from the control unit **(see illustrations)**.

5 Remove the upper and lower retaining screws and withdraw the control unit from the mounting bracket.

Refitting

6 Refitting is a reversal of removal.

Door lock motor

7 The motor is integral with the door lock assembly. Removal and refitting of the lock assembly is described in Section 12.

Tailgate lock motor

8 Removal of the tailgate lock motor is described as part of the tailgate lock removal and refitting procedure described in Section 15.

Door switches

9 Disconnect the battery negative terminal (refer to *Disconnecting the battery* in Chapter 5 Section 4).

10 Undo the retaining screw and withdraw the relevant switch from the door pillar **(see illustration)**.

11 Disconnect the wiring connector and remove the switch.

12 Refitting is a reversal of removal.

Remote control battery renewal

13 Release the securing clip and withdraw the key from the remote control body **(see illustrations)**.

14 Using a small screwdriver, carefully prise the two halves of the transmitter apart **(see illustrations)**.

15 Carefully unclip the battery from its

16.1 Electrical components behind glovebox

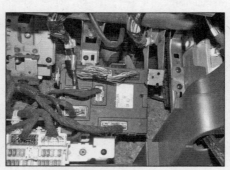

16.4a Note the location of the connectors on the BCM. . .

16.4b . . . then disconnect the wiring block connectors

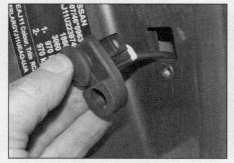

16.10 Remove the door switch from the pillar

16.13a Release the clip. . .

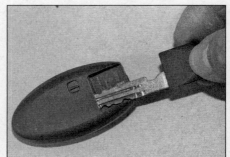

16.13b . . . and withdraw the key

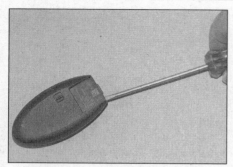

16.14a Twist a small screwdriver in the slot. . .

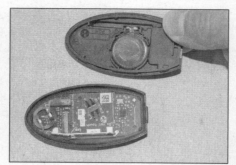

16.14b . . . and unclip one side of the transmitter

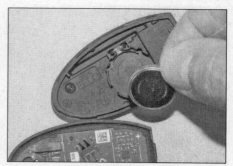

16.15 Unclip the battery from its location in the cover

position in the transmitter housing, noting its fitted position (see illustration).

16 Fit the new battery (CR2032 – 3V), observing the correct polarity, and clip the transmitter housing back together.

17 Mirrors and associated components – removal and refitting

Exterior mirror assembly

1 If working on an electric mirror, disconnect the battery negative terminal (refer to *Disconnecting the battery* in Chapter 5 Section 4).
2 Remove the door inner trim panel, as described in Section 11.
3 Carefully prise off the mirror interior trim panel (see illustration).
4 Disconnect the mirror wiring connectors, noting their routing (see illustration).
5 Support the mirror, then remove the three securing bolts, and withdraw the mirror from the outside of the door (see illustrations).
6 Refitting is a reversal of removal, ensuring that the mirror wiring is routed as noted before removal.

Exterior mirror glass

Caution: It is advisable to wear gloves to protect your hands, even if the glass is not broken, due to the risk of mirror glass breakage.

7 Carefully press the mirror glass in at the bottom, and then working through the gap at the top edge of the mirror glass, use a lever to

17.3 Unclip the plastic trim cover

release the clips that secure the mirror glass to the mirror body (see illustration).
8 Withdraw the glass, and (where applicable) disconnect the heating element wiring connectors (see illustrations).

17.5a Undo the three securing bolts. . .

17.4 Disconnect the wiring connectors

9 To refit, place a piece of cloth over the mirror glass, then carefully push the mirror glass evenly, until the securing clips lock into position on the mirror adjuster base.

17.5b . . . and remove the mirror

17.7 Carefully lever the lower edge of the mirror glass

17.8a Unclip the mirror from the mirror base. . .

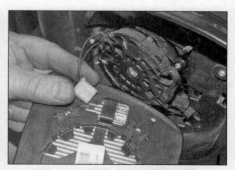

17.8b . . . and disconnect the wiring connectors

17.11a Release the retaining clips. . .

17.11b . . . around the outer edge of the mirror housing. . .

17.11c . . . and remove the mirror outer shell

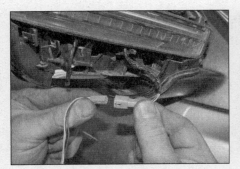

17.12 Disconnect the wiring connector

17.16 Undo the three motor retaining screws. . .

the mirror body until the securing clips lock into position.

14 Refit the mirror glass as described previously in this Section.

Exterior mirror electric motor

15 Remove the mirror glass as described previously in this Section.

16 Working from inside the mirror housing, undo the three retaining screws and withdraw the motor from the mirror body **(see illustration)**.

17 Disconnect the wiring connector as it is removed **(see illustration)**.

18 Refitting is a reversal of removal, ensuring that the mirror glass is fitted securely as described previously in this Section.

Interior mirror

19 Using a small flat-bladed screwdriver carefully prise apart the plastic covers, from around the mirror base **(see illustrations)**.

Exterior mirror outer shell

10 Remove the mirror glass as described previously in this Section.

11 Working from inside the mirror housing, release the retaining clips, and then carefully

remove the mirror shell from the mirror body **(see illustrations)**.

12 On models with camera fitted to the base of the mirror, disconnect the wiring connector, as the cover is removed **(see illustration)**.

13 To refit, carefully push the mirror shell onto

17.17 . . . and disconnect the wiring connector

17.19a Unclip the small trim. . .

17.19b . . . and then withdraw the large trim panel

17.20 Disconnect the wiring plug

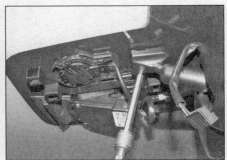

17.21a Undo the retaining screw. . .

17.21b . . . and slide the mirror upwards to remove

20 Disconnect the wiring plug at the rear of the mirror **(see illustration)**.

21 Undo the retaining screw and slide the mirror upwards, to release it from the mounting base on the windscreen **(see illustrations)**. Note the mirror can be a tight fit on the base, take care not to damage the windscreen as this is removed.

22 To refit the interior mirror to the base, offer it up and slide it downwards back into place and fit the retaining screw. Reconnect the wiring connector and refit the plastic trim covers.

18 Windscreen, tailgate glass and fixed windows –
general information

1 These areas of glass are secured by the tight fit of the weatherstrip in the body aperture, and are bonded in position with a special adhesive. Renewal of such fixed glass is a difficult, messy and time-consuming task, which is considered beyond the scope of the home mechanic. It is difficult, unless one has plenty of practice, to obtain a secure, waterproof fit. Furthermore, the task carries a high risk of breakage; this applies especially to the laminated glass windscreen. In view of this, owners are strongly advised to have this sort of work carried out by one of the many specialist windscreen fitters.

2 For those possessing the necessary skills and equipment to carry out this task, some preliminary removal of the vehicle interior trim and associated components is necessary, as follows, referring to the procedures contained in the Sections and Chapters indicated.

Windscreen

3 Remove both wiper arms (Chapter 12 Section 11).
4 Remove the windscreen scuttle grille panel (Section 20 of this Chapter).
5 Remove the front pillar trim on both sides (Section 23 of this Chapter).
6 Remove the sunvisors (Section 23 of this Chapter).

Rear fixed side window glass

7 Remove the relevant luggage compartment trim panels (Section 23 of this Chapter).

Tailgate window glass

8 Remove the tailgate trim panels (Section 23 of this Chapter).

19 Sunroof –
general information

1 Due to the complexity of the sunroof mechanism, considerable expertise is required to repair, renew or adjust the sunroof components successfully. Removal of the roof first requires the headlining to be removed, which is a tedious operation, and not a task to be undertaken lightly. Any problems with the sunroof should be referred to a Nissan dealer.

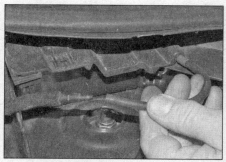
20.3 Disconnect the washer fluid hose

20.4b . . . including the ones under the sound proofing

20 Body exterior fittings –
removal and refitting

Windscreen scuttle grille panel

1 Open and support the bonnet.
2 Remove the windscreen wiper arms as described in Chapter 12 Section 11.
3 Disconnect the washer fluid hose from the right-hand side of the scuttle panel **(see illustration)**.
4 Working along the front edge of the scuttle panel, pull out the and release the scuttle panel retaining clips **(see illustrations)**.
5 Lift the scuttle grille panel away from the wiper spindles, unclipping it from the lower edge of the windscreen **(see illustration)**.
6 Refitting is a reversal of removal.

20.9a Release the plastic securing clips. . .

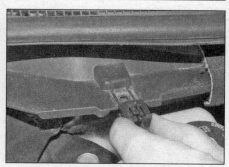
20.4a Release the retaining clips. . .

20.5 Unclip the scuttle panel

Wheel arch liners/shields

7 The wheel arch liners are secured by expanding plastic rivets, screws, nuts or bolts.
8 Firmly apply the handbrake, and then jack up the vehicle and support it securely on axle stands (see *Jacking and vehicle support*). To improve access to the fasteners, remove roadwheel(s).
9 To remove the liners, release the centre pins, and then prise the complete plastic rivet from place. Undo the retaining screws from under the lower edges of the liner. On the front, if the engine undershield is fitted undo the retaining bolts. With all the fasteners removed, manoeuvre the liner from the wheel arch **(see illustrations)**.

Body trim strips and badges

10 The various body trim strips and badges are held in position with a special adhesive

20.9b . . . and remove the inner wheel arch liner

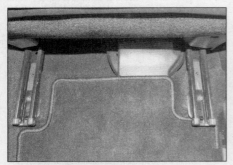

21.3 Undo the two bolts from the rear of the seat rails

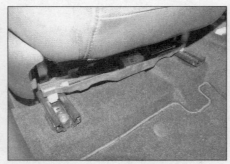

21.4 Undo the two bolts at the front of the seat rails

21.5 Disconnect the seat wiring connectors

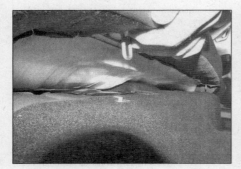

21.7 Release the front securing clip

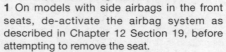

21.8 Slide the seat forwards from the locating brackets

tape. Removal requires the trim/badge to be heated, to soften the adhesive, and then cut away from the surface. Due to the high risk of damage to the vehicle paintwork during this operation, it is recommended that this task should be entrusted to a Nissan dealer.

21 Seats – removal and refitting

Front seat

⚠ **Warning: Most models are equipped with side airbags built into the outer sides of the front seats. Refer to Chapter 12 Section 19, for the precautions, which should be observed when dealing with an airbag system. Do not tamper with the airbag unit in any**

way, and do not attempt to test any airbag system components. Note that the airbag is triggered if the mechanism is supplied with an electrical current (including via an ohmmeter), or if the assembly is subjected to a temperature of greater than 100°C.

1 On models with side airbags in the front seats, de-activate the airbag system as described in Chapter 12 Section 19, before attempting to remove the seat.
2 Release the retaining clips and withdraw the headrest out from the top of the seat backrest. This will give more room, when removing the seat out through the door aperture.
3 Move the seat fully forwards and undo the two retaining bolts from the rear of the seat rails **(see illustration)**.
4 Slide the seat fully rearwards, and then unscrew the seat rail front securing bolts **(see illustration)**.

5 Tilt the seat backwards and disconnect the wiring connectors, then release the wiring loom from any retaining clips under the front of the seat base **(see illustration)**. Lift the seat, complete with the rails out from the vehicle, taking care that the seat rails do not catch on the vehicle paintwork as it is being removed.
6 Refitting is a reversal of removal, but tighten the securing bolts to the specified torque.

Rear seat cushion

7 Lift the seat cushion at the front, and then give a sharp pull upwards, to release the securing clip from the vehicle floor panel **(see illustration)**.
8 Slide the seat cushion forward, releasing the rear locating clips, then lift the seat cushion upwards and withdraw the seat belt buckles from the seat cushion **(see illustration)**.
9 Refitting is a reversal of removal.

Rear seat backs

10 Remove the rear seat cushion as described in paragraphs 7 and 8, previously in this Section.
11 Unclip the plastic trim covers at each side of the rear seat backs **(see illustration)**.
12 Undo the two nuts securing the outer part of the hinge bracket to the vehicle inner wing panel **(see illustration)**.
13 Release the upper catch on the rear seat back, then lift the right-hand seat back upwards, and pull it away from the left-hand seat back to disengage it from the inner hinge peg **(see illustration)**. Remove the right-hand seat back from the vehicle.

21.11 Unclip the trim cover

21.12 Undo the two retaining nuts. . .

21.13 . . . and remove the right-hand seat back

22.4a Insert tool to move wire clips outwards. . .

22.4b . . . then insert a thin screwdriver on the opposite side. . .

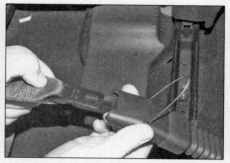

22.4c . . . to release the seat belt from the pretensioner

14 The left-hand seat back can now be removed in the same way, undo the two nuts securing the outer part of the hinge bracket to the vehicle inner wing panel.

15 Undo the centre hinge bracket bolt/nut at the join of the two seat backs, and then remove the right-hand seat back from the vehicle.

16 Refitting is a reversal of removal, tightening the hinge bolt/nut securely.

---

22 Seat belt components –
removal and refitting

22.5 Undo the seat belt lower anchor bolt

22.6 Disconnect the wiring connector from the inertia reel

Note: *Record the positions of the washers and spacers on the seat belt anchors, and ensure they are refitted in their original positions.*

Front seat belt

⚠️ **Warning: On certain models, the front seat belt inertia reels are equipped with a mechanical or pyrotechnic pretensioner mechanism. Refer to the airbag system precautions contained in Chapter 12 Section 19, which apply equally to the seat belt pretensioners. Do not tamper with the inertia reel pretensioner unit in any way, and do not attempt to test the unit.**

1 De-activate the airbag system (which will also de-activate the pyrotechnic pretensioner mechanism, where fitted) as described in Chapter 12 Section 19, before attempting to remove the seatbelt.

2 To make access easier, remove the relevant front seat as described in Section 21.

3 Remove the centre pillar trim panels as described in Section 23.

4 On models with seat belt pre-tensioners fitted, insert a u-shaped tool into the connector, then use a small screwdriver to release the lower end of the seat belt from the seat belt pre-tensioner **(see illustrations)**.

5 On models without seat belt pre-tensioners fitted, undo the seat belt lower anchorage bolt **(see illustration)**. Note the locating peg fitted to the slot in the sill panel for refitting.

6 Release the locking clip and disconnect the wiring connector from the inertia reel **(see illustration)**.

7 Unscrew the seat belt inertia reel mounting bolt **(see illustration)**, noting the fitted position of the inertial reel in the mounting bracket.

8 Undo the seat belt upper anchorage bolt, then remove the seat belt assembly from the vehicle **(see illustration)**.

9 Refitting is a reversal of removal, ensuring that all mounting bolts are tightened to the specified torque.

Front seat belt stalk

10 Remove the relevant front seat as described in Section 21.

11 Trace the wiring back from the seat belt stalk and under the seat cushion, then unclip it from the wiring securing clips **(see illustration)**.

12 Unscrew the bolt and withdraw the stalk assembly from the side of the front seat **(see illustration)**.

13 Refitting is a reversal of removal, but tighten the stalk anchor bolt to the specified torque.

Rear side seat belt

14 Remove the relevant rear seat as described in Section 21.

22.7 Undo the seat belt reel mounting bolt

22.8 Undo the seat belt upper anchor bolt

22.11 Unclip the wiring loom from the seat frame

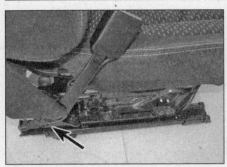

22.12 Undo the seat belt stalk anchor bolt

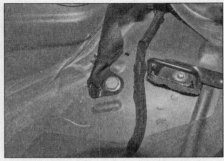

22.16 Undo the seat belt lower anchor bolt

22.17 Undo the seat belt reel mounting bolt

22.21 Undo the seat belt stalk retaining bolt

15 Working as described in Section 23, remove the relevant rear pillar trim panels for access to the inertia reel.
16 Unscrew the lower anchor bolts, from the rear floor panel **(see illustration)**.

17 Unscrew the seat belt inertia reel mounting bolt, then remove the seat belt assembly from the vehicle **(see illustration)**. Note the fitted position of the inertial reel on the mounting bracket before removal.

18 Refitting is a reversal of removal, ensuring that all mounting bolts are tightened to the specified torque.

Rear seat belt stalk

19 Remove the rear seat cushion, as described in Section 21.
20 Trace the wiring back from the seat belt stalk and disconnect the wiring connector.
21 Unscrew the bolt and withdraw the stalk assembly from the floor panel **(see illustration)**.
22 Refitting is a reversal of removal, but tighten the stalk anchor bolt to the specified torque.

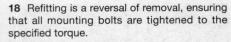

23 Interior trim panels – removal and refitting

General

1 The interior trim panels are secured by a combination of metal and plastic clips and screws. When releasing certain types of securing clips, a suitable forked tool will prove invaluable to avoid damage to the panel and clips. A degree of force will be necessary to pull some of the panels from their locations, especially where numerous internal retaining clips are used. Be prepared for some of the plastic clips to break when their relevant panel is being removed.

Door inner trim

2 Refer to Section 11.

Footwell sill trim panels

3 Unclip the front sill trim panel from the bottom of the B-pillar trim, and then from the front footwell side/kick trim panel **(see illustration)**.
4 Undo the plastic securing nut, and then unclip the footwell side/kick trim panel from the bottom of the A-pillar **(see illustrations)**.
5 Unclip the rear sill trim panel from the bottom of the B-pillar trim, and the rear inner wheel arch trim panel **(see illustration)**.
6 Refitting is a reversal of removal.

Front A-pillar trim panels

7 Carefully prise the front door weatherstrip from along the edge of the panel **(see illustration)**.

23.3 Unclip the front sill trim panel

23.4a Undo the plastic retaining nut...

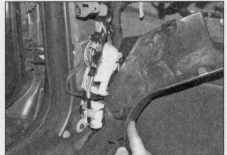

23.4b ...and unclip the kick panel trim

23.5 Unclip the rear sill trim panel

23.7 Peel back the door weather seal

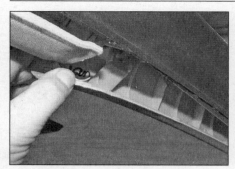

23.8a Unclip the A-pillar trim panel. . .

23.8b . . . release the securing clips. . .

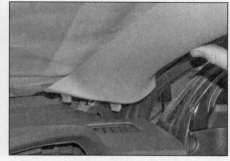

23.8c . . . then disengage the lower part from the facia

8 Pull the upper part of the panel from the pillar, release the securing clips, then lift the panel up to disengage the lower lugs from the facia and remove the trim panel **(see illustrations)**.

9 Refitting is a reversal of removal, ensuring the weatherstrip is correctly seated.

Centre B-pillar trim panels

10 To make access easier, slide the front seat as far forward as possible.

11 On models with seat belt pre-tensioners fitted, use a small screwdriver to disconnect the lower end of the seat belt from the seat belt pre-tensioner **(see illustrations 22.4a, 22.4b and 22.4c)**.

12 On models without seat belt pre-tensioners fitted, unclip the small plastic trim from around the seat belt **(see illustration 22.5)**.

13 Remove the sill trim panels from the front and rear door apertures, as described in paragraphs 3 to 5 in this Section.

14 Carefully prise the front and rear door weatherstrip from the edges of the centre B-pillar trim panels **(see illustration)**.

15 Unclip the lower trim panel from the B-pillar, and then disengage the seat belt/rubber gaiter through the slot in the lower part of the trim panel **(see illustrations)**. The lower trim panel can then be unclipped from the B-pillar.

16 Unclip the lower part of the upper trim panel from the B-pillar, and then pull it to disengage the upper part from behind the headlining **(see illustrations)**.

17 The upper trim panel can then be completely removed, by sliding the seat belt out through the slot in the panel. On models without seat belt pre-tensioners fitted, undo

the seat belt lower anchorage bolt (with reference to Section 22, paragraph 5), to remove the seat belt from the upper trim panel.

18 Refitting is a reversal of removal, ensuring that all retaining clips are fully engaged. If removed, refit the seat belt anchor bolt in the position noted during removal, then tighten to the specified torque.

Rear pillar trim panels

19 If the trim panel is to be completely removed it may be easier to remove the rear seats as described in Section 21. If required, remove the rear luggage compartment trim panel as described later in this Section.

20 Peel back the weather strip, then unclip the plastic inner wheel arch trim from each side of the vehicle **(see illustrations)**.

23.14 Pull the weather strip away from the panel

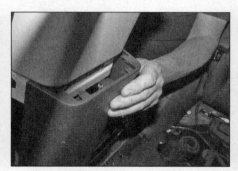

23.15a Unclip the upper part of the B-pillar. . .

23.15b . . . and remove the trim panel

23.16a Unclip the lower part of the trim. . .

23.16b . . . then pull to release it from the top of the B-pillar

23.20a Peel back the weatherstrip. . .

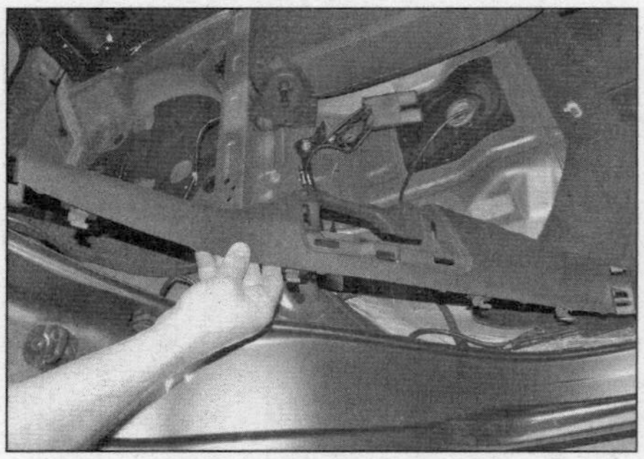

23.20b . . . then unclip the rear wheel arch trim panel

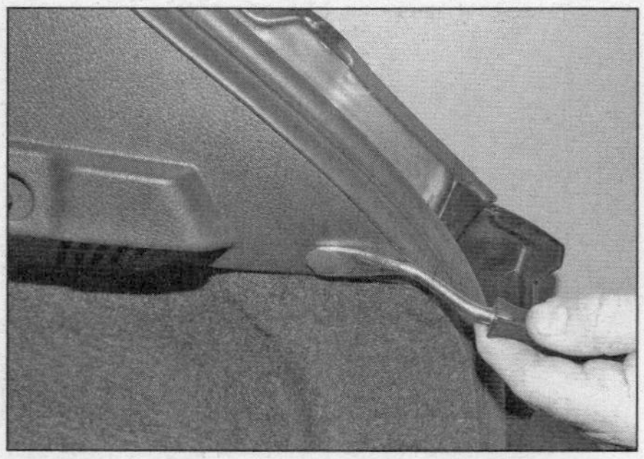

23.22a Using a lever, carefully release the retaining clips. . .

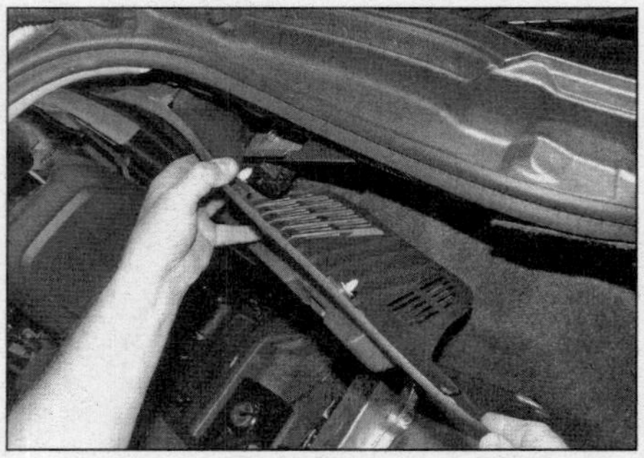

23.22b . . . and unclip the upper trim panel. . .

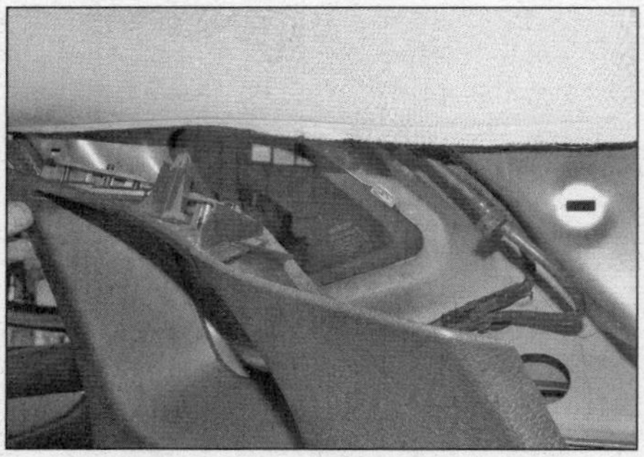

23.22c . . . and remove the trim panel

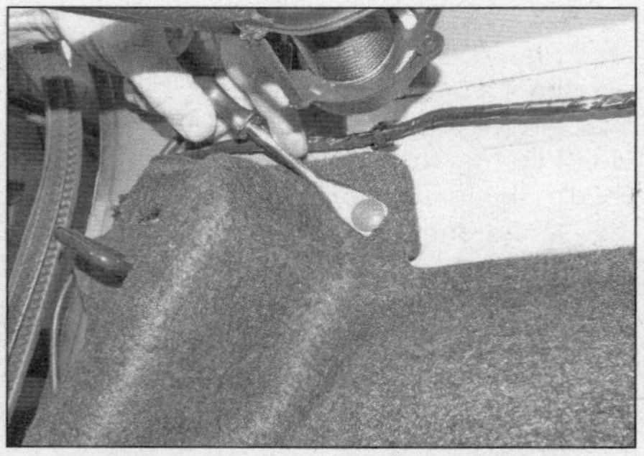

23.25a Release the retaining clips. . .

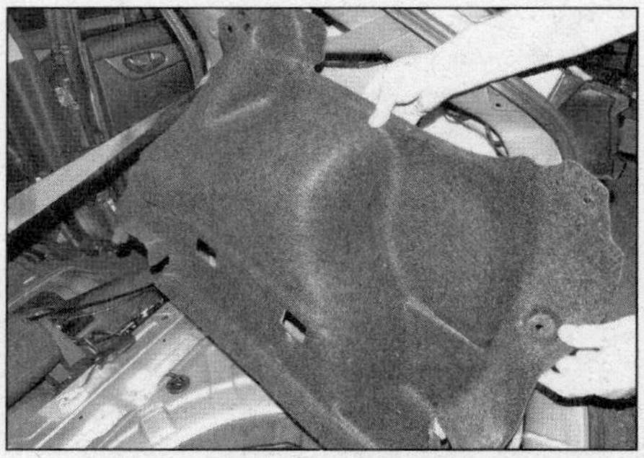

23.25b . . . and remove the lower side carpet

21 Unscrew the lower anchor bolts, from the rear floor panel **(see illustration 22.16)**.

22 Carefully prise the retaining clips, then release the upper trim panel from the rear pillar **(see illustrations)**.

23 The upper trim panel can then be completely removed, by sliding the seat belt out through the slot in the panel.

24 To remove the lower carpet trim panel, first remove the rear luggage compartment trim panels, as described in paragraphs 32 to 35 in this Section.

25 Release the retaining clips and withdraw the carpet trim from the inner rear wheel arch **(see illustrations)**.

26 Refitting is a reversal of removal, ensuring that all retaining clips are fully engaged. If removed, refit the seat belt anchor bolt in the position noted during removal, then tighten to the specified torque.

Tailgate inner trim

27 Remove the retaining screw and remove the grab handle from the lower edge of the tailgate trim **(see illustrations)**.

28 Pull out the centre pins, and then release the two securing clips, from the lower edge of the tailgate trim **(see illustrations)**.

29 Carefully working your way around the trim panel, release the retaining clips and

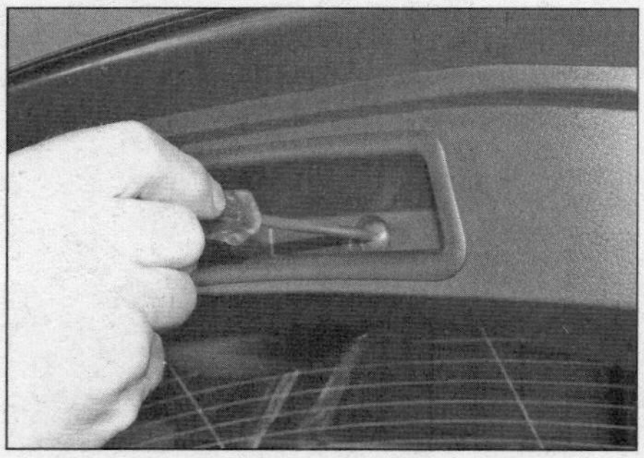

23.27a Undo the retaining screw. . .

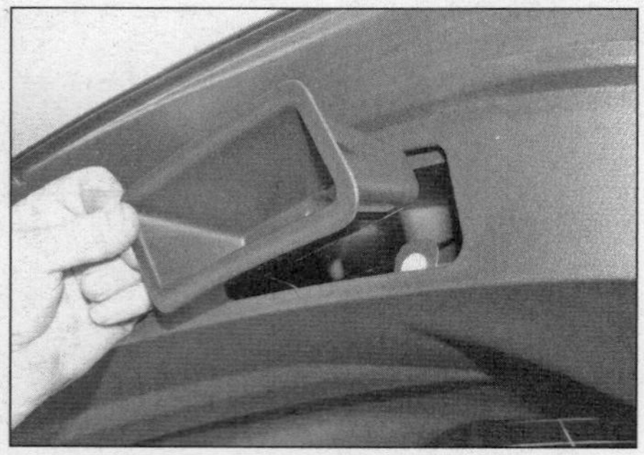

23.27b . . . and remove the grab handle trim

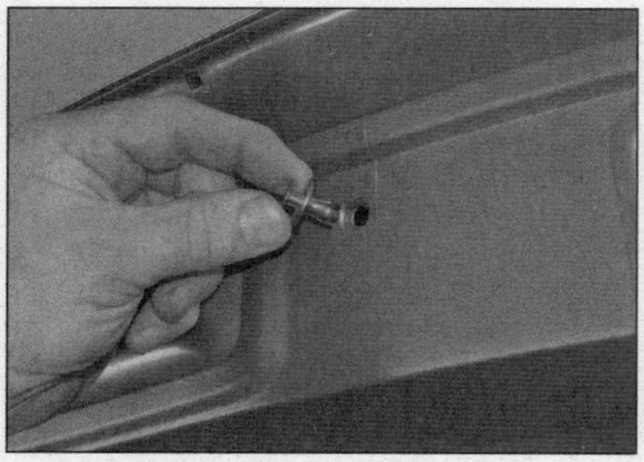

23.28a Pull out the centre pin. . .

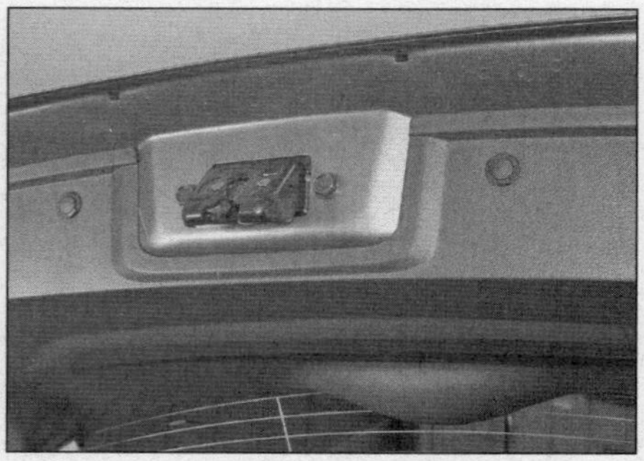

23.28b . . . and release the two retaining clips from the lower edge

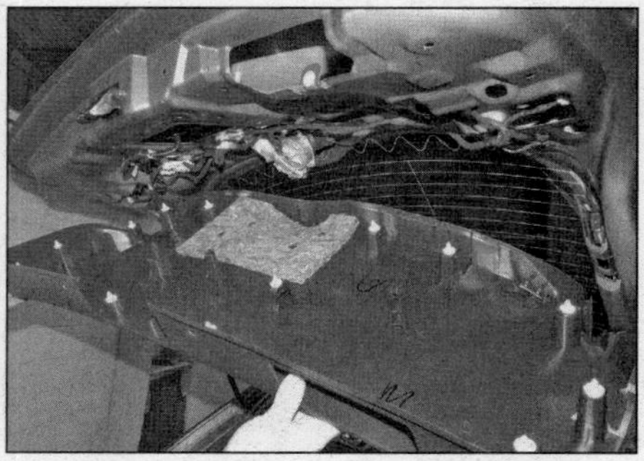

23.29 Tailgate trim retaining clips

23.30 Unclip the upper trim panel

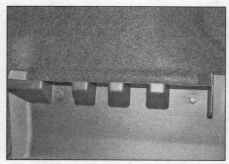

23.33a Undo the retaining bolts. . .

23.33b . . . and remove the side trim panels

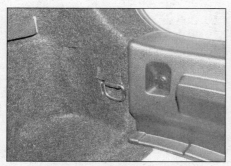

23.34 Release the retaining clips inside the rear trim panel

23.35a Remove the luggage compartment rear trim panel. . .

23.35b . . . releasing it at the centre from the body panel

remove the panel from the lower part of the tailgate (see illustration).

30 If required the upper trim panel from around the top of the rear screen, can be unclipped from the tailgate (see illustration).

31 Refitting is a reversal of removal, but ensure that all clips are securely engaged.

Rear luggage compartment trim panel

32 Open the tailgate and remove the luggage compartment floor panel.

33 Undo the retaining bolts and then ulip the plastic side trim panels from inside the luggage compartment (see illustrations).

34 Pull out the centre pins, and then release the securing clips from the inner edge of the luggage compartment rear trim (see illustration).

35 Unclip the trim panel from the rear of the luggage compartment, releasing it at the centre from the locating peg (see illustrations).

36 Refitting is a reversal of removal, but ensure that all clips are securely engaged.

Sunvisor

37 Remove the securing screw and remove the sunvisor from the roof panel (see illustration).

38 As the sunvisor is removed, disconnect the wiring connector for the vanity mirror lighting (see illustration).

39 Release the securing clip, then turn it through 90°, to remove the sunvisor retaining clip from the roof panel (see illustrations).

40 Refitting is a reversal of removal.

Grab handles

41 Using a thin screwdriver release the two plastic retaining pegs from the grab handle mounting bracket (see illustrations).

23.37 Undo the retaining screw

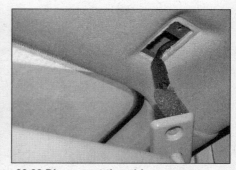

23.38 Disconnect the wiring connector as the sunvisor is withdrawn

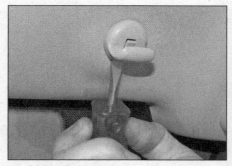

23.39a Release the securing clip. . .

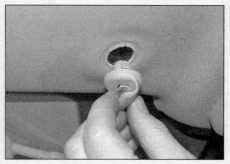

23.39b . . . then twist the retaining clip to remove

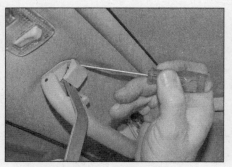

23.41a Release the retaining clip. . .

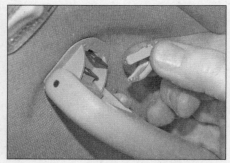

23.41b . . . and remove the plastic locking pegs. . .

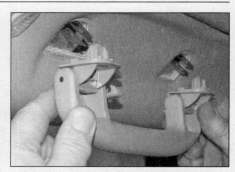

23.42 . . . and remove the grab handle from the roof panel

42 With both retaining pegs released, pull the grab handle to remove it from the roof panel **(see illustration)**.

43 Refitting is a reversal of removal, but ensure that all retaining pegs are securely engaged.

24 Centre console – removal and refitting

Removal

1 Disconnect the battery negative terminal (refer to *Disconnecting the battery* in Chapter 5 Section 4).
2 Working at the front of the centre console, unclip the two front trim panels, from inside the front footwells **(see illustrations)**.
3 Remove the retaining screws (two at each side), from the front end of the centre console **(see illustration)**.
4 Unclip the trim panel from the top of the centre console, in front of the gear lever and disconnect the wiring connectors from the switch and 12-volt supply **(see illustrations)**.
5 Undo the retaining screws, then unclip

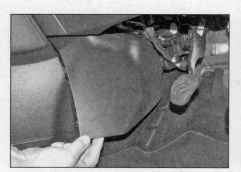

24.2a Unclip the trim covers. . .

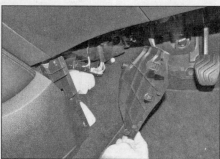

24.2b . . . from each side of the centre console

24.3 Undo the retaining screws

24.4a Unclip the trim panel. . .

24.4b . . . and disconnect the wiring connectors

24.5a Undo the retaining screws. . .

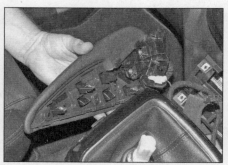

24.5b . . . unclip the side trim panels. . .

24.5c . . . then disconnect the wiring connector

24.6 Pull the gear knob from the gear lever

24.7a Unclip the gaiter trim. . .

24.7b . . . remove the securing clip. . .

the two trim panels from each side of the centre console, and disconnect the wiring connectors as they are removed **(see illustrations)**.

6 With the lever in the neutral position, pull the gear knob upwards, to release it from the top of the gear lever **(see illustration)**. Nissan recommend that a new gear knob, should be fitted on re-assembly.

7 Unclip the gear lever gaiter and trim from the top of the centre console, remove the clip and spring from the lever, then withdraw the gaiter and trim from over the gear lever **(see illustrations)**.

8 Open the lid of the armrest, then unclip the cup holder/switch panel from the top of the centre console, behind the gear lever, and then disconnect the wiring connectors as it is removed **(see illustrations)**.

9 Undo the two retaining screws from the front of the centre console and the two from

24.7c . . . and the spring. . .

24.7d . . . then withdraw the gaiter and trim

inside the rear of the gear lever aperture, at the centre **(see illustrations)**.

10 Move the front seats as far forward as possible, then working at the rear of the centre console, undo the two retaining screws

(one at each side), then unclip the rear trim panel and disconnect the wiring connectors inside the rear of the centre console **(see illustrations)**.

11 Lift the console up at the rear, manipulate

24.8a Unclip the cup holder/switch trim panel. . .

24.8b . . . and disconnect the wiring connectors

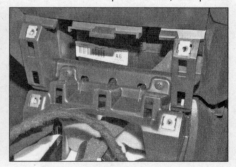

24.9a Undo the two retaining screws from the front of the console. . .

24.9b . . . and from inside the centre of the console

24.10a Undo the retaining screws (one side shown). . .

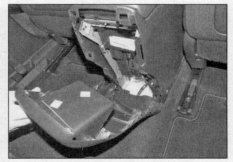

24.10b . . . unclip the trim panel from the rear of the console. . .

24.10c . . . and disconnect the wiring connectors

24.11 Remove the centre console from the vehicle

24.12a Turn the gear knob into its final position. . .

24.12b . . . insert the plastic cap. . .

24.12c . . . and lock in position with trim finisher

trim finisher fitted. Once in place twist the gear knob 30 degrees clockwise to its fitted position, then fit the plastic upper trim finisher back to the gear knob to secure it in the final position **(see illustrations)**.

25 Facia panels –
removal and refitting

⚠️ **Warning: The driver's airbag is mounted in the steering wheel centre pad and, where fitted, the passenger's airbag is mounted in the passenger's side of the facia. Make sure that the safety recommendations given in Chapter 12 Section 19 are followed, to prevent personal injury.**

Glovebox

1 Open the glovebox, and release the stay from the plastic peg on the right-hand side of the glove box **(see illustrations)**.
2 Withdraw the glovebox, releasing the hinges from the lower part of the facia **(see illustration)**.
3 If required to access the fusebox wiring and BCM (body control module), undo the retaining screws and unclip the rear trim panel from under the facia. Disconnect the wiring connectors and release the control units from the rear of the trim panel, as it is removed **(see illustrations)**.
4 Refitting is a reversal of removal.

Drivers side lower panel

5 Carefully prise the trim panel from the

it over the gear lever, and then remove the console from the vehicle **(see illustration)**. As the centre console is withdrawn, check for any retaining clips holding any of the wiring loom in place.

Refitting

12 Refitting is a reversal of removal, except when refitting the new gear knob. Fit the new gear knob at 30 degrees anti-clockwise from its fitted position, without the plastic upper

25.1a Carefully release the stay. . .

25.1b . . . from the locating peg on the glovebox

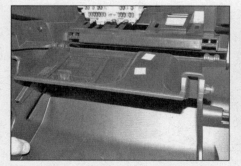

25.2 Withdraw the glovebox from the facia

25.3a Undo the three upper screws. . .

25.3b . . . withdraw the trim panel. . .

25.3c . . . then disconnect the wiring connectors. . .

25.3d . . . and remove the control units

25.6 Undo the two retaining bolts and unclip the release levers from the facia

right-hand end of the facia **(see illustrations 25.27a & 25.27b)**.

6 Undo the two retaining bolts and unclip the bonnet and fuel flap release levers, from the lower edge of the trim panel **(see illustration)**.

7 Carefully pull the trim panel from the facia to release the retaining clips, and then as the panel is withdrawn, disconnect the wiring connectors from the rear of the trim panel **(see illustrations)**.

8 Refitting is a reversal of removal.

Drivers side air ventilation grill and switch panel

9 Carefully prise the trim panel from the right-hand end of the facia **(see illustrations 25.27a & 25.27b)**.

10 Carefully unclip the heater vent trim panel from the right-hand side of the facia panel, and then withdraw the air vent grill assembly from the facia **(see illustrations)**.

11 Carefully pull the trim panel from the facia to release the retaining clips, and then as the panel is withdrawn, disconnect the wiring connectors from the rear of the switches **(see illustrations)**.

12 Refitting is a reversal of removal.

Passenger side air ventilation grill and trim panel

13 Carefully prise the trim panel from the left-hand end of the facia **(see illustrations 25.27a & 25.27b)**.

14 Undo the retaining screw and then carefully unclip the heater vent trim panel from

25.7a Unclip the trim panel. . .

25.7b . . . and disconnect the wiring connectors

the left-hand side of the facia panel, and then withdraw the air vent grill assembly from the facia **(see illustrations)**.

15 If required, the trim panel from along the

front of the facia on the left-hand side, can be removed by releasing the retaining clips **(see illustration)**.

16 Refitting is a reversal of removal.

25.10a Unclip the outer trim panel. . .

25.10b . . . release the securing clips. . .

25.10c . . . and withdraw the ventilation grill

25.11a Unclip the switch trim panel. . .

25.11b . . . and disconnect the wiring connectors

25.14a Undo the retaining screw. . .

25.14b . . . and unclip the outer trim panel

25.15 Unclip the trim panel from the facia

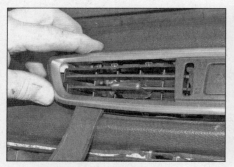

25.17a Unclip the trim panel. . .

25.17b . . . from the top of the facia. . .

25.17c . . . and disconnect the wiring connector from the switch

Centre ventilation trim panel

17 Carefully unclip the ventilation trim panel from the centre of the facia panel, and then disconnect the wiring connector from the hazard switch, as it is removed (see illustrations).

18 To refit the ventilation trim panel, it will be necessary to withdraw the air vent grill assembly from inside the top of the facia, then attach the trim panel to the grill assembly, reconnect the wiring connector to the switch, insert the complete assembly and push back into position (see illustration).

Steering column shrouds

19 Remove the steering wheel, as described in Chapter 10 Section 11.

20 Release the height adjustment lever and move the steering column downwards to its fully lowered position.

21 Undo the shroud securing screws, then release the clips securing the lower shroud to the upper shroud and remove the upper shroud from the top of the steering column, unclipping it from the trim at the lower part of the instrument panel (see illustrations).

22 Release the retaining clips securing the lower part of the shroud to the under side of the steering column and remove (see illustration).

23 Refitting is a reversal of removal, but ensure that the shroud halves engage correctly with each other.

Instrument panel surround trim

24 Using a trim tool, carefully prise the instrument panel trim, to release the retaining clips from the facia (see illustration).

25 Lift the instrument panel trim and release the securing clips from the steering column upper shroud, then remove it from the vehicle (see illustration).

26 Refitting is a reversal of removal.

25.18 Insert the complete air ventilation assembly

25.21a Undo the two retaining screws. . .

25.21b . . . then remove the upper trim panel

25.22 Unclip the lower trim panel

Facia end trim panels

27 Using a lever, carefully prise the trim panel from the end of the facia **(see illustrations)**.
28 Refitting is a reversal of removal.

Complete assembly

Note: *This is an involved procedure, and it is suggested that this Section is read through thoroughly before beginning the operation. Make careful note of all wiring connections, and the routing of all wiring, to aid refitting.*

Removal

29 Disconnect the battery negative terminal (refer to *Disconnecting the battery* in Chapter 5 Section 4).
30 Remove the front footwell trim panels as described in Section 23.
31 Remove the front A-pillar trim panels as described in Section 23.
32 Remove the centre console as described in Section 24.
33 Remove all of the components, as described previously in this Section. Note the routing of all wiring, and keep all securing screws and fixings with the relevant panels to avoid confusion on refitting.
34 Remove the heater/ventilation control unit, as described in Chapter 3 Section 11.
35 Remove the instrument panel, as described in Chapter 12 Section 9.
36 Remove the upper facia speakers as described in Chapter 12 Section 16.
37 Carefully prise out the ignition switch panel on the left-hand side of the steering wheel **(see illustrations)**, disconnect the switch wiring connectors and remove the panel.

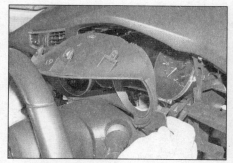

25.24 Carefully prise the trim from the facia. . .

25.25 . . . then release it from the upper shroud

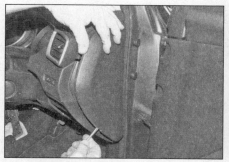

25.27a Carefully unclip the trim panel. . .

25.27b . . . from the end of the facia panel

38 Remove the radio/CD player, as described in Chapter 12 Section 15.
39 Undo the retaining screw and remove the relay mounting bracket from the centre of the facia panel **(see illustrations)**.
40 Undo the facia mounting nuts/bolts/

screws from the following locations:
a) The upper bolt at the left-hand side upper part of the facia **(see illustration)**.
b) The screws from inside the instrument panel aperture, securing the facia to the metal crossmember **(see illustration)**.

25.37a Unclip the switch panel. . .

25.37b . . . and disconnect the wiring connector

25.39a Undo the retaining screw. . .

25.39b . . . and remove the relay mounting bracket

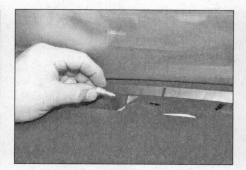

25.40a Undo the retaining bolt. . .

25.40b . . . the screws in the instrument aperture. . .

25.40c . . . one screw at right-hand side. . .

25.40d . . . one screw at the right-hand side of the centre. . .

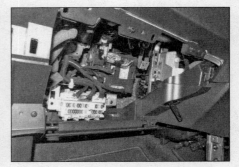

25.40e . . . two screws on the lower edge. . .

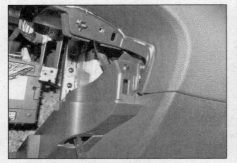

25.40f . . . one screw in the glovebox aperture. . .

25.40g . . . and the screws at each end of the facia

c) Screw on the lower part of the facia, on the right-hand side (see illustration).
d) Screw on the lower part of the facia, on the right-hand side of the centre console (see illustration).

e) Two screws securing the lower part of the facia, at the passenger side of the vehicle (see illustration).
f) One screw inside the glovebox aperture, at the top right-hand side, securing the

facia to the metal crossmember (see illustration).
g) One screw each side (see illustration), securing the top edge of the facia to the body (behind the previously removed A-pillar).

41 Make a final check to ensure that all relevant wiring has been disconnected, and any wiring loom retaining clips disconnected.

42 With the aid of an assistant, pull the upper part of the facia panel towards the rear of the car to disengage it from the scuttle – some manipulation may be required. Once the facia panel has been released, withdraw it through the door aperture.

43 If required, the metal crossmember can be removed from across the front of the vehicle. This will need to be removed to access the heating/ventilation housing.

44 Referring to Chapter 10 Section 13, remove the steering column/motor assembly from the metal crossmember.

45 Undo the retaining bolts and remove the metal brackets from the left and right-hand side of the heater housing (see illustrations).

46 Working under the bonnet, remove the scuttle panel, as described in Section 20, then undo the retaining bolt behind the wiper motor, at the top of the bulkhead (see illustration).

47 Working along the length of the metal crossmember, trace the wiring loom and disconnect the wiring plugs from any components or wiring plug connectors. Make a note, or take pictures of the connections to refer to on refitting. Wiring connectors will need to be disconnected from the following locations:
a) Along the centre console area, to the airbag ECU, handbrake warning light, console switches etc....
b) Around the heating ventilation housing to the air flap control modules and sensors.
c) At the upper and lower sides of the A-pillar on both sides of the vehicle.

48 Working at the left-hand side of the vehicle, remove the plastic covers and slacken the crossmember securing bolts (see illustrations). An open-ended spanner will be required to counter hold the crossmember adjustment nut.

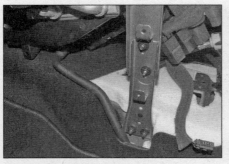

25.45a Remove the support bracket from the left. . .

25.45b . . . and right-hand side of the heater housing

25.46 Undo the bolt above the steering column

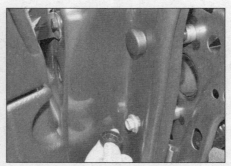

25.48a Remove the plastic caps. . .

49 Working at the right-hand side of the vehicle, remove the plastic covers and slacken the crossmember securing bolts **(see illustration)**. Note there are three bolts on the right-hand side of the crossmember.

50 The crossmember will still be held in position, as it has location pegs at each side, from the front A-pillars **(see illustration)**.

51 Make a final check along the length of the metal crossmember, to check that there is nothing still connected and lift the crossmember complete with wirng loom, out through the door aperture.

52 If required, remove the passenger's airbag from the rear of the facia, as described in Chapter 12 Section 20.

Refitting

53 Refitting is essentially a reversal of the removal procedure, bearing in mind the following points:

a) *Tighten the right-hand crossmember bolts first, and then tighten the left-hand side crossmember bolts, using an open-ended spanner to counter hold the adjustment nuts.*

b) *Ensure that all wiring is correctly reconnected, and routed.*

c) *Refit all surrounding facia panels with reference to the relevant paragraphs of this Section.*

25.48b . . . and slacken the bolts. . .

25.48c . . . leaving the adjuster nut in the left-hand side of the crossmember

25.49 Undo the crossmember mounting bolts

25.50 Crossmember locating peg – left-hand side shown

Chapter 12
Body electrical systems

Contents

Degrees of difficulty

Easy, suitable for novice with little experience	Fairly easy, suitable for beginner with some experience 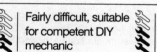	Fairly difficult, suitable for competent DIY mechanic	Difficult, suitable for experienced DIY mechanic	Very difficult, suitable for expert DIY or professional

Specifications

Bulb ratings

	Watts
Front direction indicator light (W21W)	21
Front direction indicator side repeater light	LED
Front foglight (H8)	35
Front sidelight	LED
Headlights:	
Main beam	LED
Dipped beam	LED
High-level stop-light	LED
Luggage compartment light	5
Map reading lights	5
Interior reading lights	5
Rear direction indicator light (WY21W)	21
Rear foglight – drivers side only (W21W)	21
Rear number plate light (W5W)	5
Reversing light (W16W)	16
Stop/tail light	LED

Torque wrench setting

	Nm	lbf ft
Airbag unit retaining bolts	20	15

1 General information and precautions

General information

1 The electrical system is of 12-volt negative earth type. Power for the lights and all electrical accessories is supplied by a lead-acid type battery, which is charged by the alternator.

2 This Chapter covers repair and service procedures for the various electrical components not associated with the engine. Information on the battery, alternator and starter motor can be found in Chapter 5.

3 It should be noted that, prior to working on any component in the electrical system, the battery negative terminal should first be disconnected, to prevent the possibility of electrical short-circuits and/or fires (refer to Chapter 5 Section 4).

Precautions

⚠ **Warning: Before carrying out any work on the electrical system, read through the precautions given in 'Safety first!' at the beginning of this manual, and in Chapter 5.**

⚠ **Warning: All models are equipped with an airbag system and pyrotechnic seat belt pretensioners. When working on the electrical system, refer to the precautions given in Section 19 to avoid the possibility of personal injury.**

2 Electrical fault finding – general information

Note: *Refer to the precautions given in 'Safety first!' and in Section 1 of this Chapter before starting work. The following tests relate to testing of the main electrical circuits, and should not be used to test delicate electronic circuits (such as engine management systems or anti-lock braking systems), particularly where an electronic control unit is used.*

General

1 A typical electrical circuit consists of an electrical component; any switches, relays, motors, fuses, fusible links or circuit breakers related to that component, and the wiring and connectors which link the component to both the battery and the chassis. To help to pinpoint a problem in an electrical circuit, wiring diagrams are included at the end of this chapter.

2 Before attempting to diagnose an electrical fault, first study the appropriate wiring diagram, to obtain a more complete understanding of the components included in the particular circuit concerned. The possible sources of a fault can be narrowed down by noting whether other components related to the circuit are operating properly. If several components or circuits fail at one time, the problem is likely to be related to a shared fuse or earth connection.

3 Electrical problems usually stem from simple causes, such as loose or corroded connections, a faulty earth connection, a blown fuse, a melted fusible link, or a faulty relay (refer to Section 3 for details of testing relays). Visually inspect the condition of all fuses, wires and connections in a problem circuit before testing the components. Use the wiring diagrams to determine which terminal connections will need to be checked, in order to pinpoint the trouble spot.

4 The basic tools required for electrical fault finding include a circuit tester or voltmeter (a 12 volt bulb with a set of test leads can also be used for certain tests); a self-powered test light (sometimes known as a continuity tester); an ohmmeter (to measure resistance); a battery and set of test leads; and a jumper wire, preferably with a circuit breaker or fuse incorporated, which can be used to bypass suspect wires or electrical components. Before attempting to locate a problem with test instruments, use the wiring diagram to determine where to make the connections.

5 To find the source of an intermittent wiring fault (usually due to a poor or dirty connection, or damaged wiring insulation), a 'wiggle' test can be performed on the wiring. This involves wiggling the wiring by hand, to see if the fault occurs as the wiring is moved. It should be possible to narrow down the source of the fault to a particular section of wiring. This method of testing can be used in conjunction with any of the tests described in the following sub-Sections.

6 Apart from problems due to poor connections, two basic types of fault can occur in an electrical circuit – open-circuit, or short-circuit.

7 Open-circuit faults are caused by a break somewhere in the circuit, which prevents current from flowing. An open-circuit fault will prevent a component from working, but will not cause the relevant circuit fuse to blow.

8 Short-circuit faults are normally caused by a breakdown in wiring insulation, which allows a feed wire to touch either another wire, or an earthed component such as the bodyshell. This allows the current flowing in the circuit to 'escape' along an alternative route, usually to earth. As the circuit does not now follow its original complete path, it is known as a 'short' circuit. A short-circuit fault will normally cause the relevant circuit fuse to blow.

Finding an open-circuit

9 To check for an open-circuit, connect one lead of a circuit tester or voltmeter to either the negative battery terminal or a known good earth.

10 Connect the other lead to a connector in the circuit being tested, preferably nearest to the battery or fuse.

11 Switch on the circuit, bearing in mind that some circuits are live only when the ignition switch is moved to a particular position.

12 If voltage is present (indicated either by the tester bulb lighting or a voltmeter reading, as applicable), this means that the section of the circuit between the relevant connector and the battery is problem-free.

13 Continue to check the remainder of the circuit in the same fashion.

14 When a point is reached at which no voltage is present, the problem must lie between that point and the previous test point with voltage. Most problems can be traced to a broken, corroded or loose connection.

Finding a short-circuit

15 To check for a short circuit; first disconnect the load(s) from the circuit (loads are the components which draw current from a circuit, such as bulbs, motors, heating elements, etc).

16 Remove the relevant fuse from the circuit, and connect a circuit tester or voltmeter to the fuse connections.

17 Switch on the circuit, bearing in mind that some circuits are live only when the ignition switch is moved to a particular position.

18 If voltage is present (indicated either by the tester bulb lighting or a voltmeter reading, as applicable), this means that there is a short circuit.

19 If no voltage is present, but the fuse still blows with the load(s) connected, this indicates an internal fault in the load(s).

Finding an earth fault

20 The battery negative terminal is connected to 'earth' – the metal of the engine/transmission and the car body – and most systems are wired so that they only receive a positive feed, the current returning via the metal of the car body. This means that the component mounting and the body form part of that circuit. Loose or corroded mountings can therefore cause a range of electrical faults, ranging from total failure of a circuit, to a puzzling partial fault. In particular, lights may shine dimly (especially when another circuit sharing the same earth point is in operation), motors (e.g. wiper motors or the radiator cooling fan motor) may run slowly, and the operation of one circuit may have an apparently unrelated effect on another. Note that on many vehicles, earth straps are used between certain components, such as the engine/transmission and the body, usually where there is no metal-to-metal contact between components, due to flexible rubber mountings, etc.

21 To check whether a component is properly earthed, disconnect the battery, and connect one lead of an ohmmeter to a known good earth point. Connect the other lead to the wire or earth connection being tested. The resistance reading should be zero; if not, check the connection as follows.

22 If an earth connection is thought to be faulty, dismantle the connection, and clean

3.2 Located at the right-hand end of the facia

3.3 Vehicle passenger compartment fusebox

3.4 Vehicle engine compartment fusebox

3.5a Vehicle IPDM location. . .

3.5b . . . which also has fuses on the underside

back to bare metal both the bodyshell and the wire terminal or the component earth connection mating surface. Be careful to remove all traces of dirt and corrosion, and then use a knife to trim away any paint, so that a clean metal-to-metal joint is made. On reassembly, tighten the joint fasteners securely; if a wire terminal is being refitted, use serrated washers between the terminal and the bodyshell, to ensure a clean and secure connection. When the connection is remade, prevent the onset of corrosion in the future by applying a coat of petroleum jelly or silicone-based grease, or by spraying on (at regular intervals) a proprietary ignition sealer.

3 Fuses and relays – general information

Fuses

1 Fuses are designed to break a circuit when a predetermined current is reached, in order to protect the components and wiring, which could be damaged by excessive current flow. Any excessive current flow will be due to a fault in the circuit, usually a short-circuit (see Section 2).
2 The main fuses are located in the fusebox, behind the glovebox, on the passenger side of the facia, with some fuses located at the right-hand end of the facia (see illustration).
3 For access to the fuses, remove the glovebox, as described in Chapter 11 Section 25 (see illustration).
4 Additional fuses and circuit-breakers are located in auxiliary fuseboxes around the engine compartment (see illustration).
5 The Intelligent Power Distribution Module (IPDM) is also located in the engine compartment, next to the fusebox (see illustrations).
6 It may be necessary to remove the air intake ducting, to access the engine compartment fuseboxes (see illustration).
7 A blown fuse can be recognised from its melted or broken wire. Before removing a fuse, first ensure that the relevant circuit is switched off.
8 Using the plastic tool clipped inside the main fusebox, pull the fuse from its location (see illustration).

9 Spare fuses are usually provided in the main fusebox.
10 Before renewing a blown fuse, trace and rectify the cause, and always use a fuse of the correct rating (fuse ratings are usually specified on the inside of the fusebox cover flap). Never substitute a fuse of a higher rating, or make temporary repairs using wire or metal foil; more serious damage, or even fire, could result.
11 Note that the fuses are colour-coded as follows.

Colour	Rating
Orange	5A
Red	10A
Blue	15A
Yellow	20A
Clear or White	25A
Green	30A

Relays

12 A relay is an electrically operated switch, which is used for the following reasons:
a) *A relay can switch a heavy current remotely from the circuit in which the current is flowing, therefore allowing the use of lighter-gauge wiring and switch contacts.*
b) *A relay can receive more than one control input, unlike a mechanical switch.*
c) *A relay can have a timer function – for example, the intermittent wiper relay.*
13 Various relays are located behind the facia, next to the fusebox, and in the relay box on the right-hand side of the engine compartment (see illustration 3.4).
14 If a circuit or system controlled by a relay develops a fault, and the relay is suspect, operate the system. If the relay is functioning,

3.6 Remove the air intake ducting

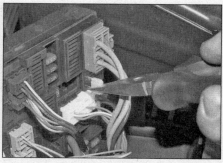

3.8 Using long nose pliers to remove the fuse from its position

4.2a Release the trim panel. . .

4.2b . . . and disconnect the wiring connector

4.3a Release the securing clips. . .

4.3b . . . and withdraw the switch from the panel

15 To remove a relay, first ensure that the relevant circuit is switched off. The relay can then simply be pulled out from the socket, and pushed back into position.

4 Switches – removal and refitting

Note: *Disconnect the battery negative terminal (refer to 'Disconnecting the battery' in Chapter 5 Section 4), before removing any switch, and reconnect the terminal after refitting the switch.*

Ignition stop/start switch

1 Remove the heater control panel, as described in Chapter 3 Section 11.
2 Release the securing clips and remove the stop/start switch trim panel from the facia panel, disconnect the wiring connector from the switch as the trim panel is removed **(see illustrations)**.
3 Release the securing clips and withdraw the switch from the trim panel **(see illustrations)**.
4 Refitting is a reversal of removal.

Steering column switches

5 Remove the steering column shrouds, as described in Chapter 11 Section 25.

Remove

6 Undo the retaining screws and withdraw the rotary switch (Spiral cable) from the top of the steering column, release the locking clips and disconnect the wiring connectors, as it is removed **(see illustrations)**.

Remove

7 Undo the retaining screws and withdraw the steering angle sensor from the top of the steering column, disconnect the wiring connector, as it is removed **(see illustrations)**.
8 Disconnect the wiring connectors from the rear of the lighting switch assembly **(see illustration)**.
9 Slacken the retaining clamp screw and withdraw the switch assembly from the top of the steering column **(see illustrations)**.
10 Refitting is a reversal of removal.

it should be possible to hear it 'click' as it is energised, If this is the case, the fault lies with the components or wiring of the system. If the relay is not being energised, then either the relay is not receiving a main supply or a switching voltage, or the relay itself is faulty. Testing is by the substitution of a known good unit, but be careful – while some relays are identical in appearance and in operation, others look similar but perform different functions.

4.6a Undo the two retaining screws. . .

4.6b . . . release the locking clip and disconnect the wiring connectors

4.7a Undo the three retaining screws. . .

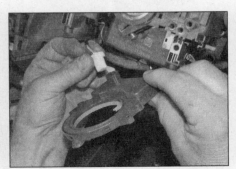

4.7b . . . and disconnect the wiring connector

4.8 Disconnect the wiring connectors

4.9a Slacken the securing screw. . .

4.9b . . . and withdraw the switch assembly

4.15a Undo the retaining screws. . .

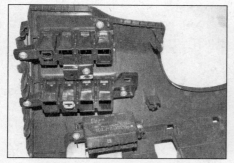

4.15b . . . to remove the switches

4.17a Using a trim tool. . .

4.17b . . . to remove the trim panel from the inner handle

Heater/ventilation switches

11 The heater/ventilation switches are integral with the heater control panel, remove the heater control panel, as described in Chapter 3 Section 11.

Heated front and rear windscreen switches

12 The heated windscreen switches are integral with the heater control panel, remove the heater control panel, as described in Chapter 3 Section 11.

Driver's side panel switches

13 Depending on model, there may a different amount of switches fitted to the drivers side trim panels.
14 Remove the trim panels from the facia, as described in Chapter 11 Section 25.
15 To remove the relevant switch, turn the trim panel over, undo the retaining screws and withdraw the switch from the trim panel (see illustrations).
16 Refit the relevant switch and trim panel, using a reversal of the removal procedure.

Electric mirror switch

17 Using a plastic trim tool carefully unclip the trim panel from around the inner door release handle (see illustrations).
18 Carefully unclip the grab handle trim panel, along with the side mirror switch assembly from the door panel and disconnect the wiring connector (see illustrations).
19 To remove the switch, undo the retaining screws and withdraw the switch from the rear

of the trim panel with the mounting bracket (see illustrations).
20 Refit the relevant switch and trim panel, using a reversal of the removal procedure.

4.18a Unclip the trim panel. . .

4.19a Undo the retaining screws. . .

Electric window switches

21 Remove the electric mirror switch trim panel, as described previously in this section.
22 Undo the three mounting bolts and

4.18b . . . and disconnect the wiring connector

4.19b . . . and remove the switch

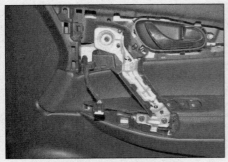

4.22a Undo the three mounting bolts. . .

4.22b . . . and remove the grab handle metal frame

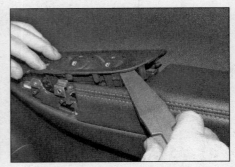

4.23a Unclip the switch panel. . .

4.23b . . . unhooking it at the front. . .

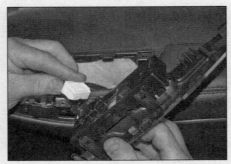

4.23c . . . then disconnect the wiring connectors

4.24 Release the securing clips and remove the switch

remove the grab handle metal frame from the door panel (see illustrations).

23 Carefully unclip the switch panel from the top of the armrest, unhooking it from the front of the door trim panel, then disconnect the wiring connectors (see illustrations).

24 Release the retaining clips and withdraw the switches from the rear of the trim panel (see illustration).

25 Refit the relevant switch and trim panel, using a reversal of the removal procedure.

Hazard warning light switch

26 The hazard warning switch is fitted to the centre ventilation trim panel, remove the ventilation trim panel, as described in Chapter 11 Section 25.

27 To remove the switch, release the retaining clips and withdraw the switch through the front of the trim panel (see illustration).

28 Refit the switch and trim panel, using a reversal of the removal procedure.

Centre console switches

29 Carefully unclip the switch panel(s) from the top of the centre console, as described in Chapter 11 Section 24.

30 To remove the relevant switch, turn the trim panel over, undo the retaining screw and withdraw the switch from the trim panel (see illustrations).

31 Refit the relevant switch and trim panel, using a reversal of the removal procedure.

Courtesy light/door warning switches

32 The door warning switches are part of the central locking system components, remove the switches as described in Chapter 11 Section 12.

Luggage area light switch

33 The switch is integral with the boot lid/tailgate lock. Removal and refitting details for the boot lid/tailgate lock are provided in Chapter 11 Section 15.

Map reading/courtesy light switches

34 The switches are integral with the interior light assembly and cannot be renewed independently. See Section 6 for interior light bulb renewal.

Steering wheel switches

35 These switches include the audio control switches to the left-hand side of the steering wheel, and cruise control system operation to the right-hand side of the steering wheel, according to model.

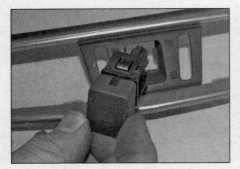

4.27 Release the switch from the front of the trim panel

4.30a Undo the retaining screws. . .

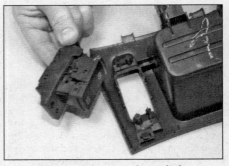

4.30b . . . to remove the switches

4.38 Unclip the rear trim cover

4.39a Undo the four switch retaining screws. . .

4.39b . . . and remove the switch assembly from the steering wheel

4.41a Carefully unclip. . .

4.41b . . . the silver trim panel. . .

4.41c . . . from the steering wheel

Warning: When working on the airbag system, refer to the precautions given in Section 19 to avoid the possibility of personal injury.

36 Remove the airbag from the centre of the steering wheel, as described in Section 20.

Type 1 steering wheel

37 Remove the Steering wheel, as described in Chapter 10 Section 11.

38 Unclip the plastic cover from the rear of the steering wheel **(see illustration)**.

39 Undo the four retaining screws, and disconnect the wiring from the retaining clips to remove the switch assembly from the steering wheel **(see illustrations)**.

40 Refitting is the reversal of the removal procedure. Refer to Section 20, when refitting the airbag.

Type 2 steering wheel

41 Carefully unclip the silver trim panel from the top of the steering wheel **(see illustrations)**.

42 Carefully unclip the two switch units from each side of the steering wheel **(see illustrations)**. Unclip the wiring from the retaining clips in the steering wheel on removal.

43 Refit the switch and trim panel, using a reversal of the removal procedure. Refer to Section 20, when refitting the airbag.

Passenger airbag switch

44 Remove the glovebox, as described in Chapter 11 Section 25.

45 Release the retaining clips and withdraw the switch from the glovebox **(see illustration)**.

46 Refit the switch and glovebox, using a reversal of the removal procedure.

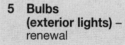

5 Bulbs (exterior lights) – renewal

General

1 Whenever a bulb is renewed, note the following points:
a) *Disconnect the battery negative terminal (refer to Chapter 5 Section 4).*
b) *Remember that, if the light has just been in use, the bulb may be extremely hot.*
c) *Always check the bulb contacts and holder, ensuring that there is clean metal-to-metal contact between the bulb and its live contact(s) and earth. Clean off any corrosion or dirt before fitting a new bulb.*
d) *Wherever bayonet-type bulbs are fitted,*

4.42a Carefully prise the switch. . .

4.42b . . . to release it from the steering wheel

4.45 Release the securing clips and remove the airbag switch

5.4 Twist the bulb holder to release it

5.5 Remove the bulb and holder from the wiring connector

5.8 Remove the plastic cover

5.9 Disconnect the wiring connector

5.10a Release the retaining clip...

5.10b ... and remove the bulb

ensure that the live contact(s) bear firmly against the bulb contact.

e) Always ensure that the new bulb is of the correct rating (see Specifications), and that it is completely clean before fitting it; this applies particularly to headlight/foglight bulbs (see following paragraphs).

⚠ **Warning: Before carrying out any operations on xenon headlight units, it is recommended that protective gloves and safety glasses be worn. It is essential that the wiring connectors are disconnected from the rear of the headlight unit, and then wait until the module and bulbs have cooled down before removal. DO NOT switch the headlights on with the bulb removed, as it is harmful to the eyes.**

Headlights

Note: *On higher specification, later models the headlights are fitted with LED's (Light Emitting Diodes), and can only be renewed as a complete headlight unit.*

2 Open the bonnet and depending on model, to improve access to the left-hand headlight, remove the air inlet ducting **(see illustration 3.6)**.

3 When handling the new bulb, use a tissue or clean cloth to avoid touching the glass with the fingers; moisture and grease from the skin can cause blackening and rapid failure of this type of bulb. If the glass is accidentally touched, wipe it clean using methylated spirit.

Dipped beam

4 Twist the bulb holder anti-clockwise and

release it from the rear of the headlight unit **(see illustration)**.

5 Disconnect the wiring connector from the bulb holder **(see illustration)**.

6 Install the new bulb, ensuring that the bulb holder is located correctly in the headlight unit. When handling the new bulb, use a tissue or clean cloth to avoid touching the glass with the fingers; moisture and grease from the skin can cause blackening and rapid failure of this type of bulb. If the glass is accidentally touched, wipe it clean using methylated spirit.

7 Refit the protective cover.

Main beam

8 Reach behind the headlamp, and rotate the plastic cover anti-clockwise to remove **(see illustration)**.

9 Disconnect the wiring connector from the headlight bulb **(see illustration)**.

5.15 Rotate the bulbholder anti-clockwise...

10 Release the retaining clip and withdraw the bulb from the headlight unit **(see illustrations)**.

11 Install the new bulb, ensuring that the bulb holder is located correctly in the headlight unit. When handling the new bulb, use a tissue or clean cloth to avoid touching the glass with the fingers; moisture and grease from the skin can cause blackening and rapid failure of this type of bulb. If the glass is accidentally touched, wipe it clean using methylated spirit.

12 Refit the protective cover.

Sidelight

13 The sidelight has LED's (Light Emitting Diodes), and can only be renewed as a complete headlight unit. Remove the light unit, as described in Section 7.

Front indicator

14 Open and support the bonnet.

15 Reaching to the inside rear of the headlight unit, twist the bulbholder anti-clockwise and withdraw it from the headlight light unit **(see illustration)**.

16 The bulb is a push in the bulbholder, pull the bulb to remove it from the holder **(see illustration)**.

17 Fit the new bulb using a reversal of the removal procedure.

Front indicator side repeater

18 Remove the exterior mirror outer shell, as described in Chapter 11 Section 17.

19 Withdraw the light unit, and disconnect

5.16 . . . and pull the bulb to remove

5.19 Remove the LED light unit

5.21 Pull back the inner wheel arch liner

5.22 Disconnect the foglight wiring plug – early model shown

5.23a Rotate the bulbholder anti-clockwise to remove – early models

5.23b Rotate the bulbholder anti-clockwise to remove – later models

the wiring connector from the LED side repeater light unit **(see illustration)**.

20 Fit the LED light unit using a reversal of the removal procedure.

Front foglight

21 Release the retaining clips and pull back the front of the inner wheel arch liner to access the rear of the front fog lights **(see illustration)**.

22 Reach behind the bumper and disconnect the wiring connector from the bulbholder **(see illustration)**.

23 Turn the bulbholder anti-clockwise and withdraw it from the rear of the foglight **(see illustrations)**.

24 Check new bulb before removing the bulb from its holder, as some new bulbs come with the bulb holder as part of the bulb. When handling the new bulb, use a tissue or clean

cloth to avoid touching the glass with the fingers; moisture and grease from the skin can cause blackening and rapid failure of this type of bulb. If the glass is accidentally touched, wipe it clean using methylated spirit.

25 Fit the new bulb using a reversal of the removal procedure.

Rear stop and tail lights

26 The stop and tail lights have LED's (Light Emitting Diodes), and can only be renewed as a complete rear light unit. Remove the light unit, as described in Section 7.

Rear indicator

27 Open the tailgate and remove the rear light unit as described in Section 7.

28 Release the retaining clips and withdraw the bulbholder from the rear of the light unit **(see illustration)**.

29 The bulbs are a bayonet fit in the bulbholder, push lightly and turn anti-clockwise to remove the relevant bulb **(see illustration)**.

30 Fit the new bulb using a reversal of the removal procedure. Note that the stop/tail light bulb has offset pins, on the side of the end cap, to ensure correct installation.

Rear fog light and reversing light

31 Open the tailgate and remove the inner tailgate trim, as described in Chapter 11 Section 23.

32 Turn the bulbholder anti-clockwise and withdraw it from the rear of the reversing light **(see illustration)**.

33 The bulb is a push fit in the bulbholder, pull the bulb to remove **(see illustration)**.

5.28 Unclip the bulb holder from the light unit

5.29 Press in the bulb and rotate it anti-clockwise to remove it

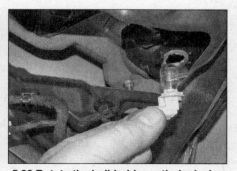

5.32 Rotate the bulbholder anti-clockwise to remove

5.33 Pull the bulb from the bulbholder

5.35a Carefully unclip the light unit. . .

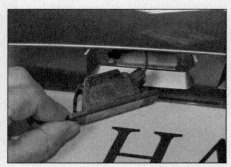

5.35b . . . and release it from the rear trim panel

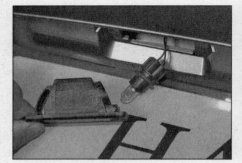

5.36 Twist the bulb holder to remove. . .

5.37 . . . then pull the bulb from its holder

34 Fit the new bulb using a reversal of the removal procedure.

Number plate light

35 Unclip the light unit from the tailgate trim **(see illustrations)**.

36 Turn the bulbholder anti-clockwise and withdraw it from the number plate light **(see illustration)**.
37 The bulb is a push-fit in the bulbholder, pull the sidelight bulb to remove it from the bulb holder **(see illustration)**.

38 Fit the new bulb using a reversal of the removal procedure.

High-level stop-light

39 Open the tailgate and remove the upper tailgate inner trim panel, as described in Chapter 11 Section 23.
40 Disconnect the wiring connector to the high level brake light and the washer pipe from the rear washer in the spoiler **(see illustration)**.
41 Undo the four bolts from inside the top of the tailgate **(see illustration 5.47)** and the four bolts (two at each side), from the outer ends of the rear spoiler **(see illustration)**.
42 Unclip the spoiler from the top of the tailgate, then withdraw the wiring connector and rear washer pipe through the tailgate, as it is removed **(see illustrations)**.
43 Working on the inside of the spoiler, release the two retaining clips and withdraw the high-level brake light **(see illustrations)**.

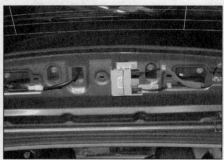

5.40 Disconnect the wiring connector and washer pipe

5.41 Undo the bolts, at each end of the spoiler

5.42a Unclip the spoiler. . .

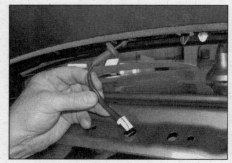

5.42b . . . and withdraw the wiring connector. . .

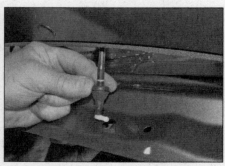

5.42c . . . and rear washer pipe

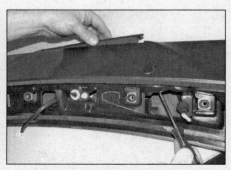

5.43a Release the retaining clips at each end. . .

If a new light unit is being fitted, disconnect the wiring connector and fit it to the new light unit.

44 The light unit has LED's (Light Emitting Diodes), and can only be renewed as a complete unit. Fit the new light unit using a reversal of the removal procedure.

6 Bulbs (interior lights) – renewal

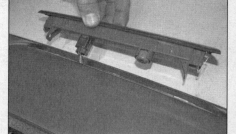

5.43b . . . remove the light unit. . .

5.43c . . . and disconnect the wiring connector

General

1 Refer to Section 5, paragraph 1.

Map reading/courtesy light (front)

2 Carefully prise the lens from the light unit (if necessary, carefully use a flat-bladed screwdriver) **(see illustrations)**.

3 Pull the bulb from the light unit; note that the bulb is a capless type **(see illustration)**.

4 If required, release the securing clips to release the light unit from the headlining **(see illustrations)**.

5 Fit the new bulb using a reversal of the removal procedure.

Courtesy light (rear)

6 Carefully prise the lens from the light unit (if necessary, carefully use a flat-bladed screwdriver) **(see illustration)**.

7 Pull the bulb from the light unit; note that the bulb is a capless type **(see illustration)**.

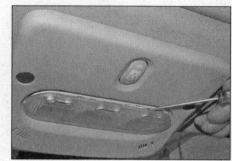

6.2a Carefully prise the light lens. . .

6.2b . . . to remove it from the light unit. . .

8 If required, release the securing clips to release the light unit from the headlining **(see illustration)**.

9 Fit the new bulb using a reversal of the removal procedure.

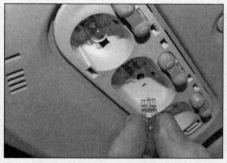

6.3 . . . then pull the bulb(s) from the light unit

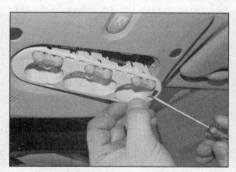

6.4a Using a thin screwdriver. . .

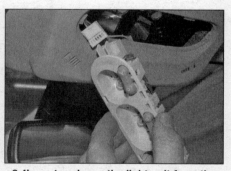

6.4b . . . to release the light unit from the roof panel

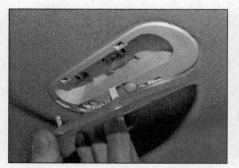

6.6 Carefully prise the light lens from the light unit

6.7 Pull the bulb from the light unit

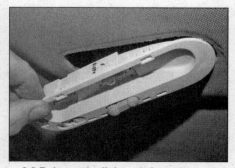

6.8 Release the light unit from the roof panel

6.10 Carefully prise the light unit from the roof panel

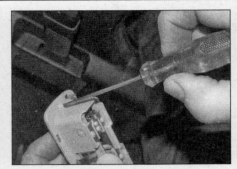

6.12a Undo the retaining screw. . .

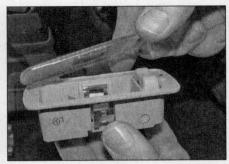

6.12b . . . unclip the light lens. . .

6.13 . . . and remove the bulb from the light unit

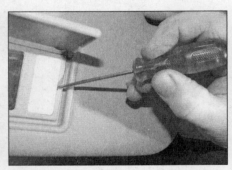

6.15 Carefully prise the light lens from place. . .

6.16 . . . and pull the bulb from the light unit

Courtesy light (side)

10 Carefully prise the light unit from the side of the roof panel **(see illustration)**.
11 Disconnect the wiring connector and remove the light unit.
12 Undo the retaining screw and remove the lens from the front of the light unit **(see illustrations)**.
13 Pull the bulb from the light unit; note that the bulb is a festoon type **(see illustration)**.
14 Fit the new bulb using a reversal of the removal procedure.

Vanity mirror light

15 Carefully prise the lens from the light unit (if necessary, carefully use a small thin screwdriver) **(see illustration)**.
16 Pull the bulb from the light unit; note that the bulb is a capless type **(see illustration)**.

17 Fit the new bulb using a reversal of the removal procedure.

Luggage area light

18 Open the tailgate.
19 Unclip the light unit from the trim panel and disconnect the wiring connector**(see illustration)**.
20 Unclip the lens and remove the bulb from the light unit, the bulb is a push-fit in the light assembly **(see illustrations)**.
21 Fit the new bulb using a reversal of the removal procedure.

Instrument panel lights

22 The instrument panel is a complete unit and is lit by LEDs. If there is a fault on the illumination of the panel the complete unit will need to be renewed, as described in Section 9.

Heater control illumination

23 The heater control panel is a complete unit and is lit by LEDs. If there is a fault on the illumination of the panel the complete unit will need to be renewed.

| 7 | Exterior light units – removal and refitting | |

Note: *Disconnect the battery negative terminal (refer to 'Disconnecting the battery' in Chapter 5 Section 4), before removing any light unit, and reconnect the terminal after refitting the light.*

Headlight unit

1 Remove the front bumper, as described in Chapter 11 Section 5.

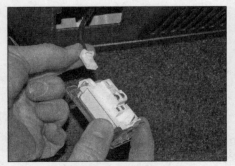

6.19 Remove the light unit

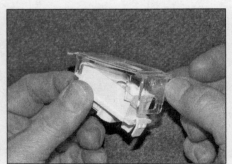

6.20a Unclip the lens. . .

6.20b . . . and remove the bulb

7.2a Undo the outer mounting bolt. . .

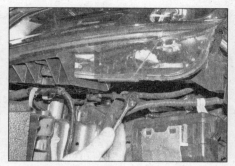

7.2b . . . and the lower mounting bolt

7.3 Remove the headlight upper mounting bolts

7.4a Withdraw the headlight unit. . .

7.4b . . . and disconnect the wiring connectors

7.5 Release the retaining clip from the light unit

2 Unscrew the two headlight lower securing bolts **(see illustrations)**.
3 Unscrew the two headlight upper securing bolts **(see illustration)**.
4 Remove the headlight unit, and disconnect the wiring connectors as the headlamp is withdrawn from the vehicle **(see illustrations)**.
5 As the headlight is withdrawn, release the wiring loom retaining clip from the base of the light unit **(see illustration)**.
6 Refitting is a reversal of removal. On completion, it is wise to have the headlight beam alignment checked (see Section 8).

Front sidelight

7 The front sidelight unit is part of the headlamp unit and cannot be renewed separately.

Front indicator

8 The indicator unit is part of the headlamp unit and cannot be renewed separately.

Front indicator side repeater

9 The procedure is described as part of the bulb renewal procedure in Section 5.

Front foglight unit

10 Release the retaining clips and pull back the front of the inner wheel arch liner to access the rear of the front fog lights **(see illustration 5.32)**.
11 Disconnect the wiring connector from the bulbholder **(see illustration 5.33)**.
12 On early models, undo the securing bolt and remove the light unit from the rear of the bumper **(see illustration)**.

13 On later models, undo the securing bolts and retaining clip, then remove the light unit from the rear of the bumper **(see**

illustrations)**. As the light unit is withdrawn, unclip the wiring loom from the mounting bracket.

7.12 Remove the fog light unit – early models

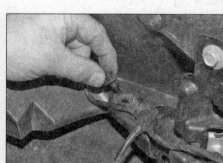

7.13a Remove the securing clip. . .

7.13b . . .undo the mounting bolts. . .

7.13c . . . and remove the fog light unit – later models

7.14 Undo the three bolts to remove light unit

7.16 Undo the rear light retaining bolts

7.17a Pull the light unit to the rear. . .

7.17b to disengage the locating pegs

7.18 Disconnect the rear light wiring connectors

14 On later models, undo the securing bolts to remove the light unit from the mounting bracket **(see illustration)**.

15 Refitting is a reversal of removal.

Rear light unit

16 Open the tailgate and working at the side of the luggage compartment aperture, undo the two rear light unit mounting bolts **(see illustration)**.

17 Withdraw the light unit from the rear of the vehicle, disengaging the two locating pegs from the rear wing panel **(see illustrations)**.

18 Disconnect the wiring connectors at the rear of the light unit as it is removed **(see illustration)**.

19 Refit the light unit using a reversal of the removal procedure.

Rear fog and reversing light unit

20 Open the tailgate and remove the inner tailgate trim, as described in Chapter 11 Section 23.

21 Remove the tailgate outer trim from across the top of the rear number plate, as described in Chapter 11 Section 15.

22 Disconnect the wiring connector at the rear of the light unit **(see illustration)**.

23 Undo the three light unit securing nuts, and then remove the light unit from the tailgate **(see illustration)**.

24 Refit the light unit using a reversal of the removal procedure.

Number plate light

25 The procedure is described as part of the bulb renewal procedure in Section 5.

High-level stop-light

26 The procedure is described as part of the bulb renewal procedure in Section 5.

8 Headlight beam adjustment components – general information, removal and refitting

General information

1 Models with Halogen headlights are equipped with a headlight beam adjustment system, controlled by a switch located on the facia, which allows the aim of the headlights to be adjusted to compensate for the varying loads carried in the vehicle. The switch should be positioned according to the load being carried in the vehicle – e.g. position 0 for driver with no passengers or luggage, then increase the position to 1, 2, or 3 as the load is increased, or when towing.

2 Models with Xenon headlights are equipped with an automatic levelling system, which is controlled from a level sensor fitted to the rear suspension. If a fault occurs in the system, a warning light will show up on the instrument panel, and the headlights will be angled down to avoid dazzling on coming traffic. If it happens, the driving speed must be adjusted accordingly to allow for decreased visibility.

⚠ **Warning: Before carrying out any operations on xenon headlight units, it is recommended that protective gloves and safety glasses be worn. It is essential that the wiring connectors are disconnected from the rear of the headlight unit, and then wait until the module and bulbs have cooled down before removal. DO NOT switch the headlights on with the bulb removed, as it is harmful to the eyes.**

3 Accurate adjustment of the headlight beam is only possible using optical beam-setting equipment, and this work should therefore be carried out by a Nissan dealer or suitably-equipped workshop. To make temporary adjustment of the headlights, position the vehicle on a level surface, 10 metres from a wall. The tyres must be all at the correct pressures, the fuel tank half full, and a person be sitting in the drivers seat. Turn on the ignition, and check that, where fitted, the manual adjustment inside the vehicle is set at 0. Measure the distance from the ground to the centre of the headlight, and then deduct

7.22 Disconnect the rear light wiring connectors

7.23 Withdraw the light unit from the tailgate

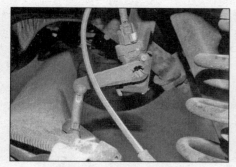

8.7 Location of level sensor

8.8 Headlight alignment manual adjustment screws

9.5a Unclip the instrument cowling. . .

5.0cm for models with halogen headlights, and 7.5cm for models with xenon headlights. Draw a mark on the wall at this height, and then adjust the headlight beam centre point onto this mark by turning the adjustment screws on the rear of the headlight unit.

Headlight adjuster switch

4 The procedure for removing the switch is described in Section 4.

Xenon headlight level sensor

5 A level sensor is fitted to the rear suspension. This forms an integral part of the headlight adjustment system for the Xenon headlights.

6 To remove sensor jack up the rear of the vehicle and support it on axle stands (see *Jacking and vehicle support*).

7 Disconnect the wiring connector from the sensor, and then undo the two retaining bolts and remove it from the rear suspension **(see illustration)**.

Manual adjustment

8 For reference, the outer adjusting screw (nearest the vehicle wing) is used to adjust the vertical alignment, and the inner screw (located nearest to the radiator) is used to adjust the horizontal alignment **(see illustration)**. Note that on models with electric headlight beam adjustment, the adjustment switch must be set to position 0 when carrying out beam alignment.

---

9 Instrument panel –
removal and refitting

Removal

1 Disconnect the battery negative terminal (refer to Chapter 5 Section 4).

2 Release the steering column adjustment lever and lower the steering column, as far as possible.

3 Remove the drivers side air ventilation trim panel, as described in Chapter 11 Section 25.

4 Remove the stop/start switch trim panel from the left-hand side of the instrument panel, as described in Section 4.

5 Unclip the instrument cowling from the

9.5b . . . releasing the lower part from the steering column shroud

9.7a Withdraw the instrument panel. . .

facia and from the upper steering column shroud **(see illustrations)**.

6 Remove the instrument panel two lower securing screws **(see illustration)**.

7 Pull the instrument panel forwards, and disconnect the wiring connectors from the rear of the panel **(see illustrations)**. Withdraw the instrument panel from the facia.

Refitting

8 Refitting is a reversal of removal.

---

10 Horn –
removal and refitting

Removal

1 Remove the front bumper, as described in Chapter 11 Section 5.

9.6 Undo the two instrument panel lower retaining screws

9.7b . . . and disconnect the wiring connector

2 There are two horns fitted to the right-hand side of the front of the vehicle, one at the top of the intercooler and one at the bottom **(see illustrations)**.

10.2a Horn located above intercooler. . .

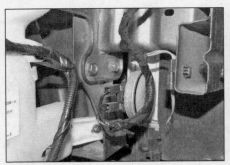

10.2b . . . and one below, behind the front bumper bar

10.3 Undo the horn mounting bracket retaining bolt

10.4 Disconnect the wiring connectors

3 Unscrew the securing bolt, and withdraw the horn complete with its mounting bracket **(see illustration)**

4 Disconnect the wiring connector from the horn **(see illustration)**.

Refitting

5 Refitting is a reversal of removal.

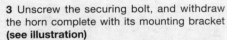

11 Wiper arm –
removal and refitting

Removal

1 Operate the wiper motor, and then switch it off so that the wiper arm returns to the at-rest/parked position.

2 If a windscreen or tailgate wiper is being removed, stick a piece of tape alongside the edge of the wiper blade, to use as an alignment aid on refitting. On some models there are marks on the screen to aid refitting.

3 Unclip the plastic cover from the wiper arm spindle nut, then slacken and remove the nut **(see illustrations)**.

4 Lift the blade off the glass, and pull the wiper arm off its spindle **(see illustration)**.

5 If necessary, the arm can be removed from the spindle, by using a suitable puller **(see illustration)**. If both windscreen wiper arms are removed, note their locations, as different arms are fitted to the driver and passenger's sides.

Refitting

6 Ensure that the wiper arm and spindle splines are clean and dry.

7 When refitting a windscreen or tailgate wiper arm, refit the arm to the spindle, aligning the wiper blade with the mark on the screen or tape fitted before removal.

8 If both front windscreen wiper arms have been removed, ensure that the arms are refitted to their correct positions as noted before removal.

9 Refit the spindle nut, tighten it securely and, clip the plastic nut cover back into position.

12 Windscreen wiper
motor and linkage –
removal and refitting

Removal

1 Disconnect the battery negative terminal (refer to *Disconnecting the battery* in Chapter 5 Section 4).

2 Remove the windscreen scuttle grille panels as described in Chapter 11 Section 20.

3 Disconnect the wiring connector from the wiper motor **(see illustration)**.

11.3a Unclip the plastic cap. . .

11.3b . . . and undo the retaining nut

11.3c Rear wiper arm retaining nut

11.4 Remove the wiper arm

11.5 If it is tight on the spindle, use a puller

12.3 Disconnect the wiper motor wiring plug

12.4 Undo the three wiper linkage retaining bolts

13.4 Disconnect the wiper motor wiring plug

13.5 Undo the rear wiper motor mounting bolts

4 Unscrew the three motor and linkage securing bolts, then withdraw it from the scuttle panel **(see illustration)**.

Refitting

5 Refitting is a reversal of removal.

13 Tailgate wiper motor – removal and refitting

Removal

1 Disconnect the battery negative terminal (refer to *Disconnecting the battery* in Chapter 5 Section 4).
2 Open the tailgate and remove the inner tailgate trim, as described in Chapter 11 Section 23.
3 Remove the rear wiper arm with reference to Section 11.
4 Disconnect the tailgate wiper motor wiring connector **(see illustration)**.
5 Unscrew the three bolts securing the wiper motor assembly to the tailgate and withdraw it from the tailgate **(see illustration)**.

Refitting

6 Refitting is a reversal of removal.

14 Windscreen/tailgate washer system components – removal and refitting

Washer fluid reservoir

Removal

1 Working in the engine compartment, release the retaining clip and then pull the filler neck upwards to remove it from the top of the reservoir **(see illustration)**. Make sure the washer fluid level is low before removing the reservoir; be prepared for some spillage.
2 Disconnect the battery negative terminal (refer to Chapter 5 Section 4).
3 Remove the front bumper, as described in Chapter 11 Section 5.
4 Release the wiring harness and fluid hoses from the retaining clips in the reservoir **(see**

illustration)**, and move the harness and hoses to one side to allow sufficient clearance to remove the reservoir.
5 Disconnect the fluid hose(s) from the washer pump – if the reservoir still contains fluid, be prepared for fluid spillage.
6 Disconnect the wiring connector(s) from the washer pump(s), and from the fluid level sensor, where applicable.
7 Remove the reservoir securing bolts, and then lower the reservoir from under the wheel arch **(see illustration)**.

Refitting

8 Refitting is a reversal of removal.

Washer pump

Removal

9 Proceed as described in paragraphs 2 to 6.

14.1 Release the securing clip from the top of the filler neck

14.7 Undo the reservoir mounting bolts

10 Pull the washer pump from the reservoir and recover the grommet **(see illustration)**. If the reservoir still contains fluid, be prepared for fluid spillage.

Refitting

11 Refitting is a reversal of removal, making sure the grommet is fitted correctly in the reservoir before refitting the washer pump.

Windscreen washer nozzle

Removal

12 Unclip the windscreen washer nozzle from the scuttle panel. Disconnect the washer fluid hose and remove washer nozzle **(see illustrations)**.
13 To adjust the position of the washer nozzle, unclip it from the scuttle panel. Then

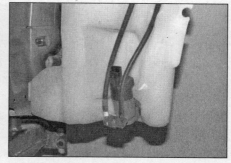

14.4 Unclip the wiring and the hoses from the reservoir

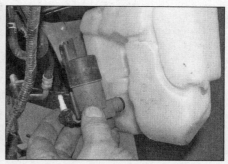

14.10 Ease the washer pump from the reservoir

14.12a Unclip the washer nozzle from the scuttle panel. . .

14.12b . . . and disconnect the washer hose

14.13 Turn the washer jet for adjustment position onto the windscreen

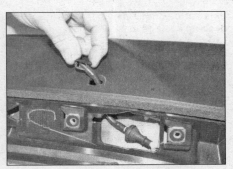

14.16 Unclip the rear washer jet from the spoiler

using a small screwdriver adjust the position of the washer nozzle **(see illustration)**.

Refitting
14 Refitting is a reversal of removal.

Tailgate washer nozzle
Removal
15 Remove the high-level brake light unit, as described in Section 5. The tailgate washer

nozzle is located in the spoiler, where the high-level brake light is fitted.
16 Carefully unclip the washer nozzle from the underside of the rear spoiler **(see illustration)**.

Refitting
17 Refitting is a reversal of removal.

15 Radio/CD player –
removal and refitting

Removal
1 Disconnect the battery negative terminal (refer to Chapter 5 Section 4).
2 Remove the stop/start switch trim panel from the right-hand side of the radio/CD player, as described in Section 4.
3 Remove the passenger side air ventilation grille from the left-hand side of the facia, as described in Chapter 11 Section 25, then carefully unclip the trim panel from across the passenger side of the facia panel **(see illustration)**.
4 Remove the four now-exposed securing screws, two at the upper corners of the audio unit and two below the unit **(see illustration)**.
5 Pull the unit forwards from the facia, and then disconnect the wiring connectors and the aerial lead from the rear of the unit **(see illustrations)**.

Refitting
6 Refitting is a reversal of removal, ensuring that the wiring is freely routed behind the unit.

16 Loudspeakers –
removal and refitting

1 Disconnect the battery negative terminal (refer to *Disconnecting the battery* in Chapter 5 Section 4).

Door-mounted loudspeakers
2 Remove the door inner trim panel as described in Chapter 11 Section 23.
3 Disconnect the wiring connector from the door speaker **(see illustration)**.

15.3 Unclip the trim panel from the facia

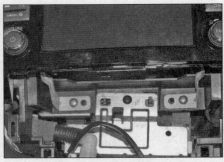

15.4 Undo the retaining screws – two lower ones shown

15.5a Withdraw audio unit from the facia. . .

15.5b . . . and disconnect the wiring plug connectors

16.3 Disconnect the speaker wiring connector

16.4 Undo the screws and remove the speaker

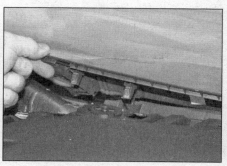

16.6 Unclip the grille panel. . .

16.7 . . . and remove the speaker

4 Undo the three securing screws, and then withdraw the loudspeaker from the door panel **(see illustration)**.

5 Refitting is a reversal of removal, but refit the inner door trim panel with reference to Chapter 11 Section 23.

Facia-mounted loudspeakers

6 Working in the top corner of the facia panel, carefully unclip the trim panel **(see illustration)**.

7 Release the loudspeaker from the top of the facia and disconnect the wiring connector **(see illustration)**.

8 Refitting is a reversal of removal.

17 Anti-theft system and engine immobiliser – general information

1 All models in the range are equipped as standard with a central locking system incorporating an electronic engine immobiliser function.

2 The electronic engine immobiliser is operated by a transponder fitted to the ignition key, in conjunction with an analogue module fitted around the ignition switch.

3 When the ignition key is inserted in the switch and turned to the ignition 'on' position, the control module sends a preprogrammed recognition code signal to the analogue module on the ignition switch. If the recognition code signal matches that of the transponder on the ignition key, an unlocking request signal is sent to the engine management ECU allowing the engine to be started. If the ignition key signal is not recognised, the engine management system remains immobilised.

4 When the ignition is switched off, a locking signal is sent to the ECU and the engine is immobilised until the unlocking request signal is again received.

18 Intelligent key system components – general information

1 The intelligent key system is a keyless entry system, which allows you to operate your vehicle without using an actual key. This can only be used when the Intelligent Key remote

is within a specified operating distance (80cm with new battery) from the antennas or ignition switch. The antennas are located in the following positions around the vehicle:

a) *Inside the rear of the centre console.*
b) *In luggage compartment, behind the rear seats on crossmember.*
c) *Left-hand front door handle.*
d) *Right-hand front door handle.*
e) *Behind rear bumper trim.*

2 As the battery discharges over time, the operating distance becomes less, so a new battery will be required. Do not hold the Intelligent Key remote too close to the door, as this may also cause it to not function correctly. If a door is not closed securely, this will cause the Intelligent Key not to function properly.

3 There is a warning buzzer, which is positioned behind the front bumper, below the right-hand side headlight unit **(see illustration)**.

19 Airbag system – general information, precautions and system de-activation

General information

1 A driver's and passenger's airbag are fitted as standard on all models. The driver's airbag is located in the steering wheel centre pad and the passenger's airbag is located above the glovebox in the facia. Side airbags are also available on certain models and are located in the front seats. Curtain airbags are also fitted to some models and are located behind the headlining around the outer edge.

18.3 Warning buzzer behind front bumper

2 The system is armed only when the ignition is switched on; however, a reserve power source maintains a power supply to the system in the event of a break in the main electrical supply. The steering wheel and facia airbags are activated by a sensor (deceleration sensor), and controlled by an electronic control unit located under the centre console. The side and curtain airbags are activated by severe side impact and operate in conjunction with the main system.

3 The airbags are inflated by a gas generator, which forces the bag out from its location in the steering wheel, facia or seat back frame.

Precautions

⚠️ **Warning: The following precautions must be observed when working on vehicles equipped with an airbag system, to prevent the possibility of personal injury.**

General precautions

a) *Do not disconnect the battery with the engine running.*
b) *Before carrying out any work in the vicinity of the airbag, removal of any of the airbag components, or any welding work on the vehicle, de-activate the system as described in the following sub-Section.*
c) *Do not attempt to test any of the airbag system circuits using test meters or any other test equipment.*
d) *If the airbag warning light comes on, or any fault in the system is suspected, consult a Nissan dealer without delay.*
e) *Do not attempt to carry out fault diagnosis, or any dismantling of the components.*

Precautions when handling an airbag

a) *Transport the airbag by itself, bag upward.*
b) *Do not put your arms around the airbag.*
c) *Carry the airbag close to the body, bag outward.*
d) *Do not drop the airbag or expose it to impacts.*
e) *Do not attempt to dismantle the airbag unit.*
f) *Do not connect any form of electrical equipment to any part of the airbag circuit.*

Precautions when storing an airbag

a) *Store the unit in a cupboard with the airbag upward.*

20.1 Airbag ECU location – behind the gear lever assembly

20.2 Disconnect the wiring connectors

20.3 Note the arrow must face forward when fitted

b) *Do not expose the airbag to temperatures above 80ºC.*
c) *Do not expose the airbag to flames.*
d) *Do not attempt to dispose of the airbag – consult a Nissan dealer.*
e) *Never refit an airbag that is known to be faulty or damaged.*

De-activation of airbag system

4 The system must be de-activated before carrying out any work on the airbag components or surrounding area:
a) *Switch on the ignition and check the operation of the airbag warning light on the instrument panel. The light should illuminate when the ignition is switched on, then extinguish.*
b) *Switch off the ignition.*
c) *Remove the ignition key.*
d) *Switch off all electrical equipment.*
e) *Disconnect the battery negative terminal (refer to Chapter 5 Section 4).*

f) *Insulate the battery negative terminal and the end of the battery negative lead to prevent any possibility of contact.*
g) *Wait for at least ten minutes before carrying out any further work.*

Activation of airbag system

5 To activate the system on completion of any work, proceed as follows:
a) *Ensure that there are no occupants in the vehicle, and that there are no loose objects around the vicinity of the steering wheel. Close the vehicle doors and windows.*
b) *Ensure that the ignition is switched off then reconnect the battery negative terminal.*
c) *Open the driver's door and switch on the ignition, without reaching in front of the steering wheel. Check that the airbag warning light illuminates briefly then extinguishes.*
d) *Switch off the ignition.*
e) *If the airbag warning light does not operate*

as described in paragraph c), consult a Nissan dealer before driving the vehicle.

20 Airbag system components
– removal and refitting

⚠️ *Warning: Refer to the precautions given in Section 19 before attempting to carry out work on any of the airbag components. Any suspected faults with the airbag system should be referred to a Nissan dealer – under no circumstances attempt to carry out any work other than removal and refitting of the front airbag unit(s) and/or the rotary connector, as described in the following paragraphs.*
Note: *Disconnect the battery negative terminal (refer to 'Disconnecting the battery' in Chapter 5 Section 4), before the removal and refitting of components in the airbag system.*

Airbag electronic control units

1 The ECU is located under the centre console in front of the handbrake **(see illustration)**, and is accessible after removal of the centre console, upper trim panels, as described in Chapter 11 Section 24.
2 Disconnect the wiring connectors from the control unit, then undo the retaining bolts and remove the control unit from the floor panel **(see illustration)**
3 The arrow on the top of the unit must face forward when refitted **(see illustration)**.

Driver's airbag unit

Type 1 steering wheel

4 De-activate the airbag system as described in Section 19.
5 Working at each side of the steering wheel, insert a screwdriver (or similar) through the holes in the rear of the steering wheel, to release the securing clips on the rear of the airbag unit **(see illustration)**.
6 Carefully lever the airbag, and release it from the steering wheel **(see illustration)**.
7 Using a thin screwdriver, release the centre retaining clips and disconnect the airbag wiring connectors from the rear of the airbag unit **(see illustrations)**.

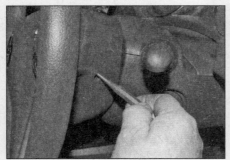

20.5 Insert a screwdriver through the sides of the steering wheel

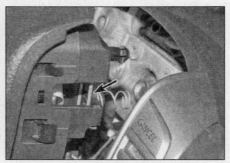

20.6 . . . to release the airbag securing spring clips

20.7a Lift up the locking clips. . .

20.7b . . . and disconnect the wiring connectors from the airbag

20.8 Disconnect the earth wiring connector

20.12a Insert a screwdriver through the rear of the steering wheel. . .

20.12b . . . to release the securing clips

8 Disconnect the earth wire connector **(see illustration)**, and then carefully remove the airbag from the steering wheel.

9 If the airbag unit is to be stored for any length of time, refer to the storage precautions given in Section 19.

10 Refitting is a reversal of removal, bearing in mind the following points:

a) *Do not strike the airbag unit, or expose it to impacts during refitting.*

b) *On completion of refitting, activate the airbag system as described in Section 19.*

Type 2 steering wheel

11 De-activate the airbag system as described in Section 19.

12 Turn the steering wheel a quarter of a turn and working at the rear of the steering wheel, insert a screwdriver (or similar) through the holes in the rear of the steering wheel, to release the securing clips on the rear of the airbag unit **(see illustrations)**.

13 Carefully lever the airbag, and release it from the steering wheel.

14 Using a thin screwdriver, release the centre retaining clips and disconnect the airbag wiring connectors from the rear of the airbag unit **(see illustrations 20.7a and 20.7b)**.

15 Disconnect the earth wire connector, and then carefully remove the airbag from the steering wheel.

16 If the airbag unit is to be stored for any length of time, refer to the storage precautions given in Section 19.

17 Refitting is a reversal of removal, bearing in mind the following points:

a) *Do not strike the airbag unit, or expose it to impacts during refitting.*

b) *On completion of refitting, activate the airbag system as described in Section 19.*

Airbag rotary switch assembly

Removal

18 Remove the steering column shrouds, as described in Chapter 11 Section 25.

19 Undo the retaining screws and withdraw the rotary switch (Spiral cable) from the top of the steering column, release the locking clips and disconnect the wiring connectors, as it is removed **(see illustrations)**.

20.19a Undo the two retaining screws. . .

20.19b . . . release the locking clip and disconnect the wiring connectors

Refitting

20 Refitting is a reversal of removal, bearing in mind the following points:

a) *Make sure the rotary switch has not been turned and is still in the position, noted on removal.*

b) *Ensure that the roadwheels are in the straight-ahead position before refitting the rotary connector and steering wheel.*

c) *Before refitting the steering column shrouds, ensure that the rotary connector wiring harness is correctly routed as noted before removal.*

d) *Refit the steering wheel as described in Chapter 10 Section 11, and refit the airbag unit as described previously in this Section.*

Passenger's airbag unit

Removal

21 The passenger's airbag is fitted to the upper part of the facia, above the glovebox.

22 De-activate the airbag system as described in Section 19.

23 Remove the glovebox as described in Chapter 11 Section 25.

24 Release the locking clip and disconnect the airbag wiring connector **(see illustration)**.

25 Undo the screws securing the airbag assembly mounting bracket to the facia support rail, and then carefully withdraw the airbag from the facia **(see illustration)**.

26 If the airbag unit is to be stored for any length of time, refer to the storage precautions given in Section 19.

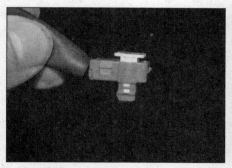

20.24 Release the centre locking clip to disconnect the wiring connector

20.25 Undo the airbag mounting bracket screws

Refitting

27 Refitting is a reversal of removal, bearing in mind the following points:

a) *Do not strike the airbag unit, or expose it to impacts during refitting.*

b) *On completion of refitting, activate the airbag system as described in Section 19.*

Side airbag units

28 The side airbags are located internally within the front seat back and no attempt should be made to remove them. Any suspected problems with the side airbag system should be referred to a Nissan dealer.

Curtain airbag units

29 The curtain airbags are located internally behind the headlining and no attempt should be made to remove them. Any suspected problems with the curtain airbag system should be referred to a Nissan dealer.

FUSE BOX IN ENGINE COMPARTMENT
IPDM E/R – INTELLIGENT POWER DISTRIBUTION MODULE ENGINE ROOM

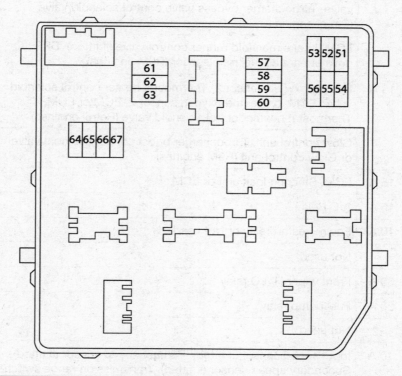

FUSE	VALUE	DESCRIPTION	OEM NAME
51	10 A	Active grille shutter or Active grille shutter, ECM	51
52	15 A	ECM, Fuel heater and water in fuel level sensor, High pressure fuel pump, NOx trap upstream air fuel ratio sensor sensor (if fitted), DPF downstream air fuel ratio sensor (if fitted), Turbocharger boost control solenoid valve (K9K engines up to May 2018)	52
		ECM, Fuel heater and water in fuel level sensor, Engine oil pressure control solenoid valve, Glow control unit, Charge air cooler cooling pump (K9K engines from June 2018)	
		Condenser, Ignition coils (up to May 2017), Heated oxygen sensor 1, Heated oxygen sensor 2, Evap canister purge volume control solenoid valve, Turbocharger wastegate control solenoid valve, ECM, (Petrol engines up to May 2018)	
		Evap canister purge volume control solenoid valve, Air fuel ratio sensor 1, Heated oxygen sensor 2, Turbocharger cooling water pump (Petrol engines from June 2018)	
		Engine coolant bypass solenoid valve, Fuel heater and water in fuel sensor, Turbocharger boost control solenoid valve, Air fuel ratio sensor, Fuel flow actuator, NOx trap upstream air fuel ratio sensor sensor (if fitted) (R9M engines)	
53	15A	Throttle control motor relay or Not used	53

54	10 A	Engine coolant bypass valve control solenoid valve, Engine oil pressure control solenoid valve, Exhaust valve timing control solenoid valve, Intake valve timing control solenoid valve, Turbocharger bypass valve control solenoid valve (Petrol engines)	54
		ECM, Intake manifold runner control valve (if fitted), DPF downstream air fuel ratio sensor (R9M engines)	
55	15 A	Heated oxygen sensor 2, Thermostat heater control solenoid valve, ECM or Heated oxygen sensor 2, ECM or ECM, Thermostat heater control solenoid valve (Petrol engines)	55
		Glow control unit, Turbocharger boost control solenoid valve or Glow control unit (R9M engines)	
56	15 A	ECM, Steering lock unit or ECM	56
57	15 A	A/C Relay	57
58	10 A	Engine restart relay or Not used	58
59	-	Not used	59
60	30 A	Front wiper HI/LO relay	60
61	20 A	Fuel pump relay	61
62	-	Not used	62
63	10 A	Input speed sensor (if fitted), Primary speed sensor (if fitted), Secondary speed sensor (if fitted), Transmission range switch (if fitted), TCM (if fitted), Output speed sender (if fitted), Fuse box in engine compartment (IPDM E/R) (up to May 2018)	63
		Transmission range switch or Park/neutral position relay	
64	-	Not used	64
65	5 A	ECM, Steering lock unit	65
66	-	Not used	66
67	10 A	Headlamp aiming motors, Transmission range switch (if fitted), Compressor, Front window defogger relays, Reverse/ neutral position switch	67

FUSE AND RELAY BOX IN PASSENGER COMPARTMENT
FUSE BLOCK-JUNCTION BOX (J/B)

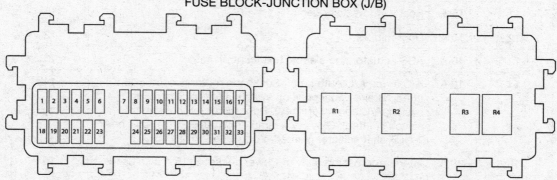

FUSE/ RELAY	VALUE	DESCRIPTION	OEM NAME
1	15 A	Combination switch, Pump control unit (if fitted), Washer switching solenoid valve (if fitted) or Combination switch	1
2	10 A	Air bag diagnosis sensor unit	2
3	5 A	Combination meter or Diode 1	3
4	10 A	Sonar control unit (if fitted), PTC relays, Fuel heater relay (for diesel engines), Data link connector, Stop lamp switch, Distance sensor (if fitted), Auto anti-dazzling mirror (if fitted), EPS control unit, Combination switch (spiral cable), Chassis control module, Front camera unit (if fitted), Option connector (illumination), Electric park brake control unit, Around view monitor control unit (if fitted), Steering angle sensor, Navi control unit, Audio unit (up to May 2017)	4
		Sonar control unit (if fitted, Fuel heater relay (for diesel engines), Data link connector, Stop lamp switch, Distance sensor (if fitted), Auto anti-dazzling mirror (if fitted), EPS control unit, Combination switch (spiral cable), Chassis control module, Option connector (illumination), Side radars (if fitted), Electric park brake control unit, Around view monitor control unit (if fitted), Steering angle sensor, Navi control unit, Audio unit, CAN Gateway, ADAS control unit, AFS control unit (if fitted), Front camera unit (if fitted), Power window switches, LDW switch, PTC relays (from June 2017)	
5	10 A	DC/DC converter or Not used	5
6	15 A	Front heated seats switches	6
7	20 A	Blower motor (with manual air conditioning), Power transistor (with automatic air conditioning), Engine restart bypass control relay (if fitted)	7
8	5 A	License plate lamps, Tail lamp LH (back door side), Glove box lamp, Headlamp aiming switch (if fitted), Audio unit, Navi control unit (up to May 2017)	8
		Headlamp aiming switch (if fitted), Audio unit, Navi control unit (from June 2017)	
9		Not used	9

10	15 A	Rear window defogger	10
11	15 A	Rear window defogger	11
12	10 A	Door mirrors	12
13	10 A	ABS actuator and electric unit (control unit)	13
14	10 A	A/C amp., A/C Auto amp., Sunshade motor assembly (if fitted), Brake pedal position switch (if fitted), Stop lamp switch, A/C control (if fitted), Door mirror remote control switch (if fitted), Glove box lamp (from June 2017), CVT or A/T DCT shift selector (if fitted, from June 2017)	14
15	20 A	Interior room lamp relay or Power socket 2, 15 A also used	15
16	15 A	Power socket 1 or Not used	16
17	20 A	Blower motor (with manual air conditioning), Power transistor (with automatic air conditioning)	17
18		Not used	18
19	20 A	Around view monitor control unit (if fitted), Navi control unit, Audio unit (up to May 2018)	19
		Navi control unit, USB connector and aux jack (from June 2018)	
20	5 A	Siren control unit (if fitted), BCM (body control module), Sensor cancel switch (if fitted), Intruder sensor (if fitted)	20
21	10 A	Combination meter	21
22	10 A	Interior room lamp relay	22
23	-	Not used or BOSE amp.	23
24	10 A	Stop lamp switch, BCM (body control module)	24
25	5 A	NATS Antenna Amp (if fitted)	25
26	5 A	Clutch interlock switch	26
27	10 A	BCM (body control module)	27
28	10 A	Electric park brake switch assembly, Data link connector, Option connector (illumination), Power window relay, Door mirror open relay (if fitted), Door mirror close relay (if fitted), CVT or AT (DCT) shift selector (from June 2017), CAN Gateway (from June 2017)	28
29	20 A	BCM (body control module), 15 A also used	29
30	15 A	BCM (body control module)	30
31	20 A	BCM (body control module), 15 A also used	31
32	20 A	Power socket 1, 15 A also used or Not used	32
33	15 A	BCM (body control module), 10 A also used	33
R1	-	Ignition relay	
R2	-	Blower relay	
R3	-	Rear window defogger relay	
R4	-	Accessory relay	

FUSE AND RELAY BOX IN PASSENGER COMPARTMENT
FUSE BLOCK-JUNCTION BOX (J/B) IS

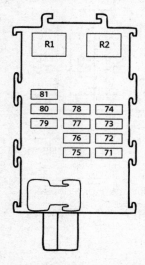

FUSE/ RELAY	VALUE	DESCRIPTION	OEM NAME
71	10 A	Steering angle sensor or Not used	71
72	10 A	Combination meter or Combination meter, Diode 2	72
73	10 A	Navi control unit, Audio unit, Around view monitor control unit (if fitted)	73
74	10 A	TCM, Primary speed sensor, Output speed, Transmission range switch (if fitted), Input speed sensor (for R9M engines), Secondary speed sensor (for HR engines)	74
75	-	Not used	75
76	10 A	A/C control (with automatic air conditioning), A/C auto amp. (with automatic air conditioning), A/C amp (with manual air conditioning)	76
77	10 A	ABS actuator and electric unit (control unit) or Not used	77
78	-	Not used	78
79	10 A	Electric oil pump relay	79
80	20 A	Navi control unit, Audio unit, Around view monitor control unit (if fitted), USB connector and aux jack (if fitted)	80
81	10 A	TCM	81

FUSE AND RELAY BOX IN PASSENGER COMPARTMENT
FUSE BLOCK-JUNCTION BOX (J/B) IS No.2 (valid up to May 2017)

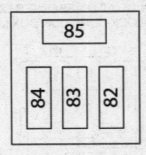

FUSE/RELAY	VALUE	DESCRIPTION	OEM NAME
82	10 A	Electric oil pump relay or Not used	82
83	10 A	TCM or Not used	83
84	-	Not used	84
85	-	Not used	85

FUSE AND RELAY BOX NEAR THE BATTERY
BATTERY TERMINAL WITH FUSIBLE LINK, FUSE AND FUSIBLE LINK BLOCK, FUSE AND FUSIBLE LINK BLOCK-1, FUSIBLE LINK HOLDER, FUSIBLE LINK HOLDER-1, FUSIBLE LINK HOLDER-2 (Up to May 2018)

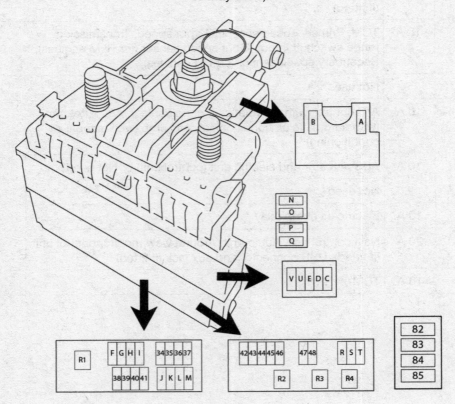

BATTERY TERMINAL WITH FUSIBLE LINK

FUSE	VALUE	DESCRIPTION	OEM NAME
A	450 A	Engine restart bypass relay or Starter motor	A
B	450 A	Alternator	B
C	100 A	Accessory power supply, Ignition power supply, Fuse and relay box in passenger compartment (Fuse block Junction box (J/B)), Fuse box in engine compartment (IPDM E/R) (for diesel engines)	C
D	100 A	Ignition supply, Fuse box in engine compartment (IPDM E/R)	D
E	50 A	Fuse and relay box on battery (Fuse and fusible link block-1)	E
V	100 A	Fuse and relay box on battery (Fuse and fusible link block), PTC relay 1	V
U	100 A	Ignition power supply, Fuse box in engine compartment (IPDM E/R) (for petrol engines), Thermoplunger control unit (for diesel engines, Glow control unit (for diesel engines)	U

FUSE AND FUSIBLE LINK BLOCK

FUSE/RELAY	VALUE	DESCRIPTION	OEM NAME
F	50 A	EPS control unit	F
G	30 A	ABS actuator and electric unit (control unit)	G
H	50 A	EPS control unit	H
I	30 A	Headlamp washer relay	I
J		Not used	J
K	40 A	ABS actuator and electric unit (control unit)	K
L	30 A	Fuse and relay box in passenger compartment (Fuse block Junction box (J/B)), Starter relay	L
M	50 A	Power window relay, Power window main switch, Sunshade motor assembly (if fitted), Power seat switch (if fitted), Power window relay (up to May 2017)	M
		Sunshade motor assembly (if fitted), Power seat switch (if fitted), Driver seat control unit (if fitted), Automatic drive positioner control unit (if fitted), Seat memory switch (if fitted) (from June 2017)	
34	15 A	Horn relay	34
35	30 A	PTC relay 2 or Not used	35
36	30 A	PTC relay 3 or PTC relay 2	36
37	30 A	PTC relay 1 or Not used	37
38	30 A	Electric park brake control unit	38

39	30 A	Option connector	39
40	-	Not used	40
41	30 A	Electric park brake control unit	41
R1	-	Horn relay	

FUSE AND FUSIBLE LINK BLOCK-1

FUSE/ RELAY	VALUE	DESCRIPTION	OEM NAME
R	60 A	Cooling fan relay-2	R
S	30 A	ECM relay	S
T	30 A	Fuse box in engine compartment (IPDM E/R)	T
42	10 A	TCM	42
43	-	Not used	43
44	20 A	Fuel heater relay or Not used	44
45	-	Not used	45
46	-	Not used	46
47	-	Not used	47
48	-	Not used	48
R2	-	Starter relay	
R3	-	Engine restart relay	
R4	-	Fuel heater relay or High pressure fuel pump relay	

FUSIBLE LINK HOLDER

FUSE	VALUE	DESCRIPTION	OEM NAME
N	30 A	DC/DC converter	N
O	30 A	DC/DC converter	O

FUSIBLE LINK HOLDER-1

FUSE	VALUE	DESCRIPTION	OEM NAME
P	40 A	Front window defogger RH relay	P
Q	40 A	Front window defogger LH relay	Q

FUSIBLE LINK HOLDER-2 (From June 2017)

FUSE	VALUE	DESCRIPTION	OEM NAME
82	20 A	Power window main switch, Front power window motor (driver side)	82
83	20 A	Rear power window switch RH, Rear power window motor RH	83
84	20 A	Rear power window switch LH, Rear power window motor LH	84
85	20 A	Front power window switch (passenger side), Front power window motor (passenger side)	85

FUSE AND RELAY BOX NEAR THE BATTERY
BATTERY TERMINAL WITH FUSIBLE LINK, FUSE AND FUSIBLE LINK BLOCK, FUSE AND FUSIBLE LINK BLOCK-1, FUSIBLE LINK HOLDER, FUSIBLE LINK HOLDER-1, FUSIBLE LINK HOLDER-2, FUSIBLE LINK HOLDER-3, FUSIBLE LINK HOLDER-4, FUSIBLE LINK HOLDER-5 (From June 2018)

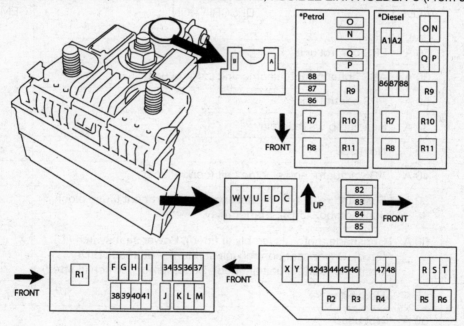

BATTERY TERMINAL WITH FUSIBLE LINK

FUSE	VALUE	DESCRIPTION	OEM NAME
A	450 A	Engine restart bypass relay	A
B	450 A	Alternator	B
C	100 A	Fuse and relay box on battery (Fuse and fusible link block), PTC relay 1	C

D	100 A	Cooling fan control module, Thermoplunger control unit, Fuses on Fusible link holder-5 (for diesel engines)	D
		Ignition supply, Fuse box in engine compartment (IPDM E/R) (for petrol engines)	
E	50 A	Fuse and relay box on battery (Fuse and fusible link block-1)	E
U	100 A	Ignition supply, Thermoplunger control unit (for diesel engines, Glow control unit (for diesel engines), Fuses on Fusible link holder-5	U
V	100 A	Ignition supply, Fuse box in engine compartment (IPDM E/R)	V
W	100 A	Accessory power supply, Ignition power supply, Fuse and relay box in passenger compartment (Fuse block Junction box (J/B)), Fuse box in engine compartment (IPDM E/R) (for diesel engines)	W

FUSE AND FUSIBLE LINK BLOCK

FUSE/ RELAY	VALUE	DESCRIPTION	OEM NAME
F	50 A	EPS control unit	F
G	30 A	ABS actuator and electric unit (control unit)	G
H	50 A	EPS control unit	H
I	30 A	Headlamp washer relay	I
J		Not used	J
K	40 A	ABS actuator and electric unit (control unit)	K
L	30 A	Fuse and relay box in passenger compartment (Fuse block Junction box (J/B)), Starter relay	L
M	50 A	Sunshade motor assembly (if fitted), Power seat switch (if fitted), Driver seat control unit (if fitted), Automatic drive positioner control unit (if fitted), Seat memory switch (if fitted)	M
34	15 A	Horn relay	34
35	30 A	Not used	35
36	30 A	PTC relay 2	36
37	30 A	Not used	37
38	30 A	Electric park brake control unit	38
39	-	Option connector	39
40	-	Not used	40
41	30 A	Electric park brake control unit	41
R1	-	Horn relay	

FUSE AND FUSIBLE LINK BLOCK-1

FUSE/RELAY	VALUE	DESCRIPTION	OEM NAME
R	60 A	Cooling fan relay-2	R
S	30 A	ECM relay	S
T	30 A	Fuse box in engine compartment (IPDM E/R)	T
42	-	Not used	42
43	-	Not used	43
44	-	Fuel heater relay or Not used	44
45	-	Not used	45
46	-	Not used	46
47	-	Not used	47
48	-	Not used	48
R2	-	Electric oil pump relay or Not used	
R3	-	Fuel heater relay or Cooling fan relay-2	
R4	-	Starter relay	
R5	-	Engine restart relay	
R6	-	Engine restart bypass control relay	

FUSIBLE LINK HOLDER

FUSE	VALUE	DESCRIPTION	OEM NAME
N	30 A	DC/DC converter	N
O	30 A	DC/DC converter	O

FUSIBLE LINK HOLDER-1

FUSE	VALUE	DESCRIPTION	OEM NAME
P	40 A	Front window defogger RH relay	P
Q	40 A	Front window defogger LH relay	Q

FUSIBLE LINK HOLDER-2

FUSE	VALUE	DESCRIPTION	OEM NAME
82	20 A	Power window main switch, Front power window motor (driver side)	82
83	20 A	Rear power window motor RH	83
84	20 A	Rear power window motor LH	84
85	20 A	Front power window motor (passenger side)	85

FUSIBLE LINK HOLDER-3

FUSE	VALUE	DESCRIPTION	OEM NAME
A1	40 A	SCR main relay or Not used	X
A2	-	Not used	Y

FUSIBLE LINK HOLDER-4

FUSE	VALUE	DESCRIPTION	OEM NAME
86	30 A	ADCM or Not used	86
87	15 A	NOx sensors or Not used	87
88	15 A	PM sensor	88

FUSIBLE LINK HOLDER-5

FUSE	VALUE	DESCRIPTION	OEM NAME
X	50 A	TCM or Not used	X or Z
Y	50 A	TCM or Not used	Y or AA

RELAYS R7-R11

RELAY	VALUE	DESCRIPTION	OEM NAME
R7	-	Park/neutral position relay	
R8	-	Back-up lamp relay	
R9	-	Headlamp washer relay	
R10	-	PTC relay 1	
R11	-	PTC relay 2	

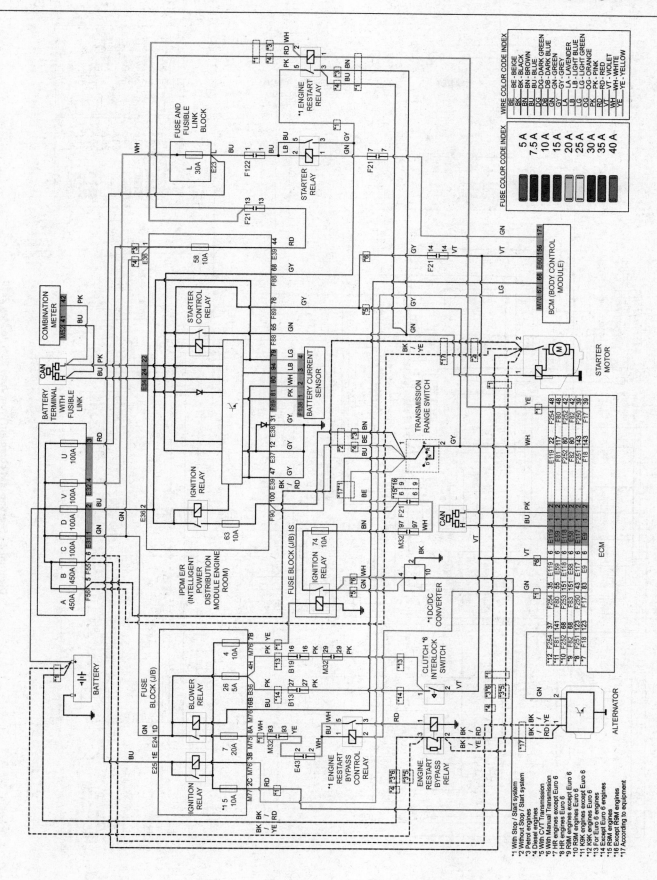

Diagram 1 – Starting and charging; Up to May 2017

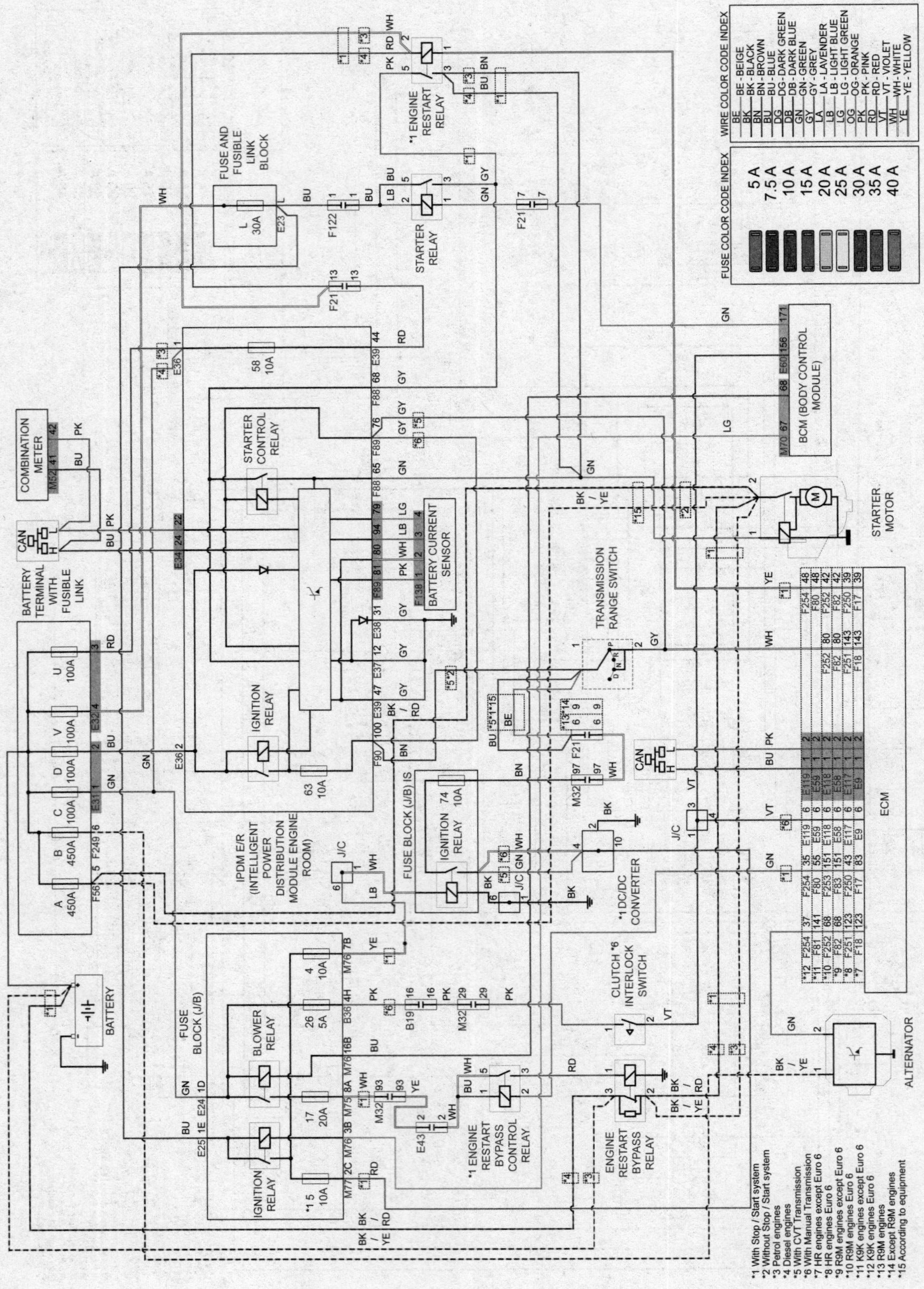

Diagram 2 – Starting and charging; From June 2017 to May 2018

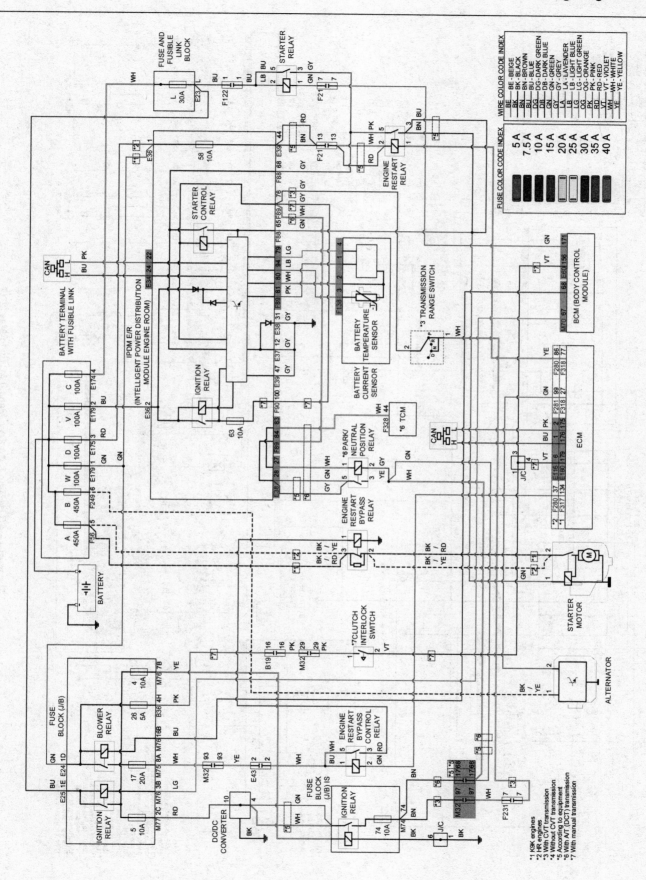

Diagram 3 – Starting and charging; From June 2018

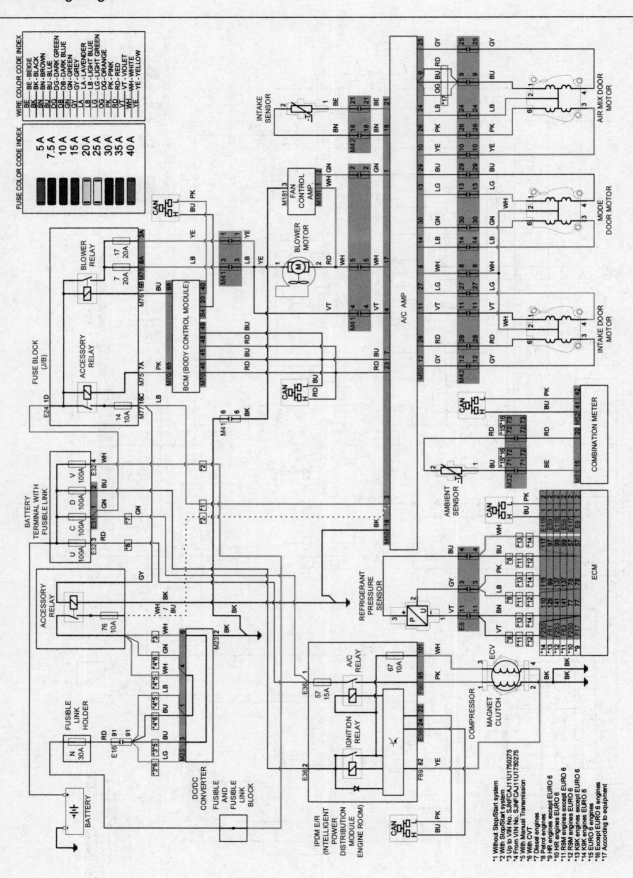

Diagram 4 – AC Heating & Cooling; Manual AC up to May 2017

Wiring diagrams 12•39

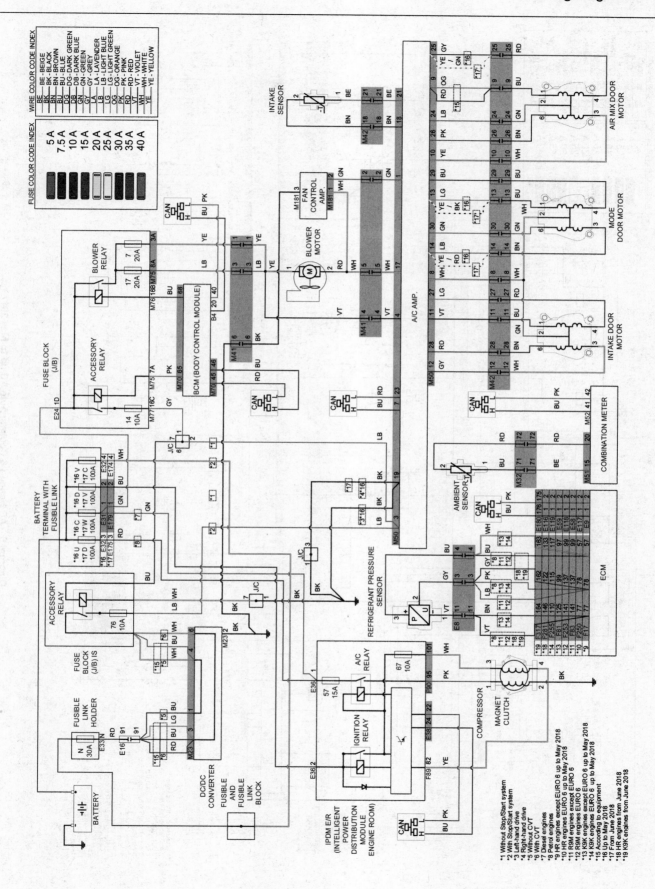

Diagram 5 – AC Heating & Cooling; Manual AC from June 2017

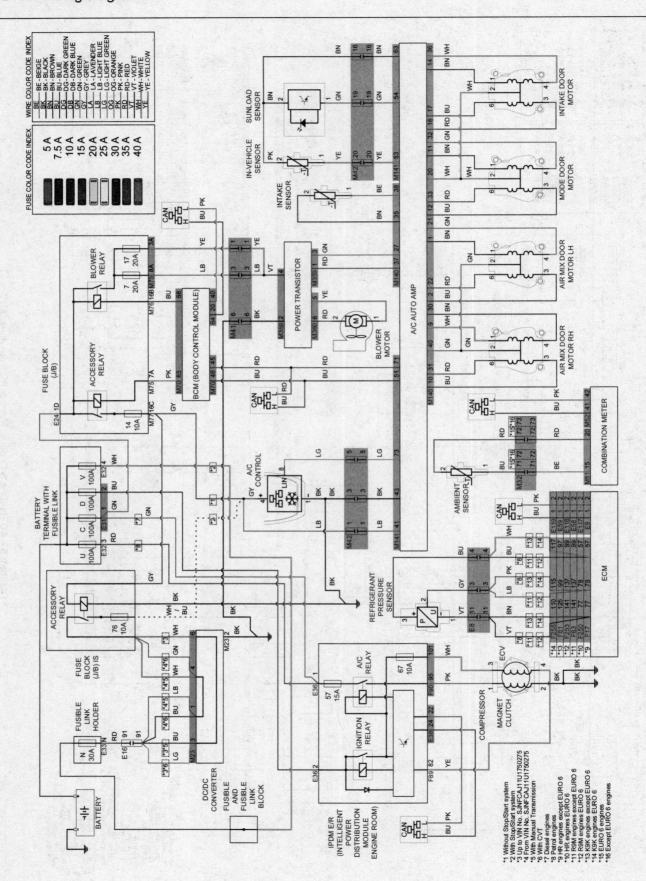

Diagram 6 – AC Heating & Cooling; Auto AC up to May 2017

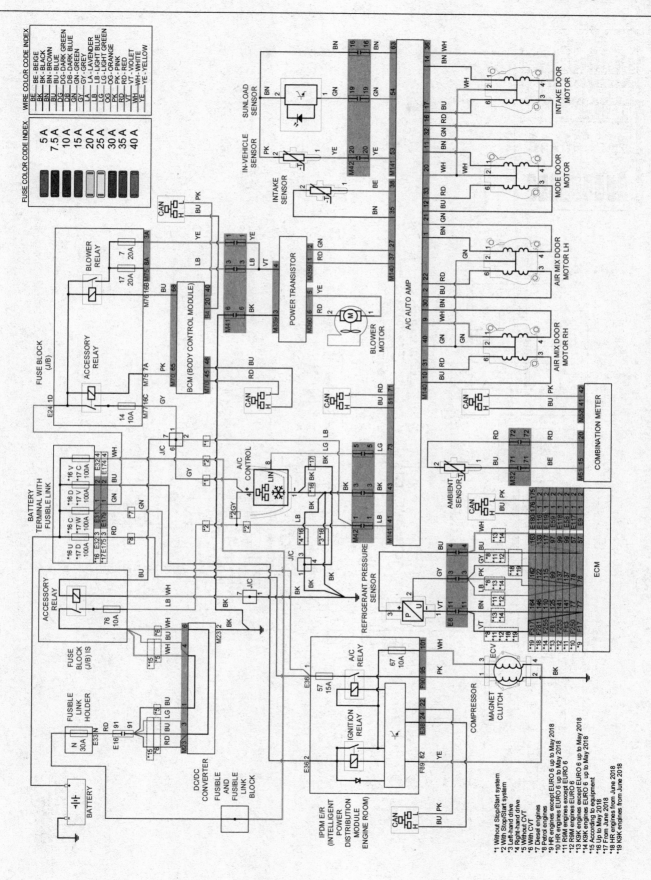

Diagram 7 – AC Heating & Cooling; Auto AC from June 2017

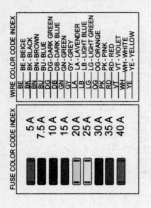

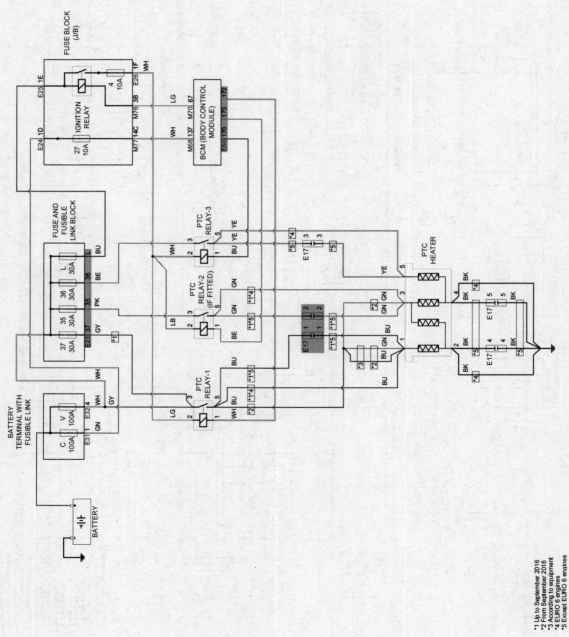

Diagram 8 – AC Heating & Cooling; PTC up to May 2017

*1 Up to September 2016
*2 From September 2016
*3 According to equipment
*4 EURO 6 engines
*5 Except EURO 6 engines

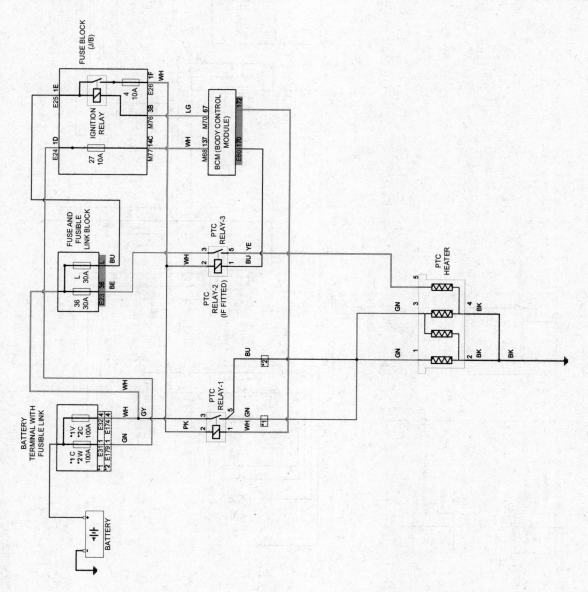

Diagram 9 – AC Heating & Cooling; PTC from June 2017

*1 Up to May 2018
*2 From June 2018

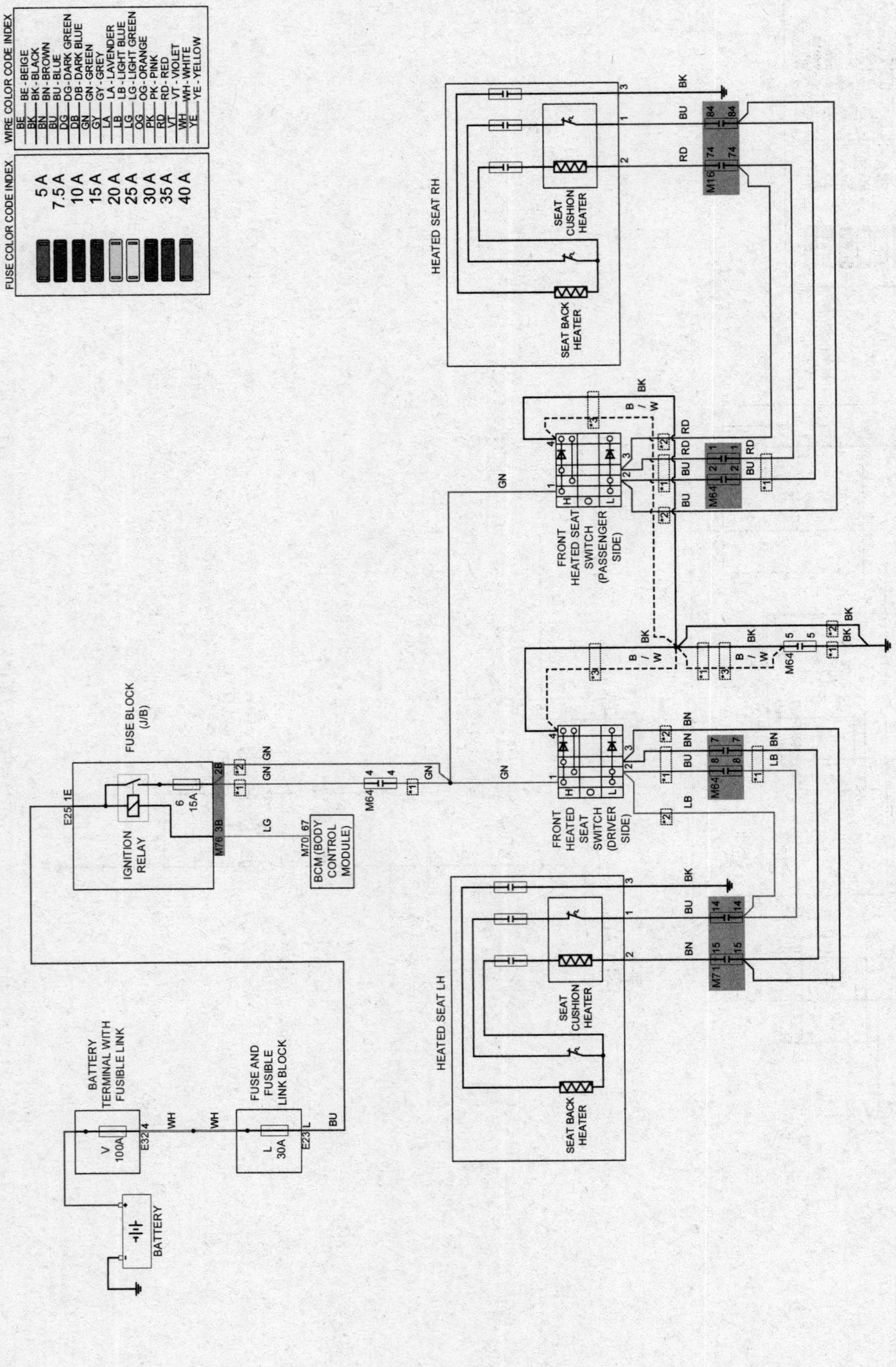

Diagram 10 – AC Heating & Cooling; Seat heater up to May 2017

*1 Up to VIN No. SJNFCAJ11U1750257
*2 From VIN No. SJNFCAJ11U1750257
*3 According to equipment

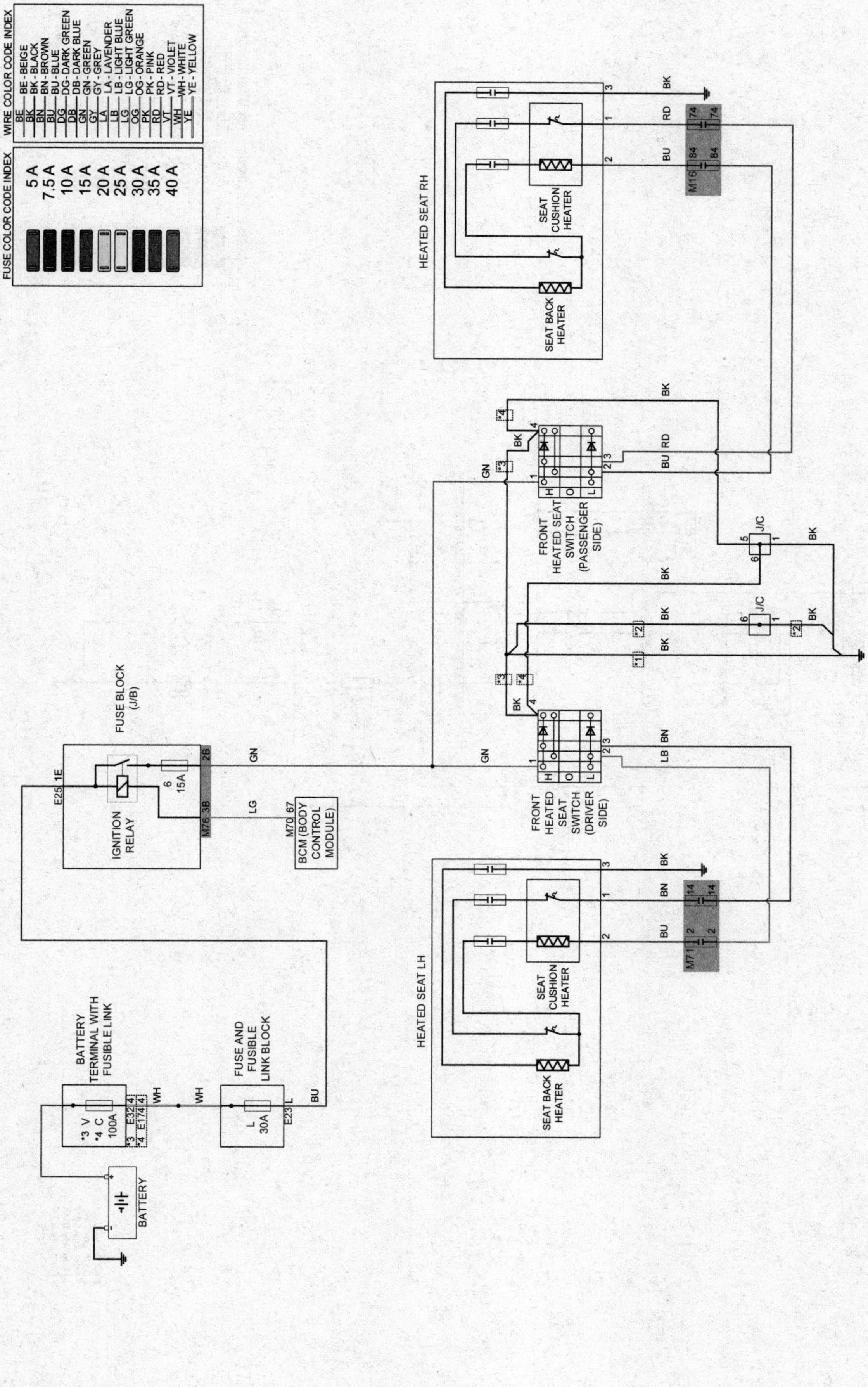

WIRE COLOR CODE INDEX

BE - BEIGE
BK - BLACK
BN - BROWN
BU - BLUE
DG - DARK GREEN
DB - DARK BLUE
GN - GREEN
GY - GREY
LA - LAVENDER
LB - LIGHT BLUE
LG - LIGHT GREEN
OG - ORANGE
PK - PINK
RD - RED
VT - VIOLET
WH - WHITE
YE - YELLOW

FUSE COLOR CODE INDEX

5 A
7.5 A
10 A
15 A
20 A
25 A
30 A
35 A
40 A

Diagram 11 – AC Heating & Cooling; Seat heater from June 2017

HEATED SEAT RH

SEAT CUSHION HEATER

SEAT BACK HEATER

FRONT HEATED SEAT SWITCH (PASSENGER SIDE)

FRONT HEATED SEAT SWITCH (DRIVER SIDE)

HEATED SEAT LH

SEAT CUSHION HEATER

SEAT BACK HEATER

FUSE BLOCK (J/B)

IGNITION RELAY

BCM (BODY CONTROL MODULE)

BATTERY TERMINAL WITH FUSIBLE LINK

FUSE AND FUSIBLE LINK BLOCK

BATTERY

*1 Left-hand drive
*2 Right-hand drive
*3 Up to May 2018
*4 From June 2018

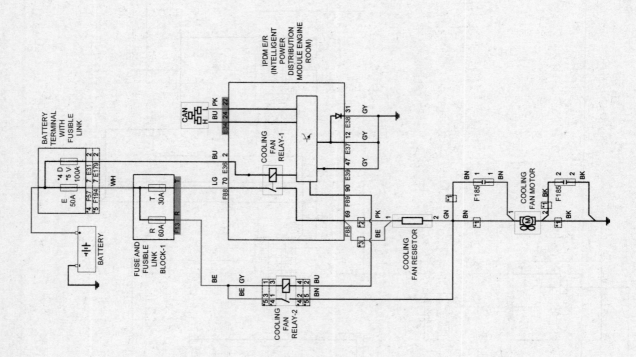

Diagram 12 – AC Heating & Cooling; Cooling fan

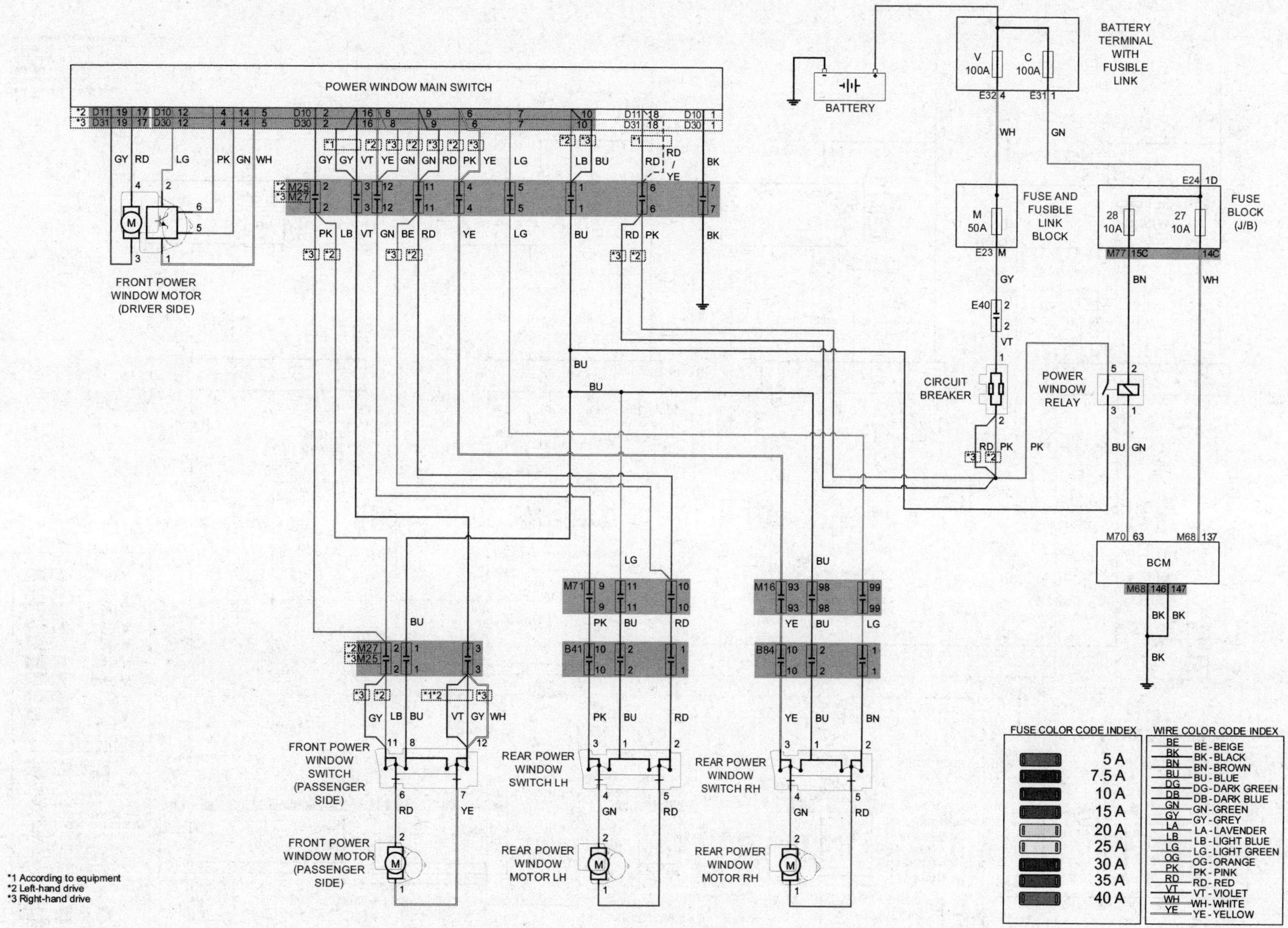
POWER WINDOW MAIN SWITCH
FRONT POWER WINDOW MOTOR (DRIVER SIDE)
BATTERY
BATTERY TERMINAL WITH FUSIBLE LINK
V 100A
C 100A
FUSE AND FUSIBLE LINK BLOCK
M 50A
FUSE BLOCK (J/B)
28 10A
27 10A
CIRCUIT BREAKER
POWER WINDOW RELAY
BCM
FRONT POWER WINDOW SWITCH (PASSENGER SIDE)
FRONT POWER WINDOW MOTOR (PASSENGER SIDE)
REAR POWER WINDOW SWITCH LH
REAR POWER WINDOW MOTOR LH
REAR POWER WINDOW SWITCH RH
REAR POWER WINDOW MOTOR RH
*1 According to equipment
*2 Left-hand drive
*3 Right-hand drive
FUSE COLOR CODE INDEX
5 A
7.5 A
10 A
15 A
20 A
25 A
30 A
35 A
40 A
WIRE COLOR CODE INDEX
BE - BEIGE
BK - BLACK
BN - BROWN
BU - BLUE
DG - DARK GREEN
DB - DARK BLUE
GN - GREEN
GY - GREY
LA - LAVENDER
LB - LIGHT BLUE
LG - LIGHT GREEN
OG - ORANGE
PK - PINK
RD - RED
VT - VIOLET
WH - WHITE
YE - YELLOW

Diagram 13 – Power Windows; Up to May 2017

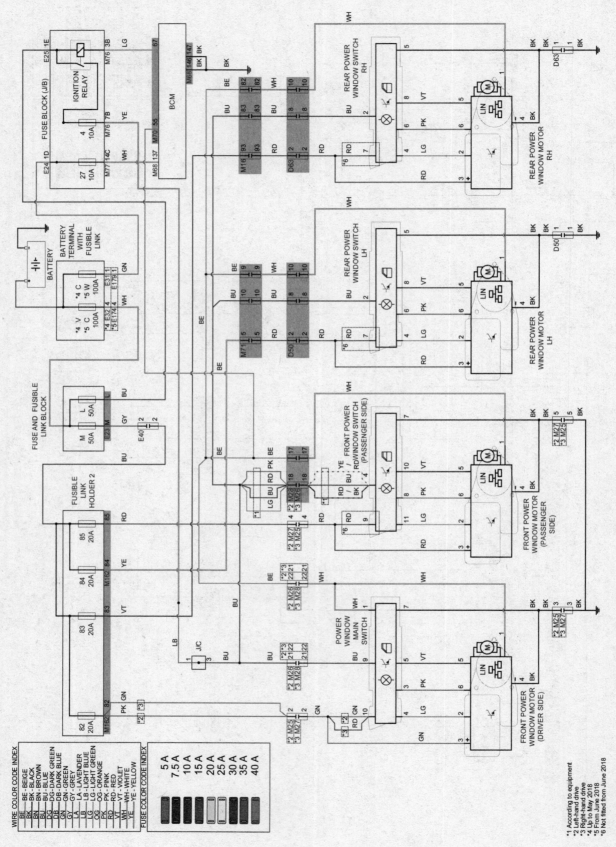

Diagram 14 – Power Windows; From June 2017

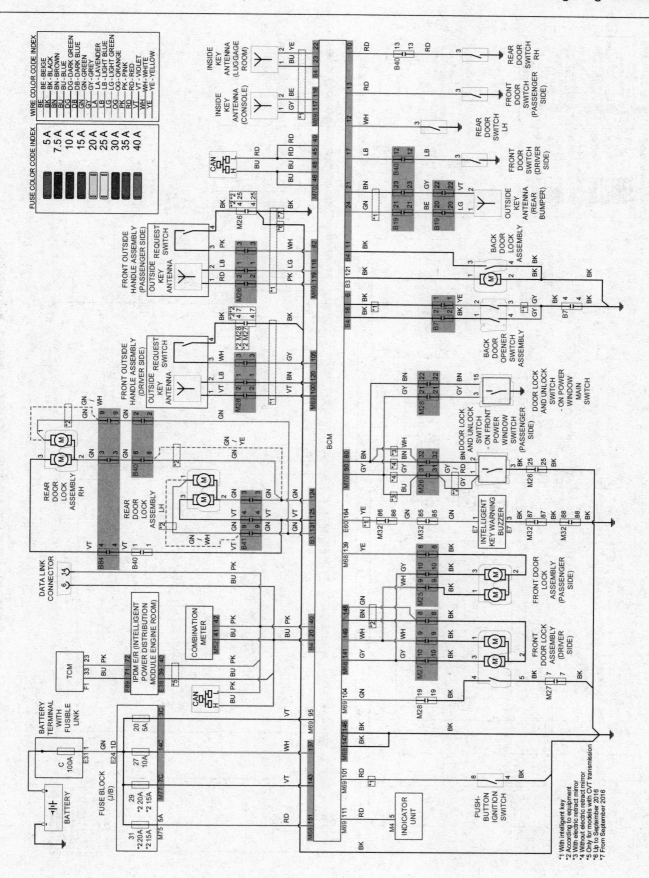

Diagram 15 – Power Door Locks; up to May 2017 – RHD with superlock

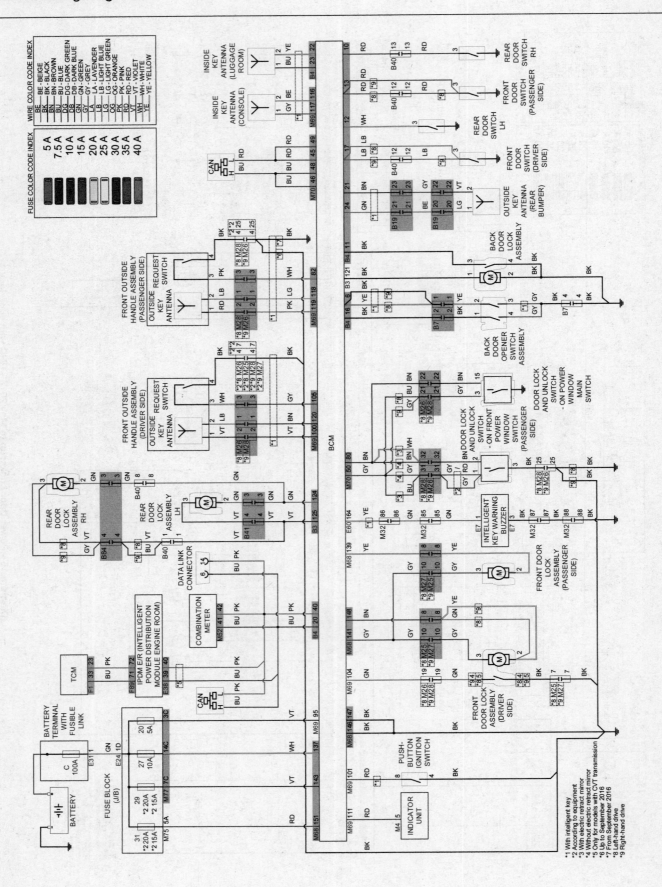

Diagram 16 – Power Door Locks; up to May 2017 – except RHD with superlock

*1 With intelligent key
*2 According to equipment
*3 With electric retract mirror
*4 Without electric retract mirror
*5 Only for models with CVT transmission
*6 Up to September 2016
*7 From September 2016
*8 Left-hand drive
*9 Right-hand drive

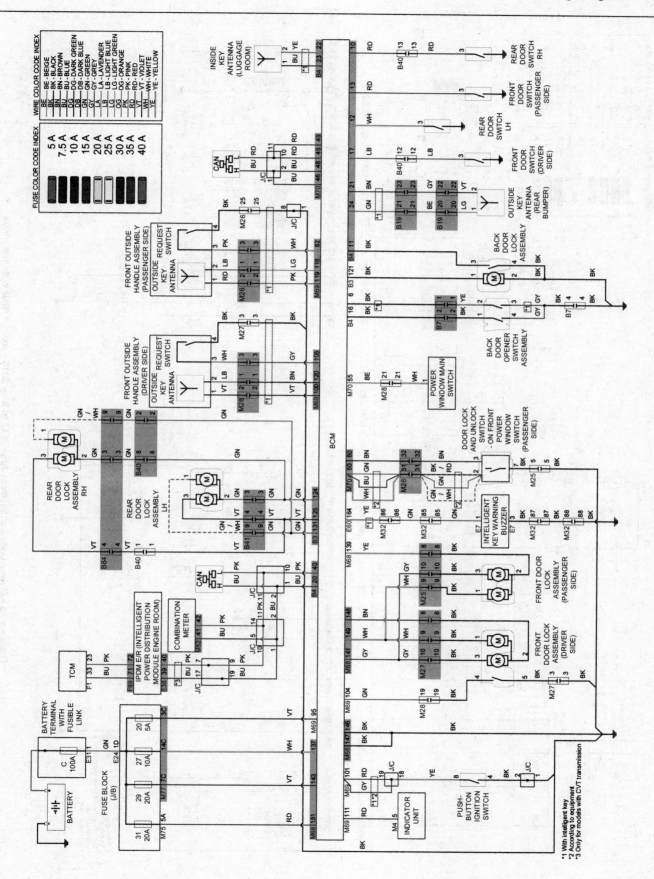

Diagram 17 – Power Door Locks; from June 2017 to May 2018 – RHD with superlock

*1 With intelligent key
*2 According to equipment
*3 Only for models with CVT transmission

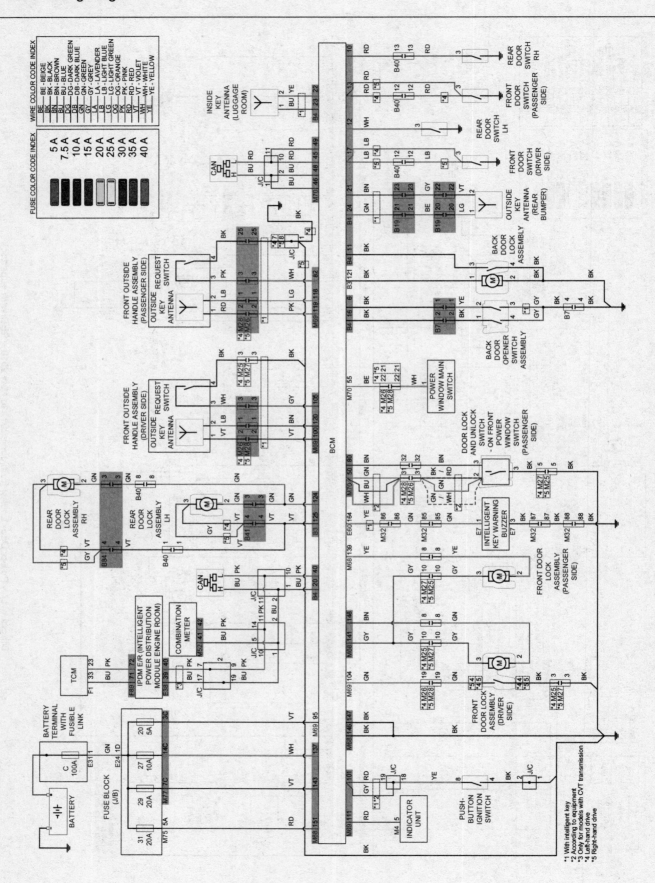

Diagram 18 – Power Door Locks; from June 2017 to May 2018 – except RHD with superlock

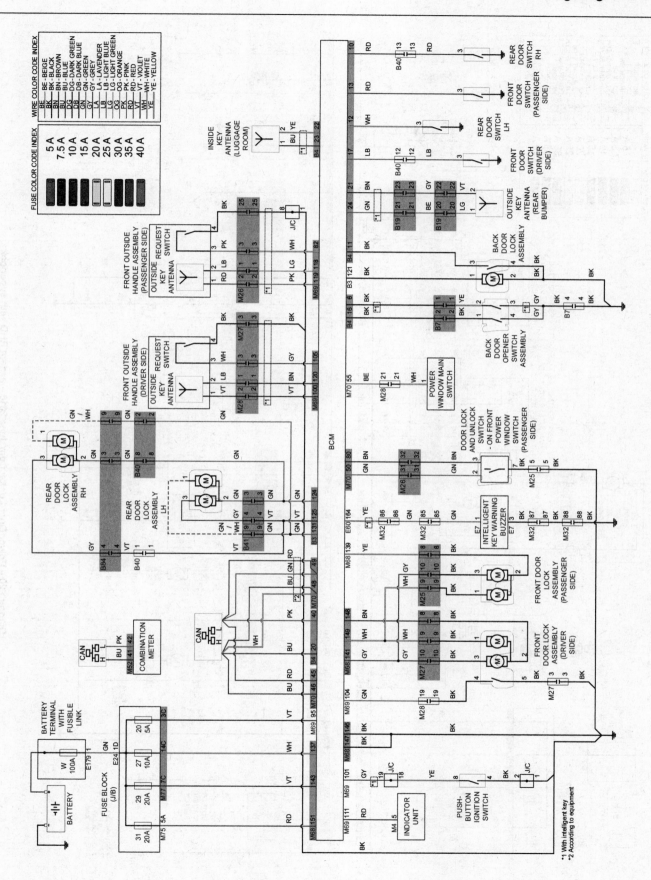

Diagram 19 – Power Door Locks; from June 2018 – RHD with superlock

*1 With intelligent key
*2 According to equipment

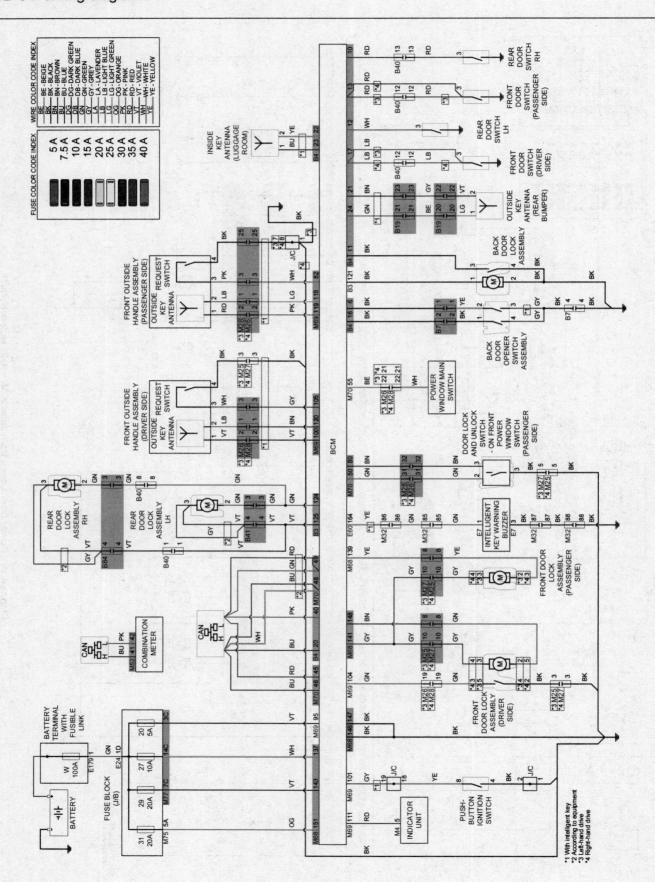

Diagram 20 – Power Door Locks; from June 2018 – except RHD with superlock

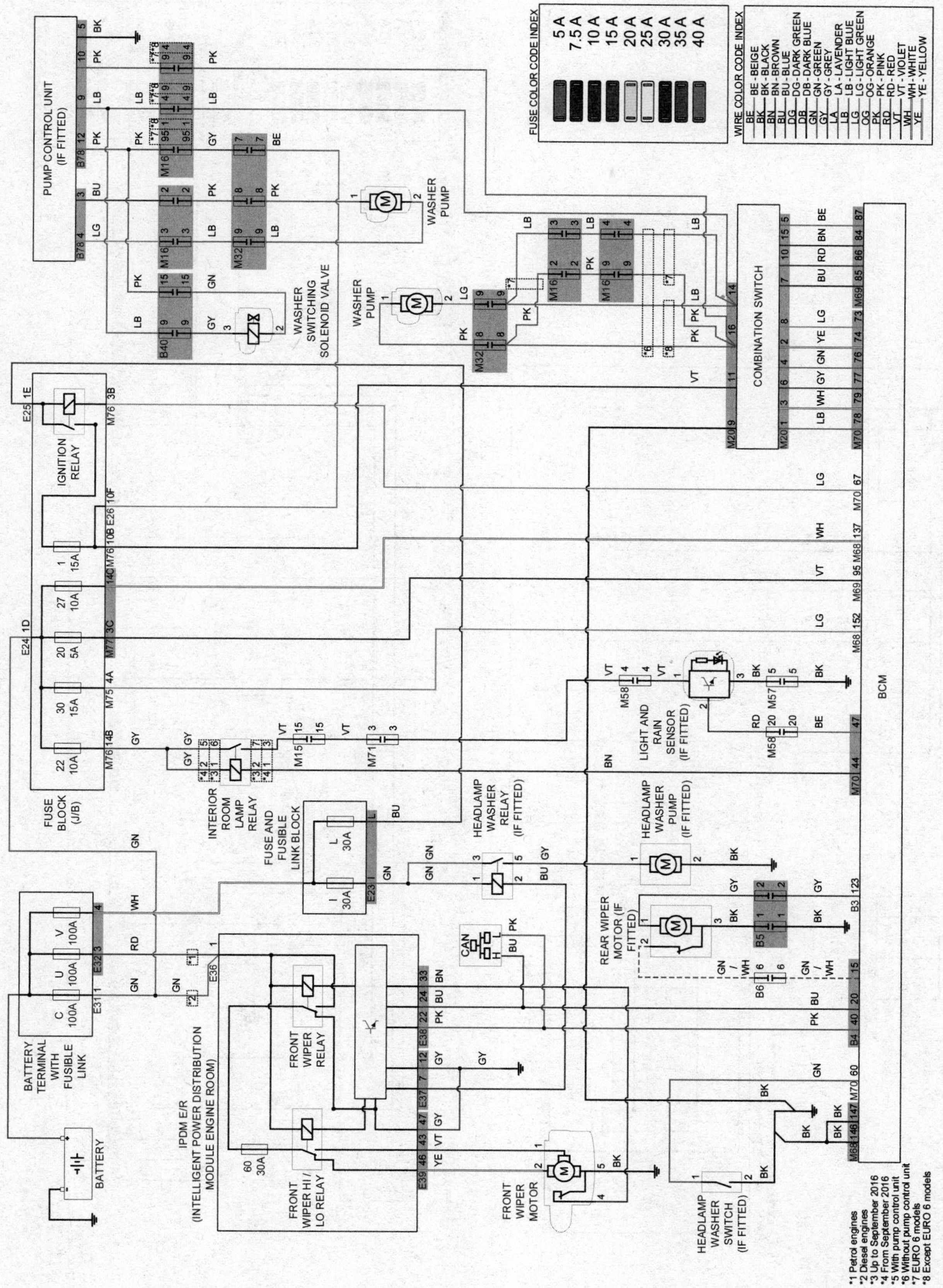

Diagram 21 – Wiper Washer; up to May 2017

FUSE COLOR CODE INDEX

5 A
7.5 A
10 A
15 A
20 A
25 A
30 A
35 A
40 A

WIRE COLOR CODE INDEX

BE - BEIGE
BK - BLACK
BN - BROWN
BU - BLUE
DG - DARK GREEN
DB - DARK BLUE
GN - GREEN
GY - GREY
LA - LAVENDER
LB - LIGHT BLUE
LG - LIGHT GREEN
OG - ORANGE
PK - PINK
RD - RED
VT - VIOLET
WH - WHITE
YE - YELLOW

PUMP CONTROL UNIT (IF FITTED)

WASHER PUMP

WASHER PUMP

WASHER PUMP

WASHER SWITCHING SOLENOID VALVE

COMBINATION SWITCH

IGNITION RELAY

FUSE BLOCK (JJB)

INTERIOR ROOM LAMP RELAY

FUSE AND FUSIBLE LINK BLOCK

LIGHT AND RAIN SENSOR (IF FITTED)

HEADLAMP WASHER RELAY (IF FITTED)

HEADLAMP WASHER PUMP (IF FITTED)

BCM

BATTERY TERMINAL WITH FUSIBLE LINK

BATTERY

IPDM E/R (INTELLIGENT POWER DISTRIBUTION MODULE ENGINE ROOM)

FRONT WIPER RELAY

FRONT WIPER HI / LO RELAY

FRONT WIPER MOTOR

REAR WIPER MOTOR (IF FITTED)

HEADLAMP WASHER SWITCH (IF FITTED)

CAN

*1 Petrol engines
*2 Diesel engines
*3 Up to September 2016
*4 From September 2016
*5 With pump control unit
*6 Without pump control unit
*7 EURO 6 models
*8 Except EURO 6 models

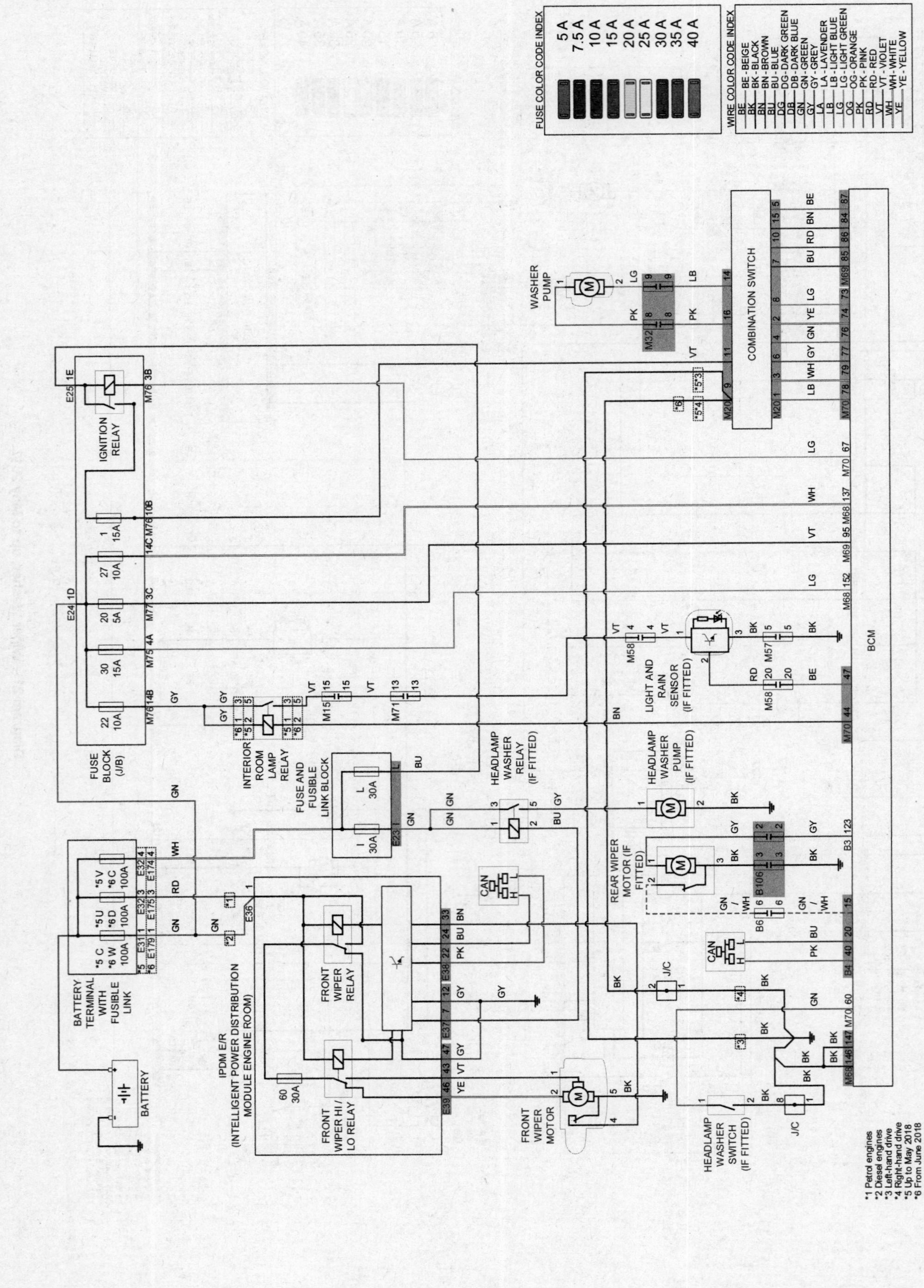

FUSE COLOR CODE INDEX

5 A	
7.5 A	
10 A	
15 A	
20 A	
25 A	
30 A	
35 A	
40 A	

WIRE COLOR CODE INDEX

BE - BEIGE
BK - BLACK
BN - BROWN
BU - BLUE
DG - DARK GREEN
DB - DARK BLUE
GN - GREEN
GY - GREY
LA - LAVENDER
LB - LIGHT BLUE
LG - LIGHT GREEN
OG - ORANGE
PK - PINK
RD - RED
VT - VIOLET
WH - WHITE
YE - YELLOW

Diagram 22 – Wiper Washer; from June 2017

IGNITION RELAY

FUSE BLOCK (J/B)

INTERIOR ROOM LAMP RELAY

FUSE AND FUSIBLE LINK BLOCK

BATTERY TERMINAL WITH FUSIBLE LINK

BATTERY

IPDM E/R (INTELLIGENT POWER DISTRIBUTION MODULE ENGINE ROOM)

FRONT WIPER RELAY

FRONT WIPER HI / LO RELAY

FRONT WIPER MOTOR

WASHER PUMP

COMBINATION SWITCH

LIGHT AND RAIN SENSOR (IF FITTED)

HEADLAMP WASHER RELAY (IF FITTED)

HEADLAMP WASHER PUMP (IF FITTED)

REAR WIPER MOTOR (IF FITTED)

HEADLAMP WASHER SWITCH (IF FITTED)

BCM

CAN H

J/C

*1 Petrol engines
*2 Diesel engines
*3 Left-hand drive
*4 Right-hand drive
*5 Up to May 2018
*6 From June 2018

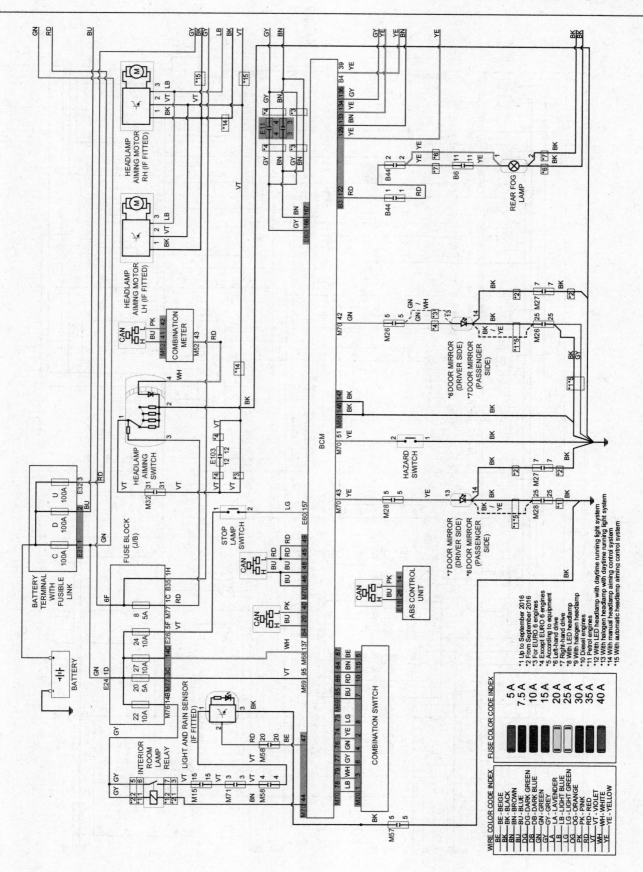

Diagram 23a – Exterior Lights; Up to May 2017 (1 of 2)

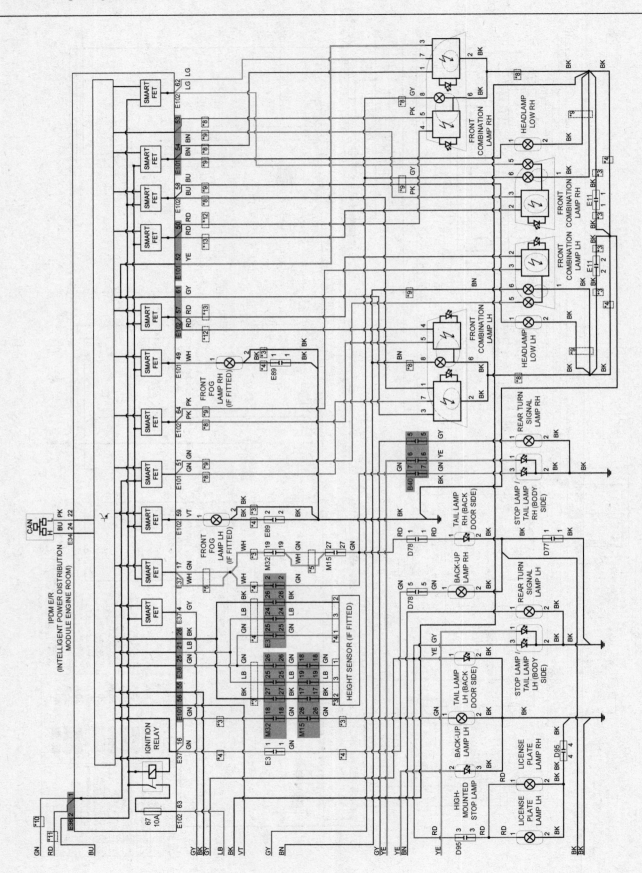

Diagram 23b – Exterior Lights; Up to May 2017 (2 of 2)

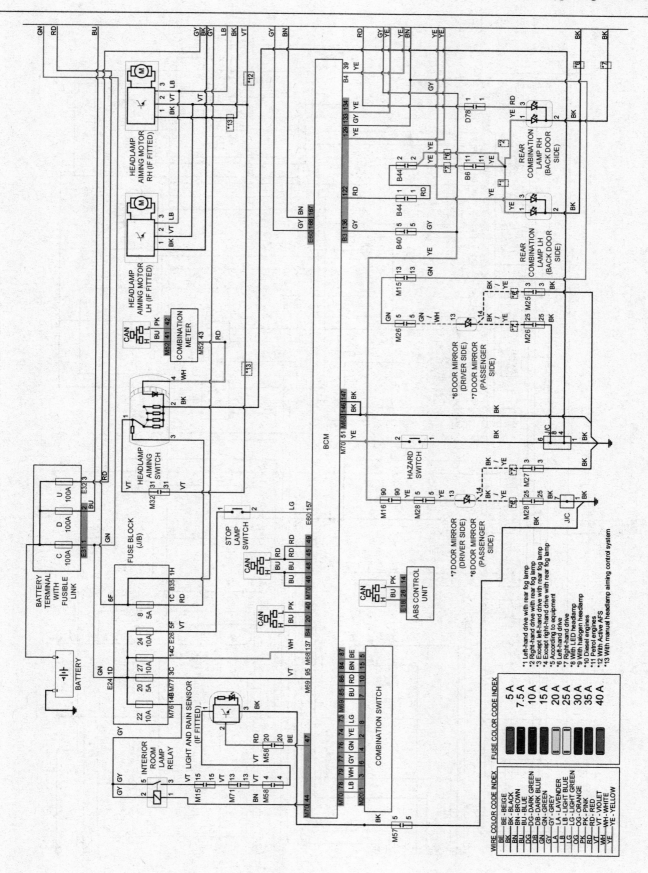

Diagram 24a – Exterior Lights; from June 2017 to May 2018 (1 of 2)

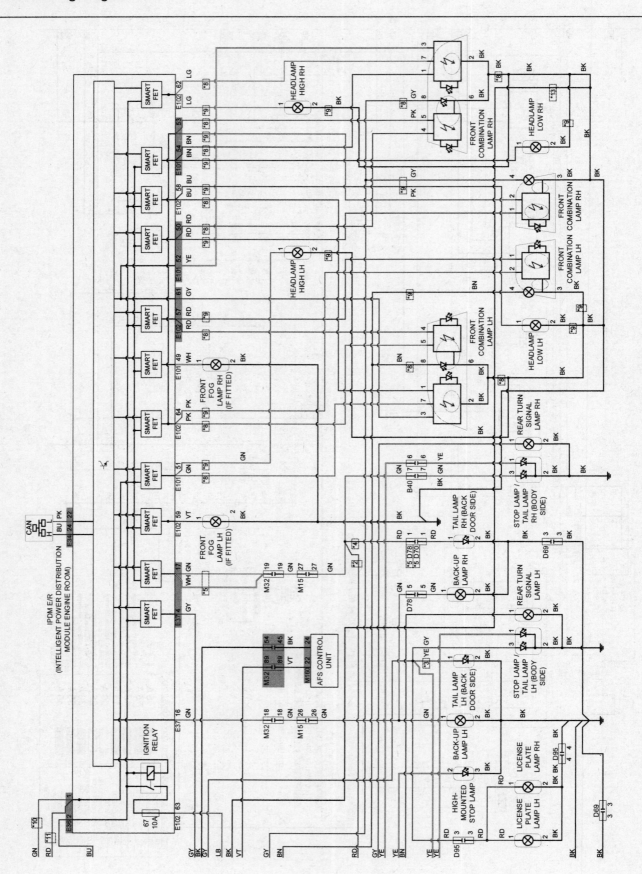

Diagram 24b – Exterior Lights; from June 2017 to May 2018 (2 of 2)

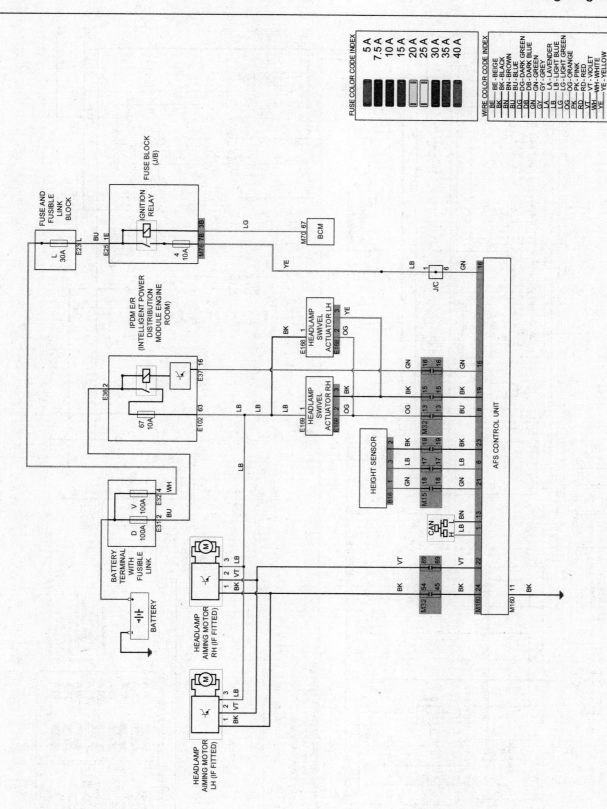

Diagram 25 – Exterior Lights; from June 2017 to May 2018 – AFS

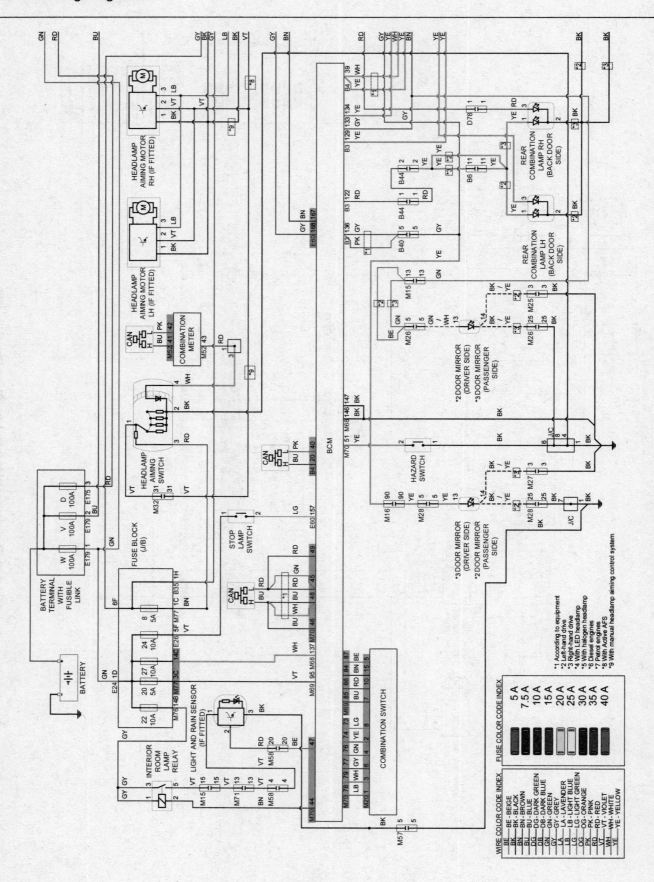

Diagram 26a – Exterior Lights; from June 2018 (1 of 2)

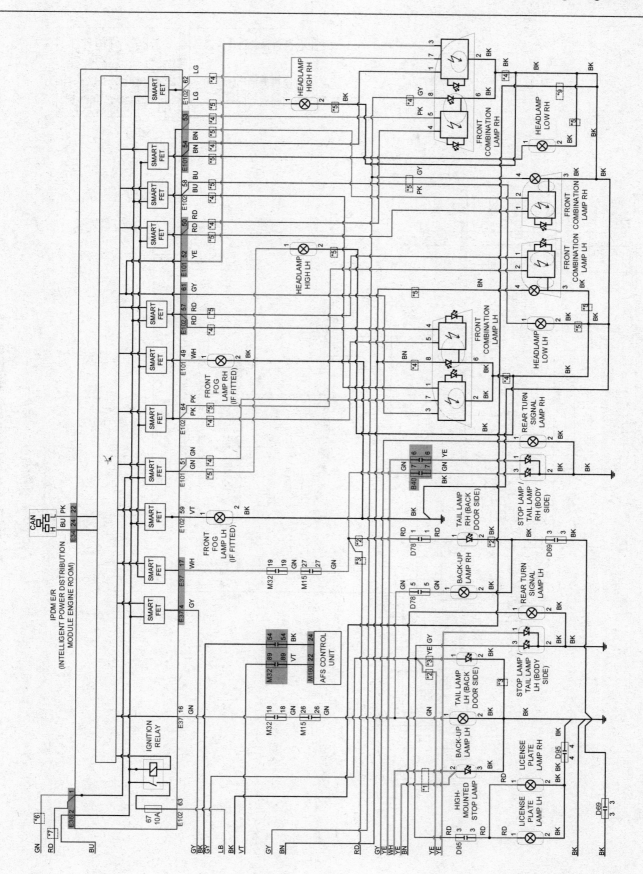

Diagram 26b – Exterior Lights; from June 2018 (2 of 2)

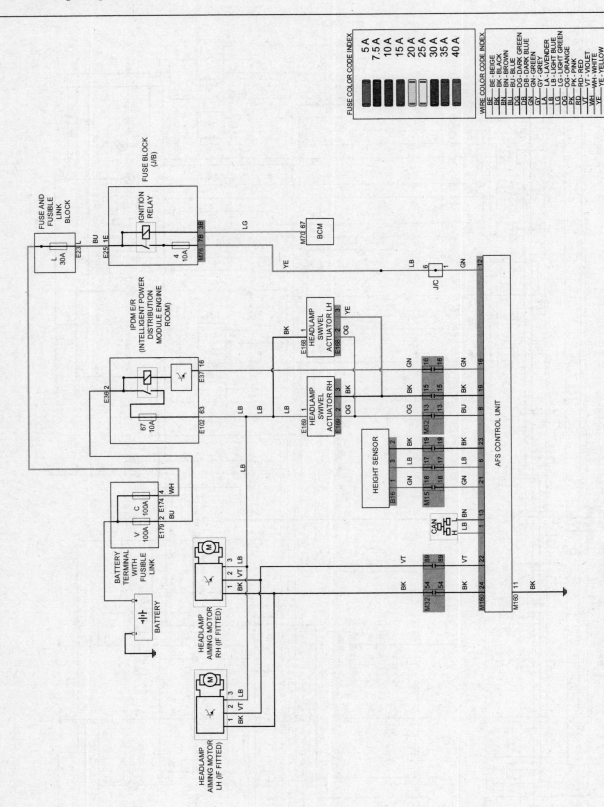

Diagram 27 – Exterior Lights; from June 2018 – AFS

FUSE COLOR CODE INDEX

5 A	
7.5 A	
10 A	
15 A	
20 A	
25 A	
30 A	
35 A	
40 A	

WIRE COLOR CODE INDEX

BE - BEIGE
BK - BLACK
BN - BROWN
BU - BLUE
DG - DARK GREEN
DB - DARK BLUE
GN - GREEN
GY - GREY
LA - LAVENDER
LB - LIGHT BLUE
LG - LIGHT GREEN
OG - ORANGE
PK - PINK
RD - RED
VT - VIOLET
WH - WHITE
YE - YELLOW

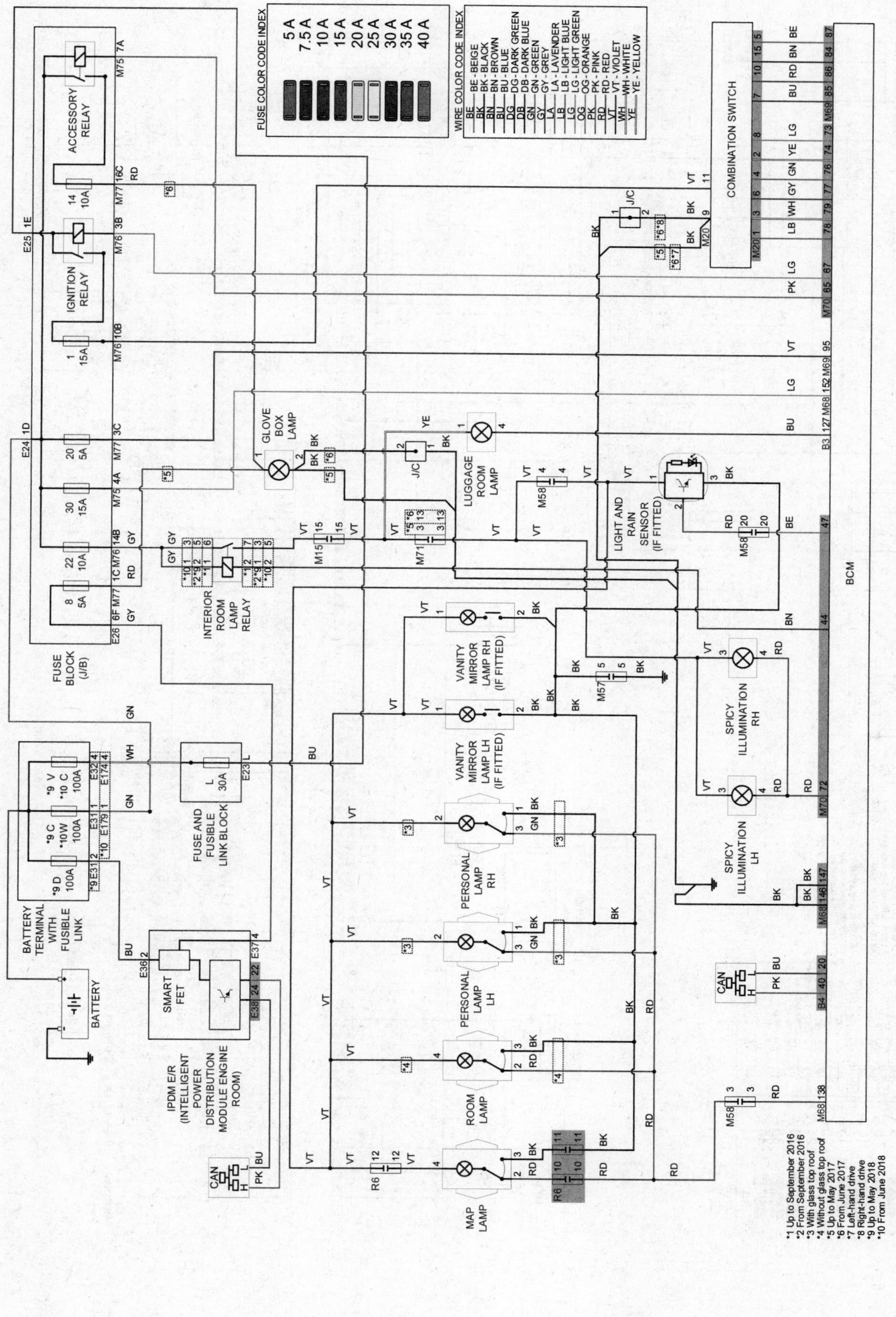

Diagram – 28 Interior Lights

*1 Up to September 2016
*2 From September 2016
*3 With glass top roof
*4 Without glass top roof
*5 Up to May 2017
*6 From June 2017
*7 Left-hand drive
*8 Right-hand drive
*9 Up to May 2018
*10 From June 2018

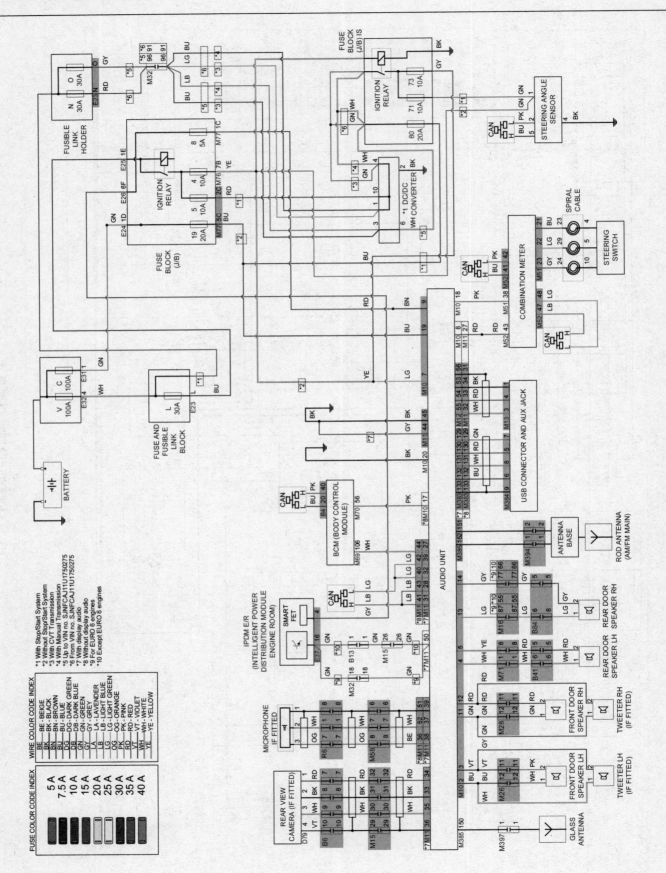

Diagram 29 – Sound System; up to May 2017 – Basic Audio or Audio Display

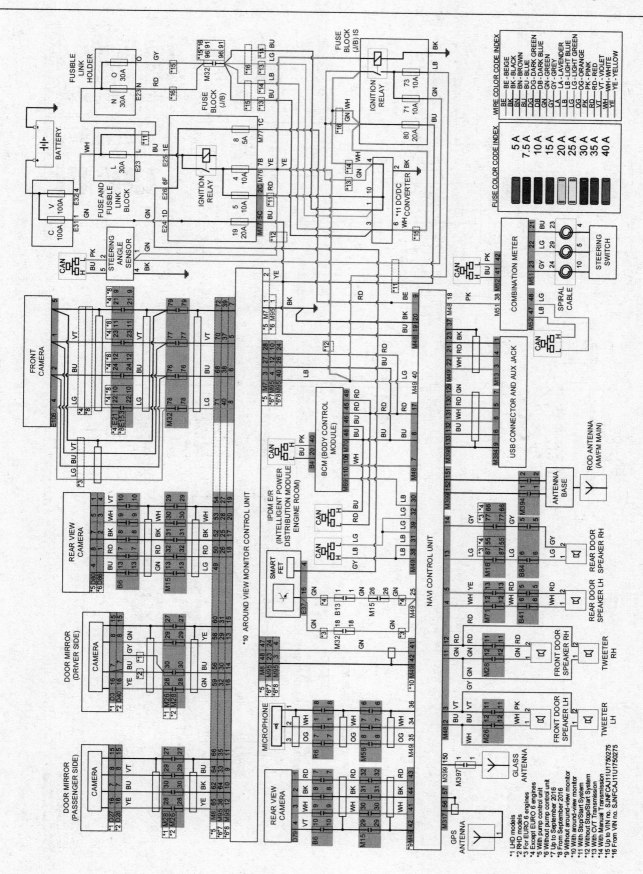

Diagram 30 – Sound System; up to May 2017 – Navigation

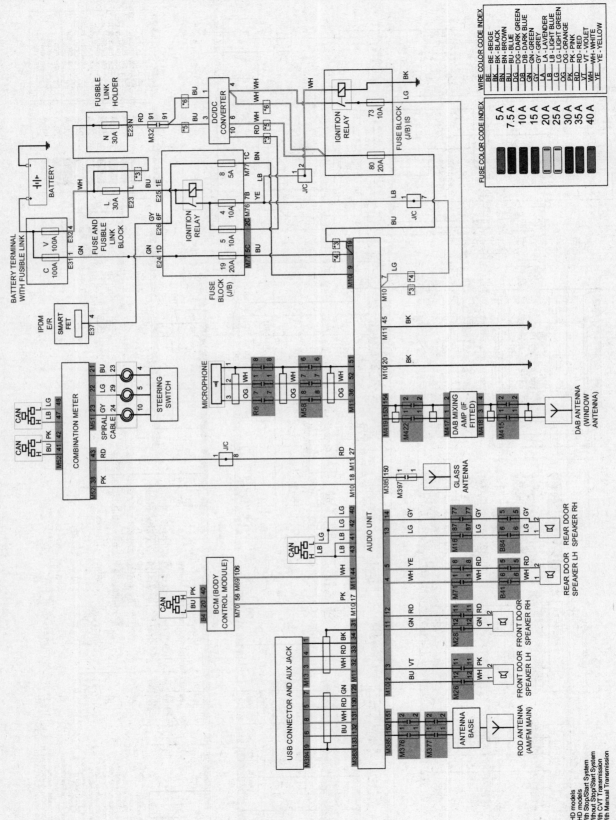

Diagram 31 – Sound System; from June 2017 – Audio

*1 LHD models
*2 RHD models
*3 With Stop/Start System
*4 Without Stop/Start System
*5 With CVT Transmission
*6 With Manual Transmission

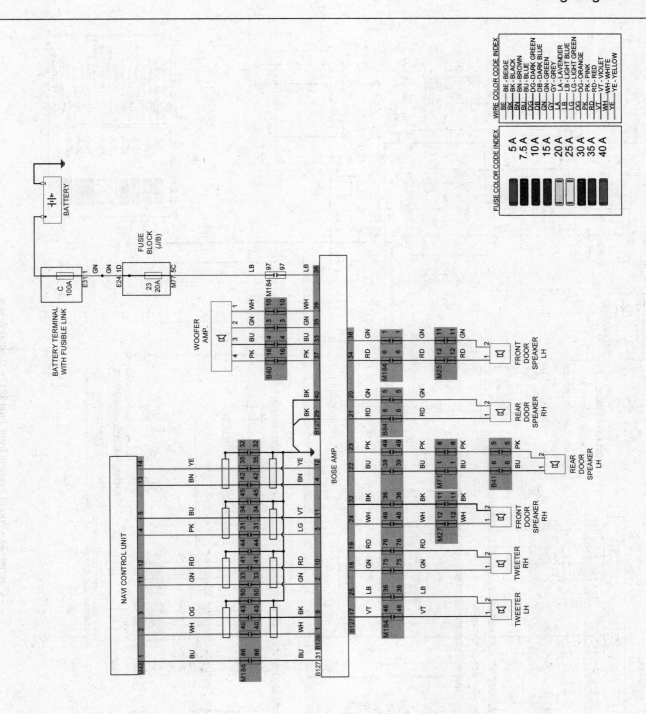

Diagram 32 – Sound System; from June 2017 – BOSE System

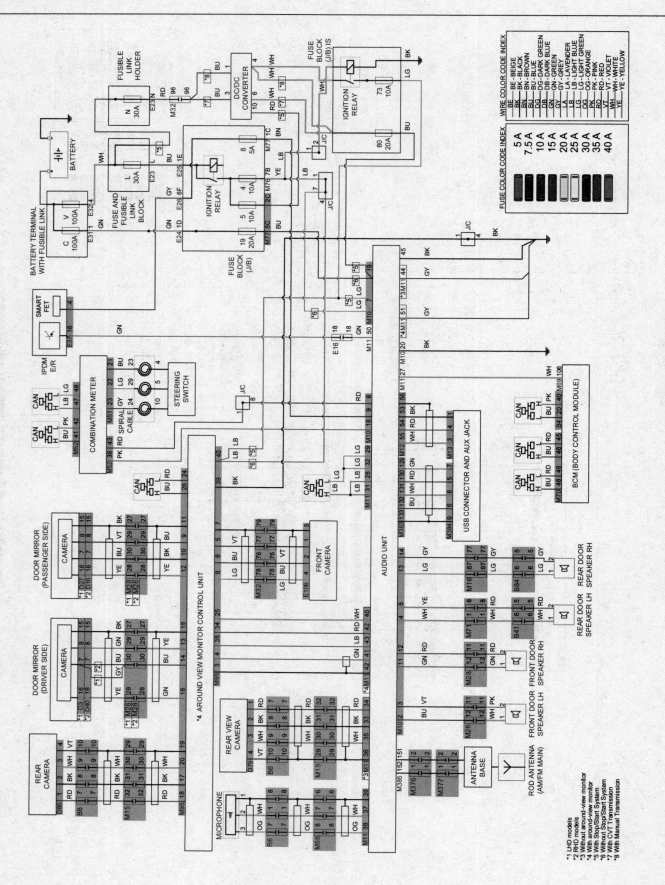

Diagram 33 – Sound System; from June 2017 – Display Audio

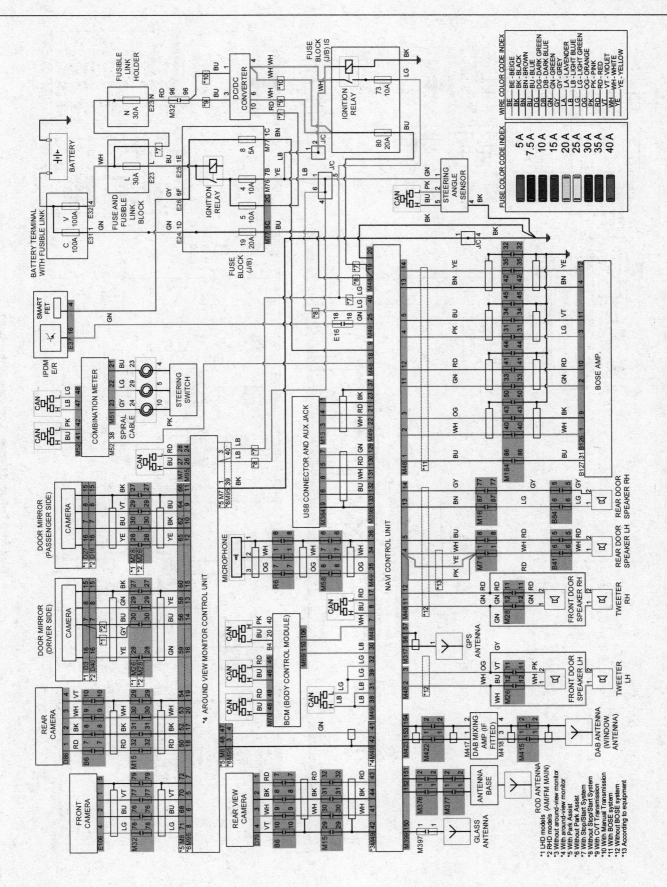

Diagram 34 – Sound System; from June 2017 – Navigation

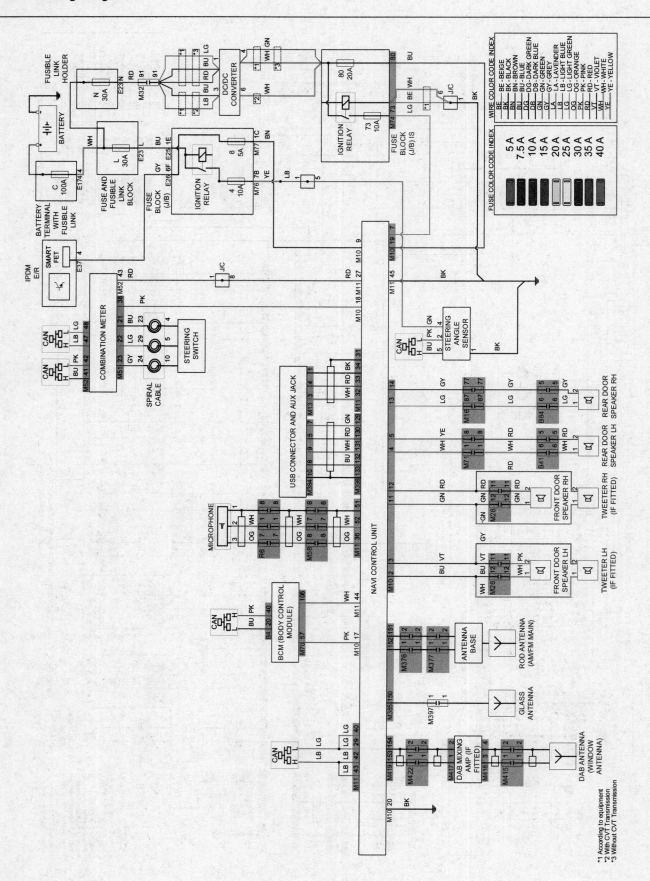

Diagram 35 – Sound System; from June 2018 – Audio

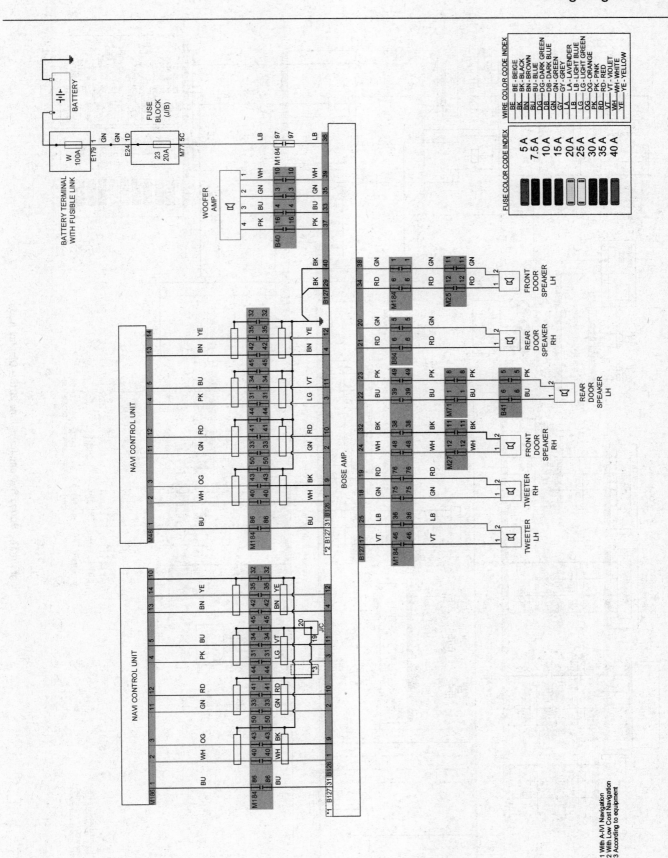

Diagram 36 – Sound System; from June 2018 – BOSE System

*1 With A-IVI Navigation
*2 With Low Cost Navigation
*3 According to equipment

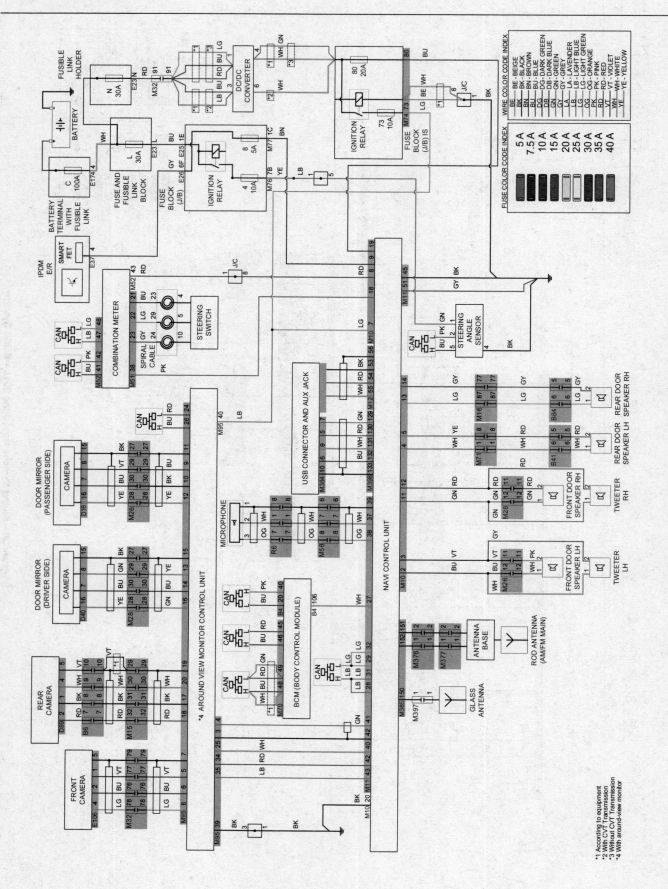

Diagram 37 – Sound System; from June 2018 – Display Audio

*1 According to equipment
*2 With CVT Transmission
*3 Without CVT Transmission
*4 With around-view monitor

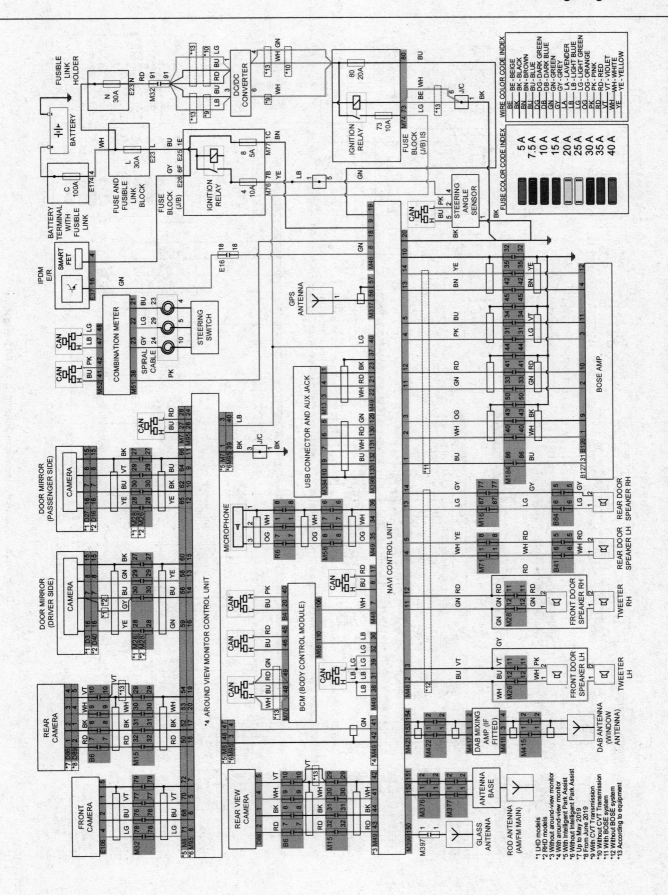

Diagram 38 – Sound System; from June 2018 – Low cost Navigation

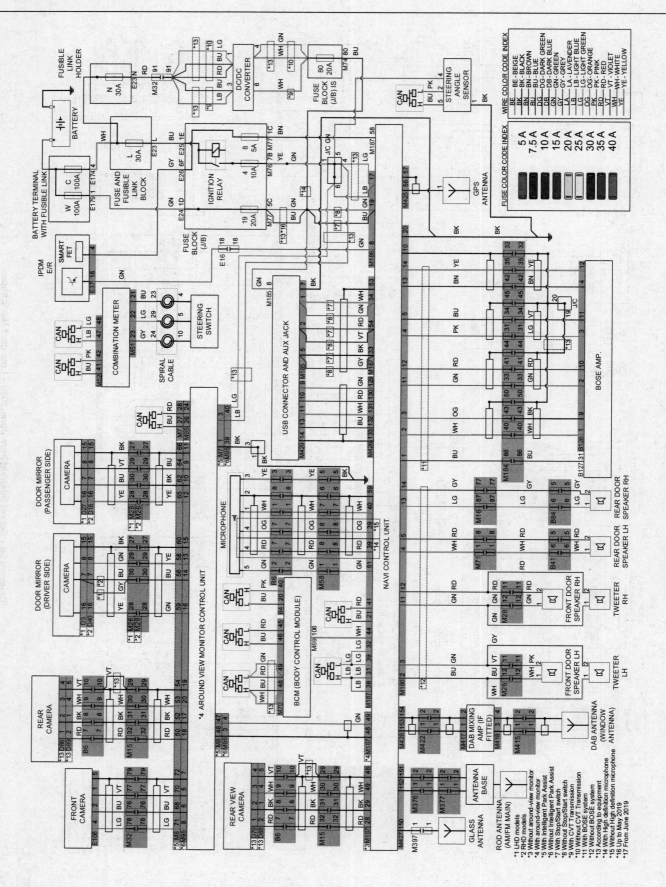

Diagram 39 – Sound System; from June 2018 – A-IVI Navigation

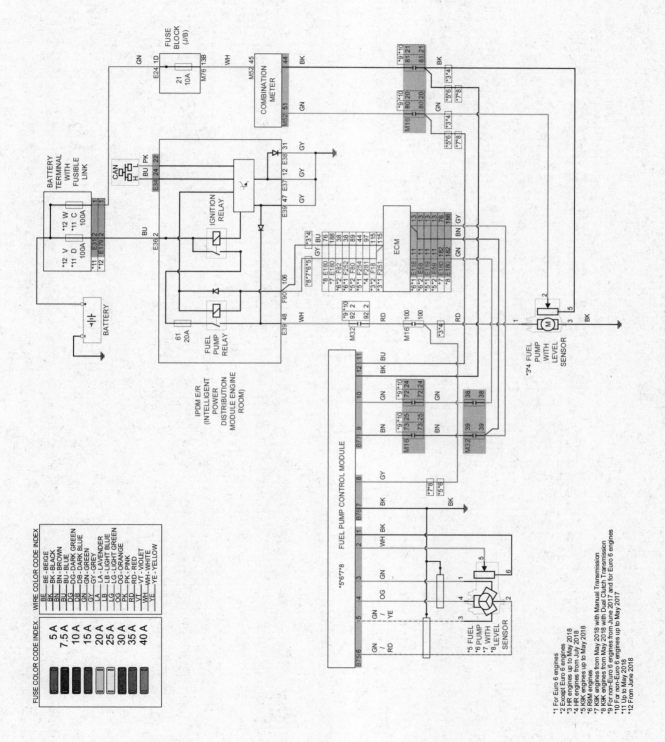

Diagram 40 – Fuel Pump

Notes

Note: *References throughout this index are in the form "Chapter number"* • *"Page number". So, for example, 2C•15 refers to page 15 of Chapter 2C.*

Note: *References throughout this index are in the form "Chapter number" • "Page number". So, for example, 2C•15 refers to page 15 of Chapter 2C.*

Note: *References throughout this index are in the form "Chapter number" • "Page number". So, for example, 2C•15 refers to page 15 of Chapter 2C.*

Note: *References throughout this index are in the form "Chapter number" • "Page number". So, for example, 2C•15 refers to page 15 of Chapter 2C.*

Note: *References throughout this index are in the form "Chapter number" • "Page number". So, for example, 2C•15 refers to page 15 of Chapter 2C.*

Preserving Our Motoring Heritage

< The Model J Duesenberg Derham Tourster. Only eight of these magnificent cars were ever built – this is the only example to be found outside the United States of America

Almost every car you've ever loved, loathed or desired is gathered under one roof at the Haynes Motor Museum. Over 300 immaculately presented cars and motorbikes represent every aspect of our motoring heritage, from elegant reminders of bygone days, such as the superb Model J Duesenberg to curiosities like the bug-eyed BMW Isetta. There are also many old friends and flames. Perhaps you remember the 1959 Ford Popular that you did your courting in? The magnificent 'Red Collection' is a spectacle of classic sports cars including AC, Alfa Romeo, Austin Healey, Ferrari, Lamborghini, Maserati, MG, Riley, Porsche and Triumph.

A Perfect Day Out

Each and every vehicle at the Haynes Motor Museum has played its part in the history and culture of Motoring. Today, they make a wonderful spectacle and a great day out for all the family. Bring the kids, bring Mum and Dad, but above all bring your camera to capture those golden memories for ever. You will also find an impressive array of motoring memorabilia, a comfortable 70 seat video cinema and one of the most extensive transport book shops in Britain. The Pit Stop Cafe serves everything from a cup of tea to wholesome, home-made meals or, if you prefer, you can enjoy the large picnic area nestled in the beautiful rural surroundings of Somerset.

John Haynes O.B.E., Founder and Chairman of the museum at the wheel of a Haynes Light 12. >

< Graham Hill's Lola Cosworth Formula 1 car next to a 1934 Riley Sports.

The Museum is situated on the A359 Yeovil to Frome road at Sparkford, just off the A303 in Somerset. It is about 40 miles south of Bristol, and 25 minutes drive from the M5 intersection at Taunton.
Open 9.30am - 5.30pm (10.00am - 4.00pm Winter) 7 days a week, *except Christmas Day, Boxing Day and New Years Day*
Special rates available for schools, coach parties and outings Charitable Trust No. 292048